CHILD AND ADOLESCENT DEVELOPMENT FOR EDUCATORS

Child
and Adolescent
Development for
Educators

MICHAEL PRESSLEY
CHRISTINE B. McCORMICK

THE GUILFORD PRESS
New York   London

© 2007 Michael Pressley and Christine B. McCormick
Published by The Guilford Press
A Division of Guilford Publications, Inc.
72 Spring Street, New York, NY 10012
www.guilford.com

Printed in the United States of America

This book is printed on acid-free paper.

Last digit is print number: 9 8 7 6 5 4 3 2 1

Library of Congress Cataloging-in-Publication Data
Pressley, Michael.
  Child and adolescent development for educators / by Michael Pressley and
Christine B. McCormick.
    p. cm.
  Includes bibliographical references and index.
  ISBN-10: 1-59385-352-1   ISBN-13: 978-1-59385-352-5 (hardcover: alk. paper)
  1. Cognition in children. 2. Adolescent psychology. I. McCormick,
Christine. II. Title.
  BF723.C5P74 2006
  370.15′2—dc22

                                                            2006012305

Photo Credits: Page 11, courtesy Laura Dwight Photography; page 41, courtesy Joel Gordon; page 62, courtesy Elizabeth Crews; page 75, courtesy Tony Freeman/Photo Edit, Inc.; page 112, courtesy Laura Dwight Photography; page 124, courtesy Laura Dwight Photography; page 130, courtesy Bob Daemmrich/The Image Works; page 148, courtesy Scott Houston/Corbis; page 158, courtesy Frank Siteman/Photo Edit, Inc.; page 178, courtesy Library of Congress; page 221, courtesy Elizabeth Crews; page 233, courtesy Bettmann/Corbis; page 245, courtesy Sara Krulwich/*The New York Times*; page 271, courtesy Peter Hvizdak/The Image Works; page 274, courtesy Creatas Images [RF]; page 276, courtesy Joel Gordon; page 310, courtesy Bob Daemmrich; page 312, courtesy Laura Dwight Photography; page 349, courtesy Laura Dwight Photography; page 378, courtesy Michael Newman/ Photo Edit; page 384, courtesy Pat Doyle/Corbis.

About the Authors

Michael Pressley, PhD, who passed away in May 2006, was University Distinguished Professor at Michigan State University, as well as Director of the Doctoral Program in Teacher Education and Director of the Literacy Achievement Research Center, with both roles part of his professorship in the Department of Teacher Education and the Department of Counseling, Educational Psychology, and Special Education. An expert on effective elementary literacy instruction, he was author or editor of more than 300 journal articles, chapters, and books. Dr. Pressley served a 6-year term as editor of *Journal of Educational Psychology*. He was honored with awards from the National Reading Conference, the International Reading Association, the American Educational Research Association, and the American Psychological Association, among others. Dr. Pressley received the 2004 E. L. Thorndike Award from Division 15 of the American Psychological Association, which is the highest award given for career research accomplishment in educational psychology.

Christine B. McCormick, PhD, is Dean of the School of Education at the University of Massachusetts, Amherst. Previously, she was a faculty member at the University of New Mexico and the University of South Carolina, where she taught undergraduate and graduate courses in human growth and development, educational psychology, learning and cognition, and classroom assessment. Dr. McCormick is author or coauthor of more than 40 publications on a variety of topics in child development and education.

Preface

This book represents the realization of our vision to create a child and adolescent development text that addresses the topics in developmental psychology of the highest priority for educators—teachers, school counselors, school psychologists, and school administrators. We have both taught the development course prospective educators are typically required to take as part of their academic programs and have not been satisfied with the focus and depth of the available texts. This book covers the classic developmental canon while being true to its educational orientation. Our intent was to produce a research-based, intelligent text that is also accessible for its audience.

The most common complaint we have heard from our students over the years as we have taught the developmental psychology course for educators at both the graduate and advanced undergraduate levels has been "I'm going into education. What do I do with all this developmental theory? What good is it to me?" Most developmental texts are designed to be all things to all people and therefore cannot address the specific needs of education students. Moreover, proposals for improving the preparation of educators have emphasized the need to develop future teachers' understandings in context. Thus, a text for one of the core courses in an educator preparation program should make explicit and repeated connections to educational contexts.

The emphasis on applications to educational contexts is informed by historically important and contemporary theories and research. We selected the most significant studies to feature, with the clear goal of focusing on the last 35–40 years of research, referencing the work that endures. Thus, this text highlights the theory and research most important for educators, and translates them to educational practices—all in what we believe is in a readable, comprehensive fashion.

The organization of this book reflects the research literature in development and education. The first part of the text, *Theoretical Perspectives in Child Development*, is organized in terms of the major theories of development. This section presents the knowledge base resultant from research directly derived from these key theoretical perspectives. Chapter 1 sets the stage by first introducing the great debates of development followed by a review of research methods commonly used by developmental researchers, including both qualitative and quantitative approaches to conducting research. This is a unique contribution of this book, for most texts in human development cover only quantitative methods and ignore methods used by many educational researchers. Chapter 2 describes the biological foundations of development, with explicit discussion of the biological foundations of academic competence. The next two chapters provide different perspectives on cognitive development: Chapter 3 highlights Piaget's theory and contributions evolving from Piaget's theory, while Chapter 4 focuses on insights in cognitive development derived from information-processing approaches. The final two chapters in this section describe theories emphasizing the social influences upon development: Chapter 5 describes some of the more traditional theories emphasizing social influences of individuals in a child's environment, while Chapter 6 describes the theories that emphasize the influence of the surrounding culture on development.

In Part II, *Key Topics in Child Development and Education*, significant topics in developmental research of importance to educators are discussed. Typically, these topics are not studied in the context of a particular theoretical perspective but are approached by researchers from varying theoretical orientations. Chapter 7 is a comprehensive discussion of language development and linguistic development, including information on bilingualism, language disorders, and deafness. The chapter on intelligence, Chapter 8, includes information on the construct and measurement of intelligence typically provided in a child development text but then adds a treatment of learner diversity designed to be more relevant for future educators. Chapter 9 provides a comprehensive view of the development of academic motivation, a topic that is vital for future educators but not adequately addressed by traditional child development textbooks. Chapter 10 describes the impact of family and peer relationships on development, while Chapter 11 explores the role of gender in developmental processes (including a discussion of factors influencing academic performance in math and science). Chapter 12, written by David G. Scherer, provides an overview of how educators can recognize and understand student mental health problems. Finally, the book concludes with an integrative review chapter where the major concepts presented in the text are combined in a longitudinal view of development. Throughout all of the chapters, explicit connections are made to the overall theme of highlighting work that is most relevant to future educators.

■ ■ ■ FEATURES OF THIS BOOK

Chapters 2–12 conclude with a *Chapter Summary and Evaluation* in which the major points of the chapter are briefly reviewed, organized around the themes of the great debates in development introduced in Chapter 1. Key terms are bolded and defined in the text where they appear, and are presented again at the end of Chapters 1–12 in a *Review of Key Terms*.

At least one *Applying Developmental Theory to Educational Contexts* special feature appears in Chapters 1–12. In this feature, specific recommendations for applying theory to practice or examples of applications to practice are given. These examples and recommendations help students make connections between theory and practice as they begin to develop the knowledge base required to generate additional applications. In addition, Chapters 1–12 contain at least one *Considering Interesting Questions* special feature focusing on an interesting question or issue that was not addressed in the text or not completely developed in the text discussion. This feature is designed to spark interest in students new to developmental topics.

■ ■ ■ ACKNOWLEDGMENTS

We have many people to thank. First, we thank Chris Jennison and his colleagues at The Guilford Press. It was a pleasure to work with you and we appreciate your patience as this project unfolded. We also thank the reviewers who gave many wonderful suggestions for the reformulation of the manuscript, as well as Karen Harrington's professional and thorough work on the test bank. Christine McCormick would like to thank her husband, David Scherer, for his support and patience and for being the applied psychologist in the family, and her daughter, Evelynn, for being the best daughter there ever was. In another book we wrote, Michael Pressley thanked his wife, Donna, for being "a good sport about all those nights of word processing," and his son, Tim, for being "a constant reminder of how important it is to educate the next generation of educators." In the time that elapsed between the first contract and the final completion of this project, life events unfolded in many different ways. Christine and David adopted a baby (Evelynn) and were privileged to witness her wonderful development. Mike's son, Tim, graduated from high school and began college—and to Mike and Donna's joy is planning to become an educator. Very early in this project, Mike was diagnosed with cancer. After amazing us all with his incredible powers of recovery for years, Mike died in May 2006. On our last visit, Mike repeated one of his favorite quotes by Joseph Campbell: "The privilege of a lifetime is being yourself." Thank you, Mike, for allowing us the privilege to experience your wisdom, wit, and indomitable spirit.

Instructors considering this book for course adoption will receive a ready-to-use test bank that includes multiple-choice and essay questions, including questions based on classroom scenarios.

Contents

PART II. KEY TOPICS IN CHILD DEVELOPMENT AND EDUCATION

PART I

THEORETICAL PERSPECTIVES IN CHILD DEVELOPMENT

CHAPTER 1

Introduction to Child Development and Education

This is a book about human development, an interdisciplinary field of study. Human development involves biological transformation: from a single cell to a fetus, then to an infant, and then to a toddler. A child matures into an adolescent, who matures into an adult, who ages and eventually dies. Human development also includes psychological changes, from a newborn who exhibits more reflexes than intentional behaviors to a child whose thinking is more concrete than abstract. In turn, the child becomes an adolescent whose thinking can be abstract and hypothetical. Teenagers are soon adults, whose intellectual powers increase across the lifespan in some ways and decline in others. Development also involves social changes—for example, from a newborn experiencing people as sensations, to an infant who is attached to his or her caregivers, to a preschooler with an expanding social world. The world of peers becomes increasingly important as the child grows older and enters adolescence.

Some basic themes have shaped the study of development. Although the intensity with which these issues are debated has waxed and waned over decades of developmental study, these debates provide a framework for considering developmental theory and research. Thus we begin this book with an overview of some of the great debates surrounding the nature of development and provide alternative perspectives concerning these debates throughout the book.

■ ■ ■ THE GREAT DEBATES ABOUT HUMAN DEVELOPMENT

At this point, we do not want readers to worry about the specific theories of development and how they contrast with one another, but rather simply to understand that debate permeates the study of human development. Thus you should read what follows with the intention of attaining a clear understanding of the major points of difference between alternative conceptions of development, rather than worrying about remembering specific details. In line with our emphasis on education, we discuss the educational implications of these great debates.

Nature versus Nurture

Today, most developmental psychologists do not believe that development is primarily due to either *nature* (determined by biology) or *nurture* (determined by experience). Instead, there is clear understanding that development is due to both nature and nurture, both biology and experience (Borkowski, Ramey, & Bristol-Power, 2002; Collins, Maccoby, Steinberg, Hetherington, & Bornstein, 2000; Lerner, 2002; Lerner, Easterbrooks, & Mistry, 2003; Rutter, 2002a, 2002b; Shonkoff & Phillips, 2000). Biology provides a range of possibilities. Which of those possibilities is realized depends greatly on the experiences available in the environment. Consider what may seem a simple example. A child inherits genes providing him or her with a biological predisposition for being taller than average. Whether this child achieves this biological potential depends upon environmental factors, such as the nutrition available and exposure to severe illness or disease.

Human intelligence provides a good example of how environmental influences act upon the range of biological possibilities. Humans do not inherit genes that result in a specific level of intelligence. Rather, they inherit the potential for a range of possibilities. Whether or not a child's level of intelligence reaches the top end of the range depends on the quality of the environment provided. Researchers debate, however, about how much **plasticity**, or sensitivity to environmental experiences, there is for intelligence (Garlick, 2002; Gottesman, 1963; Gottesman & Hanson, 2005; Lewontin, 1974; Martinez, 2000; Scarr & Kidd, 1983). Those who agree with the ideas in books like *The Bell Curve* (Herrnstein & Murray, 1994) believe the range is very narrow—that parental intelligence largely determines the intelligence of their children. Many others think the **reaction range** for intelligence is substantially broader (Jacoby & Glauberman, 1995). In this case, the reaction range is the range of all possible levels of intelligence given the biological predisposition. There is no doubt that there is some range, and that where a child ends up in his or her particular reaction range is a function of the environment he or she experiences. The goal of educators should be to make the most of the biological potential of a child. That means providing children with consistent high-quality experiences. Biological perspectives can provide insights about when particular types of experiences are crucial as well as insights about the risks of environmental deprivations at particular points in development (see Chapter 2).

Virtually all of the theories of development presented in this book have both biological and environmental components. Some theories are more biological than environmental, others emphasize environment much more than biology, but all are *both* biological and environmental. Development is complicated, an interaction between multiple components.

Stages of Development versus Continuous Development

Many theories of development specify particular stages of development (Lerner, 2002). According to these theories, children are fundamentally different depending on their stage, which generally correlates with age, and movement from one stage to another stage is rather abrupt. For example, G. Stanley Hall (1904, 1905) conceived of adolescence as a period of great "storm and stress," brought on by the sudden physical changes that accompany adolescence. According to Erik Erikson's (1968) theory of development, adolescence brings with it concerns about identity that were not important at all earlier in life (see Chapter 5). As another example, Piaget's (1970) theory of intellectual development argues that children during the grade-school years are very concrete in their thinking, with the transition into adolescence accompanied by a dramatic increase in abstract thinking skills (see Chapter 3). Thus, according to the stage perspective, development proceeds in discrete steps that may seem dramatic or sudden. The developmental change is *abrupt*. One example in nature of development occurring in discrete stages is that of the metamorphosis of a caterpillar into a cocooned pupa and its final emergence as a butterfly.

In contrast, other theories focus on *gradual* change. One example in nature is a blade of grass growing gradually with no remarkable change in its basic characteristics. According to social learning theory (Bandura, 1977, 1986), change during childhood and adolescence is accomplished largely through learning by observation, so development is much more continuous and gradual (see Chapter 5). According to yet another theory, the information-processing theory (see Chapter 4), onset of adolescence does not result in dramatic changes in intellect. Adolescents seem to be able to learn more than children because of their gradually increasing information-processing capabilities. Mental capacity increases throughout childhood and adolescence. Adolescents continue to learn new strategies as they did during childhood, and their knowledge of the world continues to expand. The result is that with increasing age during childhood and continuing into adolescence, thinking skills increase. The increases in thinking abilities do not come suddenly, but rather gradually, although the simultaneous increases in capacity, strategies, and knowledge can make it seem as if a stage-like jump in competence has occurred (Schneider & Pressley, 1996).

Our perspective on the continuity (gradual change) versus discontinuity (abrupt change) debate is that although there are some discontinuities, they are rarely as pronounced or as rapid in onset as suggested by the most extreme of stage theoretical positions (Carey & Markman, 1999). For educators, it is important to be realistic about what to expect from children of particular ages, but not to be so tied to stage thinking as to ignore inconsistencies with it. For example, although elementary-age children often do have difficulty thinking hypothetically, they can be quite hypothetical when thinking about very familiar topics. If you need convincing, ask a 10-year-old chess expert some hypothetical questions about moves in chess!

Universals in Development versus Culture-Specific Developments

Many developmental theorists have argued for universals in development, such as universal stages that all children everywhere experience (Flavell, 1971). This makes sense given that some developmental theories emphasize biological influences. At a biological level, the similarities between people from different cultures and races are much more pronounced than the differences. Indeed, from a biological perspective, the similarities between human males and females are much greater than the differences (see Chapter 11). Because of these biological similarities, similarities in physical and behavioral development are inevitable.

Some developmental theorists nonetheless emphasize that at least some aspects of development proceed differently in different cultures (Cole & Scribner, 1977; Comunian & Gielen, 2000; Dasen, 1984; Greenfield, Keller, Filigni, & Maynard, 2003; Mistry & Saraswathi, 2003; Nucci, 2003a; Snarey, 1985; Wang, 2003). To the extent that environment makes a difference in development, culture should make an impact on development. The environments children experience in one part of the world can be very different from the environments children experience in another part of the world.

Because development is both biologically determined and a function of environment, there are both universals in development and culture-specific developments. Indeed, evidence of this exists in any school district in the United States. Children in a given first-grade classroom may be very economically and culturally diverse. Nonetheless, these first graders are much more similar to one another in their behaviors and competencies than they are to eighth-grade students.

Trait-Like Consistency in Behaviors versus Situational Determination of Behavior

Are there "aggressive" children and "passive" ones or "friendly" children and "shy" ones? Some psychologists believe that powerful differences exist between children, such that some children are consistently different from others on some personality or behavior dimension (Allport & Odbert, 1936; McCrae & Allick, 2002). That is, some children are generally more aggressive than other children, others more passive, some more friendly, and others more shy. One possible explanation for such consistency is that traits are biologically determined, with differences in personality largely inherited.

Often when researchers have looked for such consistencies in personality and behavioral differences, however, they have been hard to find. One explanation for this is that behavior is primarily determined by the current environment rather than by biology. That is, no child is consistently aggressive, but rather aggressive in some situations but not in others (Mischel, 1968). According to this perspective, passivity, friendliness, and shyness vary with situations as well. So does smartness. Thus, if presented with a task matched well to their knowledge or interests, children can look very smart relative to classmates; a few minutes later, the same children may look rather typical when doing a task involving unfamiliar information (Chi, 1978).

Active versus Passive Child

Some theories portray children, including infants, as continually active in their own development (Gopnik, Meltzoff, & Kuhl, 1999; Lerner, 2002; Piaget, 1970; von Glaserfeld, 1995). They decide what they will attend to and process, seeking out things that are particularly interesting to them. Educators who subscribe to such theories tend to favor arranging learning environments to stimulate children's curiosity and exploration; they believe that the learning resulting from interactions stimulated by the child's own interests will be especially enduring. Other theories depict children as more passive, learning from stimulation that is presented to them

(Rosenshine, 1979). The educator's role according to these theories is to select to-be-learned information, present it to children, and provide feedback and reinforcement.

Our perspective is that children learn in a variety of ways (Bandura, 1986; Mahoney, 1991). Some learning results from the active efforts of the child, that is, as a consequence of the child's natural curiosity and interests. Even so, humans have a tremendous capacity to learn without effort or even interest, acquiring much information incidentally. Children learn from observation, and they learn when they are reinforced to learn. The skilled educator knows both how to stimulate children's natural activities and how to devise presentations and provide reinforcements in order to promote learning of important material. The skilled teacher also understands just how much can be learned incidentally from rich experiences and does everything possible to make certain that children experience informative worlds. Children learn through what they read, through what they are encouraged to watch on television, and by means of interactions with classmates and classroom visitors representing diverse perspectives.

Lasting Early Effects of Experience versus Transient Early Effects of Experience

A number of theories propose that experiences early in life are especially important, leading to lasting effects. One example comes from Freud's (1938) theory, which explained adult psychopathology in terms of events that occurred early in life. Other examples are theories about how language exposure and deprivation (Bortfield & Whitehurst, 2001; Neville & Bruer, 2001; Snow, 1987), perceptual experiences and deprivations (Bateson & Hinde, 1987), or loss of a mother early in life (Bowlby, 1969) can influence a child. According to this view, there are periods of time when stimulation must occur if a specific competency is to develop. This is referred to as a **critical period**. There are also times in life when stimulation has more impact on a specific competency than at other times. This is referred to as a **sensitive period**.

The concept of critical or sensitive periods has come under scrutiny in recent years. Many researchers have concluded that there are probably few critical or sensitive periods for human learning and intellectual development in that humans have high potential to learn throughout the lifespan (Bruer, 2001). In fact, in recent years, thinking about early experiences has shifted. Rather than hypothesizing that not having an experience might undermine future development, thinking has focused on how having enrichment experiences during early childhood can increase future learning. Thus an important question for educators interested in early development is whether the effects of early childhood education make a long-term positive difference. The evidence is that they, in fact, do make a difference. High-quality early childhood education positively impacts later school achievement and success—for example, in reading and math (Barnett, 2002). A key point is that program quality matters (Zigler, Finn-Stevenson, & Hall, 2002). Early childhood education is best when class sizes are smaller and long-term effects are more likely when teachers are well qualified and continue to receive professional development to increase their skills even more. Effective programs also involve parents. The best results are obtained when at-risk children (e.g., economically disadvantaged children, children who were low birthweight) experience high-quality early education for the majority of the preschool years (Barnett, 2002).

Some extreme claims about the lasting early effects of experience, however, have not been supported by research. For example, a popular belief that mother–infant contact in the first few moments and hours after childbirth is essential for mother–infant bonding to occur is not true (Goldberg, 1983). Another popular belief is that second-language acquisition is only possible during childhood. In fact, some researchers have found that adults can acquire certain aspects of second languages much more quickly than young children (McLaughlin, 1977, 1984; see Chapter 7), and some of the evidence does not support abrupt shifts in abilities to acquire a second language when moving from childhood to adulthood (Hakuta, 2001).

Finally, returning to the issue of early childhood education, some have tried to make the case that if high-quality early childhood education does not occur during the preschool years, subsequent high-quality experiences in later childhood or even adulthood will not be effective. That is not the case (Bruer, 1999; Farran, 2001). Even so, the effects of early childhood education for the least economically advantaged children and most at-risk children (children from low socioeconomic homes who were also low birthweight) are larger than for other children. Thus it is important to make high-quality early childhood education available to economically disadvantaged children (Barnett, 2002).

Environmental Influences: A Closer Look

The environment can affect development in many ways. Entire fields of study are devoted to each of the environmental factors described in this section. All that can be accomplished here is a brief introduction to each of these factors and the admonition that these components completely interrelate with one another. Scientists and writers separate them so they can simplify their description of the environment and their analysis of it. Although we must discuss one factor at a time here, keep in mind the many ways these environmental factors can relate to one another.

Historical Era

The time period in which we live is an important determinant of our development (Baltes, Lindenberger, & Staudinger, 1998). Children born in North America in 2005 are growing up in a world in which they will experience a great deal of schooling. They are growing up in a world surrounded by sophisticated technology that those born in earlier eras never could have dreamed of. Children born in North America in the 21st century are growing up in countries in which literacy is high. Literate parents can learn about factors that affect the development of their children, including how to protect their children from disease and injury (Grant, 1989). Historical era matters in development.

Culture

Culture surrounds the child, affecting every aspect of his or her development. In recent decades, developmental psychologists have studied how children's thinking is influenced by cultural factors. How culture determines mathematics achievement has been studied in especially great detail. The impact of culture can be apparent even in individual lessons. For example, when fourth-grade and sixth-grade students in Japan and in the United States experience the same mathematics lesson (in their native languages, of course), what Japanese children remember from the lesson is different than what the U.S. students remember. Japanese students tend to remember the most important parts of the lesson, whereas U.S. students are much less selective in what they remember, remembering more irrelevant information than Japanese students (Yoshida, Fernandez, & Stigler, 1993). For a more detailed analysis of this issue, see the Considering Interesting Questions special feature (Box 1.1).

Another example to illustrate this point is that Japanese middle-school teachers emphasize the development of endurance, tenacity, perseverance, and the need to formulate goals about the future more than do U.S. middle-school teachers (Letendre, 2000). Compared to their Japanese counterparts, U.S. middle-school teachers encourage students to think about personal identity issues and to develop their self-esteem. Perhaps not surprising, the self-esteem of U.S. middle-school students tends to be higher than the self-esteem of Japanese middle-school students (Letendre, 2000). Also, not surprising, however, is that U.S. adolescents often seem directionless—wanting to be successful in the future but not really knowing how to prepare for the demands they must meet to be successful (Schneider & Stevenson, 1999). Spend a day in a U.S. middle school and another in a Japanese middle school, and it will be easy to see the difference between the two school cultures: there are more arguments, rebellions, and disciplinary episodes in U.S. middle schools, greater constraint in Japanese middle schools (Letendre, 2000).

Family

Typically, a young child's family is closer to the child than anyone else. And the evidence is overwhelming that family relations make an enormous difference in children's development (see Chapter 10). For example, educational researchers have amassed considerable evidence that the family environment exerts a tremendous influence during the preschool years on children's **emergent literacy** skills. Emergent literacy skills refer to what children know about reading and writing even before they receive formal instruction in reading and writing. The development of emergent literacy is an important beginning in learning to read, permitting a good start when formal reading instruction begins in kindergarten and first grade.

What types of family environments support the development of emergent literacy? The most supportive environments are marked by (1) rich interpersonal experiences with parents, brothers and sisters, and others; (2) physical environments that include literacy materials, from plastic refrigerator letters to storybooks to writing materials; and (3) high positive regard by parents and others for literacy and its development in children (Morrow, 1989). Some preschoolers even learn how to read at home (Durkin, 1966). When that occurs, parents read to the children, helping them with their "reading" and "writing." The parents frequently read themselves, valuing reading as a source of pleasure. There are books everywhere around the home and the parents take the children to libraries and bookstores. For such children, literacy began before the first birthday, perhaps through experiences with plastic "bathtub" books filled with colorful pictures or from mothers and fathers who read nursery rhymes to their children as they rocked them to sleep. These early beginnings expand into a rich array of literacy experiences, from scribbling letters to grandma to experiencing stories on grandma's lap (Morrow, 1989; Sulzby & Teale, 1991; Teale, 1978).

Considering Interesting Questions

BOX 1.1. Why Do Students in Asian Countries Excel in Mathematics Relative to U.S. Students?

In international comparisons of mathematics achievement, U.S. students do not do as well as students in some other countries, most notably Japan and China (National Center for Education Statistics, 2003). After studying the differences between the U.S. and the Asian educational systems, Harold Stevenson (1990, 1992) eliminated some possible explanations, such as differences in innate ability and in preschool education, and produced a list of likely contributors to the Asian versus American achievement gap. They include the following factors:

Curriculum

• Many more hours are spent on mathematics in Asian classrooms compared to U.S. classrooms, and Asian mathematics curricula are more difficult in that more advanced concepts tend to be introduced earlier.

• The national mathematics curricula in Asian countries are demanding, while there is localized decision making in the United States and hence greater variability in curricular expectations across the nation.

Amount of Time/Quality of Time Spent on Mathematics Instruction

• Asian students are on-task for a greater proportion of classroom time than are U.S. students. This may be due to differences in scheduling of the school days in Asia, where students have more breaks for play during an overall longer school day.

• Asian teachers are more energetic in class because they teach fewer hours per day than U.S. teachers and have much greater opportunity for preparation.

• Asian students spend more time on homework than Americans do (Chen & Stevenson, 1989).

• Asian teachers do more to relate mathematics to the lives of their students than U.S. teachers do.

• Asian teachers question their students more about mathematical concepts and about mathematics strategies that might be used to solve problems (Perry, VanderStoep, & Yu, 1993). Questioning probably stimulates deeper thinking about mathematics in Asian classrooms, beginning in the primary grades.

Values and Beliefs

• U.S. students and parents are satisfied with lower levels of mathematics achievement than are Asian students and parents (Crystal & Stevenson, 1991). Asians value achievement in school more than Americans do.

• Asians attribute successes and failures to effort; Americans are much more likely to attribute successes and failures to ability, which does not motivate effort since ability is out of the learner's control (Hess, Chih-Mei, & McDevitt, 1987; Holloway, 1988). (See Chapter 9 for extensive discussion about the importance of beliefs in effort in motivating academic achievement.)

In short, it is impossible to single out a factor responsible for superior mathematics achievement in Asian schools. Asian culture and instruction differ from U.S. culture and instruction in many ways (see also Holloway, 1988; Stevenson, Lee, & Mu, 2000).

Emergent literacy skills develop through important family experiences such as storybook reading between parents and children.

Some educational researchers have been interested in particular family experiences that they believe might be important in the development of emergent literacy. One is **storybook reading** between parents and children. During storybook reading, the reader and the child engage in rich discussions and animated conversations. They work out the meaning of the text and have a lot of fun doing it (Morrow, 1989). There is questioning, both by adults and by children; adults praise the children's efforts to get meaning from the pictures and print; adults offer information to children and respond to children's reactions to text; and both adults and children relate what is happening in the text to their lives and the world around them (Applebee & Langer, 1983; Cochran-Smith, 1984; Flood, 1977; Pellegrini, Perlmutter, Galda, & Brody, 1990; Roser & Martinez, 1985; Taylor & Strickland, 1986). Such interactions especially impact children's language, increasing their use of vocabulary and abilities to talk about their world (Whitehurst et al., 1999; Zevenbergen, Whitehurst, & Zevenbergen, 2003).

How families communicate and interact with their children has a large effect on children's cognitive development. Preschoolers who are in families that verbally interact a great deal arrive at kindergarten with better developed language, with these same children making faster progress in learning to read during the elementary years (Hart & Risley, 1995; Storch & Whitehurst, 2001).

Extrafamilial Relationships

During the preschool years, children's range of social contacts increases (Hay, 1984; McHale, Dariotis, & Kauh, 2003). The 6-month-old is capable of the beginning of social interaction, such as looking at another child and babbling in the general direction of another baby, although 6-month-olds interact so that they hardly seem to notice each other (Hay, Nash, & Pedersen, 1983; Howes, 1987a). By the toddler years, interactions with peers are generally friendly and varied, including imitations of behaviors (Brownell & Carriger, 1990; Hanna & Meltzoff, 1993; Ross & Lollis, 1989). By the grade-school years, friends outside the family are important people (Hartup, 1983; Ladd, 1990). By adolescence, peer interactions are more extensive than interactions with parents, although excellent peer relations in adolescence are often accompanied by a happy family life (Csikszentmihalyi & Larson, 1984; Kerr, Stattin, Biesecker, & Ferrer-Wreder, 2003; Rathunde & Csikszentmihalyi, 1991).

In addition to peer relationships, children have contact with a variety of adults besides their parents, such as neighbors, teachers, and physicians. For the most part, the impact of extrafamilial adults on children's development has been neglected by researchers, with the exception of one category: many children experience early childhood education or daycare outside of the home, especially during the preschool years. Just as is the case for early childhood education, the quality of daycare can have an important effect on children's development, including their intellectual development (see Chapter 10). Just as high-quality emergent literacy and language experiences at home stimulate the development of literacy and language competencies, so do such experiences during daycare (Carew, 1980; Clarke-Stewart, Lowe-Vandell, Burchinal, O'Brien, & McCartney, 2002; Honig, 1995). When the caregiver-to-child ratio is low enough so there can be high-quality interactions, and caregivers know the importance of such interactions because they are educated about child development, children's language and intelligence can improve as a result of daycare (Barnett, 2002; Divine-Hawkins, 1981).

Institutions

A variety of institutions, such as governments, media, religions, and schools, affect the life of the developing child. Federal and state *governments* have a variety of policies that can touch the life of an individual child. Government funds can provide money for prenatal care, children's health care, housing, and daycare, all of which impact many children. Governments can pass laws that protect children from abuse or environmental contaminants, such as lead paint, and can enforce those laws. Governments can also fail to provide for the needs of children. Either way, children and their development are affected.

One significant governmental intervention in the United States for the education of young children has been Head Start, which was originally funded by the federal government in 1967. A variety of assessments have documented that in the short term, Head Start programs promote academic growth. Head Start can also have a variety of long-term positive effects, although the individual effects typically are not large (Lazar, Darlington, Murray, Royce, & Sipper, 1982; Zigler & Styfco, 1992). For example, Head Start has been shown to reduce the likelihood of a student being placed in special education, becoming pregnant during adolescence, or being processed by the criminal justice system. By being good for children, Head Start is good for the government. Every dollar spent on Head Start produced six dollars in savings over the years, reducing the need for special education, aid for dependent children, and incarceration (Weikart, 1989).

Another important institution is the *media* (Singer & Singer, 2001). Unfortunately, the media can often have negative effects. A negative relationship exists between television viewing and academic achievement during childhood (Comstock, 1991; Searls, Mead, & Ward, 1985), with these negative effects greater for students from more economically advantaged homes (Anderson, Mead, & Sullivan, 1986). The declines in achievement with increased television viewing are observed across virtually all academic subjects (California Assessment Program, 1988), with negative impacts on achievement in the early elementary years sometimes carrying over into the later elementary years and adolescence (Anderson, Huston, Schmitt, Linebarger, & Wright, 2001; Bickham, Wright, & Huston, 2001; Rice, Huston, Truglio, & Wright, 1990; Wright et al., 2001). Although elementary students tend to be heavy viewers of television regardless of their ability levels, with increasing age, brighter children are more likely than children of lower ability to engage in reading and other activities (Comstock & Paik, 1991). In short, there are clear risks of television undermining the academic achievement of at least some children, with lower ability children at greater risk than other children.

A balanced appraisal of media effects on intellect requires consideration of the positive effects of television viewing on academic achievement. When preschoolers view *Sesame Street* for an extended period of time, they learn a great deal about basic literacy and numeric concepts, such as the names of letters and the meaning of numbers (Ball & Bogatz, 1970). Positive effects on literacy development, particularly for kindergarten children, are also produced by the program *Between the Lions*, which is aimed at developing emergent literacy skills (concepts of print, phonemic awareness, letter–sound correspondences) and beginning word skills (sight-word recognition and vocabulary) (Linebarger, Kosanic, Greenwood, & Doku, 2004).

Television also exposes children to occupational roles, ethnic groups, and information about settings that they would not experience otherwise—often with improvements in understanding and acceptance of diversity. Television can be used to reverse stereotypes by presenting programming in which nontraditional roles (such as nontraditional sex roles) are portrayed in a favorable light (Comstock & Paik, 1991). Informative television in general also impacts literacy positively, improving reading achievement (Koolstra, van der Voort, & van der Kamp, 1997; Wright et al., 2001). Moreover, the effects of watching such child-informative programming during the preschool years carry over at least into adolescence, with heavier preschool viewers of child-informative programming doing better in school than other children, even controlling for alternative variables that might produce boosts in literacy achievement (Anderson et al., 2001; Rosengren & Windahl, 1989). Informative television also provides opportunity for the literacy-rich to get richer: for example, 5-year-olds who are more advanced with respect to literacy are more likely to watch informative television than less literacy-advanced 5-year-olds (Wright et al., 2001). In doing so, they gain more opportunities to learn information and skills that can affect literacy development positively. In short, the media definitely can improve children's knowledge of the world.

One interesting feature of television has been evaluated in a recent experiment. Televisions now include captioning capabilities. Turning the captioning on has positive impacts on children's literacy. For example, Linebarger (2001) asked children who had just completed second grade to watch 25 minutes of a children's television program that was either captioned or not. Then the children were asked to read 10 words that had been included in the program. The children who watched the captioned television read more of the words correctly. Captioning technology permits even entertainment television to be literacy-enhancing!

Knowledge that affects children comes from other institutions as well. *Religion* is a knowledge-building force in children's lives, with the religious exposure children receive affecting their understanding of the world (Kerestes & Youniss, 2003). For example, Lipson (1983) studied children in grades four through six, some of whom were from Jewish families steeped in Jewish tradition and some of whom were Catholic and learning Catholicism. These children read passages about a bar mitzvah and a first communion. There were striking differences in recall of passages as a function of congruency with the children's religious affiliation. Children remembered better the passage consistent with their own religious background. When reading a passage from the other religious background, recall was often distorted in that the children tended to remember the passage about the other religious tradition in terms of their own religion.

The institution most often associated with children's development is *school*. Schooling is not universal in all cultures, which permits comparisons between people who have experienced schooling and those who have not. Sometimes comparisons have been made between members of other cultures and Americans; on other occasions, comparisons have been made between members of the other culture who have experienced Western-style schools and those who have not. In general, the children in these studies were administered simple learning tasks, such as learning items on lists. Measures of memory and strategy use (e.g., did the children try to rehearse or reorganize the list?) were taken in these investigations. In general, the learning and memory strategies used by Western children were only found in other cultures when children in those cultures experienced Western-style schooling (Cole, Gay, Glick, & Sharp, 1971; Wagner, 1974, 1978).

When children in other cultures experience schooling that requires a great deal of memory, however, they develop strategies matched to the learning demands being put on them. For example, some primary-grade children in Morocco attend schools in which memorization of passages from the Quran is emphasized. The most obvious way that the memory capacities of these children differ from same-age Moroccan children receiving modern schooling is in the superiority of their serial learning, which is memory for information in order. The Quranic students have developed strategies for doing the memory task demanded of them most (Wagner & Spratt, 1987). Schooling matters in the development of strategies (see also Chapter 4).

In North America, the positive effects of schooling on development are dramatically apparent when two groups of children are compared: Consider children who just completed their first year of school, children who just made the cutoff birthdate to be in school this past year. Then consider children who did not go to school this past year, having just missed the cutoff date. Which children can read better? Of course, the ones that spent the year in school having just made the cutoff date (Crone & Whitehurst, 1999; Morrison, Griffith, & Alberts, 1997; Morrison, Smith, & Dow-Ehrensberger, 1995). Going to school has a huge effect on development as a reader.

Ecological Systems Theory

Urie Bronfenbrenner (1979, 1989) offered one of the most accepted conceptions of development, *ecological systems theory*, which is summarized in Figure 1.1. Bronfenbrenner divides the environment into the following elements: the microsystem, the mesosystem, the exosystem, and the macrosystem. The **microsystem** refers to the child's experiences at home or in the daycare center. The **mesosystem** is comprised of elements, such as community, school, church, and immediate family, that relate microsystem components to one another. The **exosystem** includes elements, such as media and extended family, affecting the child that are removed from the direct experiences of the child. Finally, the **macrosystem** embodies the cultural forces acting upon the child.

An important theme in Bronfenbrenner's ideas is that the environment not only affects the child, but the child also affects the environment, changing the world at every level. When students decide to enroll at a particular college or university, they make a huge decision about their own development, a decision that will affect everything from this point forward. Preschoolers who choose cartoons every Saturday morning impact the development of their own minds and behaviors in ways different from preschoolers who choose to spend Saturdays outside with neighborhood playmates. In elementary school, some students choose to read very little and others choose to read a lot; of those who read, some choose fiction and others nonfiction. During the high-school years, some students choose to abstain from drugs, alcohol,

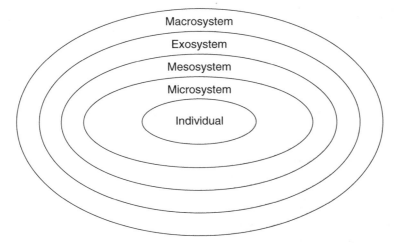

FIGURE 1.1. Bronfenbrenner's ecological systems theory divides the environment into the microsystem, the mesosystem, the exosystem, and the macrosystem, as portrayed in this figure. From McCormick and Pressley (1997). Copyright by Christine B. McCormick and Michael Pressley. Adapted by permission.

and unprotected sex, whereas others engage in one of these vices, some in two, and still others in all three. All of these choices can make a difference that affects the developing child and adolescent for life. People can have a profound effect on their own development (Bandura, 1986; Ford, 1987; Lerner & Busch-Rossnagel, 1981; Scarr, 1992; Scarr & McCartney, 1983).

Summary of the Great Debates

The debates summarized in this section have been going on for a very long time (see Table 1.1). The theorists and researchers on both sides of these issues have made excellent arguments for their perspectives. Development is very complicated. It is essential that educators appreciate and understand its complexities. Even so, the study of development often requires simplification since individual research studies are always limited in scope to remain manageable (as we will see in the next section on research methods). This is one reason why the great debates endure.

■ ■ ■ RESEARCH METHODS IN CHILD DEVELOPMENT AND EDUCATION

Since the study of child development is a scientific enterprise, every student of development must have at least a rudimentary understanding of basic research methods. It is also important for educators to be informed consumers of research. Advocates for school reform have emphasized the need for educators to employ evidence-based best practices. To do so, educators need to have at least a rudimentary understanding of how research evidence is gathered. Researchers interested in human development use diverse research methods. One reason for the diversity of methods is that not all problems can be addressed with any one method. A second reason is that some

TABLE 1.1. Summary of the Great Debates about Human Development

Nature	*Nurture*
Is development due to biology?	Is development due to environment?
Stage	*Continuous*
Is developmental change abrupt?	Is developmental change gradual?
Universal	*Culture-specific*
Does development proceed in the same way everywhere?	Does development proceed differently in different cultures?
Traits	*Situations*
Are children's behaviors consistent from one situation to the next?	Are children's behaviors determined by the situations in which they currently act?
Active	*Passive*
Do children play important roles in their own development?	Do children play insignificant roles in their own development?
Lasting effects	*Transient effects*
Do early experiences have long-term effects upon development?	Do early experiences have only short-term effects upon development?

researchers personally prefer some methods over others, perhaps because of their education or their philosophical assumptions. One way to conceptualize research methods is to distinguish between quantitative and qualitative methods.

Quantitative Methods

Quantitative approaches begin with a **hypothesis**, which is a proposed relationship between two or more variables. For example, a researcher may hypothesize that "cooperative learning is more likely to promote achievement in same-sex than mixed-sex cooperative groups." This hypothesis is then tested. Researchers often derive hypotheses from a larger theoretical orientation and/or generate them from previous studies on the topic. The investigations of the hypotheses may in turn lead to revisions and refinements of the theory or, on occasion, the discarding of a theory in favor of a new one inspired by the research results.

After researchers formulate a testable hypothesis, it is operationalized in a study. **Operationalization** refers to the process of defining variables by specifying how they will be measured or manipulated in a study. Thus, for the cooperative learning hypothesis, a cooperative learning situation is specified, perhaps mathematics classes in six fourth-grade, six fifth-grade, and six sixth-grade classrooms, each containing about 30 students. Same-sex cooperative groups are defined as four boys or four girls working together (one each per classroom). Mixed-sex groups are defined as having three boys and a girl (one per classroom), three girls and a boy (one per classroom), or two girls and two boys to a group (one per classroom). Cooperative learning could be operationalized as the teacher urging children in each small group to help one another answer the week's study problems, explaining to each other their rationales for solving problems. Cooperative learning defined in this manner might be studied for 5 weeks, comparing the learning in same-sex and mixed-sex groups, with learning defined as the mean performance of each group on end-of-week quizzes over the week's mathematics assignments.

In quantitative investigations, observations are translated into numbers that are then statistically analyzed. There are two main classes of quantitative studies. In **manipulative investigations**, usually called "experiments," researchers control variation by randomly assigning people to one educational treatment or another. **Random assignment** means that before the experiment begins, each student has an equal chance of being assigned to any treatment condition. One way to ensure random assignment of all the students in a class is to pick the names one at a time out of a hat. The first name is assigned to condition A, the second to condition B, the third to C, the fourth to D, the fifth to E, and so on.

In **nonmanipulative investigations**, researchers systematically analyze naturally occurring differences between people or settings. Comparisons of different age groups in a developmental study are necessarily nonmanipulative comparisons. We discuss nonmanipulative studies in more detail later in the chapter.

Manipulative Investigations

Often educational researchers compare a new educational intervention to conventional instruction or some other alternative instruction (Campbell & Stanley, 1966). For example, an investigator may compare typical mathematics instruction with mathematics instruction enriched by information about when and where to use the math being learned. A researcher interested in memory strategies may compare the recall performance of students taught to rehearse to learn vocabulary words to those who learned vocabulary words using their own methods. In investigations of reading strategies, the typical comparison would be between reading performances by students taught a strategy (e.g., predicting what will happen next) and those not instructed to use the strategy.

The design for a simple study in which one experimental group is contrasted with a control group contains two conditions. The factors manipulated in an experiment are the **independent variables**. In a simple, two-condition experiment, there is only one independent variable: the experimental versus control manipulation.

Independent variables are hypothesized to have effects on particular **dependent variables**, which are the performances measured in the study. Many different types of dependent variables are collected in quantitative studies. These include behavioral observations (e.g., prosocial or aggressive actions), learning measures (e.g., amount of information recalled), performances on standardized tests (e.g., achievement or intelligence tests), and responses to surveys and interviews. Sometimes dependent measures are obtained from secondary sources, such as parents or teachers. For example, parents can provide reports to researchers about the amount of homework done by their children or teachers can rate the sociability of each of the children in their classrooms.

Research studies are often much more complex than contrasting one experimental condition with one control condition. Researchers may be interested in studying several different variables, each of which can be manipulated. For example, if researchers believe that both nutritional supplements and instructional enrichment promote the learning and thinking of young children, they could conduct a factorial study. This study can be set up as a 2 (levels of nutrition) by 2 (levels of instruction) factorial design (see Figure 1.2). In one condition, children receive only the nutritional supplement; in a second condition, children receive the nutritional supplement and instructional enrichment; in a third condition, participants are given only the instructional enrichment; and in the fourth (control) condition, children receive neither the nutritional nor the instructional enrichment. This design permits evaluation of whether nutrition, instruction, or nutrition and instruction combined produce differences in children's performances measured by the researchers—perhaps on learning tasks or on an intelligence test.

STATISTICAL ANALYSES

For each condition in an experiment, two statistics are particularly important for each of the dependent variables that are collected. One is the **mean** value, which is the arithmetic average of all scores. The second is the **standard deviation**, which is an index of how much each individual score differs from the mean for the condition on average. The larger the standard deviation, the more spread out the scores are from the mean. The smaller the standard deviation, the more the scores are clustered around the mean. Thus the standard deviation is an index of the variation between scores in a condition.

How do researchers determine whether or not the differences between means are due to chance? They use the means and standard deviations in statistical tests that produce estimates of the likelihood that the experimental and control means differ at greater than a chance level. These tests determine whether there is a *statistically significant difference*—one that is unlikely to occur by chance—between the means. If there is a statistically significant difference between the experimental and the control group performances, researchers can draw the conclusion that there is a good chance the experimental treatment *caused* the difference in performance. In general, unless there is a 95% chance that the difference is not random (therefore, the chance of an error is 5%—an error rate of $p < .05$), social scientists are reluctant to conclude the difference is real. Often, researchers require even a more stringent standard, such as 99% certainty (an error rate of $p < .01$).

In addition to significance testing as just described, researchers sometimes also calculate the **effect size** that is observed in a study. Why compute effect size if the difference is statistically significant? If a study has a very large number of partici-

FIGURE 1.2. Design of a 2 (levels of nutrition) by 2 (levels of instruction) study.

pants, it is possible for even small effects to be statistically significant. Effect size, however, is not determined by the number of participants in a study. One way to determine effect size is by comparing the size of the difference between the experimental and control means with the size of the standard deviation for the control condition. For example, if the experimental students average 65% on a posttest, with a standard deviation of 15, and the controls averaged 50%, with a standard deviation of 20, the effect size would be 0.75—that is (65% – 50%) / 20. If effect size exceeds 0.9, the difference between the means is usually considered to be large; if effect size is between 0.4 and 0.9, the difference is often described as moderate in size; and if effect size is less than 0.4, the difference is considered small (Cohen, 1988). In reading reports of research studies, the informed consumer considers the effect size as well as the statistical significance.

In recent years, those interested in school reform have emphasized the value of experimentation in educational research because it provides stronger evidence for cause and effect (Mosteller & Boruch, 2002). Although some educational interventions have been evaluated in true experiments—for example, dozens of true experiments provide evidence that phonics instruction improves beginning readers' abilities to read words (National Reading Panel, 2000)—most educational interventions will only be evaluated in a few experiments at most (Cook, 2002). Experiments are expensive relative to other types of research. Moreover, sometimes it is not possible to conduct experiments. For example, some suggest Catholic schools produce better educational outcomes than public schools (see Pressley, 2002, for a review). For many reasons, however, it is impossible to assign students randomly to attend Catholic versus public schools. When random assignment is impossible, researchers employ nonmanipulative techniques. In recent years, understanding has increased about how to conduct maximally informative nonmanipulative studies (Shavelson & Towne, 2002).

Nonmanipulative Investigations

Some significant developmental questions must be studied using nonmanipulative techniques since random assignment to the variables of interest is not possible. For example, if a researcher is interested in the effects of social class, race, age, or gender on educational achievement, it is impossible to randomly assign students to these socioeconomic or biologically determined categories. People can differ in still other ways, leading to other interesting variables that can predict important outcomes. For example, psychologists have devised tests to classify people as more and less intelligent (see Chapter 8). Intelligence testing remains important to educators because it predicts success in school. Sometimes researchers conduct studies to classify people based on differences in how they process information. For instance, people differ in their use of memorization strategies, reading comprehension processes, and problem-solving tactics. People can be classified as rehearsers, elaborative rehearsers, and imagery users (see Chapter 4). These differences in how students process information also predict memory performance: rehearsers do not remember lists as well as people who integrate list items into memorable mental images.

Researchers also use individual differences in information processing to test theories. For example, suppose a researcher hypothesizes that construction of mental images during reading improves understanding of ideas in the text. If that is true, children who naturally construct mental images while they read should comprehend what they read better. In fact, they do (Sadoski, 1983, 1985). There is a relationship called a **correlation** between the two variables, use of imagery and text comprehension. In Sadoski (1983) the correlation between fifth graders' reported imagery and their comprehension and recall of text was +.37. What does this mean?

A **correlation coefficient** is used to summarize relationships between two variables and can range from –1.00 to +1.00. The greater the absolute value of the correlation coefficient, the greater the relationship between the two variables. A correlation coefficient of 0 implies no relationship between the two variables, but the closer the value is to either a –1.00 or a +1.00, the stronger the relationship. For instance, a correlation of .80 (or –.80) is high, .40 (or –.40) is moderate, and .10 (or –.10) would be low. When a correlation is positive, it means that high values on one variable are associated with high values on the other variable. For instance, time spent studying is positively correlated with test performance in that more time spent studying for a test is associated with higher test scores. When a correlation is negative, it means that high values on one variable are associated with low values on the other variable. For instance, test anxiety is negatively correlated with test performance in that more test anxiety is associated with lower test performance. So, in the case of Sadoski (1983), the relationship between mental imaging and text comprehension and recall was moderate in size and positive. The fifth graders who reported creating more images while they read comprehended and recalled more text. The presence of a correlation, however, does not prove a causal relationship. For example, in the case of the correlation between construction of mental images and text recall it is possible that children who naturally use imagery are more intelligent or deeper thinkers. If so, their greater comprehension could be due to greater intelligence or deeper thinking rather than their use of imagery. Still, many sophisticated statistical analyses use correlational techniques to create complex models showing how variables relate to each. These models increase our understanding of how developmental change takes place.

Evaluating Quality of Quantitative Investigations

How can the quality of quantitative research be evaluated? A number of characteristics define a good study described as follows:

OBJECTIVITY OF VARIABLES

Objectivity is the use of measures that are publicly observable and clearly measurable. The number of times teachers assist students is objective data; if researchers ask the teachers why they intervened, the data are more subjective and open to interpretation.

RELIABILITY OF DEPENDENT VARIABLES

Dependent measures need to be reliable. **Reliability** of a measurement means that if the measurement were to be taken again, about the same score would be obtained. One reason why behavioral measures, objective performance, and standardized tests measures are more embraced by researchers is that they often are more reliable than other kinds of dependent measures such as surveys, interviews, and adult ratings of children.

One way to increase reliability is to combine observations rather than rely on just one observation. Thus, if the dependent variable of interest is learning of text, do not study how students learn one text, but rather collect data on three or four texts and combine the performances into a single score. This combined measure will be more reliable that any of the single text scores. Reliability is critical if sound conclusions are to be drawn from a study. Yet, far too often, researchers do not make certain their measures are reliable.

"BLIND" TESTING

One way to enhance the quality of a study is to assure that those collecting the dependent variables are "blind," meaning uninformed, as to important attributes of the people being tested. For example, in an experiment, the data collectors should be blind to the participants' assignment to condition. It helps if participants in the study also are blind to the hypotheses of the study and to which condition they have been assigned. Results can be very different when such precautions are taken. For example, Harrell, Capp, Davis, Peerless, and Ravitz (1981) reported large gains in intelligence test scores of children with retardation when they were administered large doses of vitamins. Unfortunately, these researchers did not employ blind testing techniques. When others attempted to replicate the outcome using appropriate blinding (i.e., of the researchers testing the children and of the children's families), no effect of vitamin therapy manipulation on the intellectual functioning of children with retardation was found (Smith, Spiker, Peterson, Cicchetti, & Justice, 1984; Zigler & Hodapp, 1986).

INTERNAL VALIDITY

When a study has high **internal validity**, there are no other plausible competing interpretations of the results. A study with internal validity does not have confounding variables (Campbell & Stanley, 1966). **Confounding variables** are variables unrelated to the treatment of interest that may be influencing the outcome. For example, if students taught to use an imagery strategy are led to believe they are being taught this strategy because they are smart, it is impossible to know whether any performance improvement is due to the imagery instructions. The difference could simply reflect enhanced self–esteem due to the comments about intelligence made to the imagery students. In this case, self–esteem is the confounding variable.

DISCRIMINATE VALIDITY

Sometimes general motivational factors are confounding variables. An improvement attributed to an educational intervention may simply be a reaction to novel teaching, due to increases in student arousal, motivation, or interest (Smith & Glass, 1987). Perhaps the improvement is due to changes in teachers' expectations that affect student motivation (Rosenthal & Jacobson, 1968). Maybe the improvement is due to students' awareness that their performance is being used to evaluate the effectiveness of the new instruction (Campbell & Stanley, 1966). In order to eliminate such explanations, researchers can include variables that should not be affected by the independent variable or be correlated with the nonmanipulated variables of interest. Why?

Independent variables are typically hypothesized to affect particular outcomes rather than all outcomes; nonmanipulated variables are typically hypothesized to be correlated with some other variables but not all other variables. If researchers can predict in advance which outcomes measured are affected by an independent variable (and which are not), or which measures are correlated with a nonmanipulated variable (and which are not), the study can produce powerful evidence to support a hypothesis. In that case, the study has **discriminate validity** (Campbell & Fisk, 1959).

CONVERGENT VALIDITY

When researchers use more than one dependent variable and the pattern of outcomes is consistent across the dependent variables, there is said to be **convergent validity** (Campbell & Fisk, 1959) or **triangulation** (Mathison, 1988). For example, suppose that a researcher is studying a method for increasing the amount children read. If the researcher observes the classrooms in the study for an hour a week and records more reading by children receiving the intervention than children not receiving the intervention, the researcher's hypothesis that the factor being studied can increase the amount of children's reading is supported. If the researcher also has teachers provide ratings of increases in the amount of student reading, and the teachers are blind to which students are receiving the treatment intended to stimulate reading, teacher ratings is another dependent variable. If the teacher rates children who are receiving the treatment as doing more reading, convergent support exists for the researcher's hypothesis. If ratings by parents of the amount of reading occurring at home are also consistent with this pattern, there is additional convergent support of the hypothesis. Three different measures consistent with the hypothesis are better than one measure consistent with it.

REPLICABILITY

Replicability is the likelihood of obtaining the same results consistently. Replicability is high when the same results are found on different occasions, and low when results differ from occasion to occasion.

EXTERNAL VALIDITY

Studies that have **external validity** resemble the real-life issue the researcher is trying to investigate (Bracht & Glass, 1968). For instance, a study of reading in college students is externally valid to the extent typical college students are reading actual college texts. If the study participants were not representative of college students (e.g., students enrolled in a remedial English class) or if the readings were contrived (e.g., passages from the Graduate Record Exam rather than from textbooks), the study would lack external validity.

Qualitative Methods

What are the key differences between quantitative and qualitative approaches to research (Denzin & Lincoln, 2000; Guba, 1990; Hitchcock & Hughes, 1989; Howe, 1988)? Quantitative approaches emphasize hypothesis testing, whereas qualitative researchers are more interested in constructing theories, often based on the perceptions and interpretations of participants in a setting. Whereas quantitative research-ers do all possible to obtain *objectivity*, qualitative researchers are more comfortable with *subjectivity*. Qualitative researchers often are attempting to develop what is called a **grounded theory**, a theory grounded in data and interpretations of data col-lected in natural situations (Glaser & Strauss, 1967).

The distinction between quantitative and qualitative methods can be fuzzy in that an increasing number of studies have both quantitative and qualitative aspects (Tashakkori & Teddlie, 2003). One example is an experiment comparing traditional elementary science instruction with science instruction that includes reading of liter-ary pieces related to the science unit (Morrow, Pressley, Smith, & Smith, 1997). In this study, the researchers used both quantitative measures of reading and science achievement (test scores) and qualitative analysis of the differences in the interac-tions in the two conditions. Mixing of quantitative and qualitative approaches is likely to continue in future research.

Development of a Grounded Theory

Strauss and Corbin (1998) summarized how to construct grounded theories. Con-struction of a grounded theory begins with the *collection of data*. Qualitative research-ers use a number of approaches to data collection. For instance, the researcher may observe behaviors in a setting of interest. In the case of a researcher interested in constructing a theory of first-grade reading groups, this may mean many visits to first grades to observe reading groups. Alternatively, the researcher may interview many first-grade teachers about what goes on in their reading groups. In some cases, the observations may be made by the participants themselves, perhaps in the form of diaries or daily journals. Of course, the methods of data collection can be combined. Many qualitative studies combine observational and interview data.

Then, the researcher goes through the data systematically *looking for meaningful clusters and patterns*—behaviors that seem to go together logically. For example, if the teacher pairs off students to read to each other, encourages students to ask one another about difficult words, and suggests that several students read and discuss a library book, these observations suggest a meaningful cluster of activities. The researcher then names the cluster. In this case, "cooperative reading" would be a rea-sonable category name for this cluster of behaviors.

Analysis of extensive observations and interviews is likely to result in a number of categories. The next objective is to *identify support for the categories* by reviewing the data. The qualitative researcher is always open to—and actually looking for—data inconsistent with an emerging category. Qualitative researchers begin their data anal-yses early in the data collection. As tentative categories emerge, they look for support or nonsupport of categories. The researchers often take the emerging categories back to those being observed and interviewed and ask them to evaluate the credibil-ity of the emerging categories. This is called **member checking** (Lincoln & Gduba, 1985). Often the subjects of the investigation can provide important refinements and extensions of the categories. As a result of member checking, the researcher may change categories or their names.

Eventually, the researcher has established a stable set of categories based on data collected to date. The task now is to begin to *organize these categories in relation to one another*. For example, the category of "teacher modeling" seems to subsume some of the other categories of behaviors such as teachers' "thinking aloud about how to decode a word," "acting out reading processes," and "acting out deciding to read for fun." Thus the category "teacher modeling" is higher on an organizational chart than the three categories it subsumes (see Figure 1.3).

Once the researcher has identified categories and placed them in hierarchical arrangement, more data are collected and old data are reviewed again. For the first-grade reading group example, it could be time to observe some more groups, adjusting the categories and their arrangements in light of new observations, interviews, and so on. The researcher continues to collect and analyze data until no new categories emerge from new observations, no new properties of categories are identified, and no additional adjustments are made to the hierarchical arrangement of the categories.

Once enough data is collected, the researcher begins hypothesizing about causal relationships between the categories of information that have emerged as related to one another. For instance, some reflection on the teacher interviews may indicate that teacher modeling is caused by contemporary teacher education practices. That is, the teachers indicated they were running reading groups as they had learned to run them in their methods classes in college. Alternatively, reflection on the interviews may suggest that teacher modeling is due to tradition. That is, the teachers claimed they were running reading groups consistent with what they had experienced as children. Or perhaps the interviews indicate that teacher modeling is due to in-service resources, since the teachers reported that there had been many in-services on teacher modeling. Teacher modeling is not only caused but also in turn causes reactions. Thus perhaps students begin to model reading processes to one another. The qualitative researcher evaluates all the various causal possibilities, actions and reactions, against all of the available data as completely as possible. Those that are supported by the data are retained; those that are not are discarded. This continues until the point of **theoretical saturation**, when all the data are explained adequately.

Eventually, the qualitative researcher must report the data in a way that can be easily understood. The researcher must identify a key category or categories around which to tell the story. These must be in sufficient detail to reflect the richness of the data analysis. This emerging story should be member-checked as well, until there is eventually a tale that seems reasonable to researchers and participants. See the Applying Developmental Theory to Educational Contexts special feature (Box 1.2) for an example of qualitative research.

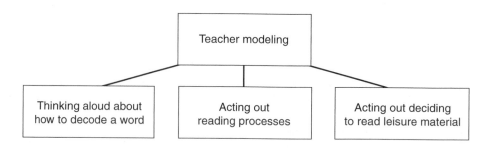

FIGURE 1.3. An organizational chart where the category of teacher modeling subsumes three categories of observations. From McCormick and Pressley (1997). Copyright 1997 by Christine B. McCormick and Michael Pressley. Adapted by permission.

Applying Developmental Theory to Educational Contexts

BOX 1.2. Difficulties in Communications between Schools and Minority-Group Parents: An Example of a Qualitative Approach

Beth Harry (1992) used a qualitative approach to study potential miscommunications between schools and minority parents, miscommunications that reduce the likelihood of positive relationships between schools and families. Harry focused on the interactions between schools and 12 Spanish-speaking, Puerto Rican American families whose children were enrolled in special education. Such intensive study of a relatively few families is consistent with the qualitative approach to research. She conducted interviews with these families, made observations, and studied the children's school records as part of a large-scale effort to understand how these families interacted with the schools and understood those interactions. Harry alternated between data collection and analyses, changing tactics to take advantage of opportunities that might be revealing. Such flexibility in method is characteristic of qualitative studies. Her findings were quite striking:

　1. The U.S. schools seemed impersonal and uncaring to the parents compared to schools they remembered in Puerto Rico. The U.S. schools often made errors in classification of the students in these families, and these errors undermined parental trust. For example, children were "promoted" by mistake and subsequently returned to their previous grade level. Because these parents tended to defer to authority figures, their concerns were not aired. Ironically, the respect of these parents for the professionals they encountered in the school, respect that resulted in the parents not challenging the professionals, increased the lack of trust felt by parents.

　2. The written communications from the schools were off-putting to these parents, in part because the letters were in English, which required finding someone to interpret them. The letters were also filled with educational jargon embedded in text that was above the readability level of many parents.

　3. Parents often felt that they had not received critical information about their children. Sometimes the information had in fact been provided but was not understood. Other times it was provided incompletely. Sometimes the messages were mixed.

　4. Many of the parents withdrew from interactions with the school and increasingly felt alienated.

　The results of this qualitative study are shocking, especially when it is recognized that the effective education of disadvantaged children is most likely to be successful when there are coordinated efforts between schools and families. The qualitative research approach can reveal important factors in child development and education.

Evaluating Quality of Qualitative Investigations

Just as it is possible to evaluate the quality of quantitative studies, it is also possible to evaluate qualitative studies and on similar dimensions. The language is different, however (Guba & Lincoln, 1982; Lincoln & Guba, 1985). Thus, rather than worrying about internal validity, qualitative researchers are concerned with **credibility**. The stronger the case that the grounded theory captures the reality of the situation studied, the greater the credibility of the study. Rather than external validity, the qualitative researcher values **transferability**, which is a measure of how representative the setting is. Evaluating transferability means deciding whether the analysis would apply somewhere else, which may require data collection in another setting. **Dependability** is the qualitative researchers' term for replicability. The qualitative researcher must convince others that most people would come to the same conclusions based on the data. **Confirmability** is the term used instead of objectivity. Confirmability is generally high when triangulation occurs in the study—that is, when multiple indicators are used to buttress conclusions.

Specific Approaches to Developmental Research

Without a doubt, the most frequent variable studied by researchers interested in development is age. Since age cannot be manipulated, causal conclusions about effects due to age are not possible. This makes conceptual sense, for age itself cannot cause anything (Wohlwill, 1973). Age can only index potential causal mechanisms, most obviously biological maturation. Thus walking is not caused by being 9 months of age (or 10 months, or 11 months, or whenever the particular child begins to walk), but, in part, because of motor maturation, which can be indexed by age.

Cross-Sectional Approach

Age differences are sometimes examined at one point in time between different people who differ in age, for example, a study of 5-year-olds, 10-year-olds, and 15-year-olds in which all data was collected in 2006. This is an example of the **cross-sectional approach** to the study of development. A strength of this approach is that data across the entire age range of interest can be collected right now. This contrasts with the most popular alternative approach to the study of development, the longitudinal approach (Baltes, Reese, & Nesselroade, 1988; Miller, 1987).

Longitudinal Approach

In the **longitudinal approach**, the same people are followed for an extended period of time, for example, from when they are 5 years of age until they are 15. The strength of this approach is that it permits study of *developmental change* rather than only age differences (Wohlwill, 1973). Thus longitudinal studies provide information about changes within people that cross-sectional studies cannot provide.

Given such an advantage, it might seem that all developmental research should be conducted using longitudinal methods. In fact, there are many more cross-sectional than longitudinal studies. The most important reason is that *it takes much longer to produce information* about relationships between age and behavior using the longitudinal approach. The greater the developmental span of interest to the researcher, the greater the problem. Thus, for researchers interested in cognitive development from middle childhood to old age, a single longitudinal study over this interval would consume more than an entire career!

Besides the longevity of the researcher, the *longevity of the participants* must be considered. In mobile societies, maintaining a sample of participants for any period of time can be a real problem. Even when people do not move, sometimes they choose to discontinue their participation in a study. On the other hand, those who are willing to remain in a longitudinal study *may not be representative of the original population sampled*. That is, those willing to undergo repeated testing may be different from people who have a lower tolerance for long-term testing or simply cannot be bothered with continuing in a study. When a large proportion of a sample is lost to a study because they have moved, it is likely that those who did not move were different from those who did. Another concern is that developmental changes in a longitudinal study may be due to *practice effects* with the tests or becoming accustomed to observation by researchers.

Even if there are no practice effects, the measures collected in a longitudinal study may become progressively more problematic as the study continues. For many issues in human development, new (and often better) measures are being developed. Moreover, the hypothesis being studied may be less exciting as a study continues. Hypotheses that seem interesting today may not be so important in the years and decades ahead. Because *a longitudinal study is tied to the measures and hypotheses that were in vogue when the study began*, it is possible that years of effort will produce results viewed as uninteresting or unimportant by the scientific community when the longitudinal study is finally completed.

Longitudinal studies are also *financially expensive* relative to cross-sectional studies. A longitudinal study must be funded for many years before there are definitive outcomes. Typically, research grants are provided for periods of 1 to 5 years, far shorter than the time needed for longitudinal studies of long-term development. In an environment in which research funds are generally scarce, only the most important of longitudinal research questions compete favorably for continuous funding. We stress, however, that some important developmental issues only can be addressed by longitudinal study. Thus some developmental researchers investigate how certain variables are related to later developmental outcomes in longitudinal studies. See the Applying Developmental Theory to Educational Contexts special feature (see Box 1.3) for an example.

Because of the disadvantages of the longitudinal approach described above, many researchers choose to conduct cross-sectional investigations of development. Researchers are aware, however, that the outcomes obtained in a cross-sectional study can be very different from the outcomes obtained in a longitudinal investigation. See the Considering Interesting Questions special feature (see Box 1.4) for an example.

Combined Longitudinal and Cross-Sectional Approach

A methodology favored by researchers interested in development across the adult lifespan is to combine cross-sectional and longitudinal methodologies (Schaie & Parham, 1977). For example, begin studying samples of 5-year-olds, 10-year-olds, and 15-year-olds today. The result is cross-sectional data (see Figure 1.4). Follow up the 5-year-olds and the 10-year-olds in 5 years, who would then be 10- and 15-year-olds, respectively. Add a new group of 5-year-olds at that point. What you will then have in 5 years is longitudinal data on two samples (on the original 5- and 10-year-olds) and a new set of cross-sectional data on 5-, 10-, and 15-year-olds. Then, 5 years later, follow up again, this time seeing the original 5-year-old sample for a third time, revisiting the new 5-year-old sample who would then be age 10, and adding still another sample of 5-year-olds. At that point, you would have 10 years of longitudinal data on the original 5-year-olds, providing longitudinal information on that group for the entire span of development of interest in the study; you would also have 5 years of longitudinal data on the original 10-year-olds (between 10 and 15 years of age) and from the 5-year-olds added at the second testing

Applying Developmental Theory to Educational Contexts

BOX 1.3. What Does High-School Underachievement Predict?: An Example of a Longitudinal Study

McCall, Evahn, and Kratzer (1992) analyzed data from a study begun in 1965–1966 in the State of Washington. They obtained achievement and ability data on more than 6,000 high-school juniors and seniors who spanned the entire range of achievement. The sample included three broad categories of students: (1) overachievers who had better grades relative to their expected ability, (2) ability-consistent achievers whose grades and abilities were consistent, and (3) underachievers whose grades were worse than would be expected on the basis of their ability. Thirteen years later, the researchers located and collected information from many of the original participants—a huge undertaking!

What happened to the underachievers? They continued to underachieve. For example, they made less money as adults than their former classmates who were ability-consistent achievers. Their jobs had less status than the jobs of ability-consistent achievers. They had obtained less postsecondary education than ability-consistent achievers. Underachievers were about 50% more likely than ability-consistent achievers to divorce in the 13 years following high school. Yes, there were exceptions to this general pattern. Underachievers who valued education, came from families that valued education, participated in high-school activities, and were confident that they could go on to complete college did seem to catch up after high school, with their incomes, job status, and marital stabilities resembling those of the ability-consistent achievers more than those of the other underachievers. Still, this was a small proportion of underachievers. In general, underachievement in high school predicts future economic and personal difficulties. This type of finding was only possible through longitudinal study. Of course, an immediate question is whether these outcomes might not be cohort-specific. That is, would the same pattern of consistent underachievement be obtained if high-school graduates from the mid-1980s were evaluated today? We cannot know from the McCall and colleagues (1992) data because they were collected on only one cohort of young adults.

(between 5 and 10 years of age). You would have a total of three cross-sectional comparisons between 5-, 10-, and 15-year-olds!

But you have something else: a way to determine whether there are cohort effects. **Cohort effects** refer to children who are born in the same time being influenced by a particular set of historical or cultural conditions. Thus research results based on one cohort may not apply to others growing up in different times. If there are no cohort effects, then 5-year-old performances should have been about equal at each testing, as should 10-year-old and 15-year-old performances. If there are cohort effects, then there would be differences between the 5-year-old means as a function of time of testing, between the 10-year-old means as a function of time of testing, and between the 15-year-old means as a function of time of testing. To the extent that there are cohort effects, the case strengthens that environmental factors play an important role in determining the behavior being studied. To the extent there are cohort effects also points out an important additional limitation of simple longitudinal studies: outcomes obtained with any particular cohort might not generalize to another cohort. If a single longitudinal sample is studied, the results could reflect development per se or development only at that historical moment. Recall the importance of historical moment in determining development, as described earlier in this chapter.

Considering Interesting Questions

BOX 1.4. Does Intelligence Decline during Adulthood?: Different Answers as a Function of Methodology

As a young adult, do you expect to be smarter as you grow older, or do you expect that your intelligence will decline with increasing age during adulthood? Perhaps it will stay the same? For many, the intuitive answer to this question is that intelligence should either stay the same (if intelligence is determined by genetic mechanisms that are insulated from other factors) or perhaps even increase (if experience really is a determinant of intelligence). When psychologists administer intelligence test items to adults across the lifespan in cross-sectional studies, however, the results are surprising. In general, with increasing age after the age of 20, the number of intelligence test items answered correctly declines (Schaie, 1959).

When intelligence is studied longitudinally, however, the results are very different. In that case, collapsing across all types of items on an intelligence test, intelligence seems not to decline or increase beyond age 20 until very late in life (Botwinick, 1977). Yes, a 35-year-old person answers fewer intelligence test items correctly from today's intelligence test than does a 25-year-old, but when today's 25-year-old is 35, she or he will answer more items than today's 35-year-old answers (Schaie & Labouvie-Vief, 1974). There is a cohort effect, such that intelligence test items are better matched to the experiences of the current young adults than to older adults. The cross-sectional differences in intelligence test performance (e.g., the difference favoring today's 25-year-old over today's 35-year-old) is due to a cohort effect. The difference today between the 25- and 35-year-old groups has nothing to do with changes in intelligence as a function of development. Only longitudinal data tap such developmental changes.

In summary, the perspective on the development of intelligence across the lifespan changed entirely once longitudinal data were contrasted with cross-sectional data. The methodology used to study a phenomenon can make a huge difference in the conclusions that are drawn.

Subjects born	Time of testing		
	Now (2006)	5 years from now (2011)	10 years from now (2016)
1991	15-year-olds	Exited study	Exited study
1996	10-year-olds	→ 15-year-olds	Exited study
2001	5-year-olds	→ 10-year-olds	→ 15-year-olds
2006	Not yet in study	5-year-olds	→ 10-year-olds
2011	Not yet born	Not yet in study	5-year-olds

FIGURE 1.4. In this combined cross-sectional longitudinal design, can you find the cross-sectional comparisons? (Hint: Look in the columns for three separate cross-sectional comparisons of 5-, 10-, and 15-year-olds.) Can you find the longitudinal comparisons? Can you find the data that allow you to conclude whether there is a cohort effect apparent at the 5-year-old level? (Hint: Look at each place in the study when 5-year-old data are collected.)

Much more information about development is generated using the combined cross-sectional and longitudinal approach than by either simple cross-sectional or longitudinal methods. Because of the expense and problems associated with the combined approach—basically all the same problems associated with the longitudinal approach plus the additional expense of continuously adding samples with each new wave of data collection—the combined method is used rarely in the study of child development despite its analytical power.

Summary of Research Methods in Development and Education

There are two major classifications of quantitative studies: manipulative and non-manipulative. Random assignment is the key characteristic of a manipulative study. Manipulation of variables, however, is sometimes not possible. The best quantitative studies are simultaneously high on internal and external validity, report outcomes proven to be reliable, and use a variety of objective measures so that triangulation is possible. Sometimes in quantitative studies a relationship between two variables is indicated in a correlation coefficient.

Quantitative research focuses on testing theories using objective techniques. In contrast, qualitative researchers use subjective interpretation to construct a grounded theory that is verified through member checking. The best qualitative studies are credible and produce outcomes that are transferable, dependable, and confirmable. Consult Table 1.2 for a list of questions to consider when reading reports of research.

Longitudinal and cross-sectional approaches to research are specific to the study development. In the cross-sectional approach, people of different ages are studied at the same point of time. In the longitudinal approach, the same people are studied for an extended period. Although the longitudinal approach allows the researcher to

---

TABLE 1.2. Questions to Ask Yourself as You Read a Description of a Research Study

What research approach was used?
   Quantitative, qualitative, or both?

Depending on your answer to the first question, select questions from the following:
   Is the study manipulative or nonmanipulative?
   Was random assignment used?
   Were any statistical tests significant?
   How large was the effect size?
   Are there any confounding variables?
   Is there evidence of blind testing?
   Are the measures and procedures reliable, valid, and objective?
   Is there evidence of triangulation?
   Can the results be generalized to real-life situations?
   If different age groups are used, is the study longitudinal or cross-sectional?
   Do the data fit the story told?
   Is there evidence of member checking?
   Are the results credible, transferable, dependable, and confirmable?

directly study developmental change (and the cross-sectional approach does not), the longitudinal approach requires a longer investment of time, has a greater likelihood of losing research participants, and is more expensive than the cross-sectional approach. Developmental researchers must always be alert to potential cohort effects, differences due to belonging to a particular *cohort* (a group of people born at the same time) rather than to other factors.

■ ■ ■ REVIEW OF KEY TERMS

cohort effects Effects due to children born in the same time being influenced by a particular set of historical or cultural conditions.

confirmability In a qualitative study, the point at which multiple indicators all support the same conclusion.

confounding variables Variables unrelated to the experimental treatment that may be influencing its outcome.

convergent validity Consistency of patterns of outcomes across more than one dependent variable.

correlation A relationship between two variables.

correlation coefficient A number, ranging between –1.00 and +1.00, that indicates the size and direction of a relationship between two variables.

credibility The degree to which the grounded theory generated by qualitative research captures the reality of the situation studied.

critical period A time period of great sensitivity to environmental input where stimulation must occur for a specific competency to develop.

cross-sectional approach The study of developmental differences carried out by examining age differences among different people at different age levels at one point in time.

dependability In qualitative research, the strength of the argument that most people would come to the same conclusion based on the data.

dependent variables Variables measured to determine the effects of the independent variable.

discriminate validity Pattern of outcome in which variables that should not be affected by the independent variable are not affected.

effect size A measure of the size of a mean difference between experimental and control conditions that allows for comparisons across studies.

emergent literacy The reading and writing behaviors observed in infancy through the preschool years that develop into literacy.

exosystem In Bronfenbrenner's ecological systems theory, environmental influences such as media that affect the child but that are removed from the direct experiences of the child.

external validity In a research study, the criterion standard of resembling closely the real-life issue the researcher is trying to investigate.

grounded theory A theory constructed from interpretations of data.

hypothesis A proposed relationship between two or more variables.

independent variables The factors that are manipulated in an experiment.

internal validity In a research study, the criterion of there being no other plausible interpretations of the results.

longitudinal approach The study of developmental differences carried out by following the same people for a period of time.

macrosystem In Bronfenbrenner's ecological systems theory, the cultural influences affecting a child.

manipulative investigations Studies in which researchers control variation by randomly assigning people to one educational treatment or another.

mean An arithmetic average of all scores.

member checking In qualitative research, the practice of taking emerging categories back to those being studied and asking them to evaluate the credibility of the categories.

mesosystem In Bronfenbrenner's ecological systems theory, environmental influences such as school and church that relate microsystems to each other.

microsystem In Bronfenbrenner's ecological systems theory, the direct experiences of the child in various settings such as home and school.

nonmanipulative investigations Studies in which researchers systematically analyze naturally occurring differences between people or settings.

objectivity The use of measures that are publicly observable and clearly measurable.

operationalization The process of defining variables by specifying how they will be measured or manipulated in a research study.

plasticity Sensitivity to environmental experiences. As used in describing the brain, having fundamental physical properties, such as the size and number of synaptic connections, vary with environmental stimulation.

random assignment A method of ensuring that before an experiment begins, each participant has an equal chance of being assigned to any treatment.

reaction range The range of all possible manifestations of a biological predisposition, the range of possible phenotypes based on a given genotype.

reliability Consistency, as in a test or measure that obtains the same results consistently.

replicability The likelihood of obtaining the same results consistently, as when studies are repeated using the same measures.

sensitive period A time period of sensitivity where stimulation has more impact on a specific competency than at other times.

standard deviation An index of how much individual scores on a test differ from the mean.

storybook reading The practice of an adult reading to a young child, which is an important emergent literacy experience during the preschool years.

theoretical saturation The point in qualitative research when all data are explained adequately.

transferability In qualitative research, an indication of the representativeness of the setting.

triangulation In research studies, multiple indications of a phenomenon.

CHAPTER 2

Biological Development

Knowledge of how biology influences all aspects of life has grown tremendously in recent years. It is likely that our understanding of biological influences on human development will continue to expand at a rapid rate. In this chapter we review the issues of biological development most relevant to educators. In addition, we distribute information about biology throughout the book to highlight how biology interacts with other factors to affect virtually all aspects of development.

■ ■ ■ FOUNDATIONS OF NEUROLOGICAL DEVELOPMENT

The human nervous system begins in the developing fetus as a single layer of cells, which thicken to form the *neural plate* (Goldman-Rakic, Isseroff, Schwartz, & Bugbee, 1983). The neural plate differentiates into separate regions shortly after its initial appearance, and as it does so it folds over to form the *neural tube*. The top of the tube begins to form into primitive forebrain and midbrain; the hindbrain and beginnings of the spinal cord are formed at the bottom of the tube (Kandel, Schwartz, & Jessell, 2000). Thus the basic structure of the human nervous system is in place about 8 weeks after fertilization (Gardner, 1975; Huttenlocher, 2002). The first behaviors, basic reflexes, appear at this time as well.

Neural cells continue to multiply through normal cell division at an extremely rapid rate at this point in development—sometimes as great as 50,000 new nerve cells a second (M. Diamond, 1992; Gottlieb, 1974; Takahashi, Nowakowski, & Caviness, 2001). Such rapid cell growth is called **neurogenesis**. Through biochemical processes not yet completely understood, neural cells move to destinations in the various parts of the nervous system (Huttenlocher, 2002; Nelson & Bosquet, 2000). Most neurons will have been formed and will have migrated to their destinations by birth (Konner, 1991). Once a neuron migrates to its appropriate location in the nervous system, it develops axons and dendrites (see Figure 2.1). Each nerve cell normally has one **axon**, a stem-like structure that conducts impulses *away* from the cell body. **Dendrites**, branch-like extensions of the cell body, transmit impulses toward the cell body from other cells. Eventually, **synaptic connections** between neurons are established. These connections involve an axon meeting a dendrite, a cell body, or another axon. Once the physical connections are formed, the physical and chemical characteristics that permit transmission of impulses develop (Bourgeois, 2001; Gibson & Petersen, 1991). Then nerve cells can send transmissions to other cells via the synapse.

Neurological Development Following Birth

Compared to other mammals, humans are neurologically immature at birth and develop substantially after birth (Gibson, 1991a, 1991b). In particular, the **cerebral cortex**, the part of the brain responsible for many complex human thought processes, expands greatly after birth. In fact, three-fourths of brain development occurs following birth (Prechtl, 1986).

Neurons take a long time to mature. Some argue that it takes as long as 10 years, whereas others think it may be as long as 18 years (Gibson & Petersen, 1991). With maturity, dendrites and axons change. Dendrites start out short, tubular, and unbranched. With development, they lengthen and develop many branches. Longer and more numerous branches provide more possible pathways for transmissions to the nerve cell.

The brain is genetically programmed to expect certain forms of experience (Black, 2003; Bourgeois, 2001). For example, some areas in the brain correspond to perceptual systems, such as the vision system or the smell system; others are specialized to support a variety of affective systems, cognitive capacities, or linguistic competencies (Anastasiow, 1990; Fodor, 1983; Panksepp, 1986). These areas of special-

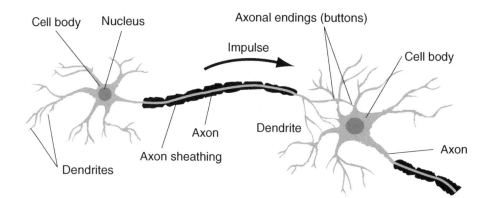

FIGURE 2.1. Axons and dendrites enable nerve cells to establish synaptic connections with other nerve cells.

ization are rich in **experience-expectant synapses** that proliferate 2–3 months following birth (Greenough & Juraska, 1986). Experience-expectant synapses are genetically programmed to respond to certain types of stimulation that are typically available in a normal environment. For example, experience-expectant synapses for the visual system are sensitive to light—a feature available in a typical environment (Horton, 2001). When light stimulation is encountered, neurons are activated and establish synaptic connections with other neurons. Experience-expectant synapses that do not make stable connections die off (Anastasiow, 1990; Black & Greenough, 1991; Crutcher, 1991).

In general, experience-expectant synapses either stabilize or die off during **critical periods,** times of great sensitivity to environmental input. For the sensory systems, these critical periods occur early in life (Bourgeois, 2001; Greenough, Black, & Wallace, 1987; Horton, 2001; Lichtman, 2001; Tychsen, 2001). For example, if particular visual experiences fail to occur early in development, visual perception is impaired for life, regardless of subsequent remediation efforts. Thus kittens who were placed in atypical environments and deprived of light for the first 8 weeks of their lives were blind once they were exposed to light (Hubel & Wiesel, 1970). Experience-expectant synapses did not function during their critical period, so they did not stabilize and eventually died off.

For humans, the critical period for some visual capabilities is considerably longer than 8 weeks. For example, if *strabismus* (a disorder involving poor muscular control of the eyes) is treated before age 5, it produces no long-term impairment (Aslin, 1981). If left untreated, however, strabismus negatively affects the visual system (Anastasiow, 1990). This happens because the sensory organs affected by the strabismus provide inaccurate information that results in the faulty stabilization of the experience-expectant synapses.

Other synapses, called **experience-dependent synapses,** are not genetically predetermined to be sensitive to particular types of information (Black, 2003; Bourgeois, 2001; Greenough & Juraska, 1986). Instead, they stabilize in reaction to whatever environmental stimulation an individual encounters. These types of synapses can be formed at any time during life and account for many of the synaptic connections made throughout life (Anastasiow, 1990). For example, the types of learning most educators are concerned with involve the creation of experience-dependent synapses.

Synaptic connections are established by repeated firing of one neuron near another (Hebb, 1949). The more often excitation of cell *A* results in the firing of cell *B*, the stronger the connection between the two and the more certain that *B* is fired whenever *A* is fired. If neuron *A* is never stimulated by the environment, it cannot fire and form a connection with neuron *B*. In most learning, more than two neurons are involved. Then **cell assemblies** are formed. Cell assemblies are closed paths, including a number of neurons synaptically connected to one another. For instance, humans can process visual information because they have formed cell assemblies that organize neurons that are sensitive to visual input. These cell assemblies are formed as a result of visual experiences during the critical period, when the cells sensitive to visual input are particularly rich with experience-expectant synapses. As noted earlier, however, if visual stimulation has not occurred within a particular period (the critical period) after the formation of the experience-expectant synapses, the synapses would have died off.

Substantial numbers of neurons die early in life. In fact, half the neurons generated before birth have already died by the time of birth. Up to half the remaining neurons in some parts of the brain die within a few years after birth (Crutcher, 1991; M. Diamond, 1992; Shonkoff & Marshall, 1990). Most of this neuron death is genetically preprogrammed: the dying cells are not critical to later functioning. Thus this phenomenon is known as *programmed neuronal death*. Loss of function, however, does not require cell death. Brain cells that continue to live undergo *synaptic pruning*. That is, the synapses that are rarely activated are lost, die off, with a great deal of synaptic pruning occurring during the childhood and adolescent years (Huttenlocher, 2002). For example, one explanation for the loss of very early childhood memories is synaptic pruning. Memories that are created before age 3 are rarely recalled, so that the synaptic connections eventually die off. Some believe that second-language acquisition may be more difficult after childhood, reflecting synaptic pruning of connections that mediate learning second languages (Huttenlocher, 2002; see also Chapters 1 and 7). It may seem counterintuitive, but the elimination of excess synapses and nerve cells might be necessary for cognitive development to proceed to maturity (Goldman-Rakic, 1987).

Maturation of the Nervous System

In addition to the physical growth of neurons, the formation of synapses, and the elimination of excess synapses and neurons, the central nervous system matures via three other mechanisms. These are myelination, the physical growth of the brain, and the development of the frontal lobe.

Myelination

Myelination is the development of a fatty sheath that envelopes a neuron (Gibson, 1991; Sampaio & Truwit, 2001). Myelin insulates nerve fibers from interference from the electrical conduction in neighboring neurons and permits increased speed of electrical conduction within the neuron (Konner, 1991). In humans, myelination begins before birth and continues for many years after birth. In general, myelination occurs first in the inner areas of the cortex and later in the outer areas of the cortex. For example, some outer layers of the cortex involved in learning associations will not myelinate until 4–8 years of age. The cortical areas of humans continue to acquire myelin at least until adolescence and may do so until about 30 years of age. Myelination occurs throughout the nervous system.

The importance of myelin becomes obvious when it is lost, such as when a person contracts Lou Gehrig's disease (amyotrophic lateral sclerosis). One result is a marked reduction in impulse speed (Konner, 1991). Since it takes longer for a nerve cell to recover after firing, the time between firings also is greater and conduction failures are more frequent. Neurological control is eventually lost.

Physical Growth

Striking changes occur in brain structure and function in the 2 years following birth (Konner, 1991). For instance, between birth and age 1, the brain doubles in volume. By age 1, it is already a little more than half the size of an adult brain. The growth rate continues to be high during the second year of life.

Is the physical growth of the brain simply a preprogrammed unfolding or does experience profoundly influence it? In other words, does environmental enrichment make a difference in brain development? Research with laboratory animals indicates that the brain is **plastic**, meaning that the fundamental physical properties of brains, including its size and the number of its synaptic connections, vary with environmental stimulation.

For example, M. Diamond (1988, 1991, 1992) demonstrated that brain weight increases when rats are stimulated appropriately. In these studies, some rats (from pups to "elderly" rats) received environmental enrichment in the form of objects to explore, climb, and sniff, and others did not. In general, environmental enrichment increased the size of the rats' brains. Enrichment also increased the number of branches in the dendrites, and thus the number of synaptic connections (Greenough, 1993). In contrast, animals raised in poor environments, lacking stimulation from other animals or objects, have retarded neurological growth.

Recent work in human cognition involving sophisticated neural imagery (e.g., positron-emission tomography [PET] scanning, which indicates which areas of the brain are functioning during various types of thinking) provides evidence for considerable plasticity in the human brain. If one part of the brain is damaged, sometimes other parts of the brain develop synaptic connections that take the place of the connections eliminated (or not made) because of the injury (Huttenlocher, 2002; Kolb & Gibb, 2001).

Development of Frontal Lobes

The neurons in the frontal lobes mature following birth (see Figure 2.2). Specifically, synaptic branching and connections become more complex by the end of the first year of life (Huttenlocher, 1979, 2002; Schade & van Groenigen, 1961). In addition,

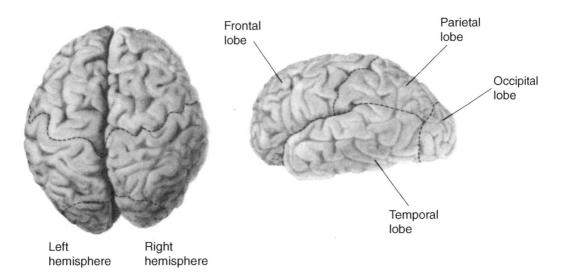

Frontal lobe

Parietal lobe

Occipital lobe

Temporal lobe

Left hemisphere

Right hemisphere

FIGURE 2.2. The human cerebral cortex is divided into left and right hemispheres, which in turn are divided into frontal, parietal, occipital, and temporal lobes. From McCormick and Pressley (1997). Copyright 1997 by Christine B. McCormick and Michael Pressley. Adapted by permission.

myelin sheathing in the frontal lobes begins to increase during the early months of life (Sampaio & Truwit, 2001; Yakovlev & Lecours, 1967).

Important changes in behaviors are associated with the development of the frontal cortex during the first year of life. For example, the human infant's ability to find an object hidden at one of two locations (A or B) is an indicator of frontal lobe development (A. Diamond, 1990a, 1990b, 1991). In a typical test of this ability, an object is hidden in full view of the infant. Then there is a delay between the hiding and when the child can retrieve the object. The object is consistently hidden in one place (either A or B) until the child is correct and then the object is hidden in the other place.

Infants under 6 months make a classic error called the "A, not B, Error." This means that they reach to the place where the object was hidden and retrieved the *last time* rather than where they saw it hidden *this time*. This error is more likely to occur the longer the delay between second hiding and when the child can retrieve the object. As children grow older, it takes a longer delay to produce the "A, not B, error" (A. Diamond, 1985). For example, the "A, not B, error" can be induced with delays of 2–5 seconds in 7½- to 9-month-old infants. By 12 months of age, the "A, not B, error" does not occur even with delays of 10 seconds. This improvement in performance occurs during the period when the frontal lobe is developing (Bell & Fox, 1992, 1997; Fox & Bell, 1990).

Discontinuities in Development

Neurological development is not continuous, changing a little bit at a time at a relatively constant rate. Rather, it occurs in fits and starts. For example, at about the time infants become less likely to make the "A, not B, error," they have a spurt in brain growth as shown by measures such as the electroencephlagram (EEG) (Bell & Fox, 1992, 1994, 1997). This growth spurt may be due to increases in the synaptic density in the frontal lobes (Diamond, Werker, & Lalonde, 1994).

Fischer and his colleagues (e.g., Fischer & Rose, 1994, 1996) have summarized the evidence that at least 13 brain growth spurts occur between birth and early adulthood. Seven of these spurts occur during the first 2 years of life. The evidence supporting these growth spurts comes from studies of EEGs and brain-imaging research. Less precise measurements, such as growth in head circumference, also support the *growth spurt hypothesis*. Importantly, each of these growth spurts is accompanied by advances in behaviors and cognition, as summarized in Table 2.1.

Throughout this book, we emphasize the idea that the development of skills depends on motivation and emotions as well as physical development. Fischer has a similar emphasis, noting that emotional development also occurs in spurts, often paralleling the brain growth spurts (Fischer, Shaver, & Carnochan, 1989, 1990). For example, separation distress (i.e., protests by children when their mothers leave) and fear develop between 4 and 8 months of age (Lewis, 1993; see also Chapter 10). What is the parallel cognitive advance (see Table 2.1)? For another example, many young children between 18 and 24 months enter the "terrible-twos," meaning that they express willfulness and anger when frustrated much more than earlier in their development. What is the parallel cognitive advance (again see Table 2.1)? Considering these parallels, Fischer's perspective on development has the potential for linking neurological, cognitive, and emotional development.

TABLE 2.1. Levels of Cognitive Development Associated with Brain Growth Spurts

Age	Behavioral-cognitive developments	Examples
3–4 weeks	New, simple reflexes develop	Infant looks at ball moving in front of face; infant grasps cloth placed in hand.
7–8 weeks	Coordination of a few reflexes	Infant hears voice and looks at eyes of speaker; infant extends arm toward ball that he or she sees.
10–11 weeks	Coordination of sets of reflexes	Infant looking at face and hearing voice smiles, coos, nods; infant opens hand while extending arm toward ball.
15–17 weeks	Coordination of reflex actions to produce single, flexible sensorimotor action	Infant looks at ball as it moves through complex trajectory; infant opens hands while extending arm toward seen ball, and in middle of reach sometimes adjusts hands to changes in ball's trajectory.
7–8 months	Coordination of a few sensorimotor relations	Infant grasps ball in order to bring it in front of face to look at it; infant looks at ball to guide reaching for it.
11–13 months	Coordination of sets of sensorimotor actions	Infant moves a rattle in different ways to see different parts of it; infant imitates pronunciation of many single words.
18–24 months	Coordination of action systems to produce concrete representations of objects, people, or events	Child pretends that doll is walking and says, "Doll walk."
3½–4½ years	Coordination of representations	Child pretends two dolls are Mommy and Daddy interacting in parental roles; child understands that self knows a secret and Daddy does not know it.
6–7 years	Coordination of subsets of representations	Child pretends that two dolls are Mommy and Daddy as well as a doctor and a teacher simultaneously.
10–12 years	Coordination of representations to produce abstract concepts	Child understands addition as general operation of joining numbers; child understands that honesty is a general quality of being truthful.
14–16 years	Simple coordination of abstractions	Teen understands how addition and subtraction are opposite operations; person integrates concepts of honesty and kindness into the complex concept of a social lie.
18–20 years	Complex coordination of subsets of abstractions	Young adult understands how operations of addition and division are related through the ways numbers are grouped and combined; person integrates several types of honesty and kindness in the complex concept of constructive criticism.
23–25 years	General principles for integrating systems of abstractions	Person understands moral principle of justice; person understands principle of reflective judgment as knowledge; person understands principle of evolution by natural selection.

Note. From Fischer and Rose (1994). Copyright 1994 by The Guilford Press. Adapted by permission.

Early Intervention

Sometimes neurological development goes terribly wrong. For instance, some children, known as "PKU babies," are born with the inability to metabolize the chemical phenylalanine, a substance commonly found in prepared foods (e.g., read the ingredients on a can of diet soda). There is a partial cure for PKU, however. It is now routine to determine at birth whether infants lack the capacity to break down phenylalanine. Once children with PKU are identified, their diets are strictly controlled so that they ingest only a very small amount of phenylalanine. With increasing age, dietary control becomes less strict (Scarr & Kidd, 1983). However, since high levels of phenylalanine can produce damage even in later childhood, dietary controls are relaxed, but not eliminated (Stern, 1985). When this intervention begins shortly after birth, general intelligence may still be mildly impaired (Diamond, 2001). For example, these children can have problems with short-term memory and self-control. If PKU is not detected until 3 years of age, however, intervention has little effect and profound retardation is the outcome (Zigler & Hodapp, 1986).

Why so much damage if the disorder is not identified early in life? Why is there less need to control diet later in life? The answer is that the myelinated nervous systems of older children are much more resistant to the biological assault from high levels of phenylalanine than the nervous systems of younger children that are not yet myelinated. Moreover, because the first several years of life are characterized by enormous growth in the central nervous system, the lack of protection that myelin provides is especially critical during these early years.

Although PKU is the best known disorder, a number of biological dietary disorders result in mental retardation if left untreated (Fernandez & Samuels, 1986). With treatment, usually involving dietary controls, the risks of retardation generally are reduced or eliminated. In addition, there are some nutritional deficiencies that can negatively impact cognitive development, especially if experienced at critical points in neurological development (Georgieff & Rao, 2001). Of course, the lesson from research on nutritional deficiencies is that children's mental development depends on adequate nutrition for pregnant mothers and children. Unfortunately, not all biological risks can be managed through early intervention—something that will become more apparent later in this chapter. The foundations of neural development are summarized in Table 2.2.

■ ■ ■ PATTERNS OF PHYSICAL DEVELOPMENT

Increases in height and weight are not linear from infancy to adulthood. In general, the rate of change in height and weight tends to be greater in the first 2 years than during the preschool and elementary-grade years. One of the most noticeable differences in the rate of change occurs in early adolescence during the **adolescent growth spurt**. This growth spurt tends to occur earlier for girls (between about 11 and 14 years of age) than for boys (between 13 and 16 years of age) (Rogol, Roemmich, & Clark, 1998; Tanner, 1970, 1989). Physical growth and development is generally completed by the end of the high-school years, with most individuals having reached close to their adult height by the time of high-school graduation. It was not always so. In the 1800s, adult height was not reached until the early 20s (Rallison, 1986).

**TABLE 2.2. Summary of Foundations
of Neural Development**

Before birth
  Production of new neurons through cell division
  Differentiation into the parts of the nervous system

After birth
  Branching of dendrites continues
  Formation of synapses between neurons continues
  Acquisition of myelin sheathing
  Death of many individual neurons
  Physical growth of the brain
  Development of the frontal lobe

Qualities of development
  Plasticity
  Discontinuity

Another indication that physical development is accelerated in comparison to earlier times is provided by data on the average age of **menarche**, the first menstruation. Over the last century or so, the age of menarche has decreased (Blythe & Rosenthal, 2000; Susman, Dorn, & Schiefelbein, 2003; Tanner & Okeefe, 1962). The average age of menarche for contemporary girls is around 12–13 years of age (Herman-Gidens et al., 1997). In contrast, in the 19th century, menarche was more likely to occur around 15 years of age (Garn, 1992; Tanner, 1962). Thus physical development varies with historical era, although our understanding of why physical development occurs earlier now is incomplete. Part of the explanation undoubtedly is due to environmental changes such as improved nutrition (Harrison, Tanner, Pilbem, & Baker, 1988).

During the adolescent growth spurt, sexual organs grow in size much more rapidly than during childhood (Brooks-Gunn & Reiter, 1990; Graber, Peterson, & Brooks-Gunn, 1996; Marshal & Tanner, 1969). In girls, breasts bud and increase in size. About 1–2 years after menarche, the ovaries begin to produce mature ova. At that point girls can first conceive children. The approach of sexual maturity during the growth spurt is accompanied by the appearance of pubic and underarm hair in girls. In boys, the testes and scrotum enlarge, with the skin of the scrotum thickening and deepening in color. The penis grows larger as well and begins to produce seminal fluid. A year or so later, the production of sperm begins (**spermarche**). Pubic hair appears, accompanied by chest, underarm, and leg hair.

In general, during infancy and throughout childhood, development tends to occur from top to bottom, with the head developing ahead of the trunk. In other

Whether or not this child reaches the maximum height predisposed by biology (nature) depends on his environment (nurture).

words, development is **cephalocaudal**, moving from head to tail. Moreover, until the end of childhood, development tends to be from the center of the body outward. That is, development is **proximodistal**, trunk development coming before the development of arms and legs, which come, in turn, before the hands and feet. During the adolescent growth spurt, however, the more distal arms and legs seem to grow at an astonishing rate (Sheehy, Gasser, Molinari, & Largo, 1999), creating havoc on the family clothes budget.

Timing of Maturation

There is considerable variability in when the adolescent growth spurt occurs (Sheehy et al., 1999). Researchers have proposed two hypotheses to explain the influence of timing of maturation upon psychological and social development (Brooks-Gunn, Peterson, & Eichhorn, 1985; Caspi, Henry, McGee, Moffit, & Silva, 1995). The first, the *maturational deviance hypothesis*, argues that adolescents who experience the onset of puberty off-time, either earlier or later than their peers, display more adjustment difficulties than their on-time peers. The second hypothesis, the *early maturational hypothesis*, suggests that developing earlier is especially a problem for girls.

It is difficult to draw clear-cut conclusions from the research exploring these hypotheses, particularly because of difficulties obtaining precise measures of the onset of puberty. In support of the maturational deviance hypothesis, adolescents who experience puberty off-time (either early or late) generally report more adjustment problems (Susman, Dorn, & Schiefelbein, 2003). In support of the early maturational hypothesis, however, early maturation does appear to be more of a problem for girls than for boys. In particular, early maturation in girls may result in stress and depression related to being unprepared for the social pressures and experiences associated with sexual maturity (Alsaker, 1992; Flannery, Row, & Gulley, 1993; Ge, Conger, & Elder, 1996, 2001; Ge et al., 2003; Ruble & Brooks-Gunn, 1982; Stice, Presnell, & Bearman, 2001). Some studies indicate that early maturation for boys can have a positive effect on their social development, in that having the body of a young man rather than that of a boy can confer positive social attention from others (Peterson, 1988: Simmons, Blyth, & McKinney, 1983).

Landmarks in Motor Development

Even more interesting than the physical changes themselves are the changes in what children can do: their *motor development*. Just as general physical development is rapid during infancy, so is motor development (Alexander, Boehme, & Cupps, 1993; Bayley, 1969; Rachat, 1989). For example, an achievement of the first 6 weeks of infancy is to be able to hold the head steady upright. In the first 6 months, babies learn to elevate themselves with their arms while lying on their tummies. They also learn to turn over and to grasp objects. In the second 6 months, infants learn to sit, to crawl, and to stand. By a year and a half, children can stand and then walk. By age 2, toddlers can scribble, begin to walk upstairs, and jump.

Motor functioning improves strikingly from ages 2 to 6. Think about the running of a 2-year-old compared to a 6-year-old. Young children run with their feet widely spaced and their running looks more like fast walking (Cratty, 1986). The running of older children is more like adult running, with the feet closer together and the running motion much smoother. Children's jumping also changes greatly in this age span. The 2½-year-old can jump a few inches in the air, but cannot coordinate his or her running with jumping, as in a broad jump. In contrast, by age 6, children can jump higher as well as run to a spot and jump forward as in a broad jump. Skills in throwing and catching also develop in this age span. By 6 years of age, children begin to use their whole bodies to throw, step forward as they throw, and begin to make subtle adjustments in the placement of their arms required to catch a moving ball (Robertson, 1984). Although 2-year-olds can scribble, by 6 years of age they can exert greater control, allowing them to print and draw pictures (Morrow, 1989). Improvements in fine motor skills during the course of the preschool years allow children to become more autonomous (Furuno et al., 1987; Newborg, Stock, & Wnek, 1984). By 6 years of age, children can use both a knife and a fork, dress themselves, and tie their shoes.

Despite this considerable progress, the motor skills of 6-year-olds are no match for those of 11-year-olds. Running, jumping, throwing, catching, and the fine motor skills required for tasks such as writing, drawing, and tool use continue to improve during the elementary-school years. Flexibility, speed, accuracy, and strength increase (Thomas, 1984). Moreover, with increasing development, coordination of skills increases. For example, skilled catching requires the coordination of running, catching, and jumping. By sixth grade, children can write in long hand and more quickly than when they were younger. Their drawings are much more complex, and they find it much easier to coordinate the skills required to play a musical instrument.

Although there are individual differences in motor competencies from infancy—with some children walking and talking much earlier than others—with increasing age, individual differences become more pronounced. It is easy to spot on the school playground the sixth graders who have better balance, are more flexible, stronger, faster, and more accurate in their throwing. In fact, the more athletic sixth graders are often better at a given sport than those who are much older (Thomas, Thomas, & Gallagher, 1993).

In adolescence, motor development continues but the differences in the motor skills of boys and girls become more apparent (Espenschade & Eckert, 1974, 1980; Haubenstricker & Seefeldt, 1986; Thomas & French, 1985). By the end of high school, boys are faster, can jump higher and longer, are stronger, and can throw farther. This is one reason why high-school physical education classes are more likely to be segregated by gender than elementary-school classes. It is important to note that the distribution of athletic abilities for males and females overlap so that there are some females who are much more athletic than many males and some males who are much less athletic than many females.

■ ■ ■ BIOLOGICAL DETERMINATION OF INDIVIDUAL DIFFERENCES: THE EXAMPLE OF INTELLIGENCE

Up until this point, we have been concentrating on the universals of human neurological development. Now we will examine individual differences in development. A number of researchers argue that individual differences of all types are genetically determined (Plomin, Defries, McClearn, & McGuffin, 2000; Plomin & McClearn, 1993). For example, some evidence indicates genetic involvement in the determination of personality differences (Bouchard & Loehlin, 2001; Markon, Krueger, Bouchard, & Gottesman, 2002; Zuckerman, 1991) as well as intellectual differences, such as individual differences in learning to read and spell (Gayan & Olson, 2003; Plomin & Walker, 2003; Stevenson, 1992; Thomson & Raskind, 2003). Intelligence, however, is the individual difference that has been most studied.

Traditionally, those who studied individual differences in intellectual functioning focused on the conceptualization and measurement of intelligence summarized as an IQ score. (Detailed discussion of IQ scores and their calculation can be found in Chapter 8.) As early as 1869, Francis Galton argued that blood relationships between geniuses were much closer than would be expected by chance. Galton concluded from these probabilities that genius was inherited. Galton's strong claims about the heritability of genius stimulated interest in individual differences in intellectual abilities.

The early years of the 20th century witnessed the proliferation of measures of intelligence (Binet & Simon, 1905a, 1905b, 1905c; Terman & Childs, 1912; Yoakum & Yerkes, 1920). Why were intelligence tests developed in the first place? Alfred Binet was trying to find a way to discriminate between normal children and children with mental retardation. Later, Terman believed the tests could also be useful in identifying feeble-minded adults. Later still, Yoakum and Yerkes designed tests to select men for officers' training from the pool of military recruits. In general, these early tests made discriminations in ability. The developers of these early intelligence tests believed that the tests were tapping biologically determined differences in functioning.

Behavior geneticists, scientists who study genetic determination of behavior, have argued that individual differences in intelligence are due more to heredity than to environment. They have used several approaches designed to separate the effects of biology and experience on intelligence (Plomin et al., 2000). We briefly review two of the most important methods.

Individual Differences in Intelligence: Heredity and the Environment

No one is much surprised if two intelligent people marry and produce intelligent offspring. But is it logical to assume that the children acquired their intelligence through the transmission of genes? Not necessarily. Gifted and talented people provide environmental opportunities to their children not available to other children. Perhaps environmental richness, not heredity, is the critical factor in stimulating the intelligence or talents of offspring. Research on twins and adopted children can help us understand the influences of environment and heredity on intelligence (Emde & Hewitt, 2001).

Twin Studies

Identical twins have the same genes because the two children were produced by a division of the same fertilized egg. When identical twins are reared together in the same family, their environments also are very similar, perhaps as similar as the environments of any two people can be. Thus the very high correlations in intelligence between identical twins (usually .80–.90 or higher) are due to both genetic and environmental determinants of intelligence. (Review the description of correlation coefficients in Chapter 1.) Sometimes, however, identical twins are reared apart. In that case, their genes are identical but their environments differ. Although the average IQ correlation (around .70) for identical twins reared apart is a little less than that for identical twins raised together, it is still a strong correlation.

Another important comparison involves fraternal twins reared together. Since fraternal twins are the product of two different fertilized eggs, they share one-half of their genes. They also have roughly comparable environments, since they are reared in the same family at the same time. The correlation of IQ scores for fraternal twins (around .60) is less than those reported for identical twins (Bouchard & McGue, 1981; Loehlin & Nichols, 1976).

Researchers use data such as these to calculate the **heritability** of intelligence, or the variation in intelligence that is due to genetic variability (Plomin, 1994; Plomin et al., 1990). The general conclusion is that roughly half the variability in intelligence is due to genes. The importance of genes is obvious from the higher correlations for identical than for fraternal twins. The importance of environment is obvious as well: the IQ scores of identical twins reared together are more similar than the IQ scores of identical twins reared apart.

Adoption Studies

What have we learned about the role of heredity and environment from adoption studies? As already noted for the study of twins, some research supports heredity as a determinant of individual differences in IQ (Bouchard & McGue, 1978). For example, the IQ correlation for parents and their biological children reared in their homes is .42. This is considerably higher than the .19 correlation between parents and their adopted children who do not have a genetic relationship to each other. In addition, the IQ correlation for biological siblings (who share 50% of their genes) reared together is .47. This is higher than the IQ correlation for biological half-siblings (who share 25% of their genes) reared together and the IQ correlation for nonbiological siblings.

On the other hand, research results also support the importance of the environment (Bouchard & McGue, 1978). For example, the IQ correlation of .47 for biological siblings reared together is larger than the IQ correlation of .24 for biological siblings reared apart. In addition, the IQ correlation of .42 between biological parents and their children when they live together is larger than the correlation of .22 when they do not live together. In general, consistent with the twin data, the adoption data indicate that about half the variability in IQ scores is due to heredity (Chipeur, Rovine, & Plomin, 1989).

The adoption data also provide support for the effects of long-term exposure to a stimulating environment. First, the longer adoptive families are together, the greater the correlations in intelligence (Plomin, DeFries, & Fulker, 1988). Second, when adopted children are raised in families with a level of intelligence higher than the adoptee's biological family, the intelligence of the adoptees tends to be higher than the biological family level. This is especially likely when the adoption occurs at an early age for the child (Scarr & Weinberg, 1976, 1983; Storfer, 1990; Weinberg, Scarr, & Waldman, 1992).

Methodological Debates Surrounding Twin and Adoption Studies

The methodology of twin and adoption studies has been criticized (Lewontin, Rose, & Kamin, 1984; Locurto, 1990; Plomin et al., 1990). For example, two key assumptions in twin studies are that identical twins reared apart experience very different environments, while fraternal twins reared together experience very similar environments (Goldberger, 1977; Grayson, 1989; Wilson, 1982). But these assumptions are not always upheld. For example, adopting families of separated identical twins often are similar in socioeconomic status to the twins' biological families. In addition, fraternal twins may lead very different lives—even during childhood. Factors such as sex, size, and physical appearance profoundly affect environmental interactions. Despite the methodological limitations of particular studies, however, replications of twin studies and adoption studies with similar results support two broad conclusions: (1) genes play an important role in determining individual differences in intelligence, and (2) the environment matters as well. The most complete behavior genetics analyses include both data from twin studies and adoption studies (Bishop et al., 2003). Table 2.3 summarizes the correlational evidence for the heritability of intelligence.

Reaction Range: Genotypes and Phenotypes

Each of us is born with a genetic heritage. The collection of genes we possess constitutes our **genotype**. The genotype specifies a potential range of possible outcomes. These outcomes, or how the genes are expressed, are called **phenotypes**. Where we end up in the **reaction range** of possible phenotypes is highly dependent on environment. According to this concept of reaction range, intelligence should be affected by the provision of high-quality environments. Let's examine these ideas in more detail.

Any given set of genes specifies a variety of outcomes, depending on the environment. For example, recall the case of children with PKU discussed earlier in this chapter. A child with PKU has the genetically determined inability to metabolize phenylalanine. If a child with PKU experiences a nutritional environment rich in phenylalanine, the result is severe retardation. If the child experiences a nutritional environment in which phenylalanine has been eliminated, normal intelligence is the outcome. Consider a second example. Heart disease has a reasonably high herit-

TABLE 2.3. Summary of Correlational Evidence for the Heritability of IQ

Identical twins, reared together	.80–.90
Identical twins, reared apart	.70
Fraternal twins	.60
Siblings, reared together	.47
Siblings, reared apart	.24
Parents and biological children, together	.42
Parents and biological children, apart	.22
Parents and adopted children	.19

ability. Suppose someone has the misfortune to be the child of parents who both suffer from heart disease. Whether this person develops coronary problems depends largely on environmental factors, such as diet, exercise, and lifestyle. That is, genes and environment interact to determine outcomes: each *genotype* has a *reaction range* of *phenotypes* associated with it (Gottesman, 1963; Gottesman & Hanson, 2005; Lewontin, 1974; Scarr & Kidd, 1983).

To summarize, humans inherit a range of possible biological outcomes. Which of the many outcomes occurs (i.e., which of the many phenotypes) depends on the environment experienced by the individual. The concept of reaction range is important for educators since teachers can help students achieve their potential—the top of their reaction range. Fortunately, we have made substantial progress in learning how to intervene to accomplish this goal.

The Effects of High-Quality Environments on Intelligence

The evidence that high-quality environmental manipulations at home and preschool increase measured intelligence, at least in the short term, is compelling (Storfer, 1990). The effective interventions include teaching parents how to read with and stimulate their children and introducing academically oriented daycare to children from economically disadvantaged homes. Gains in IQ scores are most likely to be observed at the immediate conclusion of an intervention. Typically, several years after the special intervention has ceased, the IQ scores of children participating in the intervention are no different than the IQ scores of children who did not participate, leading some to conclude that intervention programs are of little benefit (Jensen, 1969, 1972, 1973, 1980, 1992; Locurto, 1988, 1991a, 1991b, 1991c; Spitz, 1986a, 1986b, 1991a, 1991b, 1992). Others believe it is unreasonable to expect maintenance of intelligence advantages if children, as often happens, return to an environment that lacks additional intellectual stimulation. Educational interventions promoting long-lasting academic competence need to be long-term affairs (Storfer, 1990).

If intervention advantages provided during the preschool years are continued into the schooling years, intelligence gains are more likely to be maintained and school achievement increased. Some of the strongest evidence in favor of continuing interventions initiated in the preschool years was provided by the Carolina Abecedarian Project (Ramey & Campbell, 1987; Ramey, Ramey, & Lanzi, 2001). This project was aimed at increasing the intellectual competence of children who were at risk for intellectual deficiency because they came from economically impoverished environments. Children in the Abecedarian Project began their participation shortly after birth. Both those in the intervention program and those in the control group were provided nutritional support, family-counseling contacts, and medical care. The children in the intervention, however, also attended a high-quality preschool environment for the entire day throughout the year. Parent meetings were held as part of this preschool program to increase parental awareness of how to stimulate child development and use community opportunities.

Was this program successful? In general, the more total Abecedarian treatment received, the lower the failure rate and the higher the IQ at age 12 (Ramey, 1992). Moreover, those who had participated in the Abecedarian Project exhibited higher scores on both cognitive and academic measures through the age of 21 (Campbell, Pungello, Miller-Johnson, Burchinal, & Ramey, 2001). Thus the intelligence and academic achievement of at-risk children can be improved through intensive, long-term, academically oriented intervention (Ramey, Campbell, & Ramey, 1999). Does that mean biology is not a determinant of intelligence? Not at all. What it means is that children are more likely to approach the top of their reaction ranges for intelligence if they experience a high-quality environment. Humans have evolved to be sensitive to their environments, to respond to them.

■ ■ ■ DISRUPTIONS OF NORMAL BIOLOGICAL DEVELOPMENT

Sometimes biological development can go awry. Something happens in the environment that translates into a biological change that has profound, long-term implications for healthy development. Disease and injury are potential dangers from the moment of conception until old age. The study of development has increased understanding about how the timing of such trauma can determine the effects of disease or injury. Developmental psychologists have been especially interested in the effects of biological assaults during the prenatal period because it increases understanding of birth defects that make a difference for the entire life of the affected individual.

Teratogens

A critical period for adverse neurological events is the first 2–3 months of life, which corresponds to neurogenesis, when many new nerve cells are forming. **Teratogens** are environmental agents that can interfere greatly with normal development by affecting the beginnings of the nervous system. A large number of disease and chemical teratogens have been identified (Shepard, 1998; Shonkoff & Marshall, 1990; Stein, Schettler, Wallinga, & Valenti, 2002; Vorhees, 1986). In many cases, prenatal exposure to disease or chemicals will do so much damage to the developing nervous system that normal learning and development can never occur. For example, exposure to rubella during pregnancy can produce extreme retardation as well as a host of other symptoms, such as growth retardation, hearing loss, and heart disease, in the developing infant (Shonkoff & Marshall, 1990). Maternal alcoholism can result in **fetal alcohol syndrome**, which is central nervous system damage that can cause learning difficulties and even mental retardation (Abel, 1998; Streissguth & Connor, 2001). Maternal smoking during pregnancy is associated with low birthweight and expressive language difficulties (Delaney-Black et al., 2000). Children exposed to other chemical teratogens, such as lead and narcotics, experience a range of behavioral and cognitive disorders. For example, heavy marijuana use can produce fetal brain damage that affects later memory, language, and attention (Fried, 2002; Fried & Watkinson, 1990). (See Chapter 8 for a more complete discussion of the learning difficulties of children who are victims of chemical assaults.) As a general rule of thumb, substance abuse of all sorts during pregnancy is potentially teratogenic. Hence, substance abuse by pregnant women is of great concern.

Although many teratogens are most dangerous during the first trimester of a pregnancy, teratogenic effects, such as the negative effects of smoking on birthweight, can occur after the first trimester. Since teratogens can have negative effects early in a pregnancy as well as throughout the prenatal period, a woman should seek prenatal care as soon as it is clear that she is pregnant.

Malnutrition

Prenatal and postnatal malnutrition can reduce mental competency (Chase, 1973; Georgieff & Rao, 2001). Once again, the timing is important (Morgan & Gibson, 1991). Greater damage results when malnutrition occurs at critical periods corresponding to rapid development of the nervous system (Gerogieff & Rao, 2001). Children are especially vulnerable from about 6 months postconception until the second year of life, when neural cell growth via the proliferation of dendritic synapses is rapid (Dobbing, 1974; Frisancho, 1995). Furthermore, because substantial myelination occurs during the middle preschool years (3–4 years of age), this is also a period of great sensitivity to the effects of malnutrition. Children most likely to suffer malnutrition come from lower socioeconomic status (SES) homes. Long-term malnutrition is also common in developing and war-torn countries where many children exhibit lower cognitive development and reduced attentional capacity (Sigman, Neumann, Jansen, & Bwibo, 1989). Diets are not always optimal even in developed countries. It is not unusual for children to have diets deficient in important vitamins, such as A, the B complexes, C, D, and K, or in iron. Cognitive, motor, and a variety of growth problems can result from these deficiencies (Aukett & Wharton, 1995; Pollitt, 1990).

Neurological Injury

Injury can also reduce mental competency. A common form of injury is **anoxia**, the reduction of the infant's air supply during birth, resulting in a wide range of cognitive and behavioral problems (Caine & Watson, 2000). Intracranial hemorrhage is also common, especially among premature infants. Fortunately, the incidence of these types of disorders is on the decline because of better fetal-monitoring procedures and widespread dissemination of improved methods of delivery (Rosen, 1985).

For example, using ultrasound procedures, doctors can determine when an about-to-be-born baby is in a breech position. A *breech position* is any position except head-first and engaged in the birth canal. In this situation, a Caesarian birth is easiest and safest for both child and mother. Not so long ago, the delivery team only discovered the breech presentation when the baby came into view. Such deliveries took a long time, with great risk of anoxia and hemorrhage due to injury involved in pulling the baby from the womb. Technology, like ultrasound, is improving the physical and mental health of many newborns.

Premature Delivery

A number of factors cause babies to be born before they are full term, that is, before they have been in gestation for 38 weeks. The most important one is maternal malnutrition. Also, twins and triplets often are born before full term. Drug use, smoking, and poor maternal health can also contribute to the risk of premature delivery (Spreen, Risser, & Edgell, 1995).

Babies born before full term are characteristically low in birthweight relative to full-term infants, who typically weigh about 3,500 grams (7½ pounds). Any infant weighing less than 2,500 grams (5½ pounds) is considered low birthweight. It is not uncommon, because of new technologies, for babies weighing less than a 1,000 grams at birth (about 2½ pounds) to survive. Relative to full-term infants, however, very-low-birthweight infants are at risk for respiratory failure and metabolism problems. In fact, the leading cause of death among preterm infants is respiratory failure. Even when respiratory failure is not fatal, brain damage sometimes occurs due to anoxia. Premature infants are also at risk for intracranial hemorrhage and subsequent intellectual impairment caused by such hemorrhaging. The lower the birthweight, the greater the long-term risk for school failure, retardation, cerebral palsy, blindness, deafness, learning disabilities, and other health problems (Hack, Klein, & Taylor, 1995; Taylor, Klein, & Hack, 2000). One of the most frequent problems for very-low-birthweight babies is delayed development of language (Robison & Gonzalez, 1999; Vaughn & Litt, 1990). When low-birthweight children are schoolage, they exhibit delayed educational progress (Anderson et al., 2003). Prematurity is but one factor contributing to risk for low birthweight. See the Considering Interesting Questions special feature (Box 2.1) for a discussion of factors contributing to birthweight.

Interventions for Low-Birthweight Children

Children who are at biological risk at birth are more certain to thrive if they experience diverse and stimulating environments, environments with caregivers who are attentive and responsive to them (Anastasiow, 1990; Beckworth & Parmelee, 1986; Goldberg & DeVitto, 1983; Morgan & Gibson, 1991; Sameroff & Fiese, 1990; Werner, 1990; Werner & Smith, 1982). For example, a low-birthweight infant has a better chance for normal development if the parents are well educated and able to provide the advantages associated with substantial family income (Hack et al., 1995).

What might explain the benefits of high-quality early childhood environments for at-risk children? Recall that there is an overabundance of experience-expectant synapses during the early preschool years. This abundance permits greater plasticity in comparison to later in development (Anastasiow, 1990). In addition, a relationship exists between plasticity and myelination. Once myelination occurs, the nervous system is more mature and less open to change. Clearly, there are advantages to providing treatment to at-risk children early in life. Waiting until the schooling years will often mean lost opportunity, since the critical periods for stimulation will have passed.

The Infant Health and Development Project (1990) offered a compelling demonstration that a rich environment can help make up for initial biological disadvantage. This study focused on infants with low birthweights, a group at substantial risk for later academic difficulties. These infants would be more likely than their peers to have perceptual problems and learning disabilities during the schooling years (Bennett, 1987; Meisels & Plunkett, 1988; Scott, 1987). Approximately one-third of the at-risk children in this study were randomly assigned to the treatment condition and two-thirds to the control condition.

The treatment consisted of home visits during the child's first year of life. The visitor provided health and developmental information to the family, as well as other forms of support as needed. Two curricula were introduced into the home during this first year. One was a cognitive, linguistic, and social development curriculum consisting of games and activities that encouraged parent–child interaction. The sec-

Considering Interesting Questions

BOX 2.1. What Factors Contribute to Birthweight?

Whether a baby is born healthy or not depends on a number of factors in interaction. To illustrate this principle, consider the index of birthweight. There is high variability in the birthweight of infants, with many potential interacting factors (Chomitz, Cheung, & Lieberman, 1995; Frisancho, 1995):

• The most important determinant of birthweight is whether the baby is full term or not. As discussed in the text, full-term birth is determined by a number of factors, including twinning, maternal health, and substance abuse.

• Age of the mother is a critical factor in the birthweight of infants. Mothers who are less than 16-years-old are still growing themselves, and thus their growth competes with the developing fetus for nutrients. Hence, the birthweight for the children of young teens is less than the birthweight of children born to adult women. Also, the smaller, weaker pelvises of young teens increase the likelihood of premature delivery and associated low birthweight. Normal birthweight is most likely between the maternal ages of 20 and 34. Mothers who are older than 40, like very young mothers, are at risk for giving birth to a low-birthweight baby.

• A single baby has a better chance of being full term than do twins. Even if twins make it to full term, birthweight of the individual children tends to be less than single births.

• Maternal nutrition is an important determinant of birthweight.

• Maternal smoking reduces birthweight, in part because smoking reduces the amount of oxygen available to the fetus, which impairs the metabolism of proteins critical to developing tissues. Smoking dramatically affects the development of muscles.

• Maternal use of alcohol reduces birthweight, as does use of marijuana and cocaine.

• During the last trimester of pregnancy boys grow faster than girls. Hence, boys tend to be heavier than girls at birth.

• The second and third children of a mother tend to be heavier than the firstborn, with the positive effect of birth order on birthweight holding up to about the sixth-born child.

• In the United States, the incidence of low birthweight is higher among blacks than whites, with this relationship holding even when socioeconomic and prenatal care conditions are considered.

• Maternal size is more a determinant of birthweight than paternal size.

Biological determination of development is complex. Yes, the genes a child inherits can be thought of specifying a probable range of birthweight outcomes. Evidence for genetic determination of birthweight includes statistical relationships between birthweight, maternal and paternal size, and ethnicity differences that take environmental differences associated with ethnicity into account. The actual birthweight, however, depends on more than genes. It depends on many environmental factors, including maternal nutrition, age, health, and substance use.

---

ond curriculum provided child management information to parents, aimed specifically at problems parents often encounter with infants. Starting at 1 year of age, and continuing until 3 years of age, the children in the treatment group attended a child development center 5 days a week. The learning curriculum initiated at home was continued and extended at the center. The adult-to-child ratio in these centers was excellent, with one adult for each three 1-year-olds and one adult for each four 2-year-olds. The parents of the children at the center met twice a month in groups to receive information about childrearing, safety, and health.

The effects produced by this treatment were dramatic. By age 3, the intelligence test scores of treated children were substantially higher than the intelligence test scores of children in the control group. This is a dramatic demonstration of the effects of early environment on the intellectual development of biologically at-risk children. One question to ask is whether such services could be provided on a large scale. Another question is whether the gains produced by the Infant Health and Development Project treatment will persist and whether normal intelligence will translate into normal academic achievement when these children reach schoolage (Lazar, Darlington, Murray, Royce, & Snipper, 1982).

Fortunately, the Infant Health and Development Project collected longitudinal data to help answer these questions. At age 5, although there was still a positive effect of the intervention, it was not as large as it had been at age 3, immediately after the intervention. It is likely that the intervention caused the children to be at the top of their reaction range by the end of the treatment. To stay at the top of the reaction range, however, stimulation must continue. Hence the decline by age 5, 2 years after the intervention had ended. Moreover, recent analyses indicate that the positive effects of the Infant Health and Development treatment are still present at age 8, 5 years after the end of the treatment (Hill, Brooks-Gunn, & Waldfogel, 2003). Research on sustained intervention into the grade-school years, indicates that, in general, when intervention continues, the positive effects of intervention also continue (Campbell & Ramey, 1994, 1995).

Biological Risk after Infancy

Traditionally those who study human development have been more concerned with biological risks during the prenatal period and infancy than later in development. As it turns out, the world remains full of risks for children throughout their development (Bearer, 1995). They face hazards associated with food (e.g., pesticides), water (e.g., lead), and the air (e.g., secondhand smoke, asbestos). Moreover, the risks associated with these dangers are different, and often more serious, for developing children than for adults.

Virtually all organ systems continue to develop during childhood. Various hazards can disrupt normal organ development. For example, children absorb a much higher proportion of ingested lead than do adults and it accumulates to a much greater degree in the brains and bones of developing children than in the brains and bones of adults. Although there is controversy about how much lead exposure is required before there is harm, lead absorption can damage the brain and nervous system, resulting in learning problems, hearing difficulties, slowed growth, headaches, and other difficulties (Chang, 1999; Phelps, 1999; Stein, Schettler, Wallinga, & Valenti, 2002). Reducing lead levels in gasoline and paint has resulted in reduced rates of mental retardation due to lead poisoning (Alexander, 1998). Unfortunately, not as much progress has been made in curbing other environmental sources of harm for children. For example, since children consume more oxygen relative to their size than do adults, air pollutants are more dangerous for them. Children also consume more calories relative to their body weight than do adults, so food contamination is a greater risk for them than for adults. And because children eat a higher proportion of fruits, milk, and sometimes even vegetables than do adults, children are at especially great risk for pesticide poisoning.

■ ■ ■ BIOLOGICALLY DETERMINED BIASES AND CONSTRAINTS

There are many similarities in the knowledge that all people acquire and the things that people can do. The most likely explanation for these human similarities is that biology prepares humans to attend to some information more than other information and to be able to do some things and not others. Experience-expectant synapses described earlier in this chapter most likely play a large role in the development of some of these processing biases. Humans are also markedly similar in terms of certain basic constraints in cognitive processing. These constraints are linked to brain functioning.

Canalization

Some developments seem to occur in nearly all human beings. For example, motor development follows about the same time course and sequence for most babies and almost all babies develop what Piaget referred to as the "object concept," the understanding that objects continue to exist even when they are out of sight (see also Chapter 3). Waddington (1961) argued that such developments were almost completely genetically determined, or **canalized**. Imagine a ball rolling downhill in a deep canal. A great deal of pressure would be required to move the ball even a little bit up the wall of the canal. Once the pressure ended, the ball would fall back down into the depths of the canal and continue its downward course. Waddington argued that for many developments early in life, genes created something of a canal, with deviation from the canalized path very difficult to produce. Although some have challenged the concept of canalization (see Gottlieb, 1995), many human acquisitions seem to be strongly canalized, especially acquisitions early in life, including the following two examples: sensation preferences and hemispheric specialization.

Even very young babies display some forms of sensation preferences, although preferences change with development. In the case of visual stimulation, 1-month-old infants prefer stripes over a bull's-eye pattern, whereas slightly older children prefer the bull's-eye (Fantz & Nevis, 1967). With increasing age, infants increasingly prefer more complex visual stimulation (Brennan, Ames, & Moore, 1966; Hershenson, Munsinger, & Kessen, 1965; Munsinger & Weir, 1967). From birth onward, infants display a bias for contours or outlines of shapes, which is adaptive since the contour defines the shape (Banks & Salapatek, 1983). One result of these clear biases in visual perception is that from an early age humans process some types of information more than other types.

Biological preparedness is not limited to basic perceptual processing. Humans are also biologically prepared to learn the complex systems of representation that comprise language (Chomsky, 1965, 1980a, 1980b; Hoff, 2003; Tomasello, 2003). The most enduring biological claim about language is Chomsky's contention that human beings all have the competence to acquire language due to a genetically determined "language acquisition device" in the human mind. The evolution of the neural capacity to perceive and create speech also supports language and the learning of language (Lieberman, 1984, 1989). (Much more about the biological bases of language and language development is presented in Chapter 7.)

Cognitive Capacity Constraints

Short-term memory capacity, a memory store of limited capacity and duration, increases with development (Schneider & Pressley, 1997; see also Chapters 3 and 4). One way to think about short-term capacity is to consider the number of pieces of information a student can have active at any one time while working toward some cognitive goal. Or think of when you hold a telephone number in your memory while you are searching for a scratch pad to write it down. Or think of when you are juggling ideas in your head as you are trying to write a paragraph on a term paper. Case (1985, 1991) called this limited capacity **executive processing space.** Students can only perform tasks that do not require more executive processing space than they have available for use.

Case argued that executive processing space increases during development because of *practice of familiar tasks* rather than neurological maturation. As a result of practice, children can perform tasks automatically that once took considerable effort and attention. Automaticity frees up capacity for attention to tasks requiring more effort and attention. Thus, with practice, a child has greater functional capacity even if the actual neurologically determined capacity has not increased (Cowan, 2002; Kail, 2000). Children's *speed of processing* also increases with development, which in turn increases functional capacity by increasing the efficient use of available capacity. Moreover, as described in more detail in Chapter 4, as children mature, they develop *more extensive knowledge*, which also permits more efficient use of short-term capacity. That is, experiences that increase knowledge permit the more efficient and effective processing of information and thus, the more efficient and effective use of the biologically determined short-term capacity the child has. Clearly, functional capacity depends on both biology and experience! It can also depend on what a teacher does to support students as they attempt to complete complex tasks. See the Applying Developmental Theory to Educational Contexts special feature (Box 2.2) for recommendations for helping students cope with short-term capacity demands.

Hemispheric Specialization

The left and right hemispheres of the brain are specialized to perform different functions (refer to Figure 2.2). The left hemisphere is specialized for processing language and analytical information; the right hemisphere is specialized for nonverbal, visual–spatial content. Damage to the left hemisphere results in language disabilities (Bates & Roe, 2001; Foundas, 2001; McCarthy & Warrington, 1990). The left hemisphere is specialized for processing sequential and temporal content and is more logical, analytical, and rational than the right hemisphere (Springer & Deutsch, 1989). In contrast, the right hemisphere is better than the left hemisphere in processing simultaneous, spatial, and analogical information—its functioning is described by many as "intuitive."

Differences in hemispheric functioning are also associated with particular talents (Hoptman & Davidson, 1994). English majors have more blood flow to the left hemisphere than do architecture majors, who have more blood flow to the right hemisphere (Dabbs, 1980). Eye movements consistent with left hemispheric dominance are more common in English majors than engineering majors, who display eye movements more indicative of right hemispheric dominance (Bakan, 1969). Such dif-

---

Applying Developmental Theory to Educational Contexts

BOX 2.2. Helping Students Cope with Short-Term Capacity Demands

The constraint of short-term memory capacity is a fact of life. Short-term capacity difficulties, however, are more of a problem with some students, especially younger students, than others. The following are some ways for teachers to reduce the effects of their students' short-term memory constraints on performance (Case, 1985; Miller, Woody-Ramsey, & Aloise, 1991):

• *Analyze* academic tasks for the capacity demands they place on students. One way to do this is to ask students to rate how hard they had to concentrate to accomplish the task. Ask them if they were able to do other things, such as listen to music, watch TV, or talk to their mothers, while working on the task.
• *Simplify* tasks identified as complex. Break large tasks down into more easily accomplished steps that do not tax short-term memory capacity. For example, break the task of writing a term paper down into the following steps: selecting a topic, finding information on the topic, preparing an outline, writing a rough draft, revising the draft, and polishing the final draft.
• *Coach and prompt* students to help them complete complex tasks. Provide supportive materials (e.g., handouts, questions, prompts, hints) designed to reduce short-term memory load. In short, teachers can engineer materials and the learning environment to reduce short-term capacity demands.

---

ferences may have been shaped by years of processing more of one type of information over the other. If these differences predict success in some endeavors more than others, however, they could be useful in making decisions about curricular emphasis for some students. Longitudinal research on the stability of individual differences in hemispheric specialization is needed. Despite the evidence for hemispheric specialization, however, it is important to keep in mind that the two hemispheres work together (Gazzaniga, Ivry, & Mangum, 1998).

Some have argued that Western schooling focuses on developing only one side of the brain: the left hemisphere (Bogen, 1975; Ornstein, 1977, 1978). Many proposals for changes in the educational system have been made in response to this perceived bias in educational emphasis. Most approaches encourage more teaching of art, music, and intuitive interpretation in school, presumably to stimulate right hemisphere functioning. In general, however, there is little support for the theory that instructional activities designed to stimulate one side of the brain over the other are effective (Prince, 1978; Springer & Deutsch, 1989). Thus not all educational interventions inspired by biological insights are sound.

■ ■ ■ BIOLOGICAL FOUNDATIONS OF ACADEMIC COMPETENCE

Biological studies offer a tremendous opportunity to expand understanding of important academic competencies. For example, there is a great deal of active research on the brain mechanisms responsible for developing effective reading skills and successful mathematics learning (Katzir & Paré-Blagoev, 2006; Posner & Rothbart, 2005).

Reading

Reading researchers are using biological methods such as brain imaging to better understand reading processes (Casey, Thomas, & McCandliss, 2001; Shaywitz & Shaywitz, 2004, 2005). For example, the mature reading of words is determined much more by left-hemisphere processes than right-hemisphere processes (Turkeltaub, Eden, Jones, & Zeffiro, 2002). A recent, important finding based on brain-imaging data is that cognitive activity in the left hemisphere increases as students learn to read, whereas activity in some parts of the right hemisphere decreases (Turkeltaub, Gareau, Flowers, Zeffiro, & Eden, 2003). This complemented earlier research, for example, by Roberts and Kraft (1989), who studied the electrical brain activity of primary-grade and middle-grade readers (6- to 8-year-olds and 10- to 12-year-olds) as they read material that was slightly challenging for them. For the younger students, most of the comprehension activity occurred in the left hemisphere. For the older students, the activity was more evenly divided between the two hemispheres. Roberts and Kraft suggested that the predominantly left-hemispheric reading by the younger students reflected their focus on decoding during reading. On the other hand, the older students used a range of reading strategies, which resulted in the more balanced hemispheric patterns. What is becoming clear from the neural-imaging research is that, although left-hemisphere functioning is very prominent in reading, reading involves a complex coordination of brain functions (Zeffiro & Eden, 2001).

Dyslexia

Dyslexia is the failure to learn to read despite substantial reading instruction (Snowling, 2000; Wolf, 2001). If reading is defined as simply sounding out the words, then dyslexia affects a fairly small proportion of readers—at most 1–2% (Farnham-Diggory, 1992). If being a fluent reader by the middle elementary grades is the criterion for concluding a child is a reader rather than a child with dyslexia, then identifying a higher percentage of troubled readers is justified, perhaps as high as 20% (Shaywitz, 2003).

Acquired dyslexia results from some type of brain injury and *developmental dyslexia* refers to otherwise normal children experiencing difficulties in reading that are not due to obvious brain injury (Caplan, 1992; Raynor & Pollatsek, 1989). Educators encounter developmental dyslexia much more often than acquired dyslexia. Developmental dyslexia consists of a variety of symptoms (Vellutino & Fletcher, 2005). These include eye-scan patterns that do not match normal patterns; difficulties with spatial orientation, including confusing left and right; and better reading of upside-down text than right-side-up text. The particular symptoms differ from student to student. The most important characteristic is difficulty with word recognition and decoding during childhood, persisting throughout life in most cases (Bruck, 1990).

As early as 2 years of age, dyslexic children experience language difficulties not seen in children who become normal readers (Scarborough, 1990, 2001). They produce relatively short utterances and their pronunciations are less accurate. Their receptive vocabularies are not as well developed and they have more difficulties providing labels for common objects. Thus dyslexia is part of a general language-processing deficiency (Vellutino, 1979; Vellutino & Fletcher, 2005).

Some proposed explanations for dyslexia, such as dysfunctional eye movements and an underdeveloped left hemisphere, have not been supported (Vellutino, 1979). There is, however, evidence of physiological differences between developmental dyslexics and normal readers, with dyslexics having abnormal brain tissue, especially in the left hemisphere (Galaburda, 1983; Rosen, 2006; Shaywitz & Shaywitz, 2004, 2005). These findings are stimulating research to identify possible genetic causes of these brain differences.

Mathematics

The methodological tools that are shedding light on reading processes, especially brain-imaging techniques, are also being used to develop more complete models of how the brain affects mathematical thinking (Dehaene, Tzourio, Frak, Reynaud, et al., 1996; Pesenti, Thioux, Seron, & DeVolder, 2000). Certain brain structures contribute to particular mathematical competencies. Reading and understanding mathematical concepts and procedures involves the higher association areas of the individual's dominant hemisphere (Keller & Sutton, 1991). Quick mental calculation ability, abstract conceptualization, and some problem-solving skills are linked to the functioning of the frontal lobes. Finally, visual processing of mathematical symbols involves the occipital lobes, and auditory perception of numbers requires intact temporal lobes (refer to Figure 2.2).

■ ■ ■ CHAPTER SUMMARY AND EVALUATION

Neurological development reaches maturity through a number of mechanisms, particularly myelination, physical growth of the brain, and the development of the frontal lobes.Discontinuities in brain development have been described.

The plasticity of neurological development argues strongly for the importance of educational intervention. Plasticity, however, declines with age for certain acquisitions: those dependent on experience-expectant synapses. For these, the window of opportunity for educational intervention occurs during certain critical periods. On the other hand, experience-dependent synapses can continue to form all during life and much more learning and development occur via experience-dependent synapses than via experience-expectant synapses.

Patterns in physical development have been observed, with growth, in general, proceeding cephalocaudally (from top to bottom) and proximodistally (from the center outward). The adolescent growth spurt is a time of accelerated growth, with implications resulting from the timing of puberty for males and females.

Twin and adoption studies shed light on the relative roles of heredity and environment in development. Genes provide potential; whether a person reaches the high end of the reaction range of potential depends on environmental factors. Maternal malnutrition, chemical dependency, and disease can affect the biological development of an infant. The severity of resultant disability can be reduced by responsive stimulation during infancy and the preschool years.

Biology biases humans to certain types of learning over others; determines that some learning, such as language acquisition, will almost certainly occur; and constrains other learning due to factors such as limited short-term memory capacity. Performance on academic tasks, such as reading and mathematics, can be linked to physiological differences among individuals.

Developmental Debates

The research covered in this chapter can be analyzed in the context of some of the developmental debates introduced in Chapter 1. By reviewing this work with respect to those debates, the significance of much of this research can be highlighted.

Nature versus Nurture

One of the most important lessons in this chapter is that the developing nervous system is preprogrammed in many ways (nature), but its development can be affected dramatically by environmental agents (nurture). A genotype has a reaction range of phenotypes associated with it. Phenotypic expression depends on the unique environmental stimulation the organism experiences. Experience-expectant synapses are genetically programmed to respond only to certain types of environmental stimulation; experience-dependent synapses are formed in response to whatever environmental stimulation is available.

The environment children experience depends greatly on the historical era in which they live. The 1,000-gram premature infant now has a chance at life because of modern technology that permits the placement of the premature infant in an environment in which it can survive. Malnutrition is more likely during war than peace, which is one reason why healthy development is more likely during peacetime. Diseases that once ravaged developing children (such as polio and measles) are now very rare because of modern medicine. But modernity has also created environmental pollutants that were not present in earlier eras. *When* one develops does much to determine *how* one develops.

Stages versus Continuous Development

Biological research is providing powerful new ways of construing stage-like discontinuities in development. One example is the investigation of discontinuities in brain development and associated growth spurts in cognitive and emotional development described by Fischer and his colleagues. In general, biological analyses make clear that the developing nervous system differs in important ways from the mature nervous system.

Universal versus Culture-Specific Development

Some perceptual and cognitive developments, such as language acquisition, are probably universal within the human species, occurring in all but the most exceptional circumstances. Thus they are mediated by experience-expectant neurological mechanisms, with their development dependent on appropriate experience during critical periods. Deviation from the canalized perceptual development occurs only in the absence of such experience. Short of raising a child in complete social isolation, human language will develop, although the form and sophistication of language development depends on the richness and particulars of experience (as detailed in Chapter 7).

Certain brain structure–function relationships also seem universal. For example, increases in functional short-term capacity with age and hemispheric specialization have been documented in many ways.

Lasting versus Transient Effects of Early Experience

The developing nervous system is more susceptible to long-term modification than the mature nervous system. Many organ systems begin to develop during the first trimester of the prenatal period. Teratogens can devastate organ systems at this point in development and malnutrition during some critical growth periods can have long-term impacts on future cognitive functioning. Moreover, because the young nervous system is not protected by myelin, it is more susceptible to damage by metabolic by-products (such as phenylperuvic acid, which is produced by a child with PKU during metabolism of phenylalanine) than is the mature nervous system. Finally, the growing nervous system tends to be more vulnerable to chemical poisoning (e.g., lead) than is the mature nervous system.

▪▪▪ REVIEW OF KEY TERMS

adolescent growth spurt A period of rapid physical growth and development during adolescence.

anoxia The reduction of an infant's air supply during birth, which can cause brain injury.

axon A stem-like part of a cell that conducts impulses away from the cell body.

behavioral geneticists Scientists interested in the genetic determination of behavior.

canalized As used in describing development, when development is almost completely genetically determined.

cell assemblies Closed paths that include a number of neurons synaptically connected to one another.

cephalocaudal Term describing tendency for physical development to move from top to bottom.

cerebral cortex The part of the brain responsible for complex thought processes.

critical periods Time periods of great sensitivity to environmental input.

dendrites Branch-like extensions of the cell body that transmit impulses from other cells toward the cell body.

dyslexia The inability to decode words well despite substantial reading instruction.

executive processing space The number of pieces of information a student can have active in memory at any one time.

experience-dependent synapses Synapses that respond to whatever environmental stimulation an individual encounters.

experience-expectant synapses Synapses that are genetically programmed to respond only to certain kinds of stimulation.

fetal alcohol syndrome Birth defects, such as learning difficulties and mental retardation, caused by damage to the central nervous system as a result of maternal alcoholism.

genotype The genes possessed, which specify a potential range of outcomes.

heritability The variation in a characteristic (e.g., intelligence) that is due to genetic variability.

menarche Onset of first menstruation.

myelination The formation of a layer of axon sheathing that permits more rapid firing of axons.

neurogenesis A period of rapid cell growth.

phenotypes The observed outcome of the genotype, or how the genes are expressed.

plastic As used in describing the brain, having fundamental physical properties, such as the size and number of synaptic connections, vary with environmental stimulation.

proximodistal Term describing tendency for physical development to move from the center of the body outward.

reaction range The range of possible phenotypes based on a given genotype.

short-term memory capacity A memory store of limited capacity and duration; also called "working memory."

spermarche Onset of sperm production.

synaptic connections Physical connections between neurons formed through an axon meeting a dendrite, a cell body, or another axon.

teratogens Environmental agents, such as disease or chemicals, that can damage a developing fetus.

CHAPTER 3

Cognitive Development
Piaget's Stage Theory

No single individual has had as much impact on the study of children's mental capacities as Jean Piaget. Although his descriptions and explanations of development have some serious flaws, Piaget defined many important issues in the development of mental capacities and his general theory inspired a philosophy that continues to influence education. In this chapter, we first describe Piaget's original theory, and then offer a description of neo-Piagetian theories that have been proposed. Then we present Kohlberg's extension of Piaget's theory to explain the development of moral judgment. We conclude the chapter with a discussion of the constructivist approach to education, for Piaget's theory did much to inspire and inform constructivist educators (Fuhrer & Josephs, 1998; Green & Gredler, 2002).

■ ■ ■ PIAGET'S FOUR-STAGE THEORY

Piaget's (e.g., 1983) four-stage theory of development is his most visible contribution to developmental psychology. Think back to the debate between stage-like and continuous views of development described in Chapter 1. According to stage theory, development is uneven, with children fundamentally different in important ways at different times during their development. Rather than making gradual transitions, there are points of rapid development, with abrupt movement from one stage to the next.

In Piaget's stage theory of development, progress through the four stages can occur at different rates, but it is always orderly, taking place in an invariant sequence (Feldman, 2003). Each stage is characterized by the development of new cognitive structures, or schemes. A **scheme** is a coordinated pattern of thought or action that organizes an individual's interaction with the environment. The more advanced stages of cognitive development are associated with more complex and sophisticated schemes, and hence by more advanced and flexible thinking and behavior.

The schemes of infants are simple and action-oriented, such as a scheme of reaching for, grasping, and pulling an object close for careful examination. These first schemes are sensory and motor in nature. Thus the first Piagetian stage is known as the **sensorimotor stage**. According to Piaget, intelligence during this period consists in the actions of the child on the environment rather than in the child's mind. Piagetians called these actions **motor schemes**.

How do infants acquire sensorimotor schemes? Young infants possess innate reflexes, such as sucking, crying, or grasping. These reflexes serve as the basis for the first motor schemes. For example, infants initially suck their fingers instinctively. Eventually, sucking becomes a strategy for exploring new objects in the environment, a sensorimotor scheme. What are infants likely to do when handed a rattle? Their sucking response is a strategy for interacting with the rattle and other objects in their environment.

The sensorimotor schemes of infancy permit interactions with the environment that eventually lead to the development of object permanence. **Object permanence** refers to a child's understanding that objects continue to exist whether or not the child can see or touch them. Before this acquisition, children act as if objects that are out of their sight no longer exist. Once children acquire object permanence, however, they understand that objects have an existence independent of their perception of them. What do infants do if someone hides a rattle under a blanket? If they have object permanence, they will lift up the blanket to look for the rattle. If not, they'll just look away, seeming undisturbed by the object's disappearance.

The next stage, the **preoperational stage,** roughly corresponds to the preschool years. Children in this stage have developed cognitive structures called **symbolic schemes** that allow them to represent objects or events by means of symbols such as language, mental images, and gestures. The first evidence of this representational ability is often the display of **deferred imitation**. This refers to children's ability to imitate behavior long after witnessing it. For example, a child who witnessed another child's tantrum at the grocery store last week is capable of imitating the tantrum behaviors today. Another example of representational ability occurs during **symbolic play**. To a child capable of symbolic representation, an empty box can become a castle, and a stick can become a magic wand. The most powerful representational ability is demonstrated in children's use of language, arguably the most powerful symbol system for knowledge acquisition.

Despite the advances evident in preoperational children's thinking due to their use of symbolic schemes, Piaget emphasized the differences between the logic of younger children and that of older children. Preoperational children possess a logic of their own; it is just not the same logic as that found in

These children are demonstrating symbolic representation in their play by fantasizing that they are paddling a boat at sea.

older children and adults. According to Piaget, preschoolers exhibit **egocentrism**, or unawareness of the perspective of others. They view situations primarily from their own perspective and are unable to understand a situation from another person's point of view. For example, a little girl may have difficulty understanding that her grandma is her mother's mother. How can *her* mother be someone else's daughter? Another example is that preschoolers believe that others view objects in the same way as they do, regardless of the other person's viewing angle. This is why most preschoolers have to be reminded constantly during "Show and Tell" to hold the object so the other children in the class can see it. A high proportion of preschooler speech is described as egocentric since many of their utterances are not social in intent. For instance, preschoolers in conversation talk all at once, ignoring the speech of others. Preschoolers often do not communicate information to other people very well due to their egocentrism. For instance, preschoolers telling stories tend to leave out important information needed to understand the story fully.

Preschool children are also unable to solve conservation tasks. **Conservation** refers to the understanding that changes in appearance do not equal changes in amount. Preschoolers do not understand that amount can only be changed by adding or subtracting material. For example, preschoolers will claim that the amount of liquid changed because it was poured from a tall, slender glass into a short, wide glass, although nothing was added or subtracted. What is going on in this example? The children are attending to misleading perceptual cues. They might argue that there is more liquid after pouring because the water is wider after pouring, or they might claim that there is less liquid after pouring because the water is not as high in the glass after pouring. Several years later, when children understand conservation, they offer explanations about how height and width offset one another and about how the amount cannot change when nothing is added or subtracted. Failure to conserve does not mean that preschoolers are completely illogical. Many preschoolers who cannot conserve understand that it is the same water that is transferred from glass A to glass B. That is, they are beginning to understand that the **identity** of the water survives a perceptual transformation. Of course, still less cognitively mature preschoolers do not even understand that identity is preserved following a perceptual transformation.

According to Piaget, preschoolers' thought lacks some of the logical **operational schemes** (operations) that underlie mature thought, which accounts for their errors in conservation tasks (and for the name of the preoperational stage). Operations are cognitive rules. One is the identity function already described. When children completely understand identity, they realize that objects remain the same despite perceptual transformation. A second is **reversibility**. This refers to the understanding that an operation can be undone by reversing it, such as pouring the water back into the tall glass—or by doing so mentally, imagining the water being poured back. A third is **compensation**. This is the recognition that change on one dimension can be compensated for by changes on another dimension. For example, the same amount of water will be higher in a narrow glass than in a wide one.

Having these operational schemes permits conservation. Children with operational intelligence can reason that the amount of water in the wider glass is the same as it was in the taller glass because they can mentally reverse the pouring. They can also point out the reciprocal relationship between height and width of the liquid. Children in either of the next stages of operational intelligence, concrete and formal, are more powerful thinkers than preoperational preschoolers.

During the **concrete operational stage**, which corresponds roughly to the elementary-grade years, children can apply cognitive operations to problems involving concrete objects, but not to problems involving abstract manipulation or hypothetical situations. This means that children in the concrete operational stage can solve conservation tasks. Thus, if shown two rows of seven buttons lined up evenly, concrete operational children understand that the two rows contain the same number of buttons even when one of the rows is "stretched" so that a greater space lies between individual buttons. This is a number conservation problem. If two balls of clay are the same weight as indicated by a balanced scale, conserving children will predict that the scale will stay in balance even if one of the two balls is reshaped, perhaps flattened like a pancake or rolled into a snake. This is a conservation of mass problem.

Concrete operations permit the performance of other tasks as well, such as **class inclusion** problems. In these problems, children view sets of objects, some of which are subsets of each other, and they answer questions about the subset relationships. For example, if they are given a set of pictures of five cardinals and four robins and asked "Are there more cardinals or birds?," conserving children understand that there are more birds than cardinals. Preoperational children, however, are more likely to respond that there are more cardinals, since there are more cardinals than robins in the pictures they are viewing. In addition, concrete operations permit children to **seriate** items. That is, they can order objects on some dimension, such as shortest to tallest or lightest to heaviest. For example, concrete operators can correctly arrange sticks in order of increasing length.

Students at the **formal operational stage** (beginning with early adolescence) are capable of even more complex problem solving (Keating, 1990). First, they can handle problems that involve more factors. Thus, although concrete operational children can seriate on one dimension, formal operational children can seriate on several dimensions simultaneously. For example, they can correctly arrange sticks in order of color *and* increasing length. Formal operational thinkers are capable of *thinking in possibilities*, meaning that they can generate all combinations of possibilities for a given situation. For example, formal operational thinkers can infer "invisible forces," and thereby solve problems involving such forces. This allows them to solve problems such as how hydraulic presses work given some weights and several presses. Moreover, the thinking of the formal operational adolescent is not closely tied to the constraints of the "real" world. Whereas concrete operators often rely on concrete objects, called "concrete manipulatives," to aid their reasoning, formal operators can discuss complex issues without the concrete props. In addition, the formal operational adolescent routinely utilizes planning, foresight, or *thinking ahead*. Finally, the thinking ability most characteristic of formal operators is *thinking in hypotheses*. The formal operational thinker can survey a problem, formulate all potential hypothetical outcomes, and go about testing the possibilities one at a time.

This characteristic of thinking in hypotheses is a critical component of scientific reasoning. In one of the Piagetian tasks designed to elicit scientific reasoning, the pendulum problem, students are provided three lengths of string and three different weights that they can attach to the string. The students' task is to figure out which factors determine the rate at which a pendulum swings. Usually the students will conduct one of the following two actions: (1) use one of the strings and try each weight in succession, and (2) use one of the weights and try each string in succession. What students notice is that the speed of swinging varies with the length of the string, but not the weight. Good students will also systematically vary how much force they use to set the pendulum in motion, and they will note that force is not a critical factor in the speed of the pendulum swing. The students act like scientists in this situation, varying one factor at a time while holding other factors constant. Thus they are "thinking in hypotheses." In contrast, children who are not in the formal operational stage often proceed in a haphazard fashion, sometimes changing two features at once, such as the size of the weight and the length of the string. See Table 3.1 for a description of another task that elicits formal operational thinking.

Progress through the Stages

By training and by conviction, Piaget was a biologist who believed in a biological inevitability to the stages, and hence a universality to them (Brainerd, 1978b; Feldman, 2003; Piaget, 1967). The stages build upon one another, with each one a prerequisite for the next. Some individuals, however, move through the stages more rapidly than others and some do not make it all the way to formal operations.

Initially, Piaget argued that once in a stage, all thinking reflects the underlying competencies characteristic of the stage. Thus a student who is concrete operational for one task should be concrete operational for all tasks. A later version of the theory permits "stage mixture" (Brainerd, 1978b, 1978c; Flavell, 1971, 1972), so that some students might be preoperational for some tasks and concrete operational for others. Other students might be able to attack some problems in a formal operational fashion while still requiring concrete manipulatives for other problems. **Horizontal décalage** is the term used to describe that students do not master all problems requiring the same logical operations at the same time. For example, children typically acquire conservation of length (i.e., recognizing that the length of a string does not vary no matter how the string is shaped) before conservation of liquid. Moreover, Piaget suggested that individuals reach formal operations in "different areas according to their aptitudes and their professional socialization" (Piaget, 1972, p. 10). Thus successful mechanics, carpenters, or composers may use formal operational reasoning in their particular specialty, but not necessarily in other areas. See Table 3.2 for a summary of Piaget's four stages of cognitive development.

TABLE 3.1. A Question That Elicits Formal Operational Thinking: How Might Everyday Life Be Different If We All Had Tails?

College students who were asked this question as part of a classroom exercise generated a variety of responses, ranging from changes in fashion and furniture to changes in religious values and courting rituals. Their responses highlight important qualities of formal operational thought including thinking in terms of possibilities.

Fashion—tail jewelry, tail braiding, tail ribbons, tail cover-ups
Furniture—differences in chairs and beds, hooks to hang by tails
Sports—new ball games, new Olympic sports, tail workouts
Dating—Do you allow your date to see your tail on the first date?
Religion—Are tails displayed? Are there display differences for men and women?
Politics—prejudice based on length, color, degree of hairiness of tail

TABLE 3.2. Summary of Piaget's Stages of Cognitive Development

Stage	Characteristic schemes	Characteristic accomplishments	Characteristic limitations
Sensorimotor stage	Motor	Object permanence	Thinking only by doing
Preoperational stage	Motor Symbolic	Deferred imitation Symbolic play Language	Thinking dominated by perceptions Lack of awareness of others' perspectives Lack of reversibility Lack of compensation
Concrete operational stage	Motor Symbolic Operational–concrete	Class inclusion Seriation Conservation	Thinking only in concrete terms Thinking about only two attributes at once
Formal operational stage	Motor Symbolic Operational–concrete and formal	Thinking in possibilities Thinking ahead Thinking in hypotheses	

Mechanisms of Cognitive Change

How did Piaget explain progression through the stages? Piaget (1983) believed that many factors determine developmental change. The first, *maturation*, is biological. As children mature physically, new possibilities for development evolve. Although biological development is necessary for cognitive growth, it is not sufficient for such growth to occur. *Experience* plays a role as well. As children practice new cognitive acquisitions, their experiences with the physical world permit them to learn important regularities. For example, one regularity might be "as the amount of something increases, its weight increases." The *social environment* also plays a role in development. The quality of children's social environment at home and school affects the speed of movement through the stages. Environments that provide new experiences and permit practice of new skills facilitate the movement from one stage to the next.

At any given point of development, children understand the world in terms of the cognitive operations they have developed. That is, they **assimilate** new information. Children assimilate when they incorporate environmental stimuli into an existing scheme. For example, a child who sees a girl playing with a dog may be able to assimilate this observation into his or her existing scheme of household pets by thinking "That girl's dog is her pet just like my collie, Cody, is my pet." If this child walks by a training ground for guard dogs, this new information from the environment cannot be simply assimilated into an existing cognitive structure. Instead, the child must **accommodate** to the new information. Accommodation refers to the modification of existing cognitive structures in response to environmental demands. Thus the child needs to modify existing schemes about dogs to comprehend that some dogs are not pets but are trained to protect and attack. Assimilation of any stimulus involves accommodation of the learner to the stimulus, although the accommodation can be relatively minor. In the example above, the other girl's pet dog does not look and behave exactly like Cody at home, so assimilation involved some accommodation.

Here's another example. A first grader, who has observed robins and finches in the backyard for years, has little difficulty assimilating a bald eagle into his or her bird scheme when discussing the nation's symbol in first grade. Even though the bald eagle is much larger than the birds in a backyard and a predator unlike the birds typically found in a backyard, assimilation is likely with minor accommodation. This same first grader, however, would have much more difficulty assimilating the penguins observed during the class field trip to the zoo into his or her bird scheme. The child must accommodate his or her bird scheme in response to this very different example of "bird."

Finally, consider how a preoperational child, who lacks the cognitive structures that permit understanding of compensation, responds to a conservation of weight problem. When an experimenter rolls a ball of clay into a sausage shape, the child says it has less clay now than when the clay was in a ball shape because the sausage shape is "thinner." The cognitive structures a preoperational child possesses foster attention to only one dimension in making conservation judgments. If the experimenter continues to roll the sausage out, it gets longer and longer so that the length dimension becomes more salient and less easy to overlook. Some of the time the child responds on the basis of this increase in length, reporting that there is more clay when the clay is in the shape of a sausage than in the shape of a ball. The child eventually notices the inconsistency in responding one way on the basis of length and another way on the basis of width. The result is **cognitive conflict**—that is, the child has increasing difficulty making a conservation judgment based on only one dimension. For example, the child might be thinking, "If I just look at length, I answer one way. If I just look at width, I answer another way. Both answers can't be true."

Piaget used the term **disequilibrium** to refer to the realization that two ways of thinking about the world contradict each other, and thus both can't be true. This realization motivates the resolution of the contradiction through the construction of new cognitive structures. Thus the child accommodates to the environmental stimulus. Once accommodation occurs, the child's thinking returns to equilibrium. Piaget called this mechanism of cognitive change "equilibration." That is, **equilibration** is equilibrium followed by disequilibrium followed by a new equilibrium that is more powerful, because the mind has learned to do more. In the case of conservation, a child becomes a conserver through disequilibration of cognitive schemes that do not support conservation followed by new schemes that permit conservation leading to equilibrium. Cognitive development involves many cycles of equilibrium, followed by disequilibrium, followed by equilibrium at a higher level of competence (Piaget, 1983).

One of the most important ideas in Piagetian thinking is that cognitive conflict occurs most often when children are working on problems that require just a little bit more than they currently know. When children first work on such problems, they have a sense that there is something they don't understand, but that understanding is within reach. Perception of this gap between current knowledge and what needs to be known to accomplish a task motivates cognitive effort to solve the current problem (White, 1959). We will refer to this principle of the "match" when we discuss educational interventions inspired by Piaget's theory throughout this chapter. Some suggestions for applying Piaget's ideas in a classroom are presented in the Applying Developmental Theory to Educational Contexts special feature (see Box 3.1).

Applying Developmental Theory to Educational Contexts

BOX 3.1. Piaget in the Classroom

Piaget and his colleagues (Inhelder, Sinclair, & Bovet, 1974) argued that the only educational mechanisms that could produce legitimate conceptual change were ones that would mirror natural development via equilibration (i.e., cognitive conflict). How can educators design learning environments so that discovery via equilibration would be likely (Brainerd, 1978a, 1978b; Kamii, 1985)? Here are some ideas:

- Diagnose students' current developmental stages so that developmentally appropriate assignments and instruction can be given. For example, students in the formal operational stage can learn abstract scientific principles through a lecture. Students in the concrete operational stage, on the other hand, would have to see concrete applications of the scientific principles.
- Design instruction so that students are active participants in their own learning. Construct learning environments conducive to student exploration. Opportunities for student exploration, especially with concrete manipulables, increase the likelihood of learning for both concrete and formal operational students. If the objective is for students to understand the principle of compounding interest, for example, ask them to demonstrate their understanding by using Monopoly money.
- Make students aware of conflicts between their approaches to problems and features of the problems. Ask probing questions such as "What will happen if . . . ?" Present counterexamples and point out inconsistencies that may lead to disequilibrium. For example, in the case of conservation of weight, you might want to say something like "I see you are thinking about the width of the clay sausage. What have you noticed about its length?"
- Reduce adult power as much as possible, encouraging the exchange of points of view between teachers and students and between students and students. Foster student collaboration with peers who have mutual interests.
- Encourage children to think in their own ways rather than to produce the right answers in the right way as defined by a teacher. Analyze student errors to gain a better understanding of their thought processes.

Cognitive Conflict and Overcoming Scientific Misconceptions

Science educators in particular have been attracted to the idea that education at its best stimulates cognitive conflict. One of Piaget's (e.g., 1929) most important insights was that people often have ideas about the world that clash with scientific viewpoints. For example, some people believe that inanimate objects, such as the Sun, the stars, or a computer are alive! Piaget believed that such **animism** was a symptom of preoperational intelligence. He also believed that with the development of concrete and formal operations, children's ideas about what is alive versus what is not alive would reflect conventional thinking about life. A number of studies, many in the 1930s and 1940s, investigated this premise (for a brief review, see Brainerd, 1978b). The results indicated that although animism declined with development from the preoperational to the concrete and formal operational stages, it never extinguished. Animism persists throughout adulthood.

Science educators have noted that often people have important misconceptions about physical and biological relationships. Although scientific misconceptions in physics have been studied more than other misconceptions (Pfundt & Duit, 1991), people seem to have misconceptions about every scientific arena imaginable. Here are some examples of common misconceptions (Duit, 1991; Woloshyn, Paivio, & Pressley, 1994):

The Sun is a living organism—it is an animate object.
One place where water does not exist is in the air.
Molecules in solids are always still.
Plants eat soil and water.
People are not animals.

Nussbaum and Novick (1982) proposed that to overcome a misconception, students first need to be aware of their incorrect belief. Once aware, exposure to an event that cannot be explained by their belief has the potential for producing cognitive conflict. Consistent with Piagetian thinking, such conflict motivates efforts toward conflict resolution and, in particular, motivates efforts to understand the scientific concept explaining the observed event. That is, conflict motivates efforts toward *accommodation*, setting up the possibility of modification of current cognitive structures and the creation of new ones.

However, Posner, Strike, Henson, and Gertzog (1982) argued that more than just cognitive conflict is necessary for cognitive change to take place. They believed that effective instruction needs to (1) produce clear dissatisfaction with the errant belief, (2) provide an intelligible and plausible alternative conception, and (3) provide an alternative that has obvious intellectual power not permitted by the prior conception.

In addition, Posner and colleagues (1982) made three points that are critical to the conceptual conflict model. First, many scientifically valid ideas initially do not seem as plausible to students as their prior conceptions. For example, Clement, Brown, and Zeitsman (1989) noted that many students find it implausible that static objects exert forces (e.g., a table exerting an upward force equal to the weight of the items on it). Indeed, Osborne and Freyberg (1985) made the case that many ideas about force seem very counterintuitive to young students: It is hard to accept that a ball thrown upward does not have an upward force operating on it while it is on the way up. It is hard to accept that a speeding bicycle that is no longer being pedaled does not have a forward force operating on it. Second, students often find new conceptions to be unintelligible, with students exclaiming "I don't know what you're saying" or "I don't know what you mean" (Hewson & Thorley, 1989). Third, students often prefer their prior conceptions to the new conceptions offered in school, believing that their own knowledge is consistent with the "real world" even if it is not consistent with what must be learned in school (Dreyfus, Jungwirth, & Eliovitch, 1990). If new knowledge is to prove fruitful, it must prove more useful than the everyday knowledge that the student trusts because it is grounded in experience.

In general, conceptual conflict instruction is effective in promoting understanding of ideas in science not consistent with prior knowledge (Guzzetti, Snyder, Glass, & Gamas, 1993). See the Applying Developmental Theory to Educational Contexts special feature (Box 3.2) for recommendations for promoting understanding of science by inducing conceptual conflict.

Applying Developmental Theory to Educational Contexts

BOX 3.2. Inducing Cognitive Conflict

In order to promote understanding of science and conceptual change, educators should do the following:

- Develop lectures, demonstrations, problems, and labs that produce cognitive conflict in students by pointing out inconsistencies between students' prior knowledge and to-be-acquired scientific conceptions.
- Monitor students' thinking about new to-be-learned concepts, being especially alert to the defensive moves of students who resist accommodating their prior conceptions to scientific conceptions.
- Act as Socratic tutors, confronting students when they attempt to assimilate scientific concepts to their misconceptions rather than accommodate their current thinking to the scientific idea.
- Model scientific thinking, making it clear to students that their beliefs should be consistent with evidence and that it is not appropriate to "explain away" or ignore evidence inconsistent with their beliefs.
- Present content in multiple modalities (e.g., verbal, mathematical, concrete-practical, pictorial) that clarify the relationships between the various representations.
- Rely on assessments, such as interviews, that can reveal conceptual changes in students' thinking.

These suggestions were inspired by the chapters in Shantz and Hartup (1992).

Evaluation of Piaget's Theory

Does Piaget's stage theory adequately explain what we know today about cognitive development? His contribution to our understanding of cognitive development is profound, but many research outcomes have been inconsistent with various aspects of Piaget's theory (Sternberg, 2003). For example, some Piagetian conceptual acquisitions, such as the ability to solve certain abstract logical problems, appear to *develop earlier* than Piaget had described (Brainerd, 1978a). For instance, when asked to perform a conservation of number task with only three objects, preschoolers as young as age 3 can succeed (Gelman, 1972). Other acquisitions, such as the conservation of volume appear to *develop later* than specified by the theory. In addition, some behaviors reported by Piaget are not manifested like Piaget proposed. For example, Piaget's depiction of preschooler speech as extremely egocentric is not consistent with the many communicative competencies possessed by preschoolers. Preschoolers often do talk with one another and with adults in ways that suggest they do understand the other person's perspective. Also, some people never do become as logically scientific as Piaget contended (Kuhn, Amsel, & O'Loughlin, 1988).

Piaget's theory is also *limited in generalizability*. It does not take into account cultural differences. Piagetian theory only describes the development of normally functioning children. Also, it accounts for a fraction of lifespan development, rarely mentioning adult development. The highest stage Piaget described, formal operations, is attainable by adolescents. Yes, formal operational competencies can extend with additional experiences in new domains, but no real structural change occurs and no new operations are added during adulthood (Piaget, 1972).

Perhaps the most salient Piagetian claim to fall in light of scientific evidence was the claim that acquisitions such as conservation *could not be taught* and that attempts to do so would invariably disrupt natural development. Researchers had little difficulty establishing conservation using conventional learning procedures such as the following (Brainerd, 1978a; Rosenthal & Zimmerman, 1978):

Simple correction: Give nonconservers repeated trials on conservation tasks, and tell them whether their answers are right or wrong. For example, after pouring liquid from a tall glass into a wide glass, provide positive feedback if a child gives the right answer. Provide negative feedback if a child does not.

Rule learning: Teach the child a rule. For example, when correcting a failure to conserve, tell the child, "I did not add or subtract anything."

Observational learning: Expose the child to a model who performs conservation perfectly. (You will learn more about observational learning in Chapter 5.)

Although Piaget's theory is not completely consistent with our current understanding of cognitive development, many educators find the basic principles of Piagetian theory to be useful. In particular, the principle of cognitive conflict is prominent in current instructional models for science and math education. Piaget's theory also stimulated the development of other theories, including ones that are studied by contemporary researchers.

■ ■ ■ NEO-PIAGETIAN PERSPECTIVES ON DEVELOPMENT

The shortcomings of Piaget's stage theory led to rethinking of the original Piagetian theory. Neo-Piagetian theories attempt to preserve the idea of stage-like movement in development but offer alternative explanations that are grounded in contemporary theory and research.

Case's Theory of Cognitive Development

Building upon work by Juan Pascuel-Leone (1970), Robbie Case (1991, 1999) attempted to revise Piagetian theory in light of research establishing that children's ability to manipulate information in short-term memory increases greatly from birth to about age 16. As introduced in Chapter 2, **short-term memory**, often called "working memory," is a memory store of limited capacity and duration (Nairne, 2003). Short-term memory is what we use when we try to hold a telephone number in our head just long enough to dial it. The emphasis on the development of short-term capacity to explain developmental changes in thinking abilities makes this a neo-Piagetian theory rather than a Piagetian theory. Piaget believed memory changes occurred as a result of developmental stage rather than being the cause of progress through the developmental stages (Piaget & Inhelder, 1973).

Like Piaget, Case argued for four distinct stages of cognitive development, which occur in an invariant sequence. The sequencing is invariant since each stage reflects differentiation, coordination, and consolidation of schemes present in the immediately previous stage. Smaller schemes that were once separate combine to form larger, more powerful schemes. These larger schemes are increasingly coordinated with one another. More powerful schemes that are coordinated with each other permit more advanced performance.

For example, a 4-year-old can draw a human figure that has many of the global features of human beings. A slightly older child can draw a more differentiated figure and do so in relation to a larger scene. Case's explanation is that the drawings of the older child represent a differentiation not present in the younger children, with the parts of a drawing separated into figure (the human) and ground (the larger scene). The 6-year-old's systems for drawing figures and for drawing the larger scene also represent integrations of skills that are not integrated for 4-year-olds. The 6-year-old coordinates these two systems in order to produce the more complete pictures, a complex coordination not likely in 4-year-olds.

How and why does drawing ability improve according to Case's theory? Part of the explanation is practice. Only schemes that are highly practiced can be differentiated into new schemes and then integrated with other schemes. Thus a great deal of practice in drawing global figures is required before there is differentiation of drawing schemes. This practice must occur until the child can automatically perform the behaviors that once took considerable effort and attention.

Although a young 4-year-old might have to expend all available short-term mental capacity (i.e., consciousness) to draw a stick figure, a slightly older child who has drawn many such stick figures can do so automatically. Thus less short-term memory is consumed during drawing of global human figures. This frees up some short-term capacity for attention to other things, including acquisition of new understandings of how figure and ground can be separated. That is, with increasing automaticity in execution of skills, a child has more functional short-term capacity. In general, when more functional short-term capacity is available, the quality of thinking is higher (see also Chapter 4).

According to Case's perspective, multiple factors account for developmental increases in short-term memory:

1. As described in the earlier example of children's drawing, *practicing a procedure makes it more automatic*, with available capacity then used more efficiently, allowing more processes to be coordinated simultaneously and integrated in consciousness.
2. With development, children improve in their ability to *shift their attention rapidly*, getting better at moving between different sources of information and focusing attention on task-relevant information and ignoring task-irrelevant input (Bjorklund & Harnishfeger, 1990; Pearson & Lane, 1991; Tipper, Bourque, Anderson, & Brehaut, 1989).
3. In addition, as *long-term memory develops* and is better organized, information chunks are larger. Preschoolers "chunk" verbal material into single letters; teenagers use whole words and phrases.

In addition to increases in functional short-term capacity due to increases in automaticity, ability to shift attention, and extent and organization of knowledge, the *actual working memory probably increases as a function of neurological maturation*. Because both functional increases and maturational increases in short-term capacity are indexed by age, it is very difficult to determine how much of the increase in apparent short-term abilities is due to functional increases in capacity and how much is due to biological increases.

What suggestions does Case have for developing instruction that is appropriate to the developmental level of the child? In broad terms, Case (1991) argued for beginning instruction with a task the child can understand and perform. The teacher should give feedback about how well the child is performing the task and encourage the child to practice until the task becomes more automatic. Gradually the teacher increases task demands, taking care to make certain that the more demanding versions of the task do not exceed the child's capacity. Guidance is provided as the child attempts the task, with this guidance and support faded as the child is able to execute the new task independently. The amount of working memory required to execute this new task decreases with practice, as its execution becomes more automatic. Case and his colleagues have investigated such an instructional approach with respect to a variety of tasks, including learning of mathematics and everyday quantitative skills, such as telling time and working with money (see Case, 1991).

Thus, in Case's approach, Piaget's notion of stage development is translated into neo-Piagetian terms. Rather than explaining the superiority of the 8-year-old in relation to the 4-year-old on conservation as a function of acquiring concrete operations, neo-Piagetians explain it as reflecting development of capacity, with the 8-year-old having the capacity to meet the demands of conservation tasks (i.e., paying attention to several dimensions, such as the height and width of a column of liquid, and keeping track of how they covary) and 4-year-olds lacking the required capacity (Chapman & Lindenberger, 1989).

Fischer's Theories of Cognitive Development

Another neo-Piagetian, Kurt Fischer (1980; Bidell & Fischer, 2000; Mascolo, Li, Fink, & Fischer, 2002), recognized that children accomplish many tasks using a variety of skills. For example, preschoolers can solve simple addition problems by using a variety of counting strategies—from counting on fingers to counting quietly to themselves. It is difficult to explain many such skills in terms of stages or to relate them to stages. Particularly important, the skills a child has depends largely on the child's experience in a domain of competence, such as arithmetic. Moreover, different skills are used in different domains. It is hard to imagine an early reading skill that is analogous to counting, just as it is hard to imagine an early arithmetic skill that is analogous to sounding out words.

Skills are learned in context, with the specific skills children acquire largely determined by the contexts they experience. For example, children can learn counting strategies as they play house, such as when they count out four of everything to set four places at a table. At first, this skill is very much tied to context, so that the same child might have difficulty doing an abstract task that requires counting by fours. For example, when given 20 checkers, four each of five different colors, the child might not be able to construct four sets with one checker of each color. With increasing experience, however, particular skills are generalized beyond the original contexts in which they are learned and integrated with related skills (Bidell & Fischer, 1992, 2000).

Yet, for Fischer, a biologically mediated stage-like progression occurs as well (Fischer & Bidell, 1999). Recall the discussion of Fischer's thinking in Chapter 2:

Development depends on brain development, with a series of brain-growth spurts that are associated with, and may cause, cognitive and behavioral changes. Like Piaget, Fischer believes that development is discontinuous. (Review Table 2.1 if you do not recall these points.) Like Piaget, Fischer views stage-like growth in competence as something that is the stuff of youth—with the last growth spurt occurring at about age 25. The stage-like changes have profound implications for functioning, so that cognitive, behavioral, and emotional shifts occur in parallel.

■■■ MORAL JUDGMENT: AN APPROACH IN THE TRADITION OF PIAGET

As a society, we want young people to emerge from school ready to make social and ethical decisions responsibly (Wentzel, 1991a, 1991b, 2003). Providing an education supports the development of reflective participants in democracy. In fact, researchers have discovered strong correlations between academic competence and social responsibility (Hanson & Ginsburg, 1988; Schonert-Reichl, 1999; Wentzel, 1991a, 1991b). A great deal of the most credible theory-driven research on social problem solving was generated in reaction to Lawrence Kohlberg's analyses of moral judgment. Kohlberg's ideas, however, were profoundly influenced by Piaget's perspective on moral judgment.

Piaget's Theory of the Development of Moral Reasoning

Jean Piaget's (1965) theory of the development of moral judgment was informed by his observations of children playing games, especially marbles. His observations of children playing games by the rules, children in conflict over rules, children changing rules, and children cheating helped him formulate hypotheses about children's moral understandings. He then tested these hypotheses by asking children to reason about social dilemmas that he presented to them as short stories. For example, one dilemma he posed to children was whether a child who *accidentally* broke 15 cups was naughtier than a child who *intentionally* broke one cup. Piaget proposed two stages of moral development, one reflecting the conceptions about rules held by preschoolers and children in the early primary years (*stage of heteronomous morality*) and the other stage reflecting the thinking of older children (*stage of autonomous morality*).

Children in the stage of heteronomous morality focus on the objective consequences of an action, and thus conclude that the child who broke 15 cups is naughtier since more cups were destroyed by that child. In contrast, children in the stage of autonomous morality make decisions on the basis of the intentions of the actors, therefore concluding that breaking one cup intentionally is much worse than accidentally destroying many more cups. The heteronomous moral child views rules as sacred, as if they were written by the hand of God, never to be reconsidered. In contrast, the autonomously moral child recognizes that the rules have been agreed upon by the players, that they are inventions of people, and that they can be changed if people will it. For example, children who play games such as Monopoly at home may learn when they play Monopoly at someone else's house that other families have different Monopoly conventions, such as the source of the money placed in Free Parking, what deals property owners can make, or even whether or not properties

These children are playing according to the rules of the game. *Heteronomously moral* children believe that rules are absolute; *autonomously moral* children realize that rules are social contracts agreed upon by the players.

are dealt out at the beginning to make the game shorter. A heteronomously moral child would view such alterations of the official Monopoly rules as almost a sacrilege.

Like all Piagetian stages, this one has an invariant order of development, meaning that a child must manifest heteronomous morality before autonomous morality. As is the case for all of cognitive development according to the Piagetian perspective, equilibration (cognitive conflict) is the main mechanism of cognitive change, facilitating movement from heteronomous to autonomous morality. Interactions with peers that stimulate cognitive conflict, such as arguments about the rules of games, are especially helpful (DeLisi & Golbeck, 1999). Such conflicts can be real mind stretchers, moving the child from viewing rules as God-given and inalterable to seeing them as agreements that children can change by a show of hands or a chorus of protesting voices. Piaget's perspective that cognitive conflict was important in the growth of moral thinking would be preserved in Kohlberg's theory, which elaborated and expanded the two stages of moral thinking favored by Piaget.

Kohlberg's Stage Theory of Moral Reasoning

Kohlberg (1969, 1981, 1984) described the development of moral reasoning as a progression through an invariant sequence of six stages. Kohlberg developed the stages based on a research tactic similar to that of Piaget. He presented moral dilemmas in the form of stories to adolescent boys. One of these dilemmas involved a character named Heinz:

> In Europe, a woman was near death from a special kind of cancer. There was one drug that the doctors thought might save her. It was a form of radium that the druggist in the same town had recently discovered. The drug was expensive to make. He paid $400 for the radium and charged $4000 for a small dose of the drug. The sick woman's husband, Heinz, went to everyone he knew to borrow the money and tried every legal means, but he could only get together about $2000, which is half of what it cost. He told the druggist that his wife was dying, and asked him to sell it cheaper or let him pay later. But the druggist said, "No, I discovered the drug and I'm going to make money from it." So having tried every legal means, Heinz gets desperate and considers breaking into the man's store to steal the drug for his wife. (Kohlberg, 1984, p. 640)

The boys were asked to respond to questions, such as the following, about the moral dilemmas posed by the story:

1. Should Heinz steal the drug? Why or why not?
2. Is it actually right or wrong for him to steal the drug? Why is it right or wrong?

3. Does Heinz have a duty or obligation to steal the drug? Why or why not?
4. If Heinz doesn't love his wife, should he steal the drug for her? (If the boy favors not stealing the drug:) Does it make a difference in what Heinz should do whether or not he loves his wife? Why or why not?
5. Suppose the person dying is not his wife but a stranger. Should Heinz steal the drug for the stranger? Why or why not?
6. (If the boy favors stealing the drug for the stranger:) Suppose it's a pet animal that he loves. Should Heinz steal to save the pet animal? Why or why not?
7. Is it important for people to do everything they can to save another's life? Why or why not?
8. It is against the law for Heinz to steal. Does that make it morally wrong? Why or why not?
9. In general, should people do everything that they can to obey the law? Why or why not? How does this apply to what Heinz should do?
10. In thinking back over the dilemma, what would you say is the most responsible thing for Heinz to do? Why? (Kohlberg, 1984, pp. 640–641)

What mattered in the interview was not whether the boys felt Heinz should steal the drug but the *reasons* they gave for Heinz's actions. These reasons varied from stage to stage (all quotes from Kohlberg, 1984, pp. 49–53, based on Rest, 1968).

The stages of **preconventional morality**, Stages 1 and 2, focus on self-interest in decision making. The reasons given in Stage 1 centered on obedience and avoiding punishment. Staying out of trouble is the concern that is more important than all others for the Stage-1 thinker, exemplified by this rationale in favor of stealing the drug: "If you let your wife die, you will get in trouble. You'll be blamed for not spending the money to save her and there'll be an investigation of you and the druggist for your wife's death." Of course, a case also can be made that the best way to stay out of trouble is not to steal the drug: "You shouldn't steal the drug because you'll be caught and sent to jail if you do. If you do get away, your conscience would bother you thinking how the police would catch up with you at any minute." The Stage-1 thinker is only worried about protecting him- or herself—avoiding punishment.

The Stage-2 thinker has made only a slight advance: he or she is concerned only about his or her own pleasures. What is right is what brings pleasure to the self. Self-interest comes through clearly in this Stage-2 justification for stealing the drug: "If you do happen to get caught, you could give the drug back and wouldn't get much of a sentence. It wouldn't bother you much to serve a little jail term, if you have your wife when you get out." Self-interest can be used to justify not stealing as well: "He may not get much of a jail term if he steals the drug, but his wife will probably die before he gets out, so it wouldn't do him much good. If his wife dies, he shouldn't blame himself; it isn't his fault she has cancer." By now it should be obvious why Stage-1 and Stage-2 thinking is considered preconventional. An adult offering such justifications would be viewed with dismay by other adults, who long ago rejected such narrow self-interest in decision making.

The stages of **conventional morality**, Stages 3 and 4, focus on maintaining the social order. The Stage-3 thinker is sometimes thought of as displaying "good boy–good girl" thinking, which is concerned with helping and pleasing others. This is conformist thinking in the sense of wanting to go along with the majority. Consider this example in favor of stealing the drug: "No one will think you're bad if you steal the drug but your family will think you are an inhuman husband if you don't. If you let your wife die, you'll never be able to look anyone in the face again." The concern for the opinion of others comes through in this justification for not stealing the drug as well: "It isn't just the druggist who will think you're a criminal, everyone else will, too. After you steal it, you'll feel bad thinking how you've brought dishonor on your family and yourself; you won't be able to face anyone again."

Whereas the Stage-3 conventional thinker is concerned with the subjective perceptions of others, the Stage-4 thinker is concerned with being in synchrony with the established standards of his or her society. Those in Stage 4 have a deep respect for law and order. The Stage-4 person is concerned with doing his or her duty to country, God, spouse, or whatever else commands allegiance by societal standards. This rationalization in favor of stealing the drug is based on the perception of duty to family members that is expected by society: "If you have any sense of honor, you won't let your wife die because you're afraid to do the only thing that will save her. You'll always feel guilty that you caused her death if you don't do your duty to her." Consistency with the laws of society comes through in this opposition to stealing the drug offered by another Stage-4 thinker: "You're desperate and you may not know you're doing wrong when you steal the drug. But you'll know you did wrong after you're punished and sent to jail. You'll always feel guilty for your dishonesty and law-breaking."

After some experience with conventional thinking, some come to reject it. The stages of **postconventional morality**, Stages 5 and 6, are characterized by shared or potentially sharable principles and standards. The Stage-5 thinker views rules and laws in terms of a contract, which is intended to protect the will and rights of others. Those entering into a contract obey rules as part of a social understanding, rather than because of fear of retribution, respect for authority, or sense of duty. If the social purpose for the rules cannot be fulfilled by obeying them, it is all right to dispense with the rules, as reflected in this opinion that favors Heinz stealing the drug: "The law wasn't set up for these circumstances. Taking the drug in this situation isn't really right, but it's justified to do it." The social contract orientation also comes through in this Stage-5 advisement against stealing the drug: "You can't have everyone stealing when they get desperate. The end may be good, but the ends don't justify the means."

Although there was certainly room for debate over the adequacy of the data supporting Stages 1 through 5 (Kurtines & Grief, 1974), without a doubt, the greatest challenges were launched at Kohlberg's proposals about a Stage 6. The Stage-6 thinker did not compromise in respecting the sanctity of life and human freedom. Kohlberg was especially influenced by Rawls's *Theory of Justice* (1971) in his portrayal of the Stage-6 thinker, who is described as the ultimately just individual, one who could rationally make decisions without taking self-interest into account. That is, Stage-6 thinkers attempted to make decisions that would be viewed as fair as possible by all parties. That this stage was hypothetical became obvious when Kohlberg admitted that there was no convincing evidence for it (see Kohlberg, Levine, & Hewer, 1983). This Stage-6 conceptualization in terms of justice continues to be important, however, in that critics of Kohlberg point to his embrace of rationally determined justice as the highest of moral ideals to be narrow, reflecting both a masculine bias and a bias toward Western philosophies.

Most adults would find the thinking that occurs in the stages of preconventional morality unacceptable. On the other hand, the stages of conventional morality represent the type of moral thought most typically observed in adults. Stages 5 and 6, the stages of postconventional morality, are reached by some but not all adults. Thus, the stages are invariant in that to get to Stage 4, one must go through Stages 1, 2, and 3. Achieving Stage 4, however, in no way guarantees achievement of Stages 5 or 6 (nor does achieving Stage 2 assure further progress to Stage 3). A summary view of Kohlberg's six stages of moral reasoning is depicted in Table 3.3.

Classifying a person into a stage was never clear-cut and Kohlberg's scoring scheme was revised many times (Dawson, 2002). If you need evidence that the moral judgment interview approach produces ambiguous data, simply respond to the Heinz interview presented earlier. As you struggle to classify the various responses you have to the dilemma, note that Heinz was only one of nine dilemmas and interviews. Each interview resulted in a mass of data. It was not uncommon at all for the responses of a specific participant to reflect what became known as *stage mixture*, with the assignment of a research participant to one particular stage based on the most frequent response category. Using the Kohlberg manuals, arriving at a diagnosis of someone's stage level took days and weeks of scoring in some cases!

Fortunately, others such as James Rest (1979; see also Rest et al., 1986) and John C. Gibbs (Gibbs, Arnold, & Burkart, 1984; Gibbs, Basinger, & Fuller, 1992; Gibbs, Basinger, & Grime, 2003; Gibbs, Widaman, & Colby, 1982) validated adaptations of the moral judgment interview that could be scored consistently and more easily than the original Kohlberg instrument. As with the Kohlberg measure, within-person variability in responding was the norm, however, so that a person might offer Stages 3, 4, and 5 responses across dilemmas, with stage mixture even for the same dilemma not uncommon.

People may consistently use different levels of moral judgments to respond to different types of moral dilemmas (Wark & Krebs, 1996). In other words, the context of the moral dilemma may exert more influence on the moral judgment than Kohlberg originally hypothesized. Some researchers have extended the study of the influence of context on moral reasoning to the school setting. For example, Thorkildsen and her colleagues interviewed children and adolescents to assess their conceptions about the justice of typical instructional and school practices. This research revealed that students possess diverse theories about what was fair and just in the classroom context, with some evidence of developmental progression (Thorkildsen, 1989; Thorkildsen, Nolen, & Fournier, 1994; Thorkildsen, Sadonis, & White-McNulty, 2004). Kohlberg's theory continues to inspire investigations of processes related to moral judgment. See the Considering Important Questions special feature (Box 3.3) for a summary of recent research on the development of forgiveness.

TABLE 3.3. Summary of Kohlberg's Stages of Moral Reasoning

Preconventional morality: focus on self-interest
    Stage 1   Focus on obedience and avoiding punishment
    Stage 2   Focus on obtaining rewards or pleasure

Conventional morality: focus on maintaining social order
    Stage 3   Focus on being a good boy or a good girl
    Stage 4   Focus on law and order

Postconventional morality: focus on shared standards and principles
    Stage 5   Focus on social contract
    Stage 6   Focus on principle

Gender Differences in Moral Reasoning

Carol Gilligan (1982) raised concerns about the generalizability of Kohlberg's theory to women in her book *In a Different Voice: Psychological Theory and Women's Development*. Gilligan argued that females were much more likely than males to consider issues of interpersonal caring and person-to-person connections as they reasoned about moral dilemmas, consistent with other thinking that care is a much more important issue for women than for men (Brabeck, 1989; Noddings, 1984; see also Chapter 11). This conclusion was based on an examination of reasoning by males and females over many issues involving moral decisions.

The differences between reasoning based on *caring versus rationality* can be appreciated by review of some responses to the Heinz dilemma presented earlier. Female responses are more likely than male responses to include arguments such as " . . . I think he [the druggist] had the moral obligation to show compassion in this case . . . " (p. 54), " . . . if she [Heinz's wife] dies, it hurts a lot of people and it hurts her . . . " (p. 28), " . . . you have to love someone else, because you are inseparable from them . . . that other person is part of that giant collection of everybody" (p. 57), and, "Who is going to be hurt more, the druggist who loses some money or the person who loses her life?" (p. 95). The females in Gilligan's studies raised issues about compassion, connection, and concerns about minimizing hurt.

Gilligan recognized that the scoring scheme devised by Kohlberg was sensitive to thinking based on rationality and justice but insensitive to thinking strategies based on the human, interpersonal consequences of the possible actions. Gilligan contended that, at a minimum, the traditional analyses of moral judgment missed the rich diversity of thinking about moral issues, something apparent in studies conducted in response to Gilligan's (1982) book.

For example, the adult participants in one study (Lyons, 1988) were asked, "What does morality mean to you?" They were also asked to describe themselves in relation to others and to talk about their own real-life moral conflicts and issues. Consistent with Kohlberg's work, the participants in the study talked about objective relations between people, duties and obligations, rules and standards—a morality of justice. Participants also discussed a morality of response and care, however, as predicted by Gilligan's theory. Consistent with Gilligan, the morality of justice predominated in men's responses, whereas response and care predominated in women's answers. In fact, about one-third of men made no references to response and care, and about one-third of women made no references to justice issues. Two-thirds of the research participants, however, represented both moralities in their responses, so that a scoring scheme based on justice alone would have misrepresented the moral reasoning of two-thirds of the men and all of the women.

Evidence of a sex difference was also obtained in a series of studies involving upper-middle-class adolescents and adults (Gilligan & Attannucci, 1988). The participants were asked to identify an occasion when they were in a moral conflict and describe what they did, followed by reflection on whether their action was appropriate and why they thought their actions were justified or should have been different. The interview data were then analyzed for the types of moral considerations expressed by the participants. Justice considerations predominated in the responses of two-thirds of the males, with all but one of the remaining third offering a mixture of justice and care considerations. In contrast, slightly more than one-third of females focused on issues of care, a little less than one-third focused on justice con-

Considering Important Questions

BOX 3.3. How Does Forgiveness Develop?

Robert Enright and his colleagues (1994, 2001; Enright & Fitzgibbons, 2000) have studied the development of forgiveness. They asked students in grades 4, 7, and 10, and in college, as well as adults, to respond to modified versions of the types of moral dilemmas used by Kohlberg in his research. The modification involved changing the story so that the lead character was hurt emotionally by the end of the story. For example, in the Heinz story, Heinz was unable to steal the drug from the greedy druggist and his wife died. The students were asked about whether Heinz should forgive the druggist and about the role of forgiveness in the following: revenge, restitution, peer and authority pressure, and social harmony. They were also asked about unconditional forgiveness—forgiveness that occurs without getting something in exchange and without external social pressure.

Enright and his colleagues described a developmental progression moving from conditional to unconditional forgiveness. That is, granting forgiveness in exchange for something is less advanced than forgiving in response to pressure which, in turn, is less advanced than unconditional forgiveness.

Although Enright found stage mixture in the responses, the participants' answers could be related to six stages (Enright & Human Development Study Group, 1994, Table 1):

- Stage 1: *Revengeful forgiveness*. "I can forgive someone who wrongs me only if I can punish him or her to a similar degree to my own pain."
- Stage 2: *Conditional or restitutional forgiveness*. "If I get back what was taken away from me, I can forgive." Or, "If I feel guilty about withholding forgiveness, I can forgive to relieve my guilt."
- Stage 3: *Expectational forgiveness*. "I can forgive if others pressure me to forgive; I forgive because other people expect it."
- Stage 4: *Lawful expectational forgiveness*. "I forgive because my religion (or other institution) demands it." (Note this differs from Stage 2, in which forgiveness is to relieve guilt about withholding forgiveness.)
- Stage 5: *Forgiveness as social harmony*. "I forgive because it restores harmony or social relations in society." Forgiveness decreases friction and outright conflict in society; it is a way of maintaining peaceful relations.
- Stage 6: *Forgiveness as love*. "I forgive because it promotes a true sense of love. Because I must truly care for each person, a hurtful act on his or her part does not alter that sense of love." This type of relationship keeps open the possibility of reconciliation and closes the door on revenge. Forgiveness no longer depends on a social context, as at Stage 5. The forgiver does not control the other by forgiving, but he or she releases the other.

Enright found a strong relationship between stage level and age, with older participants reasoning about forgiveness at a higher level than younger participants. A modest relationship existed between the level of reasoning about forgiveness and the individual's moral reasoning in general, suggesting some overlap between the two types of reasoning but considerable independence as well.

siderations, and the remaining third offered a mixture of care and justice considerations. If the data had been scored only for consideration of justice issues, the reasoning of one-third of the males and two-thirds of the females would have been misrepresented (see also Johnson, 1988).

Gilligan and her associates believe that the identification of the two "voices" in their research on moral reasoning has far-reaching implications. Although their message of a sex difference is what has captured the most attention, the larger message seems to be that moral reasoning that is only rational, just, and attentive to rules and duties is narrow in its conceptualization of the world. There is another way to look at things, one emphasizing interconnections, caring, and responsibility for others.

Other Perspectives on "Different Voices" in Moral Reasoning

Many other analyses of conventional moral judgment data—that is, data based on typical scoring of Kohlbergian or similar dilemmas—do not reveal striking sex differences (Gibbs et al., 1984; Rest, 1979; Rest et al., 1986; Rest, Thoma, & Edwards, 1997; Walker, 1984, 1989). In a meta-analysis of many studies, Jaffee and Hyde (2000) reported small differences in the care orientation favoring females and small differences in the justice orientation favoring males. Less conventional analyses also suggest less striking differences between males and females in their reasoning than Gilligan and her colleagues observed.

For example, Galotti (1989) asked undergraduates, "When faced with a moral dilemma, what issues or concerns influence your decision?" Gallotti found little evidence of sex differences in response to this question, with both males and females including both "masculine" and "feminine" themes in their responses. In another study, Galotti, Kozberg, and Farmer (1991) administered moral judgment dilemmas to students in grades eight and 11 as well as to college sophomores. Again, male and female thinking were more similar than different, although females tended to be more concerned with what others think about their judgments and the effects of their decisions on themselves, including personal guilt and social reactions. Bebeau and Brabeck (1987) observed more similarities than differences in the moral reasoning of dental students about ethical dilemmas in their profession and they did not observe any differences between males and females with respect to their concern for care of dental patients.

Researchers focusing on the psychological development of women are not the only ones offering data challenging Kohlberg's thinking about universality, however. Cross-cultural researchers have found differences in moral thinking that reflects the socialization pressures of the culture—although the general Kohlbergian pattern of development is also observed (Baek, 2002; Gates, 1990; Iwasa, 1992; Luhmer, 1990; Maosen, 1990; Nucci, 2003; Okonkwo, 1997; Thomas, 1990; Tzuriel, 1992; Walker & Moran, 1991). For example, Chinese communists endorse practices such as capital punishment more readily than do many Westerners, emphasizing the benefits for the collective, rather than focusing on the individual rights of the victim (Walker & Moran, 1991). Also, Chinese are reluctant to claim that arguments made in response to a particular dilemma imply any general way of thinking. Even relatively sophisticated Chinese thinkers believe more in analyzing the concrete specifics of any given situation in making moral judgments than do Western thinkers. Cultural differences in responses to moral dilemmas are consistent with a general theme that culture greatly influences thinking and behavior.

Education and the Development of Moral Judgment

Can students learn to be more sophisticated in their moral reasoning? Can moral education be successful? Enright, Lapsley, and Levy (1983) summarized research on moral education that accumulated from the 1960s to the early 1980s. They concluded that the approach to moral education favored by Kohlberg works very well for older students (those in junior high and high school): have students discuss and reason among themselves about moral dilemmas. This is sometimes referred to as the **plus-one approach** because it potentially exposes each student to information from a stage beyond him or her. That is, each student in the discussion except the most advanced student would have a model who was slightly beyond his or her current functioning; the most advanced student would presumably have the teacher as a model of a higher level of moral sophistication. Kohlberg believed that a one-stage discrepancy would be likely to induce cognitive conflict, which in turn motivates reflection on the new information, reflection that often results in an understanding of the slightly more advanced position. Enright and colleagues (1983) concluded that positive effects of plus-one moral reasoning discussions can be obtained both with short interventions (a single session) and long ones (full semester courses).

This approach to moral education has been implemented in schools (Higgins, 1987; Nicholls & Nelson, 1992; Power & Power, 1992; Rulon, 1992), institutions serving emotionally disturbed adolescents (Blakeney & Blakeney, 1990), and prisons (Powell, Locke, & Sprinthall, 1991). Proponents of this type of instruction are inspired by Piagetian and Kohlbergian thinking about the cognitive growth provided by cognitive conflict, although increasingly plus-one discussions occur in the context of educational environments designed to promote moral judgment and behavior using a variety of techniques. Some of these techniques are described in the Applying Developmental Theory to Educational Contexts special feature (see Box 3.4).

It is important to acknowledge how difficult it can be to carry out Kohlbergian-type programs of moral instruction. The types of discussions required demand much of students (Sharp, 1987). Participants must be capable of all of the following: open and attentive listening to another's ideas, willing acceptance of corrections by peers, revisions of views in light of ideas from others, development of ideas without fear of rebuff or humiliation from peers, detection of underlying assumptions, the ability to ask relevant questions, sensitivity to context when discussing moral conduct, and impartial discussion of issues. Perhaps the complexity of plus-one exchanges explains why moral discussions have not been very successful with elementary-school students (Enright et al., 1983).

If plus-one is challenging for students, it is even tougher for many teachers. Many teachers do not feel comfortable serving as models of moral reasoning and/or they do not understand how to carry out Kohlberg's educational vision, identifying much more with the cultural transmission (i.e., teacher as teller of rules) approach to moral education (Bergem, 1990; Cox, 1988; Kutnick, 1988, 1990).

■ ■ ■ CONSTRUCTIVIST APPROACHES
TO EDUCATION

Kohlberg and Mayer (1972) proposed a way of thinking about three alternative methods of education. The first, *romanticism*, is based on the belief that the child is naturally good. Education should mostly leave the child alone, allowing natural develop-

BOX 3.4. Stimulating Socially Responsible Thinking and Behavior

Thomas Lickona (1991) has compiled a comprehensive sourcebook on techniques for moral education. Lickona considers cognitive conflict and just community-type interventions, along with many other approaches designed to influence moral behavior as well as moral reasoning, including the following:

- *Teacher modeling of moral behavior and reasoning.* Teachers who model moral behavior and reasoning are more likely to have students who act in moral ways and can reason in a sophisticated fashion about moral issues.
- *Guest speakers.* Teachers should expose students to real ethical models whenever possible. For example, the teacher could invite to class a whistle-blower who exposed wrongdoing at some personal cost.
- *Use of storytelling and literature.* People can learn from symbolic models, either television characters or characters in books.
- *Influencing television viewing.* Both antisocial and prosocial behaviors can be learned from television.
- *Discussion of controversial issues that concern society.* Students can learn that controversial issues are many-sided and complex by discussing them in class.
- *Using the curriculum to encourage moral growth.* Teachers should take advantage of any opportunity to teach responsibility. For example, the class's pet rabbit or hamster can be used in many ways for lessons in caring and responsibility. Ethics can be an important theme in the school day.
- *Direct teaching.* Direct explanations are often effective in changing student behavior. Teachers can make a substantial difference by communicating clearly that values matter.
- *Asking students to be more ethical in their conduct; explaining why.* Receiving explanations about why antisocial behavior is unacceptable compared to prosocial behavior increases socially acceptable behavior.
- *The institution of negative consequences for unethical conduct and positive consequences for ethical, fair, and altruistic behavior.* Teachers should use reinforcement and punishment to promote the development of positive behaviors and to discourage immoral, antisocial behaviors.
- *The fostering of cooperative learning and cooperation in general.* Evidence is growing that the ethical and mental health components in a cooperative environment are better than those in a competitive environment.
- *High expectations.* Teachers can send the message that there are high expectations about the moral, ethical, and civic development of students in the school . . . and then they should actually expect high moral, ethical, and civic responsibility.
- *Mentoring and individual guidance.* Development of close relationships between teachers and students can have a tremendous influence on moral and ethical development.
- *Rejection of the concept that ethics are simply matters of personal opinions.* One movement in moral education, *values clarification*, encourages teachers not to make value judgments about student stances on ethical issues. Lickona rejects this thinking, believing there are some clearly moral and immoral stances that are not controversial at all. Teachers should challenge students when they voice ethical positions that are contrary to stances that are acceptable in society—or when they engage in behavior that would be considered unethical by a moral person.

Lickona's perspective is consistent with the point of view favored throughout this book that effective instruction is complex and multifaceted, but understandable in terms of ideas highlighted in mainstream theories of development and instruction. Good moral education combines a variety of approaches.

ment to unfold. A permissive educational environment will permit the good in the child to come out and the bad in the child to come under control. Freedom is the prevailing theme in romantic educational settings. (One of the most famous schools consistent with the romantic approach, Summerhill School, is discussed in Chapter 5.)

The second approach, *cultural transmission*, involves direct instruction of the knowledge and values of the culture. If you are in a class in which the professor lectures and you take notes, you are experiencing the cultural transmission model. Much of conventional education in the United States is cultural transmission.

The third approach specified by Kohlberg and Mayer (1972) originated with the educational philosopher John Dewey (1933). According to *progressivism*, education at its best fosters natural interaction between the child and the environment, both the physical and the social environments. Both Piagetian and Kohlbergian approaches to education are progressive. Such natural interactions permit the child to construct understandings of the world, with such *constructivist* activities resulting in much more complete understanding than would cultural transmission of the same ideas.

According to constructivist theory, a child who constructs an understanding of conservation by playing around with beakers of water will understand conservation better than if the same child was taught the verbal rule, "It is the same amount of water unless water is added or subtracted." But recall the evidence described earlier that conservation can be acquired following instruction.

What might be going on when a child learns to conserve by learning a verbal rule? Perhaps the child does not fully understand the rule when it is expounded, but the rule permits the child to construct relatively quickly an understanding of what is going on as the water is being poured—much more quickly than if the child had to discover the rule through repeated pouring. What might be going on when a child learns conservation by observing a conserving child make judgments about water poured between beakers? Perhaps the child experiences some cognitive conflict between what he or she thought was going on and the conserving child's declarations that the amount of water is the same regardless of which beaker it is in. Observing the conserver exposed the nonconserver to a possibility not hitherto considered, producing some disequilibrium, motivating reflection on the situation and eventual reestablishment of equilibrium. Thus the possibility exists that knowledge construction can be stimulated from verbal explanations and observational learning opportunities.

Constructivism and Mathematics Education

Mathematics educators have especially embraced constructivist education, emphasizing natural engagement with tasks and the social world (see many of the chapters in Kilpatrick, Martin, & Schifter, 2003). Learning mathematics is constructivist when the learner is active and proactive during problem solving—not simply responding to directions given by someone else but rather determining his or her own direction. Such activity leads to structural change—for example, to the development of operational competence (in the Piagetian sense of "operations," cognitive rules that have some generality). Knowledge is constructed from experience. The active learner analyzes and interprets. Although construction of knowledge can occur when one individual experiments with objects in the world, knowledge construction often involves several people in interaction, bouncing ideas off one another and trying out possibilities together (Mahoney, 1991; von Glaserfeld, 1995). Mathematics educators have been carrying out experiments to test these possibilities.

Evaluation of a Problem-Centered Second-Grade Mathematics Curriculum

Paul Cobb and his colleagues at Purdue University (Cobb et al., 1991) compared performance in 10 second-grade classrooms that received arithmetic instruction consistent with constructivist principles and eight classrooms that received conventional instruction. Children in the constructivist classrooms solved challenging problems continuously. The students were encouraged to reflect on their problem-solving activities and to construct knowledge about how to solve problems. The problem solving generally took place in interactive, cooperative classroom groups, groups in which the role of the teacher was to provide support and gentle guidance in the direction of productive problem solving, rather than to provide solutions or explicit instruction about how to solve problems. The experimental curriculum focused on addition and subtraction and on the development of strategies for solving such problems. Students were encouraged to believe that success in mathematics was possible through individual and collective efforts. The experimental students were encouraged to feel successful when they solved challenging problems.

Did the constructivist approach make a difference? It did on state-administered assessments of mathematics achievement as well as on an experimenter-produced test of mathematics achievement. Differences favoring the experimental students were especially notable on items requiring application of the concepts covered in the curriculum. Moreover, the students in the experimental classes reported that they valued collaboration more than did control students. In general, constructivist mathematics approaches do seem to promote better understanding of mathematics. For example, constructivist approaches work better with fourth and fifth graders as they learn fractions (Cramer, Post, & delMas, 2002), for elementary- and middle-school students learning the content of full-year mathematics curricula (Fuson, Carroll, & Drueck, 2000; Riordan & Noyce, 2001), and in high-school algebra classes (Huntley, Rasmussen, Villarubi, Sangton, & Fey, 2000; Thompson & Senk, 2001).

Standards of the National Council of Teachers of Mathematics

The National Council of Teachers of Mathematics (2000) are so impressed with the constructivist approach that they have recommended complete revision of the mathematics curriculum to be more consistent with the constructivist model. These *Principles and Standards for School Mathematics* have had a great deal of impact on mathematics education reform across the United States. If you were to ask many contemporary mathematics educators what good mathematics instruction does—that is, how it contrasts with conventional instruction—they would tell you that it promotes understanding of mathematical concepts and procedures by encouraging student to construct those understandings. Such understanding is essential if mathematics is to be used broadly and flexibly. It entails all of the following:

- Recognizing that mathematical concepts and procedures are important ways of thinking about and organizing real experiences.
- Recognizing how mathematical concepts and procedures are related to one another and are related to information already understood by the student.

- Knowing when, why, and where to apply mathematical concepts and procedures.
- Being able to explain why particular mathematical concepts and procedures are used to solve particular problems.

These views of mathematical understanding lead to certain assumptions about the teaching of mathematics that are outlined in the Applying Developmental Theory to Educational Contexts special feature (Box 3.5).

Alternative Approaches to Constructivism

There is more than one type of constructivism. Von Glaserfeld and other mathematics educators refer to themselves as "radical constructivists," which seems appropriate given their extreme emphasis on the benefits of student discovery relative to learning from instruction. Moshman (1982) refers to this type of constructivism as *endogenous constructivism*–knowledge construction through child-determined exploration much as Piaget had originally depicted constructivism. The endogenous constructivist educator endeavors to provide the child with tasks that are just a bit beyond the child's current competence. Moreover, the endogenous educator encourages students to use what they already know about mathematics and mathematical relationships to solve such new problems.

In contrast is *dialectical constructivism*. The dialectical constructivist recognizes the inefficiencies of discovery. The dialectical constructivist educator provides hints and prompts to students as they struggle with problems. That is, he or she provides just enough support so that the child can make progress. The dialectical constructivist educator does not provide full-blown explanations or model particular strategies for problem solving, but rather reminds students about how what they already know might be applied to new problems. Like the endogenous constructivist, the dialectical constructivist educator believes that long-term internalization of problem-solving strategies and mathematical concepts is most likely if students spend time figuring out how and when to apply the mathematical ideas they know. The difference is that the dialectical constructivist is more willing to provide help.

Even more help is provided by *exogenous constructivists*, who believe much more in teaching than do either endogenous or dialectical constructivists. The exogenous constructivist educator provides explanations and models problem solving for students, in an effort to give the student a good start on problem solving. The exogenous constructivist educator knows that children do not learn how to problem solve from teacher presentations. However, they are in a better position to begin applying the methods explained and modeled, and as they struggle to apply these methods to problems they construct understanding of the procedures and how to adapt them.

Researchers interested in educational technology have found value in Moshman's distinctions pertaining to constructivism. Dalgarno (2001, 2002) concluded that many hypermedia, computer simulations, and computer microworlds that are used in instruction are consistent with endogenous constructivism. Delgarno also concluded that learner-controlled tutorials and computer-based practice modules are consistent with exogenous constructivism and that computer-supported collaborative learning is consistent with dialectical constructivism. Although many educators are attempting to devise what they consider to be endogenous constructivist curricula, other instructional perspectives that advocate for more explicit teaching can also be constructivist. The differences in the role of the teacher in these alternative constructivist approaches are summarized in Table 3.4.

Applying Developmental Theory to Educational Contexts

BOX 3.5. Assumptions about Teaching Mathematics

The *Standards* of the NCTM have lead to recommendations for teaching practice based on developmental theory.

• Learning of mathematics is best when it results from children's own mathematical activities—that is, when they construct their own understandings of problem-solving and mathematics concepts rather than when mathematics concepts are taught by a teacher or textbook.

• Often mathematical concepts can be grasped by children through manipulatives before they can be grasped symbolically (see Sowell, 1989). In general, concrete, incomplete, and unsystematic (informal) learning of mathematics precedes abstract (symbolic), complete, systematic, and formal learning. Formal learning is at its best when it is connected and related to students' informal understanding (Putnam, Lampert, & Peterson, 1990).

• Instruction should emphasize how mathematical symbols are related to events and relationships in the world, especially events and relationships already understood by the child. For example, relate the mathematical operation of division to sharing, such as when three children share six cookies, with each child receiving two cookies.

• Instruction should support student behaviors likely to motivate appropriate efforts and persistence in learning mathematics. Thus students should be encouraged to ask questions when a concept or procedure is not understood, to expect errors when doing mathematics, and to relate the mathematics learned in school to everyday life.

• Mathematics is a means for learning new ways of solving problems. Students should be encouraged to reflect in order to abstract general problem-solving principles and procedures from working particular problems.

• Students should be encouraged to use technology such as calculators as part of problem solving, since these devices eliminate much of the lower order computational demands of problem solving, permitting students to pay more attention to the higher order, executive decisions.

• Students should work on word problems from the beginning of mathematics instruction. Word problems require students to map the relationships expressed in the problems verbally to mathematical concepts, symbols, and procedures.

• Teachers should question students about how they are solving problems and listen to student answers, since such answers can be revealing about what students understand and do not yet grasp. This is part of ongoing assessment of student progress in understanding the mathematical ideas they are being taught.

• Problem solving in small groups is often effective, especially in getting students to explain their reasons for problem solving in particular ways, but also in exposing students to alternative solution methods. Small-group problem solving also permits students to experience the understanding–solving–checking cycle (Artzt & Armour-Thomas, 1992; Polya, 1954a, 1954b). According to Alan Schoenfeld (1992), real mathematics is a social and collaborative enterprise involving talking and explaining and making false starts with other people.

• Teachers should model problem solving, making obvious as they do so that problem solving is not always straightforward, but often involves false starts and consideration of many factors.

Can you detect the Piagetian influence on these recommendations? One example is teaching mathematics to young children using concrete materials. The Piagetian themes of exploration and discovery also pervade the NCTM recommendations. The Piagetian emphasis that instruction should be matched to the child's level of functioning comes through as well, with teachers urged to continually diagnose the level of functioning of the child and provide instruction just beyond the current levels of their students.

TABLE 3.4. Summary of the Role of the Teacher in Alternative Constructivist Approaches

Endogenous constructivism
    Teacher provides challenging tasks and encourages students.
Dialectical constructivism
    Teacher provides hints and prompts.
    Teacher reminds students of what they already know.
Exogenous constructivism
    Teacher provides explanations.
    Teacher models problem solving.

■ ■ ■ CHAPTER SUMMARY AND EVALUATION

Piagetian stage theory continues to have substantial impact on developmental psychology and education. Most developmental psychologists, however, recognize the limitations of the original four-stage conception of development offered by Piaget. Children acquire some acquisitions much earlier than Piaget proposed, others much later. Moreover, acquisitions such as conservation are much more teachable than Piaget believed. In addition, context matters with respect to cognitive development, with the specific skills a child acquires very much depending on the child's experiences.

Stage theory lives on in new forms, however. Perhaps most promising is the framework that Fischer is developing. As described in this chapter and in Chapter 2, Fischer and his associates are mapping how qualitative changes in physical development of the nervous system are related to cognitive, behavioral, and emotional shifts with development. In short, although the idea of clearly separable stages has given way to the idea of stage mixture, the belief that there are qualitative differences in the ways that children of different ages and stages think is enjoying renewed support. The result is a more realistic developmental psychology. For example, it is more realistic to conceive of the development of moral judgment depending on both the development of rationality and the development of caring. It is more realistic to believe that specific experiences are important in shaping specific competencies and skills than to credit the development of specific skills to cognitive development in general (i.e., the Piagetian stage the child is in).

In addition to the idea of stages, however, Piaget provided an important perspective on how development occurs: it is the result of cognitive conflict. Although cognitive conflict can lead to cognitive growth, teachers can stimulate students to construct knowledge in alternate ways. For example, explicit teaching and demonstrations can be the start of knowledge construction—discovery is not the only way to stimulate student reflection on what they know compared to what they need to understand.

Developmental Debates

The frameworks results considered in this chapter have broad implications for some of the debates introduced in Chapter 1. We revisit some of these debates to emphasize how much more we know about development because of Piagetian theory, research inspired by the theory, and other theories inspired by the original framework.

Nature versus Nurture

Although the case could be made that Piaget stressed biological unfolding of development over development based on experiences, both nature and nurture were always in the theory. The role of nurture was especially apparent in Piaget's book *The Moral Judgment of the Child* (1965), where he asserted that many arguments and conflicts with peers were key in stimulating the development of more mature moral thinking. But Piaget took various positions in his writing. Thus in *Biologie et connaissance* (Biology and knowledge; 1967), Piaget emphasizes biological regulation of development; the role of the environment was emphasized much more in *Sociological Studies* (Piaget, 1995). Of course, one way to think about environmental accommodations is that the ability to accommodate was an evolutionary advantage for humans, so that human environmental responsiveness reflects biology. Overall, Piagetian theory is typically thought of as an interactionist theory: biology interacts with environmental input.

Stages versus Continuous Development

The extreme Piagetian stage position has not survived critical scrutiny. Clear-cut stages, with abrupt onsets, are not supported by the research evidence. Recent neuropsychological research, however, confirms that some discontinuities in development do exist. In particular, brain growth spurts seem to be associated with cognitive, behavioral, and emotional reorganizations with development. Softer stage conceptions of development, such as Enright's views on forgiveness, are also flourishing. The idea of stage-like development dies hard, perhaps because the idea has some merit.

Universal versus Culture-Specific Developments

Piaget and Kohlberg both believed that they had identified universally experienced stages of development. However, their strong universalist positions fell when clear differences as a function of culture were documented in arenas like moral judgment. What may be universal, however, are the mechanisms that account for cognitive development. Cognitive conflict, explanations, and observations make a difference in the development of children growing up in a variety of circumstances.

Trait-Like Consistency versus Situational Variability in Behaviors

Piaget's original stage formulation asserts that children exhibit trait-like consistencies as a function of stage membership. Thus the thinking was that if a child were a conserver in one situation, he or she would be a conserver in all circumstances. The introduction of concepts such as horizontal décalage and stage mixture provided labels for the empirical reality of little stage-like consistency in behavior across tasks. With the development and extension of neo-Piagetian theories, which emphasize the effects of particular experiences and context on cognitive development, thinking about cognitive development is more sensitive to situational variability in cognitive performance.

Active versus Passive Child

At the heart of constructivist thinking is the belief that the child is an active self-starter. Some even suggest that when children are taught specific concepts and learn them from direct teaching, they are developing passively. New thinking about constructivism, however, argues that direct explanations and demonstrations can be the beginning of extremely active learning by children.

■ ■ ■ REVIEW OF KEY TERMS

accommodate In Piaget's theory of cognitive development, the modification of existing cognitive structures in response to environmental stimuli.

animism The belief that inanimate objects are alive.

assimilate In Piaget's theory of cognitive development, the incorporation of environmental stimuli into an existing scheme.

class inclusion The ability to answer questions about subset relationships between groups of items.

cognitive conflict According to Piaget's theory of cognitive development, the situation that occurs when a learner does not have cognitive structures that permit understanding of environmental stimuli.

compensation In conservation tasks, the recognition that change on one dimension can be compensated for by change on another dimension.

concrete operational stage The third stage of Piaget's theory of cognitive development, in which concrete operators can apply cognitive operations to problems involving concrete objects.

conservation Children's ability to realize that the transformation of a substance that changes its appearance does not alter its basic characteristics.

conventional morality According to Kohlberg's theory of moral development, the stages at which individuals focus on maintaining social order.

deferred imitation The ability to represent learned behaviors mentally so that the behavior can be imitated long after it was witnessed.

disequilibrium In Piaget's theory of cognitive development, the realization that two contradictory ways of thinking about the world cannot both be true.

egocentrism The inability to perceive the perspectives of others.

equilibration In Piaget's theory of cognitive development, the process by which a learner constructs new cognitive structures in response to disequilibrium in order to return to equilibrium.

formal operational stage The last stage of Piaget's theory of cognitive development, in which thinkers are capable of complex problem solving and of "thinking in possibilities," "thinking ahead," and "thinking in hypotheses."

horizontal décalage In Piaget's theory of cognitive development, the inability of individuals to master all problems requiring the same logical operations at the same time.

identity In conservation tasks, the realization that basic characteristics of a substance remain the same despite perceptual transformations.

motor schemes Patterns of action used to interact with the environment developed during the sensorimotor stage of cognitive development.

object permanence A child's understanding that objects continue to exist regardless of whether or not the child can see or touch them.

operational schemes The logical patterns of thinking that characterize the concrete and formal operational stages of Piaget's theory of cognitive development.

plus-one approach An approach to moral education in which students discuss moral dilemmas to induce cognitive conflict and growth in understanding.

postconventional morality According to Kohlberg's theory of moral development, the stages at which individuals focus on shared principles and standards.

preconventional morality According to Kohlberg's theory of moral development, the stages at which individuals focus on self-interest in decision making.

preoperational stage The second stage of Piaget's theory of cognitive development, in which thinking benefits from the development of symbolic schemes.

reversibility In conservation tasks, the understanding that an operation can be undone by reversing it.

scheme A coordinated pattern of thought or action that organizes an individual's interaction with the environment.

sensorimotor stage The first stage of Piaget's theory of cognitive development, in which thinking is organized by motor schemes and a major accomplishment is object permanence.

seriate The ability to order objects on some dimension.

short-term memory A memory store of limited capacity and duration; also called working memory.

symbolic play Play that incorporates children's capabilities for symbolic representation so that play objects are used to represent other items.

symbolic schemes Cognitive structures, developed during the preoperational stage of cognitive development, that allow the representation of objects or events by means of symbols such as language, mental images, and gestures.

CHAPTER 4

Cognitive Development
Information-Processing Theory

Although stage models such as Piaget's (described in Chapter 3) once prevailed as the way developmental psychologists characterized the development of thinking abilities, information-processing models of cognitive development have commanded much more attention from developmental researchers in the last two decades. The information-processing perspective is that thinking is analogous to the working of a computer (Mayer, 2003). Much like the hard drive of a computer, we have long-term memory stores, which contain our knowledge. This knowledge takes a variety of forms, such as knowledge of factual information, images of things we have seen, and knowledge of how to do things. Much of the time, we are not using the information we have stored in long-term memory. When information from our long-term memory is activated into our short-term memory (analogous to RAM, in computer terms), and then combined with information being perceived by the senses, that is when thinking occurs.

Consider the following situation. You have just picked up your boarding pass at the ticket counter of an airport. You walk toward the gate. You realize that you will need both your boarding pass and a government-issued identification (e.g., a driver's license) to pass through security. That knowledge has been in your long-term memory for a few years, although you rarely think about it. It is now being thought about in your active consciousness (i.e., your short-term memory) because you are in a setting that cues you to remember this information. You pass through security, and as you do so, the security guard tells you that you can put your identification away. This airport no longer requires an ID check at the gate. You put your ID away, and as you do so, you make a mental note that the procedure at this, your hometown airport, has changed. You have updated your long-term knowledge. Once at the gate, there is a delay, long enough that you will miss your connection. You go to the counter and ask about other connections you might make. The agent types away at the computer and then begins to read a bunch of options. After about the fourth or fifth one, you say, "Whoa!! I can't keep track of this." That is because your short-term memory, your conscious capacity, has been exceeded. Human beings can only hold a few items of information in mind at once. You ask the agent to reread the options, and this time you write down the options as she says them. You are using a strategy to overcome short-term memory limitations.

From the information-processing perspective, cognitive development is about the development of short-term memory capacity, long-term knowledge, and the use of strategies (or the ways in which we can plan to acquire knowledge). As portrayed in the anecdote about the airport, the various components of our minds are always interacting as we navigate the world. This is an enormous cognitive accomplishment. In this chapter, we present what is known about the development of short-term memory capacity, strategies, and the representation of knowledge that allow us to accomplish complex cognitive tasks.

■ ■ ■ BASIC MEMORY CAPACITIES AND MECHANISMS

One hypothesis about the development of memory and thinking skills is that memory, learning, and cognition improve with development because children's short-term memory capacity increases (Dempster, 1981, 1985; Hasselhorn, 1986; Weinert, 1979; see also Chapters 2 and 3). What do we mean by short-term memory? **Short-term memory** is a memory store of limited capacity and duration (Nairne, 2003). It is a human's active consciousness, the place where information currently activated in thinking is processed. When someone holds a telephone number in memory while searching for a scratch pad (or a list of flight options being rattled off by a frustrated gate agent), this thinking goes on in short-term memory. Short-term memory is active as an author juggles bits and pieces of ideas he or she is trying to combine into sentences and paragraphs. Close your eyes and try to keep in "view" the room you are sitting in; your image is in your short-term memory.

Short-term memory is exactly what the name implies: short term. If a person does not continue to rehearse a phone number, the number will fade from consciousness. If an author is distracted while writing, some of the ideas he or she is juggling will be lost. Moreover, short-term memory is limited in terms of the amount of information that can be attended to consciously at any one moment. Only so many numbers can be rehearsed at once. Only so many bits of information can be considered before new pieces of information literally seem to push out some of the information already in short-term memory. Thus short-term memory is limited in duration and capacity. You have probably noticed how sometimes other things compete for your limited short-term capacity when you are trying to pay attention in class. Sometimes it's a commotion in the hallway, or the person whispering next to you, or even your own plans for the weekend, but you probably shift your attention back and forth between the distractions and the task at hand since you find it difficult to hold so many things in memory at the same time.

Researchers have conceptualized short-term memory in a number of different ways. These models of short-term memory range from a rather passive "container" model (Atkinson & Shiffrin, 1968; Brown & DeLoache, 1978) to an extremely active "working memory" system, including several components in interaction such as the capacity to hold and/or to manipulate verbal information (Baddeley, 1981, 1986) as well as visual information (Logie, 1995).

Short-term memory and working memory concepts differ in that the former involves only storage and reproduction of information, but the latter includes the capacity to transform information being held in short-term memory (Case, 1978; Case & Kurland, 1980; Case, Kurland, & Goldberg, 1982; Dempster, 1985). The current trend is to focus on the active processing capacity that is captured by the working memory construct. In this chapter, however, we use the terms *short-term memory* and *working memory* somewhat interchangeably.

Short-term and working memory are usually tapped with "memory span" tasks. These typically involve presentation of a list of numbers or words. The person being tested must recall the words on the list, sometimes in order, sometimes in the reverse order of presentation, and sometimes in any order, depending on the exact aspect of short-term or working memory being assessed. In general, with increasing age, between the ages of 3 and 16, children exhibit a linear increase in the number of items that they can recall from such list presentations (see Table 4.1).

Explanations of Developmental Increases in Functional Capacity of Short-Term Memory

There are a number of possible explanations for the increases observed in children's short-term (working) memory capacity as they develop (Dempster, 1985). But as we review different explanations for this increase, it will become obvious that our understanding of short-term memory capacity is far from complete.

Neurological Development

One explanation for the increase in short-term memory capacity is that as the brain increases in size with maturity, its short-term memory capacity expands. From this perspective, the number of "slots" increase, perhaps one slot every 2 years, as a result of neurological development (Miller, 1956). Specifically, researchers are investigating how the development of the brain's frontal lobes might account for working memory development (Alvarado & Bachevalier, 2000; Fabiani & Wee, 2001).

Pascual-Leone (1970) referred to short-term capacity as "central computing space," or "mental space" (abbreviated as "M-space"), and proposed that developmental changes in short-term capacity can explain many of the stage-like shifts with

TABLE 4.1. Development of Short-Term Memory Capacity

2-year-olds	About two items
5-year-olds	About four items
7-year-olds	About five items
9-year-olds	About six items
Adolescents	About seven items

development originally described by Piaget (a neo-Piagetian perspective as described in Chapter 3). In this view, M-space is the maximum number of schemata that a person can activate and/or coordinate simultaneously. Recent evidence suggests that short-term or working memory capacity may continue to increase throughout adolescence and adulthood (Swanson, 1999; Zald & Iacono, 1998). Thus one explanation for short-term memory capacity increases is changes in brain capacity due to neurological development.

Speed of Information Processing

Other researchers maintain that developmental increases in the functional capacity of short-term memory are due to more efficient processing of stimuli (Cowan, Saults, & Elliot, 2002). Increased processing efficiency is a result of faster recognition and activation of information from long-term memory, general speed of processing, and changes in the rate of decay of information in active memory. Those who support this speed-of-processing perspective deemphasize the role of increases in actual capacity in accounting for differences in functional short-term capacity. For example, Case (1992, 1995, 1999) argued that the amount of space required to perform operations decreases with increasing age due to more rapid processing of information in working memory. This, in turn, frees up more space for storage of material and accounts for the increases in memory span performance as well as for stage-like shifts in competencies described in Piagetian theory (a neo-Piagetian perspective as described in Chapter 3). That is, formal operational thinking requires greater functional short-term capacity than concrete operational performances, which in turn require more functional capacity than preoperational thinking.

Plenty of evidence indicates that speed of processing generally increases with age during childhood. For instance, the rate of item identification (i.e., the time necessary to recognize or name to-be-remembered items when they are first presented as pictures or words) decreases with age (Chi, 1977). Memory span differences reflect developmental differences in both recognizing span items and speed in saying them (Henry & Millar, 1991; Kail, 1992, 2000; Kail & Park, 1994; Roodenrys, Hulme, & Brown, 1993). Thus short-term memory capacity increases can be explained by increased speed of processing, which allows more efficient use of a limited capacity.

Rehearsal Strategies

Yet another perspective points to the importance of verbal labeling and rehearsal in determining working memory capacity. **Rehearsal** is a strategy of repeating information in order to recall it later. For example, when Hitch, Halliday, Schaafstal, and Heffernan (1991) asked 5-year-olds to label (i.e., say the name of each picture on the list aloud) pictures in a memory span task, their performances improved, suggesting that without instruction the children would not have verbally labeled to-be-remembered items as they were presented. In contrast, when 11-year-olds were asked to label, their short-term memory performances worsened, suggesting that labeling (saying the name of each picture once) was interfering with more complex rehearsal processes the children would have used on their own. Thus short-term memory capacity increases can be explained by increased and more sophisticated use of rehearsal strategies.

Prior Knowledge and Chunking

Another explanation for increasing short-term memory capacity with development is the processing advantage of a growing knowledge base. With increasing knowledge, children can "chunk" related information together. Miller (1956) introduced the "magic" number "7 (plus or minus 2)" as the maximum number of chunks of verbal information that could be held in short-term memory at any given instant. Although capacity in terms of chunks is limited, individual differences in working memory capacity can be explained in terms of different-size chunks (Simon, 1974).

One of the most important studies supporting the chunking hypothesis was conducted by Chi (1978). She compared how well child chess experts and adult chess novices could memorize the position of pieces on a chessboard. Although the children did not perform as well as the adults on a typical memory span task (as would be expected), they did recall more of the chess positions than the adults. In interviews after the experiment, the child experts indicated that they viewed the whole chessboard as the unit of learning—a chunk. The children who knew a lot about chess were better able to create chunks than were the less knowledgeable adults. Thus short-term memory capacity increases can be explained by larger pieces of information being encoded as chunks due to an expanding knowledge base.

Inhibition and Interference

A final explanation of increasing short-term memory capacity with development is the increasing ability to reduce interference from irrelevant information. Failures to inhibit some responses can interfere with making other responses (Luria, 1961; Meichenbaum, 1977; Pressley, 1979). Children's ability to inhibit task-irrelevant responses increases with development, in part due to neuropsychological development of the frontal lobes (Dempster, 1993; Fuster, 1989; Luria, 1973).

How might developmental increases in resistance to distraction increase performance on memory span tasks—and cognitive performances more generally? As the ability to inhibit distracting thoughts increases, more of the short-term capacity is available for the task the child is focusing on (Bjorklund & Harnishfeger, 1990; Harnishfeger & Bjorklund, 1993). In addition, since distractions have the potential to interfere with performance, eliminating distractions through inhibition eliminates potential interference. Because younger children are more distractible than older children, they are more susceptible to interference from distractions (Brainerd & Reyna, 1989, 1990a, 1990b, 1993, 1995; Hale & Lewis, 1979; Reyna, 1995; Reyna & Brainerd, 1995). Thus increased short-term memory capacity can be explained by the development of inhibition and resistance to interference.

In summary, we know that children display increases in their functional short-term memory capacity and there are a variety of explanations for that increase (see Table 4.2). It is important for future educators to remember that the amount anyone can hold in memory at once—the amount anyone can think about at one time—is limited, with the limitation greater the younger the child. Thus teachers need to be aware of the memory demands of classroom tasks. When students have difficulty with classroom tasks due to working memory limitations, teachers can support their students by breaking tasks down into parts that are less memory demanding or by providing external supports that reduce the amount of information the students have to hold in their heads at one time.

TABLE 4.2. Explanations for Developmental Increase in Short-Term Memory Capacity

- Neurologically determined increases in brain capacity.
- Increases in processing speed and efficiency.
- Increased and more sophisticated use of strategies.
- Increased chunking due to expanding knowledge base.
- Increased ability to inhibit distractions and resist interference.

■ ■ ■ STRATEGIES

Increases in memory capacity clearly contribute to cognitive development but cognitive advances in childhood and adolescence are also determined in part by developmental increases in use of cognitive strategies. This idea is of enormous consequence for educators because it suggests that children's and adolescents' thinking and learning can be improved by teaching them strategies that they do not discover and use on their own.

Definition of Strategies

Strategies are plans of action designed to achieve a goal that are "potentially conscious and controllable activities" (Pressley, Forrest-Pressley, Elliott-Faust, & Miller, 1985, p. 4). Suppose you have to read a chapter for a class. What are the cognitive operations and processes that you must carry out? Of course, you must decode the words, normally by reading the article from first page to last. This is not a strategic activity according to the definition presented here, since the decoding of the words in order is pretty much obligatory in order to "read" the chapter.

What could you do that would go beyond front-to-back reading? You could employ many different strategies to understand and remember the text better (Pressley & Afflerbach, 1995). Before reading, you could skim the title, pictures, and headings to get a general idea of what the chapter is about. This might lead you to make predictions about what you will be reading. During reading, you might monitor carefully whether your predictions were correct and whether what you are reading makes sense. If it does not make sense, you might reread. Finally, after one reading of the text, you might self-test your understanding of what you read by trying to recall the content of the chapter. You might also look through the chapter, construct a summary, and note which parts of the article you did not remember during the self-test.

Teachers should teach their students to use these comprehension strategies when they read. For example, they could teach students to predict what might be in a text based on prior knowledge about the topic, to ask questions while they read (and look for answers), to construct images representing the ideas presented in text, and to test themselves by seeing if they can remember the summary of the text. Many teachers, however, experience difficulty teaching such strategies to their students (Pressley & El-Dinary, 1997). For some, the difficulty stems from the fact that they do not use such strategies themselves when they read (Keene & Zimmermann, 1997). Still, when teachers do teach their students to use comprehension strategies, the students exhibit improvements in their reading comprehension as captured by a variety of assessments, including standardized tests (Anderson, 1992; Brown, Pressley, & Van Meter, 1996; Collins, 1991).

In short, many different ways of processing text, beyond simple reading, facilitate understanding and memory of text information. These are strategies. Typically, readers execute strategies consciously and intentionally. Eventually, however, the goal is for readers to carry out these processes automatically, with great ease and little awareness. (Although strategic readers could consciously control their strategies if they chose to do so.) Several years of comprehension strategies instruction in elementary school can go a long way toward the development of skilled strategic readers (Pressley et al., 1992). The first step, however, is to understand how strategy use develops in children and adolescents.

Development of Strategy Use in Young Children

Most of the research on children's development of strategic competence has been conducted by researchers studying basic memory. This research has shaped the way educators think about how children learn new information. One of the most common strategies used by children is *rehearsal*. In many research studies investigating children's use of strategies, the children were asked to remember lists of items in a serial recall task. In a typical **serial recall task**, a researcher presents a child some items to remember: perhaps a row of picture cards, one picture to a card, with the faces turned down. After informing the child that the task was to remember the picture cards in order, the researcher would turn each card face up for a few seconds.

One strategy that more advanced learners can apply to this task is known as **cumulative rehearsal–fast finish** (Barclay, 1979; Butterfield & Belmont, 1977). In this strategy, the learner says the early- and middle-list items over and over in order of presentation. Suppose the pictures are, from left to right, a chair, a dog, a cup, a car, a radio, a book, and a tree. After seeing the picture of the chair, the learner would say "chair" several times. Then, when the picture of the chair is turned face down and a picture of a dog revealed, the learner would say "chair, dog" several times. By the time a picture of a radio is presented, the rehearsal would include saying "chair, dog, cup, car, and radio" as many times as time permits. This adding-on of rehearsed elements, the cumulative-rehearsal part of the strategy, continues during the presentation of the entire list. (In contrast, if the rehearsal is not cumulative, the learner would rehearse "chair, chair" . . . with the presentation of the first picture and then "dog, dog" with the presentation of the second picture, etc.) The fast-finish part is obvious when the learner recalls the list. The learner immediately "dumps out" the last item or two that was presented (book and tree in our example) and then recalls the earlier items in order. That is, the learner recognizes that the last two items still are in some type of shorter term memory and can be recalled effortlessly if recalled first at the time of testing.

Use of the cumulative rehearsal–fast finish strategy develops slowly (Schneider & Pressley, 1989). Preschoolers and early elementary-age student do not use it. Their most typical strategy is simply to say the name of the picture as it is displayed. This is simple rehearsal without the cumulative quality, in the case of the picture presentation—a **labeling** strategy (Flavell, Beach, & Chinsky, 1966). Children in Western cultures, however, commonly use cumulative rehearsal alone (without the fast-finish part) by the end of the grade-school years (Flavell et al., 1966; Ornstein, Naus,

& Liberty, 1975). Learners typically do not add the fast-finish component until late adolescence in Western cultures (Barclay, 1979).

What strategies a person uses is determined largely by his or her personal sociocultural history (Kurtz, 1990). For example, German parents are more likely than U.S. parents to teach learning and memory strategies at home (Carr, Kurtz, Schneider, Turner, & Borkowski, 1989). The German emphasis on teaching strategies is apparent at school as well, with more teaching of learning and memory strategies in German than U.S. schools (Kurtz, Schneider, Carr, Borkowski, & Rellinger, 1990). German children are surrounded by an interpersonal world urging them to be strategic, and this immersion affects their development, making them more strategic learners than U.S. children.

Strategy Use by Preschoolers

Even preschoolers are sometimes strategic, at least for tasks in familiar surroundings. For example, DeLoache, Cassidy, and Brown (1985) hid an object (usually a familiar toy such as a Bugs Bunny or Big Bird stuffed animal) in a living room with the children watching and aware that later they would have to retrieve the hidden object. In this situation, even 2-year-olds are strategic. Although they played in the living room during the *retention interval* (the time between when the object is hidden and when they must retrieve it), preschoolers frequently looked at the place where the object was hidden. Sometimes, they even pointed to the location and said the name of the hidden object.

These checking-back and simple rehearsal strategies are, in fact, memory strategies. Sometimes the object was hidden in the room (e.g., under a pillow); other times it was placed in about the same position, but not hidden (e.g., on top of the same pillow). Only when the object was hidden from view did preschoolers look back at the spot or say the object's name during the retention interval. That is, they used the strategies only the situation demanded for memory.

Sometimes preschoolers exhibit memory strategies that are not yet useful to them (Lange, Mackinnon, & Nida, 1989). For example, Baker-Ward, Ornstein, and Holden (1984) presented preschool children with sets of toys. In both conditions of the study, children played with the toys. In one of the conditions, the directions given to the children only mentioned playing with the toys. In the other condition, the children were asked to remember some of the toys. The addition of this memory demand changed the processing of preschoolers dramatically. The children given the memory instruction played with the toys less. Instead, they looked intensely at the to-be-remembered toys and named them. But even though these children engaged in strategic behavior more than the children who only played with the toys, they did not remember more of the toys.

Preschoolers also can select strategies that hinder their memory performances. Newman (1990) found that children who were given a memory demand actually remembered less than children in a play condition. What was going on in the play condition? The children were creating verbal stories and constructing interactions between the toys. Taking unrelated objects and placing them in a meaningful context, such as making up a story about them, facilitates memory. Such stories and pictures are elaborations. An **elaboration** is the construction of a meaningful context for the to-be-learned information that can be either verbal or visual. The children who were asked to remember the items met this memory demand by rehearsing them or repeatedly looked at them, which proved less effective than elaboration.

Thus preschoolers sometimes are strategic, although their efforts to **encode**, to create durable memories, are not always successful. Even if preschoolers have a memory trace, however, that does not mean they will **retrieve**, or access, the memory trace, later. For example, Pressley and McFadyen (1983) found that children who learned associations or elaborations between pairs of items, such as "rock and turkey," through interactive pictures (such as a picture of a turkey sitting on a rock), did not recall more pairs unless they were also given a retrieval cue to "think back to the pictures you saw. . . . " This retrieval deficiency in preschoolers is surmounted shortly with development. Unlike preschoolers, kindergarten children do not need retrieval cues to make use of elaborated pictures presented at study. Since preschoolers experience retrieval difficulties that do not occur with older children (Ritter, 1978; Sodian & Schneider, 1990), teachers working with these young children need to provide retrieval cues for optimal memory performance.

Development of Strategic Competence in the School Years

Although the use of some strategies, especially rehearsal, clearly increases during the elementary school years in Western cultures, use of other and often more effective strategies develops slowly (and, for some students, not at all). Consider, for example, how elementary-school children tackle *paired-associate learning*, that is, learning associations between two items such as a vocabulary word and its definition, states and their capitals, names of inventors and their inventions, and cities and their products. The most efficient strategies for learning paired associates involve elaborations. The elaboration to learn a paired associate (e.g., the turkey paired with rock) could be either a verbal elaboration in the form of a meaningful sentence containing both pair members (e.g., "Turkeys have rocks in their gizzards.") or a meaningful interactive image (e.g., an image of a turkey scratching at rocks in the barnyard). The research evidence is quite clear. Elementary-age children do not use elaboration strategies on their own: they do not create their own images or stories when given pairs of items to learn (Pressley & Levin, 1977a, 1977b). Even many adults fail to use elaboration strategies (Bower, 1972; Kliegl, Smith, & Baltes, 1990; Rohwer, 1980; Rohwer & Litrownik, 1983).

By the end of the grade-school years, however, children sometimes elaborate materials (i.e., make associations to them) that are more meaningful than paired associates. For example, Chan, Burtis, Scardamalia, and Bereiter (1992) asked children to think aloud as they processed texts about dinosaurs and germs. With increasing age during the elementary-school years, students were less likely to rely on superficial understandings and irrelevant associations to text (e.g., associating to a single word in the text) and more likely to relate ideas in the text to one another and to their own prior knowledge in ways that made the ideas more sensible. Even the oldest students, the sixth graders, however, could have benefited from more integration and elaboration.

A pattern of development similar to that observed with elaboration strategies has also been found for strategies requiring students to organize information. **Organization** refers to the process of grouping information into categories or patterns on the basis of relationships or connections. Younger elementary-school children are less likely than older elementary-school children to organize information in a way that helps them remember the information better but can benefit from instructions designed to promote effective organization (Bjorkland, 2000; Scheider & Pressley, 1997). Moreover, effective use of organization strategies is also dependent on an increasingly well-developed knowledge base (see the discussion of knowledge later in this chapter). See Table 4.3 for a summary of strategy development.

It is probably not surprising that many college students do not study effectively. They fail to use effective memory strategies as well as effective procedures for reading comprehension, writing, and problem solving. That is why many campuses now offer study skills courses to students. A main focus of such courses is to teach strategies supporting elaboration and organization of to-be-learned material, which is sensible, given that many strategies can be taught.

Teaching Strategies

As discussed earlier in this chapter, young children often fail to use effective rehearsal strategies when learning lists. It takes only brief instructions, however, to teach 6- and 7-year-olds how to rehearse lists so they remember them later (Keeney, Cannizzo, & Flavell, 1967). Children in the early school years (kindergarten to third grade) also often fail to make use of organizational properties of lists, such as categories, that can aid memory. Again, it is easy to teach children to sort lists into catego-

TABLE 4.3. Development of Strategy Use

Early childhood (2–6 years of age)

- Rehearsal strategies
  Primarily labeling, beginnings of simple rehearsal
- Elaboration strategies
  Preschoolers can use if elaborations are provided but need retrieval cue
  Kindergartners can use if provided, no longer need retrieval cue
- Organization strategies
  Can use if provided, constrained by limited knowledge base

Middle childhood (6–11 or 12 years of age)

- Rehearsal strategies
  Simple rehearsal (early elementary school)
  Cumulative rehearsal (by end of elementary school)
- Elaboration strategies
  Can benefit from elaboration strategies but typically don't use them on their own
- Organization strategies
  Begin to use more effectively as knowledge base expands

Adolescence (11–12 years of age to the late teen years)

- Rehearsal strategies
  Cumulative rehearsal–fast finish typically develops by the end of high school
- Elaboration strategies
  Can benefit from elaboration strategies; some students may use on their own
- Organization strategies
  Can use effectively as knowledge base expands and becomes more organized

ries (Moely, Olson, Hawles, & Flavell, 1969). There have been many demonstrations of teaching children to use memory strategies that they did not exhibit without instruction (Pressley, Heisel, McCormick, & Nakamura, 1982). Instruction in strategy use, however, is not always enough to turn nonstrategic students into strategy users.

Continued Use of Strategies Following Instruction

Teaching students how to execute a strategy does not guarantee that they will use the strategy in appropriate situations. Students sometimes fail to continue using strategies in situations *almost identical* to the ones in which they first learned the strategies. This is called failure to **maintain** strategies. **Transfer** failures occur when students do not apply strategies they have learned to *new* situations and tasks where they could be appropriate.

Why are there maintenance and transfer failures? First, sometimes students simply do not recognize that they could apply a strategy they have learned in a new situation (Gick & Holyoak, 1980, 1983; Ross, 1984). Second, students sometimes may recognize that a strategy they know is applicable, but their use of it is so mixed up that the strategy is not effective (Harris, 1988). Third, sometimes students do not use a strategy because they do not enjoy carrying it out or do not feel that the gains produced by the strategy are worth the effort (Rabinowitz, Freeman, & Cohen, 1992). Thus simply teaching a student a strategy in no way assures maintenance or generalization of the strategy.

The possibility that simple strategy instruction did not teach students to recognize when a strategy would be useful stimulated a large number of experiments (Pressley, Borkowski, & O'Sullivan, 1984, 1985). One group of students was taught a strategy for some task. A second group was taught the same strategy for the same task but also was provided information about how the strategy would benefit performance. Knowledge about the potential effects of using a strategy is called **utility knowledge**. The outcome in such experiments was always the same. Students who were informed about the utility of the strategy were more likely to maintain the strategy than students who were not provided the utility information.

To increase the likelihood of strategy transfer, strategy instruction should also include information about when and where the strategy might apply, which is sometimes called **conditional knowledge** (Paris, Lipson, & Wixson, 1983). For example, O'Sullivan and Pressley (1984) taught children in the fifth and sixth grades a strategy to learn associations between cities and the products produced in those cities. Whether the students transferred the strategy to another task—learning Latin words and their definitions—depended on how much information had been included in the instruction about when and where to use the strategy. Utility knowledge and conditional knowledge are examples of metacognition. **Metacognition** is knowledge about and awareness of thinking, including the knowledge of when and where to apply acquired strategies (McCormick, 2003). Generally, increasing students' metacognitive understanding about the strategies they are learning increases the likelihood of strategy transfer (Weed, Ryan, & Day, 1990).

Monitoring Strategy Effectiveness

Suppose that you are taught a new strategy for a familiar task and try it out. How can you know whether the strategy has worked for you, that is, whether it has improved your performance relative to an old approach with the task? If you do recognize the value of the strategy, does it affect your decision to use the strategy in the future? These questions motivated a number of studies on monitoring of strategy effectiveness that yielded some surprising but consistent results. Learners, including adults, will often fail to monitor how well a strategy is working as they use it, but they can come to realize that a strategy is effective when they are tested and they can compare how they learned with one strategy versus another (Ghatala, 1986; Hunter-Blanks, Ghatala, Pressley, & Levin, 1988; Pressley & Ghatala, 1990; Pressley, Levin, & Ghatala, 1984).

What difference does awareness of differential strategy effectiveness have on decisions to use a strategy in the future? With adults, such awareness results in a strong preference for the effective strategy when confronted with similar learning tasks. With children, especially those in the early elementary grades, awareness of strategy effectiveness is less likely to lead to commitment to the strategy in the future. Indeed, the younger the child, the less likely the child is to monitor strategy effectiveness even when tested and the less likely the child is to continue to use a strategy proven to be effective (Ghatala, 1986; Ghatala, Levin, Pressley, & Goodwin, 1986; Pressley, Ross, Levin, & Ghatala, 1984).

In summary, skilled adult learners use strategies that are well matched to the tasks they are facing. Fortunately, adults and children who do not use strategies can be taught to use them. Sometimes only brief instruction is required. In other cases, longer term instruction is necessary. Effective strategy instruction can be complicated (see Table 4.4). The failure of strategies to transfer beyond training situations is a specific instance of a general conclusion that learning often tends to be tied to the context in which it occurs (see the discussion on situated knowledge later in this chapter). The challenge for instruction is to produce learning that is not bound to specific contexts. The way educators have tackled this challenge is to do long-term teaching, as illustrated by strategy instruction for the academic tasks of writing and reading described in the Applying Developmental Theory to Educational Contexts special features (Boxes 4.1 and 4.2).

TABLE 4.4. Guidelines for Strategy Instruction

- Some children learn to use effective strategies on their own. It is important to realize that even if students do not use effective strategies already, they can be taught to use them.

- Be sure to inform students of the *utility* of the new strategy. Describe the potential benefits.

- Be sure students have *conditional knowledge* about the strategy. Describe where and when the strategy is most effective.

- Simply asking students to practice the new strategy is not enough for maintenance and transfer of the strategy. Be sure students *monitor* the effectiveness of the new strategy relative to their own methods by comparing their performance on tests.

- If working with students younger than middle-school-age, prompt them to think back to their performance using the new strategy, compared to their old performance without the strategy use. Young children often require explicit feedback on their performance in order to realize which strategies are effective.

Applying Developmental Theory to Educational Contexts

BOX 4.1. Writing Strategies Instruction

Today, in most schools, writing strategies are routinely taught beginning from the early grade-school years (Harris & Graham, 1992). Much of this instruction boils down to teaching students to plan, draft, and revise, which is what good writers do (Flower & Hayes, 1980). A number of specific strategies can be taught for each of these phases. Not surprisingly, writing strategies instruction is long term, although it is often possible to observe some benefits after a few weeks or months of some specific type of strategy instruction (Harris & Graham, 1992). Successful instruction includes a great deal of explanation and modeling of writing strategies, followed by actual writing in which students are coached in the application and adaptation of the strategies they are learning, described below.

Strategies Addressing the Planning Stage

Because students sometimes do not search their memories thoroughly for everything they might know about a topic either before or while they write (Scardamalia & Bereiter, 1986), strategies that promote more thorough search of memory for ideas can increase the quantity of material written on a topic. For example, Humes (1983) recommended providing sets of question prompts that would stimulate systematic search of memory for relevant content. Thus, if the student were writing about a sequence of events, question prompts might include the following: What happened first? What happened next? Next? What happened last? When did it happen? Where did it happen? Whom did it happen to? Similarly, Bereiter and Scardamalia (1982) provided students with sentence openers such as "One reason . . . ," "Even though . . . ," "For example, . . . ," and "I think . . . " Perhaps the most intuitively obvious prompt to search memory, however, is simply to ask the child who writes a very short essay to "Write some more!," a command that children can internalize and make to themselves if they are taught to do so (Graham, 1990; Graham & Harris, 1987).

Strategies Addressing the Writing Stage

Students can learn to instruct themselves to respond to a series of prompts that elicit the kinds of information found in the type or genre of writing they are attempting. Thus, to write a short persuasive essay, students can be taught to respond to the following four prompts in order: (1) generate a topic sentence; (2) note reasons; (3) examine the reasons and ask if readers are likely to agree with each reason; (4) come up with an ending (Graham & Harris, 1988). A second example is a set of questions for generating a story (Harris & Graham, 1992): Who is the main character? Who else is in the story? When does the story take place? Where does the story take place? What does the main character do or want to do? What do other characters do? What happens when the main character does or tries to do it? What happens with other characters? How does the story end? How does the main character feel? How do the other characters feel?

Strategies Addressing the Revision Stage

Fitzgerald and Markham (1987) taught sixth graders to approach revision as a problem-solving task, one that could be solved by making additions, deletions, substitutions, and rearrangements. Graham and MacArthur (1988) taught students to revise by adding details, examining the clarity and cohesiveness of the paper, and fixing mechanical errors. MacArthur, Schwartz, and Graham (1991) found that peers can be asked to give feedback on the content and the structure of the paper.

Applying Developmental Theory to Educational Contexts

BOX 4.2. Reading Strategies Instruction

Pressley and his colleagues studied the characteristics of effective strategies instruction for reading comprehension in elementary-school programs (El-Dinary, Pressley, & Schuder, 1992; Pressley et al., 1992; Pressley, Gaskins, Cunicelli, et al., 1991; Pressley, Gaskins, Wile, Cunicelli, & Sheridan, 1991). Students in effective programs typically are taught to *predict, visualize, and summarize* as they read. These strategies stimulate active processing of text as students react to text and make associations to background knowledge.

A lesson typically would begin with the teacher reading first, thinking aloud about how the text might relate to prior knowledge. The teacher might make predictions, report images stimulated by the text, or summarize the text while noting consistencies and inconsistencies between text content, text structure, and reader expectations. Then the teacher might invite students to try using the strategic procedures with the text. The students, in reading groups, would take turns reading aloud. Throughout the process, the teacher encourages student interpretations of text and thus exposes reading group participants to a variety of interpretations of text and the processes for constructing and evaluating those interpretations. The teacher never tells students to use a particular strategy, but rather encourages them to be active as they read, choosing for themselves the strategy they need to understand a particular part of the text. The message conveyed is that the student is in control. Students are not learning to take orders from teachers; they are learning to make the types of choices good readers make. Use of strategies over months and years provides opportunities to acquire understanding of where and when to use the strategies and how to adapt them. That is, practice provides plenty of opportunity for metacognition about the strategies to develop.

Pressley and colleagues (1992) refer to this type of instruction as *transactional strategies instruction*, so dubbed because what happens during reading group is codetermined by a teacher and a student in interaction with a text, and the interpretations of the text are codetermined by teacher–student–text transactions (Bell, 1968; Bjorklund, 1989; Rosenblatt, 1978; Sameroff, 1975). Years of transactions involving predictions, questioning, clarifications, visualizations, associations, and summaries are intended to produce independent, successful readers who employ these strategies on their own. In fact, only one school year of such instruction produces substantial gains in reading achievement (Brown et al., 1996).

■ ■ ■ REPRESENTATION OF KNOWLEDGE

Thus far we have considered two possible explanations for advances in cognitive abilities. One, cognitive development may be due to expanding short-term memory capacity. Two, cognitive development may be due to expanding use of strategies. Now we consider a third possibility, that cognitive development reflects more complete, organized, and accessible knowledge—knowledge stored in long-term memory.

Memory performance is highly dependent on the developing knowledge base. What we know has an enormous effect on what we learn and remember and what we know increases greatly in the course of development (Flavell, 1985). Researchers have established different conceptions of the nature of knowledge in children, adolescents, and adults. Long-term memory includes representations of everything from the 26 letters of the alphabet and the numbers 1–100, to the concept "mother," and to the knowledge that some animals are more closely related to one another than other animals, to images of dogs chasing cats, to an understanding of what happens when you go to McDonald's, and so on.

Why are there many different conceptions of how knowledge is represented? Some models explain some types of knowledge better than others. For example, in early childhood, you acquired the concept of "mother." You can also access a visual depiction of your mother from a knowledge representation called an "image." Your understanding of what are the key characteristics of mammals can be represented in a network of related ideas. At the most basic level, connections between ideas may be best described in knowledge representations called "neural networks." Your knowledge of how to behave in a fast-food restaurant is better characterized by a knowledge representation called a "schema." These different types of knowledge interrelate, with complex, often not very well understood, connections between them. We next examine all these different ways to represent knowledge.

Procedural Knowledge

Knowledge can be broadly categorized as being one of two types: **declarative knowledge**, which is knowledge about the world, knowledge *that* something is the case, and **procedural knowledge**, which is knowledge about *how* to do things. Many distinctions between procedural and declarative knowledge exist (Tulving, 1983). For example, procedural knowledge can be demonstrated only by performing the procedure. Evidence of declarative knowledge can come in a variety of forms such as recall, recognition, application to a situation, and association to other knowledge. Procedural knowledge is often acquired only after extensive practice. Declarative knowledge can be acquired after a single exposure. See Table 4.5 for examples of declarative and procedural knowledge.

TABLE 4.5. Examples of Declarative and Procedural Knowledge

Declarative knowledge
  Knowing what the Declaration of Independence is
  Knowing the names of all the states and their capitals
  Knowing the formula for computing area
  Knowing what a circle is
  Knowing who wrote *War and Peace*
  Knowing the genus and species of a spider
  Knowing the Pythagorean theorem

Procedural knowledge
  Knowing how to use a computer
  Knowing how to perform mathematical operations
  Knowing how to play basketball
  Knowing how to write
  Knowing how to study
  Knowing how to look up information in the library
  Knowing how to perform a laboratory procedure
  Knowing how to dissect an animal

All procedural knowledge starts as declarative knowledge (Johnson, 2003; Neves & Anderson, 1981). How to do something starts as a verbal characterization of the procedure. When a sequence of cognitive actions in a procedure is represented declaratively, carrying out the procedure proceeds slowly and requires more of the limited working memory capacity. When first learning an action sequence, we have to interpret each step one at a time. This requires cognitive capacity. With practice, we can execute the procedure automatically. The movement from declarative representation of a sequence of actions to a single procedure is known as **proceduralization**.

Let's say you are learning to use word-processing software. You may begin by reading the directions and spend some time trying to learn the basic steps. Then you struggle to use the program. Initially, you need to cue yourself to take the correct action. For instance, you may say to yourself, "When I want to save a file, I open the file menu and click the mouse on save. If I click close, I better make sure I save the file." Gradually, you will need less and less verbal cuing. Eventually, you can write an entire paper without thinking about the word-processing commands. Your knowledge of the processing software has been "proceduralized." At this point, you are no longer using much short-term capacity when you use the word-processing program and you can think more about what you are writing. We now turn to the various ways in which researchers have conceptualized the declarative knowledge base.

Concepts

A **concept** is a mental representation of a category of related items (Klausmeier, 1990). Concepts help us to organize our experiences by allowing us to group similar things together into categories. Otherwise it would be difficult to make sense of the many different things we experience in our environment. For example, your concept of "dog" helps you lump together the Labrador retriever in the neighborhood, "Lassie," and greyhounds at the race track (Bower & Clapper, 1989). When you see an animal coming toward you on the street, you can use your concept of "dog" to decide whether or not the approaching animal is a dog, rather than a rat or a lion. Children are very good at noticing essential characteristics of things (such as animals) and they are also very good at learning commonly encountered categories of things (such as dogs) and events in the world (Gelman & Koenig, 2003). Unfortunately, many other aspects of conceptual development are not so clear-cut.

Concept Formation

How people classify items into conceptual categories is not completely understood, with many competing perspectives (Murphy, 2002). One perspective, the *feature comparison theory*, is that concepts are defined according to the necessary and sufficient features, the defining features, required for an item to qualify as a representative of the concept (Stillings et al., 1987; Thibaut, 1997). For example, the defining features of a grandmother are being female and having a child who has had a child. According to the feature comparison model, learning a concept is largely a matter of learning its defining features. For example, a triangle is a closed figure in a plane with three straight sides and three interior angles. Having learned these defining features of a triangle, a student can identify examples of triangles such as a slice of pie or a side of a pyramid.

The feature comparison theory can explain the formation and representation of clear-cut concepts, ones where most people find it easy to agree whether or not an item is an example of the concept. Most of us would recognize a triangle. Most of us recognize a football game when we see it. Eleanor Gibson's (1969) theory of perceptual learning provides a framework for understanding how experience can lead to fine-tuned understanding of similarities and differences between concepts. The Considering Interesting Questions special feature (Box 4.3) explains these ideas in greater detail.

Although feature theory can handle clear-cut concepts, other concepts are "fuzzy" (Neisser, 1967; Oden, 1987). For instance, it is not clear when a person stops being a juvenile and becomes an adult or when a small business becomes a large business. Consider the fuzzy concepts of a "strike" in baseball. If you look in the rule book, a strike is carefully spelled out with respect to its features. If you watch many ball games, you know that a strike depends on the particular umpire's strike zone! Many of the concepts carried around in our heads are quite fuzzy. *Prototype theory,* an alternative to feature comparison theory as a way to think about concepts, seems to handle fuzzy concepts better than do feature theories.

Considering Interesting Questions

BOX 4.3. How Do Children Acquire Knowledge of Distinctive Features?

According to Eleanor Gibson (1969, 1991), humans enter this world active. From the beginning babies have goals. They want to touch things, to see things, to begin to understand the world. They live in a world brimming with stimulation that conveys information. For example, 6-month-olds may play with sets of rubber alphabet letters, ones that float in the bathtub. These letters have features that differentiate them, such as curves, straight lines, diagonals, and color. Although children may be able to tell that two letters are the same or different from an early age, they do not notice the features that differentiate one letter from another until quite a bit later. At first, children learn to spot particular letters such as "Mommy's letter" (*M*), "Daddy's letter" (*D*), or the letter for their own names. Still later, they can reliably spot all the letters of the alphabet and name them. There are occasional slipups, almost always involving letters that share features, such as mistaking *h* for *n*.

What is necessary for perceptual learning to occur? Repeated exposure to a set of objects differing in particular ways is essential. Thus, in order to figure out which letter was "Mommy's letter," a child has to grasp how Mommy's letter differs from other letters. Perceptual learning occurs via basic processes. One mechanism is *abstraction*, which is the finding of distinctive features or invariant relationships (i.e., relations that remain constant for a class of events). After experiencing many examples of Mommy's letter, a child can abstract the distinctive features for *M* (two vertical lines, two diagonal lines in a specified arrangement). A second mechanism, *filtering*, involves ignoring the irrelevant dimensions. For example, a student may learn to classify maple and oak leaves, now relying on shape, and filtering out color and size, which do not reliably differentiate maple and oak leaves. A third mechanism is *peripheral attention*. The processing of peripheral information is critical to determining where next to focus attention. Peripheral visual mechanisms "look ahead" and guide the eye movement from fixation at one point *A* to a next point *B* (Just & Carpenter, 1992). The selection of the next point *B* is not random. For example, if there is a noun and a function word (*a, the*) to the right of the current focus of attention during reading of a sentence, the eye is much more likely to land on the noun than on the function word. The eye moves to highly informative parts of text, not to uninformative parts, due to guidance provided by peripheral attention.

With increasing age and experience, children's attention to and processing of perceptual information becomes more efficient. For example, with increasing age, children are more likely to examine stimuli more systematically and completely. Thus they become better at deciding if two complex patterns are the same or different. In general, with increasing age, children focus on information that is pertinent to the task they are asked to perform. They are also more flexible in attending to object features, sometimes systematically examining in one way and sometimes in another, depending on the task. They learn to know what to expect and thus are better at knowing what to look for (Vurpillot, 1968).

Prototype theory suggests that people classify concepts on the basis of resemblance rather than by defining features (Rosch, 1975, 1978; Rosch & Mervis, 1975). Thus typical grandmothers are over 40 and grey-haired. There are also atypical grandmothers who are not as readily classified as grandmothers—for example, a 35-year-old, who had a child at 17, who in turn had a child at 18. Because of its typicality, we easily and quickly classify a robin as a bird but we less certainly classify a penguin as a bird. We are able to make these classifications because we construct a prototype, or a very typical member of the category. The more an animal resembles this typical bird, the more certainly and quickly we would classify the animal as a bird. We would respond faster to the question, "Is a robin a bird?" than to the same question posed about a less typical example of a bird such as a chicken (Rips, Shoben, & Smith, 1973; Rosch, 1973; Rosch & Mervis, 1975). People recall more typical category members before the atypical members and children learn the typical category members first (Smith & Medin, 1981). How are such prototypes formed? They are mental averages of the many instances of the concept previously encountered in the world. Both adults and children construct such mental averages (Lasky, 1974; Posner & Keele, 1968, 1970; Reed, 1972).

Networks of Concepts

Our conceptual understandings are related to each other in long-term memory and are stored in what are called **semantic networks**. *Concepts* are nodes in the network, with links between the nodes specifying associations between concepts. Large networks of associations are associated to each node, with many of the associations very personal. Perhaps polar bears are connected to memories of the Antarctic exhibit at a zoo you once visited. Polar bears may also bring to mind Klondike Ice Cream Bars, which have a polar bear on the wrapper.

Your knowledge of polar bears is also more general, no longer tied to particular experiences. For instance, most people have a strong association between polar bears and penguins, sea lions, and walruses, with knowledge of all of these animals tied to knowledge of the Arctic and Antarctic regions of the Earth. Semantic memories of concepts are hierarchically organized. For example, the concept of all living things can be subdivided into animals and plants. Animals can be further subdivided into reptiles, mammals, birds, and insects, and so on, each with associated features (such as hair, vertebrate, warm-blooded for mammals). Mammals can be divided by genus (such as bears, elephants, giraffes, moles, etc.), each with associated features. Each genus is further divided into species (such as bears can be polar, black, brown, speckled, etc.). Each species has its associated features. Consider the animal-concept hierarchy in Figure 4.1.

Questions requiring consideration of information at different places in the hierarchy are answered more slowly than questions requiring information coded in nearby nodes (Collins & Quillian, 1969). For example, the question "Do birds have skin?," takes longer to answer than does the question "Do robins have red breasts?," since the feature of red breasts is stored directly with "robins" and the feature of skin is stored with "animals," which is further away in the animal hierarchy.

The associations between nodes are particularly important since activation of any particular part of the network results in **spreading activation** to parts of the hierarchy that are "close" and highly associated with the activated concept (Collins & Loftus, 1975). Activating some content can make it easier to understand related material. Thus if the word *stone* is read by a person, followed by the word *rock*, *rock* is recognized more quickly than if *stone* had not been activated, since the activation of *stone* can spread to *rock*, a highly associated concept (Meyer, Schvaneveldt, & Ruddy, 1975;

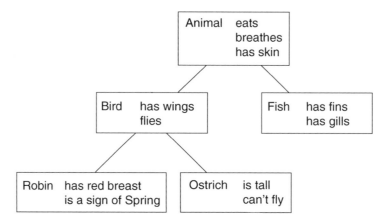

FIGURE 4.1. Sample hierarchical semantic network: animal hierarchy. From McCormick and Pressley (1997). Copyright 1997 by Christine B. McCormick and Michael Pressley. Adapted by permission.

Neely, 1976, 1977). The sentence "The lawyer is in the bank" is understood more quickly if the sentence is preceded by a sentence containing words associated with lawyer and bank, such as *judge* or *money* (Anderson, 1984; McKoon & Ratcliff, 1979).

What are the educational implications of semantic networks? Teachers often encourage students to activate background knowledge about to-be-presented material. They may remind students of what they learned yesterday or ask students to think about everyday experiences that are related to the topic at hand. This encourages spreading activation through a hierarchical network that encodes many associations between concepts. For example, a teacher may introduce a lesson on the Spanish Civil War by asking students to consider what they know about the Civil War in the United States. The students could be asked to think about the kinds of tensions and disagreements that lead to civil war. This activation should make it easier to understand new content and its relationship to the activated knowledge.

Sometimes students even reap the benefits of spreading activation while taking a test. For example, consider a student who draws a blank when reading a test question, skips the question, and decides to continue on with the test. Later on, another question on the test activates knowledge the student has. The resultant spreading activation brings to mind the answer to the question the student had skipped. A well-organized semantic network has great advantages!

Development of Semantic Networks

Do children have hierarchical conceptual networks that resemble adult networks? In general, even preschool children possess knowledge about hierarchical relations between some of the concepts they know. Infants can abstract categories from presentation of a number of examples of category members (Anglin, 1977; Bomba & Siqueland, 1983; Strauss, 1979), and 2- to 3-year-olds can sort familiar objects into appropriate categories (Carey, 1985; Gelman & Baillargeon, 1983; Horton, 1982; Markman & Callanan, 1983; Sugarman, 1983).

The knowledge of hierarchical relations possessed by preschoolers, however, is not always used by them. Children often prefer to use thematic relations rather than categories to represent categorizable content (Bruner, Olver, & Greenfield, 1966;

Kagan, Moss, & Sigel, 1972). Thus, when given a group of objects that can be sorted into categories (e.g., tiger, elephant, monkey, giraffe, banana, orange, grapes, apple), preschoolers often sort according to themes (e.g., monkeys eat bananas, elephants and giraffes live in the same house at the zoo, a tiger could eat an apple, Mommy puts oranges and grapes in her fruit salad). Unlike adults, children also *underextend*—using "duck" to refer only to one's pet duck—and *overextend*—using "duck" to refer to any bird larger than a robin—their use of concepts (Bloom, 1973; Clark, 1973).

Concepts and Cultural Experience

Cultural experience affects use of concepts and categories. Specifically, attendance in Western-style schools increases use of hierarchical categorical knowledge. Sharp, Cole, and Lave (1979) found that rural Mexicans without formal schooling classified objects on the basis of functional properties. For example, when given a triad of chicken, horse, and egg, they grouped chicken and egg together as related objects. In contrast, rural Mexicans with some formal schooling used categories comparable to Western-educated adults. They grouped chicken and horse together as examples of the conceptual category of animal.

Teaching Concepts

Although children do discover many of the most frequently encountered concepts (Gelman & Koenig, 2003), there are many others that they must be taught if they are to learn them, with a variety of ways of doing so (Klausmeier, 1990). A teacher may elect to teach a concept directly by first presenting the name and definition of the concept, including the defining features of the concept. For example, the defining rule for *square* would be a four-sided figure, with four equal sides, and four right angles. Then the teacher might present examples and nonexamples of the concept, since students can learn a concept by seeing examples of what a concept is and what it is not, pointing out the defining features and the irrelevant characteristics of the examples. This works best if the examples are presented from easy to more difficult, if examples differ in terms of irrelevant features, and if the teacher points out the similarities and differences between the examples and the nonexamples. Often it is possible to teach abstract concepts by making them more concrete through the use of analogies or illustrations in diagrams or graphs. For example, the concept of "sonar" can be explained as analogous to the movement detection system used by bats.

In contrast to this *direct explanation approach*, the teacher can elect a *discovery approach*, presenting examples and nonexamples and asking students to discover the definition of the concept and to determine its defining features and irrelevant characteristics. The students work on this independently or in groups and the teacher answers questions generated by the students. In a *guided discovery approach*, the teacher supports the students' discovery of the defining features and irrelevant characteristics of the concept through teacher questioning. Innovations in computer program design may lead to advances in supporting the discovery learning experiences of students in school contexts (de Jong & van Joolingen, 1998; Kumar & Sherwood, 1998).

Neural Networks

The importance of connections in memory, as seen in semantic networks of concepts, inspired neural network theory. According to this perspective, the most important part of long-term memory representation is the connections between units of information represented in neural networks. **Neural networks** have two basic components (Bechtel & Abrahamsen, 1991; Martindale, 1991). First, units of information, called "nodes," can be activated at various levels. If nodes are activated at a high level, we are conscious of what is activated. In general, the nodes are simpler than in concept theories (e.g., single features of letters can be nodes in neural network theory). Nodes can be activated at a low level of strength, outside of "consciousness," and still affect behavior. The second component in neural networks is the connections between nodes. Two nodes are linked either by connections resulting in simultaneous excitation of the nodes (if one is excited, the other is) or connections inhibiting joint excitement (if one is excited, excitation of the other unit cannot occur). According to neural network theory, learning is the creation of connections and the changing of the strength of connections. Connections are strengthened by simultaneous activation of nodes in a fashion analogous to strengthening of connections between neurons in the brain (Hebb, 1949).

Consider the sample neural network representing the knowledge of the letters of the alphabet (Selfridge, 1959). The nodes in this case correspond to features that letters can possess, such as a horizontal bar, a vertical bar, an acute angle, a curve bulging to the right, and a diagonal bar (i.e., what Gibson [1969] considered distinctive features). Suppose a letter is presented to the system, in this case a letter activating the vertical bar and rightward bulge features. Each of these features is strongly connected to the capital letters P and R, since adults have seen many P's and R's in their lifetime. Each exposure to these letters strengthens the connection between these two features and these capital letters. Thus the nodes representing both letters are activated. The decision that this is a P is reached, however, because a clear signal that the letter is an R requires another feature to be activated—a diagonal bar in the lower half of the letter. When the features add up to a P, inhibitory signals are sent out from the P node to the R node, as well as to all other letter nodes.

Children learning letters are building up connections between features and letters. Preschoolers often know the names of the letters before they ever have any idea what the letters look like (Adams, 1990). For example, because of listening to the "Alphabet Song," watching *Sesame Street*, playing with refrigerator letters, and reading books on Daddy's or Mommy's lap, a preschooler has many exposures to the name and shape of the letter P. With each of these exposures, the connections between the features of the letter P and the letter name strengthens. Eventually features defining the letter automatically activate the letter name. Researchers are studying the correlations between children's conceptual development and their brain functioning to increase our understanding of how the neural networks that support mature thinking develop (Posner, 2001).

Strengthening of connections also explains word recognition (McClelland & Rumelhart, 1981). Consider what happens when the word *EACH* is presented. Connections are activated between the

Young children strengthen connections between nodes of letter features through frequent exposure to letters.

individual features defining each letter and the letters as a group. Connections between each letter and its position in a word are also activated. That is, activating the E also partially activates connections with words beginning with E. Activating the A also partially activates connections with words having A in the second position, and so on. For adults who have experienced the set of connections between first-E, second-A, third-C, and fourth-H many times before, activation of the word EACH and inhibition of other words (e. g., words sharing letters with EACH) occurs.

What are the implications of the neural network model for educators? In this perspective, knowledge boils down to patterns of connections. The patterns develop slowly as reflected by the incremental nature of learning in that learners must master lower order knowledge before higher order knowledge. Thus knowledge of particular letters and associations between patterns of feature activations and their corresponding letter names and sounds must be well established before it is possible to learn to recognize words.

Practice is important for building and strengthening connections (Annett, 1989). Practice can take many forms. Teachers can help students build connections by providing multiple ways to practice in a variety of ways. For example, mental practice can be effective (Feltz, Landers, & Becker, 1988), and practice tests help strengthen connections (Glover, 1989). Whenever possible, teachers should provide feedback with practice so students have information on what they need to learn (Lhyle & Kulhavy, 1987). Teachers can encourage students to space out their practice (**distributed practice**) rather than cramming all their practice into one long episode (**massed practice**). Distributed practice is more effective than massed practice, even for young children (Toppino, Kasserman, & Mracek, 1991). Connectionist theories clarify what is meant by the idea that "practice makes perfect." What practice does is make connections and strengthen them.

Images

Could you describe where you live to your classmates? As you try to do this, you would likely access mental pictures, or **images**, from your long-term memory store. How is knowledge in the form of images represented? Allan Paivio proposed the dual-coding model (Clark & Paivio, 1991; Paivio, 1971, 1986) to articulate the difference between images and the other forms of knowledge described earlier. This model describes knowledge as associative networks of verbal and imaginal representations. The verbal system contains word-like codes for objects and events and abstract ideas that are only arbitrarily related to what they represent. For instance, the word *book* has no physical resemblance to an actual book.

The imagery system, on the other hand, contains nonverbal representations that resemble the perceptions giving rise to them. It includes visual images (e.g., of a bell), auditory images (the sound of the bell), actions (motion required to ring the bell), sensations related to emotion (your racing heart when you hear the bell ring and you are not in your classroom), and other nonverbal representations. Thus, for the book example, an image of a book shares visual and tactile qualities with the perception of an actual book.

Items in the imagery system are connected to items in the verbal system. For example, the connections between your image and verbal representations permit you to make mental images given words or to generate the names of items depicted in pictures. Connections within both the verbal and the nonverbal systems exist. In the verbal system, words are associated to other words, so that some students associate the word *school* with the words *friends, work,* and *challenge.* Categories and their instances are connected within the verbal system, so that the word *tree* is associated with the words *maple, oak,* and *pine.* In the nonverbal system, images are connected within or across sensory modalities. Thus an image of your grandmother may be associated with the warm feeling of a hug and the smell of chocolate chip cookies in the oven.

Is there research support for Paivio's dual-coding theory (Paivio, 1986)? Concrete materials, which more readily elicit images, are more memorable than abstract materials, and pictures are learned better than words. Words can be read faster than pictures can be named, suggesting that words access the verbal code directly and pictures access the verbal code only through the image. Neuropsychological evidence that left-hemisphere damage disrupts verbal processing more than nonverbal processing also supports dual-coding theory. Right-hemisphere damage has the opposite effect. Mental imagery can have a powerful effect on recall. Material that is easy to image is recalled more easily. For example, readers who construct mental images as they read facilitate their understanding of what they read (Pressley, 1976, 1977; Sadoski, 1983, 1985; Sadoski & Paivio, 2001), with much prior knowledge actually represented as images. For example, think of what you know about bears or skyscrapers—it is almost impossible to think about these concepts without activating images stored in long-term memory (Sadoski, Paivio, & Goetz, 1991).

Roger Shepard and his colleagues (Shepard & Metzler, 1971) conducted some of the most convincing research confirming the psychological reality of mental imagery. They presented adults with a complex geometric figure and a second figure, which was either the same figure (but rotated 0 to as much as 180 degrees) or a mirror image (also rotated some number of degrees). The task was to decide whether the original figure and the rotation were the "same" figure or a "different" figure. The amount of time needed to recognize the same figure as "same" was a linear function of the number of degrees of rotation required to make the figure parallel the original figure.

Since the time required for mental rotation corresponds to the physical process of rotation, this suggested that the participants were "flipping" the figures in their heads, using some kind of image. Even 4-year-olds seem to rotate figures in their heads. It takes longer for a 4-year-old to decide that a capital R and an upside-down R (i.e., an R flipped 180 degrees) are the same letter than it takes to decide that the R and an R on its side (i.e., flipped 90 degrees) are the same letter (Marmor, 1974; see Figure 4.2). With increasing age during childhood and continuing to adulthood, speed and facility in mental imagery rotation increases (Kosslyn, Margolis, Barrett, Goldknopf, & Daley, 1990; Zabalia, 2002).

Additional support for the psychological reality of images comes from people's descriptions of having and using mental images. For instance, people report flipping the cubes in their head in the Shepard and Metzler (1971) task. People report images more often when learning concrete materials than when learning abstract materials (and report relying on their images during recall of the concrete materials).

FIGURE 4.2. It takes 4-year-olds longer to decide that the figure on the left is an *R* than to decide that the figure on the right is an *R,* thus indicating that children rotate images in their heads. From McCormick and Pressley (1997). Copyright 1997 by Christine B. McCormick and Michael Pressley. Adapted by permission.

Schemata

Not all types of knowledge can be captured by the knowledge representations we have already discussed. Sometimes specific units of information commonly co-occur in particular situations, forming larger chunks of knowledge best described as schemata. **Schemata** are generalized knowledge about objects, situations, or events. For example, your knowledge of what you might expect to see when you go to a play is represented in a schema. You would expect scenery, costumes, actors, props, separate acts, and an intermission. Schemata are the skeleton structures of commonly encountered events, with the particular ways the skeleton takes on flesh varying from instance to instance.

Consider an example of a schema for an event that unfolds over time, specifically, the schema for a ship christening (Anderson & Pearson, 1984). It includes the purpose, which is the blessing of the ship. It includes information about where it is done (in dry dock), by whom (a celebrity), and when it occurs (just before launching of a new ship). The christening action is also represented (breaking a bottle of California champagne that is suspended from a rope). These parts of a schema are referred to as *variables*, or *slots*. At any particular christening, these slots are instantiated with particular instances (New Haven, CT, with the president of the United States breaking a bottle of California champagne on a new submarine). There are constraints on the instances that can occur in these slots. The celebrity is usually from government and would never be a person of ill repute (a smut publisher or a famous criminal). There are constraints on the champagne as well, with a bottle of California champagne acceptable but a rare bottle of French champagne unlikely.

Children's Use of Schemata

Do children store knowledge in schemata, and, if they do, how do schemata affect their processing of new material? Not surprisingly, the schemata that children possess are determined by events that recur in their lives. Thus children have schemata representing events such as dinner, bedtime, making cookies, and going to a museum (Hudson & Nelson, 1983; Hudson & Shapiro, 1991; McCarthy & Nelson, 1981; Nelson, 1978; Nelson & Gruendel, 1981). If children listen to a brief story pertaining to one of their schemata, they can answer inferential questions about the story. These questions require knowledge about the situation described in the text that is over and above the information specified in the text, knowledge contained in the children's schemata. Consider the following short story (Hudson & Slackman, 1999):

> Johnny and his mom and dad were going to McDonald's. Johnny's father told him he could have dessert if he ate all his dinner. They waited in line. They ate their hamburgers. And they had ice cream. (p. 378)

When presented with the question "Why did they stand in line?," the 4- to 7-year-olds had no difficulty responding since the schema for McDonalds's contains this information, even though the story did not.

The powerful effect of schemata on children's comprehension and memory is evident when children listen to stories that include information inconsistent with schemata stored by most children. Consider this story that Hudson and Nelson (1983) presented to 4- to 7-year-olds:

> One day it was Sally's birthday and Sally had a birthday party.
> Sally's friends all came to her house.

Sally opened her presents and found lots of new toys.
Everybody played pin the tail on the donkey.
Then Sally and her friends ate the cake.
They had some chocolate and vanilla ice cream.
Everybody had peppermint candy, too.
Sally blew out all the candles on the cake.
Sally's friends brought presents with them.
Then it was time for Sally's friends to go home.

Is there anything wrong about this story? You probably realized that Sally opened the presents before the friends brought them. In addition, the children ate the cake before the candles were blown out. The children in Hudson and Nelson's (1983) study used a birthday party schema to comprehend and remember this story. Some children repaired the story during recall by not mentioning either one or both of the out-of-order elements. Others reported the out-of-order acts in the schematically correct order rather than as specified in the story. In short, recall of the story was consistent with the schema for the birthday party even though the original presentation of the story was not consistent with this schema.

Text Structure Schemata

Students develop schemata for recurring intellectual tasks. For instance, texts have conventional structures that are familiar to readers (Kintsch & Greene, 1978). Both **narrative text structures** (i.e., the structures of fictional stories) and **expository text structures** (i.e., the structures of factual texts) have been identified.

Narratives, that is, stories, have a structure: a grammar. A story has a *setting* and an *event structure*, which is composed of *episodes* (Mandler, 1978, 1987). Each episode has a *beginning*, which is an event initiating a complex reaction; a *complex reaction*, which is composed of an emotional or cognitive response and a state the protagonist wishes to achieve; a *goal path*, which involves a plan of action by the character and the consequence of setting the plan of action in motion; and an *ending*, which is a reaction.

Here is a simple two-episode story adapted from Mandler (1978, p. 22):

Once there were twins, Tom and Jennifer, who had so much trouble their parents called them the unlucky twins [*setting*]. One day, Jennifer's parents gave her a dollar bill to buy a turtle she wanted, but on the way to the pet store she lost it [*beginning* of first episode]. Jennifer was worried that her parents would be angry with her so she decided to search every bit of the sidewalk where she had walked [*reaction*]. She looked in all the cracks and in the grass along the way [plan of action, part of the *goal path*]. She finally found the dollar bill in the grass [consequence, part of the *goal path*]. But when Jennifer got to the store, the pet store man told her that someone else had just bought the last turtle, and he didn't have any more [*ending*]. The same day, Tom fell off a swing and broke his leg [*beginning* of second episode]. He wanted to run and play with the other kids [*reaction*]. So he got the kids to pull him around in his wagon [plan of action, part of the *goal path*]. While they were playing, Tom fell out of his wagon and broke his arm [consequence, part of the *goal path*]. Tom's parents said he was even unluckier than Jennifer and made him sit in bed until he got well [second *ending*].

How does story grammar knowledge influence story recall? First, stories that do not conform to the story grammar structure are difficult to remember (and are processed more slowly) compared to stories that do conform. This is true for both children and adults (Kintsch, Mandel, & Kozminsky, 1977; Mandler & Johnson, 1977;

Stein & Nezworski, 1978), and also applies to stories presented on television (Collins, Wellman, Keniston, & Westby, 1978). Second, when story information is presented in an order inconsistent with conventional story grammar, both children and adults tend to "fix the story up" at recall, remembering the elements of the story in an order consistent with the story grammar (Mandler & DeForest, 1979; Stein & Glenn, 1979). Third, the probability that an element will be recalled from a story depends on the role it plays in the story as defined by story grammar (Mandler, 1984; Mandler & Johnson, 1977; Stein & Glenn, 1979). Fourth, reading times for material at the beginning of episodes are greater than for material in the middle of episodes. Content at the end of episodes is processed especially quickly (Haberlandt, 1980; Mandler & Goodman, 1982).

Just as stories have structures, so do expository texts. Perhaps an English teacher once asked you to write an expository text designed to achieve a specific purpose. Maybe you were asked to write a descriptive text or a text that compared and contrasted two perspectives or even a text that illustrated a general principle. These types of text are examples of expository text structures. Texts corresponding to well-known expository structures are easier to understand and remember (Kintsch, 1982; Kintsch & Yarbrough, 1982).

Mathematics Problem Schemata

Most of the mathematics problems presented in elementary- and high-school textbooks have typical structures. For instance, Mayer (1981) analyzed high-school algebra texts and identified about 100 common problem types. For example, an algebra textbook may contain a problem like this one:

> If a car travels 10 hours at 30 miles per hour, how far will it go?

For many students, this problem activates their schema for "distance = rate × time" problems. Here's another problem example:

> How much will be earned if $1,000 is invested at 8% interest for 1 year?

This problem activates the "interest = interest rate × principal" schema.

Students who have completed high-school math and science courses have developed schemata for the problem types in these courses and can classify problems into types (Hinsley, Hayes, & Simon, 1977). In addition, students use their problem-solving schemata as they identify the critical information in the problems (Hayes, Waterman, & Robinson, 1977; Mayer, 1982; Robinson & Hayes, 1978). This may be one reason students who possess greater knowledge of problem schemata—and hence, are more proficient at problem classification—also are better able to solve problems (Silver, 1987).

Educational Implications

What are the implications of schema theory for educators? Schemata have a powerful effect on the comprehension and recall of information in learners of all ages. Schemata focus student attention, influence the inferences students make, and have a bearing on students' recall of the information. When teachers introduce new lessons, they need to try to activate schemata that will facilitate students' understanding of the new material. Some students, however, may not have developed the text structure schemata or mathematics schemata they need to succeed. Fortunately, teachers can teach explicitly the appropriate schema to these students. For example, poor readers can be taught story grammar elements and to look for story grammar information as they read. Weak readers in the elementary grades who are taught to look for setting, character, and episodic elements of text remember more of what they read (Nolte & Singer, 1985; Short & Ryan, 1984). Lauren and Allen (1999) included story grammar instruction as part of a package of reading interventions in the elementary grades (in combination with word recognition instruction, silent reading by students, and parents reading with their children).

Situated, Distributed Knowledge

Some knowledge is not separable from the actions that give rise to it or from the culture in which those actions occur (Brown, Collins, & Duguid, 1989). That is, knowledge and thinking are not just "in-the-head" things. For instance, your knowledge of this course is in your head, but also in the notes you take in class! Consider the 747 pilot. His or her thinking involves juggling information in the head, and then combining it in meaningful ways with information on the many digital displays in the cockpit. There are manuals to consult as well, with these sometimes consulted in flight as part of decision making. Thinking involves both in-the-head activity and representations and external representations. It is distributed between the head and the environmental situation. The knowledge and thinking can be described as **situated cognition** (Moore & Rocklin, 1998).

Thinking and knowledge sometimes are also distributed in another way, across several heads in interaction or across a human head and a computer (Derry, DuRussel, & O'Donnell, 1998; Hewitt & Scardamalia, 1998; Olson & Olson, 2003). This is **distributed cognition** (sometimes referred to as "socially distributed" or "socially shared cognition"; Resnick, Levine, & Teasley, 1991). For example, distributed cognition occurs during conversations. The meaning constructed during the conversation is not a product of one head but a product of several heads in interaction with one another (Bereiter, 1990; Hutchins, 1991). By heads coming together in conversation, more powerful interpretations and understandings sometimes emerge than would have occurred to any one of the participants in the conversation thinking alone. Why? First of all, the different heads have different prior knowledge. Moreover, the different heads have attended to different aspects of the information being considered. As the talk in the group proceeds, connections are made. Something Mariah says connects with knowledge activated in Billy, who in turn responds. In doing so, Billy may combine some of what he knows in common with Mariah and something Mariah said that he did not know previously to produce a new inference. This inference might trigger something in Lukas and so it goes. . . . (The power of socially distributed cognition will be taken up further in Chapter 6.)

■ ■ ■ CHAPTER SUMMARY AND EVALUATION

Cognitive development occurs as a function of increasing short-term memory capacity, increasing use of strategies, and an increasing and more accessible knowledge base. The increasing functional capacity of short-term memory can be explained by neurological development, speed of information processing, rehearsal strategies, prior knowledge that enables chunking, and inhibition of irrelevant information.

Whether or not a child uses a memory strategy depends on the child's age and the strategy in question. Preschoolers routinely use some simple strategies, such as looking a spot where a to-be-remembered item is hidden. Familiarity of setting, materials, and task combine to permit greater strategic competence by preschoolers. Rehearsal strategies develop during the early grade-school years and elaboration strategies emerge during the later grade-school and high-school years. Many complex strategies are not always common even among university-age students. Some cultures encourage use of strategies more than other cultures. Whether parents and educators encourage and teach strategy use in children is an important determinant of whether or not children use strategies or not.

If given a small amount of instruction, students can often successfully apply strategies they do not use on their own. Unfortunately, even when children receive instructions to carry out strategic processes effectively, there is no guarantee that they will maintain and transfer strategy use. Metacognitive knowledge, such as knowledge about where and when to use a strategy (conditional knowledge) and the gains produced by a strategy (utility knowledge), increases maintenance and transfer of a strategy. Students do not always develop metacognitive knowledge on their own.

A variety of different types of representations function in thinking (see Table 4.6). Knowing how to do something is *procedural knowledge*. Knowing about something is *declarative knowledge*. By adulthood, adults have complex networks of procedural and declarative knowledge built up through experience. Procedures develop from declarative representations through repeated practice.

Features of stimuli are critical to classification in both feature comparison and prototype theories of concept formation. Prototype theories can better explain how nondefinitive features contribute to classification (such as "over-40" for grandmothers) and how people classify instances of fuzzy concepts. Concepts are related to each other in hierarchically organized semantic networks. Although some of children's knowledge probably is in categorical hierarchies like those of adults, many concepts held by children differ from those of adults. Moreover, children are less likely to rely on hierarchical concept knowledge than are adults.

TABLE 4.6. Summary of Different Representations of Knowledge

Concepts

Description: Mental representation of a category. Concepts are connected in hierarchical semantic networks.
Classroom example: Animal phyla, types of rocks.

Neural networks

Description: Connected nodes. Knowledge is in the connections.
Classroom example: Features of letters associated with letter names.

Schemata

Description: Generalized knowledge about objects, situations, and events.
Classroom example: What goes into an essay (expository schema)? What kind of math problem is this (mathematics problem schema)?

Images

Description: Nonverbal representations that resemble perceptual experience.
Classroom example: Visualizing follow-through in throwing a baseball. Visualizing a dance performance.

Connections between units of information are best represented in neural networks. Nodes in neural networks are linked by either simultaneous excitation or inhibition. Learning is the creation of connections and the strengthening of connections between nodes.

Images are nonverbal representations that resemble perceptual experience. According to Paivio's dual-coding model, items in the imagery system are connected to items in the nonverbal system. Evidence for the psychological reality of images is found in self-reports and studies of mental rotation.

Adults and children have schemata for familiar events, and these schemata determine how new information is processed, interpreted, and retrieved. The availability of this generalized representation from a very young age suggests that schematic representation is a fundamental human competency.

Developmental Debates

Research derived from the information-processing perspective has informed many of the great debates of developmental psychology introduced in Chapter 1.

Nature versus Nurture

Both short-term and long-term memories depend on human biology, with neuropsychology providing insights into the biological mechanisms underlying memory. Information-processing psychologists are increasingly allying with neuropsychologists, making the biological foundations of information-processing theory more apparent. The environment plays an important role as well. Institutions, such as school, can have a profound effect on the information-processing abilities of students. For example, many schools are teaching their students strategies that can be applied to academic tasks, such as reading and writing.

Stages versus Continuous Development

The information-processing perspective is that change is more continuous than stage-like. Some theorists (such as neo-Piagetians) have used evidence of increases in short-term memory capacity with development to explain stage-like development (such as Piaget's stages).

Universal versus Culture-Specific Development

It's a safe bet that people everywhere have the kinds of representations described in this chapter. Even so, research on cognitive development makes obvious that experience really matters. The specific strategies used by a child depend on culture and experience. The specific schemata known by children depend on experience. Children learn the strategies and the knowledge emphasized in the culture and by the family.

Active versus Passive Child

Activity, for information-processing-oriented psychologists, is use of strategies and relating current stimulation to prior knowledge. Because strategic competency and knowledge increase with development, the older child can be much more intellectually active than the younger child. How active the child is depends on a number of factors, including the child's goals and motivational beliefs (see Chapter 9). For example, children who believe that their efforts can make a difference are more likely to exert academic effort than those who believe their performance is determined by innate ability.

■■■ REVIEW OF KEY TERMS

concept A mental representation of a category of related items.

conditional knowledge Knowledge of when and where strategies are useful.

cumulative rehearsal–fast finish A strategy for remembering information in which the learner repeats all the items in a series, in order, as each new item is presented. After the last item is presented, the learner "dumps out" the last item or two and then recalls the earlier items in their given order.

declarative knowledge Knowledge about things; knowledge that something is the case.

distributed cognition Thinking that is not the product of one student but of several students in interaction with one another.

distributed practice Practice that is spaced out over a period of time, leading to better performance than the performance resulting from massed practice.

elaboration A strategy for remembering information by constructing a meaningful context, either visual or verbal.

encode To create a memory.

expository text structures Schemata for factual texts.

images Information stored in mental pictures.

labeling A strategy used by young children on serial recall tasks in which the name of an item is said as it is presented.

maintain Continue to use a strategy when it is appropriate.

massed practice Practice that is crammed into one long episode, leading to lower performance than the performance resulting from distributed practice.

metacognition Knowledge about and awareness of thinking, including the knowledge of when and where to use acquired strategies.

narrative text structures Schemata for fictional stories.

neural networks Connections linking units of information.

organization Grouping information into categories or patterns on the basis of relationships or connections.

procedural knowledge Knowledge of how to do things.

proceduralization The movement, developed with practice, from a declarative representation of a sequence of actions to a single procedure.

rehearsal A strategy of repeating information to be remembered.

retrieve To access a memory.

schemata Generalized knowledge about objects, situations, and events.

semantic networks The way in which concepts are connected to each other in a pattern of associations.

serial recall task A task in which students are asked to remember items in the order they were presented.

short-term memory A memory store of limited capacity and duration; also called "working memory."

situated cognition Knowledge that cannot be separated from the actions that give rise to it or from the culture in which those actions occur.

spreading activation The way in which concepts connected to each other in a semantic network are activated.

strategies Plans of action that may result in a solution to a problem or achievement of a goal.

transfer Apply strategies to new situations and tasks.

utility knowledge Knowledge of the potential benefits of using a strategy.

CHAPTER 5

Social Theories of Development and Learning

This chapter is about theories of development and learning emphasizing social variables affecting development. The three perspectives featured here—social learning theory, Freud's theory of psychosexual development, and Erikson's theory of psychosocial development—have all inspired research or current thinking about children's relations with others and the effects of others on children's personalities, social behaviors, and cognition.

In recent decades, social learning theory has clearly been the most influential of the three theories presented in this chapter, stimulating a great deal of research. Thus we begin the discussion with coverage of social learning theory, the preferred theoretical perspective of many contemporary developmental psychologists.

■ ■ ■ SOCIAL LEARNING THEORY

Children learn many things just from watching others. That is, other people serve as **behavioral models**. This is the main principle of **social learning theory**, proposed by Albert Bandura and his colleagues (Bandura, 1969; Bandura & Walters, 1963). Developmental psychologists have studied observational learning of a wide range of behaviors including aggression, altruism, sex-typed behaviors, caregiver–infant attachment, and social dependency. In fact, whatever the behavior, social learning theorists have been able to generate evidence supporting the conclusion that what people see and hear influences their development (e.g., alcohol abuse, Maisto, Carey, & Bradizza, 1999; spirituality, Bandura, 2003; psychopathology, Thyer & Myers, 1998).

Social learning theory began as a *behavioral theory*, meaning a theory that focuses on behavior that can be observed rather than on internal, unobservable explanatory variables (such as Piaget's operations, described in Chapter 3). It quickly became obvious that children's social learning could not be understood through studying behavior alone—cognitive processes clearly influenced behavior. Social learning theory is now very much a cognitive-behavioral approach to explaining social and personality development (Zimmerman & Schunk, 2003), one that can explain development in virtually all cultural contexts (Bandura, 2002a), as well as the effects of contexts that are only experienced at a distance, such as through the media of film and television (Bandura, 2002b).

Observational Learning of Behaviors and Expectancies

In observational learning, people learn through **vicarious experiences**. That is, when they see others experience rewards and punishments, they form expectations about the rewards or punishments they might receive for their own behaviors. For example, in a well-known study, Albert Bandura (1965) asked young children to view a film in which a child exhibited some very novel physical and verbal aggressive behaviors toward a set of toys. At the completion of the film, the child model was either punished for the aggression (spanked and verbally rebuked), reinforced for it (given soft drinks, candy, and praise), or provided no consequences. After watching the film, the children were left alone in the room where the film was made with an opportunity to play with the toys seen in the film. Children who watched the film where the child model was spanked for aggression were much less likely to exhibit the aggressive behaviors when interacting with the toys than if they watched the film depicting reward or no consequences for the aggression. Then, all children in the experiment were offered stickers and fruit juice if they would show the experimenter the aggressive behaviors that the film model had exhibited. The children had little difficulty reproducing the behaviors.

What was going on in this situation? The children had clearly learned the aggressive behaviors in question because they could reproduce those behaviors when given an incentive to do so. However, they were less likely to perform the aggressive behaviors after viewing the film in which the child model had been punished because they also learned to expect punishment for aggressive behaviors from the film. Performance of a behavior depends on knowing a response as well as the expectation of rewards. When punishments are expected, performance often will not occur unless there are offsetting rewards. For many children in the Bandura study, the fun of playing aggressively with the toys was not worth the risk of getting a spanking.

Consider another example. Although you have seen many high-speed car chases on television or at the movies, they are statistically rare. Why? People know that if they speed away from a traffic stop, they may be caught and punished. This *expectancy* has been established through years of observing the villains on television or in the movies being punished for their wicked deeds. Moreover, the punishments are usually very aversive (i.e., they have negative *value*), ranging from personal remorse and guilt to imprisonment. Whether a person executes a given behavior depends on his or her expectations of rewards or punishments for performing the behavior and the value of these rewards and punishments. In other words, the probability of performing a behavior X is a function of the expectancy of reward or punishment for X *and* the value of the reward or punishment (Rotter, 1954).

Try this little test of your understanding if you are not sure whether you understand expectancy–value theory:

1. You expect that studying for a test will make it very likely that you will pass the test. The test does not count in your grades and is on material that is boring. Will you study or not?
2. You expect that studying for a test will not increase the likelihood you will pass it or earn a better grade. Your entire semester's grade depends on this test. Will you study or not?
3. You expect that studying for a test will increase your grade, you like the content, and the grade in this course is important to you. Will you study or not?

For situation 1, you probably will not study because the value of the reward is low and there is a negative value (boredom) associated with studying. For situation 2, you probably will not study because your expectation of reward following studying behavior is low. For situation 3, however, you likely will study since the expectation of reward is high and there are two sources of positively valued reward: the pleasure of studying this material and an important course grade.

Cognitive Mechanisms of Social Learning

Imitation in its most basic form is apparently innate. Within hours of birth, infants who observe an adult opening his or her mouth or sticking out his or her tongue respond by opening their mouths or sticking out their tongues (Meltzoff, 1985, 2002; Meltzoff & Gopnik, 1989; Meltzoff & Moore, 1977, 1983). That newborns can do it does not mean that it is simple, however. There is extensive cognitive mediation of most behaviors that children learn through observation. Four cognitive processes, in particular, mediate social learning (Bandura, 1986; Meltzoff & Prinz, 2002): *attentional processes*, *retention processes*, *motor reproduction processes*, and *motivational processes*.

Even very young infants will imitate the actions and facial expressions they observe in adults.

Attentional Processes

What the learner observes or attends to depends on characteristics of the model and characteristics of the observer. For example, not everyone has equal access to the same types of models. Children who are raised in environments with gentle people have more opportunities to view gentle behaviors than children who are raised in environments filled with aggressive people. To some extent, all of us, with the exception of very young children, have some control over the social models available to us.

For example, children who elect to play soccer in a league surround themselves with models of athletic behaviors. Adolescents who elect gang life select themselves into situations where aggression is modeled. In both the soccer and the gang situations, some of the participants will command greater attention than others. Thus the best player on the soccer team is more likely to be watched and imitated than other players, both with respect to soccer behaviors and other behaviors (such as shoe styles or hair styles). The leader of a gang also is much more likely to be watched and imitated than someone who is not as respected by gang members.

Retention Processes

Once a person attends to a behavior, it must be remembered if it is to affect future behaviors. Thus processes, such as imagery and rehearsal, that enhance memory are mediators of observational learning (Bandura, Grusec, & Menlove, 1966; Bandura & Jeffery, 1973; Bandura, Jeffery, & Bachicha, 1974; Hall, Rodgers, & Barr, 1990; see also Chapter 4). For example, imaging speaking in public may improve public speaking performances and visualizing leaping over hurdles may improve performance in a race.

Motor Reproduction Processes

Not only must learners perceive and remember a behavioral sequence, they must be able to produce it themselves. In some cases, the observed sequence is readily reproducible. In other cases, the observer can carry out components but not the entire action. Sometimes individual components must be acquired before the entire sequence can be executed. For example, a very skilled gymnast can watch another gymnast's routine (e.g., on the balance beam) and copy most or all of it immediately. Less skilled gymnasts have to break the routine into segments (such as practicing the mount over and over again, practicing a particular type of handstand over and over, practicing the dismount over and over) before attempting to integrate the segments. For some of us, it would never be possible to execute a routine on a balance beam no matter how frequently we had observed it.

Motivational Processes

A child who really wants to learn how to score goals in soccer pays closer attention to the coach as he demonstrates kicking at the post than does a child who has little real interest in the game. The interested child sometimes can be observed kicking at the post of a goal gerryrigged in the backyard, motorically rehearsing what he or she saw the coach do at practice. What is learned through observational mechanisms depends on the particular motivations of the child, which determine what the child attends to, attempts to remember, and rehearses later.

A child's motivation goes far in allowing the child to be a determinant of his or her own social learning. But there is more to the child's role in controlling what he or she had opportunity to observe. There is **reciprocal determinism** (Bandura, 1986): the child's reactions to environmental events affect subsequent events. Thus the child at soccer practice who attends carefully to the coach and works hard to copy the coach's approach to kicking gets more of the coach's future attention, including additional modeling by the coach of even more advanced skills. The child's cognitive processing of modeled behaviors affects the child's subsequent behaviors, which in turn changes the future environment in ways that affect what the child sees and hears in the future. Observational learning is very complicated, determined by the environment, but also by the child, who in turn affects the environments to come (Bell, 1968; Bell & Harper, 1977; Schneirla, 1957).

Other Mechanisms of Social Learning

Social learning involves more than observational learning. It also depends on classical conditioning, operant conditioning, and punishment.

Classical Conditioning

Ivan Pavlov first explained **classical conditioning** in the late 19th century (Bower & Hilgard, 1981). Pavlov observed that when meat powder is placed in a dog's mouth, the dog salivates. The food is an **unconditioned stimulus** that elicits an **unconditioned response**: salivation. Pairing a neutral stimulus, such as the sound of a bell, with the food powder results in conditioning dogs to salivate at the sound of the bell. The bell is a **conditioned stimulus** that has acquired the power to elicit what is now the **conditioned response** of salivation. Thus neutral stimuli that accompany (usually precede) unconditioned stimuli often become conditioned stimuli (Bower & Hilgard, 1981).

Classical conditioning is not a very prominent part of what we typically think of as school learning, but humans frequently do develop emotional responses through classical conditioning. For example, fearful reactions to stimuli associated with pain are easily learned by humans via classical conditioning (Bandura, 1986; Hoffman, 1969; Watson, 1927). Thus a student who trips over a hurdle may become classically conditioned to fear gym class. Or a student who was embarrassed by knocking over a podium during a speech may become classically conditioned to fear public speaking.

Classically conditioned emotional responses often are not maintained. They can undergo a process called **extinction** by subsequent experience with the conditioned stimulus that is not followed by the unconditioned response. Thus if future experiences in gym class or speaking in front of the class are pleasant, after a while the fear subsides.

Operant Conditioning

Operant conditioning applies to more learning situations than classical conditioning. In classical conditioning the focus of learning is on the stimulus that elicits a response, typically an involuntary emotional response or reflex. In operant conditioning, the focus is on an emitted response, a behavior the learner can control. Although B. F. Skinner is the psychologist most associated with operant conditioning (Skinner, 1953), E. L. Thorndike detailed its most fundamental principle in 1913. Thorndike's Law of Effect describes the following relationship: the likelihood of an operant response being emitted is increased when it is followed by a reinforcer.

Consider an example. Suppose a teen is thirsty. She puts 75¢ in a soda machine and receives a soda. Receiving the soda is reinforcement for depositing the 75¢. When she is thirsty in the future, she will be more likely to put 75¢ in a soda machine as a result of this experience. The operant response of putting money in a soda machine can undergo the process of extinction, however. This process begins when a person makes a response and does not receive the expected reinforcement. If the same teen had put 75¢ in a soda machine and no soda came out, the best guess is that the teen would not put any more money in that machine. One trial of not receiving a soda may be enough to extinguish the response of putting money in the soda machine, at least with this particular soda machine at this particular time. Usually extinction only occurs after several instances of unreinforced operant responses.

Receiving a soda is an **unconditioned reinforcer** in that it satisfies a biological deprivation, that of thirst. Other unconditioned reinforcers include food, sex, and exposure to aesthetically pleasing stimuli, such as when a child is reinforced for correctly adjusting a telescope by seeing a vivid detailed view of the Moon. Most reinforcers that people receive are not unconditioned reinforcers, however, but **conditioned reinforcers**. Thus, for coming to work and doing your job, your employer gives you a check. No biological need is satiated by the check directly. The check allows you to purchase food, drinks, and entertainment, however, all of which do fulfill your basic needs for nourishment and stimulation. Conditioned reinforcers acquire their reinforcement properties by being paired with unconditional reinforcers. That is, money was not always valuable to you but became so because it allowed you to acquire unconditioned reinforcers.

There are two general categories of reinforcers, **positive reinforcers** and **negative reinforcers.** The occurrence of both of these types of reinforcers following a behavior increases the likelihood of that behavior. The difference between the two is in the type of consequence that causes the increase in the behavior. Many high-school students are positively reinforced for turning on the radio and hearing music that they like. When a student turns off a radio that is blaring some type of disliked music, however, that is negative reinforcement. *Positive reinforcement* involves the presentation of a stimulus following a response; *negative reinforcement* involves the cessation of an aversive stimulation following a response. That is, if polka music is aversive to a student, the student would be reinforced for the behavior of turning the radio off because cessation of the polka music occurs after the radio is turned off, and it is more likely the student will turn the radio off again next time she or he hears polka music. In other words, the student has been conditioned to escape the stimulus of polka music.

How can teachers get students to exhibit the behaviors they want by using the principles of operant conditioning? If the desired behavior sometimes is exhibited by the students, then teachers can increase its frequency through positive or negative reinforcement. How can teachers get students to exhibit behaviors they have not yet exhibited? Teachers can do this through a process called **shaping**, by reinforcing behaviors that become closer and closer to the desired behavior. Thus, when students learn to write, teachers first reinforce them for whatever they can do and keep at them to write more. Then the demands of the teachers increase. Initially, students are reinforced for forming letters correctly, but later they are only reinforced if their groups of letters form words, and eventually they are only reinforced for writing complete sentences. Finally, they have to put sentences together in coherent paragraphs. The demands increase as schooling continues. Ultimately, college students only receive reinforcement for an accurate and clearly written 15-page paper. Many patterns of response important in education are learned through shaping.

Teachers can also vary the delivery of reinforcements. Typically, reinforcements occur intermittently rather than after every response. Learning that occurs via **inter-**

mittent reinforcement is more resistant to extinction than learning that occurs under continuous reinforcement. For example, perhaps one in three football games is really exciting. Yet people keep coming back for more despite the high likelihood of a boring game. Although Skinner did not use the word *expectation*, other behaviorists have in their explanations of such behavior (Rotter, 1954). Continuous reinforcement produces an expectation of reinforcement every time, which increases vulnerability to extinction whenever a reinforcement fails to occur. In contrast, intermittent reinforcement creates an expectation that reinforcement is a sometimes occurrence, and that if a person persists reinforcement eventually occurs.

Reinforcement can be intermittent in two ways. In a **ratio reinforcement schedule**, reinforcement follows a certain number of responses. Thus children in a class who receive stickers for completing 10 worksheets are on a ratio schedule of reinforcement. Alternatively, reinforcement can be delivered at certain time intervals or on an **interval reinforcement schedule**. Some teachers reinforce a class on Fridays with extra time to talk to friends if the class has been able to get weekly work in on time. The two types of schedules lead to different patterns of response. The ratio schedule tends to produce high rates of responding that do not vary much, except perhaps for a small reduction in responding immediately after payoff. The interval schedule tends to produce a rapid decline in performance immediately after payoff that only gradually increases until it reaches a maximum just before payoff. Thus, for the teacher with the Friday reinforcement schedule, there would be fewer assignments coming in on Monday, Tuesday, and Wednesday, compared to Thursday and Friday.

Punishment

Negative reinforcement is often confused with punishment, even though negative reinforcement and punishment result in different outcomes. Negative reinforcement *increases* the likelihood of behavior; punishment *decreases* the likelihood of behavior. **Punishment** is the presentation of aversive stimulation following a response. Thus, if a preschooler darts into the parking lot at the daycare center, the teacher gives the child a stern reprimand that serves as a punishment. The response of darting away was followed by the aversive stimulation of adult disapproval. So the likelihood of the child running into the parking lot should decrease. Consider this example of negative reinforcement: if the sound of a car's warning buzzer is aversive, a high-school student taking behind-the-wheel instruction will buckle up the seatbelt in order to make the sound stop. The behavior of buckling up the seatbelt is negatively reinforced and the probability of this behavior occurring increases. In the example of negative reinforcement, the response (buckling the seat belt) resulted in the cessation of the aversive stimulus (the car buzzer) and the likelihood of the behavior (buckling the seat belt) increased. In the example of the punishment, the aversive stimulus (the reprimand) was not present until after the response and the likelihood of the behavior (darting in the parking lot) decreased.

In Skinner's view, behaviorism is a very positive approach to student learning and development. The emphasis is on catching the students doing well and reinforcing them for it. If the students cannot do well given their current competencies, then reinforce them for behaviors in the right direction and gradually shape the appropriate response. Skinner (1953) suggested that when teachers use punishment, they should also provide an alternative behavior that will be reinforced. For example, if a student is talking during a quiet study time, the teacher should remind the student firmly that this is the time to study quietly, but should also make sure the student has something interesting to work on. Skinner also argued that reductions in the frequency of undesirable behaviors using punishment were short lived and that punishment led to undesirable by-products, such as emotional responses of anxiety or anger.

Other researchers have found that punishment can have stable effects on elimination of undesirable behaviors without lasting side effects (Walters & Grusec, 1977). For example, supplementing punishment with rationales for obeying can make punishment more effective (Cheyne & Walters, 1969; LaVoie, 1973, 1974; Parke, 1969, 1974). In many cases, however, rationales alone can be as effective or more effective than punishments, and they may also help students internalize prohibitions, making it more likely that they will behave appropriately in the future (Hoffman, 1970; Kanfer & Zich, 1974). Rationales presented to young children (e.g., preschoolers) need to be concrete (e.g., "You might break this toy if you play with it because it is fragile"). Abstract rationales that focus on the rights and feelings of others (e.g., "The owner of this toy will feel bad if you play with it"), however, are increasingly effective with advancing age during childhood (LaVoie, 1974; Parke, 1974; Walters & Grusec, 1977). Thus undesirable behaviors often can often be suppressed without resorting to punishment.

Nevertheless, punishment still exists in schools. Effective school punishments are ones that have a reasonable connection to the infraction. In Blackwood (1970), junior-high students who had misbehaved copied essays as punishment. Some students copied an essay emphasizing the negative effects of classroom disobedience, while others copied an essay about steam engines. The students who copied an essay emphasizing why misbehavior was a problem were less likely to misbehave following the punishment than were students who copied the steam engine essay. MacPherson, Candee, and Hohman (1974) conducted a similar study with elementary students who had misbehaved in a cafeteria. Again, postpunishment behavior was better for students who had copied essays providing rationales for obeying school rules.

Although there is little evidence that corporal punishment leads to better behaved students (Edwards & Edwards, 1987), it is still a common practice in some schools, most commonly in the form of "paddling" (Hyman, 1990; Hyman & Wise, 1987). This practice would not meet with Skinner's (1977) approval since he believed that corporal punishment teaches that might makes right: "The punishing teacher who punishes teaches students that punishment is a way of solving problems" (p. 336). Research also indicates that children socially learn the punitive tactics they experience and observe (Parke & Slaby, 1983). Moreover, punishment has other undesirable side effects, including causing children to avoid future interactions with their punishers (Bandura, 1986). Does a disciplinary technique that causes children to learn physical aggression and to avoid their teachers really make sense?

Behavior Modification: Applied Operant Conditioning

One of the most important applications of operant conditioning is behavior modification (Bandura, 1969). The main idea of behavior modification is to reinforce behaviors that are valued. If students are not capable of the desired behaviors at present, teachers should reinforce behaviors they are capable of performing that are in the direction of the desired response. Gradually teachers increase the criterion for reinforcement until the students can produce the desired behavior. In other words, teachers shape the response. In some classrooms, children are reinforced for completing homework by receiving stickers. The stickers are a form of **token reinforcement**. Other token reinforcements sometimes include chips that can be accumulated and eventually traded in for goodies or privileges.

Teachers typically use reinforcement systems on an intermittent basis, since it is hard for a classroom teacher to monitor and reinforce every appropriate response by all of the students in a classroom and also so the student responses are less susceptible to extinction. An important goal of any behavior modification plan is to increase the ratio, or interval, between reinforcements, until the desired behaviors are occurring with only typical classroom reinforcements, such as praise. The gradual reduction in reinforcement is known as **fading**.

Good behavior modification environments often have other features as well. Correct and preferred behaviors are consistently modeled by teachers. Adult attention, which is a powerful reinforcement for many children, is provided for appropriate action rather than inappropriate action. Thus, if the teacher wishes to reduce talking out of turn in a student, the student does not get the teacher's attention when talking out of turn. Instead, the teacher responds to the student only when the student raises his or her hand and waits for acknowledgment before speaking.

Behavioral contracting is another behavior modification option. The student makes an agreement with the teacher to attempt to reach a particular goal, such as the following:

> When I _____ hand in all of my assignments on time, 5 days in a row, I will be able to (read a magazine, play a computer game, or put my head down to rest) for 10 minutes during class time. This contract will be in effect during the month of October. For every month that passes, 2 days are added to the number of days of on-time assignments necessary before I receive my reward (for example, November—7 days, December—9 days, etc.).

Usually the contract is negotiated, with students helping to decide what the goal will be, what reinforcement might be earned, and how much progress toward the goal is required before they receive any reinforcement.

This child has been removed from reinforcers in the classroom and placed in time-out, a form of punishment used in behavior modification programs.

Often parent training complements classroom behavioral programs. Parents learn how they too can use behavioral principles to provide reinforcement consistent with the school's program. Thus a teacher who is reinforcing a student for bringing homework into school also trains the parent to reinforce the student at home for doing homework.

Some forms of punishments are widely accepted in behavior modification programs. For example, one form of punishment for engaging in inappropriate behavior is **response cost.** With this technique, students are first given a number of tokens. If they engage in the unwanted behavior, they must forfeit some of these tokens. The students refrain from the unwanted behavior in order to keep the tokens. An alternative punishment acceptable in many educational settings is **time-out**, in which a student is physically removed from the other students or activities for a short period of time. Time-out can involve moving a student to an isolated corner of the classroom or to an empty room. Time-out is punishing because of the lack of reinforcers. For time-out to be effective, the area left must contain reinforcers and the time-out area must not have any reinforcers. Teachers must take care that the amount of time spent in time-out is appropriate. For elementary-school children, only a few minutes in time-out may be required.

Special educators, in particular, are interested in the application of behavioral principles to education (Kiernan, 1985). For example, behavioral principles have been used to teach everything from clearly academic tasks such as the basic arithmetic facts (Dunlap & Dunlap, 1989; Van Houten & Rolider, 1989) to life skills tasks such as banking (McDonnell & Ferguson, 1989) and acting in socially appropriate ways in employment settings (Park & Gaylord-Ross, 1989).

Cognitive-Behavior Modification

Consistent with the main tenets of behaviorism, classical behavior modification focuses on changing behaviors more than cognitions. Contemporary behavior modification also attempts to change children's thinking, largely by changing the way children talk to themselves. Arguing that self-speech could be used to organize behavior, Donald Meichenbaum (1977, p. 19) cited the following example of child speech that directed the construction of a Tinkertoy car:

> "The wheels go here, the wheels go here. Oh, we need to start it all over again. We have to close it up. See it closes up. We're starting it all over again. Do you know why we wanted to do that? Because I needed it to go a different way. Isn't it pretty clever, don't you think? But we have to cover up the motor just like a real car." (Kohlberg, Yaeger, & Hjertholm, 1968, p. 695)

Although young children often use such self-instructional speech on their own, they also benefit from explicit instructions about how to self-verbalize (Patterson & Mischel, 1976; Wozniak, 1972). Cognitive behavior modification combines self-verbalizations with modeling, reinforcement, and fading. For example, Meichenbaum and Goodman (1971) reduced the impulsive responding of hyperactive second graders by teaching them to instruct themselves to go slowly and reflect before responding. Using teacher modeling, guided practice, and the gradual fading of teacher cuing, they taught students to make self-verbalizations such as the following:

> "Okay, what is it I have to do? You want me to copy the picture with the different lines. I have to go slowly and carefully. Okay, draw the line down, down, good; then to the right, that's it; now down some more and to the left. Good, I'm doing fine so far. Remember, go slowly. Now back up again. No, I was supposed to go down. That's okay. Just erase the line carefully. . . . Good. Even if I make an error I can go on slowly and carefully. I have to go down now. Finished. I did it!" (Meichenbaum & Goodman, 1971, p. 117)

The teacher first described and modeled this kind of positive self-verbalization. Then the teacher provided external support and guidance as students attempted to apply the approach to problems. The teacher encouraged the students to internalize the self-verbalizations by guiding the students to whisper rather than to talk aloud and then eventually only to think about the problem definition, task focusing and guiding directions, and self-reinforcement as they performed the task.

An important component in the self-instructional approach is a teacher who consistently models self-control by using self-instruction (Manning, 1991). Anyone who has ever taught knows the frustration of trying to figure out what is wrong with the overhead projector. A self-instructing teacher might cope by first defining the problem verbally, followed by self-verbalizations to direct appropriate actions:

> "Why won't this overhead turn on? Let me see. I'll try all the switches again. This arrow points to the right. Did I turn left or right. Try again." When frustrated, the teacher models coping via self-instruction: "It's easy to get frustrated. Take a deep breath and relax. There must be a solution." Once a solution is found, the teacher self-reinforces: "Hey! I stuck with it and found the outlet is faulty. I'll try this other outlet. Yay! It works." If there is no success, the teacher models more coping and adapting: "I've tried all I know. I'll either show you this information by putting it on the board or call the media specialist to help fix the machine. Which would be fastest?" (Manning, 1991, p. 134)

The self-instructing teacher also models for students how to cope with problems and temptations to behave impulsively or inappropriately. Thus the teacher might model the following sequence for a student who is unprepared for a test and caught attempting to cheat. Again the teacher starts with a verbalization of the problem and then models self-direction and self-coping until a solution is achieved that can be self-reinforced:

> "I forgot to study for my test. Should I look at my friend's test? I can see her paper easily. But, is that right? Just do my best. I'll feel better about myself if I don't look. This is hard. I know my answers are wrong. That's okay. I've done the best I can. Next time I won't leave my book at school. I'm glad I didn't take answers that didn't belong to me. I feel good about that!" (Manning, 1991, p. 135)

Cognitive-behavior modification works in classrooms. Manning (1988) randomly assigned the most behaviorally inappropriate first- and third-grade children in a school to either a self-instructional treatment group or a control condition that received additional instruction and attention, but no self-instruction. For example, when the students in the experimental condition saw a teacher self-instruct to inhibit inappropriate behaviors, control students received additional explicit instruction in the school rules prohibiting the inappropriate behaviors. Both experimental and control students received 8 hours of instruction, and the classroom teachers did not know the condition assignment of the children involved in the study. The results were compelling—both immediately following training and 3 months later. The students receiving self-instructional training were perceived as more self-controlled by their teachers, were more often on-task (i.e., working when they should), and believed themselves to be more in control of their behaviors.

In another demonstration of the power of self-instruction, Manning (1990) used cognitive self-instruction to increase the on-task behavior of a fourth grader. At the beginning of the intervention, Jill (the student) was on-task during school assignments only 15% of the time. Following training in self-instruction, Jill was on-task 80% of the time. She continued to exhibit higher levels of on-task behavior 3 months after the self-instructional training.

Some specific components of self-instruction supported by research are teaching students (1) to recognize when they are at risk for behaving in a noncontrolled fashion, (2) that there are more appropriate behaviors than the ones they are using to solve problems, (3) how to interrupt impulsive responding by making comments such as "What am I supposed to do here?," (4) the standards that define effective performance of the task, (5) to self-monitor, (6) to cope, and (7) to self-reinforce (Zentall, 1989). In fact, there is now substantial evidence that self-instruction impacts students who are often out of control—children who are hyperactive, impulsive, or aggressive— with the effects of such instruction very large when students receive such instruction in school settings (Robinson, Smith, Miller, & Brownell, 1999). (Review the use of self-instruction to teach writing skills to fifth- and sixth-grade students with learning disabilities as described in Chapter 4.)

Classroom Management

Perhaps the most common application of social learning theory occurs in classroom contexts. Before it is possible to teach anything academic, the teacher must take control of the class. Principles of classroom management provide teachers with a great deal of guidance about how to maintain order in the classroom without creating an aversive environment (Doyle, 1986; Emmer, Evertson, & Worsham, 2002; Evertson, 1989; Evertson, Emmer, & Worsham, 2002), even with children who can be otherwise disruptive (Mather & Goldstein, 2002). Classroom management starts before the school year begins. One essential step is to *arrange the physical classroom so that the teacher can maintain order and monitor students easily.* In many elementary-school classrooms, small reading groups meet with the teacher in one section of the room while the rest of the class does seatwork. The classroom arrangement must allow the teacher to easily look up to scan the rest of the classroom while working with the reading group.

The teacher also needs to *establish early the rules and procedures of the classroom.* The beginning of the school day, including the opening activities and the morning's administrative activities (e.g., taking attendance, collecting lunch tickets), should become routines that are carried out automatically and quickly. The point of establishing routines is not just to promote quiet and order but also to achieve rapid transition. Time spent in transition is time lost: student achievement in school depends on the amount of time students are engaged in instruction.

In addition, the teacher needs to *clarify expectations.* Students must be made aware of what is permitted and what is prohibited. Providing students with positive reinforcement when they comply with classroom rules is a must. Teacher praise, such as "Row 2 has really been working hard this morning—way to go!", is common in well-managed classrooms. Teachers need to monitor the classroom and signal when they are concerned about classroom misconduct well before the misconduct accelerates into a situation requiring sanctions. When sanctions are necessary, the teacher needs to deal with the situation quickly and as unobtrusively as possible. For example, a teacher can dispense mild punishers, such as directive eye contact and gentle touches to move students away from distractions. Persistent misconduct should be dealt with more harshly, but efficiently and with little, if any, disruption of the class.

Teachers need to *model self-control and on-task behaviors.* They model their own enthusiasm for academic tasks, make it clear that they find their own academic competencies to be rewarding, and convey the message that students can reap the same types of rewards by learning the lessons offered in school. Students in well-managed classrooms learn a great deal about how to achieve life's long-term rewards as well as how to achieve short-term reinforcements, such as positive teacher attention for carrying out assignments in ways consistent with classroom policies.

Does classroom management work? Yes. For example, Gottfredson, Gottfredson, and Hybl (1993) demonstrated how conduct in middle schools improved when school rules were made clearer, consequences for violating them were more certain, classrooms were organized and managed more efficiently, parents were kept informed about the good behavior and misbehaviors of their children, and reinforcement was increased for good conduct. One of the most striking observations in classrooms and schools that produce high engagement and achievement is that classroom management is so good that behavior infractions rarely occur (Bohn, Roehrig, & Pressley, 2004; Dolezal, Welsh, Pressley, & Vincent, 2003; Pressley, Allington, Wharton-McDonald, Block, & Morrow, 2001; Pressley, Dolezal, Raphael, Welsh, Bogner, & Roehrig, 2003).

In summary, social learning theory is a developmental theory with tremendous practical implications. That is one of the reasons it has commanded so much attention from developmental and educational researchers. Even so, applying social learning principles well is very hard. See the Applying Developmental Theory to Educational Contexts special feature (Box 5.1) for a summary of the challenges involved in applying a seemingly simple type of classroom reinforcement, praise, which is anything but simple to use well!

Applying Developmental Theory to Educational Contexts

BOX 5.1. Praising Students

Praise is a form of reinforcement that teachers use everyday in the classroom. Unfortunately, effective use of praise is complicated (Henderlong & Lepper, 2002). All too often praise provided by teachers does not make clear what the student did well or praises behaviors that really are not praiseworthy. For example, teachers frequently offer praise for participation alone ("I'm so glad you are taking part"), rather than for participation consistent with what is being taught. Brophy (1981) described how to make praise in classrooms maximally effective. Some of the following may seem obvious but it is surprising how often teachers fail to follow these simple guidelines:

- Effective praise is delivered contingent upon desirable student behaviors.
- In delivering the praise, the teacher makes clear what the student did that was praiseworthy, focusing attention on the student behaviors leading to the praise. Students are told they are competent and why what they have done is valuable.
- Effective praise is sincere, reflecting that the teacher is attentive to the student's accomplishments.
- Effective praise implies that students can be similarly successful in the future if they exert appropriate effort.
- Effective praise conveys the message that students expended the effort that led to praise because they enjoyed the task or wanted to develop the competencies that merited the praise.

■ ■ ■ DEVELOPMENT ACCORDING TO FREUD: THE PSYCHOSEXUAL STAGE THEORY

Social learning theory emphasizes the role of the situation in determining behavior—that the way children develop depends on what they observe as well as what their culture reinforces and punishes. The contrast to a theory that emphasizes the situation would be a theory that emphasized the consistency of the individual across situations, a theory proposing that behavior is more determined by enduring characteristics of the person than by factors that vary with the situation. One of the most influential of these theories is Freud's theory of psychosexual development.

Sigmund Freud was a physician by training, but more importantly he was completely immersed in the scientific thinking of his time (Sulloway, 1992; Wollheim, 1989). Living in Vienna, a center of culture and intellect, permitted Freud to interact with contemporary thinkers who were questioning whether man's basic nature was rational—the prevailing view in the late 1800s. Freud proposed that emotions governed more than reason much of the time (Hale, 1995; Tyson & Tyson, 1990). He proposed that much of behavior was determined by unconscious processes, sexual and aggressive instinctual processes, an idea very much in contrast with the prevailing belief that behavior was rationally determined. Most shocking of all during the Victorian era, a time when sexuality was kept out of public sight and attention, Freud contended that sexually energized conflicts during childhood determined much of personality in later life. Indeed, one reason sexuality is a great concern is that society requires that it be controlled, and when it does function, it is supposed to occur out of sight (Schmidt-Hellerau, 1997).

Freud referred to the unconscious as the *primary process*; it contrasted with the *secondary process*, which was responsible for more rational and logical processes. As the names for these processes imply, Freud believed that the logical side of thinking was a very small part of mental activity compared to the unconscious primary process. Much like an iceberg, the secondary process was the tip of an iceberg, and the majority of the iceberg was primary process, below the surface.

Freud came to insights about behavior and development through working with patients who experienced a variety of psychological disorders, such as anxieties and neuroses. During psychoanalysis, the patient talked, freely associating to ideas presented by the therapist, and sometimes relating recurring dreams. Freud believed that free associations and recurring fantasies were very revealing about unconscious conflicts. As the therapist detected troubling conflicts, the therapist and the patient then worked together to replace the conflict with a story that might make the conflict less troubling for the patient.

Freud recognized that the unconscious thoughts revealed during therapy were probably not memories of objective events. One of Freud's most important insights was that when his patients reported sexual relations with parents during their childhood, they likely were reporting fantasies. Freud also realized that in helping the patient bring these fantasies to consciousness, the story that emerged was a coconstruction of the patient and the therapist, not just the patient's story. See the Considering Interesting Questions special feature (Box 5.2) for a discussion of memories recovered during therapy.

Freud studied and restudied his cases in the search for understandings about the human experience. Freud wrote about many of these cases, which continue to be

Considering Interesting Questions

BOX 5.2. Can Memories of Sexual Abuse Be Recovered through Therapy?

In the early 1990s, a number of people entered therapy for symptoms such as bulimia, depression, or low self-esteem, and exited therapy believing that their problems were caused by sexual abuse in childhood. What must be emphasized here is that when they came into therapy, they had no idea that they had been abused. Memories of abuse had been "recovered" during therapy.

How did this occur? A number of specialists in memory and its development have devoted considerable effort to understanding such memories, concluding that these memories may not be valid (Lindsay & Read, 1994, 2006; see Pressley & Grossman, 1994, for a collection of important articles on this topic). The therapist might have used any of a number of techniques to elicit memories, including hypnosis (which is a state that makes the hypnotized person susceptible to suggestions from the hypnotist) free associating, and films of explicit sexual violence. When suggestions of abuse were mentioned by patients during these sessions, the therapist pursued them. If the patient objected to an emerging interpretation of abuse, the patient may have been reassured that not remembering violence clearly is to be expected, perhaps reflecting the defense mechanism of denial. The therapist then continued to work with the patient to develop the memories, perhaps over a hundred or more sessions.

The results of this process are presented to the patient by the therapist as the patient's actual memories, previously repressed, now recovered from the unconscious. Consistent with Freudian thinking, a justification for recovering these memories is that confronting them permits better functioning in the future. But sometimes these recovered memories have been used against the alleged abusers in courts of law, with the result that parents and child caregivers have been convicted and imprisoned for heinous crimes.

Many of the therapists employing these techniques are not well qualified, with very little formal training. These therapists clearly do not understand what Freud knew, that the stories that patients and therapists construct during therapy are a product of both the patient's thinking and the therapist's interpretation of the patient's thinking. Indeed, the methods employed during memory recovery very likely distort memory (Lindsay & Read, 1994, 2006). Contemporary psychoanalysts have substantial doubts about the validity of recovered memories (Brenneis, 2000; Cohler, 1994).

That in no way suggests that people who have vivid memories of childhood abuse should be ignored. In fact, an important criticism of Freud was that he was willing to classify most such reports as fantasies. The sad truth is that many people's memories of abuse, both children's and adults' memories, reflect terrible events that actually did happen. Sexual abuse of children is real (Finkelhor, Ormrod, Turner, & Hamby, 2005; Masson, 1984).

The bottom line is that by ignoring real memories of abuse in the past, in part because of the Freudian assertion that such memories often were fantastic, harm was done; but by having confidence in recovered memories as reflections of actual events, harm was done as well. When children and adults have terrible memories, those memories should not be dismissed lightly. However, when individuals who have no memory of abuse prior to therapy discover it during therapy, it is reasonable to suspect that the conclusions constructed during therapy are not actual memories.

read and studied by contemporary students of psychoanalysis. Most of the ideas offered in this section were derived from analysis of cases, either by Freud or his followers, including his daughter, Anna Freud.

Psychosexual Stages of Development

Freud contended that the most basic force in life is instinctual energy, **id**, which is present at birth. The id seeks pleasure and immediate gratification (such as food, drink, and contact comfort), an idea Freud summarized as the *pleasure principle*. With maturation during the first few years of life, a new personality structure emerges, the **ego**. The ego is the rational side of personality and operates according to the *reality principle*. Reality demands deferring gratification as part of pursuit of more long-range goals than the hedonistic goals of the id. Later still, between age 3 and age 6 or 7, yet a third personality structure emerges, the **superego**. The superego is the conscience and as such directly conflicts with the id. The rationality of the ego balances the demands for gratification by the id with the inhibitions of the superego.

Thus Freud proposed a biologically determined invariant sequence of development, such that instinctual urgings (id) preceded the development of the rational side of the personality (ego), which began to develop before the moral aspect of personality (superego). The psychological developments paralleled physical development of the mouth, anus, and genital regions, pleasure centers in Freud's view. Sexual pleasures are important in this psychosexual stage theory of development. For example, many of the newborn's pleasures and frustrations are associated with the taking in of nourishment. Hence, the first stage of development according to Freud is the *oral stage*. If the child experiences too much frustration or unchecked pleasure during this period of time, oral fixation can occur. Freud suggested that oral fixation causes long-term problems such as overeating, drinking, smoking, and overdependency on others. It can also be the beginning of a verbally aggressive personality (Agmon & Schneider, 1998).

The ego emerges as the child is weaning and is learning to control elimination, largely because of the frustrations associated with weaning and toilet training. It develops as the mediator between the instinctual demands of the id and the demands being placed on the child during weaning and toilet training by the parent. Because so much of the development of the ego occurs as a function of the conflicts surrounding toilet training, which is enabled by the physical development of the anal region, the second stage is known as the *anal stage*. During this stage, the anal region is associated with pleasure (such as parental approval when the child eliminates at the appropriate place and time) and frustration (such as when the child does not control elimination appropriately). If the child experiences a great deal of frustration during this period, anal fixation is likely. Anal fixation can result in stubborn overattention to punctuality, neatness, and routines. Alternatively, it can play out as overmessiness. Extreme negativism or unwillingness to part with anything (individuals who hoard things) also can be indications of anal fixation.

As the genitals mature, pleasures and frustrations are centered on the reproductive organs. This is the *phallic stage*, which proceeds somewhat differently for boys and girls, a realization that Freud came to as he listened to patients talk about their childhoods. Although Freud at first believed the patients were telling him about events that actually happened, he came to believe that the patients were relating fantasies, ones reflecting unconscious desires and conflicts that occurred during childhood.

Boys experience the *Oedipus complex*. They come to desire their mothers sexually. This unconscious desire is a dangerous desire. The obvious competitor for mother—father—is much bigger and stronger than the young boy. According to Freud, this unconscious desire (a reflection of the id) conflicts with the ego-mediated recognition of the reality of the father. At the center of the reality is the possibility that the father would retaliate for any sexual advances of the son on the mother. This retaliation would take the form of castration. The resolution of this conflict between id and ego is that the son identifies with the father. In identifying with the father, the child can vicariously possess the mother. Part of the identification process is the adoption of the father's moral standards, which is the beginning of the third personality structure, the superego. Because the development of the son's superego is mediated by a great fear, the possibility of castration, the superego is very strong in boys.

In contrast, girls experience the *Electra conflict*. The preschool girl unconsciously comes to desire her father. Reality for the girl is in the form of the mother, who while threatening is not as threatening as the father is to a son. After all, the mother cannot castrate her daughter. The daughter nonetheless resolves her conflict between id and ego by identifying with the mother, permitting her vicarious possession of the father. The superego that emerges from this resolution is not as strong as the superego of a boy, however, because the threat giving rise to it was not as great. According to classical psychoanalytical theory, this is the explanation for stronger conscience in males than in females. Moreover, according to Freud, young girls experience *penis envy*, when they recognize that boys have a much more prominent sexual organ than they possess. Penis envy results in feelings of inferiority. Freud argued that penis envy is the basis for female feelings of inferiority throughout life. Not surprisingly, Freud's conceptions of female development (and his limited interest in female development) have met with more resistance than his conceptions of male development (de Fiorini, 1998). Revised conceptions of psychoanalytic theory have been offered that are not so clearly gender-biased (Horney, 1967), for instance, focusing on how females are much more concerned with interpersonal connections to others than are males (Chodorow, 1989; see also Chapter 3).

Phallic fixations were possible if the child experienced difficulties in resolving the instinctual demands of this period with external reality—that parents cannot be objects of sexual affection. According to Freud, such fixations could translate into a variety of problems later in life, including sexual identity problems and excessive guilt surrounding sexual interactions.

Once the superego emerges, the emotional turmoil subsides for awhile. There comes a period of time during which sexual desires are not much in evidence, the *latency stage*. During the latency stage, which corresponds roughly to the elementary-school years, boys prefer to interact with boys and girls prefer to interact with girls. Children's attentions during latency are directed toward acquiring intellectual and social skills. There is no latency fixation, largely because so little attention is devoted to satisfying the pleasures of the id, and hence less likelihood of frustration during this period than other periods in development.

With the onset of adolescence and puberty, the final stage, the *genital stage*, arises. The id is reenergized as the sexual organs mature, and now expressed as masturbation, sexual experimentation, and strong interest in the opposite sex. Adolescents are concerned with acting like men and women rather than like boys and girls. If the child is orally, anally, or phallically fixated because of failures to resolve instinctual and social demands during early childhood, unconscious conflicts can interfere with sexual relations during the genital stage and more generally with psychological functioning in other areas of life.

In summary, biological development is the basis for psychological development in Freudian psychoanalytic theory. There are innate sexual and aggressive instincts. As physical structures mature, these instincts seek gratifications in new ways. But these instincts meet external demands from parents and others. These demands can be frustrating, such as the frustrations surrounding weaning, toilet training, and regulation of affection with the opposite-sex parent during the preschool years. If the conflicts between instinctual and external demands are unresolved or only resolved with great difficulty, the result can be oral, anal, or phallic fixations, which are the unconscious causes of a variety of personality problems experienced later in life.

Anxiety and Defense Mechanisms

According to Freudian theory, anxiety is an omnipresent danger, capable of overwhelming the individual. There are some very good reasons to be anxious, such as when confronted with an objectively distressing or threatening situation (e.g., an ill parent, a broken favorite toy). A fact of life for Freudians is that humans are always at risk for being instinctually impulsive (e.g., overeating or drinking too much, indulging in prohibited or socially unacceptable sexual activities, or aggressing in unacceptable ways). That is, the risk of the id overwhelming the ego is always present. Anxiety results when the id prevails and individuals engage in objectionable behaviors. Such anxiety could be overwhelming if not managed. The ego manages anxiety through the use of defense mechanisms (A. Freud, 1936).

Although different psychoanalytic theorists have proposed different numbers of defense mechanisms (Plutchik, 1995), the following are commonly included in most listings, presented here roughly in their order of development, from least mature to most mature (Rohwer, Ammon, & Cramer, 1974). In general, the less mature ones are less cognitively complex than the more mature ones:

- *Repression* is the forgetting of painful or threatening events. Thus memories of Oedipal and Electra conflicts are repressed because it is so anxiety-provoking to remember having sexual feelings for a parent.
- *Denial* is simply to deny an objectionable external reality. Thus a child may deny that a pet has died by claiming that it will be coming home from the pet hospital next week.
- *Negation* is claiming to desire the exact opposite of actual desires. Thus the child who wants the teacher's attention may tell her parents that she wishes the teacher would leave her alone.
- *Projection* is attributing to another person what is actually an objectionable characteristic of the self. Thus a bully is projecting when he or she accuses the victim of being the aggressor.
- *Identification* is taking on the characteristics of a threatening person. Thus the child who fears another child may begin to imitate the threatening child. The resolution of the anxiety-ridden Oedipal and Electra conflicts is through identification with the threatening parent of the same sex, taking on their behaviors and values as part of resolving the conflict.
- *Displacement* involves venting anger toward individuals who are less threatening than the real object of anger. Thus a child may displace anger at a teacher or parents by screaming at a classmate.

- *Reaction formation* involves behavioral expressions of interest that conflict directly with actual interests. Thus the habitual consumer of pornography who publicly calls for censorship is engaging in reaction formation.
- *Sublimation* is channeling objectionable tendencies into acceptable directions. Thus someone who loves to overeat may expend great energies to be a great cook for others. A highly aggressive individual may sublimate in directing energies into competitive athletics.
- *Rationalization/intellectualization* is the development of elaborate rationales for engaging in anxiety-provoking behaviors. An adolescent girl may break up with a same-age boyfriend because she wants to explore relationships with older boys. She is engaging in rationalization if she tells the old boyfriend that the breakup is for his own good, so that he can get to know a variety of girls.

Most of the studies examining development of use of defense mechanisms have involved studies of young children (Safyer & Hauser, 1995). Even 2-year-olds evidence simple defense mechanisms like denial; by 8 years of age, a variety of defense mechanisms are used, including rationalization/ intellectualization.

Anna Freud (1936) viewed defense mechanisms as appropriate during childhood, when the ego was underdeveloped and needed protection from being overwhelmed by anxiety and instinct. When defense mechanisms persist after childhood, for the most part, the result usually is immature and neurotic thinking. The exceptions are defense mechanisms that translate into behavior that could be considered mature. For example, sublimation may result in a person directing instinctual energies into socially accepted channels, such as the lawyer who redirects sexual energies into a 70-hour-a-week law practice. In mentally healthy adults, most of the defense mechanisms give way to more mature mechanisms of coping, such as humor (Vaillant, 1971, 1975, 1976).

Defense mechanisms do not eliminate disturbing instincts and conflicts but rather relegate them to the unconscious. Because the unconscious can affect future conscious behaviors, this is problematic. Thus the sexual conflicts of the phallic stage that are repressed can interfere with mature sexual functioning later. Defensive thinking is not optimal thinking, although defense mechanisms can protect a fragile, developing ego.

Unconscious and Conscious Processing

Freud's belief that both conscious (rational, secondary process) and unconscious (emotional, primary process) thinking occurs is receiving renewed attention. Epstein (1994) reviewed a variety of evidence consistent with the idea that thinking is dualistic, that humans sometimes process information holistically rather than analytically, emotionally rather than rationally, and imagistically rather than verbally. In other words, there is evidence supporting the duality of Freud's primary and secondary processes.

Developmental psychologists have offered perspectives consistent with this division of processing. For example, as described by Piaget (1962), assimilation is intuitive thought, with judgments often made without reflection. Thus, the 4-year-old nonconserver often will answer quickly that there is "More water now," after seeing water poured from a short, fat beaker into a tall, thin beaker. In contrast, accommodation is much more reflective and rational; when a child is in transition from preoperational to concrete operational thinking, it can take a great deal of thought to conclude that "It's the same water." Thus, according to Piaget, the most important mechanism of cognitive development, equilibration, reflects the combined functioning of unconscious (assimilation) and conscious (accommodation) processes.

Certainly the most elaborate dualistic perspective offered by a developmental theorist, however, comes from Labouvie-Vief (1989, 1990, 2003), a researcher and theorist interested in development across the lifespan. She has proposed that mature thought involves both *mythos*, which is intuitive and holistic processing, and *logos*, which is rational processing. She is emphatic in making the case that both need to be balanced for healthy and creative thinking. The parallels with Freud are obvious. Freud believed that many on his couch were there because of imbalances in unconscious and conscious processing.

Cognitive scientists also are now spending a great deal of effort to understand relationships between conscious and unconscious processing. For example, researchers interested in adult memory have been extremely interested in differences between conscious, explicit versus unconscious, implicit memory, for it has become obvious that there are clear dissociations between explicit and implicit memory (Roediger, 1990). Thus, some brain-damaged amnesiacs are seriously impaired with respect to explicit memory but show no implicit memory impairment. Moreover, implicit memory seems not to vary with developmental level during childhood, whereas explicit memory definitely increases with development.

Implicit memory is measured by tasks not requiring explicit attempts to remember (Graf & Schacter, 1985; Roediger, Guynn, & Jones, 1994; Schacter, 1987, 1992; Schacter, Chiu, & Ochsner, 1993). For example, recognition priming is one task reflecting implicit memory. Suppose a child is shown a fragmented picture of something, perhaps a horse. If the child had seen the entire picture of the horse the day before, if anything, the youngster should recognize the horse picture fragment as a horse more certainly and quickly than if he or she had not seen the entire picture of a horse. That is, recognition of the horse from the fragment would have been primed by the previous exposure to a picture of a horse. Such priming is evident by age 2 and does not seem to increase after that. This contrasts with clear demonstrations that explicit memory (e.g., conscious recall of pictures seen yesterday) does develop (Carroll, Byrne, & Kirsner, 1985; Greenbaum & Graf, 1989; Lorsbach & Morris, 1991; Lorsbach & Worman, 1989; Naito, 1990; Parkin & Streete, 1988). Lorsbach and Worman (1990) offered complementary evidence of no difference in implicit memory between normal students and students with learning disabilities, which contrasted with a large difference in explicit memory favoring the normal students. Implicit, unconscious cognition seems to be very different from explicit, conscious memory. Implicit memory seems to be in place very early in life, although there are some developmental increases. For example, as world knowledge increases, implicit memory that depends on such knowledge can increase (Murphy, McKone, & Slee, 2003). Explicit memory, however, develops relatively slowly beginning with infancy (Bauer, Wiebe, Carver, Waters, & Nelson, 2003; Carver & Bauer, 2001; Murphy et al., 2003).

Neuroscientists are finding evidence that different brain structures are responsible for explicit and implicit memories (Adeyemo, 2002; Squire, 1992, 2004). Consistent with Freudian theory, brain structures that are more heavily implicated in implicit memory seem to develop earlier (i.e., in the first year of life) than those implicated in explicit memory, which develop rather slowly during the childhood years (Nelson, 1995).

Psychoanalysis and Education

Psychoanalytic theory inspired much educational reform in the first half of the 20th century (Hale, 1995). It was an important part of the mental hygiene movement. One purpose of this movement was to apply the scientific theories of psychiatry and psychology in schools in order to curb delinquency and improve the mental health of children and hence society.

The mental hygiene movement was very critical of conventional parenting, regarding parenting as generally too authoritarian. According to this perspective, homes needed to be more democratic since this would reduce the likelihood of a child experiencing too much frustration, resulting in fixation. The mental hygienists were confident that if psychoanalytic ideas were incorporated into the rearing of children, there would be less mental retardation, less childhood disease, and reduced delinquency.

The mental hygiene movement was also extremely critical of conventional schooling, especially its emphasis on orderliness, as reflected by rows of children working quietly at their desks. The mental hygiene movement advocated less discipline and reduced emphasis on academic competition, which would encourage sublimation. That is, rather than attempting to curb instinctual impulses, the goal was to redirect them into creative channels.

Although the mental hygienists worked hard to have these ideas incorporated into public schooling, the most complete translations of psychoanalytic theory into education occurred in schools set up by psychoanalytically oriented psychologists. Schools based on application of psychoanalytic theory allowed for more freedom than other schools. Masturbation was tolerated, consistent with the idea of freedom and the avoidance of frustrations that might result in fixations; scoldings were replaced by explanations to children.

Even many sympathetic to psychoanalytic theory, however, felt that the results of such schooling fell far short of the mark. Many children who attended such schools seemed unable to concentrate on school work. There were enough character disorders, behavior problems, and attention deficits in the graduates of such schools to make clear that the psychoanalytic approach was not an educational elixir (Hale, 1995). See the Applying Developmental Theory to Educational Contexts special feature (Box 5.3) for a profile of one very famous school inspired in part by the psychoanalytic emphasis on freedom.

Evaluation of Freudian Theory

Freudian theory was very vague and it has proven difficult to test definitively. Moreover, funding for testing the theory was limited (Hale, 1995). When important Freudian applications were devised and implemented, such as schools based on psychoanalytic ideas about development, formal evaluations were rare. Moreover, when others reviewed Freud's cases, they did not always come to the same conclusion that Freud drew. One example is the case of Little Hans, who was terrified of horses. Freud attributed this fear to castration anxiety. Others suggested, based in part on interviews with the original Little Hans when he was an adult, that the child may have been frightened by a horse in his youth, an event that was especially traumatic because of repeated family warnings about how horses sometimes bite (Goleman, 1990). Freud seemed ready to dismiss reports of what could have been real traumas

Applying Developmental Theory to Educational Contexts

BOX 5.3. Summerhill School

Freedom is the central governing principle at Summerhill School, a private English boarding school that was founded in the 1920s. The school came to popular attention with the publication in 1960 of the book *Summerhill*, authored by the founder of the school, A. S. Neill. Although the authors of this text do not subscribe to Neill's philosophy, we believe that every student of child development and education should know about Summerhill, for it is one of the most famous schools inspired by a psychological model. *Summerhill* is also a wonderfully interesting read, and we recommend that you borrow a copy from a library and spend some time with it.

Neill was completely committed to the idea that children are naturally good and schools should do little to interfere with that. He was extremely concerned with the mental health of Summerhill students and graduates, much more so than with their academic accomplishments. Neill was much influenced by Freud and other psychoanalytic thinkers and concluded from his study of psychology that a key factor in the development of children's mental health was freedom. He also believed that the education of children should be according to their interests:

> My view is that the child is innately wise and realistic. If left to himself without adult suggestion of any kind, he will develop as far as he is capable of developing. Logically, Summerhill is a place in which people who have the innate ability and wish to be scholars will be scholars; while those who are only fit to sweep the streets will sweep the streets. . . .
>
> What is Summerhill like? Well, for one thing, Lessons are optional. Children can go to them or stay away from them—for years if they want to. There *is* a timetable—but only for the teachers. The children have classes usually according to their age, but sometimes according to their interests. We have no new methods of teaching, because we do not consider that teaching in itself matters very much. Whether a School has or has not a special method for teaching long division is of no significance, for long division is of no importance except to those who *want* to learn it. And the child who *wants* to learn long division *will* learn it no matter how it is taught. (Neill, 1960, pp. 4–5)

But there were things much more shocking at Summerhill than optional classes. Nudity was fine and commonplace at the swimming pool, since Neill believed inhibiting student nudity might lead to warped attitudes toward the human body. Neill had little trouble with pornography and abortion. Damage of property was tolerated, since Neill had great faith in students learning from natural consequences. For example, if you break the window to your room, you sleep in the cold. Neill discouraged punishment, believing it created fear and hostility which ultimately harms psychic development. So what if Summerhill students swore a lot? Freedom was more important than forcing arbitrary rules on children. As for homework, "The homework habit is disgraceful. Children loathe homework, and that is enough to condemn it" (Neill, 1960, p. 378).

For scientifically oriented developmental and educational psychologists, the Summerhill model and other related psychoanalytic schools are frustrating because the psychoanalytic education model was never evaluated in anything like a conventional scientific study. There is simply no way of knowing whether Summerhill works or not, whether Summerhill graduates really are more emotionally healthy than if they had attended conventional school, whether Summerhill students really became all they were capable of becoming.

If, after reading *Summerhill*, you want to know more about the school, many resources are available. Extensive pictorials about the school were published, concretely depicting the translation of Neill's philosophy into educational practice (Popenoe, 1970; Snitzer, 1964). The philosophy of the school in historical perspective was described in some detail by Hemmings (1973). A number of prominent educators and psychologists provided their insightful evaluations of Summerhill in *Summerhill: For and Against* (Hart, 1970). The school also has a website: www.summerhillschool.co.uk/indexgo.html.

as fantasies. Recall Box 5.2 and the criticisms of Freud's dismissal of reports of child-hood sexual abuse.

When researchers were able to devise tests of the theory, the theory often was not supported. For example, the conflicts during the phallic period require some knowledge of differences between male and female genital structures. Many pre-school children lack this knowledge (Bem, 1989; Katcher, 1955; Tavris & Wade, 1984). According to Freudian theory, divorce before or during the preschool years, with a boy then growing up in a household lacking a father, should disrupt normal psychosocial development and result in a variety of behavioral problems. Yes, boys from families experiencing divorce exhibit more behavior problems and academic difficulties, but these problems are not confined to families in which divorce might have disrupted development during the phallic stage (Hetherington, 1989; Kline, Tschann, Johnston, & Wallerstein, 1989). Freudian theory does not explain well the problems boys experience due to the divorce of their parents.

Nonetheless, Freud identified ideas that continue to contribute to our under-standing of development (Emde, 1992, 1998):

1. The recognition that the unconscious can be important in determining behav-ior was an insight of enduring significance, with work on the cognitive uncon-scious continuing a century after Freud's initial writing on the unconscious.
2. Freud also recognized that development largely was a function of biology and environment in interaction. Specifically, during development, children expe-rience conflicts between sexual and aggressive instincts and parental and social demands that conflict with these instincts.
3. Freud proposed that development was stage-like, due largely to biological maturation. The idea of developmental stages would endure throughout the 20th century.
4. Freud recognized that what happens early in life can have implications throughout life. Although conceptions about how early development affects later life have changed considerably since Freud, the idea that a connection exists between experiences across the lifespan was an important one.
5. Specific issues that Freud emphasized became issues that were studied throughout the 20th century, including how babies relate to their mothers, the development of aggression, identification, learning of sex roles, and moral development. Freud's contribution to developmental psychology was enormous.

Freud was uncompromising about his theory. Thus, when Freud's belief in the primacy of instinctual processes was not shared by some prominent students of psy-choanalysis, who emphasized the importance of rational, conscious, realistic, and problem-oriented thinking—ego processes—these students broke away from Freud. One such ego theorist who began as a Freudian was Erik Erikson.

■ ■ ■ DEVELOPMENT ACCORDING TO ERIKSON: THE PSYCHOSOCIAL STAGE THEORY

Like Freud, Erik Erikson proposed a theory of personality development (Erikson, 1963, 1968; Erikson & Coles, 2000). Unlike Freud, who felt that the most important determinants of development occurred during early childhood, Erikson's view was that much of the most important development came later, with development continuing across the lifespan. Thus, in Erikson's theory, early experience was important but not as important as Freud's theory suggested. Moreover, Erikson based many of his ideas on analyses of the functioning of healthy people, whereas Freud studied individuals being treated for mental health problems. Over the course of his career, Erikson studied many different types of people and was struck by the adaptability of people to their surroundings.

Psychosocial Stages of Development

Freud's emphasis on instinctual energy as a determining life force resulted in his psycho*sexual* theory of development. In contrast, Erikson proposed a psycho*social* theory of development. For Erikson, what mattered were key social interactions at each stage of development. Yes, development was caused in part by biological unfolding. But the particular social, cultural, and historical environment the child experienced mattered as well, so that the social interactions that were the focus of each stage of development would vary somewhat depending on where and when the child developed. Development also depends on the individual. In particular, if social interactions during previous stages of development had proceeded well, resulting in healthy development, present development was likely to be smoother.

According to Erikson, people pass through eight stages of development. Each stage involves a central conflict, with either a positive or negative resolution of the conflict possible. Thus Erikson's theory is similar to Freud's in that the stages are defined by conflicts that can be resolved either positively or negatively, with subsequent development dependent, in part, on previous conflict resolutions. Erikson's eight stages of psychosocial development are summarized in Table 5.1.

It should be emphasized that although each of the conflicts was the focus for a particular stage, the eight conflicts occur in different forms across the lifespan (Marcia, 2002). An early conflict, such as trust versus mistrust, which is resolved poorly in infancy because of the lack of a loving mother–infant relationship, may be revisited later. Perhaps a particularly supportive and healthy loving relationship later in life will result in greater trust than was present earlier in life. Unlike Freud, who viewed fixations as insidious and irreversible without a psychoanalytic therapeutic experience, Erikson felt that adaptations across the lifespan are common.

Identity and Identity Crises

Without a doubt, the most prominent crisis in Erikson's theory is the identity crisis, with it receiving more research attention than any of the other stages (Schwartz, 2001). In part, the salience of the identity crisis in Erikson's thinking reflects how his own life proceeded. Although he was fathered by Danish parents, his stepfather was Jewish, and he was raised in a home that respected Jewish traditions. He did not realize during boyhood that his stepfather was not his biological father. Since his tall, blonde-haired presence contrasted with those of many of his father's Jewish friends and associates, he experienced identity confusion, feeling something of an outsider in his father's circles. As a Dane growing up in southern Germany in the early part of the 20th century, he experienced other tensions regarding ethnic identity, for native Germans were fiercely nationalistic. Rather than pursue university studies and a profession, as his family would have liked, Erikson chose to live the life of an artist and distinguished himself among those who knew him as someone who was trying to

TABLE 5.1. Erikson's Eight Stages

Conflict defining stage	Approximate age	What happens during stage
Trust versus mistrust	First year	During infancy, children either form a trusting relationship with an adult or they do not. Lack of interaction with an adult who can be trusted to meet the infant's needs results in long-term mistrust.
Autonomy versus shame and doubt	Second year	Children begin to do things independently, such as feeding or dressing themselves, thereby establishing some autonomy from others. Part of autonomy is self-control. During this stage much of the conflict involving self-control centers around toilet training. If children have difficultly establishing self-control and autonomy, the result may be feelings of shame in not being more independent and doubt about autonomy is possible.
Initiative versus guilt	3–6 years	As the preschool years proceed, the child has many more initiations into the world and tries new roles. If children are overly punished for their initiative, feelings of guilt result.
Industry versus inferiority	6–12 years	During the elementary-school years, children are expected to begin to master the skills of the culture. For example, in Western culture, children are expected to develop fundamental literacy and numeracy skills. Success leads to a sense of industry; failure can lead to a sense of inferiority.
Identity versus role confusion	Adolescence	During this period, people begin to establish who they are, what they believe in, and what they want to become, thus developing an identity. Successful identity achievement requires trying out various possible identities and struggling with them before making a commitment. Failure to achieve an identity results in confusion.
Intimacy versus isolation	Early adulthood	A person either achieves intimacy with others, usually a marital partner or the equivalent, or is at risk for feeling psychological isolation.
Generativity versus stagnation	Middle adulthood	Adulthood is either a period of contributing to society and to the development of the next generation, or there is a risk of stagnating.
Integrity versus despair	Late adulthood	The person who resolves all of life's crises in a positive fashion is likely to look back and feel a sense of integrity. Those who fail to resolve positively one or more life crises are at risk for disgust and despair.

find himself (Coles, 1970). Erik Erikson definitely experienced complex identity crises during his own youth, and those personal experiences obviously affected the developmental theory he would later envision and write about.

According to Erikson's theory, during adolescence and youth, the main task is developing an identity. A healthy identity can develop if the youth experiences alternative possibilities and reflects on alternative identities. A variety of identity-related specific conflicts occur during adolescence and youth that correspond to the conflicts taken up at other points in the lifespan (as presented in Table 5.1). That is, there are identity subcrises with respect to trust versus mistrust, autonomy versus shame and doubt, initiative versus guilt, industry versus inferiority, intimacy versus isolation, generativity versus stagnation, and integrity versus despair. As part of these subcrises, adolescents and youth struggle to determine what they believe with respect to sexual orientation, intellectual interests, life philosophy, vocation, religion, and so on.

Identity-related struggles are made possible by the increased intellectual power that comes with adolescence—referred to by Piaget (1983) as formal operations (see Chapter 3). What is especially important is the adolescent's new intellectual ability to think about hypothetical situations and to compare hypothetical outcomes. The ability to reflect on the possible permits adolescences to challenge themselves about what they believe (Boyes & Chandler, 1992).

One prominent researcher, James Marcia, generated substantial support for the conclusion that adolescents and youth make many choices and often come to commitments about important issues. In particular, he identified four different identity statuses (Marcia, 1966; Meeus, Iedema, Helsen, & Vollebargh, 1999), reflecting the degree to which adolescents have experienced and resolved their identity crises. In our years of teaching at the university level, we have had few students who have not been able to think of relatives, friends, and acquaintances who fit into each of the following four identity statuses:

- People in **diffusion** have not experienced crises in that they have not tried out, nor are they trying out, new roles; and have made no commitments. Youth and adolescents in diffusion often are perceived to be living lives without personal meaning. They are viewed as reluctant to make commitments to positions, avoiding close relationships, and unpredictable and changeable (Mallory, 1989).

- Youth in **foreclosure** have come to commitments without experiencing any crises. One example would be young adults who follow the life plan devised by their parents without question. The plan may be to go to a prestigious college and then on to law school, to accept a place in the family firm, and to settle down in the same community as their parents. Foreclosed individuals often have conservative values, are moralistic, conventional, sex-appropriate in their behaviors, and are satisfied with themselves (Mallory, 1989).

- People in **moratorium** are actively exploring potential identities. This is a healthy and appropriate status for adolescents and youth according to Erikson's theory. Young people who are in moratorium are perceived by others as introspective, anxious, and valuing independence (Mallory, 1989).

- Those who are **identity achieved** have gone through crises and made choices. These people are perceived as productive, consistent, and independent.

Adolescents often try on different identities when they are in moratorium.

The healthy progression according to Erikson's theory is into moratorium, with identity eventually achieved. Much less healthy is to come to an identity without conflict (as in foreclosure) or to never experience conflict or identity (as in diffusion). The danger of course is that those in the latter statuses may end up living lives very different from the ones they would have chosen if they had reflected, with the possibility later in life that they will realize they have been living the wrong life for decades.

Pascarella and Terenzini (1991) reviewed the research evidence pertaining to whether movement toward identity achievement is evident during college—that is, increasing commitments with respect to vocation, lifestyle, and philosophy from freshmen to senior years. They concluded that commitments do develop during the college years. Pascarella and Terenzini (1991) speculated that college produced movement into moratorium followed by eventual identity achievement because the college setting introduced students to diverse possibilities, a speculation supported by correlations between changes in identity status and exposure to diverse students (Henry & Renaud, 1972; Komarovsky, 1985; Madison, 1969; Newman & Newman, 1978).

Identity achievement, however, is anything but certain by the end of the college years. For example, Waterman and Goldman (1976) observed that only a little more than half of the college seniors they studied had achieved identity with respect to religious or political philosophies, a result consistent with other data reviewed by Pascarella and Terenzini (1991). Pascarella and Terenzini were especially conservative, concluding that "if identity is defined as the simultaneous achievement of an identity in the occupational, religious, political, and sexual realms, then it [identity] remains a relatively infrequent occurrence during the traditional college years" (p. 183).

Very few studies examined, however, the movement toward the identity achievement of comparably aged young adults not attending college. Thus little evidence exists to support the assumptions of many that students should know what they want to do by the end of high school. The Eriksonian perspective is that exploration is a good thing, something to be encouraged, during high school and young adulthood.

Evaluation of Eriksonian Theory

Rooted in Freudian theory, Erikson's outlook about human development was in part biologically determined. In particular, he argued that one's biological stage of life contributes to one's current conflict. Even so, resolution of the eight life crises is determined by social factors. Contextual variables are important in determining whether one's responses to a crisis are developmentally adaptive or result in long-term psychic pain.

Thus, when Erikson (1943, 1945) spent time with two Native American tribes, the Yurok and the Sioux, he recognized that their developments were very different from each other and very different from development in white America or in

Europe. Phinney (1989) demonstrated that issues of ethnic identity were much more prominent in the development of U.S. minority adolescents, who are continually confronted with issues of identity related to their ethnicity, than in the development of white Americans. Just as cultural anthropologists, such as Malinowski (1927), concluded that processes like Oedipal conflict in Freudian theory vary from culture to culture, those interested in Eriksonian theory have observed cultural variations in development. The difference is that Erikson's theory predicted such differences, whereas Freudian theory did not, predicting instead that human biology destined universal development as Freud depicted it.

Marcia (1994), in his work on identity development, also has emphasized contextual determination as important. For example, in studies in the late 1960s and early 1970s, foreclosure seemed to be a healthy identity status for females, something that is not the case now, with moratorium healthier for contemporary females than it was four decades ago. The times have changed for women, and as they have so has women's psychosocial development. It is less acceptable now for a woman simply to follow parental expectations and more acceptable for a young woman to be struggling for her identity. Some things have not changed, however: Identity achievement has been associated with healthy functioning for both males and females since Marcia began his work in the 1960s. Nevertheless, the research findings that the identity construct varies with context is consistent with Erikson's theory.

One of the more important tenets of psychoanalytically oriented theories is that what happens during early childhood affects development after that. The case in favor of that conclusion has increased greatly in recent years. For example, Sroufe, Carlson, and Schulman (1993) summarized the evidence that infants who experience trusting relationships with their mothers are more socially adept from preschool through adolescence: friendlier, more open to new friendships, and more interpersonally competent in general. Thus, as Erikson theorized, there is continuity and connection with the issues of trust and mistrust across development.

■ ■ ■ CHAPTER SUMMARY AND EVALUATION

Social learning is both a behavioral and a cognitive theory. It is biological as well, with Bandura (1986) making the case that man has evolved to be a social learner. The ability to learn from others through observation, classical conditioning, and response to reinforcements and punishments is certainly adaptive. Both parents and teachers can make use of social learning principles to promote desirable behaviors. Some of the more systematic ways of doing so are behavior modification, cognitive self-instruction, and classroom management.

Social learning researchers have generated a tremendous amount of evidence that situational variables matter. How a child behaves in any given situation depends not only on the interests, abilities, and predilections of the child but also on characteristics of the situation and the child's expectations about the situation. If the child has come to expect punishment for trying in school—for example, in the form of public teacher comments about his or her difficulties in learning—the child may be less willing to try than if the teacher has previously reinforced the student for taking chances (see Chapter 9).

In contrast, the biological bases of development suggested by Freud and Erikson seem rigid—a particular unfolding of stages. A development conflict is experienced at each stage. Freud's stages emphasize psychosexual conflicts; Erikson's stages emphasize psychosocial conflicts. In Freud's theory, the failure to resolve a conflict in the appropriate developmental period leads to issues that can only be resolved through therapy. In Erikson's theory, earlier conflicts can be revisited and resolved later in life. The lifespan approach of Erikson's theory is also evident in the inclusion of stages corresponding to middle adulthood and old age.

One way of understanding the three theories covered in this chapter is to review them in terms of the overarching model of development introduced in Chapter 1.

Developmental Debates

Nature versus Nurture

All three theories assign roles to nature and nurture, although there is a difference in emphasis across the three theories. Social learning theory is the most environmental of the three theories; Freudian theory is the most biological. Erikson believed in biological unfolding to some degree, but emphasized the social and cultural environment much more than Freud.

Stages versus Continuous Development

Social learning theory is the classic example of a theory emphasizing continuous development, with the effects of experience accumulating over time. Both Freud and Erikson proposed stage theories. In both cases, cumulative experiences matter in determining future development, although development is focused on a particular psychosexual conflict or psychosocial crisis.

Universal versus Culture-Specific Developments

According to social learning theory, the same processes of development (observation, classical and operant conditioning, punishment) operate across the human species. What the child observes and is reinforced and punished for will vary with culture, however. In contrast, Freud believed that his theory was universally applicable. One point of departure for Erikson from Freud was Erikson's understanding that development is affected by culture, although Erikson also believed that the same types of conflicts, from "trust versus mistrust" to "integrity versus despair," occur across cultures.

Trait-Like Consistency versus Situational Determination of Behavior

In social learning theory, the situation is viewed as an important determinant of development. On the other hand, both Freud and Erikson believed in trait-like consistency in human behavior, determined in large part by resolutions of psychosexual conflicts in the case of Freud and psychosocial conflicts for Erikson. That is, the anal retentive personality is anal retentive across situations; likewise, the identity-achieved individual's competence, because of success in obtaining an identity, will be obvious in many situations.

Active versus Passive Child

Although some critics of social learning theory suggest that it is a passive theory of development, in fact, children are very active in determining what they will observe. In contrast, Freudian theory suggests a more passive role of the child, with the mother largely determining the degree of frustration or indulgence the child receives with respect to oral and anal stage conflicts. The inevitability of the Oedipal and Electra conflicts make it obvious that the child is active in these conflicts only as an actor is active in a play. Yes, there is a different player on the stage, but it is the same story no matter who is playing the part. Erikson certainly plays up the importance of active decision making more than Freud does, especially with respect to the identity crisis. It is healthy to be active in seeking one's own identity and very unhealthy to be passive, accepting parentally expected values and desires.

Lasting versus Transient Early Effects of Experience

Although social learning theory recognizes that the cumulative effects of learning affect future learning and performance, new learning is always possible. Social learning theory emphasizes human plasticity as development continues. In contrast, Freudian theory suggests that fixation at any one of the stages of development affects behavior throughout the lifespan. Eriksonian theory also emphasizes the importance of early experience but allows for poorly resolved stage conflicts to be revisited later in life.

■■■ REVIEW OF KEY TERMS

behavioral contracting An agreement between teacher and student that specifies what the student's goal will be, what reinforcement might be earned, and how much progress toward the goal is required for reinforcement.

behavioral models People who display behaviors that are imitated.

classical conditioning The conditioning of a stimulus to elicit a particular response. Classical conditioning occurs when a neutral stimulus is paired with an unconditioned stimulus that elicits a response. The neutral stimulus becomes a conditioned stimulus when the conditioned stimulus presented alone elicits what is now the conditioned response.

conditioned reinforcers Reinforcers, such as money, that acquire their reinforcement properties by being paired with unconditioned reinforcers.

conditioned response The response elicited by a conditioned stimulus.

conditioned stimulus A neutral stimulus that has been paired with an unconditioned stimulus to evoke a conditioned response.

diffusion An identity status in which people have not experienced identity crisis or commitment to an identity.

ego The rational side of personality that operates according to the reality principle.

extinction The process by which classically conditioned responses cease (are extinguished) when subsequent experiences of the stimulus are not followed by the conditioned response.

fading In behavior modification programs, a gradual reduction in the use of reinforcement once the behavioral goals are reached.

foreclosure An identity status in which people have committed to an identity without experiencing an identity crisis.

id The instinctual part of personality, present at birth, which seeks pleasure and immediate gratification (pleasure principle).

identity achieved An identity status in which people have undergone identity crises and have committed to an identity.

intermittent reinforcement Reinforcers that are presented only on occasion rather than continuously, thus making behaviors more resistant to extinction.

interval reinforcement schedule Intermittent reinforcement that is provided at certain time intervals.

moratorium An identity status in which people are in ongoing crisis, actively exploring potential identities.

negative reinforcers The cessation of aversive stimulation following a response, thus increasing the likelihood of the response.

operant conditioning Conditioning that, depending on the consequences (reinforcement or punishment), increases or decreases the likelihood of a response.

positive reinforcers A stimulus that increases the future likelihood of a response when presented following the response.

punishment The presentation of aversive stimulation after a response, thus decreasing the future likelihood of the response.

ratio reinforcement schedule Intermittent reinforcement that is provided after a certain number of desired responses.

reciprocal determinism The process by which individuals through their reactions to environmental events influence future environmental events and their own subsequent development.

response cost A form of punishment used in some behavior modification programs in which unwanted behavior results in the loss of token reinforcers.

shaping Molding behavior by reinforcing closer and closer approximations of the desired response.

social learning theory A theory of learning that emphasizes learning through observation of behavioral models.

superego Conscience, the last personality structure to emerge in Freudian theory.

time-out A form of punishment sometimes used in behavior modification programs in which a student is physically removed from other students or activities (i.e., potential reinforcers) for a short period of time.

token reinforcement Reinforcement that uses symbolic reinforcers, such as chips or marbles, that can be accumulated and traded for other reinforcers.

unconditioned reinforcer Reinforcers that satisfy biological deprivation such as thirst or hunger.

unconditioned response The response elicited by an unconditioned stimulus.

unconditioned stimulus A stimulus that evokes a particular response, the unconditioned response.

vicarious experiences In social learning theory, experiences that are observed in others.

CHAPTER 6

Sociocultural Theories of Development and Education

People learn from other people. This is certainly not a new idea. For example, social learning theorists have long argued for the powerful roles of imitation and modeling in learning (see Chapter 5). People not only imitate specific models, they also respond to general influences of behavior in their surrounding culture. In this chapter we explore the role of the cultural environment in determining thinking. We begin with the most prominent contemporary theory emphasizing the role of culture in determining cognitive development, Vygotsky's theory (1962, 1978).

What will become clear in our discussion of Vygotsky's theory is that the communications a child experiences are critical in stimulating the development of his or her thinking skills. According to this perspective, instructional conversations make a big difference in the development of a child's mind. By the end of this chapter, it will also be clear that a child's cultural environment influences success in school.

■ ■ ■ VYGOTSKY'S SOCIOCULTURAL APPROACHES TO MIND

Lev Vygotsky lived in the first half of the 20th century in what was then the Soviet Union, but English translations of his works did not appear until the 1960s and 1970s. In recent years, no theorist has commanded the attention of psychologists interested in instruction as much as Vygotsky has (Brown & French, 1979; Wertsch, 1985, 1991). The main theme of Vygotsky's theory is that it is impossible to understand development without considering the culture in which development occurs, including the social institutions of a culture, such as its schools (Berk & Winsler, 1999). Cultural tools, such as language and technology, also greatly influence the development of cognitive abilities in each new generation.

The Developmental Relationship between Thought and Speech

According to Vygotsky (1978), throughout life, language plays an important role in thought. The relationship of thought to speech is different for adults than for children, however.

Thought and Speech in Adults

Vygotsky (1962) believed that inner speech plays an important role in adult thought. In contrast to outer speech, which should be readily understood by others, **inner speech** is an internal dialogue that is often abbreviated and fragmentary, with the meaning of complex thoughts captured in very few words or even in abbreviated words (Wertsch, 1991).

What is the relationship between thought and inner speech? Consider a complicated task, one that requires some thinking. For example, let's say you want to search for information on the topic of language at the library and you are unfamiliar with the databases available. Your inner speech will guide the search process. Perhaps you begin by saying to yourself something like, "How do I get to the right place? . . . OK, there's the menu. . . . What do I need?" Then you may mumble to yourself an abbreviated, "Pick it," as you select the PsychInfo database. As you gain more experience using the database, you learn to access it without any awareness of additional inner speech. Inner speech is no longer necessary, since you are solving a familiar problem.

Thought and Speech in Children

In Vygotsky's theory, much of the development of thinking is the development of inner speech. This process goes through four stages. During the first 2 years of life, in *the first stage*, thought is nonverbal and speech is nonconceptual, with no relationship between thought and speech. Beginning with the development of language at around age 2, thought and speech begin to merge in *the second stage*. During this second stage, the child labels many objects by their names and develops verbal communications with others. Children do not use speech to direct thinking during this second stage, but they will respond to the directive speech of others (Luria, 1982). For example, while 2-year-olds often live up to their "terrible" reputation, frequently they will "come" when you ask them to. Younger children typically require nonverbal cuing about the appropriateness of coming, such as an adult offering outstretched arms (Service, Lock, & Chandler, 1989).

In *the third stage*, the role of speech in directing thought and behavior begins to emerge as children exhibit **egocentric speech**. That is, preschoolers often talk to themselves about what they are doing. For example, saying "I'm going to play with the dog" before they go play with the dog, or saying "I'm going to ride my tricycle" before they go ride their tricycles. Often these utterances come when children are trying to figure out what to do. Piaget argued that preschoolers do this because of their immature understanding of communication (see Chapter 3). In contrast, Vygotsky viewed the emergence of egocentric speech as a sign of maturation, with such speech influencing what children think and do.

In one study, Vygotsky asked preschoolers to complete tasks that were complicated by some obstacle. For example, the obstacle might be that something needed to complete the task was missing. The amount of egocentric speech uttered by the preschoolers during the completion of these tasks was much greater than when preschoolers performed the same tasks without obstacles. Consider this monologue produced by a preschooler faced with a task difficulty: "Where is the pencil? I need a blue pencil now. Nothing. Instead of that I will color it red and put water on it—that will make it darker and more like blue" (Vygotsky, 1987, p. 70). This child is clearly using speech as part of thinking.

During *the fourth stage* of the development of inner speech, the egocentric speech that was overt becomes covert and abbreviated . . . becoming inner speech. For example, the egocentric speech described above would become inner speech, as follows: "Where's the pencil? Need blue. Will use red, add water." The actions are much more prominent relative to the inner speech in Stage 4 compared to Stage 3, when the egocentric speech is more obvious and clearly preceding the actions.

In Vygotsky's view, learning begins in the social world. Speech is originally external to children: they speak to address others, not to talk to themselves. Only after establishing speech for others can children internalize it. Thus children can have *monologues* with themselves only after they have developed the ability to *dialogue* with others. Internalized, or monological, speech is not egocentric in the Piagetian sense: it is social speech that has reached a higher stage, being for the self. Egocentric speech is how a person communicates with him- or herself. See the Considering Interesting Questions special feature (Box 6.1) for a discussion of children's self-speech and classroom performance.

Considering Interesting Questions

BOX 6.1. What Is the Relationship between Private Speech and Classroom Performance?

Berk (1986) observed first and third graders working on math seatwork in the naturalistic setting of their own classrooms. She was interested in exploring the relationship of "thought spoken outloud," called **private speech,** to task performance. As predicted by Vygotskian theory, Berk noted developmental differences in the students' use of private speech for self-guidance. Private speech was more common in younger students, whereas the older students were more likely to have internalized their private speech in inner speech.

The focus of the private speech also varied with development. The content of the speech changed from task-irrelevant, self-stimulating content to task-relevant content such as describing or self-guiding. The final transformation was to barely audible task-relevant speech that was only discernible through inaudible muttering or lip movement. Berk found that task-relevant private speech predicted greater attentional focus and fewer extraneous behaviors, and that the relationship of private speech to intelligence shifted with age. The total amount of private speech was positively related to intelligence for the first graders ($r = .33$), but was negatively related to intelligence for the third graders ($r = -.49$). (See Chapter 1 for a review of correlation coefficients.) Thus, in the first grade, high levels of private speech were associated with high intelligence test scores. In the third grade, however, high levels of private speech were associated with low intelligence test scores. The more intelligent third graders had internalized their private speech.

In a more recent study, Winsler, Diaz, and Montero (1997) found that performance on tasks requiring careful attention is better when preschoolers used task-relevant self-speech. Moreover, they found that adults can successfully support young children in their use of self-speech.

Development of Sophisticated Thought

Adults often assist children in thinking about problems they face. For example, they may help children solve a puzzle or help them figure out how many days there are until their next birthday. What goes on in these interactions is thinking, but thinking involving two heads. Children could not possibly think through many problems without help, but with adult assistance they make progress. After years of participating in such interactions, children internalize the types of actions they once carried out with adults (John-Steiner & Mahn, 2003; Rogoff, 1998). Vygotsky summarized this developmental progression as follows:

> Any function in the child's cultural development appears twice, or on two planes. First, it appears on the social plane, and then on the psychological plane. . . . Social relations or relations among people genetically underlie all higher functions and their relationships. . . . (1981, pp. 163–164)

According to this perspective, cognitive development moves forward largely because the child is in a world that provides aid when the child needs it and can benefit from it.

Two-year-olds can do some things for themselves. A responsive social world lets children do those things independently. For example, a parent may allow a child to pick out a T-shirt to wear, especially when the child insists that "I can do it myself." But there are other things that 2-year-olds could never do, no matter how much help they were given. The responsive social environment does not encourage children to do these sorts of things and, in fact, often discourages their attempts at overly difficult tasks. For example, a parent would try to steer a young child away from trying to put together a 500-piece jigsaw puzzle.

Most critically, however, the responsive social world provides assistance on tasks that are within what Vygotsky called the **zone of proximal development**. Tasks in the zone of proximal development are ones that children cannot accomplish independently but can accomplish with assistance (see Figure 6.1). Children learn how to perform tasks within their zone through interactions with responsive and more competent others who provide hints, prompts, and assistance to them on an as-needed basis. These hints and prompts encourage children to process a task appropriately, until they eventually can perform the task without assistance. For example, a kinder-

The most difficult task
a child can accomplish
independently

The most difficult task
a child can accomplish
with assistance

FIGURE 6.1. Zone of proximal development (ZPD). The figure shows the area between the "most difficult task a child can accomplish independently" and "the most difficult task a child can accomplish with assistance." From McCormick and Pressley (1997). Copyright 1997 by Christine B. McCormick and Michael Pressley. Adapted by permission.

gartner can write a story with help from a parent. This help may include the parent printing the words to the story as the kindergartner dictates and showing the kindergartner where to copy the words onto a page, leaving room for the child to draw an accompanying picture. The task of writing a story is within the kindergartner's zone of proximal development. The zone of proximal development is without a doubt the Vygotskian idea that has received the most attention from educators in the late 20th and early 21st centuries (Chaiklin, 2003; Tudge & Scrimsher, 2003).

A concept based on the principles of Vygotsky's theory is **scaffolding** (Wood, Bruner, & Ross, 1976). Builders use a scaffold to erect a building, gradually removing it as the building becomes self-supporting. Likewise, adults or older children who are helping younger children with a task should gradually remove their prompts and hints. That is, more capable people assist children but only enough to allow the students to get started. They should provide just enough support and assistance that the child does not fail, eventually removing that support as the child is capable of performing independently (Tharp & Gallimore, 1988).

One example of scaffolded instruction is found in Reading Recovery, which is a method for remediating the reading of primary-grade children who are experiencing reading difficulties. A Reading Recovery teacher permits children to do as much as they can independently and intervenes as needed with hints and supports that can lead children to process effectively when they stumble (Clay & Cazden, 1990). Thus children in Reading Recovery work within their zones of proximal development. The following dialogue illustrates how an adult tutor scaffolded the instruction of a tutee, Larry:

> LARRY: THE GREAT BIG ENORMOUS TURNIP. ONCE AN OLD MAN PLANTED A TURNIP.
>
> TEACHER: Good.
>
> LARRY: HE SAID GROW, GROW LITTLE TURNIP, GROW (*pauses at the next word*).
>
> TEACHER: How does that word start? Can I help you start it off? How does it start? S_____ . . . He tells it to grow sw_____ sweet . . .
>
> LARRY: GROW LITTLE TURNIP, GROW S_____ . . .
>
> TEACHER: How else does he want it to grow? He wants it to grow sweet and he wants it to grow str_____ . . .
>
> LARRY: . . . STRONG.
>
> TEACHER: Good boy, that's lovely. Grow strong.
>
> LARRY: AND THE TURNIP GREW UP SWEET AND STRONG AND . . .
>
> TEACHER: What's the other word that begins with *e*? Enor_____ . . .
>
> LARRY: ENORMOUS.
>
> TEACHER: Good.

And so it goes. The teacher continues to provide hints and support as needed. In this case, the hints encouraged the student to apply "word attack" skills to decode words. The teacher is scaffolding this instruction by providing input only when the child stumbles, never when the child can proceed on his own. During Reading Recovery, children reread a text until they are 90% successful in decoding, with teacher

Just as scaffolding supports the construction of a building, instructional scaffolding supports children's learning and development.

support decreasing at each rereading. The teacher supports independent functioning in the children by not intervening. Once a child can read a text at the 90% level, another text is selected, one that is within the child's zone of proximal development. The child will not be able to read this text fluently without support but can get through the text if provided with hints and prompts.

Instructional scaffolding means providing help to students on an as-needed basis, enough that the child can progress, with instructional support reduced as student competence increases (Wood et al., 1976). Sociocultural theorists contend that mature thought processes develop through interaction with others (Feurstein, 1980; Scrimsher & Tudge, 2003; Todorov, 1984; Vygotsky, 1962). Thus, when adults explain, model, and scaffold problem solving for children, they prompt children's attention to important dimensions of problems. Eventually, students attend to the same dimensions without prompting, having internalized the problem-solving process initially experienced in interaction with others.

Apprenticeship

Educators who agree with Vygotsky believe that excellent instruction involves social interactions between an apprentice student and a more expert adult. Apprentice carpenters learn to build houses by working with experienced builders. Airline captains learn how to fly planes from years of experience flying as first officers working with captains. Medical residencies are really apprenticeships in many ways: They are opportunities for young physicians to learn through direct contact with senior physicians.

Barbara Rogoff (1990, 1998) argued that apprenticeship occurs in many cultures and may be a universal part of human life. She believed it is the principal means for adults to pass on knowledge to children about the intellectual tools valuable in the culture, a truly Vygotskian idea. Typically, these tools are complex enough that years of apprenticeship are necessary. In some societies, apprenticeships provide education in a wide range of accomplishments such as agriculture, hunting, fishing, weaving, and healing. Rogoff contended that great similarity exists across the various types of apprenticeships.

During an apprenticeship, the master provides bridges from what an apprentice knows to what an apprentice needs to know. The master translates the task into terms the apprentice can understand, and the master makes demands on the apprentice that the apprentice can meet. As the apprentice learns, the master gradually increases the demands. Thus there is a process of **guided participation** for the apprentice, with the master providing the guidance. Gradually, the master transfers responsibility. Scaffolding is the key process here, with the master providing as much support as the apprentice needs to function until support is entirely withdrawn because the student can do it alone.

What do apprentice learners do (Collins, Brown, & Newman, 1989; Rogoff, 1990, 1998)? They *observe*, they receive *coaching* from their mentors, and they *practice* the tasks required in the profession, although always while being coached by their mentors. Good mentors "scaffold" their input, providing assistance as it is needed—not so much that the apprentices become dependent on it and not so little that they falter (Wood et al., 1976). Less is provided as the apprentice is able to go it alone.

Is it sensible to think about teaching elementary-school-age students within an apprentice relationship? Mark Lepper and his colleagues (Lepper, Aspinwall, Mumme, & Chabey, 1990) observed six expert tutors of elementary arithmetic as they worked with individual students in grades two through five. What did the expert tutors do? They consistently let their students know that the task they were trying was difficult, but also that the students had the ability to accomplish the task. There is a good reason for this. If students fail, and they blame the failure on the difficulty of the task, this attribution to task difficulty likely will not discourage their efforts on future tasks as much as other attributions could (Weiner, 1979; see also Chapter 9). For example, attributing the failure to one's own low ability is much more discouraging. After all, if a student thinks that the current failure reflects her or his low intelligence, why bother to try harder when confronted with similar tasks in the future? Thus the tutor tries to foster attributions that will encourage future efforts. For example, after a student successfully completes a problem, a tutor might say, "I guess we'll have to try to find an even harder problem for you. You tried hard and did well with this one." This is a subtle way of making the point that the last problem was hard and yet the student succeeded on it by exerting effort.

The tutors' interactions with their students included many other subtleties. They gave little direct help and rarely gave students the answers to the problems. When students made errors or had difficulties, the tutors provided hints of three sorts: (1) *questions or remarks* implying that the previous move had been an incorrect one; (2) *suggestions*, often in the form of questions, about a potential direction the student might take with the problem; and (3) *hints*, often in the form of questions, about the part of the problem the student might want to think about. That is, the tutor scaffolded the student's problem solving. For example, when a student added 36 and 36 and came up with 126, the tutor inquired, "Now how did you get that 6?" When this did not work, hints in the forms of questions became increasingly specific: "Which column do we start in? Where is the 1's column?" Good tutors know when and where to provide hints, prompts, explanations, and modeling. They realize that this assistance is contingent on the need of the student.

By studying excellent tutoring and instruction in detail, researchers have developed a more complete understanding of effective cognitive apprenticeship. See the Applying Developmental Theory to Educational Contexts special feature (Box 6.2) for an overview of the components of cognitive apprenticeship.

Research Validating Sociocultural Positions

Much of the instruction that goes on in classrooms is inconsistent with Vygotskian theory. See the Considering Interesting Questions special feature (Box 6.3) for a discussion of how typical classroom communications differ from scaffolded instruction. A reasonable question is whether instruction in the "zone of proximal development" is common at all. Do adults assume the more demanding roles in such interactions in

Applying Developmental Theory to Educational Contexts

BOX 6.2. Components of Apprenticeship

Apprenticeship can be an effective educational tool. Collins, Brown, and Newman (1989) summarized the following components of apprenticeship:

Modeling

Masters show their apprentices how to do tasks that are important and they make their actions obvious, ensuring that the apprentice sees the actions and hears a rationale for why the actions were taken. For example, an art teacher would demonstrate a specific painting technique as slowly as possible, making sure to explain all the steps of the technique.

Coaching

Masters watch students attempt a task and offer hints, feedback, and guidance. As they coach, they sometimes offer additional modeling or explanation. For example, a physical education teacher would watch students practicing a set of basketball skills, offering additional explanation or models as needed.

Scaffolding

Masters offer support, guidance, and reminders. They do not offer too much support, however, and they pull away as apprentices learn to function independently. Scaffolding requires experts to determine both when the apprentice needs help and how to offer appropriate redirection. Experts must understand many different types of errors apprentices can make and know how to deal with such errors.

Articulation

Articulation is a form of testing. Masters require their apprentices to explain what they are doing. Thus an expert math teacher may ask students how they solved a problem and why they picked a particular solution method over alternative methods.

Reflection

Masters encourage apprentices to compare their work with that of others, including the master and other apprentices (Schon, 1983, 1987). For example, young teachers often watch videotapes of themselves teaching and reflect on their work, perhaps discussing their teaching actions with more expert teachers or fellow apprentice teachers.

Exploration

Apprentices cannot be mere copies of their mentors. The apprenticeship relationship permits safe exploration. Good mentors teach their apprentices how to explore and they encourage them to do so. For example, a good writing teacher assists writers in finding their own writing voice rather than encouraging students to mimic the teacher's own writing style.

Considering Interesting Questions

BOX 6.3. How Do Typical Instructional Conversations Contrast with Scaffolded Instruction?

Conversation is probably the most common form of human interaction both inside and outside classrooms. What is the nature of classroom conversations? As it turns out, they generally tend not to be student-sensitive in ways that would be consistent with Vygotskian-inspired instruction.

Typical school conversations involve **initiate–response–evaluation (IRE)** cycles (Cazden, 2001; Mehan, 1979; Sinclair & Coulthard, 1975), as illustrated in the following dialogue:

TEACHER: Where is the Tomb of the Unknown Soldier? (Initiation)

STUDENT A: In Arlington Cemetery? (Response)

TEACHER: That's right. (Evaluation) And what might you see at that tomb? (Initiation)

STUDENT B: There's always a guard of honor there. (Response)

TEACHER: Yes. (Evaluation) Do you remember what is interesting about this guard? (Initiation) *S:* Uh, uh, no. (Failed response)

TEACHER: Someone else? (Implied evaluation, initiation)

STUDENT C: He's a member of the Old Guard. Really hard to get into the Old Guard. (Response)

TEACHER: Correct. What else is at Arlington Cemetery? (Initiation)

STUDENT B: President Kennedy's grave. (Response)

TEACHER: Anything else? (Implied acceptance, initiation)

STUDENT B: President Kennedy's brother's grave. It's over the hill, a little bit down from the turning flame. (Response)

TEACHER: *Eternal* flame. (Implied evaluation) Yes, near President Kennedy's grave. (Evaluation)

The teacher *initiates* an interaction, often with a question; the student *responds*; and the teacher *evaluates* the response before making another initiation. Teachers and students know how to interact with each other in this way. For example, teachers send clear nonverbal signals to students that a sequence of questioning is about to begin and they expect student responses (Cazden, 1988, 2001). If students are familiar with IRE cycles, they can direct their attention to the content of the academic conversation. Moreover, teachers can conduct lessons in an orderly fashion and make certain the points they consider important are "covered."

IRE cycles have strikingly negatives aspects, however (Cazden, 1988, 2001)—especially when contrasted with tutoring and teaching in the zone of proximal development as considered in this chapter. For example, questioning is usually lower level in IRE cycles, filled with literal, factual questions. In addition, because only one student can be active at a time, this is a passive approach to learning for many students (Bowers & Flinders, 1990). If the goal is for students to learn to control their thinking, IRE cycles are particularly unattractive since they are almost completely teacher-controlled. The students are powerless to do anything except answer questions they had no part in formulating (Bowers & Flinders, 1990). Students get the message that education is receiving knowledge from an authority, rather than working with knowledge to understand it in ways that are personally meaningful and that create new knowledge.

order to reduce the workload for the child? Do adults eventually cede control of tasks to their students?

Consistent with Vygotsky's ideas, adults regularly do provide instruction to children that is supportive, but not overly so (Gardner & Rogoff, 1982; Rogoff, 1998). Adults also reduce the workload for children. For example, academic tutors provide more support to younger students, such as 7-year-olds, than to older, 11-year-old students (Ludeke & Hartup, 1983). When expert weavers teach weaving, they intervene more with younger and less experienced learners (Greenfield, 1984). In addition, adults are more likely to intervene when children are having trouble with a task than at other times (Greenfield, 1984; McNamee, 1979). Also, adults control an instructional situation less as a student becomes more and more capable of doing a task independently (Childs & Greenfield, 1980; Rogoff, 1998; Wertsch, 1979). Thus, Vygotskian-like instruction seems to occur, at least in observations of naturally occurring adult–child instructional interactions.

Supporters of Vygotskian theory have made very strong claims about the superiority of scaffolding compared to other forms of instruction. Jeanne D. Day and her colleagues (1983; Day, Cordon, & Kerwin, 1989; Kerwin & Day, 1985) have examined the research supporting sociocultural instructional recommendations, however, and make some critical points about the effectiveness of the Vygotskian approach. Children who receive scaffolded instruction from a parent do not learn any faster than children who receive instruction from a parent who is less attentive to the child's competence and pattern of difficulties. Summarizing across studies, Day suggests that children probably receive a mix of types of instruction, when they are well taught. Some of this instruction is scaffolded and some not. This is not particularly surprising, since scaffolding is extremely time-consuming and difficult to do (Day et al., 1989)—a point elaborated later in this chapter. In recent analyses of exceptionally effective primary-grades instruction, researchers have confirmed that scaffolding is always part of excellent teaching, although it is only part of the instructional picture, which also includes direct instruction by teachers, whole-group and small-group instruction, cooperative learning, and discovery learning (Pressley et al., 2001, 2003).

Gelman, Massey, and McManus (1991) also recognized limits to adult scaffolding in their study of the types of instruction that parents provide to their children during museum visits. First, the types of interactions between parents and children varied with the type of exhibit. In an interactive grocery store exhibit, parents prompted, requested, and ordered their children to do things. In this setting the adults provided support for their children, although the parents rarely adjusted the support according to the level of competence of the child. In contrast, even though an exhibit intended to develop number skills was designed as a parent–child interactive activity, adults rarely helped their children with this exhibit. Gelman and colleagues speculated that the adults may have felt more competent to help their children in the more familiar grocery setting than in a math exhibit, since math is an area in which many adults do not have readily accessible knowledge of many basic concepts. Finally, even when Gelman and her colleagues themselves designed an exhibit intended to stimulate experimentation, they observed little scaffolded interaction between parents and children.

Some educators, however, are trying to apply Vygotskian ideas about education in school settings. For example, in one school in Salt Lake City, Utah, teachers and students interact collaboratively every hour of every day with teachers determined to scaffold students whom they view as apprentices (Rogoff, Turkanis, & Bartlett,

2001). Teachers and children converse about science experiments, math problems, and pieces of literature. Teachers and students question. Teachers and students do a great deal of explaining of their thinking, with teachers providing supportive hints and gentle guidance as students require it. Parents are part of this community of learning as well, often joining in the planning of instruction and the collaborative interactions that make up the instruction. Everyone in the community works hard to provide experiences that are interesting to the students, with dialogue between teachers, parents, and students with respect to every aspect of the schooling experience.

Although the Rogoff and colleagues (2001) approach to schooling is a demonstration school at this point, many individual classroom teachers are doing what they can to create communities of learners who collaborate in ways consistent with Vygotskian-based education (Duckworth, 2001; Hogan & Pressley, 1997b; Palincsar, 1998). For an example of a teacher who mastered the art of teaching mathematics in a classroom community of learners, one where students reflect on, discuss, and construct understandings of math every day, see Lampert (2001). In that classroom, as in other classrooms inspired by Vygotskian constructivist thinking, teachers listen carefully to their students' explanations as they grapple with content and do what they can to nudge them in directions that permit even better and more expansive thinking about the content. The students in Lampert's classroom are problem-solving apprentices who grow in their problem-solving competence through extensive constructive reflection about the problems that are the focus of the lessons.

In summary, while many demonstrations of adult–child apprenticeships (Rogoff, 1990, 1998) exist, parent–child and teacher–child scaffolding are anything but universal. Moreover, although some effective forms of instruction involve scaffolding, it has yet to be demonstrated as far superior to other forms of instruction, although scaffolding is prominent in the teaching of many very effective educators. Educators continue to develop educational approaches that are consistent with Vygotskian thinking, with teacher–student dialoguing and scaffolding key in such approaches. There are now Vygotskian approaches to early childhood education (Bodrova & Leong, 2003), primary education (Zuckerman, 2003), special education (Gindis, 2003), second-language education (Lantolf, 2003), and education of cultural minority students (Lee, 2003), as well as Vygotskian educational approaches in the content areas, including mathematics (Crawford, 1998; Schmittau, 2003), history (Haenen, Schrijnemakers, & Stufkens, 2003), science (Driver, Asoko, Leach, Mortimer, & Scott, 1998; Giest & Lompscher, 2003), and literacy (Miller, 2003). See the Applying Developmental Theory to Educational Contexts special feature (Box 6.4) for an example of one form of effective teaching that was developed in light of Vygotsky's theory.

The Challenges of Scaffolding and Teaching as Apprenticeship

As appealing as Vygotskian-inspired constructivist teaching is, there are real challenges that have become apparent as researchers have observed attempts to implement such teaching (Hogan, Nastasi, & Pressley, 2000; Hogan & Pressley, 1997a). For example, the apprenticeship model suggests that teachers should be real readers, writers, mathematicians, scientists, and social scientists rather than people who just

Applying Developmental Theory to Educational Contexts

BOX 6.4. Reciprocal Teaching

Reciprocal teaching is a form of instruction that is often showcased as consistent with Vygotskian principles (Brown & Palincsar, 1989; Palincsar, 1998, 2003; Palincsar & Brown, 1984; Palincsar & Herrenkohl, 1999). It involves instruction of comprehension strategies in the context of a reading group. Students learn to make predictions when reading, to question themselves about the text, to seek clarification when confused, and to summarize content. The adult teacher initially explains and models these strategies for students, but very quickly students learn to lead the group. One student is assigned the role of group leader. The group leader supervises the group's generation of predictions, questions, and summaries during reading. The group leader also solicits points that need to be clarified and either provides clarifications or elicits them from other group members. The group interactions are cooperative. The teacher provides support on an as-needed basis, that is, scaffolded instruction.

During reciprocal teaching, the students experience multiple models of cognitive processing: The teacher models and explains. Peers in the group are continuously modeling reasoning about text as part of group participation. The discussions permit students to air their perspectives and requires them to justify their claims. These discussions also allow students to review and comment about the strategies as well as the content they are learning. The teacher is progressively less involved as the students gain competence. The assumption is that by participating in the group, students will eventually internalize use of the strategies encouraged as part of reciprocal teaching. This is consistent with the Vygotskian perspective that individual cognitive development develops from participation in social groups.

The dialogue from a sample lesson should help clarify what occurs during a reciprocal reading group. The dialogue that follows (from Brown & Palincsar, 1989, pp. 421–422) is from a group of low-achieving middle-school students after 13 days of experience with the method. The students had just read the following brief text:

> In the United States, salt is produced by three basic methods: solar (sun) evaporation, mining, and artificial heat evaporation. For salt to be extracted by solar evaporation, the weather must be hot and dry. Thus, solar salt is harvested in the tropic-like areas along our southern ocean coasts and at Great Salt Lake.

STUDENT LEADER (STUDENT C): Name three different basic methods how salt is produced.

STUDENT A: Evaporation, mining, evaporation . . . artificial heat evaporation.

STUDENT LEADER: Correct, very good. My summary on this paragraph is about ways that salt is produced.

TEACHER: Very good. Could you select the next teacher. [Student C does so, selecting Student L, with the reading continuing.]

> The second oldest form of salt production is mining. Unlike early methods that made the work extremely dangerous and difficult, today's methods use special machinery, and salt mining is easier and safer. The old expression "back to the salt mine" no longer applies.

STUDENT LEADER (STUDENT L): Name two words that often describe mining salt in the old days.

STUDENT K: Back to the salt mines?

STUDENT LEADER L: No. Angela?

STUDENT A: Dangerous and difficult.

(continued)

STUDENT LEADER L: Correct. This paragraph is about comparing the old mining of salt and today's mining of salt.

TEACHER: Beautiful!

STUDENT LEADER L: I have a prediction to make.

TEACHER: Good.

STUDENT LEADER L: I think it might tell when salt was first discovered, well, it might tell what salt is made of and how it's made.

TEACHER: OK. Can we have another teacher?

Table salt is made by the third method—artificial evaporation. Pumping water into an underground salt bed dissolves the salt to make a brine that is brought to the surface. After purification at high temperatures, the salt is ready for our tables.

STUDENT LEADER K: After purification at high temperatures the salt is ready for what?

STUDENT C: Our tables.

STUDENT LEADER K: That's correct. To summarize: After its purification, the salt is put on our tables.

TEACHER: That was a fine job, Ken, and I appreciate all the work, but I think there might be something else to add to our summary. There is more important information that I think we need to include. This paragraph is mostly about what?

STUDENT A: The third method of evaporation.

STUDENT B: It mainly tells about pumping water from an underground salt bed that dissolves the salt to make a brine that is brought to the surface.

TEACHER: Angela hit it right on the money. The paragraph is mostly about the method of artificial evaporation and then everything else in the paragraph is telling us about the process. OK. Next teacher . . .

In this lesson, all students were participating, with an obvious structure to the participation. Even so, after 13 days of reciprocal teaching, the questions generated by the student leaders were all literal questions, requiring only very low-level responses. Such questions do not stimulate thinking beyond the surface structure of the text, either to formulate the question or to answer it. Moreover, no one requested clarification, although some of the students were having trouble understanding the text, nor did students monitor when they understood and when they did not understand. In addition, the teacher offered little scaffolding, but did monitor whether the students were understanding the passage and provided clarification of the content as needed. Finally, because reciprocal teaching emphasizes the teacher's fading support, lessons often included long pauses with students fumbling because the teacher was uncertain whether to enter into the conversation and provide input.

Even with these drawbacks, research evidence supports the benefits of reciprocal teaching. Rosenshine and Meister (1994) reviewed studies comparing reciprocal teaching to other forms of instruction. In general, the effects of reciprocal teaching were greater when explicit teaching of comprehension strategies occurred before participation in reciprocal teaching. Although the benefits of reciprocal teaching were very modest when measured by standardized tests, the effects were quite striking on measures assessing directly the processes stimulated by the strategies. Students of various ages and abilities benefited similarly from reciprocal teaching. Finally, teachers are able to adapt reciprocal teaching to the specific situations in their classrooms (Hacker & Tenent, 2002; Marks et al., 1993), with considerable guidance now available to teachers about how to use the approach flexibly across the language arts and school day (Oczkus, 2003).

talk about reading, writing, mathematics, science, and social science. Some teachers are real readers and let their students know how excited they are about reading particular authors. Other teachers bring real writing to the classroom. They teach writing by having everyone write a lot, including the teacher. The best writing teachers identify themselves as writers.

Even when teachers are masters, however, they must be highly motivated to teach using the Vygotskian model. Scaffolding demands much of teachers (Stone, 1998), and for teachers to work that hard, they must care about their students. According to Noddings (1984, 1996; see also Tappan, 1998), caring is at the center of teacher–student apprenticeships:

> This working together, which produces both joy in the relation and increasing competence in the cared-for . . . needs the cooperative guidance of a fully caring adult. . . . The caring teacher . . . has two major tasks: to stretch the student's world by presenting an effective selection of that world with which she is in contact, and to work cooperatively with the student in his struggle toward competence in that world. (1984, pp. 177–178)

Noddings recognizes that caring for students is difficult to foster. Teachers have many students, limited time, and numerous objectives to meet. Yet Noddings urges teachers to give up some of their control and to foster trust in their classrooms. She argues that true dialogue promotes deep contact with the ideas presented in the curriculum and stimulates the development of active thinkers who are willing to take intellectual risks.

As educators have attempted to provide instruction in the zone of proximal development, the challenges of this approach to teaching have become increasingly apparent. The following are some of the major challenges facing educators trying to apply the principles of scaffolding and apprenticeship to the classroom.

Knowledge of the Curriculum

In order to provide effective scaffolding, teachers must know the curriculum well, particularly portions of the curriculum that are troubling to students. It is easy to underestimate just how demanding this is, even for elementary-level content. For example, many teachers do not have a deep understanding of elementary mathematics and do not know the strategies that can be used to solve even simple addition and subtraction problems (Carpenter, Fennema, Peterson, & Carey, 1988; Fennema & Franke, 1992). More than knowing how to compute, scaffolding math teachers must also know their students' potential misconceptions about computing and how such misconceptions translate into observable behaviors. It may take years of experience with students to build up such knowledge.

Knowledge of Individual Students

To provide effective scaffolding, the teacher must know what a particular student already knows, what the student's misconceptions are, and what is in the student's current zone of proximal development. That is, the teacher must know what competencies are developing and which ones are far beyond the student's current level of functioning. If it is demanding to have this kind of insight into *one* student in *one* area of the curriculum, think about the enormity of this challenge for a classroom of students across the curriculum and when a class contains students with a variety of learning disabilities. Or think about how demanding it is for a high-school teacher who teaches many students.

Communication Challenges in Generating Prompts

Providing hints to students about the academic problems that they are experiencing requires great facility in generating hints and comments that provide enough assistance so that the student can make progress in solving academic problems without overdirecting them. Such prompts invite students to make the inferences a mature thinker would make, and they encourage students to construct understandings of the task at hand (Fox, 1993; Stone, 1993). Sometimes the student does not make necessary inferences at the first prompt, requiring generation of another prompt . . . and sometimes another one still . . . and then another, and so on. The scaffolding teacher is constantly required to think of new ways of prompting when initial prompts fail (Levine, 1993).

This is challenging, in part, because students' understanding of cognitive processes and the associated vocabulary develops slowly (Flavell, Miller, & Miller, 1993). For example, abstract concepts like "interpret," "infer," "conclude," and "assume" are often difficult even for high-school and college students to understand (Astington & Olsen, 1990; Booth & Hall, 1994), let alone younger students and students with cognitive disabilities. Cognitive processes must be talked about with students in very concrete ways, in terms that students can understand (Pressley et al., 1992), such as "What are you thinking as you read?," "Is this story like anything in your life?," or "Does this make sense to you?"

Another challenge is that many children experience difficulties in talking about difficulties they are having. The less a student can express precisely what his or her current difficulty is, the harder it is for an adult to scaffold the students' learning. In addition, the children who are most in need of academic help are often less likely to seek it than are other children (Karabenick & Newman, 2006; Newman & Goldin, 1990; Newman & Schwager, 1992).

Maintaining a Positive Tone

Good scaffolders are always positive and patient as they provide prompting and hinting. Sometimes this takes a great deal of patience, especially since the scaffolding teacher provides implicit messages that students do not "have it" yet. If the scaffolding is going well, the student does not construe such feedback as criticism. Unfortunately, it is hard for many adults to be unambiguously and consistently positive with children, especially when confronted with their uncertain progress. This can result in hints and tones of voice that will definitely be perceived as criticisms.

Diverse Causes of Academic Difficulties

A child may have academic difficulties for a number of reasons. How scaffolded instruction should occur and how much of it is necessary depends in part on the reason for underachievement. For some children, the problem is in their *home environment*. Their homes may be understimulating, that is, places where rich academically related experiences are rare. These children can arrive at school far behind classmates in the basic understandings critical to achievement in literacy and numeracy. These children will require intensive experiences such as one-to-one tutoring that includes much scaffolding for student progress to occur (Slavin, Karweit, & Wasik, 1994; Wasik & Slavin, 1993). Understimulation in the home environment may continue throughout the schooling years (Purcell-Gates, 1995). Thus years and years of scaffolding are needed for these children.

A variety of *biological/neurological deficiencies* also can cause learning problems. Some children experience difficulties with academics because their general cognitive abilities are low relative to those of other children. Among these children, some are more responsive to instruction than others—perhaps because they have wider zones of proximal development (Budoff, 1987). In contrast to children with general cognitive handicaps, other children have specific learning disabilities, where they are neurologically different from the norm in a way that undermines typical academic achievement with respect to some specific competency (e.g., reading, writing, mathematics; Zeffiro & Eden, 2000). For example, some children who experience difficulties in learning to read appear to have structurally and functionally different left hemispheres, which translates into difficulties mapping sound sequences to letter sequences (Galaburda, 1983; Harter, 1991; Hynd & Semrund-Clikeman, 1989; Joseph, Noble, & Eden, 2001; Rack, Snowling, & Olson, 1992; Shaywitz et al., 2003). Other children who have difficulties learning to read seem to suffer from visual-processing difficulties (Livingstone, Rosen, Drislane, & Galaburda, 1991), especially difficulties in processing visual information as rapidly as it must be processed for fluent reading to occur (Wolf & Bowers, 1999). The variety of biological differences potentially underlying academic disorders complicates educational intervention.

Finally, as helpful as scaffolding may be with some children, it may not work with all children. In some cases, the zone of proximal development may be so narrow (e.g., in the case of severely retarded children) that great tutor support and prompting are required even for little progress. Vygotsky's (1978) presumption that all students respond to stimulation in their zone of proximal development represented his socialist convictions about the power of environment in developing cognition rather than a conclusion based on research. A scientific challenge for the future is to determine when scaffolding can work, which teachers can do it, and which students can benefit from it.

■ ■ ■ CULTURAL DIFFERENCES AND THEIR IMPLICATIONS FOR CLASSROOM PRACTICE

Educational anthropologists are particularly interested in the implications of cultural differences for education. Their emphasis on *differences* in students contrasts greatly with those who assume that students who live outside the mainstream culture have *deficits*. Educational anthropologists have made enormous contributions in developing new ways of thinking about multiculturalism and education.

Anthropologists have relied heavily on qualitative methods to conduct their research, particularly ethnography (review qualitative research methodologies described in Chapter 1). Educational anthropologists distinguish between macroethnographic and microethnographic analyses. The **macroethnographic** approach considers particular cultures in relation to other cultures, both at present and historically.

In contrast to studying cultures in general, the **microethnographic** approach specifically focuses on differences in interpersonal communications as a function of culture, with the view that differences in language between cultures have profound implications for education (Hymes, 1974).

Macroethnographic Analyses

John Ogbu (1978, 1981, 1997, 2003; Ogbu & Stern, 2001) set out to explain why some minority children in the United States have more difficulties in school, are less likely to finish school, and are less likely to attain high-paying and high-status positions than majority-culture children. In doing so, he distinguished between autonomous minorities, immigrant minorities, and caste minorities.

Autonomous minorities, such as Mormons and Jewish people in the United States, have something about them that is distinct from the majority culture, such as their ethnic or religious background, and they often act to preserve that distinction. Although autonomous minorities experience some discrimination, their relationship with the dominant culture is not one of perceived inferiority. Furthermore, autonomous minorities are not economically subordinate to the majority culture and benefit from the obtainment of educational credentials at the same socioeconomic levels as the majority culture.

Immigrant minorities are recent arrivals in a geographic area. They experience some discrimination, but tolerate such treatment, largely because they are better off in the host society than in the country from which they fled. They have reason to hope for upward social and economic movement with education and across generations. Immigrant minorities are *voluntary* minorities, willingly electing themselves into their host society. They anticipate great gains from migrating to the host country. Indeed, voluntary immigrant minorities have tended to do well in the United States. The majority culture does not attempt to dominate immigrant minority groups as much as it does caste minorities.

Caste minorities, in contrast, are viewed by the majority culture as inferior. Ogbu (2003) argued that the majority culture does much to dominate members of caste minorities (see also Apple, 1979). Caste minorities typically are *involuntary* minorities. Thus African Americans were brought to North America against their will. Native Americans were conquered. Involuntary minorities tend to be preoccupied with what they have lost. As a result of the sense of loss and bad treatment by the majority culture, members of caste-like minorities often come to dislike and oppose the majority culture. For example, many blacks reject the values of U.S. public education, seeing them more as white values than as black values (Ogbu, 1981, 1987). Particularly important, even when members of caste minorities succeed in obtaining an education, is the fact that their caste limits the roles they can play. In general, caste-like, involuntary minorities have fared poorly in the United States, particularly in socioeconomic status. Caste-like minorities have not experienced the upward socioeconomic mobility across generations that other minority groups have experienced (Bowles & Gintis, 1976).

Substantial evidence from around the world supports Ogbu's portrayal of these three types of minorities (Gibson & Ogbu, 1991a). For example, consider the educational experiences of immigrant minorities in the United States (such as the Chinese, Japanese, Korean, Asian Indian, Vietnamese, Cuban, and Filipino minorities) compared to caste-like minorities in the United States (such as the black, Hawaiian, Mexican, and American Indian minorities). In general, the immigrant minorities have embraced education, including the acquisition of the English language, more than the caste-like minorities. For example, for all the immigrant minorities listed above, the majority of 18- and 19-year-olds are in school. In contrast, only about half of black American 18- to 19-year-olds and about 40% of Hawaiian, Mexican, and American Indian 18- to 19-year-olds remain in school. In general, immigrant minority parents view schooling as much more essential for their children's success than do caste-like minority parents. Yet many immigrant minority parents want their children to retain their minority identities and cultures. Although immigrant minority children sometimes face discrimination and obstacles in school, they are more likely than caste-like minorities to remain satisfied with school, and their parents continue to be determined to work with schools to better their children's future. Immigrant minority children and parents are more likely to like their school and teachers than are caste-minority children and parents. In turn, teachers and school officials have tended to appreciate immigrant minorities more than caste-like minorities.

Although Ogbu and his colleagues were interested in many minority groups in many settings, his work is most often associated with analyses of the black American experience. Ogbu was not the first to conclude that white–black relations in the United States were caste-like (Davis, Gardner, Gardner, & Warner, 1941; Dollard, 1949; Foley, 1991). However, Ogbu (2003) went farther than others in arguing that caste status does much to influence the decisions that affect minority children, which in turn influence their cognitive development and achievement both in school and the larger society. For instance, our society has made a number of decisions about the provision of nutritional, medical, and housing resources to poor people that translate into higher incidences of malnutrition, low birthweight, and lead poisoning among the children of caste-like minorities than among children from other groups (National Commission on Children, 1991).

Ogbu believed that schools make decisions that result in differential education of caste-like minority children compared to other children, differences in education that undermine the intellectual development of the former. When educational researchers have looked, they have found evidence consistent with Ogbu's concerns. For example, Rist (1970) analyzed the experiences of a classroom of ghetto kindergarten children, demonstrating that the more economically disadvantaged children received less favorable treatment from the very first days of schools. Once assigned to lower level reading groups in kindergarten, an assignment that was directly related to their socioeconomic status, no children moved to more capable groups in kindergarten or in first or second grade. Allington and McGill-Franzen (1989; Allington, 1991a, 1991b) studied the educational adaptations made for elementary-school students in programs designed for students performing poorly in school, many of whom are members of caste-like minorities. They found that the supplementary instruction provided to these students tended to be lower level than regular education, meaning that the minority students in these programs received less grade-level instruction than other students. Similar patterns also are observed at the high-school level where minorities are much more likely to be placed in lower tracks, which generally receive inferior instruction (Oakes, 1985). And, not surprisingly, caste-like minorities drop out of high school in much larger proportions than children from other groups (Waggoner, 1991).

According to Ogbu's perspective, however, blacks themselves also contribute to their lack of success in school. Fordham and Ogbu (1986; Fordham, 1988) studied black high-school students in Washington, DC. They found strong resistance in these students to many things that they perceived to be "white," including a number of behaviors that are important to success in U.S. education, such as speaking and writing standard English, visiting museums, reading literature, studying, and getting good grades in school. Although there is great peer pressure among black adolescents not to act "white" (Steinberg, Dornbusch, & Brown, 1992), such antiwhite attitudes often begin in the home (Ogbu, 1991). As Ogbu suggested, such attitudes are caused partially by an understanding among blacks, which is passed on to their children, that educational achievement is not as certain a route to success for their group as it is for other groups (Mickelson, 1990). Moreover, black children are often thrust into the larger black community at an early age through neighborhood and church contacts where they encounter many adults who encourage rejection of the mainstream white culture (Ogbu, 1974, 1978; Silverstein & Krate, 1975). It is often easier for black youths to preserve their self-esteem by orienting themselves to the black peer group rather than to school, since they are much less likely to be considered incompetent by black peers than by the institution of school (Steele, 1992). Thus a variety of factors combine to produce black students who become determiners of their own educational underachievement by embracing values that are inconsistent with success in U.S. public education.

In his last book before his death, Ogbu (Ogbu & Davis, 2003) analyzed black underachievement in Shaker Heights, Ohio. Even in this very affluent community, Ogbu found that black students distrusted the school and perceived racism in the school, as indicated by the disproportionate representation of blacks in less advanced academic courses and special education. The black students believed that counselors and teachers pushed them less intensely to do well academically than they pushed white students. They also perceived that their parents had lower academic expectations about them than did the parents of white students. Black students anticipated that they would have to work much harder than whites to get ahead economically after high school. Peer groups in Shaker Heights were racially divided, with white peer groups more encouraging of school work and academic pursuits than black peer groups. In short, just as was the case in inner-city schools, Ogbu identified many ways that black academic achievement was undermined in one of America's most economically advantaged communities.

Nevertheless, despite considerable support for Ogbu's theoretical position, many students who are members of caste-like minorities, including blacks, *do* succeed in school (Erickson, 1987; Gibson & Ogbu, 1991b; Wells & Crain, 1997). Some Mexican Americans, who are caste-like in Ogbu's framework, have experienced upward social mobility, especially across generations, with education playing an important role in their economic gains (McCarthy & Valdez, 1986; Trueba, 1988). Punjabi Sikh students in California outperform majority students, despite the fact that this group of immigrants has many caste-like characteristics. The Punjabi Sikhs, however, embrace the learning of English as the acquisition of an important cultural tool (Gibson, 1988). Thus they accommodate to the dominant culture without assimilating to it. Likewise, Latino and African American students who accommodate without assimilating also enjoy greater school success than Latino and African American students who do not accommodate (Mehan, Hubbard, & Villaneuva, 1994).

For example, consider in more detail a study establishing clear linkages between environmental support for educational achievement and actual achievement in African American families. Using qualitative methods, Clark (1983) studied economically disadvantaged high-school students, half of whom were much more successful in school than the other half of the students in the sample. There were clear differences in the homes of successful and unsuccessful students.

- The parents of successful students had *higher expectations* than the parents of unsuccessful students. Parents of successful students expected to play a major role in their children's schooling, initiated more contact with the school, expected their children to play a major role in their own schooling, and anticipated that their children would obtain postsecondary education. Parents of unsuccessful students expected much less achievement from their students.
- The parents of successful students had more *explicit achievement-oriented rules* operating in their homes. The successful students were more accepting of these rules than less successful students. The parents of successful students exercised firmer, more consistent monitoring, and more certain rule enforcement than the parents of unsuccessful students.
- Parents of successful students established *clearer role boundaries* in their homes than the parents of unsuccessful students, which resulted in calmer interactions and less family conflict.
- Parents of successful students more often *engaged in teaching their children* and were more nurturing and supportive than the parents of unsuccessful students.

The findings of Clark have been supported by more recent work. For example, Romo and Falbo (1996) described similar characteristics in the families of Latino students who succeeded in high school versus those who did not. Pressley, Raphael, Gallagher, and DiBella (2004) studied Providence–St. Mel School, a K–12 school on the West Side of Chicago, serving African American students. The school's record of success is incredible, with 100% of its graduates since 1978 being accepted into college and half of recent classes being accepted into very good colleges. Using qualitative research methods, Pressley and colleagues identified the many elements that coalesce at the school to produce such success, some of which echo those found by Clark. These include:

HUMAN COMMITMENTS
- Strong, dedicated, caring administrators.
- Capable, dedicated, caring teachers.
- Families of students who work responsively and constructively with the school.
- Supportive alumni who have succeeded after completing the school.
- Donors who provide ideas and financial backing for the school.
- Students who meet high behavioral and academic demands.
- The various players at the school trust, respect, and like one another.

CAPITAL
- A secure building, one adequate to support state-of-the-art instruction.
- Sources of funding, including the extra resources required for extensive support for economically disadvantaged and academically at-risk students (e.g., for scholarships, tutoring, test preparation classes, field trips to inspire students).

POLICIES

- High teaching standards, including efficient use of class time.
- High monitoring of teaching performance.
- Extensive monitoring of student achievement, which permits meaningful feedback to students.
- Instruction balancing learning of basic facts and skills and higher order skills and understanding.
- Deliberate use of teaching approaches and other resources known to support and motivate students, including instructional scaffolding, encouragement and demand of student self-regulation, and praise for specific accomplishments.
- A curriculum that increases students' respect of their own heritage and themselves such as the integration of African American content.

AMBIENCE

- An environment that intensely celebrates academic achievement above all else.
- A generally positive and motivating environment, one that expects much from students and offers a variety of rewards to those who do achieve.
- An environment that makes clear that a positive future depends on hard academic work during the K–12 years.
- A mentoring atmosphere that encourages dreams, builds confidence, stresses the importance of education, and shepherds the student to high goals—especially admission to a good college.

There is great trust between the school, families, and students in a school like Providence–St. Mel, one that works for disadvantaged students (Bryk & Schneider, 2002; Hilliard & Amankwatia, 2003).

A consistent pattern has emerged from studies of successful and unsuccessful minority students: The environments of educationally successful minority students, including the environments that students and their families create for themselves (e.g., through peer associations and seeking to attend schools like Providence–St. Mel), support educational achievements in ways that the environments of unsuccessful same-minority students do not—with this generalization holding for students from diverse ethnic groups (Abi-Nader, 1990; Delgado-Gaitan, 1990; Lee, 1994; Smith-Hefner, 1993). This strong association has been a powerful stimulus for intensive study of the home and school environments of minority students in microethnographic studies.

Microethnographic Research

In a qualitative study of children's lives at home and school, Snow, Barnes, Chandler, Goodman, and Hemphill (1991) followed three samples of children from low-income homes for 2 years, studying one group of students as they moved through grades two and three, a second as students traversed grades four and five, and a third as students went through grades six and seven. As did the macroethnographic researchers cited above, Snow and colleagues found that home and school influences were inextricably intertwined in determining the success of students in school. That is, whether the child did well or not depended on both the school and the family and the ability of the family to support the instruction that went on in school. An especially important finding was that the parents of many students were increasingly at a disadvantage as their children progressed through elementary school. Many well-intentioned parents could help their children with beginning reading but could not help as much with the more demanding reading required in the upper elementary grades. Thus the parents were in a better position to make up for poor instruction during the primary years than they were at later points in schooling. Therefore, the success of the students, especially after the primary school years, depended more and more on the quality of the schooling they received.

An important question for microethnographers has been whether minorities receive lower quality instruction because of cultural differences in the communication styles of minority students and their teachers, who often come from majority populations. There has been considerable support for this hypothesis (Erickson, 1987).

One of the most influential studies addressing this question was conducted between 1968 and 1973 on the Warm Springs Indian Reservation in central Oregon (Philips, 1983). Philips lived on the reservation, observing both Anglo and Native American children in grades one and six. She visited the homes of children and became thoroughly familiar with community life. Consistent with her hypothesis that communications problems were at the heart of the Native American children's difficulties in school, Philips observed that the tribal children often did not understand the teacher, frequently were inattentive, and rarely talked in class. Moreover, she noted that the teachers were not sensitive to the ways by which Native Americans communicate. The tribal children used less body language, tended not to look at others when they spoke, and tended to speak softly and slowly. Because of these communication attributes, the Native American students did not participate well in teacher-driven initiation–response–evaluation (IRE) cycles (review Box 6-3; Mehan, 1979). That is, the Native American students did not react well to being put on the spot when the teacher posed questions (initiation) that students are expected to answer quickly in front of a group (response), with a teacher evaluation following the attempted response (evaluation).

In contrast, when the Native American children were in situations more consistent with their own culture (such as one-on-one discussion with an adult or interactions within a small group of children), communications were much better (see also Lomawaima, 1995). Others have also observed that education does not go well for Native American students when teachers are insensitive to their communication styles and preferences (Erickson & Mohatt, 1982; Van Ness, 1981; Wilson, 1991). See the Considering Interesting Questions special feature (Box 6.5) for a discussion of other mismatches in communications styles that have been detected by educational researchers.

Au and Mason (1981) demonstrated that the education of minority students can be improved by providing them with instruction sensitive to and consistent with their own culturally defined communication styles and preferences. They evaluated individual lessons of two teachers at Kamehameha School, which serves native Hawaiian students. One teacher used conventional teaching—for example, teaching that included many IRE-like cycles. The other teacher used participation structures more familiar to Hawaiian children. Rather than individual children responding to the teacher, several children responded by commenting on particular points in a conversational fashion. What went on was much more like naturalistic dialogue than typically occurs during IRE cycles. The teacher was less concerned with right answers

Considering Interesting Questions

BOX 6.5. How Do Cultural Differences in Conversational Style Influence Classroom Interactions?

Although we are just beginning to learn about differences in conversational style across cultures and gender, research indicates that teachers need to be sensitive to these individual differences. For example, Heath (1989) studied African American communities in rural southeastern communities and found that older adults do not censor or simplify talk around children. Instead, they expect the young to adapt to changing contexts and speakers. Adults in these communities only ask children *real* questions, not questions the adults already know the answers to. For example, these adults would not ask a child, "What color is your shirt?," since the adult already knows the answer to that question. Also, in some cultures, it is considered inappropriate for students to show off what they know. Thus, the traditional initiate–response–evaluation cycles (Cazden, 2001), in which the teacher asks factual-level questions (what everyone should know) would be a particularly poor instructional tactic for students of some cultural backgrounds (Carlsen, 1991).

In recent years, there has been considerable debate about whether schools should allow black students to speak black English (Ebonics) in school, with wide-ranging opinions even within the African American community. At one extreme are concerns that disallowing of Ebonics attacks the very identity of African American children, sending powerful negative messages about their culture and home life; at the other extreme are concerns that Standard English is required to participate in larger U.S. life in ways that permit a bright economic future for African American students. Multilingualism is prominent in U.S. life, with it possible, desirable, and commendable to speak one form of English at home and in the neighborhood and another in educational and workplace settings (Delpit & Dowdy, 2002). We emphasize that linguists do not view black English as being inferior to Standard English or in any way reflecting on the competence of speakers of black English, although they do recognize that children whose home language is black English are often disadvantaged in U.S. schools as they attempt to learn to read Standard English (Labov, 2003).

What do we know about the differences in the conversational styles of males and females? Tannen (1990) described gender differences in communication style as being based on two different views of the world. Males engage in a hierarchical world where they are constantly jockeying for position. To them, conversations are negotiations in which they try to achieve and maintain the upper hand if they can. Their goal is to attain status and preserve independence. Women, on the other hand, engage the world as individuals in a network of connections. To them, conversations are negotiations for closeness and intimacy. Maccoby (1988) reported speech patterns in boys and girls during play that were similar to these patterns observed in adults. The boys issued more commands and interrupted each other more; the girls were more likely to take turns talking and to use the talk for social binding.

How will these gender differences emerge in the classroom (Grossman & Grossman, 1994; Tannen, 1990)? Since female students are more likely to add tag-on questions to engage their listeners, such as "Don't you think?" or "Isn't it," they will sound less decisive and certain of themselves than the male students. The female students are also more likely to let the male students choose topics, interrupt, and hold the floor, although African American females may be less likely to let the males dominate. Who interrupts more during a classroom discussion? It depends on the nature of the interruptions. Female students are more likely to display cooperative overlappings, where they show support and anticipate where the speaker is heading. Male students are more likely to interrupt to change the direction of the topic. There are also regional and cultural differences in the rate of interruptions. New Yorkers talk without pauses between speakers; Southerners pause between speakers; and Navajo Indians pause at length between speakers. Teachers who are more sensitive to the range of conversational styles are likely to be more effective in the classroom.

than with the children's interpretations, and the students were more likely to partici-pate than in typical IRE structures.

One of the most striking findings in the Au and Mason (1981) study was that academic engagement was much greater when instruction was culturally congruent. The children in the culturally congruent discussions made more reading-related responses and many more appropriate inferences than those in the more traditional reading lessons. In general, culturally congruent interactions have fared quite well in formal comparisons with more conventional teaching, including on measures such as standardized test scores (Tharp, 1982; Tharp & Gallimore, 1988).

The successes at Kamehameha School and the generally positive associations between culturally congruent communications and school participation are stimulat-ing many researchers to think about how schooling can be made more comfortable and effective for minority students. An important part of the approach is that curric-ula are constructed so that the students learn concepts that they relate to familiar concepts. For example, McCarty, Lynch, Wallace, and Benally (1991) developed social studies curricula for Navajo students in kindergarten through grade nine. In the unit on culture and community, students discuss the ideas with reference to their own culture and local community. In the unit on government, U.S. majority culture conceptions of government are related to Navajo conceptions of government. Stimu-lating students to talk and think about new information in relation to their prior knowledge is a powerful way of teaching. The Navajo students participate actively in these discussions—indeed, the entire class often joins in. Achievement, as docu-mented by improved test scores, has increased for the Navajo students experiencing this curriculum. The same approach has been adapted for Native Americans in Alaska (Lipka & McCarty, 1994).

An important goal of such teaching is to encourage learning through interac-tion. Thus instructional interventions such as these can be conceptualized in terms of Vygotsky's theory of cognitive development through social interactions. Accord-ing to Vygotsky, people learn how to think as individuals by first experiencing think-ing with others. Although research has focused most directly on the achievement of minority students, the power of conversation as a means of learning both content and how to think likely would benefit all students. See the Applying Developmental Theory to Educational Contexts special feature (Box 6.6) for some guidance about how to conduct instructional conversations that are more than IRE cycles.

Cross-Cultural Differences and the Testing of Minority Students

The anthropological research described in this chapter sensitized educators to the communications and values differences between some minorities and the majority population. This has lead to intense reflection about language and communications factors that can impact performance on standardized tests, potentially biasing against minority students (Geisinger, 2003; Valencia & Suzuki, 2001; see also Chap-ter 8).

The use of standardized tests for discriminating against minorities has a long history. Two of the earliest intelligence tests (*Army Alpha* and *Beta*) were used by the U.S. Army during World War I. After analyzing the test results of hundreds of thou-sands of young recruits and conscripts, Carl Brigham (1923) concluded that recent immigrants to the United States were less intelligent than white people born in the

Applying Developmental Theory to Educational Contexts

BOX 6.6. Factors Promoting Effective Academic Discussions

Haroutunian-Gordon (1991) suggested factors that can inhibit and promote productive class-room conversations. One way to stifle interaction is for the teacher to believe that certain issues, perspectives, or opinions must emerge during the discussion. Haroutunian-Gordon refers to conversations where the teacher tries too hard to control the discussion as "phony conversations." Although it is appropriate for teachers to gently steer conversations so students stay on topic, interpretive discussions at their best probably involve issues that the students value and ideas that the students find intriguing. Students are more likely to perceive discussions around such issues as "genuine" discussions.

Often, a real tension develops. Interpretations that the teacher feels are important do not get out on the floor, and others that the teacher might consider to be misinterpretations are embraced by the group. Consider a discussion between Haroutunian-Gordon and a teacher, Ms. Spring, about the progress of a discussion group they are "leading," on Shakespeare's *Romeo and Juliet*:

TEACHER: What is to be done if the students leave this classroom with an erroneous vision of the play and Shakespeare's message? What have they learned in such a class?

H-G: Well, one thing we can say is that they have begun to do the job that they are sup-posed to do when reading the play, right? They have begun to construct a story that allows them to connect the events in the play to one another in a meaningful way. That means they will remember those events, that the story they use to connect them will allow them to bring the events up so as to, perhaps at some point, connect them to their lives.

TEACHER: Yes, but that story about Benvolio was all wrong—

H-G: Wrong? By what criteria? It is not your story—

TEACHER: It is not Shakespeare's story!

H-G: Well perhaps not, I agree. But is yours Shakespeare's story?

TEACHER: Look, I don't claim to have any corner on his views. What I do know is that those two girls have made an interpretation of Benvolio that cannot really stand up to the text in its entirety.

H-G: You may well be right about that. But don't they now have a view to modify at least? And won't there be another class tomorrow?

TEACHER: Yes, but the question is, What should I do then? I can't tell them the truth, as we said a long time ago. They won't hear it. And they won't entertain conflicting evidence—that much we have seen. They even resist the questions I ask to get them to rethink their perspectives.

H-G: Maybe you ought to forget about Edna and Abby. Maybe things will straighten out.

TEACHER: Maybe. But what they need is a new perspective on Benvolio, another way of looking at him.

Many interesting points emerge in this conversation. Haroutunian-Gordon clearly felt the students were getting a lot from the class discussions by learning to interpret and think critically about plays. Discussions have high potential for increasing student understanding. Interpretive class discussions, however, will be difficult for teachers if they fail to accept that there are alter-native interpretations and that their own interpretations may be inadequate. Once such discussions get going, many students will find it difficult to accept "standard" interpretations, since they will have discovered alternative ways of looking at the content.

(continued)

Another important factor in classroom conversations is that it takes time for a group of students to be able to engage in interpretive discussion (Haroutunian-Gordon, 1991). Years of participating in IRE cycles have not prepared students for this. In addition, it may take a while for the students to make really interesting inferences about new content. Thus it took several sessions before the students in Ms. Spring's and Haroutunian-Gordon's *Romeo and Juliet* discussion group were making sophisticated comments about the play, ones reflecting deep understanding about the characters and their situation. As these challenges are considered, it must be emphasized that there is now considerable evidence that effective language arts instruction in middle schools and high schools is saturated with student dialoguing (Applebee, Langer, Nystrand, & Gamoran, 2003).

The fact that so many non-English-speaking immigrants were classified as being of below normal intelligence speaks to the important role of language and cultural differences in intelligence testing.

United States. He reached this conclusion because recent immigrants had not done as well on the Army tests as whites born in the United States. Imagine the communication difficulties experienced by an immigrant being tested in a unfamiliar language by a strange person who represented his new country's government. Unfair testing has occurred for generations in the United States and has been used to make unfair decisions about students' education such as placement in special education or admissions to college (Lopez, 1997).

Steele and Aronson (1995) provided a provocative analysis of why African American students perform poorly on standardized tests. They argued that such testing is threatening because of the possibility that the test will confirm the negative cultural stereotype that African American students are less intellectually able than white students. This phenomenon is known as **stereotype threat**. College students at Stanford University participated in Steele and Aronson's original experiments. The directions given before a verbal ability test emphasized either that the test was diagnostic of ability or was not diagnostic of ability. When given nondiagnostic instructions, African American students and white students performed equally on the test. When given diagnostic instructions, African American students performed more poorly than whites and more poorly than African American students given the nondiagnostic directions. The power of stereotype threat in testing situations for African American students has been confirmed in follow-up studies (Steele, 2004; Steele & Aronson, 2004).

Differences in communication styles suggest other explanations for lower performance of minority students on standardized test. One possibility is that they have different understandings about what it means to take a test and what the long-term implications of tests are. Rodriguez (1992) summarized this concern for the particular case of Hispanic students.

> Test-taking behaviors are culturally learned behaviors. Thus, at a basic level, the argument may be advanced that most Hispanics are not "test wise." Steeped as immigrants in a traditional culture where test taking is not customary, Hispanics come to the testing situation with a cultural disadvantage. Hispanics do not have a cultural knowledge of the mechanics of testing (e.g., there are several choices, but only one correct choice; the correct answer must be recorded in a given slot and within a given allotment of time), nor do they necessarily adhere to the advanced industrial norms and values encapsulated by the general belief in the legitimacy of the testing enterprise as the standard by which to assess performance.... A traditionally minded Hispanic is at a disadvantage in not understanding the implications of tests for future life chances. (pp. 13–14)

Fluency in the English language and knowledge of the majority culture also influence performance on standardized tests. Limited English speakers are at a real disadvantage when standardized tests are administered in English (American Psychological Association, 1985). Often, tests assume students have knowledge of the majority culture that many minority students do not possess (Garcia, 1991). Thus, even if a test is highly valid and interpretable with English-speaking students, it can be of little value for assessing minority students. An IQ score generated by an English-speaking examiner with a test in English means entirely different things when earned by an English-first-language student, an English-second-language student, and a student who cannot speak English at all (Donlon, 1992; Pennock-Román, 1992; Schmeiser, 1992).

In some parts of the United States, laws once required that all children be tested in English, with decisions about school placement into special education or giftedness classes based on such tests (Donlon, 1992; Rodriguez, 1992). Of course, when the same score was used to allocate special education and enriched education for all populations, disproportionately high numbers of Spanish-speaking children ended up in special education and disproportionately low numbers of Spanish-speaking children were offered accelerated programs. Fortunately, such laws have now been struck down by courts, litigation, and changing professional standards. Thus non-English-speaking students have much more protection now than ever before. For example, the ruling in *Diana v. California State Board of Education* (1970) was that students must be tested in their native language (Geisenger, 1992). In this case, an English-administered IQ test had been used to place Spanish-speaking students in special education. The court ruled that all Spanish-speaking and Chinese-speaking children in the state who were in classes intended for children with mental retardation had to be retested using procedures that did not discriminate on the basis of language. The court also ruled that the retesting had to eliminate test items tapping vocabulary and general information that might not be encountered in the minority cultures. The retesting determined that seven of the nine students who had brought the case were much more intelligent than originally assessed (Constantino, 1992). The California legislature subsequently passed new laws to prevent the abuses that had produced the *Diana* case (Geisenger, 1992), and additional court action has prevented overrepresentation of minorities in special education classes (Constantino, 1992).

Even so, when tests are reliable and valid and are not being used intentionally to discriminate, they are being upheld as appropriate, even if disproportionate numbers of minorities fail the test. In *Parents in Action on Special Education v. Hannon et al.* (1980), a federal judge upheld the use of standardized tests to classify minority children in Chicago as mentally retarded (Koocher & Keith-Spiegel, 1990; Oakland & Parmelee, 1985). Tests can be abused with minorities, but they can also be used to make valid decisions about minority students. Research on cultural differences in communication and thinking styles is being translated into better understanding about how to construct and administer culture-fair tests (Geisinger, 2003). That testing often has not served minorities well in the past does not mean that testing in the future cannot play a more constructive role in educational decision making for minority students.

■ ■ ■ CROSS-CULTURAL INSIGHTS ABOUT THE EFFECTS OF SCHOOLING ON COGNITIVE DEVELOPMENT

In Chapter 1 the impact of schooling on children's development was discussed. Ceci (1991) concluded, based on a variety of analyses, that schooling increases general intelligence. But just what does that mean? A child's IQ could increase because he or she improved on some very specific cognitive competencies tapped by IQ tests or because of generalized improvement on a variety of items covered on IQ assessments (see Chapter 8). In either case, the IQ score would increase.

In trying to unravel the effects of schooling on IQ, Scribner and Cole (1981) reported what has become a classic study. Their study focused on the Vai people of Liberia and their language skills. Many members of this culture learn to write in Vai script, a form of writing indigenous to the culture. The person who knows Vai script can engage in a variety of informal communications, such as the writing of friendly letters. Typically, Vai script is taught by family, friends, or neighbors. In addition to the informal Vai, some members of the culture learn Arabic as part of Quranic study. Such study involves a great deal of memorization of religious texts. Some members of the culture also learn to read and write English in Western-style schools. Learning to read and write English allows participation in a wide range of formal activities not permitted by learning of Vai or Arabic, such as participation in government and business beyond the village level.

Scribner and Cole (1981) administered a wide range of tasks to members of the Vai culture who had learned to read and write Vai, Arabic, or English. They also tested individuals who had not acquired any literacy skills. What they found was that *schooling had particular effects*. Performance on tasks varied depending on the type of schooling received. Thus English schooling positively effected some tasks (e.g., tasks that required giving an explanation) and made little difference on other tasks (e.g., tasks that required classifying objects on the basis of conceptual similarity).

Which group do you think did best on tasks measuring the ability to memorize the order of items? If you thought it was the students who had learned Arabic, you were right. All that practice memorizing religious texts, which requires remembering ideas in order, improved the students' serial learning ability (Wagner & Spratt, 1987).

What skills were stronger as a result of learning Vai, the indigenous language? Those who were Vai-literate were better able to use symbols than Vai-illiterates. Also, Vai-literates knew more Vai grammar than did Vai-illiterates. Still, the positive effects of learning Vai were restricted to a few measures.

So what does this study tell us about schooling? People can do what they are taught to do and what they must do often. Neither literacy nor schooling promotes cognitive development generally (Scribner & Cole, 1981). Rather, educational and cultural experiences have their own specific impacts on cognitive development. As noted in Chapter 1, the memory and learning strategies of children living in North America are only observed in non-Western countries when people experience Western-style schooling (Cole et al., 1971; Wagner, 1974, 1978). In contrast, non-Westerners who have attended Western-style school have no advantage when asked to do cognitive tasks that are common in the non-Western culture, ones familiar also to nonschooled people (Mandler, Scribner, Cole, & DeForest, 1980; Rogoff & Waddell, 1982). In African cultures in which storytelling is an important part of life, the story memory of nonschooled African students can be better than the story memory of schooled U.S. students (Ross & Millson, 1970). A variety of cross-cultural evidence supports the conclusion that cultural-specific experiences enhance cultural-specific competencies, which in turn develop additionally as the person participates in the culture that demands and supports such competencies (Cole, 1998). Moreover, when children in different cultures have comparable educational and environmental experiences, their thinking and learning skills are often comparable. Environment matters in cognitive development.

■ ■ ■ CHAPTER SUMMARY AND EVALUATION

The world in which a child is immersed affects the development of the child's mind. Vygotsky's theory was that a great deal of mature thinking is dialogic, in that the mature thinker can think about a situation much like two people seem to think about a situation as they talk about it. Such dialogical thinking skills are developed through interactions with others.

Anthropologists have also accumulated evidence that the world has a powerful effect on a child's thinking and behavior. Microanthropologists have particularly focused on how communication processes differ as a function of culture. Such differences in communication style can affect success in conventional schooling as well as performance on tests, which count heavily in the conventional educational accountability system. Macroanthropologists have substantiated that culture can affect more broadly how minority children relate to school—including how much they value it. School is not a passive player in the shaping of mind, however. Psychologists who have conducted cross-cultural studies have been able to confirm that Western schooling has particular types of effects on thinking. Other types of schooling have other effects.

Developmental Debates

Sociocultural theorists and researchers have substantiated that a variety of forces determine behavior and development.

Nature versus Nurture

Although sociocultural theories emphasize the power of the environment in determining behavior and development, they also include some strong biological assumptions. For example, the assumption of Vygotsky that social interaction is necessary for cognitive development implies that evolution has favored an organism who is sensitive to environmental input. This is in striking contrast to the position of behavior geneticists, who hold that individual differences in intelligence are genetically determined. Vygotsky's theory reflects no such presumption about biology.

Stages versus Continuous Development

Vygotsky offered an explicit stage theory. Other sociocultural theorists and researchers are less explicit about age-graded development, emphasizing more the impact of society and culture throughout the lifespan.

Universal versus Culture-Specific Developments

Vygotsky is certainly a universalist, believing that social factors operate in development across the human species. Anthropologists, while believing that humans of all cultures share a biological heritage, focus more on human differences, depending on circumstances, including the cultural pressures the individual experiences. For example, although anthropologists would agree that much development occurs because of interpersonal communications, they point out that the structures of communication differ as a function of culture.

Trait-Like Consistency versus Situational Determination of Behavior

The socioculturalists believe there is both consistency and variability within cultures. For example, although caste-like status goes far in explaining similarities in the experiences of some minority groups, how particular minority students develop depends largely on the environments they encounter. Thus, if a caste-like minority student experiences a world of schooling that is attuned to the student's preferred communication style, development in the context of schooling can be different than if schooling requires a great deal of participation in communication patterns inimical to the student's culture.

Active versus Passive Child

Although the effects of the sociocultural environment are emphasized in the theories summarized in this chapter, it is important to note that when schooling is congruent with a child's culture, the child is more active. This understanding would ideally stimulate the development of schools that are congruent with the cultures from which students come.

Lasting versus Transient Early Effects of Experience

Vygotsky certainly believed that the thinking skills developed during the preschool years had a great impact on later development. Microethnographers certainly believe in the long-term impact of the communication and learning styles developed in the home and culture before school is experienced. Cultural patterns internalized early typically affect subsequent behavior and development.

■■■ REVIEW OF KEY TERMS

attribution Explanation for behaviors, often for successes or failures.

autonomous minorities Groups of people who act to preserve some of what makes them distinct from the majority culture but who typically do not experience discrimination.

caste minorities Groups of people who are viewed by the majority culture as inferior and who experience widespread discrimination.

egocentric speech Speech of young children, directed to themselves about what they are doing.

guided participation A teaching method in which teachers explicitly direct processing done by students.

immigrant minorities Groups of people who are voluntary recent arrivals to the majority culture who may experience discrimination but have opportunities for upward mobility.

initiate–response–evaluation (IRE) cycles The typical classroom conversation structure where the teacher initiates, usually through questions; the students respond; and then the teacher evaluates the students' responses.

inner speech An abbreviated and often fragmentary internal dialogue that according to Vygotsky plays an important role in thinking.

macroethnographic An approach to studying cultural differences that considers particular cultures in relation to other cultures.

microethnographic An approach to studying cultural differences that focuses on analyses of differences in interpersonal communication as a function of culture.

private speech Thoughts spoken outloud by someone working on a task.

scaffolding An instructional technique in which teachers provide help to students on an as-needed basis.

stereotype threat A fear of minority students that a standardized test will confirm the cultural stereotype that minorities are not as intellectually able as whites, resulting in poorer performance on the test than when such threat is not present.

zone of proximal development A range of achievements that includes tasks that learners cannot accomplish independently but can accomplish with assistance.

PART II

KEY TOPICS IN CHILD DEVELOPMENT AND EDUCATION

CHAPTER 7

Language Development and Linguistic Diversity

Language development has been an area of active research in recent decades. One motivation for this work was Noam Chomsky's (1957, 1959) proposition that humans are biologically predisposed to acquire language. According to Chomsky, each human is born with a **language acquisition device**, which includes a basic understanding of the syntax of language: the rules governing the combining of words and phrases, the rules needed to express and understand the complex meanings encoded in sentences. Because all humans share this biological mechanism, Chomsky believed that language functioning should be similar across languages and cultures.

Given the strong biological claims made by Chomsky, we begin this chapter with an overview of the evidence that language is greatly determined by biology. The case for biology playing a large role in human language is strong, but so is the case that the language environment surrounding the child matters greatly.

■ ■ ■ BIOLOGICAL FOUNDATIONSOF LANGUAGE

Researchers in recent years have produced a great deal of data substantiating the critical role biology plays in language development. This section provides an overview of some of the most important work concerning the biological foundations of language.

Left-Hemisphere Involvement in Language

It has been known for a long time that particular areas of the brain are more important in language than are other areas. One form of evidence in support of this conclusion was that injuries to certain regions of the brain affected language in particular ways. In the 19th century, Carl Wernicke discovered that damage to a particular region in the left hemisphere of the brain (see Figure 7.1) resulted in verbal compre-

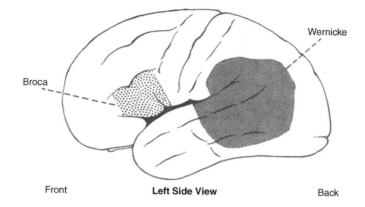

FIGURE 7.1. Side image of the left hemisphere of the brain with Wernicke's and Broca's areas labeled.

hension problems, often affecting comprehension both of speech that is heard and text that is read. The speech of patients suffering injury to Wernicke's area, however, remains relatively fluent, although some minor problems may exist such as difficulty finding the right word and adding syllables to words. The comprehension difficulties of patients with Wernicke's aphasia translate into difficulties in expressing the ideas that they have in mind (Kandel, Schwartz, & Jessel, 1995).

With damage to another part of the left hemisphere (see Figure 7.1), Broca's area (discovered in the 19th century by Paul Broca) results in a very different set of symptoms. Patients suffering Broca's aphasia comprehend, but have difficulty producing, language, either by speaking or through writing. If they can speak at all, they typically demonstrate a breakdown in syntax (Kandel et al., 1995).

Until recently, the best evidence that the left side of the brain was more responsible for language than the right side was the data on the effects of brain injuries or lesions. In recent decades, however, the development of sophisticated methods for imaging the structures and functioning of the brain has resulted in a revolution in the understanding of brain functioning (Goswami, 2004; Martin, Brust, & Hilal, 1991; Mody, 2004; Papanicolaou, Pugh, Simos, & Mencl, 2004; Shaywitz, 2003; Shaywitz & Shaywitz, 2004). Computerized tomography (CT) scanning distinguishes between the gray and the white matter in the brain, and shows many structures within the brain. Magnetic resonance imagery (MRI), a further advance in CT scanning, permits exploration of neurological structures with even higher resolution than CT scans (Mody, 2004; Papanicolaou, Pugh, Simos, & Mencl, 2004; Shaywitz, 2003; Shaywitz & Shaywitz, 2004, 2005). Although recent analyses still implicate left-side structures more than right-side structures in language functioning, language functioning involves complex articulations and interactions between parts of both the left and the right hemispheres of the brain (Eden & Zeffiro, 1998; Mody, 2004; Papanicolaou et al., 2004; Shaywitz, 2003; Shaywitz & Shaywitz, 2004; Zeffiro & Eden, 2001).

Of the new imagining procedures, positron emission tomography (PET) scans have been especially revealing about cognitive processing. With PET scanning, the subject either is injected with or inhales a substance that emits radiation. Why? Some substances that emit radiation, such as radioactive fluorine, can bind with one of the products of metabolized glucose. When neurons are active, they metabolize glucose.

The PET scan detects the accumulated radioactive glucose product, which is present in the parts of the brain that are active. The result is an image of the brain that literally glows where thinking is occurring.

What is being learned about language from use of this new imaging technology? Quite a bit. For example, studies have been conducted determining the regions of the brain activated by complex auditory input, such as a story (Mody, 2004; Phelps, Mazziotta, & Huang, 1982; Risberg, 1986; Vernon, 1991). Consistently, the left side of the brain has been more active than the right side during verbal tasks, at least when verbally normal adults have been studied (Papanicolaou et al., 2004; Shaywitz, 2003; Shaywitz & Shaywitz, 2004; Stromswald, 1995). When individuals with verbal impairment have been studied with these new imaging techniques, deviations from normality have been detected. For example, differences in structure and function (more in the left hemisphere than in the right hemisphere, but some in the right hemisphere as well) have been found in individuals with dyslexia (those who have great difficulty learning to read even with intensive instruction) as compared to normal readers (Flowers, Wood, & Naylor, 1991; Galaburda, Sherman, Rosen, Aboitz, & Geschwind, 1985; Gross-Glenn et al., 1988; Hier, LeMay, Rosenberger, & Perlo, 1978; Jernigan, Hesselink, Sowell, & Tallal, 1991; Johnson & Myklebust, 1967; Larsen, Hoien, Lundberg, & Ødegaard, 1990; Shaywitz, 2003; Shaywitz & Shaywitz, 2004; Shaywitz et al., 2002, 2003).

Genetic Studies of Language Functioning

A substantial amount of evidence suggests that individual differences in language ability are due to genetics (Stromswold, 2001). For example, the verbal abilities of identical twins are much more similar than the verbal abilities of fraternal twins (Bakwin, 1973; Gilger & Wise, 2004; Locke & Mather, 1989; Stevenson, 1992), as expected if individual differences in verbal abilities are biologically determined (see Chapter 2). Also, language disabilities tend to run in families (Eley et al., 1999; Stromswold, 1998), consistent with the conclusion that language differences are genetically determined.

Because of the great interest in reading disabilities as an educational problem, dyslexia has been studied by behavior geneticists more than other aspects of language functioning (see Chapter 2). Consistent with the hypothesis that language development is due to genetics, the co-occurrence of dyslexia in identical twins is more likely than its co-occurrence in fraternal twins (Bakwin, 1973; Dale, Dionne, Eley, & Plomin, 2000; Decker & Vandenberg, 1985; DeFries, Fulker, & LaBuda, 1987; Gilger & Wise, 2004; Pennington, 1989). Also, consistent with the genetic hypothesis, the reading abilities of adopted children and their biological parents are more highly correlated than the reading abilities of adopted children and their adopting parents (Cardon, DiLalla, Plomin, DeFries, & Fulker, 1990; Gilger & Wise, 2004). Moreover, it has been possible to locate particular genes responsible for dyslexia in some families (DeFries, Olson, Pennington, & Smith, 1991; Gilger & Wise, 2004).

Increased understanding of genetics creates difficulties for some of Chomsky's theory. For example, Chomsky's universal and invariant language acquisition device would have to be transmitted by multiple genes, with the potential for variability enormous given the many potential genetic combinations (Lieberman, 1984, 1989). The enormous variability in human language competencies (i.e., some people are more verbally facile than others), in fact, is more consistent with the conclusion that language ability varies like other genetically determined characteristics (Gilger &

Wise, 2004) than it is consistent with Chomsky's position that human language capabilities are generally invariant.

Chomsky also believed that language was "uniquely human," a claim that is not well supported. Evolution is gradual, and differences between species with respect to communications and symbolic skills tend to reflect this gradualness (Parker & Gibson, 1990). For example, research has established that the great apes share language and cognitive skills with humans. Great apes other than humans use categories to some extent (Matsuzawa, 1990), can learn to use sign language with some sophistication (Miles, 1990), and may be able to invent grammatical rules (Greenfield & Savage-Rumbaugh, 1990). Moreover, some evidence indicates that human speech and neural speech perception mechanisms continue to evolve (Lieberman, 1984, 1989). That said, no species approaches human communication competence, as even simple syntax is acquired slowly by nonhuman primates and only by means of great teaching effort by humans (Kako, 1999; Tomasello, 1994). The same holds for the language of other animals (e.g., dolphins) based on what is now known (Herman, 2002; Herman & Uyeyama, 1999).

Critical Periods for Language Development

Recall from Chapter 2 that some acquisitions, such as some visual capabilities, occur during critical periods, or they do not develop at all. That is, the human nervous system is programmed to be sensitive to certain types of input only at certain points in the life cycle. If the stimulation that is required to develop the competency in question is experienced during the critical period, the acquisition occurs. Otherwise the potential for acquiring the competency is lost.

Lenneberg (1967) proposed that there was a critical period for language, believing that language acquisition needed to occur before adolescence if it was to occur at all. For example, occasionally children are discovered who have been reared without exposure to language. These children, termed **feral children**, are typically the victims of abusive parents who have locked them away. When such children are discovered by age 7, the development of language is more likely than when they are discovered later (Skuse, 1984). Consider another example. Some deaf children are exposed to sign language from birth, whereas others experience sign language for the first time sometime during childhood. Complete language functioning using signs is more certain in children who are exposed to signing from birth. Consistent with the critical period hypothesis, for children whose first immersion in sign language is during childhood, the earlier the child begins immersion, the more complete the sign language competence in adulthood (Newport, 1990). The language development of deaf children is described more completely later in this chapter.

The acquisition of a second language also appears to occur more completely during a sensitive period. Johnson and Newport (1989) studied native Korean and Chinese adults who immigrated to the United States and found a strong correlation between the age at which people immigrated and their syntactical competence in English: Those who arrived between 3 and 7 years of age were more competent in English syntax than those who arrived between 8 and 10, who were more competent than those arriving between 11 and 15, who were more competent than those arriving at an older age. In general, the research evidence is consistent with Lenneberg's position that language proficiency is more certain if acquisition of a language begins early in life. It is unclear, however, whether the critical period for second-language acquisition is the first 5 or so years of life or the first 12 or so years of life, or even the first 20 years of life (Birdsong, 1999, 2005). Yes, acquiring a second language is easier and more certain in many ways during childhood than during adolescence (Snow, 2002). Those starting to learn a language earlier are more likely to attain native-speaker competence. But the ability to acquire a second language certainly does not disappear with the arrival of adulthood. Adults can learn much more of a second language in the first year or two of exposure than children (McLaughlin, 1978; Snow & Hoefnagel-Hohle, 1978). Bilingualism is discussed more fully later in this chapter.

Speed of Acquisition Relative to the Amount of Input for Language Development

One of the strongest arguments that biology plays a large role in language acquisition is that children acquire language with relatively little intervention. As is discussed in the next section, infants are sensitive to the particular sounds in the language they are hearing and soon begin to produce those sounds. By the end of the first year of life, infants begin to learn some vocabulary words with one exposure. Children start using syntax in the second year of life, making great progress even though they could not have experienced examples of all the subtleties that apply to syntactic constructions. Many who study child language believe that children's ability to learn language given relatively little input is proof that powerful biological mechanisms are responsible for language acquisitions (Maratsos, 1989; Meisel, 1995; Pinker, 1994). As we will see, children's language tends to be more competent when they are immersed in rich linguistic worlds, surrounded by adults who talk with them a great deal.

■ ■ ■ LANGUAGE ACQUISITION

Language acquisition is complicated in that children's comprehension and production of language involves a variety of skills, with a large body of research on each of the relevant skills (Hoff, 2001). Research on language acquisition can be organized into study of the various language competencies, which are reviewed briefly in this section.

Speech perception refers to the hearing and interpretation of speech that is encountered. Although speech perception is studied across the lifespan, work in infancy has received the most attention.

Speech production and phonological development research focuses on when and how humans can make particular speech sounds. Again, speech production and phonological development during early language development has been of special interest.

Lexical development refers to the learning of words and their meanings.

Semantic development includes lexical development but is also concerned with children's production and understanding of meanings expressed in combinations of words.

Grammatical and syntactical development focus on when and how children can combine individual words into higher order constructions, such as phrases and sentences.

Pragmatic development refers to the increasing ability to use speech and language in a variety of situations. One example is the study of children's conversational skills.

Metalinguistic development refers to children's increasing awareness and understanding of language. One aspect of metalinguistic awareness that is particularly relevant to educators is phonemic awareness (i.e., the awareness that words are composed of sounds blended together), which is a critical competency for success in beginning reading.

Cutting across many of these areas of inquiry about language is a fundamental distinction between comprehension, imitation, and generative production of language. Although there are exceptions to the general rule, typically comprehension precedes imitation, which precedes generative production (Bates, Bretherton, & Snyder, 1988). For example, infants can discriminate particular sounds in their native language long before they can imitate them or generate them on their own. Many words can be comprehended before a child uses them. Thus, although some 16-month-olds can comprehend more than 300 single words, they generally tend to use far fewer words in their utterances. Children's language production provides an underestimation of what they know about language.

Prelinguistic Development: Speech Perception and Production

A great deal of language development occurs before babies can comprehend meaning from language. Researchers have focused on infants' abilities to recognize the basic sounds in their language and infants' abilities to produce those sounds.

Speech Perception

Babies are hearing speech sounds even before they are born, which probably accounts for their very early discrimination of their mother's voice from other female voices (DeCasper & Fifer, 1980; Gibson & Spelke, 1983). Moreover, even as early as a few days of age, babies seem to be able to discriminate between the language they have been immersed in during the first few days of their lives (and during the prenatal period) and other languages. For example, French 4-day-old infants can discriminate French from Russian and prefer French, and 2-day-old infants who were immersed in Spanish could discriminate Spanish from English and prefer Spanish (Mehler et al., 1988; Moon, Panneton-Cooper, & Fifer, 1993).

During the first month of life babies can discriminate a number of the most basic sounds in their native language from one another. These most basic sounds that combine to form words are called **phonemes**. See Table 7.1 for a list of the 20 phonemic vowel sounds and 24 phonemic consonant sounds found in most English accents. (These phonemes are particularly relevant to future primary-grade teachers since these sounds are the ones that beginning readers must learn to decode from letters and letter combinations and then blend in order to pronounce printed words.)

How do researchers know that babies can make discriminations between sounds? In many studies, children have been given a nipple to suck that is rigged to equipment that records the rate and intensity of the baby's sucking. When a sound is presented to the child, for example, the "pa" sound, sucking at first increases in frequency and amplitude. Then, as the baby gets used to the sound, the sucking gradually decreases. Once sucking is slow and steady, a new sound is presented, perhaps "ba." Babies as young as 1-month-old will increase their rate of sucking when such a change occurs, thus demonstrating that they can discriminate the basic sounds in human languages (Eimas, Siqueland, Jusczyk, & Vigorito, 1971; Kent & Miolo, 1995). Between 1 and 4

TABLE 7.1. Vowel and Consonant Phonemes in English

Consonant phoneme sounds	Vowel phonemes
"p" sound in *pie* and *up*	Vowel sound in *sea, feet*
"b" sound in *by* and *ebb*	Vowel sound in *him, big*
"t" sound in *tie* and *at*	Vowel sound in *get, fetch*
"d" sound in *die* and *odd*	Vowel sound in *sat, hand*
"k" sound in *coo* and *ache*	Vowel sound in *sun, son*
"g" sound in *go* and *egg*	Vowel sound in *calm, are*
"ch" sound in *chew* and *each*	Vowel sound in *dog, cough*
"j/g" sound in *jaw* and *edge*	Vowel sound in *cord, more*
"f" sound in *fee* and *off*	Vowel sound in *put, wolf*
"v/f" sound in *view* and *of*	Vowel sound in *soon, do*
"th" sound in *thigh* and *oath*	Vowel sound in *bird, her*
"th" sound in *they* and *booth*	Vowel sound in *the, sofa*
"s" sound in *so* and *us*	Vowel sound in *ape, waist*
"z" sound in *zoo* and *ooze*	Vowel sound in *time, cry*
"sh" sound in *shoe* and *ash*	Vowel sound in *boy, toy*
"g" sound in *genre* and *rouge*	Vowel sound in *so, road*
"h" sound in *he*	Vowel sound in *out, how*
"m" sound in *me* and *am*	Vowel sound in *deer, here*
"n" sound in *no* and *in*	Vowel sound in *care, air*
"ng" sound in *hang*	Vowel sound in *poor, sure*
"l" sound in *lie* and *eel*	
"r" sound in *row* and *ear*	
"w" sound in *way*	
"y" sound in *you*	

Note. Based on Crystal (1995).

months, babies' sensitivities to these sounds increase further. They can discriminate between the same vowel said by different voices and can recognize the same phoneme even if spoken at a different speed (Jusczyk, Pisoni, & Mullenix, 1997).

Not only can babies learn much from the speech sound, they pay more attention to speech than other sounds (Vouloumanos & Werker, 2004). Thus the speech surrounding a baby has a profound effect on the child's ability to perceive sound. Six- to 8-month-old infants can discriminate between phonemes that occur in a foreign language but not their own language, but older infants, 10-month-olds, lose the ability to discriminate phonemic distinctions that occur in foreign languages but not in their own language (Jones, 2004; Werker & Pegg, 1992). Some evidence indicates that the loss of the ability to discriminate foreign phonemes from one another occurs even earlier (Mehler & Christophe, 1995). Thus babies seem to be born with the ability to discriminate many more phonemes than the ones used in their language. If the sounds do not occur in the language surrounding them, they lose their ability to discriminate them (Werker, 1995).

In addition to the sounds themselves, babies are sensitive to the rhythm or tonal structure of language. By 4–6 months of age, babies prefer to listen to speech that conforms to the pause patterns that occur in their native language (Fernald & Kuhl, 1987). In the Fernald and Kuhl (1987) study, babies were trained to turn their heads in order to activate a speaker. The babies were more likely to turn their heads for language rhythmically consistent with the language they were experiencing at home. The babies were also more likely to turn for language offered in a high-pitched tone and musical in its rhythm. That is, they preferred **motherese**, the high-pitched, sing-song speech mothers often use when interacting with their infants (Fernald, 1991). Motherese is simplified syntactically relative to the speech a mother uses when talking to adults. Such simplification makes it easier for children to understand the mother's meaning as well as to attend to the language used by the mother. Just as is the case for discrimination of phonemes, babies seem to lose the ability to discriminate between pausal patterns that do not occur in their native language (Hirsh-Pasek & Golikoff, 1991). Less than a year of immersion in a language community profoundly affects a baby's speech recognition abilities and preferences (Aslin, Jurczyk, & Pisoni, 1998).

Speech perception during infancy plays an important role in subsequent language development. The 6-month-old infant who is more sensitive to speech sounds becomes the 2-year-old who knows more words, speaks more words, and generally understands better what is being said (Tsao, Liu, & Kuhl, 2004). That, of course, makes a great deal of sense, because even during the first year of life infants seem to be able to pick out words in sound streams based on pause and stress cues (Aslin et al., 1998). Learning the perpetual characteristics that define a word begins early.

Speech Production: Babbling

Babbling begins a few months into life and continues into toddlerhood (Mowrer, 1980; Rothganger, 2003), with 2 months of age often cited as the onset of babbling. The earliest babbling, primarily a vowel sound like "uuuu" or "aaaa," is often referred to by mothers as "cooing." In the next few months, the vowel sounds give way to babbling that is filled with consonant and vowel combinations. The first consonants to be combined with vowels often are ones that are formed in the back of the mouth, such as the "g" and "k" sounds. Common combinations in the babbling of English-surrounded 6-month-olds are the "da," "ba," "wa," "deh," "ha," and "heh" sounds (Vihman, 1992). These sounds are repeated and repeated, as if the child is practicing them. The content of babbling is affected by the language the child experiences. By the end of the first year, the sounds that are more frequent in the surrounding culture definitely are more frequent in baby babbling (Boysson-Bardies, Halle, Sagart, & Durand, 1989; Boysson-Bardies et al., 1992; Oller & Eilers, 1988). A baby's babbling, however, plays a role in this shaping, since babbling increases parental attention and communication efforts. When the baby babbles, parents talk back, providing the baby with a richer language environment (Locke, 2002).

Semantic Development

Most children begin to talk at about 1 year of age, using single words as their first utterances. At first, children typically use only a few select words, adding a few new ones each month (Barrett, 1989). The rate of word learning during this early phase varies widely. For example, whereas some 16-month-olds will use 150 or more single words, others are using only five (Bates, Dale, & Thal, 1995).

During this one-word stage, children will use the single words to express meaning. For many children, most of the single words will be nouns, with nouns referring to familiar objects and objects important to the child especially favored (Goldfield & Reznick, 1990; Hart, 1991; Nelson, 1973). When nouns are more prevalent than other utterances, the child is said to have a **referential style**. That is, the child's utterances generally refer to objects (Bates et al., 1988). In contrast, other children use many one-word expressions of emotion, feeling, and action (such as, "Hi!," "Up," and "Giddeeup"). These children are said to have an **expressive style**. Bates and colleagues (1988) observed that exhibiting the referential style between ages 1 and 2 was associated with more advanced language development later.

Although single-word acquisition seems to be slow at first, toward the end of the second year the pace rapidly increases for many children (Goldfield & Reznick, 1990). Throughout much of childhood, acquisition of single vocabulary words is rapid (Anglin, 1993; Beck & McKeown, 1991; Biemiller & Slonim, 2001; Miller, 1977). How rapid? A conservative estimate is that by the end of first grade, children know 6,000 words well enough that they can recognize them; by fifth grade, the figure climbs to 20,000 (Anglin, 1993). During kindergarten and the preschool years, children learn about three or four new words a day. Between first and fifth grades, they are learning nine or 10 new words a day. An important distinction is between words and *root words*, with root words being those words that expand into whole families of words. So, *child* is a root word for *childhood*, *children*, and *childish*. The number of root words acquired increases dramatically during the elementary-school years, although there are individual differences between children (Biemiller & Slonim, 2001). Interestingly, the acquisition of root words appears to be orderly, with some words reliably acquired by younger children (e.g., *fish, flood*) and others more likely to be acquired only by older children (e.g., *sliver, knoll*).

The rate of vocabulary growth varies widely, often reflecting the actions of the child. One of the best ways to increase vocabulary is to read more (Stanovich & Cunningham, 1993). To appreciate the lexical advantages that active readers create for themselves, consider the following numbers generated by Nagy and Anderson (1984): A middle-school student who is not motivated to read may read 100,000 words a year. An average-achieving, average-motivated middle-school reader might read 1,000,000 words a year. In contrast, the best and most voracious middle-school readers will read between 10,000,000 and 50,000,000 words a year! Some children's vocabularies increase more rapidly than other children's vocabularies because they choose to read more.

A number of explanations have been proposed for how children learn vocabulary. Most vocabulary words are learned incidentally through experiencing them in contexts, both social contexts and text contexts (Sternberg, 1987). This is challenging since children often cannot discern the meaning of novel words from *context clues* (Nagy, Anderson, & Herman, 1987; Nagy, Herman, & Anderson, 1985). For example, when Schatz and Baldwin (1986) had high-school students read difficult text, they found little evidence that the students understood the meanings of new vocabulary words encountered in these texts. Contexts that provide more clues about meaning lead to more certain learning of novel vocabulary, and high-ability children are more likely to learn vocabulary from context than low-ability children (Herman, Anderson, Pearson, & Nagy, 1987; McKeown, 1985; Van Daalen-Kapteijns & Elshout-

Mohr, 1981). Beyond reading, parental interactions seem to matter a lot, as does learning of vocabulary from television. When children are immersed in vocabulary, they will acquire many words (Biemiller, 2003).

One reason is that sometimes words are learned via *fast mapping* (Carey, 1978). That is, with one exposure in context, the child understands the word somewhat, enough to recognize its meaning later in a less explicit context. For example, the child who hears a teacher refer to a "lavender" shirt may be able to select the correct color a few days later from a choice of four colors (Behrend, Scofield, & Kleinknecht, 2001; Waxman & Booth, 2000).

Fast mapping certainly does not lead to complete knowledge of a word. Complete knowledge (*extended mapping* to use Carey's [1978] term) is acquired over exposure in a number of contexts. A number of researchers besides Carey have offered evidence that children can and do refine their understandings of word meanings as they process words in multiple contexts (McGregor, 2004; McKeown, 1985; Werner & Kaplan, 1952). It is not understood exactly how children extract meaning from context, but we do know that multiple exposures to a word are necessary for a rich understanding of the word's meaning. As part of learning words from context, children get better at figuring out what words must mean by attending to meaning clues in sentences and paragraphs as well as by knowing the meanings of more root words, prefixes, and endings as their experiences with words increase (Carlisle, 2004; Sternberg & Powell, 1983). The more children read, the more they are exposed to new vocabulary in a variety of contexts, and the more opportunities they have to infer word meanings.

Since complete understanding is unlikely to occur from exposure to a word in a single context, should vocabulary be directly taught? An argument against direct teaching is that it is like attempting to fill a swimming pool with an eyedropper. Adults know so many vocabulary words, over 100,000, that direct teaching seems impractical (Nagy & Anderson, 1984). Others believe that the number of words known by literate adults has been overestimated and that the number of different words in English that need to be known is not overwhelming, perhaps more like 15,000–20,000 altogether (root words). Based on this root-word estimate, direct instruction of vocabulary over the 12 years of schooling might have quite an impact on semantic development (d'Anna, Zechmeister, & Hall, 1991), with each root word taught providing a foundation for understanding the meaning of multiple additional words. Does teaching vocabulary to children increase their reading comprehension? After reviewing all the studies related to this question, Beck and McKeown (1991) reported that sometimes teaching vocabulary increased comprehension and sometimes it did not. They noticed that comprehension increases were more likely in studies in which students not only learned new vocabulary but were provided opportunities to make deep and extensive connections between vocabulary words and their definitions. Simply memorizing new words and their meanings was not effective in promoting comprehension unless teaching also included opportunities to use and experience the words in a variety of contexts (Durso & Coggins, 1991).

As described in Chapter 4, children do not learn words as isolated bits of knowledge, but rather they develop semantic networks relating the concepts and words that they know. From infancy, children are learning how the vocabulary and concepts they know relate to one another. Children often relate words to one another in ways that are different from the ways favored by adults—for example, by using thematic relations rather than the categories adults use (Bruner, Olver, & Greenfield, 1966; Kagan et al., 1972). Do you recall the example presented in Chapter 4 of how young children sometimes group objects by themes rather than by categories? When given a pile of plastic animals and play fruit, rather than grouping the objects as animals and fruits, they come up with interesting little stories (e.g., monkeys eating bananas; elephants and giraffes going together because they live in the same house at the zoo; a bear eating apples, oranges, and grapes, consistent with the child's observation that the bears at the zoo are fed fruit). Themes and categories are both salient in children's semantic relationships.

Children's incomplete understanding of the words they "know" has been consistently noted in the literature. In particular, children often *underextend* vocabulary. If they know that the word "dog" refers to the greyhound that lives at their house, they might use the word *dog* when they see other greyhounds but not when they see other breeds of dogs. Similarly, children sometimes *overextend* vocabulary, with some children sometimes referring to a variety of four-legged animals as dogs, perhaps deer, cows, and pigs (Bloom, 1973; Clark, 1973). The presence of underextensions and overextensions in children's language simply reinforces the point that it takes a while for children to acquire complete understanding of the words they are learning. All that said, the evidence is that teaching children vocabulary does, in fact, have a positive impact, including on their reading comprehension (Kamil, 2004).

Syntactic Development

Roger Brown identified five early stages of syntactical development in his influential book, *A First Language: The Early Stages* (1973), inspiring a great deal of research. Before we present these stages, we will define some terms. **Morphemes** are the smallest units of language that convey meaning. There are two types of morphemes. *Unbound morphemes* can stand alone; that is, they are words. For example, *dog, fire, tractor,* and *stand* are all single, unbound morphemes (i.e., these are all *root words* in the way Biemiller and Slonim [2001] defined root words). In contrast, *bound morphemes* cannot stand alone; bound morphemes include prefixes, suffixes, possessives, and plurals. The length of children's utterances are calculated in morphemes, with an important measure being the **mean length of utterance** (MLU).

Roger Brown (1973) portrayed the morphemic development of three children: Adam, Eve, and Sarah. The children's MLUs as a function of age are displayed in Figure 7.2.

First, note the individual differences in the language development of the children. Eve's language development was considerably in advance of Sarah's and Adam's as indicated by examining the MLUs for each child at 28 months of age. Eve's MLU is more than 4; Adam's and Sarah's MLUs are closer to 2. Some 2-year-olds have more complex language than some 3-year-olds, as was the case for Eve compared to Adam and Sarah. The mean length of utterance and the structural and linguistic complexity used in utterances increases with each new stage of syntactic development. The stages are described as follows:

Stage 1

Once children have a speaking vocabulary of 50–100 individual words, their language changes dramatically. The first syntactic stage begins, with this stage charac-

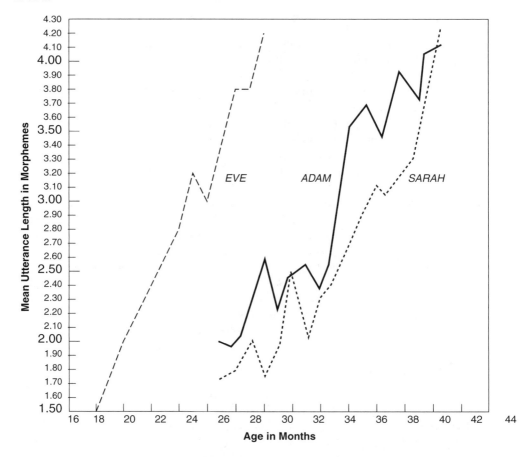

FIGURE 7.2. Children's mean length of utterance (MLU) as a function of age. From Brown (1973). Copyright 1973 by Harvard University Press. Reprinted by permission.

terized by two-word utterances, such as "See ball," "Two ball," and "Doggie run." Because Stage-1 speech is like a telegram in that it contains only important words conveying a lot of meaning, Brown (1965; Brown & Bellugi, 1964) referred to it as the period of **telegraphic speech**. Notably, the two words are not in random order, but rather in the order that would be expected in an adult sentence, except that less important morphemes are not present.

Braine (1963) noted that many times the first word in two-word utterances is an action word (i.e., a verb, such as *see* or *go*) or a preposition (e.g., *off*) or a possessive (e.g., *my*). The second word is usually a noun. Braine termed the first words "pivots" because they almost never occur alone and do not occur with other pivots, only with nouns. Many pivot-open constructions, such as "No mama," "Off bib," "More cookie," and "Alldone juice," are possible during the two-word stage (Braine, 1976). The constructions that children use during Stage 1 reflect individual differences. For example, some children use many more pivot-open relationships; some use pronouns and others do not. Yet children in Stage 1 have meanings that they intend to communicate with some elementary rules for translating those meanings into utterances. Those elementary rules are the beginning of syntax.

Stage 2

Many Stage-2 utterances are still two words, but sometimes simple, functional morphemes (e.g., prepositions, such as *in* and *on*) are added. One of the more striking phenomena in this period is the overgeneralization of syntactical rules, sometimes referred to as **overregularization**. For example, even children who have previously used the irregular past tense of go correctly ("went") may begin to say "goed" once they acquire the regular past tense rule (Marcus et al., 1992). For most children, the rate of overregularization is typically quite low, though some children produce many more overregularizations than others (Kuczaj, 1977).

Stage 3

In this stage (which occurs for many children during the third year of life), children begin to use negatives in simple sentences, sometimes with auxiliary verbs missing (e.g., "There no doggies," and "I not eating"). They also begin to form simple questions. Sometimes questions simply involve raising the voice near the end of a statement ("Doggie eat the food?"); sometimes questions involve the *wh-* elements (Who, What, Where, When, and Why). Often, the word order is not quite right in early questions. For example, it is not unusual for the Stage-3 child simply to place a *wh-*element in front of a declarative statement, such as "Why doggie sit in house?" and "Where Mommy sleeping?" During Stage 3, children also begin to utter imperatives ("Go to house doggie!").

Stages 4 and 5

Syntax begins to get much more complex, with the beginning of compound (e.g., sentences connected by *and*) and complex sentences. Passive constructions also begin to enter the child's speech. DeVillers and deVilliers (1992, pp. 379–380) provided some examples of children's speech in these stages:

> The teddy and the doll are going to play.
> I didn't catch it but Teddy did.
> After I clean my teeth can I have a story?
> Where did you say you put my doll?
> It was the man that the dog bit.

The typical 4-year-old's syntax is much more complex than the typical 2-year-old's syntax. Even so, children's syntactic skills are anything but complete by 4 years of age, although their errors always represent the use of syntactic rules. Sentences like the following, which reflect a great deal of understanding about the rules of syntax, are common among 4-year-olds (Crystal, 1987, p. 243). Each of these sentences is correct, except for the application (or lack of it) of one syntactic rule:

> You bettern't do that.
> Are there much toys in the cupboard?
> It just got brokened.
> Are we going on the bus home?

In summary, during the first 4 years of life, children utter progressively longer utterances. With increasing length, meaning is more completely expressed in the utterances, as indexed by the number of morphemes in utterances (MLUs). Moreover, sentences become more syntactically complex, with children gradually using the syntactical devices required to form compound and complex utterances, questions, passives, and imperatives. The acquisition of syntactic complexities is orderly, with Stromswald (1995) reporting that children acquire 11 complex syntactic structures in an invariant order. All of this implies a natural unfolding in normal language development, but direct instruction can also influence the process. See the Applying Developmental Theory to Educational Contexts special feature (Box 7.1) for a discussion of the role learning principles can play in language acquisition.

Pragmatics

Anyone who has ever tried to converse with a 2-year-old knows that it is challenging. Why is that so? Conversation requires connecting what you are saying with what the other person is saying. Thus, during conversation, people respond to the comment

---

Applying Developmental Theory to Educational Contexts

BOX 7.1. The Role of Learning Principles in Language Acquisition

Can principles of social learning theory (review Chapter 5), such as observation, imitation, and reinforcement, be used to facilitate language acquisition? The answer appears to be yes. For example, I. Brown (1976) established that nursery-school children could induce the grammatical rules governing the production of passive constructions if they were presented with a sample of passive sentences accompanied by enactments of the actions specified by the sentences. After hearing 50 such sentences with enactments, the children were able to understand passive constructions involving different materials than had been used during the 50-sentence training. In fact, presentation of the sentences with enactments produced about 80% correct comprehension compared to 50% comprehension for controls who did not receive the 50-sentence training. What was most impressive were the large gains due to exposure and enactment by children who had very little understanding of passives at the beginning of the study.

Parent–child interactions also can have implications for language learning. Parents often simplify speech when they talk with young children (i.e., they use motherese). If they also recast and expand the utterances of their children, they increase the likelihood that their children will induce important language rules (Ochs & Schieffelin, 1995). For example, when a child says, "Mommy sock," Mommy might reply with a recasting or expansion such as, "Yes, Mommy wears socks." The child's exclamation of "Doggie runs" might be expanded by a parent to something like "The dog is running fast." Positively reinforcing children to use language increases their competent use of it (Whitehurst & Valdez-Menchaca, 1988).

The discovery that learning mechanisms such as reinforcement and imitation can affect language acquisition has had a profound influence on the development of interventions for children whose language is not as advanced as that of their age-mates (Bos & Vaughn, 1991; I. Brown, 1979; Schiefelbusch & Bricker, 1979; Wiig, 1992). Such interventions typically involve exposing children to many examples of language structures (e.g., syntactical constructions) that the children need to acquire, sometimes explicitly reinforcing children for using these constructions (Fey et al., 1995). The theory, supported by a growing database, is that children experiencing language difficulties can extract the rules of language from exposure to multiple models of the targeted language rules, just as social learning theory would suggest.

just directed at them, often offering a response that comments on the last remark. This new remark often implies an opportunity for a response from the partner in the conversation. Although children as young as 18 months old sometimes exhibit rudimentary turn-taking skills by looking at another person when they expect them to talk (Rutter & Durkin, 1987), a typical 2-year-old's response to the remark of another is simply to repeat it (Bloom, Rocissano, & Hood, 1976; Gallagher, 1981). Conversations involving a number of turns are much more likely with 3- and 4-year-olds than with 2-year-olds. The older the preschooler, the more likely the conversation will be rich in requests, elaborative commentary on previous remarks, and clarifications (Goelman, 1986; Shatz, 1983). In short, over the preschool years, children learn how to carry on conversations, how to talk about things, and how to relate their memories and perspectives to others. See the Considering Interesting Questions special feature (Box 7.2) for a discussion of the impact language development has upon memory development.

The ability to understand the perspective of others contributes to the development of the ability to communicate with others in dialogues. Piaget believed that children communicated poorly because they could not understand the perspectives of others—that is, they were egocentric (Piaget, 1926; see also Chapter 3). For example, Krauss and Glucksberg (1969) asked 4- and 5-year-olds to provide clues to another child about the appearance of strange-looking objects, so that the other child could select the object from a group of strange-looking objects. Consistent with Piaget's ideas about children's limitations as communicators, the children were not very good at this task. This task, however, is very unusual and unfamiliar to children, which might account for the children's communications shortcomings in the study.

Researchers who have studied preschoolers' communications with tasks and in settings more familiar to them have provided evidence that children's communication skills are much more adept than Piaget believed. For example, preschoolers can look beyond the words for the meaning of an utterance. They understand that intended meaning can be expressed in a number of ways and that intended meaning is not always equivalent to the literal meaning of utterances (Garvey, 1974). Thus, by 4 years of age, children understand that, following a request for a snack, the following responses mean "No": "You've just had one" and "It will be dinner soon" (Crystal, 1995, p. 287).

In addition, preschoolers can make adjustments, reflecting understanding of the cognitive skills and perspectives of others. For example, when 4-year-olds were asked to describe a toy, either for a 2-year-old or for an adult, they spoke differently. When they addressed the 2-year-old, their utterances were shorter and simpler compared to the statements intended for adults (Shatz & Gelman, 1973; see also Tomasello & Mannle, 1985; Weeks, 1971).

In summary, conversations are more complete with increasing age during the preschool years for a number of reasons. Yes, the comments made by children are longer and more complex, both syntactically and semantically. More than that, however, when older preschoolers converse with others, their comments take into account the conversational context and the perspectives of the individual with whom they are talking.

Metalinguistic Awareness

Just as *metacognition* is cognition about thinking (see Chapter 4), *metalinguistics* is thinking about language. It is knowledge about and awareness of language. Metalinguistic theorists (e.g., Gombert, 1992) believe that metalinguistic awareness is crit-

BOX 7.2. How Does Language Affect Long-Term Memory?

For a century (Dudycha & Dudycha, 1941; Howe & Courage, 1993; Wetzler & Sweeney, 1986) there has been little dispute that adults cannot remember what happened to them during the first few years of their lives, a phenomenon referred to as "infantile amnesia." One explanation of increasing memory for particular episodes after the first 3 or 4 years of life is tied to increasing communication skills during the preschool years (Fivush, 1994; Miller, 1994; Nelson, 1993a, 1993b). That is, children need to learn how to talk about the experiences they have had before they can form enduring memories of these events.

Adults spend a great deal of time talking with their children about things that happened to them, assisting children in learning how to be "tellers of their memories." Hudson (1990) described her own daughter's experiences in talking about the past and how those experiences translated into increasing ability to describe events in her life. Their dialogues were filled with maternal questions and responses from Rachel, such as in the following *Example*:

MOM: Did you like the apartment at the beach?
RACHEL: Yeah, And I have fun in the, in the, in the water.
MOM: You had fun in the water?
RACHEL: Yeah, I come to the ocean.
MOM: You went to the ocean?
RACHEL: Yeah.
MOM: Did you play in the ocean?
RACHEL: And my sandals off.
MOM: You took your sandals off?
RACHEL: And my jamas off.
MOM: And your jamas off. And what did you wear to the beach?
RACHEL: I wear hot cocoa shirt.
MOM: Oh, your cocoa shirt, yeah. And your bathing suit?
RACHEL: Yeah. And my cocoa shirt.
MOM: Yeah. Did we walk to the beach?
RACHEL: Yeah.
MOM: Who went to the beach?
RACHEL: Mommy and Daddy.
MOM: Did you play in the sand?
RACHEL: Yeah.
MOM: What did you do in the sand?
RACHEL: Build sand castles.
MOM: Yeah, and did you go in the water?
RACHEL: [no response]
MOM: Who went in the water with you?
RACHEL: Daddy and Mommy.
MOM: Right. Did the big waves splash you?
RACHEL: Yeah.

Through such dialogues, Rachel learned how to talk about things that had happened to her. Consistent with the Vygotskian perspective (Vygotsky, 1978; Chapter 6), Hudson (1990) concluded that the important thinking skill of being able to describe events in one's life develops through social interaction. When the child cannot recall an event, the mother asks questions, providing a scaffold for the child's recall of the event. As the child becomes increasingly familiar with what should be told in recalling an event, and in fact begins to recall with greater completeness, adult scaffolding in the form of leading questions is reduced. Learning how to engage in dialogue is critical in the development of long-term memories, and the amount and quality of adult–child interaction about events is related to a child's ability to recall events (Engel, 1986; Nelson, 1993a, 1993b; Pillemer & White, 1989; Ratner, 1980, 1984; Reese, Haden, & Fivush, 1993 Tessler, 1986).

ical for the regulated use of language. For example, an accomplished author knows a great deal about how words work, how syntax can be adapted depending on linguistic context, and what is required for a written piece to communicate to various audiences.

Perhaps the most important finding with respect to development of *metasyntax* is that by the end of the preschool years children can discriminate some syntactically correct sentences from incorrect ones, something that is impossible for 2-year-olds to do (deVilliers & deVilliers, 1972; Smith & Tager-Flusberg, 1982). A striking *metalexical/metasemantic* outcome reported, thus far, is that children's understanding of the nature of a word increases dramatically between 5 and 7 years of age (Bowey & Tunmer, 1984). For example, by 6–7, children can segment some simple sentences into component words, although this ability continues to develop throughout the elementary-school years (Berthoud-Papandropoulou, 1980). From 4–8 years of age, children are becoming aware of how language must vary with social context. For example, they are beginning to understand contexts that require more polite language versus contexts that permit impolite language (Bates, 1976; Gleason, 1973).

Without a doubt, however, the most educationally important research on metalinguistic development is in the area of *metaphonological* development: Reading researchers have determined that **phonemic awareness**, which is awareness that words are composed of separable sounds (i.e., phonemes) and that phonemes are combined to say words, is a critical competency in learning to read. Think about it. Is the teacher's teaching of letter–sound associations going to make any sense if the child does not know that words are composed of such sounds blended together? This is a critical understanding for beginning reading instruction to make any sense at all. A related metalinguistic competency is understanding the *alphabetic principle* that the letters in words represent sounds (Adams, 1990), which goes hand in hand with phonemic awareness.

Phonemic awareness is one of the best predictors of success in early reading in school (Adams, 1990; Bond & Dykstra, 1967; Scarborough, 1989; Troia, 2004). Children who fail to learn to read during the first several years of schooling often lack phonemic awareness (Pennington, Groisser, & Welsh, 1993; Stanovich, 1986, 1988). Children who lack phonemic awareness have a difficult time learning to spell and developing understanding of letter–sound relationships (Griffith, 1991; Juel, Griffith, & Gough, 1986). Poor phonemic awareness at 4–6 years of age predicts reading difficulties throughout the elementary-school years (Juel, 1988; Stuart & Masterson, 1992). Poor readers at all age levels often are less phonemically aware than same-age good readers (Bruck, 1992; Pennington, Van Orden, Smith, Green, & Haith, 1990; Pratt & Brady, 1988). Just as development of phonemic awareness leads to improved reading, reading increases phonemic awareness (Perfetti, 1992; Perfetti, Beck, Bell, & Hughes, 1987; Wimmer, Landerl, Linortner, & Hummer, 1991). As summarized by Goswami and Bryant (1992), the research findings on phonemic awareness reveals "a strong (and consistent) relationship between children's ability to disentangle and to assemble the sounds in words and their progress in learning to read" (p. 49).

In normal readers, for phonemic awareness to develop, formal instruction in reading seems essential in that only a very small proportion of children develop phonemic awareness in the absence of such instruction (Lundberg, 1991). Notably, the one out-of-school literacy experience that predicts phonemic awareness is parental teaching of letters and their sounds (Crain-Thoreson & Dale, 1992). Many parents, however, do not engage in such teaching, so instruction that impacts phonemic awareness typically occurs in school. Phonemic awareness in 5- and 6-year-olds can be increased with instruction that heightens children's attention to the component sounds in words (Adams, 1990). See the Applying Development Theory to Educational Contexts special feature (Box 7.3) for a discussion of the importance of providing children experiences that develop phonemic awareness.

Concluding Comment on First-Language Development

The progress in language development during the first few years of life is impressive. During the first 6 months, children are already becoming sensitive to the sounds represented in the language surrounding them, as reflected in their babbling. In the second 6 months, babbling increasingly sounds like speech and begins to take on the rhythm of sentences. By the end of the first year, children are saying their first words, sometimes making two-word utterances. In the second year of life, children acquire many words and two-word sentences become diverse and common. Children are understanding a lot and expressing much more meaning than during the first year. In the third year, sentences get longer and more complex. Morphemes such as plurals, some past-tense markers, and *a* and *the* begin to be used. Children are better able to communicate their intentions. In the fourth year of life, sentence constructions become more complex still, with children asking questions, using negation in sentences, and often using imperatives ("Give that to me!"). They use several sentences together to express meaning, with continued growth in vocabulary. In the fifth year of life, children's communications become more sophisticated still. They adjust their speech depending on the audience and situation and are more aware of whether or not they are communicating well. Of course, language development continues for years beyond the preschool years, with the syntactical competencies of the 11-year-old far exceeding those of the 6-year-old, and many college students still learning how to wordsmith as they write, including learning how to combine sentences so they efficiently convey intended messages. Vocabulary acquisition is a life-span process, with increases in vocabulary possible even for the 90-year-old whose mind remains active. Indeed, language continues to develop in the adult years (Foley & Thompson, 2003).

None of this happens unless children are exposed to language—a lot of language. Sadly, many children do not experience frequent, high-quality language during their preschool years. Their parents do not engage them in frequent conversations and they attend preschools or daycare where conversations with adults are rare. On average, the language development of such children is impaired relative to children who experience rich conversations in their families and preschool experiences (Dickinson, McCabe, Clark-Chiarelli, & Wolf, 2004; Hart & Risley, 1995, 1999; Hoff & Naigles, 2002; Huttenlocher, Haight, Bryk, Seltzer, & Lyons, 1991; Huttenlocher, Vasilyeva, Cymerman, & Levine, 2001; Naigles & Hoff-Ginsberg, 1998; Pearson, Fernandez, Lewedeg, & Oller, 1997). Many subtleties of language cannot develop unless children experience high-quality language and have the opportunities to see how language maps to the objects and events of the world (Tomasello, 2000). A parent who converses responsively with a child promotes the child's language development (Akhtar, Dunham, & Dunham, 1991; Carpenter, Nagell, & Tomasello, 1998; Harris, Jones, Brookes, & Grant, 1986; Tamis-LeMonda, Bornstein, Kahana-Kalman, Baumwell, & Cyphers, 1998; Tomasello & Farrar, 1986; Tomasello & Todd, 1983).

Applying Developmental Theory to Educational Contexts

BOX 7.3. Instruction that Supports the Development of Phonemic Awareness

Lynette Bradley and Peter Bryant (e.g., 1983) hypothesized that providing instruction to children about how to categorize words on the basis of their sounds would increase their phonemic awareness, and hence their long-term reading achievement. An important principle emphasized in the Bradley and Bryant (1983) instruction was that the same word can be categorized in different ways on the basis of sound when it is in different sets of words. Thus, if *hen* is in a group of words that include *hat*, *hill*, *hair*, and *hand*, it would make sense to categorize all of these words together as starting with *h*, especially in contrast to other words starting with another letter. If *hen* were on a list with *men* and *sun*, however, these three words could be categorized as ones ending in *n*. If *hen* were on a list of words that included *bed* and *leg*, it would be possible to categorize the words as ones with short *e* in the middle.

The training involved 40 10-minute sessions spread out over 2 years, although another version of the instruction was implemented over a period of 4 months (Bradley, 1988). During the first 20 sessions, 5- and 6-year-olds who initially lacked phonemic awareness were taught to categorize words on the basis of common sounds using pictures of the objects. For example, in one lesson a set of pictures of objects starting with the letter *b* was shown to the child who named the objects. The child repeated the names with the teacher urging the child to listen to the sounds. The child then was asked if he or she could hear a sound common to each word. This continued until the child could identify the common sound, with the adult providing help and hints if the child experienced difficulty doing this.

This sound identification task was repeated a number of times during training, with a number of variations. For example, children were given sets of pictures, asked to group them together on the basis of common sounds, and then asked to provide justifications for their classifications. In another variation, the children were required to eliminate a word starting (or ending or containing) a sound different than the other pictures in a set. Many exercises were given for each sound, with the teacher moving on to a new sound only when children seemed to be proficient with the sound previously introduced.

The 20 sessions with pictures were followed by 20 sessions with words, with children required to determine whether words rhymed or began with the same sound (alliteration). After proficiency on this task was achieved, children were given tasks on end sounds (such as elimination of the word ending in a sound different than the others). After children could categorize on the basis of final sounds, they learned to categorize on the basis of middle sounds in words.

In this training, pictures yielded to purely aural presentations. Various discrimination exercises eventually gave way to production exercises. In the latter half of the curriculum, children were required to spell words using plastic letters, with the teacher providing help as needed, up to and including spelling the word for the child if that was what was needed to move the lesson along. Spelling exercises included sets of words sharing common features. Thus, for a set involving *hat*, *cat*, and *rat*, an efficient strategy was simply to change the first plastic letter as each new word was requested.

This training produced substantial gains in standardized reading performance—about a year advantage—relative to a control condition in which children were trained to categorize pictures and words conceptually (e.g., *cat*, *bat*, and *rat* are all animals). The sound-categorization-trained students were even further ahead of control participants who had received no categorization training. Even more striking, however, were the results of a 5-year follow-up. Although many of the students in the control condition had received substantial remediation during the 5-year interval following the study, there were still striking reading advantages for students who had experienced the sound categorization training when they were in the primary grades (Bradley, 1989; Bradley & Bryant, 1991).

Since Bradley and Bryant's classic research, there have been many demonstrations that instruction that improves phonemic awareness impacts beginning reading success (Ehri et al., 2001; National Reading Panel, 2000). Because of the consistent effectiveness of such instruction, it is one of the reading practices favored in the No Child Left Behind act (107th Congress) as worthy of federal support in schools that are receiving funds to improve. Teaching children that words are composed of sounds blended together, and helping them to practice analyzing words into their sound components and blending sounds to produce words are important aspects of language development that contribute to beginning reading competence (Ehri, 2004; Troia, 2004).

Such parents talk about topics that interest the child but also talk so the child can understand them, using simplified speech ("motherese"), which is often accompanied by gestures, facial expressions, and other hints that make it easier for the child to understand (Chong, Werker, Russell, & Carroll, 2003; Jones, 2004). Children also play an active role in this interaction. By getting their parents to talk about the toys and objects in the world that interest them and with which they interact most, children learn the names of things in the world that matter most to them (Bloom, 2000; Bloom, Margulis, Tinker, & Fujita, 1996; Bloom & Tinker, 2001).

One aspect of preschool language interaction that has received substantial attention from scholars is picture-book reading. The more that parents interact with children over books, the better developed is children's language (Ninio, 1980; Payne, Whitehurst, & Angell, 1994; for reviews, see Bus, van IJzendoorn, & Pelligrini, 1995; Scarborough & Dobrich, 1994). Moreover, parents and teachers of low-income preschool and primary-grades children can be taught to interact with children over picture books in ways that increase emergent language skills, including vocabulary development (Arnold, Lonigan, Whitehurst, & Epstein, 1994; Lonigan & Whitehurst, 1998; Valdez-Menchaca & Whitehurst, 1992; Whitehurst et al., 1988; Whitehurst, Arnold, et al., 1994; Whitehurst, Epstein, et al., 1994, 1999; Zevenbergen et al., 2003). These studies demonstrated that teaching parents and teachers to interact more responsively during storybook reading caused children to learn language.

Does acquiring language competence during the preschool years make a difference to later success in school? Absolutely. For example, learning to read depends on phonemic awareness (Adams, 1990), semantic (vocabulary) development (Kamil, 2004; McGregor, 2004), and understanding of the subtleties of syntax (Scott, 2004). In fact, just about every aspect of language that can be measured in the preschool years is associated with later reading competence, with preschoolers who have better developed language becoming better readers during the elementary years (Scarborough, 2001). If readers of this text remember nothing else from this chapter, remember that preschoolers being seen and not heard (or talked with) is a disastrous prescription, one that is played out too often by children spending hours with the television or in overcrowded daycares where there is little language interaction between adults and children. Communicating with children is at the heart of their language development.

■ ■ ■ BILINGUALISM

At least as many people in the world are bilingual as are monolingual (Garcia, 1993). Increasingly the United States is a multilingual nation, with educators needing to know about bilingualism if they are to fully understand the children in their midst. Bilinguals are a diverse group, varying in the languages they speak, their immigration status, and their socioeconomic levels, just to mention a few dimensions of difference (Cohen & Horotwitz, 2002). It helps to try and provide some simplification, however, to grasp the issues surrounding bilingual education. Romaine (1995) identified six common configurations that can result in bilingual development. These configurations are defined by the languages of the parents, the language(s) spoken to the child, and the language in the surrounding community, and are summarized in Table 7.2.

TABLE 7.2. Family and Community Configurations That Can Result in a Child Being Bilingual

Type 1: Each of the parents speaks a different language to the child. The language of one of the parents is the dominant language in the community in which the child is developing.

Example: A child being raised in St. Louis by an English-speaking father and a Greek-speaking mother.

Type 2: Each of the parents has a different native language. Although one of the parents knows the dominant language, both speak their native, nondominant language to the child. The child experiences the community-dominant language only in the community.

Example: A Spanish-speaking father and a Native American mother, who knows English, but speaks her tribal language to the child. They live in Phoenix.

Type 3: The parents share the same language, which is not the dominant language of the surrounding community. They speak with their child using the native, nondominant language.

Example: Two Spanish-speaking parents raising a child in Brooklyn.

Type 4: Each of the parents has a different native language. Neither speaks the dominant language of the community, each speaking their own language to the child.

Example: A Bosnian male and a Vietnamese female raising a child in Toronto.

Type 5: The parents share the same native language, which is the dominant language of the community. One of the parents, however, always speaks to the child in a nonnative language.

Example: Two English-speaking Canadian parents, with the father always speaking French to the child to give the child a start on English–French bilingualism, which is a valued skill in Canada

Type 6: The parents are bilingual, living in a community that is bilingual, with the child exposed to parents who regularly using both languages.

Example: Two Spanish–English bilinguals raising a child in a Texas bordertown.

Note. Based on Romaine (1995).

All of the types of bilinguals described in Table 7.2 have been studied by psycholinguists. In these in-depth, typically longitudinal case studies, the psycholinguist documented extensively the language development of a child and the contexts in which language development occurred. Sometimes these studies are referred to as "diary studies" since those conducting them invariably construct diaries about the child's language development. Such investigations are very resource-demanding in that they require years of a researcher's life to collect the data, followed by years to sort through the data, and perhaps years to write up the study. Thus not many diary studies have been conducted (Hoffmann, 1991).

For example, Werner Leopold documented the first 2 years of his daughters' language development, particularly the development of his older daughter, Hildegard. The girls were raised in the United States in a home in which their father spoke German to them and their mother spoke English. Leopold kept detailed diaries of his daughters' language. The result was four books: the first dedicated to phonological development, the second to vocabulary, the third to word formation and syntax, and the fourth to other observations (Leopold, 1939, 1947, 1949a, 1949b).

Were there difficulties for Leopold's daughters in language acquisition? Not really. Leopold reported that Hildegard acquired and used both English and German words. She seemed to have few difficulties with the sound differences between the two languages. For a while she used some German words in particular situations and their corresponding English words in other situations (e.g., using *bitte* in formal situations and *please* in less formal situations), but in general Hildegard acquired both German and English. Between 2 and 3 years of age, Hildegard was very much aware that German and English were separate languages, and she readily translated between the two languages. She learned the syntax of German and the syntax of English and seemed not to confuse them.

It was clear that community mattered. For example, Hildegard did not continue to use German words she acquired during a 3-month visit to Germany at age 1 once the family returned to the United States. As Hildegard continued to live in the United States, English became her dominant language. Karla, the younger daughter, never was as fully bilingual as her sister. However, when Karla had a chance to live in Germany during her late teen years, she rapidly acquired the German language.

One of the most important conclusions coming out of the Leopold study, and other diary studies, was that there is little evidence that learning and using two languages interfered with the development of either language. Subsequent research has confirmed that Hildegard was a typical bilingual, whose speech included a small amount of code mixing, which decreased in frequency with increasing age (Lindholm & Padilla, 1978; Redlinger & Park, 1980; Swain & Wesche, 1973).

Review of the diary studies makes it clear that language exposure dramatically affects language acquisition. For example, which of the six types of situations described in Table 7.2 should lead to the most mixing of languages by children? If you said Type 6, you were right. When two bilingual parents in the midst of a bilingual community raise children, their children tend to mix the languages more than do children raised in situations in which languages are more clearly separated (Romaine, 1995). Studies of Type-3 situations have confirmed that children can learn several languages at once. For example, Oksaar (1977) reported on a child who lived in Stockholm, in a home in which Swedish and Estonian was spoken. The child moved to Germany at age 3. The child spoke Swedish and Estonian like a monolingual and acquired German easily, with clear German pronunciation. Although the child's German syntactical development reflected the influence of Estonian and Swedish, in general the child experienced little difficulty in acquiring German.

In short, the diary studies provide a substantial amount of information about how bilingual development proceeds. When the diary study data are combined with information gathered using other research methods, a picture of bilingual language development emerges.

Bilingual Language Development

One of the best ways to understand bilingual language development is by understanding first language development, as detailed earlier in this chapter. As it turns out, the development of a particular language by a child who is also acquiring another language is not much different from the development of the same language by a child in a monolingual environment (de Houwer, 1995). Because bilingual development is not much different from monolingual development, one way to organize the research on bilingual development is to use the categories of language development described earlier.

Prelinguistic Development: Speech Perception and Production

As described earlier, children quickly develop sensitivity to phonemes that occur in the language community in which they are immersed, so that by the end of the first year of life they have difficulty hearing the differences between phonemes that occur in another language. By adulthood, people really cannot hear phoneme distinctions that are not represented in a language they know. One of the most commonly cited examples of this perceptual phenomenon is Japanese adults' inability to discriminate between /ra/ and /la/, for these two sounds, which are distinct phonemes in English, are variations of a single phoneme sound in Japanese (Strange & Jenkins, 1978).

As described earlier, the content of a baby's babbling is affected by the language the child experiences. By the end of the first year, the sounds that are more frequent in the surrounding language definitely are more frequent in baby babbling (Boysson-Bardies et al., 1989, 1992). What happens with bilingual development? Analyses of the diary studies led to the general conclusion that young bilinguals develop the sound systems for the languages they are learning in parallel. Yes, there is a little blending and the occasional mixing of sounds, but, for the most part, when a child learning German and English speaks in German, the sounds are German. When the child speaks in English, the sounds are English (Hoffmann, 1991).

One of the most important issues with respect to phonological production is whether there is a critical period for the acquisition of a language so that it is spoken without an accent. In general, the available evidence is consistent with the conclusion that the younger children are when they learn a second language, the greater the likelihood that they will not have an accent (McLaughlin, 1984). Study of immigrant populations is revealing on this issue. In general, the younger an immigrant came to the United States, the less pronounced the accent (Asher & Garcia, 1969; Oyama, 1976). Notably, the diary studies are filled with examples of children learning several languages without accents, consistent with the conclusion that learning several different sound systems is not formidable for young children.

Semantic Development

During the one-word stage, the bilingual child uses words from both languages. Sometimes words from the two languages are blended together, so that a French–English bilingual child might say "pinichon" for "pickle," blending the English word *pickle* and the French word *cornichon* (Grosjean, 1982). This mixing of vocabulary during the first-word stage is in striking contrast to slightly older bilingual children (2- to 4-year-olds) who typically do not mix words from their two languages.

Does this mean that the child has only a single lexicon (a common store of vocabulary) during the one-word stage, which then differentiates into separate lexicons for each of the languages the child knows? This is a possibility suggested by some psycholinguists (Volterra & Taeschner, 1978), but one that is debated intensely (de Houwer, 1995). Quay (1993; cited by de Houwer, 1995) suggested an alternative possibility of separate lexicons even during the one-word stage. Quay studied a 1½-year-old Spanish–English bilingual. The child was tested in a variety of linguistic contexts and with both English and Spanish speakers. Whether the child used a Spanish word or its English equivalent depended on the context, including the identity of the speaker. Quay contended that the child's differentiated use of the Spanish and English labels for the same concept might be thought of as evidence for two different lexicons developing in parallel.

The debate on the question of whether there are separate lexicons or only one lexicon is extremely technical, with much of it being studied in the context of adult bilingualism. According to the common-store model, all the vocabulary known by an individual is kept in a common store in the brain, but each item is tagged somehow with respect to language (e.g., *pickle* would be tagged English, *cornichon* would be tagged French). Those who favor separate-store models contend that each language has its own store. Critical evidence in favor of the common-store model might be that people learn lists composed of words from one of their languages at the same rate they learn otherwise comparable lists composed of words from both of their languages. Critical evidence in favor of the separate-stores model might be that learning differs when lists are composed of items from only one language versus two languages. The problem is that both types of evidence have been obtained, and, in general, the data pertaining to this issue conflict and the issue is not resolved (Hamers & Blanc, 1989).

Semantic (vocabulary) development correlates with academic achievement (especially in reading) for English-second-language students just as it does for English-first-language students (Anderson & Nagy, 1991). From fourth grade on, English-second-language students' knowledge of English vocabulary is strongly correlated to their reading achievement in English, at least as defined by standardized tests (Fitzgerald, 1995a). The more vocabulary people know in a language, the more capable they are at reading. Not surprisingly, when English-second-language students are taught English vocabulary, their comprehension improves (Carlo et al., 2004). See the Applying Developmental Theory to Educational Contexts special feature (Box 7.4) for a discussion of the reading skills of bilingual students.

Syntactic Development

A number of researchers interested in bilingualism have examined the syntactic development of bilingual compared to monolingual children (de Houwer, 1995). In general, syntactic development is the same whether a child is acquiring only one language or is an emergent bilingual (Hoffmann, 1991). The differences that do occur are subtle compared to the similarities. For example, Meisel (1984; reported in Hoffmann, 1991) studied German and French bilingual children. He noticed that the bilingual children tended to be more rigid in their adherence to German word-order conventions than monolingual German children. Even so, both the bilinguals and the monolingual German students acquired the German word-order conventions, with little difference in the rate of acquisition.

The issue of whether parallel and separate syntactic systems are being developed by the bilingual child has been considered with much more evidence in favor of separate syntactic systems than in favor of a common syntactic system (de Houwer, 1995). For example, children do not attempt to transfer syntactic rules and conventions that occur in only one of the languages they are learning to the other language. Thus, when the two languages have different ways of expressing tense, children do not use the tense conventions of one language with the other language (Schlyter, 1990). When the languages differ in how gender is marked, children do not confuse the markings in their speech (de Houwer, 1987). When one language has particular rules for expressing questions, children do not extend those rules to the other lan-

Applying Developmental Theory to Educational Contexts

BOX 7.4. Reading of Bilingual Students

Fitzgerald (1995a, 1995b) reviewed the research on the reading skills of bilingual students, providing the basis for a number of important conclusions about reading by English-second-language students. When English-second-language students read English, do they engage in fundamentally different processes than English-first-language students? Definitely not, with similarities apparent from the elementary grades on. For example, just as native English students use a variety of strategies for figuring out new words encountered in context, so do English-second-language students (e.g., sounding out, using meaning cues, analyzing syntactic relationships). Just as English-first-language students use a variety of comprehension strategies, so do English-second-language students (e.g., asking questions, rereading for clarification, imagining, using a dictionary, predicting upcoming content, varying reading speed, associating ideas in text to prior knowledge, summarizing). Just as the comprehension of English-first-language students is affected by relationships between readers' prior knowledge and text content, so it is with English-second-language students. Both types of readers make inferences as they read, based in part on their prior knowledge.

That said, the use of these processes by bilingual students often is not as extensive as their use by native English speakers. Moreover, sometimes the processes are not carried out as quickly, with the reading of bilinguals typically slower than the reading of native English speakers. The larger point, however, is that qualitatively, the reading of English seems to involve mostly the same processes, whether the reading is being done by an English-second-language or an English-first-language reader.

What is also suggested by the research with English-second-language readers is that there are many commonalities in reading across languages. Proficiency in reading of one's first language is strongly and positively correlated with reading proficiency in the second language, across age and grade levels. Moreover, the more proficient English-second-language readers are in their native language, the more active they are when reading English. The more they use comprehension strategies and relate what is being read to their prior knowledge, the more they make appropriate inferences as they read. In short, excellent reading in a language other than English predicts excellent reading in English. Reading skills transfer from one language to another.

guage when trying to form questions (de Houwer, 1990). As with sounds and vocabulary, children tend to keep the languages they use separated.

Metalinguistic Awareness

Bilingual children are more aware of language than monolingual children (Bialystok, 1997; Bialystok, Shenfield, & Codd, 2000; Levy, 1985; Romaine, 1995). They are more aware than monolinguals of the arbitrary relationship between words and things (Genesee, 1981). Bilingual children are also more knowledgeable about the properties of words, as reflected in their abilities to do tasks requiring understanding the nature of words. For example, bilingual preschoolers are more facile at identifying single words in contexts (such as sentences) than are monolinguals (Bialystock, 1987). Bilingual children know more about syntax than monolinguals (Swain & Lapkin, 1982). Bilingual children can translate from one language to another early in life (Malakoff & Hakuta, 1991). Another competency requiring a high degree of language awareness is using languages appropriately as a function of speaker and context (e.g., using Spanish when speaking to a Spanish speaker at the bus stop, using English to speak to the bus driver who is an English speaker), which bilingual preschoolers do well (Hoffmann, 1991).

It is important to realize that the development of language is a long-term process. We emphasize this point because many believe that young children acquire a second language easily in comparison to adults. McLaughlin (1984) considered the evidence pertaining to this question and offered the following comparison. In the first 6 years of life, a child experiences 9,000 or more hours of language exposure and experience, and yet the child's vocabulary and syntax are far from that of a mature adult. In contrast, during the Vietnam War, the Army Language School could develop a soldier into a native-level speaker of Vietnamese in about 1,300 hours of immersion in Vietnamese (i.e., the soldier lived and worked in a community that spoke Vietnamese). As we pointed out earlier, at least at first—during the first year or so—adults can learn a second language faster. The individual who begins learning a second language as a child, however, has a much better chance of eventually attaining native language competence, including a native accent.

Bilingualism and Cognitive Development

Researchers are extremely interested in the question of whether or not bilingualism affects cognitive development. Often the question has been posed with respect to general intelligence as measured by intelligence tests. It is difficult to draw sound conclusions on this issue, however, for bilingual experience often is correlated with development outside of the mainstream community, and IQ tests contain many items that depend on knowledge of the majority community (Hakuta, 1986; see also Chapter 8).

In an important study relevant to this issue, Peal and Lambert (1962) studied 10-year-old children in Montreal. They carefully assessed the language competencies of their participants and made sure that the bilingual and monolingual participants were comparable socioeconomically. The bilingual children outperformed the monolingual children on intelligence tests, both on items tapping verbal intelligence and on those tapping nonverbal intelligence. The superiority of the bilinguals was particularly noticeable on items requiring cognitive flexibility. Moreover, the bilinguals had a better understanding of a number of concepts. Perhaps knowing two names for a concept stimulates more reflection on it than knowing only one name (Carringer, 1974)? In general, the research since Peal and Lambert (1962) has supported their general conclusion that bilingualism is associated with more flexible intelligence than monolingualism (Hakuta, 1986). At a minimum, there is more evidence in favor of than against the positive effects of bilingualism on intelligence and creativity (Cook, 1997; Diaz, 1983; Hamers & Blanc, 1989; Hoffmann, 1991; Romaine, 1995). See the Considering Interesting Questions special feature (Box 7.5) for a discussion of how bilingualism affects private speech.

The Nature and Effects of Education
on Bilingual Students

On a variety of educational indicators, students who are not native English speakers typically perform more poorly than white, English-speaking students. Underachievement by non-English speakers is an especially pressing problem because the bilingual

---

Considering Interesting Questions

BOX 7.5. How Does Bilingualism Affect Private Speech?

Recall from Chapter 6 that young children often talk to themselves as they work on tasks ("Let's look at everything first. That's the biggest piece of the puzzle, so I use it first. . . . There's green on one side. . . . Where's another green one?"). This private speech helps children organize their behavior, assists their problem solving, and increases self-control (Meichenbaum, 1977). Private speech is absent in the early preschool years, gradually increases with age, and then decreases as children enter the elementary-school years (Kohlberg et al., 1968). According to Vygotsky, the decrease in audible private speech reflects the internalization of thinking. Private speech sometimes is discernible, however, when children encounter challenging problems (Kohlberg et al., 1968).

Diaz, Padilla, and Weathersby (1991) examined whether bilingualism affects children's private speech. They studied 34 Mexican American preschoolers between the ages of 3 and 6 who were enrolled in an additive bilingual preschool program. The children performed three tasks. One was a block design task, which involved creating a block pattern shown in a picture. The second task was a classification task, requiring children to search a set of picture cards to find pairs of pictures that relate to one another (e.g., hammer and nails, toothbrush and toothpaste, lock and key). The third task required the children to order sets of pictures that depicted the act of baking a cake, with the task to put the pictures in the correct order of events. As children performed the tasks, they were videotaped. The videotape was then transcribed and the private speech was coded as to whether it was task-relevant or not. Task-relevant remarks were further broken down into the following categories: labels and descriptions of materials, directives ("I am putting the purple one here"), planning statements ("I'll put the one with the bowl first"), transitional statements ("OK, I'm done with this one"), questions and answers ("What goes here? . . . Oh, the cow goes here"), and self-praise/self-reinforcement ("I did them all!").

The private speech of these bilingual students was very similar to the private speech of other children who have been studied. For example, they used more task-relevant private speech than task-irrelevant speech. As children's mental age increased, task-relevant private speech first increased, followed by a decline. As audible private speech declined, inaudible whispers and mutterings increased, suggesting that private speech was being internalized. When the task was more difficult, more audible private speech increased. The more bilingual children tended to emit more task-relevant private speech than the less bilingual children. This is consistent with other research suggesting that, if anything, cognition is facilitated by bilingualism.

---

population in the United States is large and growing. In some jurisdictions, such as California, up to half of the population speaks a language other than English as the primary language (Garcia, 1991). Even rural areas, such as Nebraska and Kansas, are educating more language-minority students than they have in the past. A question commonly asked by educators is "What type of instructional program works best with language-minority students?"

Program Alternatives

Educators are exploring many different ways of educating bilingual students (Genesee, Undholm-Leary, Saunders, & Christian, 2006). These programs can be fit into two major categories (Lambert, 1974, 1977). The first category of approaches, *additive programs*, has the goal of adding a second language, without eliminating the first language. The communities involved in additive programs recognize the value of the language-minority students' native languages and cultures, with the goal of helping students appreciate and develop both their native language and the majority language. Typically, some of the teaching is conducted in the native language and some in the majority language. For example, in the United States, during the primary years, English would be taught as a second language, with most content teaching occurring in the native language. As the child proceeds through school, and the child gains proficiency in both the native language and English, some content instruction is carried out in the native language and some in English.

In one type of additive program, language-minority and language-majority children are schooled together from the beginning, with the goal that both groups will emerge bilingual (these are two-way bilingual programs), with about 250 such programs now operating in the United States (Perez, 2004). This model is typical of some Canadian French–English immersion programs and has also been used in areas of the United States with large proportions of native Spanish and native English speakers (Genesee, 1985; Hakuta, 1986). Much of the enthusiasm for additive approaches involving such immersion stems from well-known success stories. For example, the success of the early 1960s immersion program in the Coral Way Elementary School near Miami, Florida (Mackey & Beebee, 1977), increased attention to immersion as an alternative in the United States (Hakuta, 1986; Moran & Hakuta, 1995). Equal numbers of native Spanish and native English speakers attended the school. Both groups of children received native language arts instruction in the morning and language arts instruction in their foreign language in the afternoon. Instruction in music, art, physical education, and other activities occurred in both languages. Participants in this program not only acquired bilingual skills but also exhibited high self-esteem and positive attitudes toward one another. In general, academic achievement in two-way programs has been as good or better as academic achievement in other programs (see Perez, 2004, for a review).

Another type of additive immersion approach also has proven successful. In this, a student is taught in the foreign language exclusively for several years before beginning to receive instruction in both the foreign language and the first language. This approach has proven successful with English-first-language students learning French in Quebec and Spanish in California (Cohen, 1974, 1975; Genesee, 1987; Snow, Galvan, & Campbell, 1983).

In contrast to additive programs, the other major category of approaches, *subtractive programs*, have the explicit goal of replacing the students' native language with the majority language, with the overarching goal of assimilating minority children to the mainstream culture (Lambert, 1974, 1977). Typically, students do not receive instruction in their native language. Hence, such programs are often referred to as "submersion programs," analogous to throwing a child into a body of water that is very much over the child's head! The majority culture is both explicitly and implicitly extolled with the subtractive approach (Romaine, 1995).

Although the most extreme subtractive approaches involve language-minority students receiving instruction entirely in the majority language, in some cases "sheltered English" instruction occurs. That is, the teachers use simplified English and consciously teach English to the students. In other cases, part of the day is spent in classes in which English is taught as a second language (i.e., ESL classes). Some programs include a transition from instruction in the native language to instruction in the majority language. In these transition programs, the child's native language is used a great deal during the primary years, but as the child proceeds through school, schooling is increasingly conducted in the majority language. The transition approach is subtractive because the primary goal is to develop the language-minority student into a competent user of the majority language. Although the effects are not always large or always obtained (Meyer & Fienberg, 1992), transitional programs tend to produce positive academic effects in comparison to submersion programs (Willig, 1985). In general, the longer instruction is provided in the native language (i.e., the longer the period of transition), the greater the achievement benefits with respect to the second language (Collier, 1992). Long-term transition makes sense, since it takes at least several years for the child who has never experienced English to become fluent enough in the language to participate fully at school (Garcia, 1993).

An important policy question is determining the advantages and disadvantages of the various approaches. Evaluating bilingual education has proven to be challenging, however (Collier, 1992; Willig, 1985). For example, researchers generally have not been able to conduct randomized experiments, and thus most of the data are correlational. The studies have varied greatly in quality, with many studies difficult to interpret. Even so, the general consensus is that additive programs such as immersion have been effective in meeting their goals (Genesee, 1985), with programs that attempt to maintain the first language while developing the second one seeming to achieve both goals (Collier, 1995; Thomas & Collier, 1997). Long-term, additive programs seem to improve the language skills of students in both languages—for example, with learning to read in two languages seeming to facilitate learning to read in both languages rather than interfering (Geva & Siegel, 1998; Geva, Wade-Wooley, & Shany, 1993). In particular, children who have learned first to read in a language other than English, such as Spanish, transfer many of the reading and language-learning strategies developed while learning to read Spanish to learning to read in English (August, Calderon, & Carlo, 2000; Carlisle & Beeman, 2000; Cohen & Horowitz, 2002; Durgunoglu, Nagy, & Hancin-Bhatt, 1993; Snow, Burns, & Griffin, 1998; Zecker, 2004), although, at least some of the time, this is more likely with strong readers compared to weaker readers (Jiménez, Garcia, & Pearson, 1995, 1996). Moreover, additive bilingual programs seem to improve the attitudes of participants toward members of the other language group.

Just as compelling a point in favor of additive programs over subtractive programs is that subtractive programs often turn students off, since their implicit message is that students should leave their first language and culture behind them (Hakuta, 1999; Nanez, Padilla, & Maez, 1992; Scollon & Scollon, 1981; Valenzuela, 1999). The best thinkers in bilingual education have recognized for some time that subtractive education can be devastating to children (Lambert, 1984).

One complicating factor in the policy debate in the United States is that a variety of political forces are opposed to conducting any instruction in U.S. schools in a language other than English (Lucas & Katz, 1994). Another complication is that increasingly, U.S. schools are dealing with many different first-language minorities. It is not unusual at all for more than 50 first languages to be represented in school districts. The presence of so many different languages almost mandates that many language minorities will experience education only in English. Still, given greater sensitivity to diversity and the value of cultural pluralism (Banks & Banks, 1995), there is reason to hope that these children's experiences often will not be as subtractive as the experiences of earlier generations who experienced submersion.

Social Consequences of Education in the Majority Language for Language-Minority Students

When language-minority students begin to learn the majority language at school, they often take it home with them, using the majority language at home rather than the minority language (Fillmore, 1991). Moreover, as students become proficient in the majority language, their minority-language skills often seem to erode, so that it is more difficult for them to communicate in their native language than it once was (Hakuta & D'Andrea, 1992). Although the shift away from the native language is often more pronounced *outside* of the home than it is *in* the home, use of the native language at home by students learning a majority language is often reduced (Fillmore, 1991; Hakuta & D'Andrea, 1992). This shift away from the native language, especially at home, has profound implications for relations with parents and other family members. In a qualitative interview study, Fillmore (1991) found that families reported increased difficulties in communications within the family as a child learned English at school. The families also expressed concern about their own abilities to pass on their cultural and ethical values to their children.

Effective Classroom Practices

Researchers interested in the nature of effective schools and classrooms analyze the instructional characteristics of settings that promote achievement (see Chapter 9). The following are characteristic of classrooms that are exceptionally effective with bilingual students (Garcia, 1991; Moran & Hakuta, 1995):

- Teachers and students communicate well. Teachers monitor whether their communications are understood, clarifying when they are not.
- Classroom work tends to take place in small, collaborative groups rather than in individual assignments. Relatively little large-group instruction occurs.
- Instruction is organized around thematic units, with students having a great deal of input about the themes studied.
- Students' home culture is incorporated into the classroom and instruction.
- Student engagement is high, with the teacher monitoring and intervening when students have difficulties.
- Although instruction in the lower grades typically is in both languages, English prevails with increasing grade level. Still, students converse in their native language, and teachers feel free to use either language, depending on what they believe is most appropriate for the situation.
- Teachers are committed to their students' development and convinced that their students can do well. They communicate these high expectations to their students.
- Parents are involved in what goes on at school.

And, as has proven true with other students, teaching cognitive strategies matched to task demands—for example, reading comprehension strategies—improves the academic performance of bilingual students (Jiménez, 1997; Muniz-Swicegood, 1994; Padron, 1992).

■ ■ ■ LANGUAGE DISORDERS

Language disorders can be found in children who exhibit no other obvious physical or mental impairment. For example, about 2.5% of preschoolers have severe problems producing the sounds of English (Shriberg, Kwiatkowski, Best, Hengst, & Tereselic-Weber, 1986). The majority of these children will continue to experience speech production problems during the schooling years (Crystal, 1987). In this section, we briefly review some of the more important language disorders.

Phonological Impairment

Some children experience difficulty saying words in their native languages. Of course, it is common for preschoolers to pronounce words differently than adults (Carroll, 1994). Preschoolers often delete some sounds (saying "puter" instead of "computer") and coalesce sounds, using one sound to express a more complex blending of sounds ("paf" for "pacifier"). In contrast to these normal pronunciation errors, phonological impairment involves more extreme speech errors. Rather than saying "sheep," the phonologically impaired child might say "teep." When the same child attempts "sleep," he or she might say "sheep." Thus, this child's difficulty in saying "sheep" was not just an inability to make the "sh" sound, but rather a difficulty saying the "sh" sound when it is required. Similarly, a child who says "dight" instead of "light" might nonetheless be able to say "lion," again reflecting that the problem is not just the inability to say the "l" sound but an inability on some occasions to organize the pronunciation of some words that begin with "l" (Leonard, 1995). Researchers in phonology believe that there are sets of rules that specify how sounds are produced in combination with one another and phonological impairments in children often represent problems in carrying out the rules for producing and combining sounds (Ingram, 1976).

Many children with language impairment during the preschool years significantly improve in their pronunciation skills even without treatment. There is little reason to take comfort in such improvement, however (Leonard, 1995; Lewis & Freebairn, 1992; Lewis, Freebairn, & Taylor, 2000). Children who experience early language impairment are likely to have difficulties in phonemic awareness, which predicts difficulties in learning to read (Ingram, 1963). Given their difficulties with sounds, it is not surprising that such children are also at risk for spelling difficulties (Aram & Nation, 1980). Children with early phonological impairment often lag behind age-mates in the development of vocabulary (Shriberg et al., 1986). Phonologically impaired preschoolers often grow up to be adolescents and adults who perform less well on speech and language measures than their peers and who have experienced a variety of educational problems throughout development (Howlin & Rutter, 1987; Leonard, 1995).

The traditional approach to phonological impairment has been to provide speech therapy, which typically involves a great deal of drill and practice on problematic sounds (Bernthal & Bankson, 1993). This approach does produce improvements in children's speech (Sommers, Logsdon, & Wright, 1992), but more research is needed to explore how to increase its effectiveness (Camarata, 1995).

Semantic (Vocabulary) Impairments

Language-impaired children often have less extensive vocabularies than other children (Kail & Leonard, 1986). In addition, they are more likely not to be able to think of a word that they want to use on a specific occasion than unimpaired children (Denckla & Rudel, 1976; Wolf, 1986, 1991). Slowness in word retrieval is a concern because of its implications for interfering with children's discourse. It also seems to impact negatively on reading, with strong correlations between word retrieval problems and poor reading comprehension (Wolf & Obregon, 1992).

Interventions for word retrieval problems focus on two processes (McGregor & Leonard, 1995): (1) developing fuller understanding of word meanings (e.g., teaching students to focus on how new words and their meanings relate to various categories of information the child knows), and (2) increasing students' strategies for retrieving words they know (e.g., teaching students to think of some sound in the word they are trying to retrieve if they cannot think of the entire word). Although children's word retrieval skills can be increased using these interventions, improvements at the word level have not translated into meaningful educational improvements (McGregor & Leonard, 1995).

Grammatical Impairments

Grammatical (syntactic) impairment generally means that some children develop syntactical rules at a much slower rate than normal children (Fletcher & Ingham, 1995; Morehead & Ingram, 1973). That is, grammatically impaired children are slow to develop the stages of syntactic development first identified by Brown (1973) and described earlier in this chapter (Leonard, Bortolini, Caselli, McGregor, & Sabbadini, 1992). Grammatical impairment in the preschool years predicts grammatical impairment in the schoolage years (Curtiss, Katz, & Tallal, 1992; Gillam & Johnston, 1992; Scarborough & Dobrich, 1990; Scott, 1995). During the schoolage years, the sentences of grammatically impaired children tend to be less syntactically complex than those of their age-mates. They tend to make grammatical errors at a much greater rate than other children, both in their speaking and in their writing. They also make many more punctuation errors than children with normal language (Newcomer & Barenbaum, 1991).

In general, there are two broad classes of intervention with grammatically impaired children (Scott, 1995). One is direct teaching of syntax; the other is more indirect, involving enrichment of children's naturalistic experiences with language. The direct approach can involve workbook exercises—for example, requiring students to combine simple sentences into more complex ones. Unfortunately, the case favoring such direct approaches with grammatically impaired students is not strong (Scott, 1995). Indirect approaches involve immersing children in language experiences, including emergent literary activities during the preschool years (e.g., book reading with parents, extensive verbal interactions with family members). With the onset of schooling, exposure to a variety of different types of texts and language experiences increases. Those favoring the indirect approach believe that it is through writing that students develop understanding and control of the grammar of language (Cordeiro, 1988; Kress, 1982), and therefore, recommend extensive writing during the elementary years for grammatically impaired students. As is the case for the direct approach, there is little evidence that such indirect approaches have substantial impact on grammatical impairment (Gillam, McFadden, & van Kleeck, 1995; Scott, 1995).

Pragmatic Impairments

Another major area of study in language impairments is the study of children's difficulties with pragmatics, that is, their ability to communicate. Much of this research has focused on conversational skills. Many, but not all, children with other language disabilities also have difficulties in carrying out conversations (Brinton & Fujiki, 1995). Several specific problems have been observed. Language-impaired children can have difficulties initiating conversations and changing topics in conversations (Conti-Ramsden & Friel-Patti, 1983; Craig & Evans, 1989). Language-impaired children are less responsive to the questions of other children (Brinton & Fujiki, 1982; Gallagher & Darnton, 1978; Rosinski-McClendon & Newhoff, 1987). Some language-impaired children are not very assertive in conversation (McTear, 1985). What must be emphasized is that such difficulties are far from universal in language-impaired children, with many language-impaired children communicating adequately with other children (Brinton & Fujiki, 1995). Unfortunately, there is very little work on interventions aimed at improving the pragmatic skills of language-disabled students (Brinton & Fujiki, 1995).

In summary, there are many different language impairments, with difficulties in one area of language functioning often associated with difficulties in other areas of language functioning. Language problems often translate into academic problems. For example, it is common for students experiencing problems learning to read to manifest a variety of language problems, from problems in basic perception of language to memory of language to development of syntax to comprehension (see Catts, 1989; Katz, Shankweiler, & Liberman, 1981; Liberman, Mann, Shankweiler, & Werfelman, 1982; Mann, 1984; Olson, Kliegl, Davidson, & Foltz, 1985; Sawyer & Butler, 1991; Scarborough, 1990; Stanovich, 1986; Vellutino, 1979). As early as 2 years of age, children who will experience later reading difficulties manifest language differences from those who will be normal readers: (1) their utterances are shorter and not as syntactically sophisticated, (2) their pronunciations are not as good, and (3) they recognize fewer words that they hear.

Although progress has been made in learning how to remediate some language disabilities, much remains to be learned. Researchers emphasize that it is especially important that children at risk for language difficulties be in rich language environments from early in life (Fey, Windsor, & Warren, 1995).

■ ■ ■ DEAFNESS

About one child in a thousand is born deaf. For a small percentage of these, the problem definitely is genetic, with deaf parents giving birth to deaf children. Others are the victims of teratogenic diseases, such as maternal German measles (see Chapter 2). Still more children become deaf during their first 2 years of life due to middle-ear infections, with profound childhood hearing loss rare after the first 2 years of life (Crystal, 1987).

It is extremely difficult to study deafness (Marschark, 1993), especially since only rarely will a researcher have a large sample of deaf children to study. Thus many studies of childhood deafness are based on just a few children. This is problematic because the childhood deaf are a diverse lot. Some children are born profoundly deaf, whereas others have significant residual hearing. Some are diagnosed early, and some are diagnosed only several years after birth. Some are the children of deaf parents, some are born to hearing parents. Of those born to hearing parents, some parents are more committed to and skillful at signing for their infant than others. Moreover, deaf children differ systematically in a variety of ways from hearing children (Marschark, 1993). For one, the socioeconomic level of families with deaf children tends to be below the average for the nation: Deaf adults, who are often the parents of deaf children, tend to earn less than other adults. Also, conditions of poverty contribute to the risk for deafness. For example, lack of appropriate prenatal care increases the odds of birth defects in the infants of economically disadvantaged mothers, with deaf children often having co-occurring disabilities (Knoors & Vervloed, 2003). For all these reasons, lack of hearing may not be the only difference between deaf children and other children. Deafness systematically relates to other economic and social variables.

Consider, for example, that even the deaf child in an economically and otherwise advantaged situation will have very different social relationships and interactions than a hearing child. Lederberg and Mobley (1990) studied the interactions of hearing-impaired and hearing-normal toddlers (1½–2 years of age) with their mothers. They observed less interaction between hearing-impaired infants and their mothers than between hearing-normal infants and their mothers. When interactions did occur, the hearing impairment affected the exchanges negatively. For example, hearing-impaired children often would cut off an interaction because they did not hear some input from the mother. Mother–child relations are different for deaf versus hearing-normal infants, which makes it very difficult to conclude that developmental differences between deaf and hearing-normal children are due to hearing loss itself rather than due to the effects of hearing loss on social interaction opportunities.

Oral Communication versus Sign Language Debate

An essential difference between deaf children is the means of communication that parents use with their children, whether oral communication or sign language. This decision affects both the quality and the quantity of the input the child receives and the communications the child can make. Debates about whether deaf children should experience oral language only or be taught to use sign language are but the most recent edition of a century-old controversy (Crystal, 1987). The creation of new technology reinvigorates the debate.

The problem with sign language is that it only allows limited social interactions, mainly, with others who know how to sign (Antia & Kriemeyer, 2003), although this is a situation favored by many who support a separate deaf culture (Woll & Ladd, 2003). The problem with the oral approach is that it typically results in a person who speaks poorly, and hence also ends up being isolated (Conrad, 1979). From the point

The decision of whether to use oral communication, sign language, or both to communicate with a deaf child has profound implications for the child's future social world.

of view of language development and school achievement, the oral communicators do not do as well as sign language users (Marschark, 1993). One point argued by those favoring the oral approach is that learning to use sign language somehow will interfere with subsequent learning of oral language. A related point is that a child who begins in an oral communication setting will stop using oral language if sign language instruction begins. Essentially, there is no evidence to support either of these suppositions (Conrad, 1979; Marschark, 1993; Quigley & Paul, 1984).

A third alternative to the exclusive oral or sign language approaches is the total, or simultaneous communication, approach in which the communicating child uses both oral communications and sign language. The research to date is supportive of this approach. The child reaps the cognitive benefits that use of sign language permits (Marschark, 1993), but also enjoys social benefits. For example, Cornelius and Hornett (1990) observed preschoolers in a total communication setting enjoying better social relations with peers than preschoolers in an oral-only setting. Given the advantages of this approach, it is not surprising that it is common relative to pure oral or manual approaches.

In recent years, a device known as a "cochlear implant" is being surgically implanted into children and adults with deafness, with the result that after a few years many recipients can understand much more oral language than they would have understood without the implant (Harkins & Bakke, 2003; Niparko & Blankenhorn, 2003; Spencer & Marschark, 2003). How much this improves the language, academic achievements, and qualities of life for recipients is an area of active research, which occurs as part of research on a number of technologies intended to improve the functioning of deaf populations, from captioned television to a variety of assistive hearing devices (Harkins & Bakke, 2003; Spencer & Marschark, 2003). Technology has great promise for changing the lives of future generations of individuals with deafness.

That deaf children do experience different communication systems, of course, complicates the study of the development of deaf children. Despite the many challenges, a great deal of progress has been made in understanding the development of deaf children. We summarize briefly here some of the most important findings of this research.

Language Development

Although the language development of deaf children has not been studied as extensively as the language development of hearing-normal children, our understanding of the language of deaf children has advanced. There are both similarities and differences between the language development of deaf and hearing-normal children.

Babbling

Although deaf children babble, their babbling tends to be much less extensive than that of hearing-normal children, with hearing-impaired infants emitting fewer sounds resembling native language syllables than hearing-normal infants (Oller & Eilers, 1988). Indeed, one indication to parents and physicians that an infant may be deaf is that the child does not babble as hearing-normal children babble.

An intriguing observation is that deaf infants who have sign-language-using deaf parents exhibit manual babbling (Lederberg, 2003; Schick, 2003). The deaf, signing parent communicates extensively with the infant, using a form of "signing motherese," with the signs presented slowly and in a somewhat simplified fashion (Bloom, 1998; Erting, Prezioso, & O'Grady Hynes, 1990). Just as the syllable, which occurs in vocal babbling, is part of a word, signs can be decomposed into parts. Deaf infants have been observed producing such part signs (Petitto & Marantette, 1991). The first years of life are a time when children practice the basic elements of communications that they will eventually employ to construct words and more complex messages, whether those elements are syllables, as they are for hearing children, or parts of signs, as they are for deaf children in signing families. The power of exposure to signs to elicit infant manual babbling comes through when hearing infants are exposed to signing during their first year of life: Their hands babble (Petitto, Holowka, Sergio, Levy, & Ostry, 2004; Petitto, Holowka, Sergio, & Ostry, 2001). From the first months of life, all children, regardless of hearing status, attend to and respond to communications they encounter repeatedly.

Gestures

All children gesture, including deaf children (Lederberg, 2003; Schick, 2003). The most common gesture is pointing, but other gestures have some physical resemblance to their referents (e.g., a child making a spiral upward motion to draw attention to a bear spiraling up a tree on television; Marschark, 1993). Some deaf children, whose parents do not sign to them, come to use gesturing extensively. By 2 years of age, these children can be combining several gestures to express their meaning, somewhat parallel to hearing 2-year-olds who are beginning to combine words to form sentences. Such gestural systems do not seem to develop further, however (Goldin-Meadow, 1985; Goldin-Meadow & Mylander, 1984).

First Signs and the Development of Vocabulary

Early vocabulary development can be quite advanced for the deaf child relative to hearing children (Lederberg, 2003; Marschark, 1993). The first signs of deaf children with deaf parents often are acquired several months earlier than the first words of hearing-normal infants (Goodwyn & Acredolo, 1993). At a minimum, deaf children with deaf-signing parents produce their first signs no later than hearing-normal children produce their first spoken words (Meier & Newport, 1990).

The advantage of deaf signers over hearing-normal children continues into the second year of life (Lederberg, 2003). During the second year, deaf signers acquire vocabulary at a much faster pace than hearing-normal children, with some evaluations suggesting as much as a 4:1 advantage in the number of vocabulary words used for deaf signers over hearing-normal children by the end of the second year (McIntire, 1974, cited in Marschark, 1993). Within deaf children, one of the biggest differences in favor of sign language over oral communication approaches is in vocabulary development. The vocabulary development of deaf 2- and 3-year-old oral communicators lags far behind that of deaf signing and hearing-normal 2- and 3-year-olds (Meadow-Orlans, 1987).

Unfortunately, the vocabulary advantage of the deaf toddler eventually gives way to a long-term vocabulary disadvantage for deaf children compared to hearing-normal children (Blarney, 2003; Lederberg, 2003). During the schooling years, deaf children have less extensive vocabularies. Moreover, they have less knowledge of the relationships between words. Undoubtedly, an important factor accounting for the less extensive vocabularies of deaf compared to hearing-normal schoolage children is that hearing-normal children de facto are exposed to much more content than deaf children (Marschark, 1993). A lot of information communicated aurally—over television, radio, and around the dinner table—is missed by the child who cannot hear.

In summary, language development in deaf children depends very much on the input they receive. The healthiest situation seems to be when deaf parents begin early to sign to their infants, which results in early use of sign and rapid vocabulary development during the first 2 years (Gallaway & Woll, 1994). Only a small proportion of deaf children, however, are in this category. Most deaf children have hearing parents, who either cannot sign, cannot do so fluently, or simply do not do so. Moreover, deafness often is diagnosed late (Marschark, 1993). In addition, little is known about the language development of deaf children relative to what is known about normal language acquisition. For example, there is little systematic work on the syntactic, metalinguistic, or pragmatic development of deaf children, although what does exists suggests strong parallels between normal language acquisition and the language acquisition of both deaf who communicate orally and those who use sign language (Blarney, 2003; Schick, 2003). What should be emphasized, however, is that like language acquisition in hearing children, acquisition of language by deaf children very much depends on social interactions that are filled with high-quality language that, in the case of deaf children, they can see (Lederberg, 2003).

Cognitive Differences in Deaf and Hearing-Normal Individuals

Although there are some inconsistencies in the evidence, in general, deaf children perform below hearing-normal children on a variety of conventional assessments of general intelligence, including nonverbal measures (Marschark, 1993). Moreover, when tested on some theoretically derived measures of intellectual development, such as Piagetian measures of conservation, deaf children do less well than hearing-normal children (Furth, 1964, 1966; Watts, 1979).

Deaf children typically experience difficulties in school, as reflected by achievement test data (Karchmer & Mitchell, 2003). A number of studies suggest that deaf children's lack of knowledge of vocabulary and English language syntax, relative to hearing-normal students, contributes to their difficulties in learning to read and write, in particular, but also to achieve more generally in school (Conrad, 1979; Laybaert & Alegria, 2003; Marschark, 1993; Paul, 2003; Power & Leigh, 2003; Quigley & Paul, 1984). An important advance in understanding in the past quarter century is that many of the instructional techniques that work with regular education populations can be adapted to increase the reading and writing skills of deaf students. For example, deaf students can be taught to use reading and writing strategies and their prior knowledge as they read and write (Albertini & Schley, 2003; Schirmer & Williams, 2003; see Chapter 4).

■ ■ ■ CHAPTER SUMMARY AND EVALUATION

Researchers identifying with a number of different disciplines and perspectives study children's language. Chomsky's theory inspired many biologically oriented researchers to evaluate the neurological and genetic determinants of language. Much is now understood about which brain structures support particular language competencies. Language functioning depends greatly on an intact left hemisphere, and individual differences in language ability are associated with individual differences in left-hemisphere structure and function. Such work is being carried out at an accelerated pace today because of technological advances in brain-imaging techniques, particularly techniques that permit localization of cognitive processing. Advances in behavior genetics methodologies have lead to increased understanding that individual differences in language functioning are largely determined by genetic differences, with language acquisition more certain during childhood than during later life. Despite the support for Chomsky's conviction that language is biologically determined, genetic and evolutionary analyses have not supported Chomsky's formulation of an invariant language acquisition device unique to humans. The symbolic capacities of the great apes are greater than Chomsky imagined. The individual differences between people in their language competencies are also greater than Chomsky originally supposed. When genes determine biology, there is always variation in biology!

The effects of immersion in a language are apparent from the earliest days of life, with babies a few days old clearly differentially sensitive to sounds from the language surrounding them. Children's earliest babbles reflect the sound structure of the language they have been hearing. Their awareness of that sound system will take years to develop and depends on particular types of experiences. Six months of experience in school playing games that require analysis of the sounds of words increases phonemic awareness, which increases the likelihood that the child will learn to decode well. Children also learn vocabulary from contextual experiences, including explicit teaching of vocabulary.

Bilingual language development is not all that much different from monolingual language development. The differences that do occur are small compared to the similarities. Most critically, acquisition of a language does not appear to be negatively affected by acquiring a second language at the same time. Indeed, bilingual children have some language capabilities not possessed by monolingual children, including greater awareness of language.

Language difference often translates into academic difficulties. English-second-language children's achievement does seem to depend, in part, on educational programs that transition them from education mostly in the native language to education in English. Additive immersion as practiced in Canada and some parts of the United States that are Spanish–English bilingual seems more effective than subtractive approaches. Even if a teacher is not in a district with additive options, much can be done at the classroom level to improve the experience of language-minority children.

Children can exhibit language disorders in every aspect of language, with it often the case that children who experience one impairment suffer other impairments as well. For example, phonological-processing problems undermine reading, which undermines semantic development. Although treatments for most language disorders exist, we are far from having cures for most language problems.

Deafness significantly impacts language development, although much of the language development of deaf children parallels normal language development. With the advent of technologies such as cochlear implants, there is definitely going to be new thinking about how deaf children can communicate to maximize their language development. The new technologies offer great promise for much better language outcomes for individuals with deafness than have occurred in the past.

Developmental Debates

The work on language development has proven fundamentally important to understanding many issues regarding development. We revisit them in closing this chapter, as we have revisited them at the end of each chapter.

Nature versus Nurture

Language depends on and is determined by biology. But experience matters too. At the extreme, children do not develop language unless they are exposed to it. Beyond exposure, however, rich language experiences in the home and explicit educational experiences do promote important aspects of language development, including development of phonemic awareness, learning of new syntactic structures, lexical development, and learning to decode. Both nature and nurture affect language development.

The similarities in language development across a range of language competencies—babbling, first words, gradual development of syntactic competence—suggest that biology plays a very great role in language. Even so, language development also depends greatly on experience. The sounds that children can hear and produce depend in part on the languages they experience during their first year of life. For some language-impaired children, production of certain sounds depends on intensive therapeutic experience. Whether a deaf child becomes an adult with some degree of oral language depends on his or her oral experience during childhood.

Stages versus Continuous Development

Childhood probably is a critical period for language development. The stage-like progression for the development of syntax proposed by Roger Brown decades ago still seems sensible. The data on accent in bilinguals strongly suggests that there is a sensitive period for acquiring the ability to produce the sounds of a language.

Lasting versus Transient Early Effects of Experience

Extreme language deprivation during childhood has lasting effects. So can less extreme forms of deprivation, however. For example, an impoverished language environment during the preschool years can devastate future academic achievement. Failing to have the educational experiences that promote phonemic awareness leaves a child at risk for long-term reading failure. The second-language acquisition literature is especially telling on this point, with early exposure leading to more complete acquisition given its effect on basic linguistic perceptual skills. The lack of exposure to sign language or oral language during the first 2 years of life, generally because of late detection of deafness, negatively impacts development. With respect to language, early experience very much matters.

■■■ REVIEW OF KEY TERMS

deep structure The underlying meaning of an utterance.

expressive style Refers to using many expressions of emotion, feeling, and action during the one-word stage of language acquision.

feral children Children who have been reared in isolation, without exposure to language.

language acquisition device According to Chomsky, an innate biological mechanism that allows us to understand the syntax of language.

mean length of utterance (MLU) A measure of the length of children's utterances used to track language acquisition.

morphemes The smallest units of language that convey meaning.

motherese The high-pitched, singsong speech often used by mothers to interact with their infants.

overregularization Refers to when children overgeneralize syntactic rules, thereby making grammatical errors that they had not made previously.

phonemes The most basic sounds of a language that combine to form words.

phonemic awareness Awareness that separate sounds (phonemes) are combined to make words.

referential style Refers to using many nouns during the one-word stage of language acquisition.

telegraphic speech Speech in which only the most important words are expressed.

CHAPTER 8

Intelligence and Individual Differences in Academic Competence

People differ in ways that influence their academic competence. Traditionally, psychologists and educators have measured such individual differences using standardized instruments, including intelligence tests or achievement tests. Thus this chapter begins with a discussion of standardized tests and consideration of two important characteristics of tests: their reliability and their validity. This section is followed by an extended discussion of the assessment of intelligence, including potential biases in intelligence assessment. Since intelligence tests often figure prominently in the intellectual classification of students, this sets the stage for discussion of learner diversity. The potential threats to intellectual capacity, including living in poverty, exposure to harmful substances, and disease, are also taken up briefly.

■ ■ ■ STANDARDIZED TESTS

Standardized tests are given under controlled conditions so that every person taking the test has approximately the same examination experience. Developers of standardized tests also provide test norms. A **norm** is the typical level of performance for a clearly defined reference group. For example, norms might be provided for students of various ages or for students in different grades. An individual score can then be interpreted by comparing it to the norm, the typical performance, for the group to which the individual belongs. It is important for norms to be up-to-date and truly representative of the reference group. For example, a norm obtained in 1975 from a white, middle-class suburban population is not appropriate for interpreting scores obtained in 2006 in a culturally diverse urban school.

It is very likely you have taken a standardized test. Perhaps your performance on that test influenced decisions about your future. For example, admission to college or graduate school often involves standardized testing of academic achievement (Calvin, 2000). Many readers of this book have taken the Scholastic Aptitude Test (SAT), which was revised in 1994 and renamed the Scholastic Assessment Test I: Reasoning Test (Viadero, 1994). In 2005, the SAT was revised again, adding a writing section. Other readers have taken the American College Test (ACT), which is similar to the SAT. In addition, states may use standardized tests to assess student progress—and may use the student test results as a measure of school accountability. In fact, the No Child Left Behind legislation, which passed Congress in 2002, requires much more testing in schools than has occurred in the past (107th Congress, Public Law 107-110). Clearly, educators need to be informed about the important qualities of standardized tests, especially about what to look for to determine a test's usefulness for the purpose it is being used for and how to address issues concerning potential test bias.

Two important characteristics of tests are reliability and validity. A first requirement of a test is that it have **reliability**, which means that it measure consistently. Without reliability, a test cannot possibly have **validity**, that is, measure what it is presumed to measure (Anastasi & Urbina, 1997; Cronbach, 1990; Sattler, 2002).

Reliability

The first step in understanding reliability is to grasp that any *observed score* on a test is actually comprised of two scores: the *true score* and *error*. Thus, *observed score = true score + error*. Error represents the part of the score that is due to irrelevant and chance factors. On some occasions performance is higher than it typically would be, such as when the tester is lucky guessing between two responses, and on other occasions it is lower than it typically would be. Some typical sources of testing error that may lower the scores of students taking any test are lack of sleep, illness, and an unusual level of anxiety. The greater the error, the lower the reliability.

One way to reduce error and to increase the reliability of a test is to make testing conditions as consistent as possible for all people taking the test. In other words, follow the standardization procedures. For instance, SAT reliabilities were calculated with group administration of the tests, under particular time constraints, and when students were not permitted to interact with one another or to consult notes or textbooks. If a student took the SAT with notes and open books, the reported reliability and validity would not hold under these circumstances. See Figure 8.1 for ways to increase the reliability of tests.

- Use test questions that can be scored objectively. The more subjective the scoring of the test items, the lower the reliability.
- Make certain that some questions on the test do not suggest the answers to other questions.
- Eliminate tricky questions. Tricky questions reduce the reliability of a test.
- Make certain the questions can be understood. Poorly worded questions reduce the reliability of a test.
- Make certain directions are clear. Poor directions reduce the reliability of a test.

FIGURE 8.1. Some ways to increase the reliability of tests.

How is reliability estimated? One method of establishing a test's reliability, **test–retest reliability**, is simply to administer the same test twice to a group of test-takers. The correlation between the two scores earned on each testing occasion indicates whether or not the test is measuring consistently (see the discussion of correlation in Chapter 1). If the students' relative performance on one test occasion is highly correlated with his or her relative performance on another testing occasion, the test is reliable.

Another form of reliability, **alternate-forms reliability**, measures the consistency of performance between two, supposedly equivalent, forms of the test. In this method of estimating reliability, students take two forms of the measurement. The correlation between performances on one form of the test and on the other form is the reliability of the test. The more similar the alternative forms of a test, the higher the reliability. Similar alternative forms cover the same content with the same number of roughly equally difficult items for each topic. Standardized tests often have multiple forms.

It is possible to estimate the reliability of a test even if the test is administered only once. This type of reliability measures the internal consistency of the items on the test. To calculate **split-half reliability**, a test is literally split in half. For example, scores for the odd and even items on the test are computed, and the correlation between the score on the odd items with the score on the even items is the "estimate of reliability." The problem with this approach is that the reliability estimate will vary depending on how the items are split. In most cases the correlation between odd–even halves would differ from a correlation based on halves produced by randomly assigning items to half-test scores. One solution to this problem is **coefficient alpha**, which is the average of all possible split-half reliabilities (Cronbach, 1951).

Validity

The reliability of a measurement is not enough. The measurement must also be valid for its purpose. Thus, although we can measure the circumferences of children's heads with high reliability, head circumference is not a valid measure of intelligence (an example from Gould, 1981). A measurement can be no more valid than it is reliable, however, so test developers must consider issues of validity and reliability simultaneously.

Does this test measure what it is supposed to measure? That is the main validity question. More specific validity questions depend somewhat on what is being assessed. Three common types of validity are *construct*, *criterion*, and *content* validity.

Construct Validity

The question addressed by **construct validity** is, Does this test measure the construct it is intended to measure? To understand this question, it is first necessary to define *construct*. Many psychological variables are abstract rather than concrete. For example, "ability" cannot be directly observed, nor can "intelligence." Such constructs must be inferred from behavioral observations. Thus "mathematical ability" is inferred from consistent, exceptional performance in mathematics. "Anxious personality" is inferred when an individual exhibits anxiety in situations that do not provoke anxiety in others. "Intelligence" is inferred from performances on academic tasks.

If test developers are attempting to create a new test for a construct measured by existing instruments, construct validation requires demonstrating that the new test correlates with the accepted tests measuring the construct. For example, if test developers were trying to create a short intelligence test that can be given in groups, they must demonstrate high correlations between their new measure and standard measures of intelligence.

Content Validity

The question addressed by **content validity** is, Does this test include the content it is supposed to cover? Suppose a national testing agency wishes to devise a test of high-school mathematics achievement. What should the test include? A content-valid assessment would include items from general mathematics, algebra, geometry, trigonometry, and calculus. Depending on the test's purpose, the proportions of these items might vary. If the purpose is to determine whether students have obtained basic numerical competencies, the test might consist primarily of general math items. If the purpose is to decide who should be selected as a finalist for scholarship consideration in mathematics, the test would include a much greater proportion of calculus and trigonometry items than general math items.

Content validity is an important concern for an educational achievement test. When test developers are devising a subject area test to assess knowledge in some undergraduate major area, they first must decide what should be covered and in what proportions. For example, developers of the Graduate Record Examination (GRE) in psychology might lay out all of the subfields of psychology that they wish to cover, such as developmental, social, clinical, physiological, educational, and experimental psychology. Then they must decide on the proportions of items for each subfield, based on their conception about which areas deserve emphasis relative to others. For example, areas that all psychology majors would have studied would receive more emphasis than completely elective areas.

Criterion Validity

The question addressed by **criterion validity** is, Does this test make the distinctions it is supposed to make? Does it predict performance on some criterion measure? For example, does the SAT discriminate between students who will be successful in college and those who will not be successful? It does in that SAT performance is positively correlated with college grades (Lawlor, Richman, & Richman, 1997; Pearson, 1993). When the criterion is in the future, as it is when the SAT is used to predict college grades, the criterion-related validity is referred to as *predictive validity*. When both a measure and its criterion can be collected close in time, criterion-related validity is sometimes referred to as *concurrent validity*. For example, when the extent of brain damage evident from using medical technology such as a CAT (computerized axial tomography) scan correlates highly with a behavioral measure of neurological damage, this would be evidence of concurrent validity for the two measures.

Questions Educators Should Ask about Tests

Educators should ask themselves some important questions about measurements and tests that they encounter:

- Is this test reliable?
    Does it measure consistently and how was this consistency determined?
        Test–retest? Alternate forms? Split-half?
    Does the test have many questions?
    Is the scoring relatively objective?
    Are the test-takers prepared?
- Is this test valid?
    Does it measure what the test developers indicate?
    How are the test results being used?
    What is the evidence of test validity?
        Construct validity? Content validity? Criterion validity?
- Are the norms appropriate?
    Is the norming group representative?
    Is the norming up to date?
- Are standardized testing procedures followed?

These questions can be answered by seeking out information provided in testing manuals for the tests in question. In addition, test consumers can consult publications found in reference libraries, such as the *Mental Measurements Yearbook* (Plake, Impara, & Spies, 2003), and *Tests in Print* (Murphy, Plake, Impara, & Spies, 2002), which review published tests and discuss how well they perform their purposes. A test should only be given great weight in decision making if it is reliable, valid for the intended purpose, appropriately normed, and has been administered as it was intended to be administered.

■ ■ ■ INTELLIGENCE TESTING

For well over a century, theorists and researchers who were interested in exploring the nature of intelligence focused not only on the conceptualization of what intelligence might be, but also investigated techniques for measuring it. This history is a rich one, although charged with controversy from its beginning. In his book *The Mismeasurement of Man* (1981), anthropologist Stephen Jay Gould provides an exceptionally interesting history of intelligence testing.

The origins of intelligence theory can be traced back to Francis Galton's (1869) *Hereditary Genius: An Inquiry into Its Laws and Consequences*. Galton's contributions to the scientific analysis of intelligence were enormous. For example, he devised a rudimentary individual-differences test based on reaction time, strength, eyesight, and motor abilities. He also devised rudimentary correlation coefficients to analyze the data he collected. Galton performed the first twin studies in an attempt to separate the contributions of heredity and environment in determination of individual differences (see also Chapter 2). Galton's thinking was a source of stimulation for both European and U.S. researchers who were interested in individual differences in intellectual abilities.

An extremely important advance in the study of intelligence was Spearman's (1904) conceptualization of intelligence as consisting of multiple factors, one general factor (*g*) and the others more specific (*s*), such as mathematical abilities or verbal competence. Every item on an intelligence test was assumed somehow to be related to general intelligence, with the degree of correlation to *g* varying among individual items. Every measure of intelligence also tapped specific functions, *s*, independent of *g*. Spearman definitely understood that intelligence was a construct, something that had to be inferred. He also understood that powerful inferences could be made based on correlations between measurements, and he developed the statistical methods that permitted the identification of patterns of correlations that indicated *g*. See the Considering Interesting Questions special feature (Box 8.1) for a discussion of the process to identify patterns of correlation indicating *g*.

Why were the first intelligence tests developed? Early in the 20th century, Alfred Binet was charged by the Minister of Public Instruction in Paris to find a way to discriminate between normal children and those with mental retardation. The result was Binet and Simon's intelligence scale for children (1905a, 1905b, 1905c). Lewis Terman shared Binet's vision that useful discriminations could be made between normal and low intelligent children, but he also felt that the tests could be useful in identifying unintelligent adults. Terman's revision of the Binet–Simon scale, the Stanford–Binet scale, was carefully normed on U.S. children (Terman & Childs, 1912). In the United States, Yoakum and Yerkes (1920) designed tests for the U.S. Army to help it to discriminate between the mentally unfit and those who attempted to fake stupidity to avoid World War I. These U.S. Army tests were able to make discriminations in ability in that higher ranking troops generally performed better than lower ranking troops (Yoakum & Yerkes, 1920).

It is impressive that these early tests resemble contemporary intelligence assessments, although a number of other tests of intelligence were proposed and dismissed or discontinued after a short period of use. What follows is a description of the most influential contemporary measures of intelligence (Reynolds & Kamphaus, 2003; Wasserman, 2003).

Considering Interesting Questions

BOX 8.1. How Do We Know There Is a *g* Factor in Intelligence?

Sometimes tests assess more than one process or knowledge domain. How do test-makers determine which items on the test are assessing the same construct? When items test the same construct, performances on these items correlate more highly with one another than performances on other items (see the discussion of *correlation* in Chapter 1). **Factor analysis** is a way of making sense of the correlations between items (Gorsuch, 1983). The starting point for factor analysis is identifying how performance on each item of a test correlates with performance on each other item on the test. For example, if every time a student is correct on item 12, he or she is correct on item 16, and every time a student is wrong on 12, he or she is wrong on 16, the correlation between 12 and 16 would be 1. If this is the case, performance on 16 can be predicted perfectly from performance on 12. If there is a 50/50 chance a person who gets 12 correct will get 16 correct and a 50/50 chance that a person who gets 12 wrong will get 16 right, the correlation between 12 and 16 would be 0. If this is the case, it is impossible to predict performance on 16 from knowing performance on 12. If there are 50 items on a test, there will be 1,225 (50 × 50) correlations to review, a difficult task made easier through factor analysis.

Factor analysis identifies clusters of items, or "factors," that correlate with one another. Then the investigator examines items in each factor to identify what might be causing the correlations. When intelligence test data are factor-analyzed, most or all of the items or subtests frequently cluster in one common factor, which has become known as *g* for general intelligence.

The reasons for developing intelligence tests in the early 20th century were varied. The Army tests were designed to discriminate the mentally unfit from those faking stupidity to avoid serving in World War I.

Wechsler Intelligence Scales

In the 1930s, David Wechsler began work on the test that would become the standard for the assessment of adult intelligence, the *Wechsler Adult Intelligence Scale (WAIS)*. He borrowed liberally from previously validated tests, although his instrument was unique in its balance of nonverbal and verbal items (verbal items had predominated in most previous assessments). The test has been revised three times, most recently in 1997 as the Wechsler Adult Intelligence Scale–III (WAIS-III). See Figure 8.2 for a description of the Verbal and Performance scales of the WAIS-III. One of the strengths of the WAIS-III is that it has high test–retest reliability (.97). The concurrent validity (and to some extent the construct validity as well) of the WAIS-III is supported by high correlations of WAIS-III scores with scores obtained from other intelligence tests (Ryan & Smith, 2003; Thorndike, Hagen, & Sattler, 1986).

The WAIS-III was adapted for use with children. The *Wechsler Intelligence Scale for Children (WISC-IV)*, published in 2003, can be administered to children ages 6 years, 0 months to 16 years, 11 months (Weiss, Saklofske, & Prifitera, 2003). The test–retest reliability is high (0.91 and above for all age groups), as is the concurrent validity, with the test correlating with other standardized measures of intelligence. Because sometimes information is needed about preschool children, the *Wechsler Preschool and Primary Scale of Intelligence–Revised (WPPSI; 1991)* was developed for use

Verbal Scales of the WAIS-III

- *Information*: questions tapping general knowledge from such fields as literature, history, and geography
- *Digit Span*: lists of digits to recall either in order of presentation (forward span) or reverse order of presentation (backward span)
- *Vocabulary*: words to define
- *Arithmetic*: problems to solve
- *Comprehension*: questions dealing with everyday problems requiring understanding of social rules and concepts
- *Similarities*: pairs of words, with the examinee asked to explain the similarity between the words in each pair

Performance Scales of the WAIS-III

- *Picture Completion*: drawings of common objects, each of which is missing some essential component, with the examinee asked to indicate the missing part (timed)
- *Picture Arrangement*: series of pictures to place in a logical sequence (timed)
- *Block Design*: red-and-white pictures of designs, with the examinee asked to construct a matching design with red-and-white plastic blocks (timed)
- *Object Assembly*: jigsaw puzzles to solve that produce pictures of well-known objects (timed)
- *Digit Symbol*: number–symbol pairings to remember, with the examinee asked to copy the appropriate symbol when presented with numbers alone (timed)

FIGURE 8.2. Verbal and Performance scales of the WAIS-III.

with children 4 to 6½ years of age (Saye, 2003). The test–retest reliability is .91 and the test also has good concurrent validity, correlating highly with other intelligence scales used with children.

Other Intelligence Tests for Children

Two other important intelligence assessments with normal children, the Stanford–Binet and the Kaufman Assessment Battery for children, are described in the following sections.

Stanford–Binet

The *Stanford–Binet, Fifth Edition*, can be used for a wide age range (norms are available for 2- to 23-year-olds; Youngstrom, Glutting, & Watkins, 2003). It provides a general score (*g*), along with scores in four specific areas: verbal reasoning, quantitative reasoning, abstract/visual reasoning, and short-term memory. The Stanford–Binet is based upon the conceptualization of intelligence described by Cattell (as described later in this chapter; see also Kamphaus, 1993; Reynolds & Kamphaus, 2003). Test–retest reliability for the composite score is .90 and concurrent validity for the composite score is fairly high, with correlations with other intelligence ranging from .71 to .91.

Kaufman Assessment Battery for Children

Although the Wechsler scales are the most commonly used measures of intelligence, the Kaufman Assessment Battery for Children (K-ABC; Kaufman & Kaufman, 1983) is also widely used (Kamphaus, 1993, 2003). Based on theories of intelligence derived from information-processing perspectives (see Chapter 4), this scale focuses on measuring mental processes, "how" children tackle intellectual problems rather than simply whether they are successful or not. The original K-ABC scales (for children ages 3–12) differentiate between simultaneous and sequential processing. *Simultaneous processing* refers to the ability to integrate information all at once to solve a problem correctly. *Sequential processing* refers to the ability to arrange information in sequential or serial order for successful problem solving. The K-ABC has good test–retest reliability, predictive validity for school achievement, and the content of the test items were carefully designed to provide a fair assessment of minorities, bilinguals, and children with language difficulties (Anastasi & Urbina, 1997; Kamphaus, Kaufman, & Harrison, 1990). A 2004 revision of the test, the KABC-II, maintains the original version's emphasis on processing (Simultaneous and Sequential) but adds a Learning Ability scale (long-term storage and retrieval). For older children, Planning Ability and Knowledge scales can be added. A Nonverbal Index is also available to test nonnative English speakers and children with hearing impairments. The KABC-II can be administered to a wider age range (ages 3–18) than the original (ages 3–12).

Group Measures of Intelligence

All intelligence tests with excellent reliability and validity are individually administered, although some tests of mental ability that can be administered to groups of children have acceptable reliability and validity. Since group measures are not as reliable as individual measures of intelligence, they are not used for placing children in special programs. Tests such as the Otis–Lennon School Ability Test (OLSAT), the Cognitive Abilities Test (CogAT), the Detroit Tests of Learning Aptitude (DTLA), and the School and College Ability Tests (SCAT) provide helpful information to teachers and school personnel at low cost (Sattler, 2002; Braden, 2003). Typically, students are provided a response book or answer sheet and mark their answers in the booklet or on the sheet. The directions for these tests have been carefully prepared so that most students can understand them. Items on these tests call for students to make classifications and to solve analogies, number series, and problems (Anastasi & Urbina, 1997). Educators should take care to read the manuals and supporting materials carefully before they administer such tests or attempt to interpret the scores. See the Applying Developmental Theory to Educational Contexts special feature (Box 8.2) for more information on how to interpret test scores.

Intellectual Competencies across the Lifespan

Does intellectual functioning change much across the lifespan? Do IQ scores at childhood correlate with scores at adulthood? Yes, IQ scores at age 7 correlate at least .60 with IQ scores at age 18 (Brody, 1992; Brody & Brody, 1978). Test designed to measure intelligence in infants, however, do not predict adult intelligence very well (Francis, Self, & Horowitz, 1987; Goodman, 1990) or even intelligence in later childhood (Tasbihsazan, Nettelbeck, & Kirby, 2003).

Applying Developmental Theory to Educational Contexts

BOX 8.2. Interpreting Standardized Test Scores

Many different standardized tests, such as intelligence tests or achievement tests, are used routinely in today's classrooms. It is important that future educators (and future parents and taxpayers) understand better what a standardized test score means. Simply reporting the number of items a student got correct on a standardized test gives little information about the student. In contrast, comparing a student's raw score to a measure of central tendency for the distribution of scores provides more information about the student's performance in relationship to the performance of others. The most commonly used measure of central tendency in reporting standardized test results is the mean.

The **mean** of a distribution of scores is the average score. The mean is computed by adding up the scores and dividing the sum of scores by the number of scores. For example,

If there are raw scores of 2, 4, 5, 7, 1, 3, 8, 9, 1, 10

The sum of scores = 50; number of scores = 10

Therefore, the mean is 5.

In this set of scores, six of the students (those scoring 2, 4, 5, 1, 3, and 1) scored at or below the mean. The other students (those scoring 7, 8, 9, and 10) scored above the mean.

Measures of variation, such as the **standard deviation**, provide still more information. The standard deviation is a measure of how widely scores vary from the mean. The larger the standard deviation is, the more spread out from the mean the scores are. The smaller the standard deviation, the more the scores are clustered around the mean.

The norms for standardized tests are typically normally distributed. In a **normal distribution**, most of the scores fall near the mean, that is, fewer scores are further away from the mean (see Box Figure 8.1). Using the mean and the standard deviation, the normal distribution can

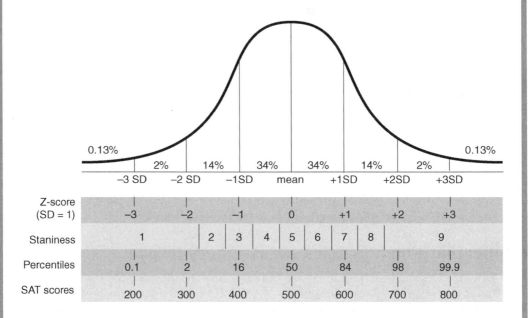

BOX FIGURE 8.1. Normal distribution, with percentiles, z-scores, stanines, and SAT scores clearly indicated.

(continued)

be divided into parts. Approximately two-thirds of the scores (68%) fall within 1 standard deviation of the mean. Fewer scores (28%) fall between 1 and 2 standard deviations from the mean, and very few scores (4%) are over 2 standard deviations from the mean. For example, scores on the SAT are normally distributed with a mean of 500 and a standard deviation of 100. In all the Wechsler intelligence scales, the mean performance is 100 with a standard deviation of 15.

Scores on standardized tests are often expressed in **standard scores**. A very common standard score, the **z-score**, tells how many standard deviations above or below the mean a raw score is (see Box Figure 8.1):

$$z\text{-score} = (X - M)/SD$$

where X is any raw score, M is the mean of the raw scores, and SD is the standard deviation of the raw scores.

Scores on standardized tests are also often expressed in terms of stanines. **Stanines** are standard scores with only 9 possible categories corresponding to ordered regions of the normal distribution. The mean is 5, and the standard deviation is 2. As you can see from Box Figure 8.1, each stanine corresponds to a band of raw scores with the width of half a standard deviation except for stanines 1 and 9, which include the ends of the distribution. Although stanines are less precise measures for the extreme scores, one advantage of this method of scoring is that performance can be expressed in only one digit, from a low of 1 to a high of 9.

Finally, perhaps the most easily communicated method of expressing standardized test scores is in terms of percentile ranks. **Percentile ranks** are expressed in terms of relative position within a norm group. The percentile rank shows the percentage of students in the norming sample who scored at or below a particular raw score. For example, a percentile rank of 75 means the student scored the same or better than 75% of the other students in the norm group. Percentile ranks are often more easily understood by parents and teachers than the other methods of reporting standardized test scores.

Do IQ scores change across the adult lifespan? For many years, psychologists reported that intelligence test scores decrease with increasing age during adulthood. After age 20, it was all downhill! This conclusion, however, was generated via cross-sectional studies. That is, different people provided the intelligence data at each age level. Cross-sectional studies confound age level and the cohort of people providing the data. (Recall the discussion of *cohort effects* in Chapter 1.) This confounding is particularly important in this case because of the differences in educational and cultural experiences found in older and younger adults, which influence their performance on intelligence tests (Baltes, 1968; Baltes et al., 1988; Kaufman, 1990; Schaie, 1980; Schaie & Labouvie-Vief, 1974). Intelligence data collected longitudinally suggest that the decline in IQ is much less dramatic than it seems when cross-sectional data are examined (Schaie, 1990, 2002).

Cattell and Horn's Theory of Intelligence across the Lifespan

In recent decades, researchers have broken down general intelligence into different factors, with aging affecting some aspects of intelligence differently than other aspects. Many intelligence tests have items that can be thought of as tapping either knowledge or ability to process quickly and adeptly. Knowledge and the ability to process correspond to Cattell's two factors of intelligence: crystallized and fluid ability (Cattell, 1987; Cattell & Horn, 1978; Horn, 1985; Horn & Cattell, 1967; Horn &

Hofer, 1992; Horn & Stankov, 1982). **Crystallized intelligence** is measured by intelligence test items indicating breadth and depth of cultural knowledge, such as vocabulary knowledge. **Fluid intelligence** is measured by items requiring reasoning abilities, such as inductive and deductive reasoning, to understand relations among stimuli, comprehend implications, and draw inferences.

During the childhood and adolescent years, both fluid and crystallized abilities increase (Sattler, 2002). During adulthood, however, there are important differences in the course of fluid and crystallized intelligence (see Figure 8.3). Why? The nervous system naturally deteriorates with advancing age during adulthood. For example, adults lose something like 50,000 neurons a day during adulthood due to normal cell death. Unlike other cells that die, neurons do not regenerate. Thus fluid intelligence, which is strongly dependent on biological wholeness, declines with advancing age (Brody, 1992; Kaufman, 1990). This means that older adults exhibit dramatic reductions in their ability to quickly execute steps in problem solving (Salthouse, 1982, 1985, 1988, 1992, 2005). On the other hand, life experiences accumulate with advancing age. Thus knowledge continues to grow through most of the adult lifespan. Not surprisingly, crystallized intelligence, which is determined by knowledge, increases with advancing years. When individual differences in speed of processing (fluid intelligence) and differences in amount of education are taken into account, there is evidence that crystallized abilities can increase until age 70 (Hertzog, 1989; Kaufman, 1990; Kaufman, Reynolds, & McLean, 1989; Schaie & Labouvie-Vief, 1974).

Continuing Debates about the Nature of Intelligence

Theorists have offered alternatives to the traditional *g*-theory of intelligence as measured by traditional intelligence tests. For example, in two sets of essays on *What Is Intelligence?* (Khalfa, 1994; Sternberg & Detterman, 1986), intelligence was variously

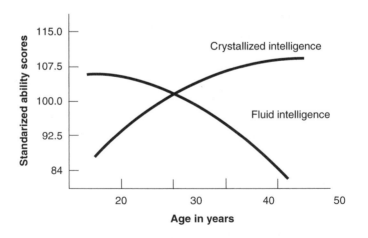

FIGURE 8.3. Fluid and crystallized intelligence across the lifespan. From "Major abilities and development in the adult period" by J. L. Horn and S. M. Hofer, 1992. In R. J. Sternberg and C. A. Berg (Eds.), *Intellectual Development*, New York: Cambridge University Press. Copyright 1992 by Cambridge University Press. Reprinted with permission of Cambridge University Press.

defined as acting appropriately and responsibly, being skilled in problem solving, having and being able to apply a great deal of knowledge, knowing and being able to do what is valued in one's culture, possessing the ability to learn, possessing the ability to make inferences, and having the ability to make and use tools. The *Encyclopedia of Intelligence* (Sternberg, 1994) included 250 articles about intelligence, showcasing a vast array of alternative conceptions of the construct. Two of the most cited alternative conceptions to the traditional view—the triarchic theory of intelligence and the theory of multiple intelligence—are described in the next sections.

Triarchic Theory of Intelligence

Robert Sternberg (1985, 2003) proposed a process-oriented theory of intelligence called the *triarchic theory*. The triarchic theory is composed of three subtheories: contextual, experiential, and componential. The *contextual* subtheory highlights the sociocultural context of an individual's life. Intelligent individuals adapt in order to maximize the fit between themselves and their environment. They may also shape their environment to increase the fit or, if a satisfactory fit is not possible, they select an alternative environment. According to this perspective, what is intelligent behavior depends on the cultural context.

The second subtheory, the *experiential* subtheory, emphasizes the role of experience in intelligent behavior. Sternberg argues that intelligent behavior sometimes reflects the ability to deal with novel experiences by drawing upon past experiences but also refers to the ability to deal with familiar situations quickly and efficiently. Thus intelligent behavior involves accessing prior knowledge and developing automaticity (these concepts were introduced in Chapter 4).

The third subtheory, the *componential* subtheory, specifies the mental structures that underlie intelligent behavior. These components correspond well to the characteristics of information processing described in Chapter 4. "*Metacomponents* are higher-order executive processes used in planning, monitoring, and decision making in task performance" (Sternberg, 1985, p. 99). These include processes such as deciding what the problem is, selecting a strategy, and monitoring a solution.

"*Performance components* are processes used in the execution of a task" (Sternberg, 1985, p. 99). These include recall of new information, integrating and comparing pieces of information, and outputting solutions once they are determined.

"*Knowledge-acquisition components* are processes used in gaining new knowledge" (Sternberg, 1985, p. 107). These include distinguishing relevant from irrelevant information, combining encoded information into a coherent whole, and comparing new information with information acquired in the past.

Theory of Multiple Intelligences

In his *theory of multiple intelligences*, Howard Gardner (1983, 1993, 1999) argues that people have a set of specific intelligences that are biologically determined. These include linguistic intelligence, musical intelligence, logic–mathematical intelligence, spatial intelligence, body–kinesthetic intelligence, interpersonal intelligence (i.e., the ability to notice and make distinctions among other individuals), and intrapersonal intelligence (i.e., access to one's own feelings). People with high linguistic abilities may excel in fields requiring verbal skills, such as journalism. People with high musical intelligence may excel as musicians or composers. High logic–mathematical intelligence would predict success as a mathematician or engineer. Those high in spatial intelligence may excel in fields such as sculpting or architecture. Body–kinesthetic intelligence is necessary for athletes. Interpersonal intelligence is a key characteristic of salesman and therapists and intrapersonal intelligence is important for successful actors. Almost every human endeavor, of course, requires more than one type of intelligence. For instance, dancers would need to be high in musical as well as in body–kinesthetic intelligence. Trial attorneys would need to be high in linguistic and in interpersonal intelligence. Engineers would need spatial intelligence as well as logic–mathematical intelligence.

One of the most critical features of this theory is that people vary in the strength of their particular faculties. Gardner argues that it makes no sense to think of someone as smart or not-so-smart in general, as is implied in traditional views of intelligence. Rather, people with musical intelligence would be expected to excel in music given appropriate stimulation; while those who have superior capacity in mathematics would be expected to do well given appropriate exposure to mathematics.

Gardner believes that one of the problems with contemporary schooling is that linguistic, and logic–mathematical intelligences are emphasized to the exclusion of others. Schools do little to gauge the strengths and weaknesses of students in terms of the various intelligences. He argues that educators should realize the multiple nature of abilities. This awareness would lead them to help students discover their own patterns of strengths and weaknesses. Then teachers could encourage students to accentuate their strengths as well as help their students to learn to compensate for their weaknesses or even teach them ways of remediating their weaknesses.

■ ■ ■ BIAS IN MENTAL TESTING

As introduced in Chapter 6, there has been a historic tendency in the United States to denigrate the intelligence of minorities and to conclude that their minds are somehow biologically inferior. For example, intelligence data collected during World War I was interpreted to mean that recent immigrants (e.g., Irish, Italian, and Swiss) were not as intelligent as people born in the United States. Many Americans are aware that the IQ scores of blacks are on average approximately 15 points lower than the IQ scores of whites. For all of this century, there have been those who have pointed to such differences as indicative of biological differences between races, with the most recent example being *The Bell Curve* (Herrnstein & Murray, 1994). There are many reasons to object to such a conclusion, most of which boil down to potential systematic biases in intellectual testing that put some groups at a disadvantage relative to others (Fraser, 1995; Jacoby & Glauberman, 1995; Reynolds & Kaiser, 2003; Reynolds & Ramsay, 2003).

Differences in Test Performance Related to Socioeconomic Level

Socioeconomic status is correlated with IQ scores. Specifically, those from socioeconomically inferior environments score lower (Jensen, 1973; Mensh & Mensh, 1991; Sattler, 2002). Socioeconomic differences between blacks and whites almost certainly account for some of the difference (perhaps a third) in intelligence scores between blacks and whites (Jensen, 1973). Other minority groups, such as Hispanics, are also disproportionately represented at the poverty levels of U.S. society, which is reflected by lower IQ scores.

Although some of the white-minority difference in intelligence test scores is due to socioeconomic differences between the populations, not all of it is. What might account for IQ score discrepancies ·that cannot be explained as due to socioeconomic-mediated differences? Are intelligence tests biased against various ethnic and racial groups?

Other Potential Sources of Test Bias

Bias can be introduced in tests in a number of ways (Reynolds & Kaiser, 1990a, 1990b). First, the content of items can tap concepts and experiences more familiar to some groups than to others. For example, the vocabulary used to test a concept may be unfamiliar to some people taking the test. Although test constructors attempt to eliminate "content bias," even experts in a culture cannot reliably identify items that will pose difficulty for children in their culture (Jensen, 1976; Sandoval & Mille, 1980). Fortunately, in well-constructed intelligence tests, high correlations in the difficulty level of items across populations are found (Reynolds & Kaiser, 1990b, 2003), thereby reducing the likelihood that some items are particularly difficult for minority groups.

A second possible bias concerns the predictive validity of the tests. Some tests may predict educational or other types of successes better for some groups than for others. Well-constructed tests, however, predict equally well across racial and cultural groups. For example, if the purpose of the test is to predict "Will this person do well in this college?," it is unbiased if the answer it generates is "correct" about the *same* proportion of times for *all* groups.

A third potential source of bias is in the samples (i.e., predominantly white, English-speaking) used to norm standardized tests. In particular, there may be sociocultural differences in understanding what it means to take a test and what the long-term implications of tests are (Rodriguez, 1992). Producers of well-constructed tests are aware of the need for representative national norming samples, however, and they make the effort to generate such samples (Sattler, 2002; Reynolds & Kaiser, 2003).

A fourth potential source of bias is mismatch between the test language and the primary language of the test-taker (Geisinger, 2003; Ochoa, 2003). As discussed in Chapter 6, laws in some parts of the United States required that all children be tested in English and decisions about school placement into special education or giftedness classes were based on these tests (Donlon, 1992; Rodriguez, 1992). When that was the case, disproportionately high numbers of Spanish-speaking children ended up in special education classes and disproportionately low numbers of Spanish-speaking children experienced accelerated offerings (Pennock-Román, 1992; Schmeiser, 1992). Ability tests administered in English to Spanish-speaking students sometimes do not correlate at all with ability tests administered in Spanish and may grossly underestimate intelligence.

A fifth potential source of bias is mismatch between the race and/or culture of the examiner and the test-taker (Geisinger, 2003; Ochoa, 2003). The race of an examiner, however, apparently does not make a difference in the test score earned by a person being examined (Graziano, Varca, & Levy, 1982). What does seem to matter is "familiarity" between the examiner and the person being tested, with personal familiarity between them boosting the performance of the examinee slightly. The "familiarity effect" seems to be especially large for lower socioeconomic populations (Fuchs & Fuchs, 1986).

In summary, there is a group of "usual suspects" in the bias debate, ones that are always on the mind of excellent test constructors who are determined to produced technically adequate and fair tests. Still, there are many tests on the market that are biased in the ways we have discussed, and educators should be on guard with respect to these sources of bias when selecting tests for use in assessing people and in interpreting test data already collected. Although it is possible to devise tests on which minority students perform better (such as Mercer's [1979] *System of Multicultural Pluralistic Assessement* [*SOMPA*] and Williams's [1972] *Black Intelligence Test of Cultural Homogeneity* [*BITCH-100*]), these tests have not proven to be valid predictors of academic achievement (Constantino, 1992; Sattler, 2002).

Testing and the Law

Arguments about test bias have appeared in our nation's court system. In *Larry P. v. Riles* (1979), a federal judge ruled that California's mandated use of intelligence tests to decide special education placements for minorities was inappropriate. Tests that have been normed without sufficient samples of minorities are rejected as a reasonable basis for making decisions about minorities (e.g., *Rivera v. City of Wichita Falls*, 1982).

Despite all the concerns with potential test bias, when tests are reliable and valid and are not being used intentionally to discriminate, they are being upheld as appropriate, even if disproportionate numbers of minorities fail the test (e.g., *United States of America v. State of South Carolina*, 1978). The courts are not rejecting the use of tests wholesale. Court decisions support tests that clearly tap competencies that are relevant to the selection process, such as competencies unquestionably required to do a job (*Washington v. Davis*, 1978). The more the test clearly reflects the requirements for a particular job, the more certain it is that the court will consider it valid. Thus, an in-the-cockpit test of flying skill would probably be considered valid for determining airline hiring, even if there were vast differences in the proportions of whites and minorities or men and women who passed the test.

In conclusion, we are more sensitive now than ever before about how intelligence tests and other standardized measures can be misused in their application with minorities. Minorities have greater legal protection than ever before, which is possible because of research that clarifies when tests are valid and when they are not valid, when they are biased and when they are not biased.

■ ■ ■ LEARNER DIVERSITY

Children can differ in many ways as learners. First, we introduce three common classifications of exceptional learners: (1) gifted students, (2) those with learning disabilities, and (3) individuals with mental retardation. Then we provide an overview of students who exhibit general characteristics that make them at risk for school difficulties. These include students living in poverty, students with a serious disease or medical condition, students who have been victims of environmental assaults, and substance abusers. Another very large group of students at risk for school failure, students who are non-native-English speakers, are considered in detail in Chapter 7. Practices for including these diverse learners in schools are described in the Applying Develomental Theory to Educational Contexts special feature (see Box 8.3).

Giftedness

The intellectually gifted are a great societal resource. Some of the gifted become great writers, physicians, statesmen, and business, academic, and industrial leaders. The gifted are a diverse group. One distinction is between **prodigies**, those who are very talented in one particular domain, and those who are generally smart but not exceptionally talented in any one area. Thus the gifted include both specialists and generalists (Feldman, 1986).

So who is gifted? What defines a gifted student? One criterion is IQ score, although many different IQ cutoff points have been used as the starting point for giftedness. Often scores of 130–140 are considered the lower part of the gifted range. In many school districts, however, scores as low as 115 are taken as the beginning of the gifted range, which means that approximately 10% of all children would be considered "gifted" (Grinder, 1985). Of course, a high IQ score alone does not define giftedness. For example, there are underachievers who perform well below what they are capable of based on their IQ scores. Some students are much stronger on some subscales of intelligence tests than on other subscales, so their overall IQ score does not adequately represent their giftedness. Not surprisingly, some have argued in favor of expanding the definition of giftedness beyond being a label for the upper end of the IQ distribution (Richert, 1991). Consider, for example, the discussion of Gardner's multiple intelligences earlier in this chapter. A person can have much greater intelligence in music, or math, or for physical activities than for other competencies.

Prodigies

Who is a prodigy? John Radford offers one definition (1990, p. 200): "Statistically, a prodigy comes at the extreme end of a distribution of achievement in a particular activity." For example, Wayne Gretsky was clearly the best of the best, a hockey prodigy if there ever was one, with his overwhelming talent apparent since he first showed up at the neighborhood rinks in Brantford, Ontario. Liona Boyd received a guitar for Christmas when she was 12 and as a young adult had established herself as the first lady of classical guitar. Stevie Wonder was a successful songwriter and singer at age 12 and has since had a long and distinguished career.

A main question posed by many studying prodigious genius is how to foster the giftedness of such individuals. What environmental variables influence whether a person with a great talent becomes a leading figure in a field of specialization? If the talent is there, how can we increase the odds of producing a great mathematician, scientist, or artist? The following are mentioned often as important to the development of prodigious genius (Bloom, 1985; Feldhusen, 1986; Feldman, 1988; Pleiss & Feldhusen, 1995; Radford, 1990; Renzulli, 1986; Tannenbaum, 1986):

Applying Developmental Theory to Educational Contexts

BOX 8.3. Inclusion of Diverse Learners in U.S. Classrooms

In the past, some students with disabilities were placed in regular classrooms where they received few if any special services. More students with disabilities, however, were placed in **self-contained classrooms** where they were taught by special education specialists and had little contact with regular instructional programs, or they attended separate schools designed for students with particular special needs (such as schools for the visually or hearing impaired, or schools for students with mental retardation). Today, students with disabilities often take their place next to nondisabled students in regular education classrooms. Educational practices for students with disabilities have changed greatly in response to criticisms of the failure to maximize the educational opportunities for all students and the passage of a series of laws beginning with Public Law 94-142.

Public Law 94-142 stipulates that students with disabilities be provided a free, appropriate education in the **least restrictive environment**. The term "least restrictive environment" is interpreted as meaning that students with disabilities must be educated with their nondisabled peers to the maximum extent appropriate. This provision has led to **mainstreaming**, or the practice of placing students with disabilities as often as possible in regular classrooms with their nondisabled peers, rather than in separate classrooms or schools. Implementation of the principle of least restrictive environment can range from **inclusion**, in which all instruction is received in the regular classroom (often including consultation or collaboration with special education teachers or other specialists), through temporary removal to a **resource room** for special services, to placement in a self-contained special education classroom.

Public Law 94-142 also calls for development of an **individualized education program (IEP).** The IEP describes a particular student's disability and outlines an educational plan to address the student's learning difficulties. The team who draws up the IEP is typically comprised of the special education teacher, the regular education teacher, the school principal, and the parent(s). An IEP has the following components:

- A summary of the student's present level of educational performance, based on sources such as standardized tests and classroom observations.
- A listing of both long-term goals and short-term instructional objectives for the student. The short-term objectives are steps progressing toward the long-term goals.
- A plan for support services the student needs to reach the goals and objectives. This plan also specifies the extent to which the student will participate in regular education programs.
- A method for evaluating whether or not the student attains the objectives and goals.

Thus, in today's classrooms, many educators work in teams to provide appropriate instruction for students with a wide range of special needs. These include physical and sensory disabilities, such as visual and hearing impairments; speech and communication disorders, such as articulation difficulties and stuttering; and emotional and behavioral problems, such as conduct disorders, including aggressiveness and withdrawal. The three common classifications of learning differences—giftedness, learning disabilities, and mental retardation—are discussed more fully in this chapter.

- Instruction related to exceptional abilities. Prodigies benefit from a series of teachers of increasing sophistication who coach the student in the area of his or her giftedness.
- Parents who are generally nurturing, but who are also supportive of the development of their child's particular talent.
- The child's long-term motivation to develop his or her ability, often to the point of obsession where it is as much play as work.
- For the child, multiple rewards for engaging in the activity, such as attention, applause, evident progress, and the opportunity to distinguish him- or herself from his or her peers.
- For the child, a great deal of practice of his or her special ability or abilities.
- For the child, confidence in his or her special ability.

This list makes it clear that the development of prodigious talent is the happy coincidence of many factors. A child with the right genes is born into a supportive family; the child is excited by his or her special competency and dedicated to developing it; and the talent is one that is needed by society, in that it is matched to the needs of the world at the moment.

For the child who does not have parents who are committed to developing his or her talent, school usually is society's best shot at directing the talent appropriately. Emerging genius requires some creative linking of resources to educate well. For example, conventional educational options may not serve well the brilliant fifth-grade computer programmer. Perhaps a solution for this child would be to match him or her with community members who are excellent programmers. Such individuals may be able to introduce an exceptional student to a much larger world of computer technology than anyone in the school could offer.

Whether or not this child prodigy's talent becomes fully developed will depend on many factors. Talent alone is not enough.

People Who Are Generally Highly Intelligent

Suppose we accept an IQ score of 130 as the cutoff for high general ability. Since that figure represents roughly only 2½% of the population, it is obvious that general intelligence is a scarce resource, yet not so rare that most educators are not going to be dealing with it on a regular basis. If a person is teaching 125 students a day at a high school with an average group of students, three or four of that teacher's students would have IQ scores exceeding 130. Thus all educators should have a working understanding of such students.

Terman's Study of the Gifted

Genius fascinated Lewis Terman, a professor at Stanford University. During the years when he was developing the Stanford–Binet test (as mentioned earlier in this chapter), Terman encountered a number of children who scored in the 140 range or higher. He was absorbed by the tales the parents of these children told of their sons and daughters reading and writing early. Terman knew of the stereotypes: Geniuses were quirky, eccentric, and even unhealthy. He also realized, however, that most of the geniuses he was meeting were well adjusted and happy (Shurkin, 1992; Terman, 1925; Terman & Oden, 1947, 1959).

In the early 1920s he began a longitudinal study of very bright children. He administered intelligence tests and other assessments to a large number of children throughout California. A sample of 643 children was identified as gifted in the sense of having IQ scores of 135 or higher. Eventually, other children from outside the geographical areas searched were added to the sample, as was a group of children with special talents, so that the final sample was over 1,500 children.

Contrary to the stereotypes, Terman's gifted children were more healthy and slightly superior physically to the population as a whole. They excelled in school and often moved ahead in the curriculum. Half of the sample was able to read before they began school. They tended to graduate from high school early and entered college at a young age. The Terman kids excelled in college and a high proportion were elected to the honorary society Phi Beta Kappa. In addition to being academically successful, these gifted people were also socially adept and accepted by their peers.

As adults, those in Terman's study were more likely to earn doctorates and professional degrees than members of the general population, with the majority eventually earning some kind of graduate degrees. Quite a few excelled in their fields, and their incomes were also well above population averages. (Not surprisingly, given the era of the study, the majority of Terman's women became non-income-producing homemakers.) The majority of Terman's adults reported being very satisfied with their life and life's work. In general, they reported that personal satisfaction was more important than occupational satisfaction. In addition, alcoholism was low for the group; so was criminality. Terman's adults married other bright people and gave birth to children with IQ scores that were well above average. In the twilight of their lives, the surviving Terman men and women appear happy and mentally active. Terman's study is one of the most visible pieces of evidence that gifted people tend to be happy and to be socioemotionally healthy (Reis & Renzulli, 2004).

One interesting comparison is between the very successful Terman children and the minority who were less successful. The successes had parents who really pushed them to achieve in school and to go to college. Thus, as with prodigies, parents seemed to play a guiding, shaping role in the lives of successful people with high intelligence. Ability alone does not guarantee great success.

Terman's study is sometimes criticized on the basis of how the children were selected to participate. Many of the children had been nominated by their teachers as exceptionally bright. These teachers may have been biased toward the nomination of well-adjusted children, those children doing well in a conventional school. Some very intelligent children may not have been nominated because they did not do well in school. Other children were nominated in a haphazard fashion by those familiar with the study, such as the brothers and sisters of nominated children. Although some precautions were supposedly taken to reduce bias due to language and cultural differences, the total sample included much lower proportions of minorities than were present in California in the 1920s. The initial sample was also biased toward the inclusion of boys and children from middle-class and upper-middle-class families.

Other researchers have added to our understanding of the gifted by analyzing specific aspects of the information processing of gifted individuals compared to the population at large (see also Chapter 4). This research has illuminated ways in which the intellectually gifted differ from other children.

Strategies and Metacognition

The gifted use more advanced strategies than peers of average intelligence on memory and problem-solving tasks (Jackson & Butterfield, 1986; Robinson & Kingsley, 1977; Steiner & Carr, 2003). They also have superior metacognition (Alonso, 1999; Hannah & Shore, 1995; Sternberg, 1981). Gifted children are more likely to continue to use effective strategies and to transfer them from one task to another task where the strategies might be useful (Borkowski & Peck, 1986; Chan, 1996; Cho & Ahn, 2003; Coyle, Read, Gaultney, & Bjorklund, 1998; Jackson & Butterfield, 1986). Even so, underachieving gifted children can benefit from instruction in strategies for accomplishing academic tasks (Jausovec, 1994; Manning, Glasner, & Smith, 1996; Muir-Broaddus, 1995).

Processing Efficiency: Interactions between Working Memory, Speed of Processing, and Knowledge

Gifted people process information more efficiently than do other people (Jausovec, 1998; Kanevsky, 1995; Saccuzzo, Johnson, & Guertin, 1994). For example, they can scan a set of items being held in memory more rapidly than people of average intelligence (Keating & Bobbitt, 1978; McCauley, Kellas, Dugas, & DeVillis, 1976). They also can retrieve information more rapidly than can people of average intelligence (Borkowski & Peck, 1986; Hunt, Lunneborg, & Lewis, 1975; Jackson & Myers, 1982). Gifted students process information more efficiently than do less talented people, with their superior efficiency freeing up more of their short-term memory capacity for consideration and manipulation of strategies and other knowledge.

The gifted also have great facility in combining information and working with knowledge to produce new ideas and solve problems (Feldman, 1982; Geary & Brown, 1991; MacKinnon, 1978; Sternberg & Davidson, 1983). They acquire early mastery of knowledge in the field in which they are gifted and their knowledge is deeper and broader than that of people of normal intelligence (Feldhusen, 1986; Gagné & Dick, 1983; Rabinowitz & Glaser, 1985; Tannenbaum, 1983).

Motivation

The gifted have a strong commitment to excellent performance in one or more fields (Feldman, 1979; Terman & Oden, 1959). They also have high self-concepts (Feldhusen, 1986; Feldhusen & Kolloff, 1981; Ketcham & Snyder, 1977; Ringness, 1961).

One possibility that continues to be explored is that gifted boys may be more motivated than gifted girls in academic settings, although this probably depends on the specific academic task and how academic tasks are presented (Dai, 2002).

Learning Disabilities

Debates over the definition of learning disabilities continue to rage (Kavale & Forness, 1992, 1995; Torgesen, 1991). Students with learning disabilities perform below expected levels in some academic area but otherwise perform within expected levels of achievement for age and grade. Learning disabilities may be specific to one or two competencies or to a cluster of closely related competencies, such as reading and writing.

Many people think of dyslexia when they hear the term "learning disability." **Dyslexia**, which is the inability to decode words well despite intensive educational efforts, accounts for only a small proportion of all learning disabilities. Probably no more than 1% of all people suffer from dyslexia. Learning disabilities are more wide ranging than dyslexia, including difficulties in comprehending once decoding is accomplished, difficulties in remembering what has been read, and nonverbal disabilities such as extreme difficulties in calculating (see also Chapter 2).

It is difficult to determine how many students have learning disabilities. The percentage of students classified as LD in schools is typically reported as between 4 and 5% of the population of children in school (Kavale & Forness, 1992). It is likely, however, that too many students are being classified as learning-disabled. Sometimes the only way to obtain needed services (and financial resources for the services) for some students is to have them classified as learning-disabled. Moreover, parents are less likely to protest their child being diagnosed as having learning disabilities than as having mental retardation. Since the federal government has increased pressure to identify no more than 2% of the total schoolage population as learning-disabled, the number of students classified as learning-disabled has declined.

Progress has been made in identifying neurological abnormalities, especially for reading disabilities. For example, using a variety of techniques—from studies of cerebral blood flow to autopsies—abnormal structures and dysfunctions of the left hemisphere have been detected in the reading-disabled (Flowers et al., 1991; Galaburda et al., 1985; Hier et al., 1978; Shaywitz, 2003; Shaywitz et al., 2003; Zeffiro & Eden, 2003). The use of brain-imagery techniques, such as MRI technology, has revealed that regions of the brain implicated in language processing tend to be smaller in reading-disabled students (Hynd & Semrud-Clikeman, 1989; Shaywitz, 2003). MRI studies have also detected abnormal brain structures at the back of the left hemisphere of dyslexics (Jernigan et al., 1991; Larsen et al., 1990; Shaywitz, 2003). In addition, there also are abnormalities of blood flow in the frontal lobes of children with attention-deficit/hyperactivity disorder (Lou, Henriksen, & Bruhn, 1984), which is not surprising given that the frontal lobes are critical for self-control and self-regulation.

Although learning disabilities were not first defined in terms of information processing, analyzing the information-processing characteristics of students with learning disabilities compared to normal learners has increased our understanding of learning disabilities. The results of this research have influenced the design of instructional interventions that increase the academic performance of learning-disabled students (Larson & Gerber, 1992).

Strategies and Metacognition

Students with learning disabilities are less likely than normally achieving students to use strategies for performing academic tasks (Bauer, 1977a; Torgesen & Goldman, 1977). Fortunately, students with learning disabilities are able to carry out strategies when instructed to do so (Bauer, 1977b; Mastropieri, Sweda, & Scruggs, 2000; Tarver, Hallahan, Kauffman, & Ball, 1976; Torgesen, 1977). For example, students with reading disabilities benefit from learning prediction, questioning, clarification, and summarization strategies, with the result of improved comprehension (Anderson, 1992; Gersten, Fuchs, Williams, & Baker, 2001; Klingner, Vaughn, & Schumm, 1998). Students who have difficulties in language arts can learn to use writing interventions such as the plan–write–revise approach to composition (Gersten & Baker, 2001; Graham & Harris, 2003; see also Chapter 4). Students who struggle to learn mathematics benefit from instruction in problem-solving strategies (Fuchs & Fuchs, 2003).

Strategy instruction for students with learning disabilities includes extensive attention to metacognition, including efforts to increase student awareness of when and where the strategies can be used, and many prompts encouraging students to monitor their own performance (Swanson & Sáez, 2003; Wong, Harris, Graham, & Butler, 2003). The reason for this is that students with learning disabilities often are not as aware as normally achieving students of their cognition (Larson & Gerber, 1992). Such instruction can be very effective in developing strategic competence in students with learning disabilities (Meichenbaum & Biemiller, 1998).

Processing Efficiency: Interactions between Working Memory, Speed of Processing, and Knowledge

Students with learning disabilities make less efficient use of their limited-capacity working memory than normally achieving students (Hulme & Mackenzie, 1992; Swanson, 2003; Swanson & Cooney, 1991; Swanson & Sáez, 2003). It is impossible, however, to be certain that there is really less capacity. Rather, it may only seem that way because of processing inefficiencies. Many students with learning disabilities are easily distractible, and so much of their attention may be diverted away from the task that little of the total capacity is used for the memory demand (Cutting & Denckla, 2003; Shaywitz & Shaywitz, 1992). Moreover, lacking prior knowledge possessed by many others prohibits the learning-disabled from forming meaningful "chunks," which are easier to hold in working memory. Also, students with learning disabilities do not readily use strategies to reduce capacity demands, such as taking notes. See the Applying Developmental Theory to Educational Contexts special feature (Box 8.4) for a discussion of students who display attentional deficits in classroom contexts.

Motivation

Students with learning disabilities are more passive than other students (Torgesen, 1975, 1977). They often are caught in a terrible cycle. Because they have done poorly in school, they think of themselves as academic failures—they begin to believe they are stupid. Such a belief does nothing to motivate academic effort, which results in additional failure, which in turn strengthens the perception of low ability (Borkowski, Carr, Rellinger, & Pressley, 1990; Licht, 1983, 1992; Torgesen, 1977; see also Chapter 9). Consequently, compared to normally achieving children, students with learning disabilities lack academic self-esteem and they expect to do poorly in school (Butkowski & Willows, 1980; Rogers & Saklofske, 1985; Winne, Woodlands, & Wong, 1982).

Conventional schooling often reinforces the negative academic self-esteem of children with learning disabilities. Classrooms are filled with reminders to students who are doing poorly that they are doing so. Their papers are not displayed with the "A" papers, their names are not displayed in the "Geographer of the Week" display, and they are not members of the reading group that includes all the smartest children in the class. The more the classroom publicly honors its high achievers, the

Applying Developmental Theory to Educational Contexts

BOX 8.4. Attention-Deficit/Hyperactivity Disorder

Students with specific learning disabilities quite often exhibit difficulties maintaining attention. Sometimes these attentional deficits are paired with other behavioral symptoms (Lerner, Lowenthal, & Lerner, 1995; Stein, Efron, Schiff, & Glanzman, 2002). Students who display attentional deficits, impulsivity, and hyperactivity are identified as having **attention-deficit/ hyperactivity disorder** (ADHD). The attentional-deficit component of ADHD refers to difficulties sustaining attention. Phrases used to describe ADHD students include "fails to finish tasks," "can't concentrate," and is "easily distracted." The impulsivity component of ADHD refers to difficulties students with ADHD experience inhibiting responses. These students respond without considering alternatives, are careless and inaccurate, and appear unable to suppress inappropriate behavior. The hyperactivity component of ADHD refers to frequent and intense excessive body movements and vocalizations. Descriptions of students with ADHD relevant to this component are "squirmy and fidgety," "hums or talks incessantly," and "can't sit still." In an accurate diagnosis of ADHD, these symptoms are observed in different situations, such as both home and school, and should appear early in life (typically by age 7). ADHD is more often identified in boys than in girls.

Many students identified as having ADHD are treated with medications, most often stimulants such as Ritalin or Dexedrine (Lerner et al., 1995). These medications stimulate areas of the brain that control attention and can improve classroom performance. Some students experience side effects such as insomnia and loss of appetite. Some also experience a "rebound effect," where their behavior deteriorates later in the school day as the medication wears off (Lerner et al., 1995).

Treatment with medications, however, does not teach students how to control their behavior or promote self-regulation. Teachers can also employ a variety of techniques in the classroom that help students with ADHD to focus and sustain their attention. For example, they can make sure that the directions they give students are brief, clear, and simple. They can also limit the number of distractions in the student's work area. They can surround the student with ADHD with good role models or place the student near the teacher's position. It is also important for teachers to prepare students for transition and reduce transition time by establishing routines. Recognizing that all students (especially students with ADHD) have difficulty focusing attention for long periods of time, teachers can schedule frequent breaks between demanding tasks. Finally, teachers can promote self-regulation in students with ADHD through self-instruction techniques described in this chapter, as well as in Chapter 5 (see Chapter 12 for additional discussion of ADHD).

worse the social comparison for the low achievers (Ames & Archer, 1988; Stipek & Daniels, 1988).

This situation is not hopeless. Students with learning disabilities can learn to attribute their successes and failures to effort rather than to factors that are out of their control, such as ability or luck. When they do make "effort attributions," their motivation improves (Dev, 1998). As students are taught strategies that improve their task-related performances, they can also learn to attribute their task performances to use of the strategies (Borkowski et al., 1990; Licht, 1992). The long-term commitment of students with learning disabilities to the use of new strategies is increased when they understand that their performances are improving because of this strategy use (see also Chapter 4).

Other instructional procedures also increase learning-disabled students' sense of competence and control (Licht, 1992). Focusing students' attention on successful attainment of concrete and immediate goals, such as getting today's problems correct, increases student self-efficacy. **Self-efficacy** refers to students' beliefs that their performances are under their own control (Bandura & Schunk, 1981; see also Chapter 9). In contrast, focusing on progress toward long-term goals, such as on how many more days it will take to cover the entire unit of material, has much less of an impact on sense of self-efficacy. In addition, modeling can increase the sense of self-efficacy. When students see another student like themselves struggling with a task, but finally accomplishing it, their self-efficacy is likely to improve (Schunk, Hanson, & Cox, 1987). In addition, students seem to have greater self-efficacy, more positive feelings of competence, and better performance in classrooms emphasizing improvement rather than performance relative to peers (Nicholls, 1989).

Mental Retardation

"Mental retardation is a disability characterized by significant limitations both in intellectual functioning and in adaptive behavior as expressed in conceptual, social, and practical adaptive skills. This disability originates before age 18" (American Association on Mental Retardation, 2002; www.aamr.org/Policies/faq_mental_retardation.shtml). Thus individuals with mental retardation exhibit both limitations in intelligence and problems adapting to the environment beginning when they are young.

In general, the long-term prospects for independent functioning vary with the degree of retardation. A common convention is to consider individuals with IQ scores between 50 and 70 to have *mild retardation* and those with IQ scores below 50 to have *severe retardation* (Richardson & Koller, 1985). Most individuals with severe retardation require substantial social services and support for their entire lives. But many individuals with mild retardation manage to live reasonably independent lives as adults (Batshaw & Shapiro, 2002).

There is nothing magical about the IQ of 70 as a cutoff (Burns, 2003). In fact, there is a long history of considering people who have IQ scores between 70 and 85 as borderline for retardation, with these students at greater risk for failure in school than students with average intelligence (IQ scores around 100). Four times as many people are in this borderline group, with IQ scores between 70 and 85, as people in the group with IQ scores of 70 or less (Zetlin & Murtaugh, 1990).

An important distinction is between retardation caused by known organic causes and retardation due to sociocultural factors (Batshaw & Shapiro, 2002; Burack, 1990). The organic causes of retardation include the following:

- Chromosomal anomalies, including Down syndrome, which usually is due to an extra copy of chromosome 21. Other chromosomal abnormalities associated with mental retardation include abnormal genes and "fragile" sites on chromosomes (Batshaw & Tuchman, 2002; Evans & Hamerton, 1985; Roizen, 2002).
- Prenatal factors, including disease and infection, such as syphilis and rubella; exposure to radiation; malnutrition; and exposure to alcohol and other drugs (Beker, Farber, & Yanni, 2002; Berg, 1985; Spiegel & Bonwit, 2002; Stern, 1985; Wunsch, Conlon, & Scheidt, 2002).

- Injury at birth, including oxygen deprivation (Berg, 1985; Ward & McCune, 2002).
- Premature birth, which results in greater susceptibility to injury such as brain hemorrhage (Berg, 1985; Rais-Bahramai, Short, & Batshaw, 2002).
- Neonatal hazards, including head injury, disease (e.g., meningitis), chemical assault (e.g., lead exposure), and malnutrition (Berg, 1985; Stern, 1985).

Distinguishing retardation due to organic causes from sociocultural retardation is difficult (Batshaw & Shapiro, 2002). Sociocultural retardation tends to run in families, but explanations for this developmental problem vary. One obvious possibility is heredity. Perhaps parents of below-average intelligence simply provide their children with a genetic endowment that places them at the lower end of the range of intelligence. Sociocultural retardation, however, could also be due to some inherited, but undetected, organic disorder. In addition, parents of lower intelligence may provide less stimulating environments for their children than do parents of higher intelligence. In short, it is likely that familial retardation is multiply determined.

Determining the prevalence of retardation is also extremely difficult (MacMillan & Reschly, 1997; Zigler & Hodapp, 1986). About 75% of all retardations are of the sociocultural type that results in much less severe impairment than organic retardation. One good ballpark estimate is to remember is that at most 1 in 100 people have severe retardation, mostly organically caused. Another 2–3 people per 100 have mild retardation, with more of these having sociocultural retardation than organic retardation.

Although mental retardation continues to be defined in terms of performances on intelligence tests, mental retardation has proven to be more comprehensible in terms of the components of information processing. Thus we describe briefly the information-processing characteristics of children with mental retardation.

Strategies and Metacognition

Individuals with mental retardation are less likely to develop learning strategies than are normally intelligent individuals (Ellis, 1979). When given strategy instruction, however, students with mental retardation can learn to use a variety of strategies, such as rehearsal, categorization, and elaboration (Blackman & Lin, 1984; Bray, Fletcher, & Turner, 1997; Brown, 1978).

Students with mental retardation, however, do not regulate their use of the strategies that they know, at least not as well as children with normal intelligence (Bebko & Luhaorg, 1998; Brown, 1974; Brown & Campione, 1978). That is, although they can carry out strategies, they often do not do so on appropriate occasions. Fortunately, with more elaborate instruction, students with mental retardation can learn to regulate their use of strategies. One way they can learn to do so is through self-instruction (see Chapter 5). For example, these students can learn to self-instruct as follows (Belmont, Butterfield, & Ferretti, 1982):

- Decide on a goal.
- Make a plan to reach the goal.
- Try the plan.
- Ask themselves after their attempt, "Did the plan work?"
- If yes, no more is required; if no, ask, "Did I actually follow the plan?" If this

answer is no, the students try to follow the plan. If the answer is yes, the students ask themselves, "What was wrong with the plan?" and devise a new plan and try it.

Why does self-instruction like this work? Students with mental retardation are often impulsive. **Impulsivity** refers to the tendency to respond quickly without considering alternatives. Self-instruction forces students to plan and reflect on their actions and the characteristics of the situation. When students check their performance following use of a strategy, they are attending to utility information, or how well the strategy works, which is important in promoting maintenance of strategy use (see also Chapter 4). The attempt to devise a new plan when an old plan fails also forces attention to information about when and where strategies are helpful. Thus self-instruction affects long-term self-regulation by increasing metacognition about strategies such as knowledge of when and where strategies work (Borkowski & Kurtz, 1984).

Processing Efficiency: Interactions between Working Memory, Speed of Processing, and Knowledge

Working memory capacity probably is more limited in students with mental retardation than in normal achievers (Hulme & Mackenzie, 1992; Rosenquist, Conners, & Roskos-Ewoldsen, 2003). It is uncertain whether students with mental retardation really have less neurological capacity or if it only seems so because they use their capacity inefficiently (Brewer, 1987; Detterman, 1979; Henry & MacLean, 2002; Numminen, Service, & Ruoppila, 2002). Although students with mental retardation can learn to do many tasks faster with practice, they remain far slower than normally intelligent students who are given equivalent practice (Brewer, 1987; Nettlebeck & Wilson, 1997). They are also often less attentive than normally achieving students to task-relevant information (Ross & Ross, 1984; Tomporowski & Tinsley, 1997; Zeamon & House, 1979), although attentional deficiencies in children with mental retardation are often very mild and sometimes nonexistent (Iarocci & Burack, 1998). In addition, students with mental retardation do not possess as much knowledge of the world and academic content areas as normally intelligent students. This means that they are less able than normally intelligent students to "chunk" information into larger units that are more easily held in working memory, such as recoding the sequence of numbers 7–4–7 as "747 jet" or 4–1–1 as "directory assistance." In summary, a variety of factors, such as working memory capacity, knowledge, motivation, and strategies, combine to reduce the efficiency of processing by students with mental retardation compared to normally achieving students (Bray, Fletcher, & Turner, 1997).

Motivation

Students with mental retardation often undermine their own learning by making attributions that reduce future effort (see also Chapter 9; Merighi, Edison, & Zigler, 1990; Zigler & Hodapp, 1986). When students with retardation fail at tasks, they tend to blame themselves more than do normally intelligent students (MacMillan & Knopf, 1971). Their failures lead them to doubt whether they could possibly solve problems presented to them and increase their dependency on others to provide solutions to them (Achenbach & Zigler, 1968; Zigler & Balla, 1982). Ironically, this dependency is particularly a problem for students with mental retardation since they tend to be more wary of helpful adults than other students (Merighi et al., 1990). Students with retardation often have little confidence in themselves as learners or problem solvers.

Fortunately, some motivational interventions work extremely well with the retarded (Kiernan, 1985). Behavior modification, which involves the provision of reinforcement for appropriate behaviors (see also Chapter 5), is often successful with retarded populations. Behavior modification can improve communication skills, increase attention span, decrease hyperactivity, decrease aggression, and increase social interaction. A variety of reinforcers, ranging from opportunities to interact with others to earning money, are powerful motivators for behavior changes in individuals with mental retardation.

Motivation is critical if individuals with mental retardation are going to learn to self-regulate (Whitman, 1990). They need to understand that they can experience success if they exert effort by executing effective strategies—and that failure often results from lack of effort and failure to use appropriate strategies. They need to acquire beliefs that are likely to motivate cognitive effort and strategy use, such as "I can do this, if I try hard and use a plan," rather than persist with beliefs that support passivity, such as "I am dumb, so why try?"

Other Students at Risk for School Difficulties and Failure

Students, other than those with identified learning disabilities or mental retardation, are also at risk for school failure. Many different classifications of students who are at risk for school difficulties exist, and within every one of these categories individual differences can be found with some students functioning much better than others. However, at-risk students are more likely than typical students to be noncompliant; they are also less likely to self-regulate their behaviors. This means that they fail to attend to and process information as efficiently as normal children, are less likely to be calm and organized, and are less likely to adapt to new situations (Stevens & Price, 1992). At-risk students also are more likely to have language problems, to experience difficulties in social relations, and to be slow to acquire problem-solving and decision-making skills (Stevens & Price, 1992). Fortunately, the functioning of at-risk students can often be improved through environmental interventions. A broad generalization is that the earlier the interventions are introduced, the better the results (Stevens & Price, 1992).

Children Living in Poverty

One in five U.S. children and one in 10 Canadian children live in poverty. Economic conditions have not only increased the number of poor but have also made it more difficult to escape poverty (Eitzen, 1992). The more successful programs for poor children, such as Head Start, can only provide a fraction of the service that pre-schoolers living in poverty need (Gilliam & Zigler, 2000; Reynolds, 2000; Ripple & Zigler, 2003). Poor children fare worse in school than children living well above the poverty line. They are less likely than age-mates to master basic skills and less likely to be orderly in the classroom—and much more likely to be classified with intellectual disability (Birenbaum, 2002). The traditional approach to these disadvantaged students has been to provide them with more instruction in basic skills, which reduces the amount of instruction devoted to grade-level skills and knowledge (Allington, 1991a, 1991b). The current emphasis is to provide high-quality instruction aimed at developing higher order competencies (Hilliard & Amankwatia, 2003; Hrabowski, Maton, Greene, & Greif, 2002; Hrabowski, Maton, & Greif, 1998; Knapp & Associates, 1995; Porter, 1991; Secada, 1991).

Children with Medical Conditions

Some students who attend school are seriously ill. For some of these students, their illness will be terminal; others will experience complete recovery; and some will live with lifelong disabilities caused by their childhood sickness or injury. Some diseases and injuries cause mental impairment, and some treatments produce side effects that affect participation and progress in school.

One disease that can affect school performance is AIDS. Many babies will be born this year infected with HIV (human immunodeficiency virus) that may eventually lead to AIDS (Stevens & Price, 1992). A critically important effect of AIDS early in life is that it causes central nervous system damage, including the possibility of mental retardation (Seidel, 1992), although that risk has been reduced by treatment advances in recent years. Nonetheless, more subtle nuerological impairments are still common, including ones affecting intelligence and communications skills (Spiegel & Bonwit, 2002).

Children who have recovered from cancer are also at risk for school failure (Langeveld, Ubbink, Last, Grootenhuis, Voute, & De Haan, 2003). The most common childhood cancer is leukemia (Bartel & Thurman, 1992). Because of great advances in treatment, most childhood leukemia victims do survive. Brain tumors are the next most common form of childhood cancer, and although the survival probabilities are not as great as for leukemia, the chances of survival are increasing steadily with new understandings about effective treatments. At a minimum, students with cancer are at risk for falling behind in school at the time they are treated. The illness and treatment dramatically disrupt normal life and school attendance (Vance & Eiser, 2002). Often the treatment produces side effects, such as fatigue, that hamper normal academic activities (Zebrack & Chesler, 2002). The treatments also can affect long-term cognitive development negatively (Espy et al., 2001). For example, radiation to the brain because of a brain tumor is likely to impair long-term functioning. How much impairment occurs depends on a number of factors, including the age of the child when the cancer occurs and how much radiation therapy he or she receives (Kieffer-Renaux et al., 2000; Palmer et al., 2003). Brain tumors during the preschool years, when the brain is developing rapidly, produce more impairment than brain tumors later in childhood (Bartel & Thurman, 1992).

Children Exposed to Environmental Hazards

One type of environmental hazard is lead exposure. About 8% of children under the age of 6 have at least low levels of lead in their blood, with poor children much more likely to be exposed to dangerous levels of lead in their environment (Centers for Disease Control and Prevention, 2000). Herbert L. Needleman (1992; Needleman & Bellinger, 1991) argued that even low levels of lead exposure pose a long-term risk to neurological functioning. Lead exposure can reduce IQ scores, impair language, and decrease self-regulation and attention (Canfield, Kreher, Cornwell, & Henderson, 2003; Coscia, Ris, Succop, & Dietrich, 2003; Wasserman et al., 2003).

What is the source of this lead? Flaking, chipping lead paint is common in the homes of poor children and common in the homes of children with high blood-lead levels. Paint chips end up being nibbled; flaking paint produces dust that can be inhaled. The costs of repairing homes with lead paint are quite small relative to the long-term savings in medical and special education costs if the repairs are not made.

Another type of environmental assault is through parents who abuse chemical substances, especially mothers who drink or take drugs during pregnancy (Wunsch et al., 2002). More people have mental retardation because of prenatal exposure to alcohol than for any other reason (Burgess & Streissguth, 1992). The child experiencing the full effects of **fetal alcohol syndrome (FAS)** is subject to low birthweight (itself a risk factor), facial disfigurations, and central nervous system damage that can translate into behavioral disorders ranging from retardation to learning disabilities (Lockhart, 2001). The mean IQ score for individuals with fetal alcohol syndrome is about 65–70, with a range of 30 to a little more than 100, which is significantly lower than the distribution of IQ scores in the normal population. Children with FAS often have limited communication abilities, which impact their school performance and their social relationships.

In a school of 1,000 students, approximately three of the students might be expected to have experienced fetal alcohol effects. At present, educators understand little about how to intervene with children with FAS, except for the general consensus that early intervention is better than later measures and the recognition of the great need to improve the social and communications skills of children with FAS.

Firm conclusions about the effects of maternal addiction to illegal drugs on the developing fetus are difficult to produce because drug users rarely rely on one drug exclusively. Thus we need to focus on prenatal polydrug exposure (Griffith, 1992; Johnson & Leff, 1999; Wunsch et al., 2002). Moreover, children who are drug-exposed frequently are living in poverty and with parents who do not parent well, making it impossible to know for certain that any behavioral or cognitive problems are due to the drug exposure (Inciardi, Surratt, & Saum, 1997). That said, the apparent effects of drug exposure are evident from birth, with poor self-regulation a major problem. These children do not display the "quiet alert" state as often as other children, a state that permits information from the environment to be processed. Much more swaddling, rocking, and pacification is required to induce quiet alertness in these children than in normal children. Moreover, these children can be easily overstimulated. They then use disorganized crying and extended sleeping as ways of reacting to their overstimulation. Great care must be taken to avoid overstimulation if drug-exposed babies are to be able to attend to their environments for prolonged periods of time, which is absolutely essential for cognitive growth (Griffith, 1992).

Little is known about the long-term effects of exposure to illegal drugs (such as crack cocaine) during the prenatal period on mental functioning (Inciardi et al., 1997). For some children whose mothers sought treatment during pregnancy and who experience appropriate levels of stimulation, the long-term effects may be much less than initially suggested by reports in the media. Still, even some children who receive the best treatments manifest communications and attentional problems at age 3. They are less likely to be able to control themselves and are easily overwhelmed by the environment, resulting in them withdrawing when challenged or going out of control (Eghbalieh, Crinella, Hunt, & Swanson, 2000). Although we do not yet know how to treat such symptoms, the best advice available is to adjust the environment as much as possible to eliminate overstimulation by reducing distractions and transition times. It is possible that the approaches to increasing self-regulation that work with other students, such as teaching students to self-instruct, will work with drug-exposed children.

Children and Adolescents Who Are Substance Abusers

Substantial numbers of adolescents are substance abusers, including use of alcohol, marihuana, and cocaine (Brown, Schulenberg, O'Malley, Bachman, & Johnston, 2001; Bukstein, 1995; Pagliaro & Pagliaro, 1996; see also Chapter 12). Experimenting with such substances by children is also increasing (Norwood, 1985; Swadi, 1992; Westermeyer, 1992). Educational failure is common in children and adolescents who use drugs and alcohol since the drugs and alcohol impact negatively on cognition, learning, and memory (Bryant, Schulenberg, O'Malley, Bachman, & Johnston, 2003). For example, alcohol, benzodiazepines, and marijuana impair long-term memory (Pagliaro & Pagliaro, 1996). Drug and alcohol abuse also undermine motivation to learn and to participate as fully in life as other adolescents. More positively, teens are less likely to abuse substances when home and school discourage substance abuse (Kumar et al., 2002).

■ ■ ■ CHAPTER SUMMARY AND EVALUATION

It is difficult to grow up in the United States without experiencing standardized achievement tests, such as the SAT or tests used by public school systems to assess student progress. Indeed, the No Child Left Behind act (107th Congress, 2002) requires much more testing than has occurred in most schools previously. Consumers of information generated by tests must always verify whether the test measures what it claims to measure (*validity*) and whether the test does what it claims to do consistently (*reliability*).

Intelligent functioning is described in a variety of ways, with a great deal of debate about the nature of intelligence. Initial theories differed in the degree to which they emphasize general and specific factors in intelligence, which informed the development of measures of intelligence. Shifts in the nature of thinking abilities across the lifespan are illuminated from analyses of intelligence test data. The quick and somewhat contentless reasoning skills that are the endowment of the young (fluid intelligence) give way with advancing age to content-filled knowledge acquired throughout the lifespan (crystallized intelligence).

Minorities often perform at lower levels than members of the majority population on intelligence tests. Much of this lower performance, however, can be traced to a number of factors, including socioeconomic status and potential sources of test bias.

Although it is something of an oversimplification, in general, evidence of strategy use increases going from students with retardation, to students with learning disabilities, to normally achieving students, to gifted students, as does evidence of metacognition, extensive world knowledge, and motivation supporting academic behaviors. In addition, there is increasingly efficient information processing in terms of speed moving from students with retardation to gifted students. Although it is not possible to know if the amount of neurological capacity allocated for short-term processing differs between these classifications, functional short-term capacity certainly does, with performance on short-term memory tasks improving steadily, going from retarded, to learning-disabled, to normally achieving, to gifted classifications.

We know less about the many types of learners who are at risk for school failure. For the most part, we have been better at documenting the existence of learning problems for economically disadvantaged students, students with serious illnesses, and students exposed to environmental hazards than we have been at understanding their cognitive problems in ways that might lead to more effective education of these children.

Developmental Debates

Theory and research on intelligence and intellectual diversity contributes to understanding many of the larger issues in developmental psychology.

Nature versus Nurture

The nature versus nurture debate has been played out most fiercely with respect to intelligence. In general, most psychologists agree that individual differences in intelligence are largely heritable, although what is inherited is a reaction range of intellectual outcomes rather than a specific intelligence quotient (see Chapter 3). Where a person falls in the reaction range depends on the quality of environment that the person experiences. Of course, extreme environmental experiences, such as serious injury or disease, can result in great intellectual decrement.

Trait-Like Consistency versus Situational Determination of Behavior

An important assumption of most theories of intelligence is that there are great consistencies in an individual's intellectual competence relative to others, consistencies that will be apparent in many settings. This consistency is the basis of the prevalence of intelligence testing—performance on intelligence tests predicts success in school.

Active versus Passive Child

People do play a role in determining their own intelligence. Adolescents can choose to be substance abusers or choose to abstain, or at least indulge in moderation. If they do elect heavy use of drugs or alcohol, there are potentially profound effects on their development, including the possibility of diminished intelligence. Students can also make choices likely to increase intelligence. Children and adolescents can choose to spend their free time with more capable and academically oriented peers, ones who reinforce an emphasis on academic activities (see also Chapter 10). Children who are already doing well in school, for example, in reading, are the ones most likely to read more, which increases their academic competence further. In general, smarter people make choices leading to experiences that make them smarter still, so that the intellectually rich get richer (Stanovich, 1986).

■■■ REVIEW OF KEY TERMS

alternative-forms reliability A measure of a test's reliability established by administering two forms of the test to test-takers. The correlation between performance on one form of the test and performance on the other form measures the test's reliability.

attention-deficit/hyperactivity disorder (ADHD) A syndrome of learning and behavioral problems that makes it difficult for students to sustain attention and inhibit responses.

coefficient alpha The average of all possible split-half reliabilities for a given test.

construct validity The standard of a test that establishes how well the test measures the construct it is intended to measure.

content validity The standard of a test that establishes how well the test measures the content it is purported to cover.

criterion validity The standard of a test that establishes whether or not the test makes the distinctions it is supposed to make, such as whether or not the test predicts scores on some criterion measure.

crystallized intelligence The knowledge acquired through the processes of intelligence.

dyslexia The inability to decode words despite substantial reading instruction.

factor analysis A statistical technique that identifies clusters of items, or "factors," that correlate with one another.

fetal alcohol syndrome (FAS) Birth defects, such as learning difficulties and mental retardation, caused by damage to the central nervous system as a result of maternal alcoholism.

fluid intelligence The reasoning ability that allows the acquisition of knowledge.

habituation The tendency of familiar stimuli to attract less attention after frequent exposure. Susceptibility to habituation is one way to measure intelligence in infants.

impulsivity The tendency to respond quickly without considering alternatives.

inclusion An implementation of the principle of least restrictive environment in which students with disabilities receive all instruction in the regular classroom, often in collaboration with special education teachers or other specialists.

individualized education program (IEP) A program that describes a student's disability and outlines an educational plan to address the student's learning difficulties.

least restrictive environment A term interpreted as meaning that students with disabilities must be educated with their nondisabled peers to the maximum extent appropriate.

mainstreaming The practice of placing students with disabilities as often as possible in regular classrooms with their nondisabled peers.

mean An arithmetic average.

norm A typical level of performance for a clearly defined reference group.

normal distribution A frequency distribution of scores on a test that resembles a bell-shaped curve, with most scores falling near the mean and fewer scores falling further away from the mean.

percentile ranks An expression of scores in terms of relative position within a norm group.

prodigies Those who display extremely high aptitude for a particular activity.

reliability Consistency, as in a test that obtains the same results consistently.

resource room A place where a student with disabilities can go to receive special services.

self-contained classrooms Classrooms where student with disabilities are taught by special education specialists and where these students have little contact with regular instructional programs.

self-efficacy A learner's perception of his or her capability of reaching a desired goal or a certain level of performance.

split-half reliability A measure of a test's reliability established by correlating the scores for half the items on the test with the scores on the other half of the test items.

standard deviation An index of how much individual scores on a test differ from the mean.

standard scores An expression of scores on standardized tests that can be compared across contexts.

standardized tests Tests that are given under controlled conditions so that every student taking the test has the same examination experience.

stanines Standard scores with only nine possible categories, corresponding to ordered regions of the normal distribution.

test–retest reliability A test's reliability that is established by administering the same test twice to a group of test-takers. The correlation between the two scores earned by test-takers on each testing occasion indicates whether the test is measuring consistently.

validity Relevance and meaningfulness, as a test that measures what it is purported to measure.

z-score A type of standard score that tells how many standard deviations above or below the mean a raw score is.

CHAPTER 9

The Development
of Academic Motivation

An important goal of many educators is to keep students motivated. You have already been exposed to some important ideas about motivation in the other chapters in this textbook. For example, as described in Chapter 5, behaviorists such as Skinner emphasized the effects of reinforcements and punishments upon behavior. Recall also from Chapter 5 that the expectancy of reinforcement influences motivation in that people are more likely to be motivated to do something if they expect that the activity will be reward*ing* and reward*ed*. Contemporary developmental and educational psychologists focus much more on cognitive factors affecting motivation, including what children think as a consequence of being reinforced or punished. An important theme in this chapter is that cognitions in reaction to reinforcements and punishments vary somewhat, depending on the developmental level of the child. In addition, we discuss many other factors besides developmental level that are correlated with children's motivational beliefs, motivation, and achievement.

One of the most disturbing findings of developmental psychologists who are interested in motivation is that with increasing age during the schooling years, academic motivation declines. In general, students tend to like school and academic tasks less with each additional year in school. They value school less, and they are less interested in school and what is studied in school the more that they experience school (e.g., Eccles & Midgley, 1989; Eccles et al., 1989; Lepper, Corpus, & Iyengar, 2005; Wigfield, 1994; Wigfield & Eccles, 1992; Wigfield, Eccles, Mac Iver, Reuman, & Midgley, 1991). We begin this chapter with a discussion of explanations for the developmental decline in academic motivation as students advance in school. Then we introduce general ideas and specific methods for promoting motivation in schools. Finally we discuss the influence of contextual variables upon motivation.

■ ■ ■ WHY DOES ACADEMIC MOTIVATION DECLINE WITH INCREASING GRADE IN SCHOOL?

We consider two important factors in explaining *declining* motivation with *increasing* grade in school. First, children's reactions to and thinking about reinforcements and punishments changes with increasing age during the elementary-school years. Thus we examine a number of different theoretical perspectives on children's cognitions about their own performance. Second, reinforcement contingencies change with advancing grade level, such that competition for grades and other rewards becomes keener and more obvious. Thus we also examine changes in classroom context that influence motivation.

Self-Efficacy

One of the best predictors of student academic achievement is student perceptions of their own academic abilities (Bandura, Barbaranelli, Caprara, & Pastorelli, 1996; Eccles, 1983; Wigfield, 1994; Wigfield & Eccles, 1992; Zimmerman & Bandura, 1994). Even though, in general, academic motivation declines with advancing grade level in school, some students do remain interested in school and do stay motivated to do their best in school. Such students approach the academic demands placed on them with confidence and resourcefulness. They are very diligent, sticking with a task until they complete it. One of the most important characteristics of motivated students is that they have high academic self-efficacy (Bandura, 1977, 1986, 1993, 1997; Schunk, 1990, 1991; Zimmerman, 1989a, 1989b, 1990a, 1990b, 2002; Zimmerman, Bandura, & Martinez-Pons, 1992). That is, they believe that they are capable of doing well on academic tasks. Students develop a sense of **self-efficacy**, or beliefs about their competence or ability to perform a task. High self-efficacy in a subject area is important because it motivates students to attempt tasks in the same and related subjects in the future, and thus is a causal factor of future academic achievement (Marsh, 1990a; Marsh & Yeung, 1997b; Schunk & Pajares, 2004; Zimmerman et al., 1992). What children and adolescents believe they can do goes far in shaping their academic aspirations and even their career aspirations (Bandura, Barbaranelli, Vittorio-Caprara, & Pastorelli, 2001).

For example, one motivation for a high-school student to enroll in Algebra 2 is his or her previous success in Algebra 1. Suppose that the student does well in Algebra 2: Now his or her self-efficacy with respect to mathematics is increased even more, which in turn can motivate his or her future choice of mathematics courses and even thinking about an engineering career. What if the student did poorly in Algebra 2? His or her sense of self-efficacy with respect to mathematics should decline, reducing the likelihood of his or her seeking mathematics courses in the future and the careers that require mathematics, like engineering. Self-efficacy is determined in part by present attempts at learning and performance, which in turn affect future attempts at learning and performance and life pursuits as well as actual achievement. That is, believing that you can do well in math based on your past performance contributes to your future successes in mathematics performance (Chen, 2002; Guay, Marsh, & Boiven, 2003; Marsh & Yeung, 1997a).

What else shapes self-efficacy besides previous success or failure in the domain? First, *social models* can influence self-efficacy (see Chapter 5). When people who are similar to us can do something, we are more likely to believe that we could do it too and should attempt to do so (Schunk, 1991). For example, that social models are important is one of the reasons that hiring female math teachers is important for the goal of encouraging female adolescents to take math courses and consider careers that require mathematics (American Association of University Women, 1995). Second, the *opinions of others* can persuade us of our competencies. So teachers who want to encourage females to be confident in their math abilities try to promote the message that women can do well in math; teachers who want to encourage females to think about occupations requiring math communicate that women can become engineers, accountants, and math teachers. Third, although modeling and the opinions of others have an impact on self-efficacy, *feedback* resulting from one's own efforts has a greater impact (Schunk, 1990, 1991). For example, nothing will convince an adolescent female that she can *do* math like *doing well* in math classes, which happens a lot, since gender differences in mathematics achievement are small when they occur at all (Hyde, Fennema, & Lamon, 1990). Fourth, when students attend a selective school with lots of high-performing classmates (or a gifted and talented program), a student's own self-efficacy is likely to be lower than if the same student attends a less-selective school or program with generally weaker students, a phenomenon known as the "*big fish in the little pond*" effect (Marsh, Chessor, Craven, & Roche, 1995; Marsh & Hau, 2003).

Self-efficacy is subject-specific. For example, students can have high self-efficacy with respect to math and low self-efficacy with respect to composition—and this self-knowledge is generally accurate. People know their own academic strengths and weaknesses (Marsh, 1990b, 1992). Although students get better at understanding their own strengths and weaknesses with age, even elementary-grade students understand a great deal about their capabilities and weaknesses (Marsh & Ayotte, 2003; Marsh & Craven, 1991; Marsh, Cravens, & Debus, 1991, 1999; Stipek & Mac Iver, 1989).

Even within specific domains, differences in self-efficacy can exist. For example, in gymnastics, some students have high self-efficacy with respect to tumbling and low self-efficacy with respect to the parallel bars. Ask a track team member who consistently wins the 440-yard dash about the 440, and that runner will have great confidence in his or her ability in the 440. Ask that same athlete about the 100-yard dash, and the answer may be surprising—No confidence! In fact, many runners move up to the 440 because they have the stamina for the longer dash but not the incredible short-term speed required for the 100—and they know it, so that their self-efficacies for the 440 and 100 are very different. All of us possess detailed knowledge about what we can do well, with the detailed perceptions of self-efficacy playing a large role in determining our future efforts (Schunk, 1989, 1990, 1991; Shell, Murphy, & Bruning, 1989). With respect to athletics, skilled athletes know what they can do and cannot do, and they are very strategic—planning their moves, attributing their successes to selecting and using the right strategies, and consigning their failures to using the wrong strategies. They know they can do well by using the right approaches (i.e., their self-efficacy beliefs mix with their strategy beliefs; see Cleary & Zimmerman, 2001). The next time you see a skilled volleyball player make an unbelievable serve, recognize that there was much going through her head as she served, including knowing that she could make the serve (Kitsantas & Zimmerman, 2002). Recognize the same when you see a darts player get a high score, including a bull's-eye or two (Kitsantas & Zimmerman, 1998).

So far we have made it sound as if every attempt at doing something has great consequences for self-efficacy, but this is not the case when a person already has a very strong sense of self-efficacy built up over years. Consider a high-school senior who has made straight A's in mathematics throughout high school, including up to this point in calculus. Then this student gets a C on one test. Is there an effect on the student's sense of self-efficacy with respect to mathematics? Probably not, or if it is, it is likely to be a very specific shift, such as "I have a lot of trouble with Simpson's rule—which was what was covered on this test." Thus performing below-par on one occasion in a subject area in which one enjoys a long record of accomplishment does not significantly impact one's sense of self-efficacy with respect to that subject (Bandura, 1986; Schunk, 1991).

Development of Self-Efficacy Beliefs

If academic self-efficacy is important in determining academic motivation, and academic motivation declines with advancing grade level, then it would make sense that academic self-efficacy declines with advancing grade level. In fact, students' expectancies for academic success do decline with advancing grade level. Particularly striking are the declines with the transition from elementary-school to middle- or junior-high school (Eccles, 1993; Eccles & Midgley, 1989; Harter, 1990; Marsh, 1989; Stipek & MacIver, 1989). Compared to elementary-school, middle-school or junior-high school life involves more hassles, less social support, and less extracurricular involvement, which can translate into decreased academic self-efficacy, less preparing for school, and lower grades (Seidman, Allen, Aber, Mitchell, & Feinman, 1994).

For example, Wigfield and colleagues (1991) asked sixth graders to rate how good they were at English, math, and sports just before they entered junior-high school. The same students completed a similar questionnaire during the first year of junior-high school. Although the declines in perceived competence were not great, perceived competence did decline for each of the three domains. These longitudinal findings support cross-sectional evidence that as students proceed through school, they come to believe less in themselves. By the middle- and upper-elementary grades, students are more aware of their failures than their successes (Kloosterman, 1988). Students, especially poorer students, often perceive that they are doing worse academically than they actually are doing (Juvonen, 1988; Renick & Harter, 1989). There are increased feelings of "learned helplessness" in reaction to failures—feelings that it is impossible to do better—during early adolescence than during childhood (Roeser, Eccles, & Sameroff, 2000). Once a student comes to believe that success is unlikely, it is hard to change his or her belief (Fincham, Hokoda, & Sanders, 1989). The "can't-do attitudes" that are so well known by high-school teachers have been developing for years. Such attitudes are disastrous since "can't-do" perceptions translate into "won't-try" students!

Matching Academic Tasks to Student Competencies

Do you recall from Chapter 3 the Piagetian idea that students should be provided tasks just a bit beyond their current competence, as well as the related Vygotskian (Chapter 6) idea that teaching should be in the zone of proximal development and scaffolded? This idea of providing students with tasks that are just a bit beyond them is also supported by the self-efficacy perspective. If students attempt an easy goal, they make progress rapidly, but they do not acquire information about their abilities to tackle more ambitious tasks. If students attempt too difficult a task, they experience little progress toward meeting the goal, resulting in diminished self-efficacy and motivation to continue with the task. Only tasks that are challenging for the learner, but not so challenging as to prevent progress, are capable of providing information to students that increases their sense of self-efficacy and promote their future attempts to meet challenging tasks. Teachers need to encourage students to select appropriate goals, ones that are not too easy and not too hard.

We emphasize that teachers need to encourage students to challenge themselves appropriately, because some students do not do so, and there are big differences between students who seek challenge and those who avoid challenge. There are also big consequences for seeking challenge versus avoiding it (Meyer, Turner, & Spencer, 1997). Students who seek challenge generally are more confident in their ability to do a task, and, if they struggle, they do not get upset but instead rebound, confident that they'll make progress and learn something with additional effort. Any initial frustration might prompt deeper thinking in such students. Those students who avoid challenge often lack confidence that they can make progress, and, if they experience a little failure, react negatively to it, perhaps giving up. They tend not to expend the effort to use strategies that get below the surface of a problem, and hence do not learn as much as those who challenge themselves. One of the best ways to encourage the challenge avoider to accept a challenge is to scaffold the student's attempt at learning.

Does teacher scaffolding of learning, consistent with Vygotskian theory, impact self-efficacy? The answer is a loud and definite yes. For example, if students are learning how to use an electronic search engine, learning goes better and is more satisfactory when a teacher scaffolds the instruction rather than requires students to discover how to search on their own. Most important here, students' self-efficacy with respect to their search skills is greater when such learning is scaffolded rather than when it is left to discovery and chance (Debowski, Wood, & Bandura, 2001).

Self-Efficacy and Expectancy–Value Theory

Although self-efficacy theory can be related to a variety of theoretical perspectives (see Pintrich & De Groot, 1990; Schunk, 1991; Skinner, Wellborn, & Connell, 1990), one that seems particularly appropriate to consider is its relationship to expectancy–value theory. As described in Chapter 5, expectancy–value theory specifies when people will perform behaviors that they are capable of performing. If self-efficacy is high in a subject area, the expectancy of reinforcement contingent on performing in the subject area is also high. If, in addition, the potential reinforcements for performing in the subject area are also valued, then the likelihood of a student working hard in the subject is high. If the student works hard in the subject and experiences success, then expectancy of reinforcement remains high. In contrast, if the student experiences failure in the subject, expectancy of reinforcement for the subject area declines, as does the likelihood of working hard in the subject in the future (Schunk, 1991; Eccles & Wigfield, 2002; Wigfield & Eccles, 1992. 2000).

A critical assumption of expectancy–value theory is that successful students *both expect and value* academic success. Berndt and Miller (1990) observed that the success of seventh-grade students in English and math was linked strongly both to expectations of success in these subjects and to valuation of potential rewards for success in

English and math. That is, successful students both expected and valued academic success. It is a little disturbing that even very good teachers sometimes do not make clear to students that the tasks being assigned are valuable (Green, 2002). Moreover, even if students can do the homework they are assigned, they often do not understand the value of it (Trautwein & Koeller, 2003). As students advance through the grades, they are given more and more assignments that they perceive as boring (Gentry, Gable, & Rizza, 2002). From the perspective of expectancy–value theory, should we be surprised that sometimes students do not do assignments (or do them haphazardly) if the value of doing the assignment is not made clear? Also, one possible explanation why some groups have historically underachieved in schools is that the value of doing schoolwork is not as apparent to them as to other more mainstream groups who have historically achieved highly in school (Graham & Taylor, 2002; Van Laar, 2000).

Attributions for Success and Failure

When students succeed or fail, they can explain their success or failure to themselves in various ways—that is, they can attribute their achievements to what they believe to be causal factors. These explanations for performances are called **attributions**. Weiner (1979, 2001; Graham & Weiner, 1996) specified four types of attributions, with each of these having different motivational consequences. Students can explain outcomes by referring to their *efforts*—success was due to their hard work and working effectively, and failure was due to their lack of effort; *abilities*—success was due to their high ability and failure to their low ability; *task factors*—success occurred because the task was easy, but failure occurred because the task was difficult; or *luck*—success reflected good luck, while failure reflected bad luck.

Only the first of these attributions—effort—is likely to promote adaptive motivational tendencies. If students believe that their successes and failures are due to effort, then they believe that their fate is personally controllable. Learners who attribute their successes and failures to high and low efforts respectively *expect* that reinforcement will occur if they work hard. The other explanatory possibilities—ability, task difficulty, and luck—are all out of personal control, due to genes, teacher task selection, or the whimsical nature of supernatural forces.

Believing that one's fate is under personal control is an important type of self-efficacy, sometimes referred to as "belief in personal causation" (deCharms, 1968, 1992) or "self-agency" (Martin & Martin, 1983). People who believe that they can control their destinies are likely to be more motivated to exert great effort in pursuit of goals than are those who believe their achievements are out of their control. For example, students with high mathematics self-efficacy have more positive attitudes about mathematics, which translates into higher mathematics achievement (Randhawa, Beamer, & Lundberg, 1993). Why? They *expect* to do well in mathematics.

Attributions, Learning Difficulties, and Learning Disabilities

Researchers have studied the role of attributions in motivating the academic efforts of students who have experienced difficulties in school. For example, Jacobsen, Lowery, and DuCette (1986; see also Borkowski et al., 1990; Palladino, Poli, Masi, & Marcheschi, 2000) determined that children with learning disabilities were much more likely than their normally achieving classmates to believe that their achievements reflected low ability. Normally achieving children were more likely to believe that with effort they would be able to succeed in school. Within a group of low achievers, those who believe that they can control their academic progress through effort, *in fact*, do achieve at higher levels than those who believe that their low achievement reflects low ability (Kistner, Osborne, & LeVerrier, 1988). What is going on here? Failure following great effort leads to negative affect and decreasing expectancies for future success (Covington & Omelich, 1979a, 1979b). Observing other students experiencing success following their efforts does not help, and, in fact, probably intensifies feelings of personal incapacity (Covington, 1987). **Learned helplessness**—that is, the belief that nothing one can do could lead to success—develops in such a situation (Dweck, 1987). Doing nothing becomes a preferred choice for these children, for at least failure following lack of effort does not lead to the conclusion that one is stupid (Covington & Omelich, 1981, 1984). Is it any surprise that children with learning disabilities often seem passive in school (Fulk, 1996a, 1996b)? Trying gets them nowhere; not trying permits them to offer themselves an explanation of failure that is not as damaging to their self-esteem as failure following effort.

Can a teacher make a difference with respect to such attribution? *Yes*. Students with learning disabilities often receive more assistance with their work than other students. If a great deal of teacher support is given, students with learning disabilities may not attribute the success to their own efforts but to the help they received. On the other hand, just enough help that gets the student moving in the right direction—the amount of help that is "scaffolding"—can result in the student attributing success to his or her own effort, and, hence, presumably increase his or her long-term motivation (Ring & Reetz, 2000).

Developmental Differences in Attributions

How do children's attributions explain the increasing tendency with advancing grade in school not to like things academic (Anderman & Maehr, 1994; Eccles et al., 1993; Midgley, 1993)? Why is it that with increasing age during the elementary- and middle-school years, feelings of learning helplessness in response to failures increases?

Nicholls (1978, 1990) offered an explanation, one that reflects that young elementary students think very differently than do older students. Preschoolers, kindergarten, and first-grade students do not differentiate between *effort* and *ability*. Thus a positive academic outcome is viewed as reflecting their effort, and young children believe that success following high effort is an indication of high ability. What does failure after effort imply? The young child may believe that she or he simply did not try hard enough. With increasing age during the elementary years, students more clearly differentiate effort and ability. For example, they begin to believe that if students who experience equal outcomes differed in their efforts, the one expending less effort probably has higher ability. As they grow older, children increasingly begin to explain accomplishments in terms of ability, with poor outcomes reflecting low ability and positive outcomes reflecting high ability. That is, with increasing age students are less likely to think that they can improve by trying hard (Freedman-Doan et al., 2000; Stipek & Mac Iver, 1989).

Another factor explaining developmental differences in response to academic difficulties is that, as children progress through school, they become more accurate in their self-appraisals since they are better able to understand evaluative feedback (Nicholls, 1984). These changes in self-assessments are corroborated by children's increasing reliance on social information to understand their own performance—that is, they rely more on what teachers, parents, and peers say to them about their own achievement (Altermatt, Pomerantz, Ruble, & Greulick, 2002). And, with increasing age, such evaluations tend to be more realistic, adding to the likelihood of much more realistic self-appraisals, but also potentially to the addition of more negative ones.

Similar developments occur with respect to children's understanding of task difficulty (Nicholls & Miller, 1983, 1985). If a young child can do a task, it must be easy and the child believes that she or he is smart. If a child at this age performs poorly on a task, the task is difficult, and the child concludes that she or he lacks ability. With increasing age during the elementary years, children become more sophisticated in their thinking about the relationships between task difficulty and ability. For example, they come to recognize that good performance on very difficult tasks is indicative of high ability, but that good performance on a task that is performed competently by most people indicates little about ability.

Children also come to understand the difference between *luck* and *skill* with increasing age during the elementary years (Nicholls, 1990; Nicholls & Miller, 1985). Very young children believe that task performance is due to effort and/or ability even when the task outcome truly depends on chance (such as winning a coin toss). With development, children come to understand that performance on tasks involving chance has nothing to do with effort or ability.

In summary, with increasing age, students are increasingly at risk for a sense of low self-efficacy, due in part to the attributions they make about their own successes and failures. Thus, early in the grade-school years, thinking about task outcomes in terms of effort, ability, task difficulty, and luck is fuzzy. As children come to differentiate these alternative explanations of task performance, they are increasingly likely to explain outcomes, including academic performances, in ways that undermine motivation. For example, they interpret failures as indicative of low ability. Even success can be taken as an indication of low ability, if such success comes after much greater effort than that expended by others to achieve at the same level. Such insights undermine children's academic self-esteem, encouraging the conclusion that if ability is low, there really is not much reason to try hard, for ultimately failure is inevitable. With so many converging developmental factors that increase the likelihood of students being more doubtful about their performances and abilities, is it any wonder that older children are less confident about their competencies and have lower expectancies for success than younger children (Covington, 2000; Nicholls, 1984, 1989)? *No*, especially when differences in the nature of school with advancing grades is considered.

Classroom Competition

Competition is a way of life in many classrooms. Some teachers grade on the curve, so that only a very few students can receive the highest grades. Worse yet, grades are often public and salient in the classroom, as when students look through all the papers in the "graded bin" before finding their own. Other forces beyond the schoolhouse door also support competitiveness. Many parents respond to their children's report card by asking how "So-and-so" did, followed by remarks about how it would be nice if their son or daughter were more like "So-and-So"? Local papers carry news about the academic achievements in schools—for example, by publishing honor rolls. Bumper stickers on family cars proclaim the academic success of a child on the honor roll.

What is the result of this focus on identifying publicly the highest academic performers? Nicholls (1989) argued that this practice probably undermines the academic motivation of many children He contended that such classroom competition and evaluation fosters what he called **ego involvement**. This means that students interpret success in the classroom (especially relative to peers) as indicating high intellectual ability and failure indicating low intellectual ability. Since most students will not end up doing "best" in the class, feelings of failure, self-criticism, and negative self-esteem often occur (Ames, 1984). Emphasizing competition has high potential for undermining effort when success is not certain (e.g., a new task), for trying and failing leads to feelings of low ability. The research indicates that competitive classroom environments do much to undermine student motivation and achievement (e.g., Anderman, Austin, & Johnson, 2002; Anderman et al., 2001; Anderman, Maehr, & Midgley, 1999; Anderman & Midgley, 1997; Maehr & Anderman, 1993; Midgley, Anderman, & Hicks, 1995; Turner et al., 2002; Urdan & Midgley, 2003).

Students will often go to great lengths to avoid having to try something that is academically risky in order to avoid feelings of failure relative to other students who succeed at the task. See the Considering Interesting Questions special feature (Box 9.1) for a discussion of how students maintain their feelings of academic self-worth.

Grade-Level Differences in Classroom Reward Structures

One reason for the decline in perceptions of academic self-efficacy and academic motivation from kindergarten to the middle grades is that comparative evaluations are more frequent in the later elementary- and middle-grades than in the early-elementary-grades (Harter, Whitesell, & Kowalski, 1992; Stipek & Daniels, 1988). With increasing age, children also become more aware of the competitiveness in their classrooms (see Harter et al., 1992; see also Schmidt, Ollendick, & Stanowicz, 1988) and of the implications of not succeeding. Paying attention to how one does compared to others affects perceptions of one's own competency, with these perceptions affecting expectancies about future success and having the potential to affect school performance. Shifts with increasing grade level in the saliency of competition are accompanied by developmental shifts in making comparisons between self and other, which contributes to the impact of classroom competitiveness.

Developmental Differences in the Making of Social Comparisons

The cognitive egocentrism of young children (see Chapter 3) has some advantages. Young children tend not to compare themselves much with others, especially with respect to psychological characteristics—such as intelligence or reading ability or extent of prior knowledge. Yes, preschool children can and do compare the tangible "goodies" they have with the tangible "goodies" another child has (Ruble, Boggiano, Feldman, & Loebl, 1980): "I have more orange juice than you" "Do not!"—"Do too!" But they do not make much of differences or similarities in performance on aca-

---

Considering Interesting Questions

BOX 9.1. How Do Students Preserve Feelings of Academic Self-Worth?

Martin Covington (1992, 2004; Covington & Roberts, 1994) proposed that academic motivations can be broken down into motives to try for success and motives to avoid failure. In order to understand students' academic behaviors and motivations, both of these motives need to be considered. Covington identified four types of students:

- *Overstrivers*: These students are highly motivated to go for success, but they are also very highly motivated to avoid failure. They put in a great deal of effort, often preparing extensively—indeed, much more than is necessary to achieve success. The anxiety produced by their many thoughts of failure and the perceived horror of failure are so motivating that they keep on studying and studying.
- *Success-oriented students*: These students value academic achievement, but are not particularly worried about failing. These students work hard, but not because they are motivated by anxiety (as are the overstrivers).
- *Failure avoiders*: These students are not motivated to work hard, for academic success means little to them. However, they also want to preserve their sense of academic self-worth— their feelings that they are intelligent and capable. If a failure avoider does fail, it must be in a way that the failure cannot be attributed to low ability. How is that managed? Don't study!! A failure avoider can then attribute failure to low effort (Covington & Omelich, 1979a, 1979b). If a student is sick, does drugs or alcohol, or stays up all night before the exam, there's no reason for the student to attribute the failure to lack of ability. Of course, procrastinating, altering consciousness with chemicals, and intentionally losing sleep are all self-handicapping strategies (see Urdan & Midgley, 2001), so that the failure-avoiding student is actually increasing the likelihood of failure but avoiding the conclusion that failure was due to low ability.
- *Failure acceptors*: These students care little about either academic success or failure. They are the students who have rejected the academic system. For example, recall the minority high-school students studied by Fordham and Ogbu (1986) as discussed in Chapter 6. Minority students who reject majority academic values can be thought of as failure acceptors (Covington, 1992).

An important idea emerging from Covington's work is that effort is a double-edged sword. If a student must expend a great deal of effort to achieve success that comes easier to others, the student is at risk of coming to the conclusion that he or she is low in ability. Which of the four types of students face this type of risk? The other edge of the sword is that not expending effort also is a self-worth-preserving strategy, with failure following low effort not attributable to low ability. Which of the four student types is on this edge of the sword? From a self-worth perspective, which two of the four types of students are in the best position for academic success?

---

demic tasks. Thus a first grader who feels badly because she or he is having difficulty with two-column addition is unlikely to feel better if the teacher mentions that the other children in the class are experiencing the same difficulty. With increasing age during the elementary-grades years, students become more concerned with how they are doing academically relative to others (Eccles, 1999; Ruble, 1983). Again, because for most students other students in the classroom will be doing better, the increasing focus on comparing one's own achievement with others has the potential for leading to negative conclusions about one's own ability. Such conclusions can then translate into reduced motivation to achieve.

Other Characteristics of Classrooms That Undermine Achievement

In addition to increased competitiveness, school changes in other ways with advancing grade, most of which probably do more to undermine student motivation than support it. As children get older during the elementary years, they can feel less accepted by their teachers, possibly because the teachers are less accepting than their primary-grade teachers, which can undermine academic motivation and engagement (Furrer & Skinner, 2003). Middle schools are larger and less personal than schools serving primary-level students and students in the middle-elementary grades (i.e., fourth and fifth grades; Anderman & Maehr, 1994). Rather than spending the day with the same teacher and the same group of 20–25 students, middle-school students move from teacher to teacher and classroom to classroom over the course of the day, encountering many more people for less time than was the case in elementary school. This provides fewer opportunities to form meaningful relationships with teachers and peers, at a time in child development when a child's needs for belongingness are especially important (Osterman, 2000). Compared to elementary-school teachers, middle-school teachers tend to exert more control (e.g., discipline is more certain and firmer) and permit less student decision making, with this occurring at a time in development when students desire more autonomy (Brophy & Evertson, 1976; Deci & Ryan, 1985; Eccles, Wigfield et al., 1993).

An Alternative to Competition

Rather than rewarding students for *being better than one another*, it is possible to reward students for *doing better than they did previously*, that is, to reward personal

Young children's expectations of their school performance are very high. Later in elementary school these expectations decrease.

improvement on academic tasks. Nicholls refers to such classrooms as fostering **task involvement**. Nicholls and Thorkildsen (1987) found that work avoidance is much more commonly reported in ego-involved (competitive) classrooms than in task-involved (noncompetitive) classrooms. Students in ego-involved classrooms were much more likely than students in task-involved classrooms to endorse claims such as "I don't have to do any homework," "I don't have to work hard—all the work is easy," "I don't have any tough tests," and "The teacher doesn't ask hard questions." The students in the task-oriented classrooms believed that success in school depended on interest, effort, and attempting to learn, whereas the students in the ego-involved classrooms believed that success depended on being smarter than other kids and trying to beat out other students.

Nicholls and Thorkildsen (1987) also found that students in the task-oriented classrooms were much more satisfied with school and learning in school than students in the ego-oriented classrooms (see also Duda & Nicholls, 1992; Weinstein, 2002). Task-oriented classrooms are much more likely to keep students interested in and committed to school than are ego-oriented classrooms (Nicholls, 1989). The problem is that many more classrooms are ego-involved than task-involved. In far too many classrooms the goal is to get better grades than the ones earned by peers rather than to actually learn (Ames, 1992; Blumenfeld, 1992). This has big consequences for students.

For example, Nolen (1988) provided evidence that classroom competition can undermine the quality of thinking that occurs in the classroom. She assessed whether eighth-grade students were task- or ego-oriented. In addition, Nolen asked the students to indicate whether they would use particular strategies for reading and understanding textbook material. Students' reported strategy use was then compared to their actual strategy use as observed when they studied some text material. Although both task- and ego-oriented students endorsed and used surface-level strategies for processing text (e.g., "Read the whole thing over and over"), the task-oriented students were much more likely than the ego-oriented students to endorse and use strategies that involved deeper processing of text (e.g., "Try to see how this fits with what I've learned in class"). Thus task orientation, academic effort, and use of sophisticated strategies are linked (Covington, 1998).

Cultural Differences in Reactions to Classroom Competition

Consistent with the multicultural differences in classroom participation styles described in Chapter 8, classroom competition is more compatible with the styles of students from some cultures than others. Farkas, Sheehan, and Grobe (1990) analyzed the grades given in grades seven and eight of one urban school district, taking into account whether the students knew the material as reflected on course mastery tests and their rate of absenteeism. Even with mastery and absenteeism controlled, some students still earned better grades than others: In particular, Asians were graded higher than Anglos, and more affluent students received better marks than students in poverty. Farkas and colleagues speculated that either the behaviors of Asians and more affluent children suggest to their teachers that they are working harder or that their behaviors are somehow more pleasing to their teachers. Because students from Asian cultures believe more strongly than members of many other cultures that effort largely determines achievement, Asian students are more likely to work hard and achieve at high levels in school (Salili, Chiu, & Lai, 2001). Working hard does more than promote achievement, it brings positive attention to the student. If the teacher perceives that a student is working hard, the teacher is more likely to provide rewards and support than if the teacher feels the student is not trying (Weiner, 2003). Regardless, if grades are important as long-term motivators—and they are in competitive classrooms—Asians and other hard-working students may have an advantage over other students in such competitive environments.

Views of Intelligence

Dweck and Leggett (1988; Dweck, 2002a, 2002b; Henderson & Dweck, 1990) have proposed that a critical determinant of achievement motivation is whether a person believes that intelligence is *fixed* biologically, and hence not affected by environmental variables, or *malleable*. People who believe intelligence is fixed are said to possess an **entity theory of intelligence**. That is, they believe that intelligence is a thing that one either has in great quantity or does not. Those who believe intelligence is modifiable subscribe to an **incremental theory of intelligence**.

The particular view of intelligence held by an individual has a powerful impact on his or her achievement behaviors (Dweck & Leggett, 1988; Elliott & Dweck, 1988; Henderson & Dweck, 1990; Jones, Slate, Blake, & Sloas, 1995; Meece, Blumenfeld, & Hoyle, 1988; Strage, 1997; Wood & Bandura, 1989). First, consider academic goals. Entity theorists are oriented to seek positive evaluations of their abilities and to avoid negative evaluations. This perspective can be damaging when negative feedback occurs, as it inevitably does in school. Such students are likely to interpret failures as indications of low intelligence, and hence to be discouraged by failures. In contrast, incremental theorists are much more oriented to increasing their abilities, believing that daily efforts lead to small gains. Such students keep trying when obstacles occur because they see obstacles as a natural part of the learning process.

In short, students who are entity theorists are more likely to experience negative emotion when confronted with failure, believing that failure signals low ability, with that belief undermining future attempts at the academic task in question. Indeed, the entity theorist may be motivated not to engage in the task in the future to avoid additional evidence of low ability. (Recall the idea of effort as a double-edged sword as described in Box 9.1.) Incremental theorists experience much less negative affect in response to failure, interpreting the failure as part of the improvement process, which motivates high persistence. As long as there is success, little difference exists in the behaviors of entity and incremental theorists. It is when failure occurs that the differences in their outlooks become apparent, with the entity theorists much more at risk for believing that they are helpless when they experience difficulties during challenging tasks, with low persistence and task avoidance the likely outcomes. Incremental theorists just keep plugging away following a failure.

To the extent that classrooms foster competition rather than improvement, students are discouraged from trying hard, using potentially effective learning procedures, or being optimistic in the face of academic difficulties. That is, to the extent that classrooms are "ego-oriented," to use Nicholls (1989) term, or foster "entity views of mind," to use Dweck's vernacular, motivation is undermined. Students are better off in classrooms in which the mentally healthy messages associated with non-competitive classrooms are prominent. These include the following:

- Trying hard fosters achievement and intelligence.
- Failure is a natural part of learning.
- Being best is not what school is about; getting better is.

In short, the incremental view of intelligence is more likely to be sustained in non-competitive rather than in competitive classrooms.

Overjustification Effects

According to White (1959), people have an inherent need to feel competent and to interact effectively with their environment. Thus we can have **intrinsic motivation** to engage in some activities for their own sake. Often rewards are used to get children to complete tasks that are not intrinsically motivating. Rewards, however, have the potential for undermining performance of behaviors that children would do in the absence of reward, tasks that are intrinsically motivating to them. That is, even though a task was previously done for its own sake, once it is rewarded, there is less likelihood that it will be done for its own sake in the future.

Lepper, Greene, and Nisbett (1973) provided the classic demonstration of this effect. They asked preschoolers to do an art activity, one that was very interesting to preschoolers when they did it as part of class activities. Some children were rewarded for completing the activity and others received no reward. When given an opportunity to do the art activity in class later, the nonrewarded children were more interested in the activity than the rewarded children. The goal of the research following this initial demonstration was to determine when and why rewards undermine performance. Rewards can undermine motivation when initial interest in the rewarded activity is high and when the reward to perform the behavior is so salient that it could be construed as controlling (Deci & Ryan, 1985; Lepper, 1995; Lepper & Hodell, 1989; Lepper, Keaveney, & Drake, 1996). When students can justify their willingness to do something in terms of an extrinsic reward, it is harder in the long term to justify doing the same activity in the absence of reward—an outcome that Lepper and colleagues (1973) dubbed the **overjustification effect**. Rewards can be effective even when intrinsic motivation is high, however, if the situation is arranged so that the rewards come after the performance occurs as an unanticipated bonus (Lepper, 1983; Lepper & Hodell, 1989). In that case, the reward cannot be interpreted as controlling or as coercing the student to perform the task.

Although the winner of this spelling bee is clearly happy, the expressions of the other students emphasize the possible negative effects of a competitive environment.

Even so, teachers give many rewards, including grades, in a coercive fashion. Students know that positive outcomes depend on them doing tasks that the teacher wants them to do. One additional factor for some of the decline with advancing grades in intrinsic motivation to perform academic tasks is that students are becoming more oriented to the extrinsic rewards that are more emphasized with advancing grade. Hence,with increasing grade level, students increasingly believe that what should be done in school are those activities that are explicitly rewarded (Bacon, 1993; Harter, 1992). A corollary of this belief is that in the absence of rewards, there is no reason to perform, and hence declining intrinsic motivation to do things academic.

Given this pattern of outcomes, why would anyone ever use rewards to motivate performance? One reason is that students often are not intrinsically motivated to perform tasks that are good for them! When initial interest in a task is low, rewards can increase the likelihood of academic engagement and performance of important academic tasks (Bandura & Schunk, 1981; Lepper & Hodell, 1989; Loveland & Olley, 1979; McLoyd, 1979). This is a principle that has been understood for many years by behavior modification theorists (see Chapter 5).

In summary, competition undermines student motivation because many students end up feeling they can never make the grade. Those who coast to high grades have no incentive to do better, so it is hard to make the case that classroom competition for grades is good for anyone. We do not know how much of the developmental decline in academic motivation could be eliminated by replacing competition with an approach that emphasizes improvement. But some classroom characteristics—such as perceived control and choice for students and caring, supportive teachers—are associated with greater classroom motivation. Teachers can do much more to promote achievement.

■ ■ ■ PROMOTING MOTIVATION IN SCHOOL

Some ideas about promoting motivation proposed and explored by psychologists have been translated into educational practice. For example, cooperative learning, which will be considered first in this section, is now commonplace in U.S. schools. Other approaches to promoting motivation in schools are also considered in this section.

Cooperative Learning

As discussed already in this chapter, classroom environments can be structured so that they have devastating effects on the motivation of many students. Researchers interested in cooperative learning believe that much can be done to improve student motivation in classrooms, even if the classroom has competitive grading.

Johnson and Johnson (1985b) describe three types of social structures found in classrooms: A *cooperative* social situation exists when the goals of the separate individuals are linked together so that an individual can obtain his or her goal only if the other participants can achieve their goals. A *competitive* social situation exists when the goals of the separate individuals are in opposition, so an individual can obtain his or her goal only if the other participants cannot obtain their goals. Finally, an *individualistic* social situation exists when there is no relationship among the goal attainments of the participants—that is, whether an individual accomplishes his or her goal has no influence on whether other individuals achieve their goals (Johnson & Johnson, 1985b, p. 251).

Students can be more successful problem solvers in cooperative learning contexts.

For example, when students work together to put on a play, they are participating in a cooperative situation: The play is a success only if all students do their part. A spelling bee is an example of a competitive situation: Only one student can win, the others must lose. Finally, a student working to master the multiplication tables is an example of an individualistic situation—whether or not the student accomplishes this task has no bearing on the other students in the class.

Cooperative learning produces better learning and more motivated learners than competitive learning and individualistic learning (Johnson, Maruyama, Johnson, Nelson, & Skon, 1981; Marr, 1997; O'Donnell & King, 1999). Moreover, the approach has been demonstrated to facilitate learning at *all* grade levels, for *all* subjects, and for *all* achievement levels (Slavin, 1995; Slavin, Hurley, & Chamberlain, 2003). Cooperative learning also produces many positive social effects including increases in self-esteem, attitudes toward school, and acceptance of handicapped persons. In general, cooperative learning seems to improve problem solving for students of all ages and for a variety of problems (Qin, Johnson, & Johnson, 1995; Saab, van Joolingen, & van Hout-Walters, 2005; Stevens & Slavin, 1995a, 1995b). Slavin (e.g., 1985a, 1985b) emphasizes that cooperative learning is most likely to be effective if there are both *group rewards and individual accountability*. It is important to note, however, that more research on cooperative learning has been conducted in elementary schools than in high schools.

Peer Tutoring

Often students can learn a great deal just by working together. Sometimes this involves something as simple as having one student tutor another. Both the student tutor and the tutee (i.e., the student being tutored) benefit from this interaction (Allen, 1976). If anything, peer tutoring is an even more positive educational opportunity for the tutor than the tutee, since learning of material often is improved more by being a tutor than a tutee (Semb, Ellis, & Araujo, 1993).

Greenwood, Delquadri, and Hall (1989) compared a group of low-socioeconomic-status (SES) students who had been in classrooms emphasizing peer tutoring all through grades one to four with a similar group of students in more conventional classrooms. At the end of fourth grade, the students experiencing peer tutoring achieved at higher levels than the control students in reading, math, and language arts. Tutoring produced other benefits as well. The peer-tutored students were better behaved in class and spent a higher proportion of class time engaged in academic activities. The students themselves also readily accepted peer tutoring and considered it to be fair (Thorkildsen, 1993). Given the many times we have seen classrooms in which students are seated in twos as "partners," we know that individual children helping one another fits into many classrooms and can be used for many purposes. For example, as technology becomes more available in classrooms, peers can teach new programs to classmates, a demand that many teachers otherwise could not work into the class day (Hoysniemi, Hamalainen, & Turkki, 2003). Peer-assisted learning also works with the math and reading that occurs in every elementary classroom, as well as with instruction at the secondary level, even with students who struggle academically (Calhoon & Fuchs, 2003; Fuchs, Fuchs, Yazdian, & Powell, 2002; Mastropieri, Scruggs, & Graetz, 2003; Mastropieri, Scruggs, Spencer, & Fontana, 2003; McMaster, Fuchs, & Fuchs, 2002).

Cooperative Learning Groups

Cooperative learning also can take place in the context of small groups. Such cooperative learning in groups requires four essential characteristics (Johnson & Johnson, 1985b):

- Learning should be *interdependent*. Tasks should be divided so that different students can take on different parts of tasks. Moreover, task completion must require everyone's help. Rewards need to be structured so that everyone has an incentive to pitch in and help.
- The small learning groups should involve *face-to-face interactions among students*. The likelihood that all students will participate is greater with small groups than with large groups.
- *Individual accountability* is essential. Students can assist one another effectively only if they realize who knows how to perform a given task and who needs help. One reason individual accountability is so crucial is that many students are tempted to coast when they are in small learning groups, with only one or two participants working hard (Hogan et al., 2000; Lindauer & Petrie, 1997).
- Students need to be taught *interpersonal and small-group skills*. Students who do not interact well in groups naturally need to learn the social skills that permit more productive interactions (e.g., Johnson & Johnson, 1985a).

One cooperative learning approach, Student Teams–Achievement Divisions (STAD), is adaptable to most subjects and grade levels (Slavin, 1991). Students are assigned to four member teams, mixed in performance level, sex, and ethnicity. The teacher presents the lesson, and the teams work together to make sure all students master the lesson. The students take individual quizzes, without the assistance of team members, to assess what they have learned. The teacher compares the students' quiz scores to their own past averages and computes a team average based on student improvement. Perfect performances always receive a maximum score no matter what the previous performance.

In this approach, every student must know the material. Thus there is *individual accountability*. The teams can also earn *team rewards* if they achieve at or above a designated criterion. The teams are not in competition with each other in that all teams could earn a team reward. Since team averages are computed in consideration of student past averages, all students have *equal opportunity for success* and can contribute to the team performance by improving on their past performances.

Cooperative learning makes sense from many theoretical perspectives, involving the types of active peer interactions embraced by Piaget and Vygotsky. The assumption is that by students thinking together—dialoguing about challenging academic tasks—students learn how to think, eventually internalizing as their own the approaches to thinking tried in the group. There now exists a substantial amount of research on how teachers can structure cooperative learning situations and support their students as they do cooperative learning in order to maximize the benefits for learners (O'Donnell & King, 1999). One set of guidelines for creating cooperative learning groups is provided in the Applying Developmental Theory to Educational Contexts special feature (Box 9.2).

Attribution Retraining

Given that many low-achieving children attribute their failures to uncontrollable ability factors, and hence are not motivated to exert academic effort, some researchers, especially John Borkowski and his colleagues, have developed interventions aimed at shifting the attributions of low achievers in order to promote their academic performances (Borkowski, Weyhing, & Carr, 1988; Carr, Borkowski, & Maxwell, 1991; Reid & Borkowski, 1987). Since skilled academic performance depends on a variety of factors—at a minimum, strategies, metacognition, and conceptual knowledge (see Chapter 4)—Borkowski recognized that merely getting students to attribute success to effort would probably do little for low-functioning students. Thus, Borkowski and his colleagues per-

---

Applying Development Theory to Educational Contexts

BOX 9.2. Creating Cooperative Learning Groups

Research on cooperative learning has been enlightening about how to structure cooperative learning groups so as to maximize student achievement. Here are some of the best teaching tips emerging from this work.

- Be sure to use both *group rewards and individual accountability*. Individual accountability helps to eliminate freeloading and a group reward provides incentive for the students to work together.
- As in peer tutoring, students who do the explaining often learn the most, so it is important to structure groups so that a high percentage of students participate (Webb, 1989).
- Make sure the students in each cooperative group represent a *range of ability,* although cooperative learning seems to work better if groups do not include the full range of ability (Webb, 1989, 1992). For example, place high-ability and medium-ability students together. Similarly, place medium-ability and low-ability students together.
- Make sure the groups are *gender-balanced* as well. Girls are more likely to be interactive and have higher achievement in cooperative learning groups if there are equal numbers of boys and girls (Webb, 1984). If there's a majority of boys, girls are more likely to be ignored. If there's a majority of girls, proportionately more interactions are directed at the few boys.
- If at all possible, try to make the groups racially or ethnically balanced as well.
- As much as possible, *monitor* group interactions. Make sure groups stay on task and that all students have equal opportunities for learning.
- Teach students appropriate social skills for academic interactions, such as how it often makes sense to compromise and that disagreements are all right so long as students who disagree are respectful in their disagreements. Recall the discussions in Chapter 3 about how Piagetian-oriented theorists interested in education consistently encourage cognitive conflict as a means of cognitive growth. An important point here is that engaging in such conflict can be highly motivating. Respectful discussions involving students arguing for their perspectives does much to promote cognitive growth. Such discussion is often engaging.

suaded students as they learned strategies that they were acquiring tools that would permit them to improve their academic performances, which was a powerful motivation for them to use the strategies (Chapman, Skinner, & Baltes, 1990).

For example, in one study (Carr & Borkowski, 1989), underachieving elementary students were assigned to one of three conditions: (1) In the Strategies + Attribution Training condition, students were taught comprehension strategies. They were instructed to read paragraphs and to self-test whether they understood the content. The students were also taught summarization, topic sentence, and questioning strategies as means of understanding text. The attributional part of the training consisted of emphasizing to students that they could understand text by applying the comprehension strategies. They learned that their comprehension of text was a function of how they approached text rather than of any inherent comprehension abilities. (2) Students in the Strategies-Only condition were taught the same strategies, but without the benefit of attributional training. (3) Students in the Control condition were provided neither strategies instruction nor attributional training. Children in all conditions participated in six half-hour sessions.

What a difference in the Strategies + Attributional Training condition! When tested 3 weeks following the conclusion of the training sessions, the students in the Strategies + Attribution condition were more likely to use the strategies than other participants in the study, and they also recalled more text information than students in the other conditions of the study. In addition, the Strategies + Attributions students were using the training strategies in the classroom much more than the students in the other conditions of the study.

Many who work with students with learning disabilities are including attributional retraining in their instruction. For example, a key ingredient in the strategies instructional model developed at the University of Kansas is promoting the understanding in students that they can do better if they master strategies matched to the demands of school (Deshler & Schumaker, 1988). As students with learning disabilities are taught comprehension, writing, and memory strategies, the use of strategies is emphasized as a determinant of performance, one that is under the control of the students themselves. Other researchers also have documented that attribution retraining can make a substantial difference in the motivations of students who otherwise tend to attribute their poor performances to factors other than effort (Foersterling, 1985; Stipek & Kowalski, 1989). Attribution retraining can do much more than affect academic achievement, however. See the Considering Interesting Questions special feature (Box 9.3) for an example of attribution retraining addressing a social problem.

Making Academic Tasks More Interesting

John Dewey (1913) was the first educational philosopher to emphasize the critical role of interest in learning. Unfortunately, many students find that what they are asked to learn in school is boring (e.g., Farrell, Peguero, Lindsey, & White, 1988). Of course, this is a problem, since students pay more attention to content that is interesting and remember interesting material better (Anderson, Mason, & Shirey, 1984: Hidi, 1990; Renninger, 1990; Renninger & Wozniak, 1985; Schiefele, 1992).

Richard Anderson and his colleagues (e.g., 1982) conducted studies to determine the mechanisms underlying the "interest effect." Students spent more time reading interesting texts as compared to less interesting texts. In addition, interesting texts were so absorbing that readers failed to respond to an external signal as quickly

Considering Interesting Questions

BOX 9.3. Can Aggressive Boys Benefit from Attribution Retraining?

Inappropriately aggressive children's aggression can be understood by the attributions they make. Thus, if a child in a lunchroom accidentally spills milk on an extremely aggressive child, the aggressive child is likely to believe that the milk spilling was intentional (Dodge & Crick, 1990). In contrast, most children would correctly interpret the spilling of milk as an accident. Making the attribution that somebody has intentionally spilled milk on him (overly aggressive children are more likely to be boys than girls) can set off a chain of events. The attribution causes the overly aggressive child to get angry, with the anger causing the child to retaliate for the intentional milk spilling, perhaps by hitting the milk spiller (Weiner, 1991). Graham, Hudley, and Williams (1992) found that aggressive African American boys, were, in fact, more likely than nonaggressive children to attribute hostility to other children, to be angered by perceptions of aggression against them, and to act on their anger by retaliating.

To address this problem, Hudley and Graham (1993) developed a 12-session, 4-month attribution retraining curriculum for aggressive African American boys in grades 3 to 5. The boys were taught how to make more accurate intentionality attributions. For example, they learned to look for facial cues that tip off whether another child's action is accidental or intentional. The children practiced in small groups to identify the intentions of other children. They were taught rules of conduct to reduce the likelihood of hostility—for example, "When I don't have the information to tell what he meant, I should act as if it were an accident" (p. 128).

After the training, the students who received the attribution retraining intervention demonstrated improved performance compared to control students on a number of measures. These included reactions to hypothetical situations described on a questionnaire: behaviors in a game-like situation in which another child provided poor directions, resulting in the target child not winning a prize: and teacher ratings of classroom behavior. The intervention, however, did not result in decreased disciplinary referrals at school. What do these data suggest? The children who received the attribution retraining did seem to increase their understanding of the intentionality of others but a short-term intervention cannot eliminate a behavior pattern developed over years of growing up.

---

as they did when reading uninteresting texts (e.g., by pressing a button in response to a sound heard while reading). Even so, greater attention alone did not account for the greater learning of the interesting materials, for when differences in attention and effort were factored out of learning data (i.e., amount of time spent reading sentences was controlled statistically), there were still large differences due to interest (e.g., Shirey & Reynolds, 1988). Thus interest can directly affect both attention and learning, with only some of the increases in learning due to interest because of the effects of interest on attention to academic content.

When Anderson, Shirey, Wilson, and Fielding (1987) analyzed school textbooks, they found that one of the most frequent approaches to make texts interesting is to add interesting anecdotes. Unfortunately, texts filled with anecdotes may lack coherence (e.g., Armbruster, 1984; Sadoski, 2001). In addition, often the personal anecdotes or interesting bits of information, **seductive details**, are recalled, but memory of the abstract and general points is unaffected (Garner, 1992; Garner, Alexander, Gillingham, Kulikowich, & Brown, 1991; Garner, Gillingham, & White, 1989; Hidi & Baird, 1988; Wade & Adams, 1990). That is, students might remember well that John F. Kennedy played football on the White House lawn with his family but this interesting detail does not help them remember key facts about the Kennedy administration.

Trying to find out how to make classroom texts more interesting and to increase student interest in school materials has generated a great deal of research (Hidi, 2001; Schraw, Flowerday, & Lehman, 2001; Schraw & Lehman, 2001; Wade, 2001). There are several ways that teachers can increase student interest (Schraw et al., 2001). These include the following: (1) offering meaningful choices to students by allowing them to select some texts themselves; (2) selecting well-organized, vivid, and relevant texts to use in the classroom—a text can't be interesting if it isn't coherent; (3) considering student prior knowledge—use classroom materials on topics that students already know about, or, if the topic is completely novel, provide some background before the materials are introduced; and (4) encouraging students to be active learners. There is increasing evidence that when students read texts that interest them, they like to read more, and they persist at reading longer (Ainley, Hidi, & Berndorff, 2002).

How to make classroom materials more interesting extends beyond textbooks, however. For example, most classrooms contain computers and they are used on a regular basis. Some educational software programs are dressed-up drill-and-practice routines, which involve little more than presentation of electronic flashcards, whereas others incorporate all the bells and whistles of the most elaborate arcade games. Are these programs interesting and motivating (Lepper & Malone, 1997)?:

1. Interesting programs are appropriately *challenging*—not too easy but not so difficult that they cannot be played competently with some effort. (Think about the concept of this "match" in instruction relative to Piagetian and Vygotskian ideas about the tasks that should be given to students.)
2. These programs also *provoke curiosity*—"I wonder how doing this will affect the lights and sounds this program makes."
3. These programs *provide a sense of control* to players, feelings that their actions determine what happens in the miniature world of the computer program, which is critical since controlling events is a powerful intrinsic motivator. (Think back to the overjustification effect and what happens to motivation when it seems that reinforcements are controlling behaviors.)
4. In addition, some of the games offer opportunities to cooperate with others that can be interpersonally motivating; other games increase motivation by providing opportunities to compete.

The problem with many computer programs, however, is that they were designed to be motivating with less attention to facilitating learning of the educationally relevant content (Lepper & Malone, 1987). It is all too easy to have a lot of fun with many of the programs without learning much. Fortunately, some programs are well designed and do motivate attention to the intended content (Parker & Lepper, 1992; Traynor, 2003).

Nurturing Possible Selves

Ask yourself the following question: What am I going to be in 10 years? This question is tapping your conception of the **possible selves** that you might become, which is another way to conceptualize your perceptions and expectations about yourself (Cantor, Markus, Niedenthal, & Nurius, 1986; Markus & Nurius, 1986). Students reading this book who are enrolled in teacher preparation programs may anticipate that they will be teachers, administrators, or curriculum developers. Students in music programs may envision themselves as concert soloists, conductors, or teachers. Functional possible selves are not frivolous fantasies but realistic goals. Possible selves provide direction and the energy for behaviors that reduce the distance between the current true self and the possible self that one aspires to become (Markus & Nurius, 1986).

Unfortunately, many students do not have desirable possible selves. For example, consider a 10-year-old boy who expects to become a drug dealer because that is all he sees older boys doing in his neighborhood, or a little girl who suspects she will never have a job because she knows no woman who has one.

It is important to have a realistic possible self. Many students believe that they have a high probability of becoming professional athletes. In fact the odds of attaining such a possible self are extremely low. This unrealistic possible self motivates effort directed toward athletic accomplishment, effort that could have been expended in pursuit of a self that is a more realistic possibility.

Attainable "dreams" can be powerful motivators. For example, Gooden (1989) reported the case of a dishwasher whose dream was to become a chef, a dream that motivated him to make it through cooking school. Gooden also described cases of young black males whose lofty goals, such as becoming a famous scientist or physician, kept them on track academically so that they did eventually become professionals, although they did not attain their specific dreams.

Given the potential of possible selves for motivating interest in and commitment to academic attainment, Day, Borkowski, Dietmeyer, Howsepian, and Saenz (1994) designed an intervention to encourage possible selves that are more likely to keep Mexican American students in grades three through seven on track. Most of the students come from neighborhoods with few, if any, professionals. Thus these students did not see neighborhood models in high-status occupations, models that could inspire these children to believe that they themselves could become professionals. Even so, these children highly valued success in school and had ambitious possible selves: 92% expected to graduate from high school, 75% expected to graduate from college, and 17% expected to graduate from a postcollege professional school. On the other hand, they also feared that these dreams might not come true. Half of the children feared that they would end up in jobs that required less than a high-school education.

Day and colleagues (1994) developed a training package designed to help the children maintain their dreams through the many, potentially frustrating, steps of the educational process. This training package was aimed at increasing awareness of the many types of jobs these students might attain in their lives and to make it clear that completion of high school is essential for many vocations. In addition, the training package focused on how to cope with negative feedback and failure, including the unjustified reactions of others. Consistent with the principles of attribution theory described earlier in this chapter, the training was designed to increase student understanding that their successes were under their control—that is, that their own academic efforts would pay off.

The results of this intervention were promising. In comparison to control students not receiving the intervention, students participating in the possible-selves training had greater expectations of success in the future. They were more likely to believe they might attain especially high-status occupations, such as judge or physician, and showed modest improvements in grades (Estrada, 1990).

Hock, Schumaker, and Deshler (2003) have developed a set of materials that any teacher could use to promote healthy possible selves in their classrooms. These include exercises for thinking about *hoped-for* possible selves, *expected* possible selves, and *feared* possible selves. The approach is also filled with suggestions for encouraging students to set healthy goals for the short and long term.

How Do Really Motivating Teachers Motivate Their Students?

Despite the fact that motivation declines during the elementary-school years and beyond for many students, many other students stay motivated. There are huge individual differences in student motivation, with the difference in enthusiasm between the most and the least motivated increasing as students get older and make it into the advanced grades (Lee & Brophy, 1996). What can teachers do to increase the likelihood that their students will be motivated?

Wentzel (1998) observed that students were more motivated when they perceived that their teachers were supportive. It also helps if students feel that they are somewhat in control of their achievement, that their effort matters. When students perceive that their teachers are warm and supportive, they are also likely to perceive that their efforts will pay off—that they are in control of their academic outcomes (Connell & Wellborn, 1991; Skinner, 1991; Skinner et al., 1990; Skinner, Zimmer-Gembeck, & Connell, 1998). If anything, promoting the feeling that they themselves are in control is more important in motivating students as they grow older (Chapman et al., 1990). Motivating and engagement also increases if students believe that they are exerting effort because *they want to do so*, not because *they are being forced to do so* (Patrick, Skinner, & Connell, 1993; Skinner & Belmont, 1993). Of course, there is some reciprocity here. If caring and supportive teachers succeed in motivating students to engage more, when students do engage their teachers are likely to react with greater support and warmth, which has the potential to increase motivation even more (Skinner & Belmont, 1993). Consistent with a long history of research that teachers' expectations matter (Weinstein, 2002), exceptionally engaging teachers let their students know that they can do what is asked of them and then support students appropriately so that success is likely.

Pressley's research group, in particular, has been doing research to observe just what is different in the teaching of very-motivating and less-motivating teachers, that is, between teachers who produce consistent high engagement in their students and those who fail to do so. From first-grade through middle-school grades, they have found a very consistent pattern (Bogner, Raphael, & Pressley, 2002; Dolezal et al., 2003; Pressley, Dolezal, Raphael, Welsh, & Bogner, 2003; Pressley, Dolezal, Raphael, Welsh, Bogner, & Roehrig, 2003). Engaging teachers *flood* their classrooms with motivating instruction, doing something to motivate students *every* minute of *every* hour of *every* day, using all of the positive motivational mechanisms covered in this chapter. That is, these teachers communicate high expectations about today's work and students' long-term futures, praise specific accomplishments, use cooperative learning, permit choices for students, and much, much more. Teachers who motivate their students care deeply about their students (Noddings, 1984). From the very first days of school, they send the message that students need to self-regulate themselves, making certain they know what they are supposed to do and are doing it without the teacher reminding them constantly—although the most effective teachers provide just enough scaffolding on an as-needed basis to individual students that no one flounders (Bohn et al., 2004). Many educational psychologists interested in motivation have concluded that teachers should use diverse strategies to motivate students (Brophy, 1998; Stipek, 1996), focusing consistently on positive motivation rather than punishment or other aversive approaches.

A major question that follows from this work is whether teachers can be taught to be so motivating. In Chapter 6, we described Jere Brophy's analysis of how teachers use praise in the classroom. A major implication of that research was that teachers often do not behave in ways that support the learning, achievement, and development of their students. Brophy (1986, 1987) suggested that many teachers do not understand all that they *could* do and *need* to do to maximize motivation in their classrooms. Brophy then proposed his own "greatest hits" list of motivational interventions, ones most defensible from classical conceptions of motivation. These are summarized in the Applying Developmental Theory to Educational Contexts special feature (Box 9.4).

Brophy (1987) discussed a preliminary study in which seventh- and eighth-grade social studies teachers were provided brief training in the various ways for making instruction more motivating. The teachers in the study used the motivational tactics they had learned in one of their classes and continued to teach another section in their customary fashion. Although the positive effects of the intervention were not large, and the effects were obscured somewhat by teachers carrying over what they had learned about motivation into their "control" classes, the outcomes were in the right direction, indicating that teachers can develop more motivating classrooms when provided with the right kinds of information about motivation. We think it is time to go well beyond a pilot study and to evaluate the consequences of teaching teachers to be more motivating, to "flood" their classrooms with instruction that is motivating.

It is heartening that individual classrooms can be identified where encouragement of academic motivation occurs consistently, but are there whole schools that do that? The Pressley group is now studying this issue. For example, they identified Providence–St. Mel School in Chicago as producing high-achieving students. Over the course of a semester, just about every way of motivating students described in this chapter was observed at Providence–St. Mel (Pressley et al., 2004).

■ ■ ■ CONTEXTUAL DETERMINATION OF ACADEMIC MOTIVATION

Recall Bronfenbrenner's (1979, 1989, 1992) *ecological systems theory*, introduced in Chapter 1. Bronfenbrenner contends that children's proximal environments (i.e., the **microsystem**: community, school, church, immediate family) have great impact on children, but so do more distant environmental factors and cultural forces (i.e., the **macrosystem**). These forces operate simultaneously and interactively.

Research evidence indicates that academic achievement is associated with students' social environments. Virtually all of this research is correlational, and thus determining cause and effect is often very difficult. Of course, if Bronfenbrenner is correct, it should be impossible to determine whether the environment causes a

Applying Developmental Theory to Educational Contexts

BOX 9.4. Brophy's "Greatest Hits" List of What Teachers Can Do to Motivate Students

To motivate students, classrooms should have the following characteristics:

- They should be orderly and well managed.
- What is being taught should be worth learning.
- Content should be at an appropriate level of content, not too easy, but not so difficult that most students will not be able to meet task demands with reasonable effort.
- A teacher's repertoire of motivational devices should be extensive enough so that none must be used so frequently that it becomes "old hat."

This repertoire of motivational tricks can and should include the following:

- Teachers should model interest in learning, letting students know that they like learning and find academic activities rewarding and generally satisfying.
- Teachers should let students know about especially interesting aspects of upcoming content and why people value the knowledge covered in school.
- Teachers should model thinking and problem solving as they occur. This can be a powerful way of conveying both how to approach tasks and that academic tasks are engaging and meaningful.
- Classrooms should be low anxiety places. What goes on in school should be presented as learning experiences, rather than tests. The more classrooms are improvement-oriented rather than competitive, the better.
- Send the message that what is occurring in school deserves intense attention. Teachers need to stage their presentations so that their words, tone, and manner sends the message that "This stuff is important." Of course, this approach must be used selectively and be reserved for really important material.
- Induce curiosity and suspense. This can be done, for example, by encouraging students to make predictions about what might be in an upcoming text or lesson, stimulating students to want to determine whether their prediction holds. Sometimes this can be accomplished by demonstrating to students that their current knowledge is inadequate. One effective mechanism is to induce cognitive conflict, pointing out apparent contradictions in materials, stimulating students to come up with ways to resolve the contradictions.
- Include games as part of learning.

In short, Brophy recognized that effective instruction is not informed simply by one or even a few perspectives but by many traditions, including motivational theories and research, research on classroom management, and understanding of age-/grade-appropriate curricula.

child's academic achievement or if the child's achievement affects the environment. Children and the social context reciprocally interact. For example, parents affect children, who in turn affect their parents.

Microsystem

There are probably few simple effects of the environment. For example, parents can affect cognitive development and achievement in complex ways (Fan & Chen, 2001;

Steinberg, 1997, 2001). Parents who are accepting of their children, who supervise them appropriately, and who grant them autonomy as their children can handle it (i.e., authoritative parents; see also Chapter 10) are more likely to have academically motivated and successful adolescents, other things equal, than are parents who are more dictatorial, indulgent, neglectful (Steinberg, Lamborn, Darling, Mounts, & Dornbusch, 1994), or abusive (Eckenrode, Laird, & Doris, 1993). Parental involvement in schooling is more likely to make an impact in authoritative families compared to other families (Steinberg, Lamborn, Dornbusch, & Darling, 1992). Indeed, authoritative parents not only impact on the positive behaviors of adolescents in their own families, but also on the behavior of their teenagers' friends (Fletcher, Darling, Steinberg, & Dornbusch, 1995).

Educational progress is more certain in intact families than in single-parent families—again, other things being equal (Blair, Blair, & Madamba, 1999; McLanahan & Teitler, 1999; Thompson, Entwisle, Alexander, & Sundius, 1992; Weisner & Garnier, 1992; Zimiles & Lee, 1991). Helpless and depressed mothers send children to school who are less willing to try than other children (Nolen-Hoeksema, Wolfson, Mumme, & Guskin, 1995). Parents who are effective disciplinarians are more likely to have children who are academically engaged in school than are parents who are ineffective disciplinarians (DeBaryshe, Patterson, & Capaldi, 1993). Clearly, the family matters with respect to student motivation and achievement.

Peers are also prominent in the microsystem of children—again using Bronfenbrenner's term for factors that affect a child's life through direct contact (see also Chapter 10). Peers become increasingly important as children grow older (Levitt, Guacci-Franco, & Levitt, 1993). Better peer relations are associated with better academic motivation and performance (Wentzel, 1991a, 1991b, 1998, 2003). For example, good students are more likely to have supportive peers than weaker students (Levitt, Guacci-Franco, & Levitt, 1994).

School and the various elements of instruction encountered there are salient in the child's microsystem, with the motivational effects of what happens at school very much depending on a variety of contextual variables. For example, some gifted students' academic motivations are much better maintained when they remain in regular classrooms, where they can be "big academic fish" in the regular classroom pond, than if put in gifted classes that are filled with "big fish" (Marsh et al., 1995; Marsh & Hau, 2003). Many of the variables that are associated with schools that can make a positive impact on student motivation and achievement are showcased in the Considering Interesting Questions special feature (Box 9.5). A point made throughout this chapter is that academic motivation depends very much on what school is like . . . whether school is motivating *depends*!

Macrosystem

Culture exerts an impact on students, affecting their motivations by affecting elements of the microstructure. Japanese culture's emphasis on effort translates rather directly into familial and schooling support of student effort, with the role of uncontrollable factors that might determine achievement downplayed (Heine et al., 2001; Holloway, 1988; Tuss, Zimmer, & Ho, 1995). German parents and teachers emphasize the teaching of strategies, consistent with German cultural norms about the determinants of achievement (Kurtz et al., 1990; see also Chapter 4). Mexican American culture places great value on schooling, which translates into strong familial sup-

BOX 9.5. What Are the Characteristics of Schools That Especially Promote Intellectual Competence?

Some schools work surprisingly well, producing high achievement in places where high achievement often does not occur, such as in U.S. inner cities. These schools that succeed more than expected have been studied (Edmonds, 1979; Firestone, 1991). At the elementary level, such schools have the following characteristics (Firestone, 1991):

- Strong administrative leadership
- High expectations for all children
- A safe, orderly, but not rigid environment
- Top priority given to student acquisition of basic school skills
- Willingness to divert resources from other tasks to development of basic school skills
- Frequent monitoring of pupil progress

A similar list of characteristics emerges from studies of effective secondary schools (Newmann, 1991, p. 58):

- A shared sense of academic purpose by faculty, parents, and community
- Recognition of student accomplishments
- Recognition of good teaching
- High involvement by parents and community in school affairs
- A sense of caring and community
- Academic emphasis (and coursework) for all students
- Homework
- High expectations that students can learn
- Most class time is on-task
- School environment is orderly
- Discipline is fair-minded
- Strong leadership that actively recognizes problems in the school and seeks to solve them
- Teachers and administrators believe they are in control of the school and teaching
- Staff collegiality

Some researchers concerned with quality in education focused on what goes on in particular classrooms, rather than with the ecology of the entire school. Newmann (1991) believes that effective classrooms are ones that permit and foster a high degree of pupil engagement in learning, a defensible perspective based on a great deal of research (Fredricks, Blumenfeld, & Paris, 2004). Engaged students are really invested in and committed to learning, understanding, and mastering what is presented in school. Engaged students concentrate on their work, are enthusiastic about it, and are deeply interested in academic content. They care about whether they are doing well in school. They are motivated.

Effective teachers present tasks that seem authentic to the students, lead them to inquire about important academic issues, require integration of knowledge, and produce outcomes that mean something besides the grade that results. They present their students with tasks that they "own" in part because they are involved in deciding what is done in school and how it is evaluated. The pace and methods of teaching are flexible, with many opportunities for students to ask questions that are important to them, frequent occasions to pursue issues that students see as important, and many demands that students invent their own work. That is, students create new understandings rather than simply parrot back what the teacher has said. Engagement is fostered by academic environments that encourage risk taking. There is no disrespect for trying and failing, but rather great respect for making an effort and support for making new attempts following a failure. Engagement is fostered by environments that respect student dignity and project a message that young people are important. Not least of all, engaging environments are fun.

port of student effort with respect to schoolwork and clear commitment in many Mexican American students to do well in school (Delgado-Gaitan, 1992; Duran & Weffer, 1992). Costa Rican cultural values contribute to high positive regard for teachers by Costa Rican children (DeRossier & Kupersmidt, 1991). Although children living in the West and in Moscow share many beliefs about school and school performance, Russian girls are more likely to believe that they can control their academic outcomes (Stetsenko, Little, Oettingen, & Baltes, 1995). Thus striking cultural variations in academic motivation exist. In Bronfenbrenner's terms, these are striking macrocontextual effects.

Microsystem–Macrosystem Interactions

Contextual variables and their effects on achievement also have been obvious when relationships between microsystem and macrosystem variables have been studied. For example, how the state of the economy (a *macrosystem* variable) affects families in ways that impact their children, their children's academic motivations, and their children's academic achievements is a problem that has attracted a number of social scientists.

How does maternal employment, which is often required in the contemporary U.S. culture and economy, affect children's intellectual development? It depends, with maternal employment during the child's first year of life possibly having a negative impact on intellectual development (Baydar & Brooks-Gunn, 1991). Any negative effects of maternal employment on student achievement during the preschool and early elementary years are small (Harvey, 1999). More positive associations between maternal employment and achievement are more likely when the child is older (Vandell & Ramanan, 1992). The effects of employment on the family and children's schooling depends too on the nature of the work, with parents who hold stimulating jobs more likely to be appropriately supportive parents than those with less-fulfilling occupations (Castellino, Lerner, Lerner, & von Eye, 1998; Greenberger, O'Neil, & Nagel, 1994). For some families and some children, parental work may reduce monitoring of their children's academic involvement, which undermines their children's academic progress (Crouter, MacDermid, McHale, & Perry-Jenkins, 1990; Jacobson & Crockett, 2000), for the degree of parental involvement and monitoring of children's academic progress is associated with academic motivation and performance (Ginsburg & Bronstein, 1993).

On the other hand, however, when parents experience unemployment and associated economic hardship, this often translates into reduced academic motivation for students in the family, with this effect especially well documented for adolescents (Conger et al., 1992, 1993; Flanagan & Eccles, 1993). A booming economy can have pejorative effects too, however. Consider student achievement when students have opportunities for after-school employment. High-school students who are employed for long hours have less academic motivation and lower achievement than other students (Steinberg & Dornbusch, 1991). Yes, weaker students often are more likely than motivated and successful students to seek such employment, but the employment further undermines their possible achievement (Steinberg, Fegley, & Dornbusch, 1993), negatively effecting adolescents in many ways that affect schooling—for example, reducing their sleep, undermining their heathy eating habits, reducing their exercising, and shortening their leisure time (Bachman & Schulenberg, 1993). In short, family effects on academic achievement are determined somewhat by the economic context. The economy has indirect effects on students through effects on the family. The economy also can have direct effects on student motivation and achievement, such as when part-time jobs divert attention from schoolwork and school activities (Steinberg & Cauffman, 1995). The larger economic context, such as the economic health of the community in which a family resides, can affect motivation by affecting family dynamics. Or, in other words, the macrosystem a child or adolescent lives in can affect his or her microsystem.

Biological Contextual Effects

Social context is only part of the story. Bronfenbrenner's perspective neglects biological factors affecting motivation. For example, chronic middle ear infections can undermine young children's attention (Feagans, Kipp, & Blood, 1994), as can the treatments for more serious illnesses (e.g., treatments for brain cancers; see Butler & Copeland, 2002). Childhood cancer can drain the energies of a child, who is already disadvantaged because of school absence caused by the illness (Bartel & Thurman, 1992), resulting in long-term underachievement (Langeveld et al., 2003). Self-concept can be affected very negatively by severe chronic illness (Silver, Bauman, Coupey, Doctors, & Boeck, 1990), although staying on track despite illness and treatment can have a very positive impact on a child's self-esteem (Fottland, 2000).

Even variations in normal biological development can have motivational implications. Thus early-maturing girls are more likely to have opportunities for social involvements outside of school than later-maturing girls, sometimes in ways that really interfere with healthy development in that early-maturing girls are more at risk for delinquency behaviors and internalizing disorders, such as depression and eating disorders (Ge, Conger, & Elder, 1996; Hayward, Killen, Wilson, & Hammer, 1997; see Chapter 2). Biological contextual and social contextual variables interact.

Role of the Individual Child

The individual child is part of the context and as such a determiner of his or her own motivation and achievement, although always in interaction with other factors. For example, researchers have documented how the naturally shy kindergarten student or first grader, or the 5- or 6-year-old who is afraid of taking academic risks, succeeds in isolating her- or himself in the classroom, setting off a cycle of increasing isolation, that undermines participation, that is so critical to high achievement in school (Evans, Fitzsimmons, & McDermid, 1995; Finn & Cox, 1992; Jones & Gerrig, 1994). Teachers often do not push shy children to participate, perhaps believing that participation may be too stressful for the child. Thus the child's nonparticipation can shape the teacher's behavior in ways that support the continued nonparticipation of the child, although through gentle encouragement teachers can sometimes increase the participation of shy children (Evans, 2001).

■ ■ ■ CHAPTER SUMMARY AND EVALUATION

The research conducted in the past few decades to map out the development of academic motivation and identify the causes of developmental shifts in motivation and achievement has been impressive. On the one hand, the work links well with the experiences of educators and parents. Every high-school teacher knows that many secondary students are not motivated. Every kindergarten teacher senses enthusiasm for learning in most of her students. Teachers' perceptions are not illusions but rather correspond with developmental declines in academic motivation. These declines can be explained in part to declines in self-efficacy, shifts in attributional tendencies, and increasing competitiveness moving from the primary to the middle grades and into high school.

Understanding of motivation occurred in the last two decades because researchers focused largely on students' thinking about themselves as learners (i.e., self-efficacy) and their thinking about the causes of achievement (i.e., a function of effort, ability, task difficulty, or luck) as a function of various types of experiences (e.g., participation in competitive vs. cooperative classrooms). What the child thinks often affects what the child does . . . and what the child is motivated to do.

Understanding of developmental declines in motivation also occurred because researchers mapped out how schooling changed with increasing age in ways that affect motivation. Most critically, school becomes more competitive with "winners" and "losers" more apparent. Since most children do not consistently come out on top, their self-efficacy and related motivational beliefs can be affected negatively.

More positively, much has also been learned about increasing motivation in school. Various cooperative learning methods have been developed and have been linked to greater achievement by students. As students are taught new intellectual skills, instruction can be engineered to make it clear that effort pays off. Thus students can be encouraged to attribute their academic performances to the controllable factor of *effort*, rather than to factors that are out of the control of the student, such as *ability*, *task difficulty*, or *luck*. Academic tasks can be made more interesting. Teachers can be taught about student motivation and how to apply insights from research on motivation to their classrooms. With respect to long-term motivation, teachers can foster healthy "possible selves" as part of encouraging students to try hard in school. By doing so, they are developing a set of expectations about how academic effort today can translate into lifelong success. The importance of success expectations has been discussed in detail in this chapter. Without expectations of success through expenditure of effort, there is no reason to expend effort. In classrooms where there is high academic engagement, teachers flood the classroom with motivating instruction, using all of the positively motivating mechanisms reviewed in this chapter and doing nothing that could undermine academic achievement.

Research on academic motivation highlights the contextual determination of motivation and achievement. A student's academic motivation is very much determined by family, peer, and school factors in interaction, all of which are embedded in a complex larger society and world. The down side of the contextualist perspective is that prediction of motivation and achievement will always be iffy, for motivation depends on so many forces in interaction. The positive side of contextualist approaches is that there are many ways to intervene in order to affect student motivation positively: through the family, the peer system, the school, and/or by attending to the biological health and individual needs of the child.

Developmental Debates

Research on motivation has produced much evidence that informs the great debates about development.

Nature versus Nurture

A perspective supported by a great deal of data is that humans are born with an intrinsic motivation to be more competent, to try hard to improve. Whether such intrinsic motivation translates into high academic motivation depends a great deal on experience, however. As frustrations accumulate in school, intrinsic motivation to do school-like things seems to decline in general. Intrinsic motivation is fostered better in cooperative than in competitive academic environments and depends in part on how interesting new material is. In short, environmental variables are extremely important in determining academic motivation, with recent evidence making clear that the most effective and engaging classrooms are those in which the teacher creates a motivating environment. As we have concluded again and again in this text, nature and nurture interact to determine development and behavior.

Stages of Development versus Continuous Development

Theorists and researchers interested in academic motivation do not identify much with stage models. Developmental regularities are more often attributed to shifts in the environment experienced by all children with advancing age or to gradually changing biological factors (e.g., mental capacity) than to any biologically mediated, stage-like progression.

Universal versus Culture-Specific Developments

The universal most often referred to in discussions of student motivation is that children are born with an intrinsic interest to improve themselves (White, 1959). Whether that motivation is maintained and how that motivation translates into behavior depends largely on the child's culture, which affects the behaviors of families and peers as well as going far in determining the nature of important institutions making contact with the child, such as school.

Trait-Like Consistency versus Situational Determination of Behavior

The contextualistic perspective is that motivation will vary from situation to situation, which should reduce trait-like consistency. For example, a naturally shy child might not seem shy at all in an appropriately supportive classroom context. On the other hand, that is not to say that there is no consistency. It is the trait-like decline in academic motivation as schooling proceeds that has been of such great concern to many educators.

Active versus Passive Child

Although children seem to be born to be naturally active and motivated, the developmental declines in motivation suggest increasing passivity with advancing age and grade. Alternatively, with increasing age there is increasing motivation for other things besides school, including motivation to be with friends and to make money. It is not that high-school students are not motivated or that they are passive, it is that they are not motivated to do school things!

■ ■ ■ REVIEW OF KEY TERMS

attributions Explanations for behavior, often for successes or failures.

ego involvement A determination of success whereby students compare their performances to those of others.

entity theory of intelligence The belief that intelligence is fixed.

incremental theory of intelligence The belief that intelligence is modifiable by experience.

intrinsic motivation Motivation generated within the learner.

learned helplessness The belief that there is nothing one can do that will lead to success.

macrosystem In ecological systems theory, the cultural influences affecting a child.

microsytem In ecological systems theory, the direct experiences of the child in various settings such as home and school.

overjustification effect The effect of extrinsic rewards perceived as controlling upon intrinsic motivation.

possible selves Envisioning what one might become. Learners are motivating to reduce the difference between their current selves and their possible selves.

seductive details Interesting bits of information that may distract attention from the main idea.

self-efficacy A learner's perception of his or her capability of reaching a desired goal or a certain level of performance.

task involvement A determination of success whereby students evaluate their own improvement.

CHAPTER 10

Family and Peer Relationships

Typically, a child's earliest social relationships are in the context of a family, and his or her earliest social relationship is with an adult primary caregiver, very often the mother. Thus we begin this chapter with the development of adult–infant attachment. Family life extends beyond infancy, however, with the second section of this chapter devoted to the development of familial relationships during childhood and adolescence, including parenting style and sibling relationships. Since family functioning depends in part on the amount of stress the family is experiencing (e.g., divorce, economic duress), we also consider these variables.

The quality of adult–infant attachment and family life affects social relations with peers, with peers playing an increasingly important part in development with increasing age. Thus we devote the third section of this chapter to peer relationships and their impact on development. Given that so many children spend significant time with peers in daycare or after-school care settings, we summarize the research on how social and academic development are influenced by these experiences. Finally, we end the chapter with a discussion of how social relationships affect academic achievement, with the conclusion that social development and cognitive development are strongly related.

■ ■ ■ THE CHILD'S FIRST RELATIONSHIP: ADULT–INFANT ATTACHMENT

Babies form strong emotional ties with their caregivers. The attached baby interacts extensively with the adult attachment object—typically, the child's mother. Once attachment occurs, babies do what they can to maintain proximity to their mothers, clinging hard to them, crawling toward them, and crying when they are out of sight (Bowlby, 1969; Marvin & Britner, 1999).

The developmental course of infant–caregiver attachment has been studied extensively since Bowlby's (1969) book *Attachment* first appeared (Ainsworth & Bowlby, 1991; Cassidy & Shaver, 1999; Thompson, Easterbrooks, & Walker, 2003). Bowlby provided a comprehensive theory about both the course of attachment and the biological and social mechanisms that might account for attachment. Bowlby was a psychiatrist whose experiences with children who were separated from their parents stimulated his interest in child–parent attachment and child–parent separation following attachment. In particular, he studied children separated from their parents because of hospitalization.

Bowlby was influenced by *ethological theory*. One important tenet of this theory is that humans have evolved to be sensitive to signals that elicit particular behaviors. Particularly relevant to the formation of adult–infant relationships is that the Kewpie-doll appearance of babies elicits affectionate responses from adults (Alley, 1981). The role biology plays in this has been substantiated in studies showing that postmenarchal girls exhibit greater interest in babies than premenarchal girls (Goldberg, Blumberg, & Kriger, 1982). According to Bowlby (1969), and confirmed by research (Keller & Scholmerich, 1987), adult humans react instinctively to babies' smiles, vocalizations, and cries, attending to and interacting with infants appropriately when they signal adults with a grin, by babbling, or with a wail of distress. Adult humans are innately sensitive to the signals that babies emit.

Moreover, infants are innately disposed to emit signals to adults. Even very young babies cry differently depending on what they are trying to signal. They have one cry that means they are hungry, another to express anger, and a third to signal pain (Wolff, 1969). The presence of other people elicits smiles from 2-month-olds (Spitz & Wolf, 1946). Hearing human voices can elicit a smile during the first month of life (Wolff, 1963). Babies are hard-wired to act in ways that elicit adult attention.

Babies are also innately disposed to pay attention to adults. From very early in infancy, babies prefer voices over other auditory stimulation (Columbo & Bundy, 1981), and they are especially sensitive to high-pitched voices, sound frequencies more characteristic of female than male voices (Aslin, 1987). In addition, babies come into this world ready to attend to perceptual displays like the human face, preferring faces to displays that have similar visual qualities (Johnson, Dziurawiec, Ellis, & Morton, 1991). The baby's biological endowment has prepared it to seek out stimulation from adults and to prefer adult humans to other stimuli.

Why would it make sense for humans to have evolved to be sensitive to infant signals and for infants to be responsive to the adults around them? Such sensitivities must have had a survival advantage in ancient times. Parents who were sensitive to infant signals that caused them to stay in contact with the infant should have been more likely to have babies that survived and grew up to be adults, who, in turn, reproduced. Similarly, babies who signaled their parents when they needed parental attention should have been more likely to grow up and produce children of their own. Parents not so sensitive to signals given by their babies might have ignored their wails just before a dangerous event, such as a wild animal attack. Similarly, babies who failed to wail when in danger would have been less likely to live long enough to reproduce. In either case, if the result was the death of the infant, the parents' genes would not have been passed on and their characteristics would not have been favored by evolution.

During the first 6 months of life, infants emit signals that lead adults to respond, caring for their needs. Although such signals are indiscriminate at first, increasingly during the first 6 months of life, infants come to prefer adults who have been responsive in the past (Schaffer & Emerson, 1964). The more responsive the adult, the more secure the emerging attachment. The more secure the attachment, the more effective the parent is in serving as a secure base from which the infant can explore the world (Ainsworth, 1967; Schaffer & Emerson, 1964). On many occasions, when researchers have measured parental sensitivity early in the first year of a baby's life and security of attachment later in the first year of life, parental sensitivity was clearly associated with secure attachment (Sroufe, 1996).

Infant Cognitive Development and Attachment

The development of an infant's attachment to an adult probably depends somewhat on the level of cognitive development of the infant. For example, it would be hard for infants to become attached to someone if they did not understand that the attachment object continues to exist, even when out of sight. That is, attachment depends somewhat on infants having what Piaget referred to as the "object concept" (Lester, Kotelchuck, Spelke, Sellers, & Klein, 1974; Schaffer, 1971; see Chapter 3).

Bowlby (1973, 1980) recognized that attachment requires more than simply recognizing the continuing existence of other people. It also involves the development of mental representations of the self and the attachment object. The more responsive the adult has been to the child, the more likely that the infant develops a representation of the self as valuable and self-reliant. If the adult has been less responsive or rejecting, the infant comes to view the self as less worthy and incompetent. Infants begin to have expectations about the future based on the primary caretakers' previous responses, anticipating the primary caretakers' likely reactions to situations and planning their own responses accordingly (Bretherton, 1995). Thus the securely attached infant recognizes that the primary caretaker will be there to lend a hand if something scary is encountered as the child crawls around an unfamiliar room, and the child's plan to crawl around emerges with this assurance in mind. In contrast, a less securely attached infant does not expect parental help in the event that a crawl around a strange room proves frightening, and thus may be less likely to explore.

Recall the discussion in Chapter 4 about how even young children form schematic representations of the world. These representations of recurring events in their world serve as the basis for future expectations about what will happen in similar situations. That is what the attachment theorists are claiming. During the first year of life, infants form schemata about how their primary caretakers respond in various situations. When infants form the schemata that their primary caretakers are responsive, this mediates the development of secure adult–infant attachment. When infants form the schemata that their primary caretakers are unresponsive, it contributes to the development of an insecure attachment.

Measurement of Attachment: The Strange Situation

Individual differences in the quality of infant–mother attachment have been documented, with general agreement among researchers as to the types of attachment relations that occur between parents and infants (Weinfield, Sroufe, Egeland, & Carlson, 1999). These individual differences have been studied most extensively in what Ainsworth and her colleagues (Ainsworth, Blehar, Waters, & Wall, 1978) dubbed the "Strange Situation." The situation involves eight episodes that take place in an experimental room that is set up like a living room. Like many living rooms, this one has a variety of interesting toys scattered on the carpet. Except for the first episode, which is only a half-minute in duration, each episode lasts 3 minutes. The episodes are as follows:

1. A researcher introduces the mother and baby to the experimental room and then leaves.
2. The baby is free to explore the room with the mother present. The mother is inactive, unless the baby does not begin to explore in the first 2 minutes. At that point, she encourages the baby to play with the toys that are in the room.
3. A second researcher (a stranger) enters the room, remaining silent for about a minute. Then the stranger talks to the mother. In the third minute, the stranger approaches the baby. At the end of the third minute, the mother slips out of the room.
4. The second researcher and the baby are left alone in the room for the entire 3-minute episode.
5. The mother returns, greeting and comforting the baby. The second researcher leaves. Then the mother encourages the baby to play some more with the toys. At the end of this 3-minute reunion between the mother and baby, the mother leaves again.
6. The baby is alone for 3 minutes.
7. The separation from the mother continues for 3 more minutes, as the second researcher enters the room for 3 minutes with the baby.
8. The mother reunites with the baby as the second researcher slips out of the room. Mother greets and picks up the baby.

The critical data in Strange Situation research are the baby's responses to the various episodes, especially the behaviors during the reunion with the mother. Researchers have observed five different types of reactions, which are summarized in Table 10.1.

Of course, type B, secure attachment, is considered the most healthy of the attachment statuses summarized in Table 10.1. Mothers of securely attached infants are sensitive to their children's needs and encourage their children to explore (Ainsworth, 1979; Isabella & Belsky, 1991; Teti, Nakagawa, Das, & Wirth, 1991). Mothers of securely attached infants (type Bs) react promptly to their children's distress and stimulate their children appropriately (Belsky, Rosenberger, & Crnic, 1995). Mothers of avoidant infants (type As) tend to intrude on their children's exploration more than do mothers of secure infants; mothers of resistant infants (type Cs) tend to ignore their infants more than do mothers of securely attached infants (Belsky et al., 1995; Moran, Pederson, Pettit, & Krupka, 1992; Pederson et al., 1990). The association between responsiveness and security of attachment is not always large, but maternal responsiveness is clearly associated with attachment security (Belsky et al., 1995; Goldsmith & Alansky, 1987; Nicholls & Kirkland, 1996; Stevenson-Hinde & Shouldice, 1995).

If attachment security follows from maternal responsiveness to the needs of the child, then what should follow from dysfunctional parental patterns, such as those manifested by abusive parents? When Carlson, Cicchetti, Barnett, and Braunwald (1989) examined the reactions of abused 12-month-olds to the Strange Situation,

TABLE 10.1. Patterns of Attachment

Secure (type B)

- Prevalence in population: 55–65%
- Uses caregiver as a "secure base," explores freely when the caregiver is available, may or may not be distressed at separation but greets positively on reunion, seeks contact if distressed, settles down, returns to exploration.

Avoidant (type A)

- Prevalence in population: 20–25%
- Appears minimally interested in caregiver, explores busily, minimal distress at separation, ignores or avoids caregiver on reunion.

Resistant/ambivalent (type C)

- Prevalence in population: 10–15%
- Minimal exploration, preoccupied with caregiver, has difficulty settling down, both seeks and resists contact on reunion, may be angry or very passive.

Disorganized/disoriented (type D)

- Prevalence in population: 15–20%
- Disorganized and/or disoriented behavior in the caregiver's presence, approaches with head averted, trance-like freezing, anomalous postures

Other

- Although rare, some children do not fit any of the other patterns.

Note. Based on Goldberg (1995).

they found than most (82%) manifested the type-D profile. Their behaviors in the Strange Situation were confused and disorganized. This makes sense from the perspective of attachment theory, for such children's lives are often characterized by inconsistent care, including overstimulation at some times, which produces avoidance in the Strange Situation (type-A responses), and lack of attention at other times, which is associated with resistance (type-C responses) in the Strange Situation (Cicchetti, Cummings, Greenberg, & Marvin, 1990). Small wonder that these children exhibit inconsistent responses to parental separation and reunion in the Strange Situation! The freezing responses and uncertainties exhibited by type-D children may represent fear, a natural reaction of a child when interacting with an abusive adult in a Strange Situation (Main & Hesse, 1990).

The Strange Situation has been adapted so that it also can be used to assess children between 2½ and 4½ years of age (Solomon & George, 1999) and 5–6 years of age (Main & Cassidy, 1988; Solomon & George, 1999; Stevenson-Hinde & Verschueren, 2002).

Other Measures of Attachment

Obviously, the Strange Situation is a labor- and time-intensive way to measure attachment in infants. Fortunately, other measures of attachment have been developed that can be used more efficiently and are appropriate for other parts of the lifespan (Waters, Vaughn, Posada, & Kondo-Ikemura, 1995).

Q-Sort Procedure

In the Q-sort procedure (Waters, 1995), a person who knows a child well is asked to sort 90 statements into one of nine piles, from "9" for statements describing the child well to "1" for statements that do not describe the child. Each of the statements refers to a behavior that is characteristic of either secure, avoidant, or resistant attachment. Thus, for a securely attached child, the following items would be placed in the high-end piles (Waters, 1995, pp. 236–237):

- Child clearly shows a pattern of using mother as a base from which to explore. Moves out to play; returns or plays near her; moves out to play again, etc.
- Child will approach or play with things that initially made him or her cautious or afraid if receives reassurance from mother.
- Child keeps track of mother's location when playing at home. Calls to her now and then; notices when she changes activities.
- When frightened or upset, the child stops crying and quickly recovers when held.
- Child recognizes when mother is upset. Tries to comfort her; asks what is wrong.

Conversely, for a securely attached child, the following items would be placed in the low-end pile, for they represent insecurity of attachment (Waters, 1995, pp. 244–246):

- Child easily becomes angry at mother.
- When upset, the child stays put and cries, rarely asks mother for help.
- At home, child gets upset or cries when mother walks out of the room.
- Child sometimes signals that she or he wants to be put down and then fusses or wants to be picked right back up.

The Q-sort procedure can be used appropriately with infants or preschoolers (Waters & Deane, 1985). Some universality to the measure has been demonstrated in that when mothers and child development experts in seven different countries (China, Colombia, Germany, Israel, Japan, Norway, and the United States) were asked to sort the 90 Q-sort items so as to describe the ideal child, they tended to sort them in the same way (Posada et al., 1995). In addition, the measure seems to be reliable, with stable Q-sort ratings reported from 2 to 5 years of age (Symons, Clark, Isaksen, & Marshall, 1998).

Measurement of Attachment in Older Children

Main, Kaplan, and Cassidy (1985) developed a strange situation procedure for use with older children. A family was first visited in the home. About a week later, they came to the laboratory, which was a playroom. The session lasted about 2 hours. The interactions in the playroom between the child and the parents were videotaped. Then the parents left for an hour. A researcher remained with the child. After about 15 minutes of the researcher and the child interacting informally, the researcher interviewed the child to evaluate the child's separation anxiety. After the interview, the child played until the parents returned. The parents returned one at a time, with a 3-minute reunion period with the mother and another 3-minute reunion period with the father. Security of attachment was assessed from the child's reactions during these reunion episodes.

Since this approach can assess attachment in older children, the stability of attachment security can be measured. For example, Main and colleagues (1985) reported very high reliability between attachment to mother as measured during infancy with the Strange Situation and attachment at 6 years of age as measured with the method just described. In general, infants who are securely attached to their mothers are likely to become children who have secure relationships with their mothers.

Measurement of Attachment in Adults

Can attachment be measured in adults? Main and colleagues (1985) reported the first use of the Adult Attachment Interview. During the interview, adults are asked to select five adjectives to describe their childhood relationships with their parents. The adults are asked what their parents did when they were upset in childhood, whether they felt rejected by parents during childhood, and, if yes, why their parents rejected them. During the Adult Attachment Interview, the adults are asked whether their parents had ever threatened separation from them. They are also asked about any changes in their relationships with their parents from childhood to adulthood. Finally, the adults are asked to comment on how their relationships with their parents affected their adult personalities.

The interview responses are rated in terms of security themes. Some adults clearly value secure attachment relationships, believing that secure attachments are important in the development of a healthy personality. They see their own parents as warm, responsive, available, and sensitive. In contrast, some adults do not believe that attachment relationships are valuable or influential. Sometimes adults express extreme dependency themes during the interview, including the desire to continue to please their parents. Sometimes they lost a parent early in life and continue to mourn. In short, adults with beliefs reflecting insecure attachments also tend to believe that they had less than optimal rearing.

One of the most important findings with the Adult Attachment Interview is that women who value secure attachments and reported secure attachments during their childhood tend to have securely attached infants compared to women whose interviews lacked secure attachment themes (Fonagy, Steele, & Steele, 1991; Main et al., 1985; Steele, Steele, & Fonagy, 1996; van IJzendoorn, 1995; Ward & Carlson, 1995). The Adult Attachment Interview has been a powerful tool for studying connections between attachment in childhood and social relations in adulthood.

Although other measures of attachment in adulthood have been developed, they are more related to patterns of social behavior not emphasized in this chapter—for example, focusing on romantic attachments (Crowell, Fraley, & Shaver, 1999). As the Adult Attachment Interview has continued to evolve, how responses are evaluated has changed. For example, how the interviewee engages in discourse with the interviewer is now emphasized, such as whether the interviewee is self-absorbed during the interview and whether the interviewee seems to monitor consistency of comments (Hesse, 1999; Hesse & van IJzendoorn, 1999).

In summary, attachment can be measured from infancy to adulthood. The measurement of attachment over the course of development is important, because attachment theory proposes that early attachment predicts later attachment and healthy functioning. As this discussion of attachment continues, the long-term relationship between attachment and other aspects of human development is explored.

The Nature of Maternal Responsiveness

Pederson and Moran (1995; Bailey, Waters, Pederson, & Moran, 1999) reflected extensively on the attachment literature in order to develop a Q-sort instrument that could be used to identify mothers who were responsive to their infants, and thus likely to foster secure attachment in their infants. Readers can get a good sense of the nature of responsive motherhood by reflecting on some of the items *most* descriptive of responsive mothering (Pederson & Moran, 1995, pp. 249–250). A responsive mother does the following:

- Interprets cues correctly as evidenced by baby's response.
- Responds consistently to baby's signals.
- Slows pace down; waits for baby's response in face-to-face interactions.
- Monitors and responds to baby even when engaged in some other activity.
- When baby is distressed, able to quickly and accurately identify the source.
- Aware of baby's moods and fluctuations in state.
- Respects baby as individual; accepting of baby's behavior.
- Aware of how her mood affects baby.

The nature of mothering that produces insecure attachment according to Bowlby's theory also can be understood from reflection on Pederson and Moran's (1995) items. The following are some of the scale items *least* characteristic of mothers who foster secure attachments (Pederson & Moran, 1995, p. 254):

- Unaware of or insensitive to baby's signs of distress.
- Subjects baby to constant stimulation overwhelming the baby.
- Responds inconsistently and unpredictably to baby's communications.
- Sets content and pace of interactions without noting baby's responses.
- Teases baby beyond point where baby seems to enjoy it.

A great deal of evidence indicates that maternal sensitivity is an important factor in the development of mother–infant attachment (Barnett, Kidwell, & Leung, 1998; Braungart-Rieker, Garwood, Powers, & Wang, 2001; De Wolff & van IJzendoorn, 1997; Goldsmith & Alansky, 1987; NICHD Early Child Care Research Network, 2001; Pederson, Gleason, Moran, & Bento, 1998). See the Considering Interesting Questions special feature (Box 10.1) for a discussion of another variable that might have a large impact on attachment: infant temperament.

Attachment and Subsequent Social Relations

Bowlby (1969) contended that secure attachment was a precursor of mental health, and believed that securely attached infants are more likely to be well adjusted and sociable when they are older. Often preschoolers who were securely attached infants are indeed more outgoing, more sensitive to the needs of other children, and more popular than preschoolers who were insecurely attached during infancy (Jacobson &

BOX 10.1. Does Infant Temperament Affect Attachment Security?

A person's temperament is defined by activity level, emotionality, degree of self-regulation, fearfulness, and sociability (Buss & Plomin, 1984). Thomas and Chess (1977; Chess & Thomas, 1987) identified three different temperamental patterns in infancy:

- *Easy temperament*: These babies positively approach novel stimuli, are highly adaptable to new circumstances, and predominantly positive in mood. Their sleep and feeding cycles are regular and they accept new types of foods without a fuss. In addition, they smile at strangers, and accept frustrations without getting very upset. The parents of children with easy temperaments enjoy their babies. About 40% of the participants in the Thomas and Chess study were easy infants.
- *Difficult temperament*: The biological functions of these babies tend to be irregular. Such children tend to withdraw and react negatively to new stimulation. They are slow to adapt to change. Often they have intense and negative moods. These children do not accept new foods readily. Although they may laugh loudly, they also have extreme and negative reactions to frustration. Parents with such children often have a difficult time. About 10% of the children in the Thomas and Chess study were difficult.
- *Slow-to-warm-up temperament*: These children sometimes offer mildly negative reactions to new stimuli but their emotions are not nearly as intense as those expressed by difficult children. Moreover, as they warm up to new things and activities, they often come to like them and react positively to them. About 15% of the babies in the Thomas and Chess sample could be classified as slow to warm up.

A number of developmental researchers believe that infant temperament, which is inherited to some degree (Buss & Plomin, 1984), is an important determinant of infant attachment classification (Crockenberg, 1981; Kagan, 1982; Mangeldorf, Gunnar, Kestenbaum, Lang, & Andreas, 1990). Think about it. How is a difficult child going to react to the Strange Situation? Or a slow-to-warm-up child? Certainly, such children are more likely to be resistant or avoidant than children with easy temperaments. Is it more likely that a mother will be sensitive to an easy child compared to a difficult child? Often, it is so. This raises a key question. Is it the mother's sensitivity that results in a secure attachment or the affect of the child's temperament on maternal sensitivity, which in turn affects the security of attachment? Of course, if a difficult infant has a mother who provides a "good fit" (Chess & Thomas, 1987; Thomas & Chess, 1986) in that she remains calm and accepting as the child reacts negatively to new situations, then mother–infant attachment might be more secure and the child more adaptable in the long run (Chess & Thomas, 1984). Debate continues on just how much security of attachment is determined by maternal sensitivity, infant temperament, and the goodness of fit between a mother and an infant (Mangelsdorf & Frosch, 2000; Park, 2001; Seifer, Schiller, Sameroff, Resnick, & Riordan, 1996).

When a child has both an insecure attachment and a difficult temperament, there is reason for real concern, for this predicts problems in later childhood such as unacceptable aggression as a preschooler and less advanced cognitive development (Burgess, Marshall, Rubin, & Fox, 2003; Stams, Juffer, & van IJzendoorn, 2002). Some developmental researchers even believe that insecure attachment and difficult temperament early in life predict juvenile delinquency and antisocial behaviors in adolescence and adulthood (Saltaris, 2002).

Wille, 1986; Park & Waters, 1989; Pastor, 1981; Sroufe, Fox, & Pancake, 1983; Waters, Wippman, & Sroufe, 1979).

An interpretation of this data based on Erikson's theory (see Chapter 5) is that a secure attachment during infancy reflects the development of basic trust, whereas an insecure attachment reflects basic mistrust. Basic trust in infancy is linked to later security and trust in interacting with other children, which is necessary for effective social relationships during the preschool years and beyond. Secure attachment early in life also seems to be linked with the development of autonomy in adolescence (Allen & Land, 1999), an important part of identity development, which is central to Eriksonian thinking. Throughout childhood and into adulthood, security of child–mother attachment is associated with better social and emotional functioning with peers (Cohn, 1990; DeMulder, Denham, Schmidt, & Mitchell, 2000; Elicker, Englund, & Sroufe, 1992; Feeney & Noller, 1990; Hazan & Shaver, 1987; Kobak & Sceery, 1988; Kochanska, 2001; Lieberman, Doyle, & Markiewicz, 1999; McElwain, Cox, Burchinal, & Macfie, 2003; Sroufe, Egeland, & Kreutzer, 1990; Starns, Juffer, & van IJzendoorn, 2002). On the other hand, insecurity of child–parent attachments are associated with dysfunctional peer relationships, including aggression, withdrawal from peer relations, and acting out inappropriately (Erickson, Sroufe, & Egeland, 1985; Greenburg, 1999; Lyons-Ruth, Alpern, & Repacholi, 1993). Although the relationships between parent–infant attachment and later social functioning tend to be small to moderate, they are striking in their consistency (Schneider, Atkinson, & Tardif, 2001).

One very interesting possibility is that if child–parent attachment is not as secure as it could be, subsequent relationships with educators might compensate. In fact, some support for this possibility exists. When preschoolers who have insecure parental attachments experience a secure, trusting attachment relationship with a preschool teacher, their social interactions in preschool go better than when they have not experienced such a compensatory relationship with an educator (Copeland-Mitchell, Denham, & DeMulder, 1997). The possibility that secure relationships with educators can make up to some extent for the experience of insecure relationships with parents is a compelling one for future educators to consider.

In closing, we emphasize that considerable evidence indicates that early attachment status predicts later attachment status for many individuals. That is, parent–child socioemotional relationships tend to be stable from early childhood to later childhood, adolescence, and even adulthood (Hamilton, 2000; Waters, Merrick, Treboux, Crowell, & Albsersheim, 2000; Waters, Weinfield, & Hamilton, 2000). That said, under some circumstances child–parent attachment is not stable. Parents sometimes change so that the mother and father who were always there and responsive to their children when infants become parents who are less concerned with their schoolage children than other issues in their lives, perhaps because of divorce (Lewis, Feiring, & Rosenthal, 2000). Mental health difficulties experienced by the parent also could cause a change in child–parent attachments (Weinfield, Sroufe, & Egeland, 2000). Much can happen in a child's life after infancy and early childhood that impacts later socioemotional functioning (Thompson, 1999; Waters, Merrick, et al., 2000).

Attachment and Subsequent Cognitive Interactions

Correlations between secure attachment during infancy and subsequent cognitive interactions with parents also have been noted. Matas, Arend, and Sroufe (1978) observed that secure attachment during infancy predicted the quality of problem-solving undertaken by 2-year-olds and their mothers working together. The mothers of children who had been securely attached infants offered higher quality support to their children during the problem-solving tasks. The problem-solving process was more pleasant for the securely attached children compared to the less securely attached children, who more often rejected their mothers' suggestions, even responding aggressively when suggestions were offered. Frankel and Bates (1990) were able to replicate the Matas and colleagues finding that the quality of child–adult problem solving can be predicted from the security of infant–mother attachment during infancy. In general, when there is a secure attachment, parental directions and support are more likely to be at an appropriate level, neither too little nor too much (Fagot & Kavanagh, 1993).

Experiences during mother–child emergent literacy interactions during the preschool years also reflect the quality of attachment (Bus, 2001). Bus and van IJzendoorn (1988) observed 1½-year-olds, 3½-year-olds, and 5½-year-olds and their mothers as they watched *Sesame Street*, read a picture book together, and went through an alphabet book. The attachment status of the participating children was established during the study, using the Strange Situation with the 1½-year-olds and the procedure devised by Main and colleagues (1985) for assessing attachment in older children. Consistently, the interactions during emergent literacy tasks were more positive for securely attached compared to less securely attached children. Securely attached children were more attentive and less distractible during emergent literacy interactions. The mothers of the securely attached children demanded more of their children, and the children met these demands.

Bus and van IJzendoorn (1988) studied a group of 3-year-olds who varied in security of their attachments to their mothers. One important finding was that the frequency of reading that mothers reported doing with their children was related to security of attachment, with more securely attached children and mothers doing more reading together than less securely attached child–mother dyads. During the study, the researchers observed children and their mothers as they engaged in storybook reading. Insecure dyads exhibited less engagement during reading than securely attached children and mothers. The less secure the attachment, the more the children were inattentive, the more the discussion digressed from the story, and the harder it seemed for the children to get the message of the text.

In short, security in attachment predicts healthy interactions as parents and children tackle intellectual challenges together, including reading with one another. Some children, however, are at substantially greater risk than others for not developing secure relationships with parents during infancy—for example, because of their difficult temperaments (Chess & Thomas, 1987; Thomas & Chess, 1977). Even in those cases, intervention can increase the likelihood of secure attachment and cognitively productive interactions. See the Considering Interesting Questions special feature (Box 10.2) for a discussion of such interventions.

Recall from Chapter 6 the sociocultural perspective that social interactions, particularly between caregivers and children, are critical to mature cognitive development. Much of what secure attachment is about is responsive interaction between mother and infant. These responsive interactions continue into early childhood and extend to interactions in problem-solving situations. Recall that, according to Vygotsky, much of thinking is the internalization of social interactions by the child. Thus the better the interactions, the better should be the internalizations that form

Considering Interesting Questions

BOX 10.2. Can Attachment Security Be Increased Through Intervention?

Given that secure attachments are associated with a variety of long-term social and intellectual benefits, a reasonable question is whether it is possible to intervene so as to increase the likelihood of secure attachments developing. The answer seems to be yes (Belsky, Rosenberger, & Crnic, 1995). For example, van den Boom (1994) studied poor families in Holland who had irritable infants, in other words, temperamentally difficult infants. Fifty families were assigned to an experimental group and 50 to a control group. During three home visits (one when the child was 6 months of age and one in each of the next 2 months), mothers were coached about how to be responsive both to negative and positive signals provided by their child. When security of attachment was assessed (using the Strange Situation) 4 months after the intervention, 38% of the experimental infants were insecurely attached compared to 78% of the control infants.

Van den Boom (1995) conducted a follow-up study of the children who had participated in the experiment. When they were toddlers, the children in the experimental group exhibited greater security in the mother–infant relationship than children in the control condition. Moreover, when the children were 3½, the parents of experimental children continued to be more responsive to their children and their children exhibited fewer behavioral problems and interacted more constructively with peers than did children in the control condition. Thus even the brief intervention in van den Boom (1994) heightened parental sensitivity to cues emitted by children, with differences in sensitivity between experimental and control parents still evident 3 years later. More sensitive parental interactions translated into more secure attachment, which, in turn, resulted in more positive social behaviors and interactions in the preschool years.

Other experiments have been conducted in which support has been defined more broadly than by van den Boom, but always including instruction of parents about how to interact more responsively with their infants (van IJzendoorn, Juffer, & Duyvesteyn, 1995). In general, such interventions have reduced the incidence of insecure attachment (Jacobson & Frye, 1991; Lieberman, Weston, & Pawl, 1991; Lyons-Ruth, Connell, & Grunebaum, 1990). The data from such true experiments are among the most powerful in establishing the importance of maternal responsiveness to secure attachment. (Recall from Chapter 1 the powerful cause-and-effect inferences that are possible from a true experiment.) Moreover, these studies indicate that much can be done to encourage parents to be more responsive to their children in ways that promote attachment security.

the basis of thought. Although the evidence is not yet definitive, preliminary data indicate that secure attachment relates to long-term cognitive development and academic achievement (Borkowski & Dukewich, 1996; Laible & Thompson, 2000; Moss, 1992; Moss & St. Laurent, 2001; Starns, Juffer, & van IJzendoorn, 2002). Thus those wishing to optimize intellectual development should target children's social interactions, beginning with parent–child interactions during the first year of life.

■ ■ ■ FAMILY AND DEVELOPMENT AFTER INFANCY

Those who study development in the context of the family have focused on different issues at different times in the history of the field. Research on parental style has proven to be particularly useful for predicting important developmental outcomes.

Thus we begin with a discussion of the research on parental style and then move on to discussion of other factors that influence familial effects on the development of children and adolescents.

Parental Style

Diana Baumrind (1972) conducted a longitudinal study of parent–child relationships, beginning in the preschool years and continuing into the middle-elementary years. She observed children in school settings as well as at home with their parents, taking special note of how parents interacted with their children. The observational data were complemented by interviews of the parents. Based on these observations and interviews, Baumrind identified two dimensions characterizing parenting style. One dimension was the *degree of parental responsiveness*, which varied from highly responsive and child-centered to rejecting and parent-centered. The second dimension was the *degree of demand* on the child by the parent, which ranged from demanding to undemanding. Considering degree of responsiveness and demand together, Baumrind defined four different types of parenting styles:

- Highly responsive, highly demanding, **authoritative** parenting. Authoritative parents expect much from their children and reward their children for meeting expectations rather than punishing them for failing to meet expectations. Parent–child interactions are warm and communication is good, with parents making their high expectations and standards clear to children. Parents also explained the reasons for their expectations, providing these explanations in the context of dialogues in which the children's voices and perspectives were heard and taken seriously.
- Highly responsive, low demanding, **permissive** parenting. Permissive parents allow children to make up their own minds about most daily events: snacks, TV viewing, going to bed, and so on. Permissive parents tend to be mildly warm to neutral in the affect they direct toward their children.
- Low responsive, high demanding, **authoritarian** parenting. Authoritarian parents demand strict obedience. They use punishment frequently and threaten often. Authoritarian parents do not engage in the parental–child dialoguing that characterizes authoritative parenting.
- Low responsive, low demanding, **uninvolved** parenting. Uninvolved parents are neglectful of their children.

Authoritative parenting is associated with more positive developmental outcomes than the other parenting styles (Baumrind, 1991; Parke & Buriel, 1998). Children raised by authoritative parents tend to be responsibly independent, mature in their social interactions, cooperative with adults and other children, and have high self-esteem (Baumrind, 1989, 1991; Darling & Steinberg, 1993). The authoritative style is associated with greater academic achievement as well (Steinberg, Elman, & Mounts, 1989; Weiss & Schwartz, 1996). In fact, authoritative parenting promotes achievement relative to authoritarian parenting in most ethnic/racial groups, although the advantages of authoritative parenting on achievement are greater for some groups than for others (Dornbusch, Ritter, Leiderman, Roberts, & Fraleigh, 1987; Steinberg, Lamborn, Dornbusch, & Darling, 1992). For example, first-generation Chinese Americans do not seem to benefit as much as other Americans from authoritative parenting (Chao, 2001). In fact, the children of many Asian Americans and African Americans seem to do better academically if parents exert considerable control in their lives (Avenevoli, Sessa, & Steinberg, 1999; Glasgow, Dornbusch, Troyer, Steinberg, & Ritter, 1997; Leung, Lau, & Lam, 1998).

In contrast to the positive benefits associated with authoritative parenting, children raised by authoritarian parents are more likely to exhibit poor peer relations, social anxiety, and antisocial behaviors (Maccoby & Martin, 1983; Putallez, 1987; Rubin, Stewart, & Chen, 1995). Difficulty in social adjustments (e.g., to the social constraints and demands in school) tend to characterize the children of permissive parents as well (Lamborn, Mounts, Steinberg, & Dornbusch, 1991; Pulkkinen, 1982). Children of uninvolved parents suffer socioemotionally as well as with respect to cognitive development and academic achievement (Cummings & Davies, 1994; Kurdek & Fine, 1994).

Why do parenting styles produce such results? To answer this question, researchers have studied the specific mechanisms that parents can use to socialize their children. In general, the findings on specific socialization mechanisms complement the research on overall style.

Specific Socialization Mechanisms
Secure Base

Recall the importance of a secure base to mother–infant attachment. Research on the importance of a secure base as children grow older suggests that relationships between parents and their children are healthier when children can explore ideas and the world, confident of their parents' help and support when it is needed (Allen et al., 2003). For example, adolescence is a period of great exploration for children and a secure attachment to a parent provides a secure base for the adolescent to try new and different roles and activities (Kerr, Stattin, Biesecker, & Ferrer-Wreder, 2003; Marvin & Britner, 1999). Parents support their adolescents' development simply by being there when their teenagers need them, helping them talk through problems and find solutions to the growing challenges of life. Closeness to parents truly matters (Chao, 2001). Authoritative parents are more likely to provide a secure base and to encourage exploration than authoritarian parents.

Specific Disciplinary/Teaching/Learning Mechanisms

One of the major goals of parenting is to foster the development of long-term self-control in children. This is more likely to happen when parental discipline is characterized by the use of a method known as induction (Hoffman, 1989) than if parents rely mostly on punishment. **Induction** involves explaining to a child the potential harm of the misdeed, especially the consequence of making another person feel bad: "Don't push your brother. Think about how he'll feel if he gets hurt." At the center of an inductive approach is encouraging children to be empathetic, to think about other people and their feelings (Hoffman, 2001). Providing children with explanations about why they should behave a particular way helps assure children's long-term compliance with sanctions (Kanfer & Zich, 1974; Parke & Walters, 1967). Even if parents use punishment, providing explanations can increase the effectiveness of punishment (Cheyne & Walters, 1969; Parke, 1969, 1974; LaVoie, 1973, 1974). In order for rationales to work, however, children must understand the message being delivered by their parents (Grusec & Goodnow, 1994). Because children in elementary school are better able to understand the perspective of others (see Chapter 3), rationales emphasizing potential harm to others have more of an impact among elementary compared to preschool children (Parke, 1974). Yet the evidence indicates that reasoning works better than force even with 2-year-olds (Crockenberg & Litman, 1990).

Although physical punishment, such as spanking, can immediately reduce behaviors that are not wanted by parents, it can produce side effects that argue against its use (Gershoff, 2002). Recall from Chapter 5 the power of social models. Children often do imitate what they see. When a parent asserts control by hitting a child, the parent is modeling physical aggression (Coie & Dodge, 1998). Social modeling of aggression increases children's aggression, especially in the case of boys (Bandura, 1977, 1986; Martin, 1975; Olweus, 1980; Rollins & Thomas, 1979; Weiss, Dodge, Bates, & Pettit, 1992). The child who is spanked at home is more likely to be an aggressive child at school than the child who is not spanked, with aggression accompanied by poorer peer relations in general (George & Main, 1979; Loeber & Dishion, 1984; MacKinnon-Lewis et al., 1994; Olweus, 1993; Rohner, Kean, & Cournoyer, 1991). Punishment-oriented homes often are cold and rejecting (Dishion, 1990; Parke & Slaby, 1983; Redd, Morris, & Martin, 1975), with this pattern producing children who are more aggressive than prosocial in their interactions with others. One of the most critical potential negative side effects of parental punishment is that it has the potential of driving a wedge between children and parents, encouraging children to distance themselves from their parents.

Aggression begets aggression and punishing a child can escalate until the situation is out of control. The child, frustrated by the punishment, retaliates against the parent, with the result that the adult is even more harsh with the child (Patterson, 1976, 1986, 1996). Many cycles of such aggression lead to habits of aggression extending beyond the home. Cycles of aggression often can be broken by teaching the parent how to discipline more positively, including teaching the parent to use reasoning with the child (Patterson & Fleischman, 1979). In general, it makes sense to intervene as soon as such a pattern develops in a family and to treat the entire family, teaching all members of the family to encourage peaceful resolutions of problems and to discourage aggression against other family members (Patterson, 1982; Patterson, DeBaryshe, & Ramsey, 1989).

Parents can be taught specific ways to decelerate aggression in the family. One is to teach the power of reinforcement, and, in particular, the power of reinforcing a desired behavior that is incompatible with the undesired behavior (Slaby & Crowley, 1977), an approach technically known as **differential reinforcement of other behavior (DRO)** (Ross, 1981). Thus, rather than simply punishing a 5-year-old for aggressing against little sister, reinforce the 5-year-old for positive play with the little sister. Another very good approach is to use **time-out**. The offending child is physically removed from the setting, perhaps to a particular corner of the house or a time-out box. The child stays there for a set period of time or until she or he calms down. Time-out can be especially powerful when combined with differential reinforcement of other behavior and with providing the child with an explanation for the sanction, including why the child's misbehavior hurts others (Parke & Slaby, 1983).

In summary, the social learning processes of modeling, reinforcement, and punishment commonly occur in families. Effective parenting is characterized by more reinforcement than punishment, by more modeling of persuasiveness and reasonableness than punitiveness. Authoritative parenting has a clear positive reinforcement orientation, whereas authoritarian parenting has much more of a punishment orientation. The disciplinary mechanism of induction is completely consistent with authoritative parenting, which involves a great deal of parent–child communication. It is completely consistent with the knowledge that children must understand and accept disciplinary prescriptions if it is to be effective (Grusec & Goodnow, 1994). It is probably as effective as punishment in eliminating undesired behaviors without the negative side effects often associated with punishment.

Stress

When families are under stress, positive parent–child interactions often decrease and more punitive and authoritarian tactics increase. Parent–child relations tend to be more positive when spouses are mutually supportive, since stress is much less in such homes compared to ones in which parents are at odds with one another (Simons, Lorenz, Wu, & Conger, 1993). Marital breakup and divorce create high stress, and authoritarian parenting styles increase as families dissolve and during the immediate period following dissolution (Block, Block, & Gjerde, 1986; Buchanen, Maccoby, & Dornbusch, 1991; Hetherington, 1989). Alternatively, parents can become more uninvolved with their children as they become more absorbed in their problems with their spouses (Katz & Gottman, 1991). The financial difficulties and transitions during breakup and divorce often are overwhelming and distressing, all of which can affect parenting style negatively (Fauber, Forehand, Thomas, & Wierson, 1990). Not surprisingly, adverse child outcomes are associated with divorce. Family breakup is associated with increased behavioral problems (e.g., aggression, poor peer relations, substance abuse), affective problems (e.g., depression), and academic problems in children (Allison & Furstenberg, 1989; Camara & Resnick, 1988; Doherty & Needle, 1991; Fauber et al., 1990; Stolberg & Anker, 1984; Wallerstein, Corbin, & Lewis, 1988; Wallerstein & Kelly, 1980; Wallerstein & Lewis, 2004). In general, the negative effects of divorce seem to be more pronounced and long term with boys compared to girls (Hetherington, Clingempeel, & Associates, 1992; Wallerstein & Kelly, 1980).

Divorce is not the only stressor that can negatively affect parenting behaviors, however. Some children place more stress on their parents than do other children (Johnson & Moore, 1968). For example, parents have more difficulties being positive with temperamentally difficult children (Crockenberg, 1981; Eisenberg & Fabes, 1994). Premature children also are often irritable and demanding of parents, which can undermine parental style so much that the parent becomes abusive of the infant (Parke & Collmer, 1975).

Economics factors matter in family life. Severe financial problems increase parental stress, which affects parental behaviors, thereby affecting children's functioning and development (Conger et al., 1992; McLoyd & Wilson, 1990). Parental employment also can impact on parental style. Having to work when one does not want to work, having to work at a job one does not like, and not being able to work when one would like to work (e.g., during layoffs) are all sources of stress that can negatively affect parenting style (Conger et al., 1992; DeMeis, Hock, & McBride, 1986; Flanagan & Eccles, 1993; Gottfried, Gottfriend, & Bathurst, 1988; Hock & DeMeis, 1990; Greenberger & Goldberg, 1989; Lerner & Galambos, 1985, 1986, 1988). Although the data are not as definitive as for other issues, a heavy workload that reduces parental monitoring and support of children sometimes has been associated with academic and social problems for children (Cole & Rodman, 1987; Crouter, MacDermid, McHale, & Perry-Jenkins, 1990; Rodman & Cole, 1987).

At least some of the negative effects of stress are sometimes offset by social supports of various sorts (Melson, Ladd, & Hsu, 1993; Taylor, Casten, & Flickinger, 1993). Single parents and married couples who are experiencing financial difficulties sometimes receive support for their children from members of their extended family (Beck & Beck, 1989; Brooks-Gunn & Chase-Lansdale, 1995; Taylor et al., 1993; Wilson, 1986). Single parents sometimes marry, resulting in the addition of a stepparent who can provide support for the previously single parent and guidance for the child (Santrock & Warshak, 1979; Santrock, Warshak, Lindbergh, & Meadows, 1982). Supportive friends can help, as can the availability of counseling that provides guidance about how to manage children in a positive fashion (Hetherington, 1989; Wahler & Dumas, 1989).

In summary, both stress and social support can impact on parents so as to affect their parenting behaviors in ways that affect their children. Whether a child experiences a positive and more authoritative environment or a more negative, authoritarian (or neglectful) environment depends on a variety of contextual factors—biological, economic, and social.

Presence of Siblings

A huge contextual variable affecting parent–child interactions is the presence or absence of siblings. Some important questions regarding the nature and effects of siblings on development have been addressed by researchers.

One of these questions is, Are "only" children spoiled or disadvantaged relative to other children? The answer is "Not at all" (Falbo & Polit, 1986; Polit & Falbo, 1987; Thompson, 1974). Indeed, if anything, only children have better peer relations than children with siblings. Moreover, they tend to be a little smarter (Glass, Neulinger, & Brim, 1974; Sutton-Smith & Rosenberg, 1970; Zajonc, Marcus, & Marcus, 1979). The most likely explanation for these effects is that only children's intensive involvement with parents provides more experience with mature social and intellectual stimulation (Belsky, Gilstrap, & Rovine, 1984; Belsky, Rovine, & Taylor, 1984; Falbo & Polit, 1986). The only child is surrounded by mature models of thinking and interaction, whereas the child who is a member of a large family is exposed to models varying in maturity, from baby sister to parents (Zajonc et al., 1979). The social advantages of being an only child, however, are small, especially in comparison to children raised in a small, two-child family (Furman, 1995).

How does life change for a child when a new member of the family arrives? Dunn and Kendrick (1982; Dunn, 1993) studied 40 families. A new child was born into each family, which was comprised previously of a mother, a father, and one child between 1 and 4 years of age. Observations continued for about a year and a half, beginning about 2 months before the new baby was born and continuing into the new baby's second year. After the birth of the new baby, mothers and their firstborn children interacted less often and the interactions were less positive than before the birth of the new child. Typically, the firstborn received more prohibitions, in part because the firstborn tended to be less well behaved, especially when the mothers were taking care of the new baby. The arrival of a second child often decreased the quality of parent–first child interaction (Dunn, 2002). Thus authoritative parenting

Typically, the arrival of a new baby decreases the amount of time parents interact with their older child(ren). Sometimes the interactions that do occur with older child(ren) are less positive.

becomes more difficult since additional children sometimes decrease how much a parent will negotiate with the older children in the family rather than make demands on them (Dunn, 1993, 2002; Teti, 2001).

How do siblings interact with one another? As the children in a family increase in age, their interactions tend to be more positive (Dunn, 1992, 2002; Dunn & McGuire, 1992; Vandell, Minnett, & Santrock, 1987). As any parent knows, siblings sometimes quarrel with one another. The degree of sibling hostility is determined, in part, by parenting style, with authoritative parents producing children who are more positive in their interactions than authoritarian parents (Collins, Harris, & Susman, 1995; Stocker, Dunn, & Plomin, 1989).

Do parents treat their children the same? In general, there is more evidence of consistency in parental treatment of their children than evidence against it (Furman, 1995). Even so, children are treated very differently in some families (Dunn & McGuire, 1994). For example, siblings with handicaps are treated very differently compared to normally developing siblings (McHale & Pawletko, 1992). When one child is treated much more favorably in a family than another child, the potential for rivalry and hostility between peers increases (Brody, Stoneman, & McCoy, 1992).

In summary, family dynamics and parental style vary with family composition. In general, in smaller families each child receives more parental attention (and the associated cognitive and social benefits) than in big families. The addition of a new child to a family stresses the relationship between the parent and the older child. The long-term prognosis is more favorable, however, with comparable treatment of children more likely than differential treatment as children mature, and more evidence of friendly sibling relations than negative ones. Siblings model behaviors for one another and explicitly teach each other new things. They often provide emotional support for one another, as when an older sibling serves as a secure base for a younger child's exploration when a parent is not around (Samuels, 1980; Stewart & Marvin, 1984).

■ ■ ■ BEYOND THE FAMILY: PEER RELATIONSHIPS

Children really do love being with other children. Even 3-month-old infants get excited when another child is present (Field, 1979). Given children's desires for peer relationships from an early age, it is not surprising that peer relationships are important in development (Hartup, 2005; Rubin, Bukowski, & Parker, 1998). Next, we discuss what is known about children's interactions with their peers and the effects of those interactions on development.

Development of Peer Relations

If you put two 6-month-old infants together, they do not ignore one another (Field, 1979; Fogel, 1979). Rather, they seem to explore, looking at and touching each other. The children smile and babble as they do so (Vandell & Mueller, 1980). Six-month-olds are not very interactive, however, in the sense of being clearly responsive to one another, although responsiveness is beginning (Hay, Nash, & Pedersen, 1983; Vandell, Wilson, & Buchanen, 1980).

As the first year of life continues, children are increasingly sociable when they are together. The touches, smiles, babbles, and gestures are much more coordinated (Bronson, 1981; Vandell et al., 1980). Children begin to play with toys together (Bakeman & Adamson, 1984). Even so, year-old infants can be together and completely ignore one another, or at most interact only a little bit (Eckerman & Stein, 1982; Hartup, 1983). During the second year of life, children's interactions increase, with 2-year-olds often chasing each other around and playing together with toys, even complicated toys that require the coordinated efforts of two children (Brownell & Brown, 1992; Brownell & Carriger, 1990; Howes, 1987a, 1987b). Two-year-olds imitate one another quite a bit (Eckerman & Stein, 1990; Howes & Matheson, 1992), and they take turns in games such as tag (Howes, 1987a, 1987b). By 2 years of age, and certainly by 3, children clearly prefer some children over others. That is, they are beginning to have friends (Brownell & Brown, 1992; Hartup, 1989; Howes, 1988).

Peer relations develop a great deal during the preschool-age years. In a classic study, Mildred Parten (1932) observed preschoolers and identified six different patterns of play:

- *Unoccupied*: The child does not play with others but notices some of what is going on around her or him.
- *Solitary play*: The child plays alone, oblivious to other children.
- *Onlooking*: The child watches other children playing. If the child speaks to others, she or he does not join in the play.
- *Parallel play*: Children play at similar activities, but play on their own as they do so. The children are close together, and each is doing something that could be coordinated with the activities of the other children, but no coordination takes place.
- *Associative play*: Children interact as they play, but they do not cooperate in pursuit of a shared goal. For example, they share toys, but do not cooperate to use toys together as part of a common scenario.
- *Cooperative play*: Children play with one another, pursuing common goals such as building something or playing house.

Parten observed that parallel play was common throughout the preschool years. Although unoccupied play and solitary play were prevalent in the early preschool years, cooperative play increased with increasing age. The more important conclusion, however, is that preschoolers tend to engage in more than one type of play, including solitary, parallel, and cooperative play (Hartup, 1983; Rubin, Maioni, & Hornung, 1976).

Developmental shifts in preschoolers' play also were examined by Howes and Matheson (1992). In this longitudinal observational study of children between 1 and 4 years of age, the more complex forms of play were observed more frequently with increasing age. Parallel play developed before more social, interactive play. Howes and Matheson (1992) also observed that simpler forms of parallel play develop before more complex forms. Thus parallel play that requires only involvement with the task develops earlier than parallel play that involves focusing on both the task *and* paying attention to the other child. Similarly, social play can involve simple interactions or complex coordination of roles (e.g., role reversals in hide-and-seek). Games of simple interaction are not as complex as play involving role playing (e.g., playing house), which is not as complex as role playing that is planned and carried out deliberately (e.g., as when children plan and carry out a play around the "playing house" theme). Playing "make-believe" requires sophisticated language, cognitive, and social skills, ones more likely in 4-year-olds than in 2-year-olds (Howes, 1996; Howes et al., 1992 Rubin & Coplan, 1992).

Attendance at nursery school provides opportunities for preschoolers to have expanded social interactions compared to children who are cared for at home by their parents. Children who attend nursery school probably are ahead of other children in their readiness for the social and cognitive demands of kindergarten (Ladd, 1990). It takes awhile to learn how to negotiate a culture filled with many peers. The nursery school graduate has made progress on this learning curve that the child who stayed at home for the first 5 years of life has not made (Harper & Huie, 1985; Shea, 1981). The exception to the generalization that nursery-school or daycare attendance promotes social skills is when the quality of the care is so poor that a great deal of interpersonal aggression occurs, which is then transferred into the kindergarten setting (Howes, 1990; Vandell, Henderson, & Wilson, 1988). A more complete discussion of daycare and its effects is provided later in this chapter.

"Playing house" is complex social play involving role playing.

Although play researchers interested in early childhood education have emphasized positive changes in preschoolers' play patterns and social interactions, some other characteristics also deserve attention. Most preschoolers spend the majority of free playtime alone rather than in interaction with other children (Rubin & Coplan, 1992), so peer interactions are not the centerpiece of the preschool experience. The absolute amount of aggression increases during the preschool years, although proportional to all interactions aggression goes down relative to more prosocial interactions (Hartup, 1983; Pepler & Rubin, 1991). Aggression by other preschoolers—both physical and relational aggression—is very annoying and salient to young children (French, Jansen, & Pidada, 2002).

During the elementary-school years, peer interactions become even more complex; the games children play with peers also are more sophisticated (Hartup, 1983; Piaget, 1965). School plays an important role in this, assuring that children spend a great deal of time with each other. Children spend a lot of time talking with their friends, exploring many ideas with those who are at a similar level of development, curious about similar issues, and share similar interests (Zarbatany, Hartmann, & Rankin, 1990). Increasingly during the grade-school years, children are spending time with the children they want to be with, rather than spending time with the children who happen to live next door (Hartup, 1983). Physical fighting and quarrels decrease during the elementary years; sharing and helping increase (Hartup, 1983).

Peers are increasingly important with approach and entry into adolescence (Brown & Klute, 2003; Brown, Mounts, Lamborn, & Steinberg, 1993). The intensity of friendships and the importance of them also increase with the onset of adolescence (Buhrmester, 1996). Adolescents often are part of a 5- to 10-person peer group, called a **clique**, which is important to them (Brown, 1989; Palmonari, Pombeni, & Kirchler, 1989). Clique members are the people the teen spends the most time with and trusts the most. Often, teens have one or two very special friends in a clique, people with whom they feel they can be especially honest (Berndt, 1982; Furman & Bierman, 1984; Youniss & Smollar, 1985). For most adolescents, having and just being with friends is the best part of life (Csikszentmihalyi & Larson, 1984). Cliques tend to be a subset of a larger **crowd**, with the crowd members defined by salient characteristics. For example, some typical crowds found in high schools may be identified as the jocks, the brains, the druggies, and the nerds. There are also some kids who are not distinguishable as members of the aforementioned categories—they're just regular teens (Brown, 1990). Hanging out with other teens is healthy, with the lonely teen much more likely to be maladjusted and depressed than the teen who has close friends (Buhrmester, 1992). That said, the potential for falling into a bad crowd that can lead to participation in delinquent behaviors is also real (Morizot & LeBlanc, 2000), although something that is not inevitable, with children of nurturing and involved parents less likely to fall into such a crowd than children with less caring and involved parents, even in community situations where the risk of encountering wrong-crowd peers is great (Brody et al., 2001; Mason, Cauce, Gonzales, & Hiraga, 1996).

Crowd membership is not a life-defining identity, however. Recall from Chapter 5 Erickson's portrayal of adolescence as a period of time for experimenting with identities. Peers, including crowds of them, play a great role in such experimentation. The intellectual power that comes with formal operational thought, to use Piaget's explanation for the expansion of thinking skills during adolescence compared to childhood, permits teens to think about things they have never thought about before. Often, they try their ideas out on their intimates, their closest friends. It is safe to do so, for even if the idea is ridiculous, the close friend is not hard on the teenage philosopher! Close friends help teens think out situations and figure out who they are (Youniss & Smollar, 1985).

In summary, peer interactions and friendships clearly progress from infancy to adolescence. With increasing age, interactions are more complex and more decidedly social. Although even very young children have friends versus acquaintances, the distinction between a close friend and a member of the larger crowd becomes more salient with increasing age. By adolescence, teens participate in hierarchies of relationships, being members of crowds who share lifestyles and general interests as well as part of cliques who are closer friends. Some members of a teen's clique are closer than others, with especially close friends becoming confidants as adolescents explore who they are, what they want to be, what they think, and how they want to live.

Development of Social-Cognitive Abilities

Cognitive development plays an important role in mediating the development of children's abilities to interact with others. In particular, there is a great deal of development of children's **social cognition** (Flavell & Miller, 1998; Lewis & Carpendale, 2002). Social cognition refers to the understanding of other people and the nature of the social world (Flavell, Miller, & Miller, 1993). One example of social cognition is the understanding that people have intentions that can drive their behavior, an understanding that increases during the preschool years (Feinfeld, Lee, Flavell, Green, & Flavell, 1999). As we shall see, much development needs to take place before a child can size up other people and the world like an adult thinker can.

Selman's Theory of Social-Cognitive Development

Robert Selman (1976) proposed a complex developmental sequence for social perspective taking. His thinking was influenced by Piaget and Kohlberg, and, in the end, he offered a stage theory paralleling the Piagetian and Kohlbergian stage theories described in Chapter 3. Much like Kohlberg, Selman asked children to reason about dilemmas. One was about Holly, who was good at climbing trees, but had promised her father, who feared for her safety, that she would not climb trees. When confronted with a kitten stuck in a tree, Holly faced a dilemma, whether to climb the tree in defiance of her father's direction and save the kitten, or obey her father and leave the kitten in the tree. Selman asked children to make the choice for Holly and explain the choice.

At Selman's Stage 0 (preschool years; *egocentric stage*), children have difficulty understanding other perspectives and recognizing that others may interpret situations differently than they do. The Stage-0 thinker might defend Holly's decision to climb the tree and save the cat by arguing that Holly's father would agree with Holly's decision, seeing the situation precisely as Holly saw it. (How does Stage 0 relate to Piaget's notion of egocentrism during the preschool years?)

Children in Stage 1 (6- to 8-year-olds; *social-informational role-taking stage*) recognize that others have different perspectives but experience difficulties thinking about several perspectives at once. Thus, when talking about Holly, they may mention her father's concern as well as the welfare of the kitten but not recognize the conflict between these perspectives. (Is it unusual from the point of view of Piagetian theory for children of this age to have difficulty juggling several pieces of information in mind at one time? Think about the neo-Piagetian reformulation of Piaget's theory, which emphasizes the development of functional short-term memory abilities as a mediator of cognitive development.)

Stage-2 children (8- to 10-year-olds; *self-reflection stage*) are more attuned to their own perspectives and those of others, but still experience difficulties thinking about both their own perspectives and those of others at the same time.

Stage-3 children (10- to 12-year-olds; *mutual role-taking*) can consider two viewpoints at once and recognize that other people can do so as well. Thus, in talking about Holly, such children might argue that the father could be concerned with Holly's safety, but also be pleased that Holly succeeded in saving the kitten.

The highest stage in Selman's theory is Stage 4 (beginning at ages 12–15; *social and conventional system role taking*), with adolescents able to think about the situation from a third party's (as well as society's) perspective. In reasoning about Holly's dilemma, the young teen can weigh the perspectives of the different characters in the dilemma, but also can think about what makes sense from the larger perspective of the society. Thus, after detailing Holly's thinking, her father's concern and directive, the Stage-4 thinker might decide to leave the cat in the tree, recognizing that the risks of injury and the societal costs of injury to a child far outweigh the risks of losing the kitten. Alternatively, the Stage-4 thinker might factor in the animal rights perspective, which could result in the decision that Holly should rescue the kitten. (Is Selman's Stage 4 sensible given what is known about thinking during adolescence according to Piaget? Which of Kohlberg's moral development stages most resembles Selman's Stage 4?)

In general, Selman's (1980; Selman, Schorin, Stone, & Phelps, 1983) theory of the development of perspective taking has been confirmed in the sense that as children mature, their thinking about social dilemmas shifts much as Selman proposed. That is, children do increase in their abilities to reflect on alternative perspectives, considering both their own ideas, those of other people, and those of the larger society. Such increasing ability to think about and interact with others about social dilemmas should contribute to improved interactions with others.

In fact, Selman (1981) has also proposed a theory of friendship based on his perspective-taking model and roughly paralleling it. At Stage 0, preschoolers conceive of friendship as depending only on proximity rather than on any psychological basis. At Stage 1, children talk about friends as helpers. At Stage 2, children's descriptions of friendship include reciprocity, but still a good deal of self-centeredness, so that Stage-2 children believe that an argument can end friendly relations. The sharing reported by Stage-2 children involves concrete objects more than personal ideas. By Stage 3, children view friendships as being more enduring, with friends intimately open to one another about many issues. By Stage 4, children portray friends as providing a great deal of psychological support for one another, with adolescents finding and testing their identities with one another.

Theory-of-Mind Research

Much work on social cognition has focused on children's developing *theory of mind*, which refers to children's increasing understanding about how minds function (Lewis & Carpendale, 2002; Taylor, 1996; Wellman, 2002). Researchers studying children's theory of mind have demonstrated substantial social-cognitive development during the preschool years and beyond (Leekam, 1993). For example, although 3-year-olds understand that people only can see things that are in their unobstructed line of sight, 4- and 5-year-olds have more subtle understandings about perspective. They realize that the line of sight between an object and the eyes perceiving it must necessarily be straight (Flavell, Green, Herrera, & Flavell, 1991). They also realize that people viewing objects from different angles will see different things (Flavell, Everett, Croft, & Flavell, 1981).

If children can pretend, they must understand the distinction between the real world and the imaginary, mental-only world. Theory-of-mind researchers have established that children younger than age 3 sometimes pretend, but they do not understand the properties of imaginary compared to real objects as well as do older preschoolers. For example, 3-year-olds know that it is impossible to touch an imaginary cup and they understand that they can flip such a cup over in their head (Estes, Wellman, & Woolley, 1989; Wellman & Estes, 1986). On the other hand, preschoolers' understanding of the distinction between real and imagined objects is not complete. Thus, when Harris, Brown, Marriott, Whittall, and Harmer (1991) asked 4- to 6-year-olds to imagine a monster, they recognized that no one else could see the monster and reported that it was not real. Even so, they also were apprehensive that it might become real!

During the preschool years, the understanding that people have desires, beliefs, and intentions also increases (Feinfield et al., 1999). Moreover, the ability to differentiate these states of mind substantially improves. Thus, with increasing age during the preschool years, children understand that people can wish for one thing and believe that a different outcome will occur. In contrast, younger children focus on wishes, believing that a person's wishes reflect the individual's belief about what is going to happen (Bartsch & Wellman, 1989).

In short, theory-of-mind researchers have generated evidence that children's understanding of how the mind functions and how the mind's functioning differs from functioning in the physical world increases during the preschool years. Understanding how one's own mind and that of other's works is important social-cognitive knowledge. A mature theory of mind will facilitate children's interactions with others. For example, children increasingly understand that emotions such as happiness and surprise depend in part on a person's desires and beliefs. That is, someone cannot be happy about something unless they desired it, and someone cannot be surprised unless they expected something else to happen (Hadwin & Perner, 1991; Wellman & Banerjee, 1991). Such knowledge is essential for a child who is trying to make another person happy, perhaps by planning a pleasant surprise. Knowing how other people's minds work is essential knowledge for dealing with other people, knowledge that increases dramatically during the preschool years (Perner, 1991; Wellman, 1990).

During the preschool years children increasingly recognize that they can affect the emotions of another person by acting one way or another way and that emotional states vary with situations (Barden, Zelko, Duncan, & Masters, 1980; Terwogt & Harris, 1993). For example, preschoolers learn how to comfort others in distress, which requires clear understanding of the perspective of others (Dunn, Kendrick, & MacNamee, 1981; Stewart & Marvin, 1984). It is not until the early grade-school years, however, before children have an understanding of the wide range of emotions and how the many human emotions vary depending on the situation (Harris, Olthof, Terwogt, & Hardman, 1987). During the elementary years, children come to understand that they can hide their emotions and should on some occasions so as not to hurt the feelings of another person (Harris & Gross, 1988; Harris, Olthof, & Terwogt, 1981). It is easy to see how understanding of emotion is critical to effective peer interactions. Part of peer interaction is comforting others; part of it is also hiding how one feels so that others do not feel badly. Emotional regulation of self and others very much depends on children developing theories of mind.

Theory-of-mind perspectives may offer an important window on one group of children who have puzzled researchers for a long time. One of the most defining characteristics of children with autism is that they do not relate to other people. There is growing evidence that such children lack a theory of mind or at least have much less complete understanding than normal children about the existence of others' thoughts, feelings, and desires, as well as a less complete understanding of themselves as thinkers and doers (Baron-Cohen, 2001; Baron-Cohen, Wheelwright, Lawson, Griffin, & Hill, 2002). See Chapter 12 for a more complete discussion of autism.

Increases in Other Understandings about People and Social Situations

During the grade-school years, children begin to understand that other people have enduring characteristics—they have traits such as friendliness, shyness, or aggressiveness (Livesley & Bromley, 1973; Yuill, 1993). They begin to understand that males and females exhibit some differences in their social interactions (Markovits, Benenson, & Dolenszky, 2001). With increasing age, children understand that other people are better defined by their internal characteristics (i.e., feelings, knowledge, thought) than by their external characteristics (i.e., possessions, dress; Mohr, 1978).

Children's understanding of the social world and how it is organized also increases during the preschool and elementary years. Children acquire understandings of many social rules (Smetana, 1993). They learn who to address politely and when, how dress varies with occasions (e.g., clothes for "dress up" vs. clothes for play), and how to negotiate the world safely (e.g., waiting for the walk light). Children also learn about status differences and how these translate into differences in human interaction and power (Emler & Dickinson, 1993). In short, as children develop, they acquire a great deal of information about how to act, when, and with whom, knowledge required for effective social interactions with others.

In summary, the work on social cognition makes clear that social development occurs in tandem with cognitive development. That is, social-cognitive knowledge and skills are correlated with social competence (Gnepp, 1989; Hudson, Forman, & Brion-Meisels, 1982; Kurdek & Krile, 1982; LeMare & Rubin, 1987; McGuire & Weisz, 1982). There is a chicken-and-egg problem, however. Do social interactions lead to increases in social-cognitive understandings, or do increases in social-cognitive understandings enable social interactions? Most likely, the answer is both. Social behavior and cognitive development are probably reciprocally causative. See the Applying Developmental Theory to Educational Contexts special feature (Box 10.3) for an illustration of the difficulty children may have displaying social cognition in their writing.

The Gender of Friends

Children tend to play and interact with children who are about the same age and of the same sex. This tendency holds through childhood and adolescence, with the same-sex preference growing stronger from early childhood into the elementary years (Bukowski, Gauze, Hoza, & Newcomb, 1993; Gottman, 1986; Maccoby & Jacklin, 1987). It holds across a variety of cultures (Harkness & Super, 1985). By middle school, children spend more time with their same-sex friends than with either their mother or their father (Buhrmester & Furman, 1986).

Boys tend to have more friends and to engage in activities involving more people than do girls—that is, they engage in *extensive relationships*; girls have fewer friends, with girls tending to have *intensive relationships* (Waldrop & Halverson, 1975). Another way of thinking about it is with respect to boys' greater tendency to do things to shorten one-to-one interactions versus girls' tendency to do things to increase the length of interactions; Maccoby (1990) referred to these as, respectively, *constricting* and *enabling* styles. Yet another way of characterizing this gender difference is to think of males as *domineering* and females as *cooperative* (Leaper, 1991). In

Applying Developmental Theory to Educational Contexts

BOX 10.3. Children's Social Cognition as Reflected in Their Narrative Writing

Some changes in children's writing can be understood in terms of the development of children's knowledge about how minds work. Fox (1991) asked 7-, 9-, 11-, and 13-year-old school children to write two stories, one about "The Visitor," and the other about "The Day I Ran Away from Home." The essays were scored in terms of the social interactions and the thoughts about social interactions of the characters in the story.

Older children included much more information in their stories about the inner world of their characters. In the stories of 7-year-olds, inner feelings were simple, with the child telling the reader what the character saw, knew, or wanted, but little else. The 9-year-olds were much more able to link desires with emotions in their stories than the 7-year-olds. With increasing age, children increasingly referred to more complex mental states and character reflection on their own behavior relative to their mental states. Moreover, with increasing age children wrote more about how characters made inferences about the mental states of others. Thus, 13-year-olds wrote more about how one character thought about the thinking of another character and related the thinking of characters to their attitudes and actions than did 7- or 9-year-olds.

If preschoolers know so much about states of mind, as reflected by the theory-of-mind research, why don't they express that knowledge in their writing? Writing is very difficult for children. It requires planning and organizing ideas, sentence creation to translate the ideas into prose, and physically penning the composition, which is a demanding task during the early elementary years. In contrast, preschoolers' theories of mind have been tapped in tasks that are relatively easy for them, such as orally answering specific questions. It is very likely that the writing of students in the early elementary grades reflects so little of their theories of characters' minds because writing demands much more than answering questions. It is not that the children lack the competence to think about their characters' minds, but rather the performance demands of the task are so high that developing competencies are not apparent.

short, boys compete with one another more than do girls, with attempts at dominance and aggression much more common in groups of boys than in groups of girls (Black, 2000; Maccoby & Jacklin, 1974; Parke & Slaby, 1983).

By early adolescence, the increased mixing of the sexes begins, with adolescence being the traditional time when dating begins. A seventh-grade boy is unlikely to share the same intimacies with a girl as he would with his best male friend, nor would a seventh-grade girl share her deepest secrets with a boy rather than a girl. By grade 11, however, boys and girls are sharing their most personal thoughts with members of the opposite sex (Sharabany, Gershoni, & Hofman, 1981). Such intimate relationships are important testing grounds for identity development during adolescence and for learning important life skills, such as negotiation and compromise (Douvan & Adelson, 1966; Shulman, Bar-Ilan, & Ramat-Gan, 2003). These intimate relationships can become so important that they result in the exclusion and ignoring of old friends, in favor of spending time with the girlfriend or boyfriend (Roth & Parker, 2001). The romantic relationship, however, can have an ugly side—for example, resulting in inappropriate aggression and abuse of a romantic partner (Florsheim, 2003).

Popular and Unpopular Children

When researchers ask children in a class to evaluate who they like and who they do not like, individual children receive vastly different scores (Asher & Dodge, 1986; Cilleson & Bukowski, 2000; Coie, Dodge, & Coppotelli, 1982; Hymel, Rubin, Rowden, & LeMare, 1990; Hymel, Vaillancourt, McDougall, & Renshaw, 2002). *Popular children* receive positive votes from many of their classmates. In contrast are *rejected children* who receive many negative votes. *Controversial children* receive quite a few positive and quite a few negative votes. *Average children* do not elicit extremely positive or negative votes, but are rated as okay by their peers. Then, there are the *neglected children*, who are just ignored in the polling!

What makes a child popular? It is a mix of qualities. The popular child has very good social cognition, which translates into constructive communications and interactions with other children (Newcomb, Bukowski, & Pattee, 1993). It helps to be physically attractive and athletic, too (Hops & Finch, 1985; Lerner & Lerner, 1977).

Why are some children rejected by their peers? Some rejected children do things that other kids do not like. They are disruptive or simply hard to get along with, perhaps because they are socially awkward. High aggression is an almost certain route to rejection (Bierman, Smoot, & Aumiller, 1993; Gottmann, 1977; Newcomb et al., 1993). As discussed in Chapter 9, some children are quick to aggress against other children because they perceive neutral behaviors as hostile (Dodge, Coie, Pettit, & Price, 1990; Quiggle, Garber, Panak, & Dodge, 1992). Other rejected children show another pattern, however. It is not unusual for a rejected boy, for example, to be submissive and withdrawn, and thus end up being the target of aggression from other boys (Schwartz, Dodge, & Coie, 1993). Rejected-aggressive children have more academic difficulties than rejected-submissive children (Wentzel & Asher, 1995). That is, bullies are more at risk for academic problems than children who are withdrawn.

Neglected children also tend to be withdrawn (Coie, Dodge, & Kupersmidt, 1990). They have a lot of social anxiety and can be very unsure of their skills in negotiating social situations (Cassidy & Asher, 1992; Younger & Daniels, 1992). Academically, neglected children can do quite well. Wentzel and Asher (1995) evaluated a sample of sixth- and seventh-graders and concluded that the rejected-submissive children were motivated academically. They were better liked by teachers, who perceived them to be self-regulated relative to other children. Although often avoiding other children, with just a little nudge such children often will engage in normal social interactions (Ladd & Burgess, 1999).

Unpopular children may grow up to experience problems as adults, with the prognosis especially unfavorable for children who are unpopular for a long period of time. Poor school outcomes, social and emotional adjustment problems, and legal charges in adolescence and adulthood often await the overly aggressive elementary student (Bagwell, Newcomb, & Bukowski, 1998; Caspi, Elder, & Bem, 1987; Eron, 1987; Kupersmidt & Coie, 1990; Lerner, Hertzog, Hooker, Hassibi, & Thomas, 1988). Overly shy and withdrawn children are more likely to suffer depression and anxiety as adults (Rubin, LeMare, & Lollis, 1990). Years of being victimized because of lack of assertiveness may translate into pathological withdrawal.

Controversial children have a mix of qualities (Newcomb et al., 1993). We think about Eddie, a little boy we observed for some time. Eddie was good looking, and much of the time was extremely personable, a great conversationalist, and a terrific athlete. Eddie could also be quite aggressive, however, and was especially willing to victimize the withdrawn children in the class. Then there was Cathy, who was extremely attractive physically and a social star with other physically attractive kids. Cathy simply ignored the rest of the class. It is easy to understand why some children are controversial. Perhaps we worry about controversial youngsters less because some of their peers do like them (Parkhurst & Hopmeyer, 1998), even though such children are bullies or very nasty at times (DeRosier & Thomas, 2003). Life is worse in so many ways for rejected and neglected children.

Why do children end up being so socially unskilled, either hyperaggressive or extremely withdrawn, that they are singled out by peers for rejection or are completely ignored. It is probably due to a number of factors (Kazdin, 1994). Some of the possibilities in the mix of potential causes include biological factors (e.g., possible prenatal neurological damage, genetically determined differences in temperament) and family characteristics (e.g., parental discipline, parental psychopathology, marital discord, family size). One of the reasons it is hard to pinpoint the factors that might be more important than others is that risk factors tend to come in packages. That is, children at biological risk are often reared in families with characteristics that influence social behavior. For example, psychopathologically aggressive parents provide both the genes and the environment for their children, who are often more aggressive than other children.

Researchers have studied a number of ways to successfully intervene with children who lack social skills, although more for the treatment of aggressive behaviors than withdrawal. Some of these efforts are designed at affecting parenting behavior, teaching parents how to interact with their children to promote social skills. Often, these efforts are combined with ones directed at reducing other stressors in the family's life, so that assistance is provided to families in obtaining community and social services. Such programs have proven their worth in that when the children in the families are evaluated 10 years after the intervention was delivered, they are doing better than comparison children. They display less antisocial behavior, are achieving at higher levels in school, and have had fewer encounters with law enforcement (Lally, Mangione, & Honig, 1988; Seitz, Rosenbaum, & Apfel, 1985).

Other interventions are school-based, although they often include parent components. When such programs are successful in the long term, they tend to be implemented over a number of years. These include placement of at-risk children in high-quality preschool environments (Weikart & Schweinhart, 1992) or in programs during junior high aimed at teaching children social skills and rewarding them for using the skills they are learning (Bry, 1982). Other programs are carried out in recreational centers and other community-based facilities, and also involve direct teaching of social skills and reinforcement for using the skills (O'Donnell, Lydgate, & Fo, 1979).

One of the most important approaches to the instruction of social skills is the problem-solving approach (Camp & Bash, 1985; Spivack & Shure, 1982). Students are taught to recognize when they are in a situation in which they might behave inappropriately. They are taught to think before acting and to generate alternative ways that they might deal with the situation and to reflect on the consequences for behaving appropriately and inappropriately. The children are typically taught to approach situations in a step-by-step fashion, and to verbally self-instruct themselves along the way to size up the situation, think of appropriate ways to act and the benefits of doing so, and then carrying out the action. (These treatments are examples of cognitive behavior modification, as described in Chapter 5.) The teacher working with a child will introduce the skills gradually, with the child using them in game-like situations before attempting to apply them in the real world of peer interactions and school. In general, the track record for such interventions is good (Kazdin, 1994; Kendall, 1991; Pepler & Rubin, 1991).

In recent years, bullying at school has received a great deal of attention, for bullying is a common problem in schools. The case is strong for monitoring children to detect bullying when it occurs, for example, by observing playground behavior carefully. The case is also strong for school policies that demand parents of bullies work with the school to change the objectionable behaviors of their children, with administrative policies that permit drastic measures to stop bullying such as moving a student to another class or school where the staff are more skilled at working with bullies. Central to dealing with bullies is to teach them appropriate social skills, reinforcing them when they behave appropriately, and providing consequences when they do bully. By using a variety of approaches, schools can reduce the incidence of bullying and its negative effects on the school environment (Olweus, 2003; Rigby, 2002).

Teaching children how to act skillfully with other people makes a great deal of conceptual sense. The study of popular children reveals that they know how to begin, sustain, and end an interaction, such as a conversation (Dodge et al., 1983). Children who cannot do this are much more likely to be rejected by peers (Black & Hazen, 1990; Ladd, Price, & Hart, 1988). Intervention programs simply teach socially unskilled children to do what works for popular children.

In closing this discussion of popularity, we note that popularity and academic outcomes are related. For example, the incidence of social skills deficits in children with learning disabilities is much higher than the incidence of social skills problems in normally achieving students and they are much more likely to be rejected by classmates than normally achieving students (Kavale & Forness, 1996). Again, it is difficult to figure out the cause-and-effect here. Do academic difficulties affect social skills, or does lack of social skills impact negatively on cognitive development? Or does it work both ways, such that academic and social difficulties feed on one another?

Parental and Peer Pressures

Developmental psychologists have investigated the possibility that parents and peers place conflicting pressures on children and adolescents, with parents attempting to get their kids to do certain things and peers urging them to do otherwise. The time spent with peers increases with development, so the opportunity for peers to have influence increases. With adolescence comes a change in schooling, with many children leaving smaller, personal elementary schools and entering larger, more impersonal middle schools and high schools. Middle-school and high-school students are under pressure to make friends in what can be an intimidating context. Moreover, some adolescents engage in risky behaviors such as substance abuse, sexual activity and its consequences (e.g., teenage pregnancy and parenting), and acts of delinquency. There are a lot of reasons to believe that peers must be exerting much more pressure and influence during adolescence than childhood.

As it turns out, when children and adolescents are polled about the pressures on them, they do report increasing peer pressure with the onset of adolescence (Berndt,

1979; Brown, Lohr, & McClenahan, 1986; Hartup, 1983; Steinberg & Silverberg, 1986). Reported conformity to peer pressure, however, only increases slightly at adolescence, mostly with respect to antisocial behaviors such as illicit substance use (Berndt, 1979; Urberg, Luo, Pilgrim, & Degirmencioglu, 2003). Moreover, after the increase in conformity to peers in moving from childhood to early adolescence, peer conformity declines somewhat with age during the teen years, probably reflecting the fact that older adolescents have a much better sense of themselves than do young teens (Brown, 1989).

That said, conformity to peer pressure during adolescence depends on a variety of factors. For example, whether specific adolescents conform to peer pressure depends somewhat on their personalities (e.g., whether their self-esteem is low, increasing vulnerability to peer pressure to gain acceptance) and their relationship with their parents (Fuligni & Eccles, 1993; Hartup, 1983). It also depends on the issue (Huebner & Mancini, 2003; Sim & Koh, 2003). In matters of dress and style, peers are increasingly important with increasing age during the teen years. This is not the case with other issues, however, with parents' viewpoints highly valued with respect to moral values and life goals (Brown et al., 1986; Sebald & White, 1980; Wilks, 1986). In addition, the relationship with parents matters greatly. For example, adolescents with authoritative parents are less likely to cave in to pressure to use illicit substances than adolescents with more authoritarian parents (Adamczyk-Robinette, Fletcher, & Wright, 2002).

Finally, peers and parents are often not far apart on the big issues, with peer pressures and family pressures very similar (Huebner & Mancini, 2003). Researchers no longer think that it is either peers or parents that determine adolescents' behaviors, but rather a particular adolescent in interaction with peers *and* parents (Kerr, Stattin, Biesecker, & Ferrer-Wreder, 2003), with all of these players typically sharing more common perspectives than differing perspectives.

Why Have Friends?: The Developmental Significance of Friendship

Friendship promotes healthy development in a variety of ways (Hartup, 1996a). Friends often grease the wheels of the world for each other. Thus, it is not uncommon for one child to usher a friend into new activities (Howes, 1988). It is often easier to face new situations, such as a new school, surrounded by supportive friends than when going it alone (Hartup, 1996a; Ladd, 1990; Simmons, Burgeson, & Reif, 1988). By adolescence, friends are a primary source of social support when confronting new situations, including new ideas about the self, the world, and one's place in the world (Buhrmester, 1996).

Friendships also provide a context in which children can learn and practice social skills, with friends providing corrective feedback for one another about the many social do's and don'ts that children must learn in order to get along well in the world. Competent children model competent behaviors for less competent children in their company; they also reinforce the social competence of other children, through positive comments and approval, as they punish social incompetence, through mild disapproval (Hartup, 1983). Friendship also is an arena in which children can learn to manage conflict. A hallmark of social competence in adolescence and adulthood is the ability to resolve conflicts (Hartup, 1989).

Beyond gains in social competence, having friends also predicts cognitive competence. Although it is not possible to do a true experiment in which having friends can be experimentally manipulated, having friends and success in school are positively correlated (Ladd, 1990; Newcomb & Bagwell, 1996). See the Applying Developmental Theory to Educational Contexts special feature (Box 10.4) for some ideas on how friends facilitate cognitive development in the context of cooperative learning.

A related question is does the way a teacher teaches impact the way children relate to one another in a classroom? A group at the University of California–Berkeley (Donohue, Perry, & Weinstein, 2003) examined this issue in first-grade classrooms. As you might recall from Chapter 9, the Pressley research group has established that effective and engaging first-grade classrooms are very different from other classrooms. In effective classrooms, instruction is more individualized, with the teacher monitoring individual children's needs and teaching to those needs. In these classrooms, children are encouraged to be self-regulated from the first day. Does such teaching impact the way that children feel about one another in such a classroom? The answer seems to be yes. Donohue and colleagues (2003) found that

---

Applying Developmental Theory to Educational Contexts

BOX 10.4. Friends Working Together at School

At several points in this text we make the point that cooperative learning increases learning. Are academic interactions more productive when it is friends interacting and cooperating than when children work with nonfriends (Hartup, 1996a)? The answer seems to be a definite yes in favor of friends. When elementary-school friends work together, they explore more, talk more about the exploration, and complete the task with greater enthusiasm. Moreover, children seem to learn more when friends explore than when nonfriends carry out the same task (Newcomb & Brady, 1982).

When 11-year-olds worked on problems together (Azmitia & Montgomery, 1993), friends, more than acquaintances, provided more justifications for their attempts at solving the problem, reacted to the ideas of others more completely, engaged in more productive cognitive conflict about the problem and its solution, and monitored progress. Friends were also more likely to solve tough problems than were nonfriends.

When 11-year-old friends wrote together (Hartup, Daiute, Zajac, & Sholl, 1995), they wrote better stories than nonfriends writing together. They also spent a lot more time interacting about the emerging story, and engaged in richer interactions about the content of the story, than did nonfriends.

Hartup (1996a, 1996b) provided the following explanations for why academic interactions between friends are more likely to be engaging and successful than interactions between acquaintances:

- Friends communicate better than nonfriends because they know one another better.
- Friends expect more assistance from one another than do nonfriends.
- Interactions tend to be more positive between friends than nonfriends, with friends able to find points of agreement and common ground more quickly than nonfriends.
- When disagreements occur, friends are better able to iron them out than are nonfriends.

In short, when friends interact in doing academic tasks, they are more likely to be positive with one another, freely exchange ideas, manage their conflicts, and stay on task than are acquaintances (Newcomb & Bagwell, 1995).

first graders in such classrooms were more empathetic toward a classmate compared to students in classrooms that are less learner-centered and less motivating. By the end of the year, there were also fewer interpersonal behavior problems in effective classrooms. That is, the students got along better, with fewer cases of children rejected by their classmates.

■ ■ ■ HOW DOES DAYCARE AFFECT SOCIAL AND ACADEMIC DEVELOPMENT?

The majority of North American preschoolers experience some form of daycare (Lamb, 1998). Often, this means that the child spends time at a relative's home. Many children, however, are cared for by nonrelatives. Sometimes the nonrelative comes to the child's home, but also some caregivers open their homes to other people's young children. Still other children go to daycare centers. Daycare varies tremendously with the age of children, with infants and 1-year-olds requiring more intensive support from adults than do 3-, 4-, and 5-year-olds.

Beginning in the early 1990s, the National Institute of Child Health and Human Development (NICHD) organized a group of early childhood researchers to conduct a large, national evaluation of early childcare. The commitment was to collect data on the early childcare experiences of 1,100 children with follow-up analyses of their cognitive and socioemotional characteristics through the sixth grade. Our tactic for dealing with this treasure trove of data is to discuss the most important findings in the context of other studies about daycare. Rather than attempting to cite the many studies that have been produced by this NICHD Early Child Care Research Network, we simply refer to their efforts as the NICHD study. A complete bibliography of research from this project is available at secc.rti.org.

The Characteristics Determining the Quality of Daycare

One of the most salient outcomes produced by the NICHD group is that the quality of early childcare matters, with better cognitive and socioemotional outcomes associated with higher quality daycare. Sizing up the quality of a daycare environment requires paying attention to what is in the environment (i.e., *structure*) and what goes on in the environment (i.e., *process*) (Abbott-Shim & Sibley, 1987; Arnett, 1989; Harms & Clifford, 1989; Harms, Cryer, & Clifford, 1990).

Structure

When you walk around a high-quality daycare environment, you should encounter the following:

- The setting includes furnishings that support routine care (e.g., a changing table for infants).
- Furnishings permit the children to relax and be comfortable (e.g., beanbag chairs, large pillows).
- Materials to support learning activities (e.g., books, games, art supplies, musical toys, sand and water, dress-up clothes).

- Materials supporting both fine (e.g., drawing) and gross (e.g., playground equipment) motor activities.
- Space for free play and group activities (e.g., a rug for whole-group meetings).
- A sufficient number of adults to care for the children in the setting. The number of adults needed depends on the ages of the children. The Panel on Child Care Policy of the National Research Council (Meadows, 1991) recommended one adult for every four infants and 1-year-olds, one adult for very four to six 2-year-olds, one for every five to 10 3-year-olds, and one for every 16 to 20 4- and 5-year-olds.
- Caregivers are educated in early childhood development and education.
- A space where adults can meet (e.g., an office where teachers can interact with parents).

Beyond having adequate personnel and supplies, the furnishings, equipment, and materials at a good childcare facility are clean and safe. Moreover, the available supplies and space accommodate comfortably all children who are present in the setting. In addition, the space is arranged so that children can self-regulate their activities to a large degree (e.g., all toys and books are within reach).

Process

Although the quality of a setting's structure can be evaluated fairly quickly, the quality of the process that occurs in a daycare setting requires more prolonged visitation. Here are some of the behaviors that can be observed in high-quality daycare:

- The adult caregiver greets children on arrival and says good-bye when the children depart.
- A regular snack and meal schedule, with food served in a positive atmosphere.
- A regular schedule of activities.
- Nap or rest periods are part of the routine.
- Diapering and toileting are uneventful.
- The children keep themselves clean (e.g., they wash up before meals).
- The adults talk with the children a great deal and provide ample opportunities for the children to talk with them. The caregiver's language is at a child-appropriate level.
- The adults reason with the children, for example, explaining to a child the reason for a rule when a rule violation occurs.
- Adult supervision of motor activities (e.g., playing on playground equipment) and creative activities (e.g., art, music, building blocks).
- The tone of the interaction between children and adults is positive. The caregivers clearly like children and are enthusiastic when they are around children. They initiate interactions with the children rather than simply responding when children seek them out.
- When children want to speak to an adult, there are adults who listen.
- The center activities reflect the cultural diversity of the children in attendance, with all of the cultures that are present treated with respect.
- The caregivers encourage the children to try new experiences.

- The caregivers encourage prosocial behavior by the children.
- The caregivers are aware of individual differences between children, and accommodate to such differences and to special needs when planning activities.
- Regular conferences with parents.

Unfortunately, not all childcare environments are high quality. An environment can be filled with expensive equipment and be immaculate, and yet the process in that environment does not support the healthy development of the child (Scarr, Eisenberg, & Dieter-Deckard, 1994). Some of the signs of a setting that is not appropriately supportive of children are the following:

- The caregivers are critical of the children and are often irritated by the children.
- Punishment and threats of punishment are salient. Many activities are not allowed, with an emphasis on what the children should not be doing rather than on what the children should be doing.
- The caregivers are detached from the children and they are often unsupervised.

Development of High-Quality Childcare Environments

Development of high-quality daycare is facilitated by substantial knowledge about child development, especially during the preschool years. That is, the quality of childcare environments and the training of the individuals running them are correlated (Cost, Quality, and Child Outcomes in Child Care Centers, 1995; Galinsky, Howes, & Kontos, 1995; Galinsky, Howes, Kontos, & Shinn, 1994; also, see the NICHD study). Individuals with substantial training in early childhood recognize the importance of providing a favorable caregiver-to-child ratio, and they are aware of the need for a stimulating environment as part of children's social and intellectual development. The processes that occur in good environments can only occur when there are enough adults relative to the number of children, and these adults both care enough to interact with the children constructively and have the know-how about constructive caregiver–child interactions.

Daycare Effects on Attachment

As we have learned, some infants are more securely attached to their parents than are other infants. A hallmark of secure parent–child attachment can be observed when a parent leaves a child and then returns. On return, the securely attached infant will greet the parent warmly, approaching the parent with a smile or laughter, perhaps indicating that she or he would like to be picked up. Less securely attached infants avoid their parents upon their return or perhaps are ambivalent, showing some signs of wanting renewed contact with the parent and some signs of not wanting such contact. One possibility considered by early childhood education researchers is that daycare, especially during infancy, undermines secure attachment (Belsky, 1988).

As described earlier, one way attachment can is assessed is by the "Strange Situation." The Strange Situation involves the mother leaving the baby in a strange room (sometimes alone, sometimes with a stranger). This situation might not be so unusual for daycare infants compared to homecare infants. After all, daycare infants have had quite a bit of experience with mother leaving them in a room and with strangers. When all of the data using the Strange Situation are analyzed, the difference in reactions to the strange situation of daycare and parental-care infants proved to be rather small (i.e., 36–37% of daycare infants were insecurely attached vs. 29% of homecare infants; Clarke-Stewart, 1988, 1989, 1992; Lamb, Sternberg, & Prodromidis, 1992). Moreover, when other measures of attachment security—besides the Strange Situation—have been used (e.g., observer ratings of infants' typical behaviors), differences in the security of attachment for daycare and parental-care infants have not been obtained (Belsky & Rovine, 1990; Weinraub, Jaeger, & Hoffman, 1988). In the NICHD study, attachment security did not reliably differ as a function of daycare experience (e.g., NICHD Early Child Care Research Network, 1997). Moreover, when the attachment question has been addressed in older children (i.e., 2- to 4-year-olds), the security of attachment of daycare and parental-care children have not differed, typically, as assessed with the Strange Situation (Kagan, Kearsley, & Zelazo, 1978; Moskowitz, Schwarz, & Corsini, 1977; Portnoy & Simmons, 1978; Ragozin, 1980; Roopnarine & Lamb, 1978, 1980).

The NICHD study also found associations between the quality of daycare provided to children and children's social competence in general, with higher quality daycare associated with more socially competent children. This is consistent with findings in the larger literature on early childcare. When infants and preschoolers experience high-quality daycare, they seem to be more social, interacting more with peers and in a more constructive manner when they interact (Field, Masi, Goldstein, Perry, & Parl, 1988; Howes, 1988, 1990; Howes, Smith, & Galinsky, 1995; Lamb, 1998; Rosenthal, 1994). Indeed, a particularly good predictor of positive peer relations is a positive relationship with a daycare provider (Howes, Hamilton, & Matheson, 1994; Howes, Phillips, & Whitebrook, 1992; Pianta & Nimetz, 1991; Sroufe, Fox, & Pancake, 1983). Children experiencing high-quality daycare seem to have more mature personalities than other children (Lamb, 1998). The positive effects of daycare during the preschool years have been detected with respect to social interactions even during the teenage years (Andersson, 1992).

Do infants in daycare become attached to their care providers? Often, they do, especially if the caregiver is in the life of the child for some period of time and is sensitive to the child's needs (Goosens & van IJzendoorn, 1990; Howes & Hamilton, 1992a, 1992b; Sagi et al., 1985). Importantly, daycaregivers who are not naturally responsive can be taught to be so, with this positively impacting their attachments to the infants and children in their care (Galinsky et al., 1995; Howes, Smith, & Galinski, 1995). With improved attachment to the daycaregiver, the interactions between the caregiver and the child are richer, for example, as reflected in more play and more sophisticated play between the caregiver and the child (Howes, Matheson, & Hamilton, 1994). As described earlier, the quality of infant–parent attachment depends greatly on the responsiveness of the parent. So it is with respect to attachment to caregivers, with interactions in general improving as caregiver–child attachment is more secure. In the NICHD study, parental responsiveness was a more important predictor of child outcomes than any of the variables associated with out-of-home care. The message is clear: responsivity to children matters.

On the negative side, participation in daycare has been associated with noncompliance to parental requests (Lamb, 1998). This outcome makes sense to those who believe that attachment is undermined by daycare, for noncompliance with parental directions can be a symptom of weakened parental–child attachment (Ainsworth,

Blehar, Waters, & Wall, 1978; Arend, Gove, & Sroufe, 1979; Louderville & Main, 1981). Moreover, low-quality daycare is associated with poorer social relations with other children (Howes, 1988, 1990) and more immature personalities (Lamb, 1998). Daycare participation has also been associated with increased aggression and other behavior problems (e.g., temper tantrums; Bates et al., 1994; Burchinal, Ramey, Reid, & Jaccard, 1995; Lamb, 1998). The NICHD study has added data to this concern, with greater daycare participation associated with more aggression and acting out at the end of the preschool and beginning of the kindergarten experience.

If attachment security and social functioning differ as a function of daycare, however, the differences are not great. With the evidence presently on hand, it is not justifiable to criticize daycare, even infant daycare, because of its negative effects on attachment or children's social relationships (Lamb, 1998; the NICHD study). Indeed, daycare can provide an opportunity for children to become attached to nonparental adults who can provide the child with exposure to different activities than the ones occurring at home, with this more likely with high-quality daycare. For withdrawn children, daycare has the potential for bringing them out, increasing their sociability (Egeland & Hester, 1995). Low-quality daycare, however, has its perils. For example, the more lax and inattentive the preschool teacher, the more misbehaved the preschoolers (Arnold, McWilliams, & Arnold, 1998). Also, the NICHD study found better daycare outcomes when childcare providers had more training.

Finally, the NICHD study found that home life mattered more than the quality of daycare in determining long-term social adjustment and cognitive outcomes. Although when home life was problematic—for example, mothers were not sensitive to their children, poverty stressed the family—the risk of adverse outcomes in daycare increased. This finding is consistent with other research findings that children from unfavorable family situations are less likely to thrive in daycare (Belsky, Woodworth, & Crnic, 1996; Stifter, Coulehan, & Fish, 1993).

Daycare Effects on Cognitive Competence

When all forms of daycare are considered, daycare has a positive impact on the cognitive development of preschoolers—for example, as indexed by performance on IQ assessments—although the impact is very small. Development of cognitive competence in daycare, however, depends very much on the quality of the daycare, with higher quality daycare settings more likely to produce cognitive gains in children than lower quality daycare settings (Broberg, Wessels, Lamb, & Hwang, 1997; Bryant, Burchinal, Lau, & Sperling, 1994; also see the NICHD study).

When disadvantaged children have been provided high-quality, educationally oriented daycare (e.g., Head Start), more striking positive effects on cognitive competence have been observed (Burchinal, Roberts, Nabors, & Bryant, 1996; Zigler & Styfco, 1993, 1994, 2003). Recall the Abecedarian Intervention Project, discussed in Chapter 2, which provided intervention for economically disadvantaged African American children, beginning at 3 months of age, including enrollment in high-quality daycare by age 1 (Ramey, 1992; Ramey & Smith, 1977). The program participants exhibited clear IQ advantages relative to control participants, with the advantages continuing into the elementary years (Burchinal, Campbell, Bryant, Wasik, & Ramey, 1997).

The Abecedarian approach formed the basis for an intervention targeted at low birthweight infants created and evaluated by the Infant Health and Development

Program (1990; Ramey et al., 1992), which was also described in Chapter 2. As in the original Abecedarian work, at the end of the preschool intervention, program participants enjoyed a significant IQ advantage over control participants.

One consistent criticism of the daycare studies documenting intellectual advantages for participants is that IQ and related cognitive competence gains made during the preschool years often disappear after the child enters school (Lamb, 1998; Lee & Loeb, 1995; Zigler & Styfco, 1993, 1994). Although that is true, a broader range of measures of cognitive competence than IQ provide evidence of long-term benefits. Thus disadvantaged preschoolers who attend high-quality, educationally oriented daycare are less likely to fail a grade in school, less likely to require special education intervention, and more likely to complete high school (Bennett, 1987; Consortium of Longitudinal Studies, 1978, 1983; Schweinhart, Barnes, & Weikart, 1993). In addition, academic gains obtained in the preschool years can be maintained if supplementary academic support is provided during the primary grades (Ramey, 1992; Seitz, Apfel, Rosenbaum, & Zigler, 1983), including long after intervention ends, such as in junior and senior high school (Campbell & Ramey, 1995). For example, Reynolds and Temple (1998) examined the consequences of continuing to provide educational supplement into the primary grades. When students were assessed at grade seven, those students who had experienced continuing intervention until grade three were better readers and better at math. The children receiving supplementary instruction also were less likely to have been retained in a grade during the elementary years.

Another criticism of effective educationally oriented daycare is that its positive impact is not enough: Populations of at-risk children who receive such daycare do better than similar children who do not receive it; nonetheless, their intellectual performances remain below those of more advantaged populations (e.g., middle-class children; McLoyd, 1998; Zigler & Styfco, 1993, 1994). Although academically oriented daycare can do some good, a preschool intervention cannot make up for the cumulative impact of long-term disadvantages (Stipek & Ryan, 1997).

Still another concern about academically oriented daycare is that even though it promotes academic progress, this comes at a cost. Stipek, Feiler, Daniels, and Milburn (1995) observed that preschoolers experiencing academically oriented preschools had less confidence in themselves (e.g., they took less pride in their academic abilities) than preschoolers in more child- and play-centered care settings. Children in academic settings also tended to be more dependent on adults, for example, seeking their permission to do things that children in play-oriented settings do without worrying about getting permission. The preschoolers in academic settings tended to worry about their academic skills, whereas children in child-centered settings had no such concerns. This study raises a specter that needs to be evaluated more fully. How can preschools promote academic competence without undermining children's motivation? (See Chapter 9 for a further discussion of how school can undermine student motivation.)

Finally, the possibility exists that daycare can impact negatively the academic advance of children coming from advantaged environments. That is, some children with responsive parents who have resources to enrich them might be getting less stimulation in daycare, and hence not grow as much cognitively as if they had remained in the home environment (Caughy, DiPietro, & Strobino, 1994).

In summary, high-quality daycare can stimulate academic competence, especially for disadvantaged preschoolers. Such care is not a cure-all for such children, however.

For example, if children who experienced high-quality daycare are subsequently enrolled in a regular public school that provides no extra support for at-risk children, some cognitive gains from the preschool years will not be maintained. Children who are at risk need long-term supplementary academic support. Even in the absence of such support, however, children who experienced high-quality daycare during the preschool years exhibit fewer problems during the schooling years and beyond.

Daycare for School-Age Children

Many parents work into the late afternoon and sometimes even into the evening. The result is that many children are "latchkey" children, who come home from school and are unsupervised. Perhaps worse, many such children do not come home at all but rather hang out in unsupervised public places, such as malls. Various forms of after-school care are the alternative, including school-based after-school programs, center-based care, supervision in another family's home, and home-based babysitters.

Although the evaluations of latchkey children have produced mixed outcomes (i.e., some have detected personality and cognitive difficulties as more prevalent in latchkey children than in other children, and some have reported no differences between latchkey and other children; Lamb, 1998), the reports of reduced academic achievement, poorer social relationships, and greater substance abuse in latchkey populations cause concern (Long & Long, 1983, 1984; Richardson et al., 1989; Woods, 1972). The types of structural and process features that distinguish good from not-so-good preschool daycare also distinguish good from not-so-good after-school care. For example, Rosenthal and Vandell (1996) reported that programs received favorably by children and their parents were characterized by a low staff-to-child ratio, a wide variety of activities, and many more positive interactions between staff and children than negative interactions. Unfortunately, the effects of after-school care have not been studied enough, although there is some evidence that much after-school care is not effective in preventing intellectual, social, and emotional problems (Posner & Vandell, 1994; Vandell & Shumow, 1999). Research on how after-school care can be effective in promoting the intellectual, emotional, and social development of children is needed, with many communities how attempting to develop after-school options for children (Noam & Miller, 2002).

■ ■ ■ HOW DO SOCIAL RELATIONSHIPS AFFECT ACADEMIC ACHIEVEMENT?

Lawrence Steinberg, Bradford Brown, and Sanford Dornbusch have investigated adolescent relationships with their families and peers. In the course of their program of research, they surveyed more than 20,000 adolescents, interviewed many parents, and analyzed student achievement data. This research led to the development of a comprehensive model of how social relationships explain academic achievement, particularly underachievement. Most who attempt to explain student underachievement put the blame on schools, concluding that school reform is the way to increase the achievement of U.S. students. Not so, according to Steinberg, Brown, and

Dornbusch (1996) who argue that social relationships can explain much of under-achievement, and who conclude that increasing student achievement would require a wide range of social changes. How do they explain underachievement?

Parenting style has an effect. A significant proportion of parents (perhaps 25%) have a disturbing parenting style. They neglect their kids. They do not monitor their children's progress in school, nor do they take an active role in regulating their children's participation in school, such as by supervising homework. Parental disengagement is associated with lower student achievement. On the other hand, authoritative parenting improves academic achievement largely through parental involvement in school. When children in authoritative homes experience difficulties at school, the parents get busy and help get the student back on track. They interact with the school to identify sources of support for their student. Unfortunately, far too few parents are so proactive and involved.

Peers also greatly affect the achievement orientations of a student. Fewer than 5% of adolescents consider their crowd to be the "brains," and most students are members of crowds who are not oriented to academic matters. Steinberg and colleagues (1996) found that when peers encourage social activities—and even delinquent activities—rather than academics, they succeed. More positively, when students do have academically oriented friends, their academic orientation does encourage more academic involvement. For example, Steinberg and colleagues argued that much of the high achievement of Asian American students can be explained by the high academic orientation of Asian American peer groups. Conversely, much of the underachievement of black students can be attributed to the lack of academic orientation of black adolescent crowds. Recall the discussion of Fordham and Ogbu's (1986; Fordham, 1988) work in Chapter 9.

U.S. students also spend too much time in part-time jobs. Extensive after-school work is associated with poorer school performance, more psychological distress, substance abuse, and delinquency. The more a student works, the less the student is involved with school, with underachievement the result.

Although Steinberg and colleagues (1996) suggest many ways to improve school achievement, three suggestions follow directly from their analyses:

- Parents need to be involved in their children's schooling. As a society, Americans must become increasingly aware of the enormous role of the family in determining academic success.
- Parents can do much to influence their children's peer group, for example, by choosing carefully their neighborhood and school. Parents should do all possible to encourage their children to interact with peers who are "into" academics. Moving to place children in a school in which the students are more academically oriented is not too extreme a measure for a parent to take.
- Parents should limit the amount of time that their students spend in after-school employment.

In short, Steinberg and colleagues' (1996) message is that family and peer relations are extremely critical in determining school achievement. Parents should not expect schools to do it all, but rather be involved with schools and with their children, exerting influence in every way possible for their children to make decisions that support their academic development.

■ ■ ■ CHAPTER SUMMARY AND EVALUATION

Although parents and infants interact from the first day of life, attachment, in the sense of strongly preferred contact for one or two adults in particular, is not obvious until about the middle of the infant's first year of life. In part, this probably reflects the need for extended social relations in order for attachment to occur; in part, it probably reflects cognitive development, especially the development of object permanence.

A secure attachment between children and their caretakers is not guaranteed. Differences in maternal responsiveness may explain security of attachment. The baby's temperament also may play a large role. Perhaps it is easier for mothers to respond to a temperamentally easy than to a temperamentally difficult baby. A secure attachment during infancy predicts good things to come, not only with respect to the child's social relations, but also with respect to future cognitive interactions. Attachment not only depends on cognitive development but probably contributes to later cognitive development.

Authoritative parenting produces better social and cognitive outcomes than other parenting styles. The most effective socialization mechanisms are consistent with authoritative parenting. Authoritative parenting demands much of parents, however, so that when parents are under stress, parenting often becomes less authoritative. Support for families experiencing stress may be effective because it would permit a return to parental behaviors more consistent with the authoritative style.

A child's experience in the family depends not only on parents but also on siblings. Although the effects of differing numbers of siblings on child development tend not to be large, they do exist.

Peer interactions begin in infancy, probably the first time a child encounters another child. They increase in frequency, diversity, and complexity with increasing age until adolescence, when the majority of social interactions are with peers. As with most of development, peer relations depend in part on cognitive development; they also probably determine cognitive development to some extent.

Good parental relationships predict healthy peer relations. Parental–child and child–peer interactions thus are complementary to one another. They remain so through adolescence. When parental–child relationships are healthy, parent versus peer pressures are less likely to conflict than when parental–child relationships are less cordial.

The majority of U.S. children experience some kind of daycare at some point during their childhood. The impact of such care depends greatly on the quality of the care received, as defined by the structural resources that are available and the processes occurring during care. When resources are good and the process includes many educationally oriented activities, the outcomes are typically good. The benefits of high-quality, educationally oriented daycare especially have been demonstrated with at-risk populations. Creating such high-quality settings requires know-how, especially knowledge about child development.

Much of the research on family and peer effects on development was intended to test claims made in major developmental theories. Not surprisingly, then, this research literature informs many of the enduring issues in developmental psychology.

Developmental Debates
Nature versus Nurture

Attachment theorists have strong assumptions about the biological foundations of mother–infant relationships, believing that human attachment evolved because of its adaptive significance to the human organism. That is, humans who attached to their infants were more likely to have infants who would mature and reproduce. That said, environment matters greatly to the attachment theorists, for the mother's responsiveness to the infant goes far in determining the security of infant–mother attachment. Infant temperament, most likely determined by biology, also greatly impacts infant–parent attachment.

Stages versus Continuous Development

Clearly, social interactions evolve through the qualitatively different periods of development: infancy, childhood, and adolescence. The newborn is social only in a rudimentary fashion compared to the securely attached 1-year-old, whose social relations are limited relative to the preschooler and the elementary-age youngster. With the passage from childhood to adolescence, the peer group becomes more salient. But is any of this really discontinuous, really stage-like?

Well, some of it is. The developments during infancy seem to follow a developmental timetable that is governed by maturation: perceptual, cognitive, and physical maturation. Also, some social relations during childhood seem to depend on cognitive development in a stage-like fashion. For example, increases in perspective-taking skills are often used to explain children's increasing social interactions between 4 and 8 years of age. The adolescent's formal operational competence is sometimes offered as an explanation for the increased intensity of friendships at adolescence, especially with respect to increased attention to psychological characteristics of friends.

Even so, most changes in social relationships seem gradual rather than sudden. The qualitative differences between adolescents and preschoolers can be traced to gradual changes in number of friends and types of interactions with friends. In short, the developments described in this chapter have both stage-like and non-stage-like properties.

Trait-Like Consistency versus Situational Determination of Behavior

Although, in general, securely attached infants act very differently than insecurely attached infants, at times insecurities come through even for a securely attached infant. Parental style research provides another example of how there can be consistency, yet situational determination of behavior. Even parents who are generally authoritative can act other than authoritatively if stressed.

Lasting versus Transient Early Effects of Experience

Attachment research has provided a good deal of evidence that early experience matters. Secure attachment predicts healthy social relations and cognitive interactions during the preschool years and perhaps beyond; insecure attachment predicts less favorable outcomes during preschool and perhaps beyond. Parental style in early childhood has an effect on the immediate behavior of the child and on the child's long-term development.

Active versus Passive Child

Children's behaviors affect social relations, and thus development more generally. The temperamental infant may contribute to the development of an insecure attachment to mother. The socially unskilled child is excluded from many social relations that contribute to the positive development of children who experience them. By selecting membership in one crowd or another (e.g., "brains" vs. "druggies"), adolescents greatly alter much in their everyday lives.

■ ■ ■ REVIEW OF KEY TERMS

authoritarian parenting A parenting style where the parents are highly responsive to their children and highly demanding of their children.

authoritative parenting A parenting style where the parents are highly demanding of their children but not responsive to their children.

clique For adolescents, a peer group of intimate friends, ranging in size from 5 to 10 people.

crowd A large group of adolescent friends defined by salient characteristics (e.g., jocks, brains, etc.).

differential reinforcement of other behavior (DRO) Reinforcing a desired behavior that is incompatible with an undesired behavior.

induction A type of parental discipline in which parents provide reasons to a child on why certain behaviors are not desired, with a focus on developing empathy in the child.

permissive parenting A parenting style where parents are responsive to their children but not demanding of them.

social cognition The understanding of other people and the nature of the social world.

time-out A type of discipline in which a child is physically removed from a setting where misbehavior is being exhibited for a short period of time.

uninvolved parenting A parenting style where parents are neither responsive to their children nor demanding of them.

CHAPTER 11

Gender Role Development

Probably the foremost way people identify themselves is in terms of being female or male. Our gender affects much of what happens in our lives, including our experiences in educational institutions. Nearly any person on the street "knows" a lot about what women and men are like. One thing we have learned from the scientific study of gender is that much of what the person in the street knows is wrong. People hold many misconceptions about the differences between males and females.

The chapter opens with a discussion of societal stereotypes versus verified gender differences. As you might expect, the supposed stereotypical differences outnumber the actual differences. We then discuss the various ways psychologists have attempted to account for gender role development and associated gender differences, including gender differences in academic motivation. The chapter concludes with a discussion of the development of sexuality. Again, although the onset of sexuality is often explained as a function of the biological changes associated with puberty, it turns out to be more complicated and influenced by social factors.

■ ■ ■ GENDER STEREOTYPES VERSUS GENDER DIFFERENCES

There are many folk beliefs about gender differences (Ruble & Martin, 1998), with many stereotypes favoring "masculine" qualities over "feminine" qualities. Males are strong, tough, aggressive, and competitive, whereas females are weak, passive, nurturing, caring, and sympathetic. Little boys are adventurous in their play, whereas little girls are quiet. Sports are for boys, and the arts for girls. Boys are boisterous, girls are chatty. Boys are good at math and science, girls excel in reading and language arts. Males respond to reason, and girls are more suggestible. Is there any truth to these stereotypes, which have persisted for centuries and continue today (Lueptow, Garovich, & Lueptow, 2001; Powlishta, Sen, Serbin, Poulin-Dubois, & Eichstedt, 2001)?

Social and Personality Differences

One of the most surprising research findings is that few verifiable social and personality differences between females and males exist. That is, female and male personalities are more similar than different; females and males are more similar than different in their social interactions.

What are the differences supported by research evidence? One is that males are more physically aggressive than females on average (Maccoby & Jacklin, 1974). Even so, when it comes to indirect aggression and verbal aggression, girls and boys, women and men, are probably more even (Maccoby & Jacklin, 1974; Underwood, 2002). What must be kept in mind is that a group difference in aggression does not predict aggression in individual children. Why? Observe all the males on an elementary-school playground and give each a score for physical aggression on a 1 (never aggressive) to 10 (frequently physically aggressive) scale. Chart the result. Visit enough playgrounds and you will get a bell-shaped distribution, centered around an average value. Score all the females on the same playgrounds on the same scale and graph the data. Again, you will obtain a bell-shaped distribution, centered around an average value. Yes, the male average will be greater than the female average (that is the group difference), but plenty of females will have higher scores than many of the males! Graphing physical aggression observed in boys and girls on the playground would produce overlapping distributions, as shown in Figure 11.1.

It is important to realize that the female and male distributions for any characteristic will always overlap. Moreover, average female versus average male differences are typically small. What this means is that it is impossible to know, based on knowing an individual person's gender, whether they are more or less aggressive (or more verbal or mathematical) than a person of the opposite gender.

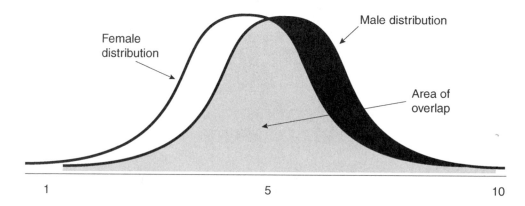

FIGURE 11.1. Hypothetical distributions showing overlap.

The following gender differences in social and personality characteristics have been demonstrated:

- Boys are slightly more physically aggressive than girls.
- Boys and girls are both verbally aggressive. If there is a difference between the sexes, boys tend to be more direct and openly insulting, whereas girls gossip more and engage in exclusionary tactics. That is, boys prefer direct and overt verbal aggression and girls prefer more subtle tactics (Crick & Werner, 1998). Again, such differences are not large.
- Boys are more active than girls (Eaton & Enns, 1986).
- Females are slightly more altruistic, caring, and nurturing than males (Chodorow, 1978; Gilligan, 1982; Radke-Yarrow, Zahn-Waxler, & Chapman, 1983).
- Females are more anxious and more cautious than males (Christopherson, 1989; Ginsburg & Miller, 1982; Last, 1989; Miller, Boyer, & Rodoletz, 1990).
- Girls are more likely to be obedient in response to requests of adults (Maccoby, 1988).
- Girls are more likely to use persuasion rather than force to get their way with peers, a tactic that is more effective with other little girls than with little boys (Borja-Alvarez, Zarbatany, & Pepper, 1991; Leaper, 1994; Leaper, Tenenbaum, & Shaffer, 1999).

Remember that these average differences between males and females are fairly small and that there is great deal of overlap in the distributions (as displayed in Figure 11.1) so that many boys are not physically aggressive; many females are not anxious; many males are altruistic, caring, and nurturing; many girls are active; and so on.

Cognitive Differences

A great deal of research evidence supports the conclusion of no overall difference in the intelligence of males and females as measured by psychometric tests of intelligence. That is, the mean IQ scores for males and females are both about 100; intelligence is normally distributed for both males and females, with the standard deviation for IQs equal to 15 for both sexes (see Chapter 8).

When cognitive processing and abilities are examined more closely, however, some differences have been noted (Eccles, Wigfield, & Schiefele, 1998; Halpern, 1992, 2000; Shea, Lubinski, & Benbow, 2001). Females are favored with respect to one important competency:

> • **Verbal ability**, including word fluency, grammatical competence, spelling skills, reading, vocabulary, and oral comprehension is greater in females than in males. Dysfunctions in verbal abilities are more common in males than females, with most stutterers and dyslexics being male. Verbal differences favoring females are apparent from early childhood, with females exhibiting more proficiency in language earlier than boys. Differences are apparent throughout the schooling years as well, although not as pronounced as during preschool nor as pronounced as they will be in adulthood. Consistent with the effect size for most gender differences, gender differences in verbal abilities are small on aver-

age (see also Hyde & Linn, 1988; Hyde & Plant, 1995). It is certainly not inconsequential, however, that clinically significant verbal impairments, including acquisition of the critical skill of reading, are much more likely in males than females (Campbell, Hombo, & Mazzeo, 2000; Halpern, 2000). Is this difference in verbal ability due to genetics? Probably not entirely, for from infancy onward parents interact verbally more with daughters than with sons (Leaper, Anderson, & Sanders, 1998).

Males are superior to females in the following processes and tasks:

- **Visual–spatial tasks**, which involve the ability to imagine figures, including moving them around "in the head" in order to envision relationships between various objects (Levine, Huttenloch, Taylor, & Langrock, 1999). Differences in visual–spatial ability can be detected during childhood. Although the effect size varies with the task, it is not at all unusual for gender differences on visual–spatial tasks to be large—indeed, much larger than the typical gender difference. Although practicing spatial tasks improves the performance of both boys and girls, gender differences persist even after practice (Ben-Chaim, Lappan, & Houang, 1988). What this suggests is that spatial skills are affected by both biology and experience but that biologically determined individual differences persist even if males and females receive comparable experiences. Notably, the girls who practice spatial skills perform better than boys who do not, making clear that females can improve their performances on spatial tasks, just as boys improve on such tasks with practice (Subrahmanyam, Greenfield, Kraut, & Gross, 2001).
- **Field independence** is more common in males than females. "Field independence" refers to the ability to perceive an object separate from its background (Witkin, Moore, Goodenough, & Cox, 1977). For example, if presented a picture of a figure embedded in a more complex form, males are more certain to locate the figure quickly than females (see Figure 11.2). Females are more likely to perceive the pattern holistically than analytically and have more difficulty picking out the figure in the complex pattern. Field independence, however, may only reflect male superiority on visual–spatial tasks, since all tests that produce male–female differences in field independence have a large spatial component.
- **Quantitative skills** as measured by the mathematical portions of standardized tests typically favor males over females when gender differences are

FIGURE 11.2. An example of a figure used in a test of field independence. The task is to find the figure on the left in the pattern on the right. People who are field-independent can find such embedded figures easily. From Witkin, Moore, Goodenough, and Cox (1977). Copyright 1977 by the American Educational Research Association. Reprinted by permission.

detected. Particularly striking is that males are much more likely to score high on tests like the SAT mathematics sections than are females, as reflected by scores in excess of 700. That is, males outnumber females 17 to 1 among 700+ test scorers (Stanley & Benbow, 1986).

One striking aspect of this list of cognitive differences is that it is so short! Many aspects of performance produce no gender differences. The shortness of the list is even more impressive when it is realized that many of the differences favoring males might be accounted for by visual–spatial factors in measurements of field independence and mathematics abilities. Cognitive similarities between the sexes are greater than differences (Halpern, 1992, 2000). See the Considering Interesting Questions special feature (Box 11.1) for a discussion of gender differences in vulnerability to intellectual disorders.

As we reflect on the few and often small gender differences, we think about the many classrooms we have seen where beliefs about gender differences and stereotypes are quite apparent, with some teachers clearly signaling that there are boy things and girl things (Koch, 2003; Ruble & Martin, 1998). This is a concern because of evidence that when powerful adults, such as teachers, model and reinforce such thinking, it does cause some children to become more gender-stereotyped in their own thinking (Bigler, 1995). It is important for teachers to realize that gender differences are few and often small, with individual differences in virtually all skills much greater *within* each gender than *between* genders (again review Figure 11.1).

Androgyny

Although there is a long tradition in psychology of thinking of people as more masculine or feminine, other possibilities have been advanced in recent decades. For example, Sandra Bem (1974, 1975, 1993, 1998) theorized that people can be categorized into four types:

- Undifferentiated individuals are not high on either masculine or feminine characteristics.
- Masculine individuals are high on masculine characteristics and low on feminine characteristics.
- Feminine individuals are high on feminine characteristics but not on masculine characteristics.
- **Androgynous** individuals are high on both masculine and feminine characteristics.

How can undifferentiated, masculine, feminine, and androgynous individuals be identified? One way is to complete a questionnaire, such as the Bem Sex Role Inventory (Bem, 1974, 1977) or the Personal Attributes Questionnaire (PAQ; Spence, Helmreich, & Stapp, 1975). To take the Bem Sex Role Inventory, a person rates 60 different attributes in terms of whether the attribute applies to them. Twenty of the attributes are "masculine" (e.g., aggressive, forceful); 20 are "feminine" (e.g., tender, soft-spoken); and 20 are equally masculine and feminine (e.g., friendly, jealous). How people are classified depends on their pattern of responding on these scales.

BOX 11.1. Are Males or Females More Vulnerable to Intellectual Disorders?

Although societal stereotypes may favor males, many developmental psychologists believe that biology is not so kind. Males seem to be at much greater risk than females for a wide range of disorders that have a large biological component. The disorders include mental retardation, learning and language disabilities, autism, hyperactivity, and schizophrenia (Zachau-Christiansen & Ross, 1975). We cannot yet explain why males and females differ in their risk for learning and behavioral disorders, although researchers are exploring some important hypotheses.

Consider a study by Raz and colleagues (1995). They studied premature infants who had suffered intracranial hemorrhage. Such hemorrhaging can and often does cause cognitive, language, and behavioral impairments. Raz and colleagues (1995) hypothesized that because the nervous systems of infant females are more advanced in neurological development than are the nervous systems of infant males, females may be more resilient to neurological injury. Specifically, Raz and colleagues studied a sample of males and females who experienced intracranial hemorrhaging as a complication of premature birth as well as control premature infants who had not experienced intracranial hemorrhage. The children were given intelligence tests at age 3.

At age 3, the premature children who had not experienced intracranial hemorrhage had typical IQs (i.e., their mean IQ was about 98, just 2 points below children in general, with a standard deviation of about 16 IQ points; see Chapter 8), with no gender difference. Among the premature children who experienced intracranial hemorrhage, the girls at age 3 had normal IQs (mean = 101, standard deviation = 13 IQ points). In contrast, the boys had below-average IQs (mean = 92, standard deviation = 13 points). Consistent with the general pattern of male–female differences in vulnerability, boys who had experienced intracranial hemorrhage as a result of prematurity were more likely to experience intellectual impairment than females who had experienced intracranial hemorrhage. Raz and colleagues (1995), however, would have had stronger support for their hypothesis that female–male differences were due to neural maturational differences at the time of injury had they taken direct measures of neurological development during infancy.

Although males do seem to be more vulnerable than girls to intellectual disabilities, educators must be cautious that they do not classify too many boys as having disabilities relative to girls. Shaywitz, Shaywitz, Fletcher, and Escobar (1990) carried out extensive and sensitive diagnostic testing of children who had been identified as having reading disabilities by school authorities, with many more boys than girls so labeled by the school. Shaywitz and colleagues concluded that the school authorities were too quick to classify a boy as having learning disabilities, so that many boys were being referred for treatment of learning disabilities who did not really have learning disabilities. On the other hand, Shaywitz and colleagues determined that some girls who should have been classified as having learning disabilities and should have been referred for treatment were not. What seemed to be going on was that boys who have learning disabilities also tend to exhibit behavior problems. Such behavior problems make their learning disability more salient to teachers. Moreover, school authorities have begun to blur the distinction between learning and behavioral disabilities because of their correlation. Thus some boys who only have behavior problems end up classified as having learning disabilities.

In contrast, girls tend not to be behavior problems. It is very easy for teachers to overlook well-behaved little girls who are experiencing severe problems in learning to read. If Shaywitz and colleagues (1990) are correct, male vulnerability with respect to learning disabilities may not be as great as suggested earlier. In contrast, girls may be more vulnerable to learning disabilities than once thought, as well as being more vulnerable to not receiving appropriate referral to an educational specialist.

What behaviors might be seen in a person identified as androgynous by questionnaires like these? Consider an individual who is aggressive on the athletic field, although always playing within the rules. After the game, this individual sticks around to give some pointers to younger children who watched the game, encouraging them in their efforts to learn the sport. This same individual is kind to animals to the point of taking charge and organizing a school club that provides support to the local Humane Society, cooperating productively with other students to raise funds. On other occasions, such as during a class debate, the person is decisive and competitively assertive, determined for her or his perspective to prevail. Is this person a contradiction in characteristics or androgynous? Androgynous people's behaviors vary as a function of the situation, sometimes behaving in more masculine ways in some situations and in more feminine ways in others. Thus the behaviors of androgynous people are often more adaptively appropriate than the behaviors of others who are stereotypically masculine or feminine.

The case supporting androgyny as being more adaptive revolves around correlations between androgyny, as defined by responses to the Bem Sex Role Inventory or the PAQ, and desirable psychological outcomes, including being well liked and adjusted (Boldizar, 1991; O'Heron & Orlofsky, 1990). The actual meaning of these relationships continues to be disputed, however. As it turns out, the items on gender role scales that correlate most highly with good adjustment are ones tapping masculine traits. Thus some believe that masculinity produces psychological health rather than a mix of masculinity and femininity (Orlofsky & O'Heron, 1987; Taylor & Hall, 1982; Whitely, 1983). Even so, many believe that androgynous people function better in the world than people who are extremely masculine or feminine. Moreover, whether children become androgynous or not is susceptible to environmental pressure, with children raised in environments that emphasize traditional gender roles less androgynous and those raised in environments downplaying gender stereotypes being more androgynous (Weisner & Wilson-Mitchell, 1990). Giving children encouragement to think in less gender-stereotyped ways, has impact (Bigler & Liben, 1990, 1992). Educators need to think hard about whether their classroom environment is filled with gender stereotypes and to send the message to students to be more flexible and less stereotyped in their thinking.

One important advance for educators was the development of a version of the Bem Scale that could be used with children (Boldizar, 1991). See Table 11.1 for a short version of the *Children's Sex Role Inventory*.

■ ■ ■ THEORETICAL EXPLANATIONS OF GENDER DIFFERENCES

Psychologists have been long interested in understanding gender differences and have produced a great deal of psychological theory about gender differences. None of the individual theories can account for gender differences. Instead, gender differences reflect the interaction of biological, social, and cognitive mechanisms. What each of these theories does is attempt to explain some aspect of gender differences, rather than provide comprehensive explanation of gender differences. A fuller understanding of gender differences requires integrating across these theoretical perspectives (Maccoby, 2002).

TABLE 11.1. Short-Form Items from the Children's Sex Role Inventory

Masculine items

I can control a lot of the kids in my class.
When a decision has to be made, it's easy for me to take a stand.
I am a leader among my friends.
When I play games, I really like to win.
I am sure of my abilities.
I stand up for what I believe in.
I am good at sports.
It's easy for me to tell people what I think, even when I know they will
    probably disagree with me.
I make a strong impression on most people I meet.
I am good at taking charge of things.

Feminine items

I care about what happens to others.
When someone's feelings have been hurt, I try to make them feel better.
I am a warm person.
I am a kind and caring person.
I like babies and small children a lot.
I am a gentle person.
I am a cheerful person.
When I like someone, I do nice things for them to show them how I feel.
I like to do things that girls and women do.
It makes me feel bad when someone else is feeling bad.

Neutral items

People like me.
I have many friends.
It's easy for me to fit into new places.
I'm always losing things.
I like to do things that other people do.
I am a moody person.
I like acting in front of other people.
I never know what I am going to do from one minute to the next.
I always do what I say I will do.
I feel bad when other people have something that I don't have.

Note. All items rated on a 4-point scale: 4 = very true of me, 3 = mostly true of me, 2 = a
little true of me, 1 = not at all true of me. From Boldizar (1991, Table 1). Copyright 1991
by the American Psychological Association. Adapted by permission.

Biological Theories

Males and females are unambiguously biologically different, from the moment of
conception, with females having two X chromosomes (XX) and males having an X
and a Y chromosome (XY). That is only the start of the biological story, however,
with multiple biological mechanisms contributing to gender development and differences (Zucker, 2001).

Hormones and Development

The sex chromosomes cause the development of ovaries in females and testes in males. These sex organs secrete hormones even during the prenatal period. The testes secrete hormones referred to as **androgens**, and the ovaries secrete **estrogen**. One androgen, **testosterone**, is particularly important in masculine development. Typically, males produce testosterone in sufficient quantities to stimulate the development of the male's external sex organs, the penis and the scrotum. Another hormone inhibits the development of female sexual organs in the boy. In females, the low levels of testosterone experienced prenatally result in the development of female genitalia.

The sex hormones also affect development of the nervous system and hence thinking abilities, although the relationships are not always strong or predictable (Geary, 1998). For example, prenatal hormonal exposure may account for the gender difference in visual–spatial abilities. What is the evidence for this conclusion? Not all humans experience the levels of hormones typical for their gender. In general, cognitive skills tend to differ from the norm for such individuals, depending on the hormonal levels they experienced prenatally. Females with congenital adrenal hyperplasia experienced higher levels of androgen prenatally than normal females. They also do better on spatial tests than females in general (Collaer & Hines, 1995; Perlman, 1973; Resnick, Berenbaum, Gottesman, & Bouchard, 1986). Individuals with Turner's syndrome have one X chromosome only. These individuals have low levels of both androgen and estrogen prenatally and tend to do very poorly on tests of spatial cognition (Alexander, Walker, & Money, 1964; Rovet & Netley, 1982). Males with Klinefelter's syndrome have an extra X chromosome (two X chromosomes and a Y chromosome). These individuals experience low levels of androgen prenatally and exhibit lower levels of spatial functioning relative to normal males (Hier & Crowley, 1982). In addition, manipulating androgen levels prenatally in animals results in direct effects on spatial abilities, with this experimental data permitting cause-and-effect conclusions regarding the role of androgen in the development of spatial skills (Gaulin, 1995; see also Chapter 1 for a discussion of experiments). All of these outcomes converge on the conclusion that prenatal hormonal exposure affects the development of visual–spatial cognitive abilities, specifically, that exposure to androgens increases visual–spatial cognitive abilities.

Manipulation of prenatal hormones in animals also has resulted in changes in social behavior. Thus, when female monkeys were exposed to high levels of testosterone prenatally, they were more aggressive than normal female monkeys (Young, Goy, & Phoenix, 1964). Again, experimental data such as this permits a cause-and-effect conclusion, although it must always be remembered that the studies were conducted with monkeys rather than with humans. Even so, one explanation for very clear differences in the behaviors of males and females from infancy through old age is that the differences are caused at least in part by hormonal differences between males and females (Maccoby, 1998). This is supported especially in females by increasing evidence that high levels of prenatal exposure to the male hormones results in more masculine social behaviors (Golombok & Hines, 2002; Hines et al., 2002).

When Biology and Environment Conflict

Sometimes prenatal hormonal irregularities occur, resulting in children who have sexual organs that are not consistent with their biological sex. Thus a prenatal girl can experience high levels of prenatal androgens because her mother has an adrenal gland disorder. Also, in the 1940s and 1950s, pregnant women were sometimes administered high levels of progesterone to prevent miscarriage, so that their *in utero* daughters were also exposed to abnormal levels of progesterone. Both adrenal gland disorders and maternal progesterone administrations can result in girls who have external genitalia that look like a penis and a scrotum. The clitoris is larger than usual so that it looks like a penis, and the labia are fused, resembling a scrotum. Biological males sometimes develop what appear to be female genitalia—for example, because of a lack of sensitivity to male sex hormones. These children have internal sexual organs that are consistent with their biological sex even though their external organs are not. If the problem is not detected earlier, it becomes apparent at adolescence. The female who looks like a male develops breasts at puberty and the male who looks like a female does not begin to menstruate. Fortunately, these abnormalities typically are detected early in life and corrected.

Although it is always possible to correct the external genitalia surgically, the timing of such surgery may determine whether the child grows up psychologically as a girl or a boy. Money and Ehrhardt (1972) concluded that if the problem with the external genitalia was detected in the first year of life and corrected surgically, few problems emerged. After the first couple of years of life, however, surgical corrections are not so straightforward and psychological adjustment is much more difficult. Once the child understands her- or himself to be a girl or a boy, it is very difficult to change the way the child thinks about her- or himself. How might medical treatment proceed for adolescents who have been mislabeled because of anomalous genitalia? Treatment can be designed to permit them to live their psychological gender. For example, the biological girl who has grown up believing she is a boy might be given hormonal therapy to inhibit breast development; the biological boy who has grown up psychologically as a girl may take estrogen to inhibit masculine development.

For a long time, Money and Ehrhardt's (1972) conclusion that the first few years were a critical period for development of gender identity was generally accepted. There are now serious doubts, however. For example, some surgical gender corrections at adolescence have been accompanied by successful gender identity shifts (Herdt & Davidson, 1988; Imperato-McGinley, Peterson, Gautier, & Sturla, 1979). In addition, some cases of surgical and psychological gender changes during the first 2 years of life have created severe problems later in life. The most famous case involved a boy whose penis was accidentally severed, whose sex was then changed surgically. Although raised as a girl and psychologically a girl during childhood (Money & Tucker, 1975), this child developed great identity confusion in adolescence and was very unhappy as a girl (Diamond, 1982). This individual later returned to the male role (Colapinto, 2001; Diamond & Sigmundson, 1999; Unger & Crawford, 1992). Indeed, it not unusual at all for biological males who are raised as females to display many more male-appropriate behaviors than do biological females (Hines & Kaufman, 1994; Zucker, Bradley, & Lowry-Sullivan, 1996). Gender role identification is clearly very complex, with children varying in their response to biological and socialization pressures.

Prenatal Hormones and Development of Sexuality

What about eventual sexuality? When females experience high levels of androgens prenatally, they are likely to have a sexual preference for females, even if they were raised as psychological females (Dittman, Kappes, & Kappes, 1992). Males who are completely androgen-insensitive tend to develop a sexual preference for males (Money, Schwartz, & Lewis, 1984). Money (1987, 1988) contended, based on such data, that prenatal androgen exposure predisposes both males and females to desire females as sexual partners. Alternatively, low levels of prenatal androgen exposure predisposes the desire for males as sexual partners. More recent research on the effects of prenatal estrogen provides additional evidence to support the conclusion that prenatal exposure to sex hormones determines sexual orientation to some extent. When females are exposed to high levels of prenatal estrogens, they are more likely to be bisexual or homosexual (Meyer-Bahlburg et al., 1995).

The assumption is that prenatal exposure to sex hormones causes structural and functional differences in the brain, which mediates the development of sexual orientation. Neuroscientists are trying to determine how the brain may be affected by prenatal exposure to sex hormones (Allen & Gorski, 1992; LeVay, 1991; Swaab, Gooren, & Hofman, 1992). As they do, the evidence is increasing that males and females differ in neurologically fundamental ways. For example, females are much more likely to use the left and right side of their brains for a variety of tasks than males, who tend to use more left hemispheric processing as they perform verbal tasks and more right hemispheric processing as they do tasks with a visual–spatial component (Halpern, 2000).

Social Learning Theories of Gender Role Development

The role of social forces in gender role development has been recognized since the earliest theory of gender role development, Freud's psychosexual theory. As you might recall, Freud portrayed the preschool years as key in this development, with the development, of castration anxiety in boys—and the lack of it in girls (see Chapter 5). Freud believed that children identify with the same-sex parent, adopting many of that parent's behaviors, after recognizing the impossibility of sexually possessing the opposite-sex parent. Thus, according to Freud, gender role socialization occurred within the family structure.

Although Freud's recognition that gender role development had a social component and could not be explained by biology alone was an enormous contribution, the specific mechanisms of development he proposed do not explain gender role development adequately. For Freud's theory to be credible, preschoolers would have to have a clear understanding on how males and females differ physically. They do not (Bem, 1989). Moreover, children do not seem to identify with parents who are seen as aggressors but rather with parents who are nurturing and responsive (Hetherington & Frankie, 1967).

In contrast to the failure of Freudian theory to account for gender role development, social learning theory has been more successful. Recall that the three main mechanisms of social learning theory are reinforcement, punishment, and observational learning (review Chapter 5). All three of these mechanisms operate to promote the development of gender-related behaviors.

Reinforcement and Punishment

In many ways, parents and peers treat daughters and sons similarly (Lytton & Romney, 1991; Maccoby & Jacklin, 1974). Even so, they influence gender role development by reinforcing appropriate and punishing inappropriate gender role behaviors (Brody, 1999; Turner & Gervai, 1995). For example, parents in traditional gender roles raise children who are very consistent with traditional gender roles (Turner & Gervai, 1995). A variety of differential reinforcements and punishments for gender-appropriate behavior are apparent from early in life:

- Parents, especially fathers, play more roughly with their sons beginning in infancy than they do with their daughters and encourage gross motor activity more in males than in females (Parke, 2002; Parke & Suomi, 1980; Smith & Lloyd, 1978; Stern & Karraker, 1989).
- Parents and other adults, such as teachers, provide children with gender-appropriate toys and encourage their children to play with gender-appropriate toys and in gender-appropriate ways (Eisenberg, Wolchick, Hernandez, & Pasternack, 1985; Fagot, 1978; Fagot & Hagan, 1991; Fagot & Leinbach, 1989; Frisch, 1977; Schau, Kahn, Diepold, & Cherry, 1980; Sidorowicz & Lunney, 1980; Snow, Jacklin, & Maccoby, 1983; Weisner & Wilson-Mitchell, 1990). Before 2 years of age, children understand which toys are appropriate for their gender (Levy, 1999).
- Children's peers send clear messages about the appropriateness of play behaviors. For example, boys are quick to criticize other boys who play with girls' toys (Langlois & Downs, 1980).
- Children are encouraged to dress in gender-appropriate clothing (Fagot, 1978; Shakin, Shakin, & Sternglanz, 1985).
- Males are encouraged in many ways to be more independent and far ranging in their explorations than females, and mothers are more tolerant of their little girls following them around the house and relying on them than they are of their little boys doing the same (Fagot, 1974, 1978; Leaper, 2000; Leaper et al., 1998; Pomerantz & Ruble, 1998). Girls are encouraged to play closer to home, with boys given more freedom to go to parks, playgrounds, and other public areas (Hoffman, 1977; Huston, 1983; Newson & Newson, 1986). Boys are encouraged to keep plugging away at cognitive tasks in contrast to girls, who are given assistance much more quickly (Rothbart & Rothbart, 1976).
- Parents expect greater academic achievement from males than from females (Block, 1977; Brooks-Gunn & Matthews, 1979). They also provide more support for male achievement, doing much more teaching of boys than girls in a variety of activities, both social and academic (Weitzman, Birns, & Friend, 1985).
- Boys receive more attention in the classroom from teachers—both encouragement when they are doing well academically and discouragement away from unproductive directions—than do girls. Girls receive less feedback about the quality of their academic work than do boys (Dweck, Davidson, Nelson, & Enna, 1978; Sadker & Sadker, 1994). A much higher proportion of the feedback given to girls relative to that given to boys focuses on academic problems the girls are experiencing, while boys receive a higher proportion of comments about their misbehavior. Thus more of a girl's interactions with teachers involve the message that they are experiencing academic problems (Dweck, 1978; Meece, 1987; Minuchin & Shapiro, 1983).

One point that comes through clearly in reviewing the research on reinforcement and punishment of gender-appropriate behaviors is that the pressure is higher on boys to conform to the male gender role than for girls to conform to the female gender stereotype (Sandnabba & Ahlberg, 1999). For example, fathers react especially strongly and negatively to inappropriate gender role play in sons (Langlois & Downs, 1980). Parents place greater expectations on males than females to consider practical careers (Newson & Newson, 1986). In general, males are discouraged much more strongly not to do things feminine than girls are discouraged for doing things masculine (Fagot, 1978; Langlois & Downs, 1980; Maccoby & Jacklin, 1974).

Something else that comes through is that teachers of young children in schools more often encourage feminine characteristics, especially passiveness and conformity, than male characteristics (Brophy & Good, 1974; Fagot, 1981). Indeed, primary-grades teachers especially discourage the rambunctious behavior in boys, even when merely playful (Serbin & O'Leary, 1975). A result is that early elementary school can seem especially unwelcoming to boys, with the potential of undermining boys' commitments to do things valued by school (McCall, Beach, & Lan, 2000; Ruble & Martin, 1998). Reinforcement patterns change as children progress through school. See the Applying Developmental Theory to Educational Contexts special feature (Box 11.2) for a discussion of gender roles in middle school.

Observational Learning

The world is filled with models of women and men behaving as women and men do, all of which provide observational learning opportunities for the child. Yes, there is variability in the way women behave, with some much more feminine than others, and there is variability within men, with some much more masculine than others. Children seem to be able to keep track of the behaviors most often associated with women and those most often associated with men, learning both female and male behaviors and roles in the process (Huston, 1983; Perry & Bussey, 1979). Children learn the sex role appropriateness of behaviors from exposure to multiple examples of females doing the feminine things and males doing the masculine things (Bussey & Bandura, 1984; Bussey & Perry, 1982).

Given the intensity of children's relationships with their parents, it might be expected that mothers and fathers would be gender role models. They are, although the effects of maternal and paternal behaviors on gender role development are not always large. Consider a few findings supportive of the point that mothers and fathers affect gender role learning in their children:

- Daughters of working mothers are less traditionally gender-typed than daughters of mothers who do not work outside the home (Hoffman, 1979, 1989, 2000; Weinraub, Jaeger, & Hoffman, 1988). Daughters of working mothers are more likely to aspire to work and careers themselves (Gold & Andres, 1978; Hoffman, 2000; Marantz & Mansfield, 1977).
- Males who grow up without a father exhibit lower levels of behaviors such as aggressiveness, independence, and self-control (Biller, 1970; Biller & Bahm, 1971; Kurdek & Siesky, 1980; Ruble & Martin, 1998; Santrock & Warshak, 1979; Stevenson & Black, 1988).
- Females who grow up without a father at home seem less able to interact appropriately with males when they reach adolescence (Hetherington, 1972; Stevenson & Black, 1988). When the mothers of fatherless girls are socially and sexually active, the adolescent girls tend to be more affectionately active with

Applying Developmental Theory to Educational Contexts

BOX 11.2. Reinforcement and Gender Roles in Middle School

Eder, Evans, and Parker (1995) spent 3 years in a middle school in the Midwest of the United States, conducting a qualitative study of life in middle school, focusing on gender role development and gender inequalities. What they found was that male experiences were more valued and reinforced than female experiences:

- Male athletic events were important in the school, a source of prestige for the male athletes and a focus of many social interactions. In contrast, girls' athletic events were all but ignored. The high-status male athletic activities were reinforced by virtually everyone in the school—faculty, administrators, and students alike.
- Cheerleading was the female counterpart to athletics. What was striking was that many of the males, especially the male athletes, mocked and ridiculed the cheerleaders. Females who were not cheerleaders often questioned the value of cheerleading and the way in which cheerleaders were selected. The result was that many of the cheerleaders were socially isolated because they were considered "stuck up" by other girls. (In contrast, the male athletes seemed to be valued by nearly everyone.) The highest status female activity was not much admired nor reinforced in the school, nor did it lead to the benefits that the high-status male activity produced.
- Physical attractiveness was an important determinant of social success for females. Physical unattractiveness in girls was much more likely to lead to social rejection than physical unattractiveness in males. Physically unattractive females were often the target of ridicule and vicious teasing. Although extremely unattractive males also experienced ridicule, only the most unattractive of males were targeted for abuse on the basis of their unattractiveness. Both boys and girls sent powerful messages to girls who were attractive, reinforcing them for their physical appearance, and to girls who were unattractive, punishing them for their looks.
- Heterosexual orientation was the only acceptable orientation in this community. The students had extremely negative views of homosexuality.
- Gender role deviancy led to rejection. Students who deviated were often ridiculed by other students, who called them derogatory names.
- Males were encouraged in many ways to be aggressive, both by peers and by teachers. Although much of this took place in the context of athletics, much of it also occurred in day-to-day interactions.
- The emerging sexual interest of males tended to depersonalize females, with competition for high-status females another aspect of the general competitiveness among boys in the school. Engaging in verbal exchanges involving sexual vulgarities was part of being one of the boys. Males tended to be aggressive with females. Physical advances that the boys would consider to be just teasing would be seen as much more disturbing by the girls. The boys definitely tended to see the girls as sexual objects rather than as sexual actors. They had little concern for the girls' feelings and tended to believe they "owned" the girls with whom they went steady.
- Girls who tried to be attractive to boys, especially if they engaged in sexual activity, were often referred to by derogatory terms. Again, this negative evaluation of any sexual activity by females was in contrast to the generally positive social evaluation of sexual activity by boys, at least within the peer culture. Worse yet, however, was that there was a double bind for girls, with low social status associated with being perceived as sexually innocent!

(continued)

In short, Eders and colleagues (1995) provided powerful evidence that the middle-school students they studied were under great pressure to conform to traditional gender roles. The penalties for deviation were great, including a great deal of ridicule. Highly masculine, athletically successful boys had the run of the social world in this school, dominating other boys and the girls. Even the most successful girls, the cheerleaders, were living in a world of sharks compared to the successful boys. The cheerleaders were surrounded by less attractive girls who were ready to devalue their status and boys who made sexual advances that often were unwelcome. The gender role pressures in middle school can be tough, probably more so for girls than for boys.

males and affectionately active earlier than girls from homes in which a father was present (Belsky, Steinberg, & Draper, 1991; Booth, Brinkerhoff, & White, 1984; Hetherington, 1972; Wallerstein & Corbin, 1989). Of course, the inference based on social learning theory is that the daughters are doing as their mothers have modeled.

Finally, peers and playmates are role models. Children play more with same-sex peers and accept feedback from same-sex peers which assures that boys will pick up much from other boys and girls from girls (Benenson, Apostoleris, & Parnass, 1997; Fagot, 1985; Maccoby, 1998; Underwood, Schockner, & Hurley, 2001). By choosing same-sex playmates, children go far in controlling their gender role development by immersing themselves in same-sex peer groups who model and reinforce boys being boys and girls being girls.

Observational Learning from Symbolic Models

Beyond the family, culture provides many symbolic models to children, with most symbolic models that children experience being gender-stereotyped. Popular television is gender-stereotyped (Coltrane, 1998; Huston & Wright, 1998), with many male television characters behaving as males are supposed to behave and many female characters behaving as females are supposed to behave. Television commercials also are filled with gender-stereotyped figures (Bretl & Cantor, 1988; Coltrane, 1998; Singer & Singer, 2001). Not surprisingly, children who watch a lot of television are more gender-stereotyped in their thinking and behaviors than those who watch little television (Berry, 2000; Calvert & Huston, 1987; Morgan, 1987; Signorielli & Lears, 1992). Davidson, Yasuna, and Tower (1979) exposed 5- to 6-year-old children to gender-stereotyped cartoons or more neutral cartoons. Following this exposure, the children who saw the gender-stereotyped cartoons were more gender-stereotyped in answers they provided to specific questions about male and female roles.

Peers do much to reinforce gender role appropriate behaviors.

The symbolic models that children encounter in the textbooks and literature they read are also gender-stereotyped (McDonald, 1989; Sadker & Sadker, 1994; Tepper & Cassidy, 1999; Turner-Bowker, 1996), although there certainly are efforts to reduce gender stereotyping in textbooks and children's trade books (Purcell & Stewart, 1990). Do gender-stereotypic characters in books make a difference? They sure do. For example, children are less gender-stereotyped in their behaviors and thinking after reading or hearing stories that involve nonstereotyped characters (Ashton, 1983; Flerx, Fidler, & Rodgers, 1976).

Cognitive Theories

Recent formulations of social learning theory have emphasized how cognitive observational learning is, with observational learning of gender roles requiring a great deal of memory, the classification of behaviors as female or male, and the comparison of one's own characteristics and behaviors with those of social models (Bandura, 1986). Two cognitive theories have been prominent in debates concerning the development of gender role. One was part of the Piagetian revolution that swept developmental psychology in the 1960s; the other reflects the information-processing perspective that prevails today.

Kohlberg's Theory

Lawrence Kohlberg (1966), whose work on the development of moral thinking was described in Chapter 3, proposed what was for some time the most influential of the cognitive developmental conceptions of gender development. Kohlberg's theory of moral judgment was an extension of Piaget's theory. Not surprisingly, his theory of gender role development also was informed by Piaget's thinking.

Infants during the first year of life can discriminate females from males, on the basis of what males and females sound and look like (Fagot & Leinbach, 1993). The first couple of years of life provide a baby with a great deal of information about maleness and femaleness, about how she or he should behave, and about how males and females in the world behave (Fagot & Leinbach, 1993). At about 2–3 years of age, however, according to Kohlberg, a child comes to an important insight. That insight for girls is, "I am a girl." For boys, it is, "I am a boy." Understanding of gender is anything but complete at that point, however. Femaleness and maleness are defined by physical features—such as length of hair or wearing of gender-appropriate clothing—that correlate with biological sex, but do not define it in a biological sense (Emmerich, Goldman, Kirsh, & Sharabany, 1977; McConaghy, 1979; Thompson & Bentler, 1971). Thus, a 2- to 3-year-old child sometimes believes that if a lady gets a buzzcut, she becomes a he! With advancing age during the grade-school years, children understand that an individual's gender is stable. That is, the person who is a boy today was a boy yesterday and will be a man someday. The child comes to understand that gender is consistent, that it does not change with appearances. Progressing from labeling gender to understanding its stability and consistency across situations takes 3–5 years, with a mature understanding of gender consistency often not present until the early elementary-grade years (Slaby & Frey, 1975).

Kohlberg argued that once a child understood that she or he was a girl or a boy and that was not going to change, this understanding motivated the child to learn how to be a girl or a boy, resulting in differential attention to information pertaining to one's own gender rather than to the opposite gender. Kohlberg believed that the development of the understanding of gender consistency was related to the development of the understanding of conservation as Piaget defined it (see Chapter 3). Recall that conservation is the understanding that the amount of something remains constant, despite superficial changes in appearance, unless material is added to or subtracted from it. Analogously, **gender consistency** is the understanding that gender does not change with superficial changes in appearance. In fact, understanding of gender consistency does correlate with development of conservation abilities (Marcus & Overton, 1978).

There are problems with Kohlberg's theory, however. First, other cognitive understandings besides conservation, such as knowledge of female and male genitalia, are strongly related to understanding of gender consistency. Bem (1989) showed preschool children pictures of nude male and female children and asked them to identify the gender of each photographed child and to explain their answers. Some preschoolers did better than others, labeling females as females and males as males and doing so with reference to possession of sex-defining genitals. The children who were so knowledgeable also continued to label the male as male and the female as female even when the same children were depicted as cross-dressed! Children who did not classify the nude photos correctly, using sex organs in their justifications, were more likely to believe that clothing defined gender. Thus, even if they recognized the boy was a boy when he was pictured nude, they would claim that the boy was a girl when he was pictured wearing a dress. Bem (1989) demonstrated that understanding gender consistency was tied to understanding the biological basis of gender.

Second, children make much progress in their gender role development before they are 5–7 years of age (Bussey & Bandura, 1992). That is, it does not seem to be necessary for children to understand that gender is stable and consistent for them to acquire a great deal of knowledge about gender and to be motivated to learn behaviors appropriate to their own gender. For example, the behaviors of children who can label themselves as boy or girl during the early preschool years are more gender-stereotypical than are the behaviors of children who are not yet referring to themselves as boy or girl (Fagot, 1985; Fagot & Leinbach, 1989, 1993; Hort, Leinbach, & Fagot, 1991). The implication is that once children label themselves, they are motivated to learn gender-appropriate behaviors and behave in more gender-appropriate ways (Fagot & Leinbach, 1989). Not surprisingly, by 5–7 years of age, children know a great deal about maleness and femaleness and generally pay more attention to and know more about behaviors associated with their own gender than with the other gender (Boston & Levy, 1991; Bradbard & Endsley, 1983; Levy & Fivush, 1993). A specific information-processing theory, *gender schemata theory*, provides a basis for understanding the development of knowledge about gender and gender-appropriate behaviors well before children can conserve or understand the consistency of gender.

Gender Schema Theory

Recall from Chapter 4 that even 1- to 2-year-old children are capable of acquiring schema pertaining to situations that they encounter often. Thus, 2-year-olds know about birthday parties and going to McDonald's. Particularly pertinent here, they also have schemas for "boyness" and "girlness," schemas that continue to develop over the preschool years, but schemas that are present from the time when children first learn to label boys and girls, men and women (i.e., between 1 and 2 years of age). Martin and Halverson (1981, 1987) referred to such organized knowledge of gender as **gender schemas**.

Like Kohlberg, the proponents of gender schema theory believe that thinking and knowledge play a big role in motivation to learn about gender-appropriate behavior (Martin, 2000; Martin, Ruble, & Szjrybalo, 2002). Gender schema theorists believe that labeling is the critical knowledge that motivates children to learn about and act like members of one sex versus the other. That is, once a boy begins to label himself as a boy, the boy is motivated to acquire knowledge about "boy things." There is so much to learn that is part of gender schematic knowledge (Martin, 1993; Signorella, Bigler, & Liben, 1993), such as which toys are considered girl toys and which ones are considered boy toys, which specific behaviors are considered female versus male behaviors, which roles and occupations are more typically feminine versus masculine, and which traits are more often feminine traits and which more masculine. As Levy and Fivush (1993, p. 132) put it, gender schemas are "packets of gender-relevant information, understanding, knowledge, and beliefs."

For the young preschooler, the gender schema is powerful. Once children know that someone is a male, they are making inferences that the person acts and thinks like males do. Once they know someone is female, they automatically believe that the individual is female in everything she does. Also, if all they know is that a person did something stereotypically associated with males (e.g., kicked a football), young preschoolers are firm in their belief that the person is a male. If an activity is labeled as consistent with one's own gender, young children like the activity more and are more interested in it (Martin, Eisenbud, & Rose, 1995). Gender schemas are an overwhelming force in thinking about gender-related issues (Martin, 1989; Martin, Wood, & Little, 1990), with children making many inferences about the personalities of other children on the basis of whether the other child behaves in gender-appropriate or gender-inappropriate ways (Lobel, Bempechat, Gewirtz, Shoken-Topaz, & Bashe, 1993). It is very hard, for instance, for the preschooler to understand that males are not always rougher than females, that males can be better cooks than females, or that females can command cockpits and operating rooms (Serbin & Sprafkin, 1986; Urberg, 1982).

Gender schemas affect children's learning as well. When preschoolers are presented information consistent with gender-stereotyped knowledge (e.g., a picture of a male firefighter, a female nurse), they remember it better than information not consistent with gender conventions (e.g., a picture of a female firefighter, a male nurse; Liben & Signorella, 1993; Martin & Halverson, 1983; Signorella & Liben, 1984). Gender schemas probably affect children's memory beginning at about 2–3 years of age (Bauer, 1993; Cherney & Ryalls, 1999).

In closing this section, we want to emphasize that the ascent of gender schema theory does not mean that Kohlberg's position was entirely wrong or without value. Indeed, his theory continues to stimulate research that is suggestive about the role of cognitive development in gender role development. Luecke-Aleksa, Anderson, Collins, and Schmitt (1995) studied the television viewing of 5-year-olds, some of whom had attained gender consistency and others who had not. Boys who had attained gender consistency were much more likely to watch programs with salient male characters than were boys who did not yet recognize the constancy of gender. Gender-consistent boys were more likely to watch sports and action programs than were boys who did not understand the consistency of gender. Of course, these outcomes with boys are consistent with Kohlberg's position. The data with the girls, however, indicated that gender consistency did not make a great impact on girl's television viewing. Thus more than understanding of gender consistency must be at work in mediating gender role development.

■ ■ ■ MOTIVATION AND GENDER DIFFERENCES IN ACADEMIC PERFORMANCES

U.S. females historically have not achieved at the same level in mathematics and science as U.S. males, especially when the benchmark was achievement on standardized assessments. The result is that females are underrepresented in the pool of mathematics and science majors and in professions that require mathematics and science competency (Maple & Stage, 1991). This is a real dilemma, since occupations requiring math and science are among the more prestigious and rewarding of vocational possibilities. Thus gender differences in mathematics and science achievement are an enormous concern for policymakers and educators (e.g., American Association of University Women, 1992; Research Advisory Committee, 1989).

On the positive side, as far as classroom grades in mathematics are concerned, females do better than males. Women who take college mathematics do better in it than do men (Bridgeman & Wendler, 1991). Although males outperform females on standardized math and science tests (Bielinski & Davison, 1998; Comber & Keeves, 1973; Erickson & Erickson, 1984; Kimball, 1989; Levin, Saber, & Libman, 1991), the differences generally are not large. Male–female differences on standardized mathematics tests in particular have declined in recent years (Friedman, 1989; Hyde et al., 1990), although, as discussed earlier in this chapter, the top math scores on tests such as the math SAT are predominantly obtained by males. When the top 1% of people taking the math SAT test are excluded, the test scores of females and males differ little. In addition, international comparisons in cultures where males and females perform comparably on mathematics assessments make it obvious that there is no inherent biological reason for female underachievement (Walberg, Harnisch, & Tsai, 1986).

Given that females obtain better math course grades, it is especially disturbing that many more females than males stop taking mathematics and mathematics-related courses (e.g., computer science) in high school, even females who exhibit great talent in mathematics (Eccles, 1989). Developmental psychologists have made progress in understanding why females are less interested in and less persistent at mathematics and less willing to take science courses requiring a great deal of mathematics, such as physics. As we shall see, it is a long complicated story, with many converging forces undermining the motivation of females to continue in mathematics and quantitative areas of science.

Expectancies about Academic Success and Reactions to Failures

Even when boys and girls perform equivalently—or when girls outperform boys—boys tend to believe that they did much better than they actually did and girls tend to be less confident about their performances (Crandall, 1969; Entwisle & Hayduk, 1978;

Frey & Ruble, 1987; Parsons & Ruble, 1977; Pressley & Ghatala, 1989; Pressley, Levin, Ghatala, & Ahmad, 1987; Stipek & Hoffman, 1980; Whitley, McHugh, & Frieze, 1986). Boys are more certain they do well than girls (even when it is not true), and hence more confident (even when there is no justification for the confidence). That said, there is some evidence that the confidence of boys and girls in high school is more comparable than earlier in their lives (Jacobs, Lanza, Osgood, Eccles, & Wigfield, 2002).

Males and females react differently to failure experiences. Dweck (1986) reported a study in which otherwise high-achieving boys and girls reacted differently to a failure experience on a concept formation task. The high-ability girls tended to be devastated by the failure much more than the high-ability boys and this affected subsequent performances: the high-ability boys outperformed the high-ability girls on subsequent trials of the same task. High-ability girls seemed to be especially disadvantaged, with initial failures and difficulties disrupting their subsequent performances more than the performances of less able girls (Licht & Dweck, 1984). In this same program of research, Dweck determined that girls are more likely than boys to prefer tasks they are good at. In contrast, boys prefer tasks that present some challenge for mastery. Moreover, girls are more likely than boys to attribute any difficulties they have to unchanging abilities (rather than to low effort, high task difficulty, or bad luck; see Chapter 9).

In summary, how girls think about task performances and task difficulties makes it likely that they will reduce their motivation to continue a task when it proves difficult. That is, when they experience frustration, girls tend to believe it is because of low ability. Given a choice, they elect tasks that are not so frustrating, ones that are already familiar to them. Boys, on the other hand, tend to shrug off initial failures, attributing them to something other than their own ability. Since they prefer some challenge and novelty anyway, they are more likely to forge onward.

Dweck (1986) reasoned that secondary-school mathematics is more likely than other content to present difficulties to students at a first encounter. Moreover, it is likely to look very different from elementary-school arithmetic, with algebra, geometry, and calculus full of new terms, symbols, and concepts. Thus, for girls who are more disrupted by frustration and more likely to avoid the unfamiliar, deciding not to pursue mathematics could be a motivating option for them in secondary school. Because, if anything, bright girls seem to be more disrupted by initial difficulties than less able girls, the girls most likely to gain from advanced mathematics instruction are also at special risk to flee from math when they experience difficulties with it. These girls are much more likely to think of themselves as having difficulties in mathematics than are much less mathematically able boys, who are not daunted by initial difficulties (see Fennema, 1974). More specifically, girls are less likely to attribute their successes in mathematics to ability and their failures to bad luck than do same-age boys; elementary-age girls are less likely to be confident that mathematics success can be achieved through effort than elementary-age boys; girls take less pride in their math successes than do male classmates; and girls are more likely to want to hide following a math failure than are boys (Hyde et al., 1990; Stipek & Gralinski, 1991).

Believing that one is able can be extremely motivating even when it is not true! Believing one is not able can undermine motivation to try new and challenging tasks even when ability is high. That boys have more confidence in themselves in general relative to girls probably has a profound impact on their willingness to take on domains like mathematics. That boys think they are better at math and science, even when male and female performances are comparable, probably contributes to the underrepresentation of females in math and science (Andre, Whigham, Hendrickson, & Chambers, 1999; Freedman-Doan et al., 2000). The evidence is accumulating that female beliefs that math is difficult contribute to female underachievement in mathematics (Ethington, 1992).

Societal, Parental, and Teacher Input and Reactions

Males and females are treated differently from the moment the delivery room nurse reaches for a blue blanket for a boy or a pink one for a girl. The pervasiveness of such sexism can affect behavior if internalized, so that much of the reason girls might have less interest in math and careers requiring mathematics is that they have internalized societal, stereotypical beliefs such as "Math is for boys," "Engineers and scientists are men," and "Science requires cold objectivity"—a male stereotypic trait—rather than interpersonal warmth and human contact, female stereotypic traits. Western society does much to discourage female interest in mathematics and science (see Halpern, 2000, for a review).

Parents also tend to have gender-stereotypic expectations about math and science achievement and valuation. That is, they do not expect their daughters to do as well in mathematics and science as their sons. Parents also are much more concerned that sons do well in mathematics and science than daughters. Moreover, parents communicate their beliefs very clearly to their sons and daughters (Eccles & Jacob, 1986; Eccles-Parson, Adler, & Kaczala, 1982). Thus sons are more likely to receive help in math than daughters, with this negatively impacting on the achievement of females (Ethington, 1992). Parental input about the importance of math and science has a great impact on students. For example, in Koballa (1988), eighth-grade girls indicated that they considered their parents as important sources of information about whether they should be taking science seriously. Unfortunately, parents do their share to undermine their daughters' confidence in their mathematical and science abilities, probably impacting short- and long-term motivation and achievement (Eccles, Freedman-Doan, Frome, Jacobs, & Yoon, 2000).

Teachers also undermine female confidence in mathematical and scientific abilities (Campbell, 1995). Many math teachers expect more from boys than from girls and are more responsive to male achievements in mathematics than to female achievements. Math and science classes foster boys more than girls in a number of ways. Boys ask more questions in these classes and they get more answers, with males generally dominating science and math discussions in school (Morse & Handley, 1985). Males receive more total interactions and more academic interactions with their science teachers than do females (Becker, 1982; Jones & Wheatley, 1990; Sabar & Levin, 1989; Taber, 1992; Walford, 1983), largely because boys assert themselves in science classes more than girls do (Sabar & Levin, 1989; Taber, 1992). When volunteering is a main mechanism for determining who participates, when competitive grading is the norm, and when public recitation is a large part of the culture of the math and science classroom (and it often is), male patterns of aggression and competitiveness are favored more than female patterns of cooperation (Eccles & Blumenfeld, 1985; Ruble & Martin, 1998).

When male and female children work on math and science problems together, males dominate the interactions and the decisions that are reached (Lockheed,

1985). After several years of such gender differences in interaction, males are better able to pose questions to other group members that produce assistance and are more likely to seek assistance when they need it (Webb & Kenderski, 1985). This is very distressing, for when male students provide supportive input to female students, indicating to them that a female can do well in science, it has a positive impact (Koballa, 1988). The problem is that classrooms are not set up to foster such supportive interactions.

More positively, there are classrooms in which both females and males continue to believe in their mathematical and scientific abilities (Eccles, 1989; Eccles, MacIver, & Lange, 1986; see also Casserly, 1980: Koch, 2003). Girls fared better in classrooms that were not competitive, ones where ability comparisons were played down. Girls fared better when the teacher emphasized the value of mathematics. Girls did better with warmer teachers, ones who were fairer in their distribution of attention to students. Part of the classroom formula for high math self-efficacy in females is (1) low classroom competition, (2) private and personal contact with the teacher, and (3) little public drill and practice. Much of the rest involves sending the message that math is important for males and females alike, regardless of race or socioeconomic status (Kahle, 1984). In classrooms in which females do well in mathematics, they are exposed to the message that they can do mathematics and they should "go for it" (Metz & Campbell, 1987).

Classrooms that foster high self-efficacy with respect to math and science achievement also tend to involve a great deal of hands-on, cooperative activity between students over math and science problems (see Eccles, 1989, for a review; see also Kahle, 1984; Koch, 2003; Wilkinson & Marrett, 1985). Students feel that they can answer questions without being regarded as stupid, and that student questions are an important part of instruction (Campbell, 1995). Teachers that foster high self-efficacy in females do not give into attention-demanding tactics from males (and males are more likely to engage in such tactics), but rather they make certain that all students are involved in class discussion, interacting productively with one another and with the teacher. Understanding is emphasized more than covering large volumes of material (Campbell, 1995). Lest anyone feel that encouraging such classrooms would encourage a sort of reverse discrimination, girl-friendly classrooms are supportive of minorities and lower achieving boys as well (Kahle, 1984; Malcolm, 1984).

Lifestyle Preferences

Lubinski and Benbow (e.g., 1994) have been studying males and females who turn in the very best performances on the math SAT, in order to understand better why so few women choose careers in math and physics. They have found that even females who are strong in mathematics are less likely to aspire to scientific careers. Females want more social contact than they perceive is permitted by work in mathematics and the physical sciences. Even females who are justifiably confident they could do scientific or mathematical work simply do not want to do such work. Successful scientists and mathematicians often are portrayed as masculine: They are seen as independent, self-assertive, competitive, aggressive, dominant, and aloof. For many females, who have been socialized to be interpersonal, cautious, and cooperative, becoming the stereotypical scientist has little appeal.

Interpretive Summary

Recall the discussion of expectancy-value theory in Chapters 5 and 9. In order for people to be motivated to do something, they must expect that they can succeed at doing that something, and the reward they will receive will be one that they value. Expectancy–value theory can be used to summarize the information in the previous section.

Young women are less confident in their mathematics and scientific abilities than young men (Eccles, 1985), translating to lower expectations with respect to success in mathematics. In addition, females are less likely than males to value careers involving mathematics and sciences (Eccles, 1985; Lubinski & Benbow, 1994). With lower expectancies of reward for taking math and science and lower interest in the potential rewards associated with mathematics and scientific achievement, both components of the expectancy × value product are lower for females than for males, and hence the probabilities of taking mathematics and science are lower for females than for males.

There are many ways that boys are led to believe that they can do mathematics and science and that mathematics and science are valuable for males. Important adults in children's worlds (e.g., parents, teachers) often believe that science and/or math is not for females, with these beliefs negatively affecting the self-perceptions of females about their scientific and mathematical abilities, which in turn negatively affects their performance in these areas (Jacobs, 1991).

One way to react to what has been presented in this section would be to conclude that the forces converging to shape gender differences in science and mathematics achievement and interest are overwhelming. Another way is to recognize that these multiple determinants permit multiple opportunities for intervention. Educational decision makers at all levels can elect options that decrease gender discrimination (Jacobs & Wigfield, 1989). For example, Jones and Wheatley (1988) catalogued many ways that teachers can make their teaching less gender-biased (see also Koch, 2003). These include projecting clear expectations for science achievement by both girls and boys, doing all possible to assure comparable interactions with girls and boys (e. g., making certain both girls and boys play active roles in science laboratory activities), and referring to scientific contributions by both females and males. To the extent educators encourage female submissiveness, they undermine science achievement. When teachers encourage female independence, self-reliance, and exploration, they encourage the development of scientific traits. Providing females with opportunities to experience science and mathematics hands-on through clubs and field trips is consistent with the development of science and mathematics participation. Teachers, counselors, and school administrators need to send the message that females can achieve in science and mathematics.

What is particularly encouraging is that interventions seem to work (Campbell, 1995). For example, Mason and Kahle (1988) studied the effects of teaching science teachers how to create a more gender-free learning environment, largely as described in the last paragraph. The treatment did boost the interest of female students in science, with self-reported increases in participation in science activities outside of school. Martinez (1992) provided evidence that modifying science materials and activities to enhance the interestingness of the activity and its social appeal promotes the interest of girls in the activities. The modifications included posing questions as part of the activity that elicit discussion, requiring sharing and joint answers, and using personal references in the materials. Burbules and Linn (1988) observed that providing junior-high girls with additional experiences during laboratory exercises (e.g., enriched opportunities to examine the laboratory equipment and to generate hypotheses based on these examinations) improved their learning of scientific ideas that clashed with their misconceptions.

Societies in which schools encourage girls to take science and mathematics (such as Finland and Thailand) provide evidence that girls achieve and participate at the same high levels as boys when the educational system supports the view that females can achieve in science (Klainen & Fensham, 1987; Klainen, Fensham, & West, 1989; Skaalvik, 1990). For example, in Thailand, 80% of the chemistry and 50% of the physics teachers are female; girls often participate more actively than boys in Thai science classrooms. See the Considering Interesting Questions special feature (Box 11.3) for a portrayal of the educational experience of girls in the United States.

■ ■ ■ DEVELOPMENT OF SEXUALITY

One of the most striking human developments is the onset of puberty, including maturation of the sexual organs. For girls, there is first menstruation and for boys the new experience of ejaculation. Physical maturation of the sex organs is accompanied by hormonal activities not previously experienced. The result, according to G. Stanley Hall (1904), is "storm and stress" during adolescence, with biological upheaval resulting in psychological upheaval. As we shall see, the traditional concept of inherent storm and stress during adolescence has been called into question.

One biological development during adolescence that has received more attention than others is adolescent intercourse. Although there has always been a need for sex education in order to provide adolescents with an informed perspective about their own biological functions and those of the other sex, the urgency seems greater when it is understood that sexual intercourse can result in the contraction of sexually transmitted diseases such as AIDS.

When does first intercourse occur? It varies from individual to individual. A very small percentage (i.e., 1–2%) experience first intercourse at 11–12 years of age. By age 17, the majority of males report that they have had intercourse; it is another year or two before the majority of females report that they have had intercourse. Even by age 20, a nontrivial proportion of both males (approximately 20%) and females (approximately 25%) report that they have not yet had intercourse. Some will not experience intercourse for another decade. That is, first intercourse occurs for the majority of people during adolescence, defined as the teenage years, but a substantial number of people do not engage in intercourse until early adulthood (Alan Guttmacher Institute, 1994, 2001; Udry & Campbell, 1994).

Some groups experience first intercourse earlier than other groups, on average. Thus, on average, males are sexually active before females; on average, blacks have sex earlier than whites; and, on average, adolescents from lower-class homes experience sex before adolescents from middle- and upper-class homes (Alan Guttmacher Institute, 1994, 2001). What should be remembered, however, is that the differences are small, with great overlap in the distributions. It is impossible to predict the age of first intercourse based only on knowledge of an individual's gender, race, or socioeconomic status.

BOX 11.3. Do Girls Experience Lower-Quality Education Than Boys?

In 1992 the American Association of University Women (AAUW) issued a report summarizing the experiences of girls in school. The report was compiled by social scientists who surveyed all the available research relating gender to quality and quantity issues. They made the case that females were receiving less education than males and that the education females were receiving was of lower quality. Myra and David Sadker, who had participated in the preparation of the AAUW report, provided an elaboration of the AAUW report perspective in a 1994 book, *Failing at Fairness: How America's Schools Cheat Girls*.

The many points made in support of the conclusions that females receive poorer education than males included the following:

- Preschool experiences tend to target competencies that are less developed in boys than in girls, such as impulse control, small muscle development, and language use. Activities matched to areas in which girls need to develop, such as ones involving large motor activities, tend to be played down in many preschool settings.
- Girls are more likely than boys not to be identified for special education services when, in fact, they need them.
- Girls are reading less nonfiction and taking less math and science than are boys.
- Schools and society do not do enough to assure that girls who become pregnant and bear children continue their education.
- Vocational education tends to have a more positive impact on males than on females, with vocational education for girls pointing them in the direction of gender-stereotyped office and support positions.
- Males have more opportunities to participate in extracurricular activities and sports.
- Gender bias, favoring males over females, can be found in standardized tests. For example, SAT tests predict higher grades for males than the grades they actually obtain; the same tests predict lower grades for females than the grades they obtain.
- Males are represented much more favorably than females in the curriculum (e.g., the number of males covered in history relative to females), with girls receiving the message that female lives count less than male lives.
- In many ways the interactions that go on in school favor males, with males interacting more with their teachers. Interactions between teachers and students often occur in ways that are more comfortable for males than for females. For example, competitive classroom environments are better matched to male preferences than to female preferences.
- Female students experience harassment. Schools tolerate behaviors such as rating girls as they enter a room or teasing girls to the point of tears if they are enrolled in courses taken predominantly by boys. These types of behaviors can be seen as harmless instances of "boys being boys" (AAUW, 1992, p. 73).

At the beginning of the 21st century, the case is still strong that female students are not treated as fairly in schools as males (American Association of University Women Educational Foundation, 1998, 2000, 2001). We urge the future educators who are reading this book to think hard about what they can do to make schools more gender-equitable.

Individual differences in the age of first intercourse suggest that more than physical maturity determines the age of first intercourse or sexual behavior in general. In fact, social and personality factors play a considerable role in adolescent sexual behavior (Udry & Campbell, 1994). Whether an adolescent is religious has an effect; more religious adolescents wait longer to begin sexual activity relative to less religious students. Adolescents who are shy experience sexual relations later than more assertive adolescents. Weaker students tend to experience intercourse earlier than better students (McAnarney & Schreider, 1984). An adolescent who has friends who have had sex is more likely to engage in intercourse than an adolescent surrounded by virginal peers, with the effect of peer sexuality probably stronger for females than for males (Billy & Udry, 1987; Miller & Moore, 1990). Overall social context also makes a difference as reflected by shifts in sexual behavior as a functional of historical era: Adolescents at the beginning of the 21st century are more sexually active and sexually active earlier than adolescents throughout most of the 20th century (Alan Guttmacher Institute, 1994, 2001).

That sexual socialization depends on social context is a position that stands in contrast to G. Stanley Hall's (1904) assumption that biological developments during adolescence inevitably lead to psychosocial turmoil centering on sexuality. One of the great studies in the social sciences was Margaret Mead's *Coming of Age in Samoa* (1961), originally published in 1928. Mead studied adolescence in a primitive society as a window on the universality of the adolescent experience. Specifically, Mead wanted to know if adolescence in other cultures was similar to adolescence in the United States. The prevailing sentiment at the time followed from Hall's line of reasoning that the adolescent experience was a consequence of biological changes during adolescence. From that perspective, it would be expected that adolescence and the development of sexuality would be similar across cultures.

As a woman, Mead felt that she has a better chance of studying female development in a foreign culture than male development. Hence, she focused on the development of Samoan girls. What Mead observed was that puberty for Samoan girls was not stressful. Whereas Hall (1904) had written long chapters on new faults and immoralities at adolescence that did not occur in childhood, Mead found little of the sort. Hall offered many pages reflecting on adolescent delinquency, whereas Mead found few girls that were delinquent relative to Samoan standards. Whereas Hall portrayed adolescence as a period of painful wrestling with conflicting possibilities, for everything from religious beliefs to social integration with society, Mead found little psychological conflict. In particular, with respect to budding sexuality, the adolescents accepted Samoan practices, with no storm and stress about when and how to be sexual. Adolescence was not a difficult period of time in life, certainly not the anxiety-ridden period that Hall had portrayed.

So why was Samoan adolescence so different than adolescence in Western culture? According to Mead (1961), the "stress is in our civilization, not in the physical changes through which our children pass" (p. 235). In the West, adolescence is the period of time when society expects choices that were not expected during childhood, with various groups pressuring adolescents to make choices consistent with their viewpoints. (Recall from Chapter 5 Erik Erikson's conception of adolescence as a period of moratorium.)

After Samoa, Mead continued studying gender roles as a function of culture and found a great deal of support for the conclusion that gender roles were largely culturally determined. Mead (1963; first published in 1935) studied three tribal societies in New Guinea. What she found was that gender roles varied tremendously between the three societies. One of the tribes socialized the feminine role for both sexes; the second tribe socialized the masculine role for both sexes; and in the third tribe, males were socialized to be feminine by Western standards, whereas females were socialized to be masculine. Such a pattern of differences defies the conclusion that biology is destiny with respect to gender roles, attitudes, and behaviors. Some have challenged Mead's conclusions and her methods (Freeman, 1983; Goodman, 1983; in response, see Coté, 1994), but Mead made a major contribution by presenting evidence and a position that sharply contrasted with the prevailing biological-deterministic sentiment of the early 20th century regarding gender and sexual development.

We close by noting that developmental psychologists recently have had great interest in another potential contemporary, cultural influence on gender role development: whether being raised in an alternative family (e.g., two gay or lesbian partners who raise a child) impacts sexual orientation. The general conclusion that emerges from this work is that both boys and girls raised in such homes are more likely to be gender-consistent in their behaviors and sexual orientation than not (Patterson, 2002, 2003). See the Considering Interesting Questions special feature (Box 11.4) for further discussion on this topic.

■ ■ ■ CHAPTER SUMMARY AND EVALUATION

Gender differences do exist. However, the differences between the sexes are much smaller than the person in the street supposes and there is a great deal of overlap in the male and female distributions on almost any characteristic measured.

Chromosomes alone do not tell much of the story with respect to gender identity and gender-related behaviors, except to the extent that they determine prenatal hormonal exposure and levels. Hormones certainly affect genital development and probably affect development of the central nervous system to some extent. But biology does not operate alone in determining gender identity, for when biology and socialization forces conflict, socialization forces can have a powerful impact.

The world reinforces boys for being like boys and girls for being like girls! Moreover, many live and symbolic models surround the developing child. All of the observational learning opportunities provide plenty of information about what boys are like and what girls are like. There is powerful consistency in the world with respect to the pressures on children to develop in gender-stereotypical ways. Cognition plays a large role in that the learning of gender roles require a great deal of memory, classification of behaviors as female or male, and comparing of one's own characteristics and behaviors with those of social models.

Then comes schooling, and, with it, the social world changes. A great deal of effort has been made in the past two decades to understand how school affects females and males differently. Much of this work has focused on striking differences in the eventual math and science achievement of females and males. Much of the gender difference in achievement seems to be due to gender differences in motivation, ones determined in part by the structure of conventional schooling.

The work summarized in this chapter is exceptionally informative with respect to the great debates in human development and factors affecting development.

Considering Interesting Questions

BOX 11.4. Does Being a Child of Homosexual Parents Affect Sex Role Development and Sexual Orientation?

If environmental theories of gender role acquisition are the entire story, it would make sense that children of homosexual parents would be more likely to be homosexual than children of heterosexual parents. In fact, that is not the case. Research evidence indicates no difference in the sexual orientation of children raised by homosexual versus heterosexual parents. For example, Bailey, Bobrow, Wolfe, and Mikach (1995) studied the adult sons of gay or bisexual men. They asked both the fathers and the sons about the son's sexual orientation. Ninety percent of the sons were heterosexual in their orientation, a figure consistent with other studies of the sexuality of children fathered and/or reared by homosexual men (Patterson, 1992). Moreover, the fathers were aware of their sons' orientation. On the basis of environmental theories, it might be expected that the longer a child had lived with a homosexual father, the greater the likelihood that the child would be homosexual. That also proved not to be the case.

Golombok and Tasker (1996) conducted a longitudinal study of 25 children raised by lesbian mothers and 21 children raised by heterosexual single mothers. The children were studied roughly between 9 and 24 years of age. As young adults, a minority of children from both types of homes reported same-gender sexual attraction. The children raised by lesbians were more likely to have explored same-gender sexual relationships. Even so, all but two of the children raised by lesbians were heterosexual in early adulthood. Although none of the young adults raised by heterosexual women were homosexual, in general, there was far more evidence of similarity than difference in the gender role and sexual development of the two groups of young adults. One factor predictive of children exploring homosexuality was that their lesbian mothers were openly active sexually, with children witnessing great affection between their mothers and their mothers' lovers. Thus this study provided some support for environmental contributions to gender role development, although the larger message was that there was really little difference in outcome for children raised by homosexual compared to heterosexual mothers.

In summary, researchers have found little or no differences in the gender role development or sexual orientation of children raised in homes with gay or lesbian parents (Patterson, 1992, 2002, 2003). Moreover, there is no credible evidence of differences in other areas of personal development between children raised in gay versus straight homes—no differences with respect to self-concept, morality, intelligence, peer relationships, and so on.

Developmental Debates

Nature versus Nurture

Although there have been claims about gender role development based on nature and others based on nurture, it is clear that both biology and environment play a role. This holds for a variety of issues pertaining to gender role development, from basic issues of gender identity to the timing of first intercourse.

Stages versus Continuous Development

Traditional thinking about gender role development has been stage-like, with Kohlberg's theory being one example (i.e., gender role development depends on stage of cognitive development). More recent thinking indicates that from early in life, children have powerful schematic representational abilities that permit them to organize their thinking about gender, which in turn leads to more continuous gender role development.

Universals versus Culture-Specific Developments

The work of Margaret Mead and other cross-cultural researchers argues for the powerful influence of culture on gender role development. Much of the research summarized in this chapter was produced in the West. We wonder whether any universal generalizations about gender role development will survive as additional cross-cultural data accumulate.

Trait-Like Consistency versus Situational Variation in Behavior

An assumption of many persons in the street is that a lot of people are consistently masculine and others are consistently feminine. What the work on androgyny suggests is that there are some people who are more consistent than others, and, indeed, varying responses as a function of the situation (i.e., behaving in a more masculine fashion in some situations, in a more feminine fashion in other situations) is probably psychologically healthy.

Active versus Passive Child

As soon as a child gets the idea that he or she is a boy or a girl, it stimulates active attention to male or female things. The child is certainly active in gender role development. Even so, there is a great deal of environmental press, so that some of gender role development probably occurs passively.

Lasting Early Effects versus Transient Early Effects of Experience

Some of the strongest evidence for the effects of early experience on long-term development was presented in this chapter. Perhaps most striking is the evidence that prenatal hormones affect brain development that in turn affects gender role development. Also, as Money and Eherhardt documented, several years of experience being reared as a boy or a girl can be difficult to reverse.

■■■ REVIEW OF KEY TERMS

androgens Hormones secreted by the testes.

androgynous Refers to individuals who are high on both masculine and feminine characteristics.

estrogen A hormone secreted by the ovaries.

field independence The ability to perceive an object separate from its background.

gender consistency The understanding that gender does not change with superficial changes in appearance.

gender schemas Organized knowledge about gender.

quantitative skills Mathematical skills and reasoning.

testosterone A hormone secreted by the testes that is particularly important in the development of masculine characteristics.

verbal ability Skills such as word fluency, grammatical competence, spelling, reading, and oral comprehension.

visual–spatial tasks tasks requiring the ability to imagine figures, including figure manipulation "in the head."

CHAPTER 12

Recognizing and Understanding Student Mental Health Problems

David G. Scherer

A broad spectrum of mental health problems is present in schoolage children. Estimates indicate that as many as one in 10 children and adolescents suffer from a diagnosable psychological disorder (Mash & Dozois, 2003). Educators associate with a wide variety of children, especially because of recent efforts to include children with serious learning, emotional, and behavioral problems in mainstream classrooms. It's inevitable that teachers will work with children who have mental health problems that can be challenging to cope with in the classroom and quite debilitating to a child's overall development. Some of these children will already have been identified as having psychological problems, although many others will not. Teachers and other education professionals, because of their experience with applied developmental psychology and their extensive contact with and insight about children, are in a unique position to detect and report mental health problems that need immediate attention before they worsen.

The intent of this chapter is to introduce some of the developmental psychopathologies educators may encounter among their students. The chapter begins with descriptions of psychological and developmental disorders that are first evident in preschoolers, followed by explanations of mental health problems most noted in elementary-schoolage children, and concludes with a brief rendering of some of the mental health issues that are prevalent among teenagers. Some of these problems are rare and teachers may never observe a child with some of these diagnoses unless they are engaged in educating children with special needs. Other mental health prob-

David G. Scherer, PhD, received his doctoral degree from the University of Virginia in 1989. He is a family/child and adolescent clinical psychologist currently teaching at the University of Massachusetts in Amherst.

lems, unfortunately, are quite common and a teacher will almost certainly encounter them at some point in his or her career. We hope that reading this chapter will help you recognize when a child is suffering from a serious mental health problem and to understand that child and his or her behavior a little better.

■ ■ ■ THEMES TO KEEP IN MIND

Before we can delve into the particulars about the kinds of developmental psycho-pathologies found in children, a few key concepts and ideas need to be covered first. In particular, we need to discuss some introductory, but vitally important, themes that mental health professional use to distinguish healthy and acceptable behavior from behavioral patterns that are maladaptive. Sometimes there is a fine line between what is "normal" and what is "dysfunctional." To be helpful, teachers and educators need to remember and use these themes when deciding how to respond to the unusual behaviors they may observe in the children with whom they work.

The Quantity and Quality of the Problem Behavior

All children, at some time or another, exhibit behaviors and emotions that are symptoms of mental health problems. For example, most children have temper tantrums or outbursts of anger, most children behave impulsively from time to time, most children have difficulty sustaining attention at times, and most children have overwhelming fears and feel helpless and unhappy on occasion. In fact, most adults exhibit these behaviors and feelings now and then too. One thing that distinguishes healthy children from those who are suffering from a mental health problem is the *quantity or frequency* of the symptomatic behavior (Campbell, 2002). Healthy individuals experience and express these emotions and behaviors periodically. The behavior or mood occurs and may even endure for a couple of days, but soon enough the feeling or behavior subsides and the person returns to normal. Actually, children frequently cycle in and out of phases in which they are naughty or excited or worried or unhappy. Children with psychological problems, however, experience negative moods and express problematic behaviors frequently, often multiple times a day. Children with serious psychological problems never really bounce back to their "normal" selves—in fact, their usual way of being is troubled and the times when they act and feel fine is the exception, not the rule.

Another factor that separates healthy individuals from those who are struggling with the vicissitudes of life is the *quality* of the symptomatic behavior. When healthy children experience negative moods or exhibit problematic behavior, it's usually in a milder and more manageable form. Healthy children will try to respond to encouragement and limit setting from adults and seem to learn what the boundaries of acceptable behavior are. Psychologically troubled children experience more extreme manifestations of problematic moods and behaviors. Their tantrums may be horrific and destructive; they may be exceedingly defiant, not just naughty; their worries are extreme, even bizarre; and when they are unhappy they are morose and inconsolable. They don't seem to respond to the directives from adults to control their behavior and often assert they just can't control their feelings and behavior.

In short, two things that often distinguish healthy children from psychologically troubled children are the quantity and quality of their problematic moods and behavior. Healthy children exhibit problem behaviors episodically and generally at a more manageable level. Symptomatic emotions and behaviors in troubled children are persistent. They occur frequently and with a surprising level of intensity. The troubling feelings and behaviors last longer and are seemingly uncontrollable. As a rule of thumb, teachers should expect that all children will exhibit problematic moods and behaviors. Avoid "jumping the gun" and assuming the worst at the first sight of problem behavior. The risk is that you will begin to develop a bias and "see what you believe." If that happens, then every behavior the child exhibits could be interpreted as part of the child's "pathology." Even worse, you might create a "self-fulfilling prophecy" in which a child lives up to your expectation: if you expect him or her to be a problem child, he or she will become a problem. It's better to begin with the assumption that children are trying hard to be on their best behavior and that sometimes they lapse or struggle with their feelings and behavior. Instead of jumping to premature conclusions about a child's psychological condition, look for enduring patterns of moods and behavior that far exceed what you ordinarily encounter, because this is what will confirm or refute the presence of a more serious psychological problem.

The Context in Which the Problem Behavior Occurs

People live within and move between social environments. Each of these environments has different rules or expectations for what is appropriate behavior. The demand characteristics of an environment and the circumstances that lead to the creation of these environments provide the setting or context for interpreting emotional expressions and behavior. We generally think of many emotions and behaviors, like humor and laughing, as prosocial and enhancing of our lives. However, laughing during a solemn occasion, like a funeral, or joking around when you are supposed to be concentrating on a school assignment, is not appropriate and may be indicative of a more serious emotional or behavioral problem. Alternatively, we often consider anger, aggression, and fighting as negative emotions and behaviors, but if they are expressed in reaction to unprovoked aggression from others or in self-defense, these behaviors might be deemed appropriate for the circumstances. The point is, whether an emotion or a behavior is symptomatic of a serious psychological problem or not depends a great deal on the context in which the behavior occurs.

Ordinarily, when children and adults shift from one social setting to another, they alter their behavior and emotional expressions accordingly. Children with serious psychological problems may have a difficult time adjusting their behavior and emotions to match the social context. The symptoms of a serious emotional or behavioral disorder are not easily turned on and turned off. Consequently, as a general rule of thumb (there are some notable exceptions to this rule), when a child has a serious mental health problem, the symptoms of that disorder get expressed no matter what the context or social environment is. So, for example, an adolescent suffering from a serious depression will act and feel depressed at home, at school, and while hanging out with friends. Similarly, a child who has attention-deficit/hyperactivity disorder (ADHD) is likely to manifest those symptoms across contexts. On the other hand, when a child expresses psychological problems in one context but not others, there is probably something about that particular context that accounts for the child's behavior, rather than something endemic to the child (Eccles, Midgley, & Wigfield, 1993). Sometimes teachers take advantage of these environmental and contextual effects. For example, a teacher may make a small change in a social environment, like moving where a child sits, from the back to the front of a classroom, to make a difference in how a child behaves.

One kind of mistake that people frequently make is dismissing the effects of context and environment and assuming that the reason a child is behaving inappropriately is because of something wrong with the child. It is really important for teachers not to make this error and to take note of the circumstances in which a child's problem mood or behavior is expressed. It may be very difficult for a mental health professional to make an accurate diagnosis if he or she doesn't know the context in which the problem is occurring. When reporting on a child's psychological adjustment, it is useful to note the physical, social, and demand characteristics of the environment. For example, how stimulating is the environment? Is it noisy and overstimulating or is it bland and boring? Is the child comfortable with the people in his or her midst, or is he or she being teased or tormented? Does the problem emerge during particular times, like during lessons that are really challenging or difficult for the child and not during lessons the child enjoys and feels competent doing? Also, it is very useful to observe whether the child is exhibiting symptoms of a psychological disorder in more than one setting. Do symptoms of a serious psychological disorder show up in the classroom, during recess, and on the bus to and from school? Is more than one adult observing these problems in different contexts? Finding answers to these kinds of questions will make a big difference when it comes time for a professional to diagnose the child's problems and often to figure out how to best treat these issues.

The "It's Probably Not a Zebra!" Issue

One wonderful aspect of human nature is that people are always curious about why something is happening, try to figure out what's going on, and look for cause-and-effect relationships. As noted in the previous paragraph, we often make mistakes when we do this. Another of the more common mistakes is assuming that something rare and exotic is causing a phenomenon, when in fact it's caused by something common and mundane. For example, a person might feel some nausea and a slight pain in his or her side and think, "Oh my god, I have appendicitis!" (a low-frequency event) when it's much more likely that he or she has a touch of food poisoning because he or she ate old leftovers (a high-frequency event). Well, the same is true in child and adolescent clinical psychology. People are apt to attribute a child's problematic behavior to some relatively low-prevalence psychopathology when there are much more common and frequent factors in a child's life that may be causing his or her difficulties.

Many of the developmental psychopathologies we discuss in this chapter occur in a small percentage of children (often less than 1%; usually less than 2–3%; sometimes as many as 5–10%, but rarely more). On the other hand, there are some very-high-frequency events in children's lives that are quite disruptive and can cause psychological symptoms. For example, nearly one in five children (a high-frequency event) in the United States lives in poverty (Child Trends DataBank, 2004; U.S. Census Bureau). Consequently, they are often malnourished, exposed to more environmental toxins, have less access to medical care, have less social support, receive less cognitive stimulation, and are subject to more social and familial turmoil (Evans, 2004; McLoyd, 1998; see also Chapter 2). Moreover, there is some evidence to suggest that when poverty is alleviated, psychopathology diminishes (Costello, Compton, Keeler, & Angold, 2003). Similarly, a substantial number of children in the United States experience dramatic family upheaval and transition (e.g., marital separation, parental divorce, remarriage), and as many as one-third live in stepfamilies (Doyle, Wolchik, Dawson-McClure, & Sandler, 2003). While there is some controversy about how traumatic and enduring the effects of this may be on children, there is no doubt that it is stressful and emotionally destabilizing for children for a period of time preceding and following the transition (Hetherington, Bridges, & Insabella, 1998; see also Chapter 10) and causes disruptions in children's behavior. Many children (depending on who you ask, estimates range from 7 to 13%) live in homes with family violence (Fantuzzo et al., 1997; Finkelhor, 1991). Twelve in every 1,000 children in the United States are confirmed victims of child abuse and twice that number are suspected victims of abuse (Department of Health and Human Services, Administration for Children and Families, 2002). Perhaps even more common and insidious are the effects of sleep deprivation. Recent reports have suggested that many, perhaps most, children and adolescents (and maybe lots of adults too) are getting too little sleep, which has dramatic effects on their behavior, including mimicking psychopathology or exacerbating already existing emotional and behavioral problems (Carskadon, 2002; Sadeh, Gruber, & Raviv, 2002).

These examples are used to highlight the fact that symptomatic behavior can be caused by many factors. Consequently, when a teacher is trying to understand a child's problematic behavior, he or she should consider more frequent and common causes of problematic behavior before assuming that a child has developed a psychological pathology. In fact, for most educators, unless they have received advanced training in abnormal child psychology, it is best to avoid making any kind of diagnosis at all of a child's behavior.

What's an Educator to Do?

Making psychological diagnoses is complicated, there are many ways to make mistakes, and sometimes having just a little knowledge can cause a lot of troubles. So as you read through the following pages about the kinds of psychological problems that plague some children, keep the preceding cautions in mind. Remember that all children exhibit problematic behaviors some of the time. Think first about how a child's social and physical environment may be contributing to his or her problems. Consider whether his or her troubled emotions and problem behavior may be in response to common and frequent events in the lives of children and families and avoid jumping to diagnostic conclusions about a child.

On the other hand, your observations about a child are invaluable to psychodiagnosticians and other mental health professionals. The more precise and specific your observations are, the more useful they will be. For example, reporting that a child gets out of his seat, on average, five times an hour regardless of what subject is being taught, is much more useful than complaining that a child is "hyperactive." Similarly, stating that the child "acts weird" will communicate less than if you observe that a child rarely makes eye contact and laughs or giggles at inappropriate times. Look for enduring patterns of disturbing behavior, try to avoid allowing any single or brief episode of emotional or behavioral problems to bias your perception of a child, and, above all, look for times when the child behaves competently which might disconfirm your suspicions of a more serious problem.

■ ■ ■ PSYCHOLOGICAL PROBLEMS OFTEN FIRST DETECTED IN EARLY CHILDHOOD

Pervasive Developmental Disorders

Pervasive developmental disorders (PDDs) are exactly that. They are debilitating illnesses that impact a child's social, emotional, cognitive, educational, and behavioral development—in other words, all aspects of a child's psychological development. There are several different types of PDDs, and they range in the types, severity, and the manner in which the symptoms develop. At one time PDDs were thought to be exceedingly rare, but more recent studies have detected higher rates of PDDs in the general population, somewhere between 16 and 63 per 10,000 children (Klinger, Dawson, & Renner, 2003). It's not clear whether the population of children with PDDs is increasing or people are getting better at detecting them (Klinger et al., 2003); either way educators are finding they have more contact with children with these serious disorders, especially the types that are less debilitating.

Autistic Disorder

Autistic disorder is a devastating mental disorder characterized by a variety of symptoms including dramatic deficits in social interaction, severe impairments in communications, and a markedly limited repertoire of activity and interests (American Psychiatric Association, 1994). Children with autism seem to cope with social situations in ways that are quite different than other children. They seem either not to attend to social stimuli (e.g., responding to faces) or attend to social stimuli in unusual ways from an early age (Klinger et al., 2003). As babies, they seem aloof and passive. They decline to reach out for their caretakers, sometimes stiffen when held, and often fail to smile or make eye contact like healthier babies do. This hinders their ability to imitate and learn social behavior and to respond emotionally. As a consequence, children with autism may seem oblivious to the presence or feelings of others and are unlikely to seek comfort from others. Many children with autism are mute, and those who aren't frequently use language in peculiar ways. They often use *echolalia* (repeating words or phrases they previously heard), *pronoun reversals* (e.g., saying "you" instead of "I" when talking about themselves), *unusual rhythms and intonations*, and *odd nonverbal communications*. Children with autism typically engage in repetitive and stereotypic movements (e.g., rocking or flapping of hands or arms), may become preoccupied and inordinately attached to inanimate objects, and experience extreme distress even to the slightest changes in their environment. Some children with autism adopt self-injurious behaviors like head banging or finger biting. In the 1988 movie *Rain Man*, Dustin Hoffman portrayed an autistic man who had unique mathematical skills. On rare occasions, children with autism will demonstrate extraordinary memory skills or savant behavior in math, drawing, or music. However, the reality for most children with autism is much grimmer; the disorder is so crippling that their overall intellectually abilities are severely impaired.

The cause of autism is still a mystery. We know it is *not* caused by poor parenting. Concerns that childhood immunizations may be responsible for some types of autism have been refuted by recent research. Most explanations of the cause of autism are physiological in nature. Advances in genetic and neuroanatomical research have identified potential genes that may contribute to the development of autism and variations in neuroanatomy and how the brain develops in people with autism (Klinger et al., 2003).

There also may be different types of autism: some appear to begin very early in infancy while others seem to begin after a period of 1–2 years of seemingly normal development. As we have gained more knowledge about autism, researchers and clinicians have begun to speculate there is a spectrum of autism-like disorders in which individuals have all or only some of the symptoms of autism, depending perhaps on their genetic makeup. This has led to the concept of "high-functioning autism." The big difference between children with severe autism and those with high-functioning autism seems to be the acquisition of language skills—although the latters' language skill development is still delayed and they often still have notable expressive and receptive language deficits. Because of the rarity of autism and the severely debilitating nature of its symptoms, most teachers will not be called on to educate autistic children unless they seek out that opportunity. However, teachers are having more contact with children with high-functioning autism and the related disorder of Asperger's syndrome.

Asperger's Syndrome and Nonverbal Learning Disorder

It can be quite difficult to distinguish between a child with high-functioning autism and one with **Asperger's syndrome**. In turn, it can be challenging to distinguish a child with Asperger's syndrome from one with nonverbal learning disorder (NLD). Developmental psychopathologists continue to debate whether these are separate and distinct diagnoses (Klinger et al., 2003; Rourke, 1995; Rourke, Ahmad, & Collins, 2002; Stewart, 2002). Many of the symptoms that characterize Asperger's syndrome, particularly the social deficits, are similar to the symptoms found in children with autism. Recently, the pendulum seems to be swinging toward the idea that Asperger's syndrome is really a form of nonverbal learning disorder (NLD), although there are children with NLD who have the same kinds of cognitive impairments found in children with Asperger's syndrome, but absent the serious social interaction difficulties (Rourke, 1995; Rourke et al., 2002). The important issue for educators is for them to realize they are apt to have contact with children who have complex and serious difficulties with learning and social interaction, but who do not have deficits severe enough to warrant a diagnosis of autism.

In general, children with NLD syndrome disorders will have problems with tactile perception, visual perception, and motor coordination, and they will also have difficulty processing and retrieving information, particularly tactile and visual memory, which makes it hard for them to use past experiences to cope with unique or novel situations. These problems, in turn, lead to deficits in attention and exploration, which lead to deficits in organization, higher order reasoning, abstract thinking, emotional regulation, and social interaction (Rourke et al., 2002; Stewart, 2002).

More specifically, children with Asperger's syndrome usually do not have the kinds of substantial impairments of language and intellectual functioning found in children with autism—in fact, they are often above average in some intellectual abilities. Children with Asperger's syndrome are usually proficient in the technical aspects of language (e.g., word recognition, spelling, grammar, articulation), often have excellent auditory or rote memory recall, and frequently have a superior fund of knowledge in some idiosyncratic topic. Still, their perception and expression of nonverbal communications may be odd and uncomfortable. Also, they use language in fairly concrete ways; metaphor, analogy, and humorous plays on words may confuse them, and their comprehension of written language and ability to problem solve are often impaired.

Although their intellectual abilities may be better than those found in children with autism, children with Asperger's syndrome are awkward in social interactions in ways that are reminiscent of the kinds of social deficits found in children with autism. Similar to children with autism, children with Asperger's syndrome tend to develop a fixation or obsessive interest in some activity. However, in children with Asperger's syndrome, unlike their autistic counterparts, this activity is usually socially acceptable (e.g., playing with Legos). Conversations with children with Asperger's syndrome tend to be one-sided; they are often verbose and don't seem to grasp the reciprocal and social nature of conversing. Sometimes children with Asperger's syndrome lack physical coordination. Because of these unusual and socially awkward behaviors, children with Asperger's syndrome often are socially isolated and their peers may refer to them as "geeky" or "nerds." Unlike children with autism, though, children with Asperger's syndrome seem to be aware of being social outcasts and it bothers them, but they have difficulty in adjusting their social behavior enough to remedy this.

At present, NLD syndrome disorders are thought to be caused by irregularities in the "white matter" of the brain (Rourke, 1995). Nerve cells are called "neurons," and they have "arms" that extend from them called "axons" that connect to other neurons. These axons are often coated with white globules of tissue called "myelin" that make nerve signals travel along the axon faster (see also Chapter 2). So *white matter* is the myelinated axons that make connections across various brain structures (*gray matter* is the granular appearance of the neuronal cell bodies). Theoretically, the white matter or neuronal connections in the brains of children with Asperger's syndrome or NLD either didn't develop correctly, doesn't function correctly, or were damaged in some way. These problems could occur for genetic reasons, or as a consequence of prenatal conditions, or because of postnatal illness or trauma.

What Can Teachers Do When Working with Children with PDDs?

Teachers not involved in special education or in teaching young children may be inclined to think they won't have to work with children with PPDs and NLDs because they don't teach young children. The reality is that children with high-functioning autism, Asperger's syndrome, and other NLDs are increasingly found in mainstream classrooms. Nor do children grow out of these disorders; so elementary-school, middle-school, and high-school teachers are finding they need to understand what these disorders are about and how they can best contribute to these children's education.

There are some general strategies teachers can follow when faced with children who have a PPD or an NLD. Because children with PPDs and NLDs have difficulty responding to novelty and unique situations, they do best when they have consistent and predictable routines. Children with PDDs and NLDs need more time to accomplish tasks, so schedule fewer activities and "do more of less" rather than trying to expose these children to a "little bit of a lot." Keep directions simple and short and provide children with PPDs and NLDs places to work that are free from distraction.

Teach these children how to focus attention on the main idea and how to organize their work by prebriefing them on how to distinguish between important ideas and superfluous details and how to organize using color codes, notebooks, schedules, and time awareness. Then debrief them at the end of a task about what worked and what didn't work in helping them get their assignment done. These are children who, in general, are better at auditory learning; who do better with scaffolding and when things are divided into steps; and who work well with facts and logical explanations. They usually don't do well with teaching strategies that emphasize visual learning, learning the gestalt (or whole) and working backward to discover the parts, problem solving, and self-discovery. Furthermore, because children with PDDs and NLDs have difficulty understanding and responding to social stimuli, teachers may need to adapt their lessons accordingly. For example, children with PPDs and NLDs may have difficulty working in groups, so the group activities they are asked to do should be highly structured and well supervised. Also, teachers can look for opportunities to teach about the intricacies and nuances of social interaction, and to model and practice effective social and communication skills (e.g., making eye contact, making appropriate greetings, reading facial expressions, using polite words, developing listening skills). Lastly, because feelings are difficult for children with PDD and NLD to process, it's best to mute emotional expressions, especially strong negative feelings; otherwise children with PPDs and NLDs will focus on the emotion and not the message and will quickly become overstimulated and frustrated. An excellent resource about Asperger's syndrome and NLDs, written for parents, although teachers may find it very useful, is Stewart (2002).

■ ■ ■ PSYCHOLOGICAL PROBLEMS PRESENT DURING THE ELEMENTARY-SCHOOL YEARS

Children's Anxieties

As adults, we have a tendency to idealize childhood. It seems to us that the life of a child is carefree and full of fun, but the reality is that children experience a great deal of stress. In fact, feeling stressed and anxious is a normative experience and a necessary part of our development (Albano, Chorpita, & Barlow, 2003). Each time children or adolescents strike out on their own and assume more autonomy or engage in new and challenging activities, they experience and learn to cope with the unpleasant physiological arousal we label "anxiety" and "dread." That arousal, assuming that it's not overwhelming, serves to focus attention and concentration and to facilitate learning. Moreover, there is evidence that suggests that anxiety levels in children, adolescents, and young adults in the United States have been increasing over the past 50 years (Twenge, 2000). Some of this has to do with the genetic transmission of the predisposition for worry and anxiety. However, a substantial portion also has to do with social trends such as the increasing instability in family life and changes in our social environment, most particularly from the perception of greater danger in the world that follows from increased access to media coverage of worldwide crime, war, terrorism, and disease; and from the erosion of social connectedness that stems from the increasing mobility of people in our society, and peoples' relative isolation and lack of involvement in developing a sense of community.

Unfortunately, many children lack the experience, insight, and adult guidance they need to cope with the tensions of life and the strong emotional conditions that accompany them. They become confused by their feelings, have difficulty explaining why they feel the way they do, and feel their emotions are in control of them rather than the other way around. Sometimes, as a consequence, their anxieties and fears become overwhelming, and instead of being transitory experiences that focus attention and facilitate learning, they become chronic, encompassing, and debilitating conditions. This is a very serious problem because chronic anxieties in children interfere with healthy development and learning, and may lead to a proclivity for even more serious anxiety disorders, depression, substance use, and suicide in adulthood (Albano et al., 2003).

The first step in addressing anxiety problems in children is determining whether the problem is a normal fear or anxiety, a transitory state-related anxiety, or a more debilitating psychological condition. There are a variety of very common fears that children express in the course of normal development: for example, things like stranger anxiety, fear of loud noises, fear of falling, fear of the dark, and even some specific phobia-like fears such as fear of snakes, spiders, or storms. Although these fears are practically universal, there are considerable individual differences in how much or in what way any particular child may express them. Some children have a temperament that is more robust, and so they tolerate anxiety better; other children are more timid, and so they ruminate over anxieties. Generally, the more a child has control over the situation, the less intense the fears.

However, while there is a wide range of estimates, more than 10% of children manifest a degree of anxiety that qualifies as a diagnosable anxiety disorder (Albano et al., 2003). In fact, anxiety disorders are the most common mental health problem in children and adolescents. When children experience debilitating anxiety, their symptoms may look quite different than when adults express anxiety. Anxious children tend to get fidgety and restless. They may become impulsive, distracted, and preoccupied (which may look a lot like ADHD). They may become irritable, moody, and look and act depressed (indeed, they may be depressed in addition to having an anxiety disorder). The most prevalent symptoms involve withdrawal, dependency, somatic complaints, and developmental regression. For example, younger children may become clingy, may become enuretic after years of bladder control, or may start sucking their thumb again; adolescents may withdraw from the family and revert to more childish behaviors; and children of all ages may complain about stomachaches, fatigue, or headaches as their anxiety increases. Currently, only one anxiety disorder is diagnosed in children (i.e., separation anxiety disorder), but children and adolescents develop other kinds of anxiety disorders (e.g., generalized anxiety disorder, social phobias, specific phobias, obsessive–compulsive disorder, posttraumatic stress disorder). The following is a description of the most commonly diagnosed anxiety disorders in children and adolescents.

Separation Anxiety Disorder

The main symptom of **separation anxiety disorder (SAD)** is the expression of extreme anxiety and agitation when separated, or even anticipating separation, from home or from the people to whom a child is most attached (e.g., parents, other important caregivers) (American Psychiatric Association, 1994). Children with SAD worry excessively that something cataclysmic or harmful will happen to those they love and depend on; alternatively, they worry they themselves will be kidnapped or lost and in that way lose their loved ones.

These fears are so overwhelming to the child that he or she begins to avoid being alone or to engage in any activity that would require him or her to be away from the caretakers to whom they are attached. This avoidance behavior often begins with small reasonable requests for parental comforting, but gradually these requests escalate in frequency and intensity till the child is unwilling to sleep alone, go to school, or allow a parent out of his or her sight even for a moment. Children with SAD often have recurrent nightmares and frequently complain they feel physically ill. As these symptoms intensify, children with SAD encounter greater limitations in where they can go and what they can do. Over time children with SAD lose friends and the opportunity for enriching social interaction, they begin to lag behind their peers in academic achievement because of missed school, and they encounter more family discord as their parents struggle with how to comfort their child, but also set limits on their anxious child's desperate attempts to be omnipresent in their lives. It is important to note that separation anxiety is one cause of school refusal behavior. In the past people erroneously referred to this as "school phobia," but it is neither a "fear of school" nor a "phobia." Also, sometimes kids engage in school refusal for reasons unrelated to anxiety, because refusing to go to school provides gratification (e.g., it's a way to get attention, it's a way to be passively resistant to parents, it results in being able to watch TV and play video games at home).

Social Phobias

Social phobias in children and adolescents generally are expressed as excessive shyness and overwhelming anxiety in social circumstances where the child has to interact with or perform for children and/or adults that he or she doesn't know. Children and adolescents with social phobias tend to be quite self-deprecating and anticipate they will humiliate themselves and be rejected in social circumstances. Consequently, children with social phobia will do anything to avoid social situations. In school, they tend to be reclusive at recess and at mealtimes in the cafeteria, and when forced into social engagement, like during group activities or when asked to read or talk in front of the class, they may experience panic (Albano et al., 2003).

The fears that are characteristic of social phobia are pervasive. In other words, they are not occasional or temporary, nor do they just show up in some situations and not in others. Moreover, these fears are quite debilitating and impair healthy social, psychological, and educational development. Children with social phobia become isolated; they lack friends, won't join social groups or sports teams, and feel very lonely. Even at home or while with their family, children with social phobia tend to avoid any activity that might require social discourse, like picking up a ringing phone, responding to the doorbell, or visiting with extended family members (Albano et al., 2003). Similar to children with SAD, children and adolescents with social phobia frequently develop school refusal. Even when they force themselves to attend school, their anxiety hinders their ability to learn and achieve academically.

Generalized Anxiety Disorder

Unlike SAD and social phobia, **generalized anxiety disorder (GAD)** doesn't occur in response to any particular situation. As the name implies, it is a more global and indiscriminant type of anxiety. Children and adolescents with GAD worry *a lot*, in ways that are disproportionate and unrealistic, and they have a very hard time controlling or limiting their worries. In particular, children with GAD view life and the world as capricious and expect catastrophic consequences if they don't perform flawlessly. They lack security, are excessively concerned about the future and future events, and fear that their academic, athletic, and/or social accomplishments will be inadequate. These worries are accompanied by physical distress like headaches, stomachaches, fatigue, restlessness, muscle tension and cramps, and disturbed sleep; and by psychological discomforts like difficulty concentrating and irritability.

In school, children and adolescents with GAD are perfectionists—so much so that they drive themselves and those that care about them crazy with their obsessive need to be faultless. Nothing seems to console or reassure them, not even their own history of superb accomplishment. In spite of receiving frequent excellent grades, they continue to fear failure and are exceedingly self-punitive should they slip below their own standards (Albano et al., 2003). Eventually, the worry, the physical ailments, and the perfectionism intensify and handicap the child's ability to perform academically, socially, and psychologically.

What Can Teachers Do to Attend to Children's Anxiety?

Treating child anxieties can be quite complicated and frequently involves attending to maladaptive family dynamics. Many interventions employ behavioral or cognitive-behavioral strategies. As a teacher, you may be asked to cooperate with mental health professionals and parents by helping a child to monitor his or her anxious thoughts and feelings, to dispute his or her irrational beliefs, to accurately evaluate his or her performance, and to reinforce thoughts and behaviors that counter his or her anxiety and help to build adaptive social, psychological, and academic functioning. Also, as a teacher, you might be called upon to examine your own behavior to guard against unwittingly doing things that might be reinforcing the child's anxiety and the maladaptive behaviors that stem from it.

Teachers also find themselves having to contend with the realistic worries and concerns that children and adolescents have when traumatic events strike a community. Schools and educators are invaluable resources in these times. There are strategies that teachers can adopt, and recommend to parents, to help children and adolescents cope with their realistic concerns about the risks and dangers of today's world. For starters, restoring children's and adolescents' usual school routines following a disaster or crisis can help to reestablish a sense of regularity and predictability. Moreover, it is useful to encourage children and adolescents to reengage in recreational activities (e.g., playing, art, music, sports) because these are natural ways that children and adolescents use to "blow off steam" and cope with their anxieties.

Second, teachers need to assess to what extent they intend to address dramatic current events in their classrooms. Depending on the developmental maturity of a teacher's students, it may be useful to limit students' exposure in the classroom to repetitious news coverage and gory details. When it is appropriate and necessary to discuss anxiety-provoking events in the classroom, teachers need to remember that children and adolescents look to them (and other respected adults) for cues on how to respond to crises, and will respond more positively when their teachers are composed and reassuring. Validate children's and adolescents' feelings (don't dismiss or discount them) and especially respond with empathy. Answer questions simply and honestly, and address concerns in fairly concrete words and examples. But also express a positive and hopeful perspective: when talking about bad times, balance that out by also talking about the good times you expect in the future and how things can get better. Remind children and adolescents of ways and times in the past when they mastered challenges and worries, and encourage children to think of things they can do to contribute to improving the situation.

Lastly, teachers should look for opportunities to reassure children and adolescents during times of crisis. Sometimes it's useful to review and discuss safety plans and contingencies for what a child can do if he or she is at school or home alone when an emergency occurs (e.g., responding to fire drills, knowing a safe place to go to, making sure kids have proper identity and phone numbers of people they can call in an emergency). The good news is that most children have instinctive capacities for coping with stress and a little help will foster their natural buoyancy in the face of adversity.

Disruptive Behavior Disorders

Child and adolescent mental health problems are often classified as either internalizing or externalizing (Mash & Dozois, 2003). *Internalizing disorders* have symptomatic thoughts, feelings, behaviors, and physical complaints that are experienced primarily within the individual and include anxiety disorders (discussed previously) and mood disorders (to be discussed below, in the adolescence section). Because they are more privately experienced, other people often do not detect that a child with an internalizing disorder is having troubles until the problems become severe. Disruptive behavior disorders are *externalizing disorders*. Their primary symptoms are expressed in the social environment. Consequently, disruptive behavior disorders are quite public and relatively quickly detected. They are unique, in that the symptoms of disruptive behavior disorders are generally more troubling to other people than to the child who has the disorder. There are three types of disruptive behavior disorders; attention-deficit/hyperactivity disorder (ADHD), oppositional defiant disorder (ODD), and conduct disorder (CD).

Attention-Deficit/Hyperactivity Disorder

Perhaps no other child and adolescent mental health issue elicits more controversy than the diagnosis of **attention-deficit/hyperactivity disorder (ADHD).** Debates rage about whether the condition actually *exists* or whether it's a bias held by a society that is intolerant to people who are different; whether the condition is over- or underdiagnosed and treated (see the Considering Interesting Questions special feature [Box 12.1] for a discussion of this issue); and whether or not it is appropriate to use medications to control children's activity levels and other behaviors that are more troublesome to others than to the children diagnosed with ADHD. These and other controversies have become complicated and even muddled over the past 50 years as the diagnostic criteria for the condition has changed, as the theories of what causes ADHD have evolved, and as who is being asked to supply the information needed to confirm and validate the diagnosis is chosen.

ADHD-like conditions have been documented for over 100 years. There is little doubt that some children manifest considerable difficulties with attention and impulsivity that significantly detract from their ability to learn and develop optimal psy-

Considering Interesting Questions

BOX 12.1. Are Stimulant Medications Overprescribed for Attention-Deficit/Hyperactivity Disorder?

Recently, questions have been raised about whether or not children are overprescribed medications for attention-deficit/hyperactivity disorder (ADHD). Some authors (Breggin, 2001) argue that stimulant medications are not all always necessary and vastly overused for young children. Others argue just the opposite is true: that many children need medication as treatment for ADHD and don't receive it. It's quite possible that both of these positions are correct.

In some communities in the United States, particularly affluent communities with abundant health care, significant percentages of children are taking stimulant medication as a treatment for ADHD—sometimes far more than even the highest proposed incidence of ADHD. On the other hand, some communities in the United States, most notably poor, rural, and ethnic communities, lack adequate health care for children and families. Frequently, in these communities, stimulant medication to treat ADHD is not available to the children who could benefit from it. Estimates of stimulant medication treatment rates for ADHD in the United States range from 1.6% of children's prescriptions in the Washington, DC, area to 6.5% in the state of Louisiana

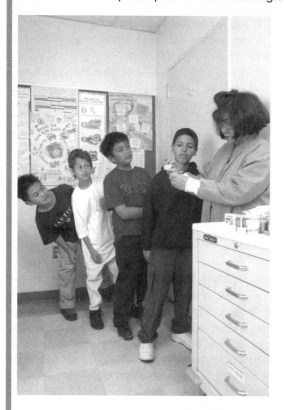

(Cox, Motheral, Henderson, & Mager, 2003). In general, significantly higher rates of medication for ADHD are reported in the South and the Midwest than in the West. Use of stimulant medication to treat ADHD is also higher in white children and children living in higher income areas (Cox, et al., 2003). Rate of medication as treatment for ADHD is effected by a range of factors including advertising by drug manufacturers, regional standards of physician practice, and parents' and teachers' values.

What is the role of teachers in this important and controversial issue? Clearly, teachers play a vital role in the diagnosis of ADHD. Medical professionals rely on detailed information about children's behavior in the classroom to help them make accurate diagnoses. Teachers are the best source for this information. It is important, however, for teachers to leave the decision to medicate to medical professionals. It is also important for educators to advocate for children and to help them receive the health care they need. Moreover, once a child is on medication, teachers need to carefully monitor and observe the child's behavior and possible side effects, provide appropriate instructional support, and be in close communication with parents.

Are stimulant medications overprescribed for attention-deficit/hyperactivity disorder?

chological functioning (Barkley, 2003). Currently, ADHD has two main classes of symptoms: developmentally inappropriate and sustained inattentiveness and developmentally inappropriate and sustained disinhibition in the form of impulsivity and hyperactivity (American Psychiatric Association, 1994). Inattentiveness may manifest itself in difficulty listening to and following through on instructions, carelessly done and/or incomplete work assignments, forgetfulness, distractibility, and disorganization. Hyperactivity and impulsivity are evident in the ADHD child's fidgeting, difficulty remaining seated, impulsive speech (talking excessively and frequently interrupting others), and inability to wait for his (or more rarely, her) turn. According to the current diagnostic standards (American Psychiatric Association, 1994), these symptoms must be present for at least 6 months to be relatively certain that the symptoms are an enduring pattern of behavior and not the consequence of some transitory developmental or environmental factor, and exist before the age of 7, since the developmental pathology is theoretically present by then and so the ADHD diagnosis does not get confused with other conditions that may occur later in life. Barkley (2003) argues that the age limit should be raised since some symptoms may not develop or be recognized until later than childhood and recommends that the symptoms be present for 12 months.

It's important to keep in mind that most children are not as attentive and are more active and impulsive than most adults. The ADHD diagnosis is based on whether the child's inattentiveness and activity level exceeds the norm of similarly aged children, not on whether adults feel the child's behavior is more than they can tolerate. The diagnosis can be complicated because children with ADHD don't display their symptoms in some situations. For example, during free play or at times when an adult is intensely monitoring or structuring behavior, many children with ADHD will be indistinguishable from non-ADHD children. On the other hand, the symptoms of a child with ADHD may be very noticeable in settings that require people to behave within restricted limits (e.g., fine arts performances, at church, while dining in restaurants). Also complicating the diagnosis are indications that some symptoms, principally those that have to do with disinhibition, may develop earlier or be noticed sooner than symptoms related to inattentiveness (Barkley, 2003). Consequently, some children who have ADHD may be mistaken for children who are oppositional or who have conduct disorder, and then, of course, some children with ADHD do qualify for these diagnoses.

Estimates of the prevalence rate for ADHD vary dramatically because different researchers use different diagnostic criteria, different sampling techniques, sample different populations and age groups, and use reports from different observers. The best guess is that ADHD occurs in about 4–6% of the population and is probably three times more common in boys (Barkley, 2003). ADHD has been found across socioeconomic status (SES) populations and cultural groups, although people of different cultures and nationalities are probably more or less tolerant of some ADHD symptoms and interpret the symptom criteria differently (Barkley, 2003).

Barkley (2003) has advanced a reconceptualization of what ADHD entails that theoretically explains the disparate symptoms seen in children with ADHD. Barkley's theory deemphasizes the role previously assigned to attention in describing the disorder and instead focuses on deficits in metacognitive and neurological executive functions that regulate self-control (see also Chapter 4). Briefly, Barkley hypothesizes that deficits in behavioral inhibition hinder the development of nonverbal working memory and the ability to use past experience to inform current behavior, the internalization of speech and hence verbal working memory, the use of language to self-regulate emotion and motivation, and the ability to mentally manipulate concepts that aids in organization and planning. These impairments, in turn, result in reduced motor control and reduced ability to sustain goal-directed activity.

As our theoretical and empirical understanding of ADHD advances, research on the etiology or cause of ADHD is also improving. The evidence to date suggests that ADHD develops as a consequence of neurological dysfunction that comes about largely hereditarily, but may also occur because of prenatal complications, exposure to environmental toxins, or some other disease process (Barkley, 2003). At one time people thought that children would outgrow or compensate for these neurological failings, but current research suggests that as many as 80% of children with ADHD continue to be symptomatic in adolescence and a substantial proportion of children diagnosed with ADHD continue to manifest symptoms into adulthood (Barkley, 2003). Even when specific ADHD symptoms abate as a child develops, many of the sequelae of ADHD persist, including poorer academic and vocational achievement, social difficulties, parental conflict, and poorer physical health.

Earl-Onset Conduct Disorder and Oppositional Defiant Disorder

Conduct disorder (CD) is defined as a persistent pattern of unacceptable social behavior that violates the rights of others and basic societal norms and rules. Children with conduct disorder are not simply naughty or troublesome; they are children who consistently commit delinquent acts. In many respects they are incorrigible and often a menace to other children and adults. The symptoms that characterize CD vary some depending on the age of the child. Elementary school-age children with CD are constantly disobedient and defiant; they may lie and steal, and they may be especially aggressive, bulling other children and tormenting animals. Older children and adolescents with conduct disorder will exhibit these behaviors in addition to engaging in truancy, running away from home, destruction of property, substance abuse, and inappropriate sexual behavior. It is important to keep in mind that many children may engage in some of these behaviors from time to time, but they will only warrant a diagnosis of CD if they *repeatedly* engage in these behaviors for longer than 6 months.

There are two types of CD: one type begins in adolescence, and the second type begins prior to age 10. Developmental psychopathologists suspect that the two types of CD often have different etiologies and outcomes (Compas, Hinden, & Gerhardt, 1995) and that early-onset CD may be especially insidious (Christophersen & Mortweet, 2001; Hinshaw & Lee, 2003). It is hard to pin down exactly how many children have CD, in part because researchers from different disciplines use different definitions and interpret the criteria for CD differently. However, prior to puberty, 2–8% of boys and up to 2% of girls may qualify for a diagnosis of CD. In adolescence, 3–11% of boys and 1–8% of girls may have CD (Christophersen & Mortweet, 2001; Hinshaw & Lee, 2003). More boys than girls are diagnosed with CD, although we are only beginning to learn about CD in girls (Chamberlain & Moore, 2002; Hoyt & Scherer, 1998).

In contrast to CD, the symptoms of **oppositional defiant disorder (ODD)** are less severe, although just as pervasive. The disobedience that characterizes ODD is exhibited in the form of uncooperativeness, argumentativeness, disrespect, and/or insolence toward authority, and a generally negative mood (e.g., frequently angry, easily annoyed). Children with ODD have difficulty controlling their temper, frequently become enraged, and sometimes tantrum wildly. Other children sometimes avoid children with ODD because they perceive them as difficult to get along with, stubborn, and mean. Once again, these symptoms must be consistently present for more than 6 months to warrant this diagnosis. Because it is quite common for *some* children to have *some* of these symptoms *some* of the time, the symptoms must be far in excess of what similarly aged children exhibit, and not just attributable to a normal developmental phase like the "terrible twos" or adolescent "rebellion" and autonomy seeking.

Once again the prevalence rates for ODD are inexact. Some say 5–10% (Fonagy & Kurtz, 2002), others say 2–16% (American Psychiatric Association, 1994) of children warrant a diagnosis of ODD. Some developmental psychopathologists suspect that ODD is a mild variant or an incipient form of CD since about 80% of children with CD qualified for a diagnosis of ODD (Hinshaw & Lee, 2003). However, only about 25% of children with ODD ever develop CD (Barkley, 1997). Also, keep in mind that many children with ODD and CD also have other mental health conditions and qualify for ADHD, learning disability, mood disorder, anxiety disorder, and substance abuse disorder diagnoses (Barkley, 1997; Hinshaw & Lee, 2003).

A child can acquire or develop ODD or CD in a variety of ways. Some children, particularly those with early onset of these disorders, may be genetically or temperamentally inclined toward behavioral problems. For others, it's the consequence of exposure to familial or community risk factors like poverty; parental inadequacies due to criminality or parental mental illness; abusive, critical, hostile, and/or inconsistent parenting; and/or antisocial gang or peer influence. Regardless of the cause, untreated ODD and CD can have serious negative lifetime consequences including poor academic and vocational achievement, rejection by peers, addictions, depression, and suicide (Barkley, 1997).

What Can Teachers Do to Assess and Intervene for Disruptive Behavior Disorders?

A proper assessment and intervention plan for disruptive behavior disorders will be multimodal in nature. That means that the evaluator will use a variety of assessment tools and seek input from several sources familiar with the child, including the child, his or her parent, and his or her teacher(s). Teachers are typically interviewed by evaluators, and asked to complete some rating scales. The evaluator may ask to come to the classroom to observe the targeted child and may ask to see examples of the child's work. The evaluator typically ask teachers to provide examples of the child's problem behavior and the context in which it occurs, what precedes the problem behavior, how often it happens, and what the teacher has done in response to the child's behavior.

When a child is diagnosed with a disruptive behavior disorder, teachers have an important role in implementing the treatment plan. One effective means of treating the symptoms of ADHD is through the use of stimulant medications (Fonagy, Target, Cottrell, Phillips, & Kurtz, 2002). Still, some children do not respond favorably to stimulant medications, and for some children with ADHD medications are not enough to change some of the academic and social consequences of ADHD. For children who have just ODD/CD there are few, if any, pharmacological options. So teachers are called upon to cooperate with the child's parents and other treatment team members in implementing a behavioral intervention. A good behavioral intervention will take a positive approach that emphasizes building the child's academic and social competence by recognizing and praising the child when target behaviors are generated. A number of techniques may be employed such as a token reinforcement system that prescribes how to monitor and respond to targeted competencies as well as maladaptive behaviors (see also Chapter 5), frequent teaching and review of classroom rules and expectations, and strategy training, in addition to developing individualized instructional strategies (Christopherson & Mortweet, 2001; DuPaul & Stoner, 2003; Fonagy et al., 2002). Two books written for parents of children with ADHD and ODD that teachers may find useful themselves or may want to recommend to parents are Barkley (2000) and Barkley and Benton (1998), respectively.

Finally, as outlined in Chapter 9, teachers can employ instructional practices that are supportive of students with behavior disorders such as ADHD (McConnell, Ryser, & Higgins, 2000; Rief, 2003). Fortunately, these instructional techniques are also effective with all students. These include the following:

- Provide clear, simple directions.
- Limit distractions.
- Include frequent breaks (particularly ones allowing physical outlets).
- Reduce transition time.
- Promote self-regulation and self-instruction.
- Provide structure for presented content (graphic organizers, visual information, etc.).

Educators looking for in-depth discussion of assessment and intervention with students with disruptive behavior disorders should consult Barkley (1997) and/or Barkley, Edwards, and Robin (1999) regarding ODD/CD and DuPaul and Stoner (2003) and/or view DuPaul and Stoner's (1999a, 1999b) videos regarding ADHD.

■ ■ ■ PSYCHOLOGICAL PROBLEMS THAT ARE PREVALENT DURING ADOLESCENCE

Adolescence has been characterized as a period of storm and stress. Adolescents frequently are depicted as addled by hormones, fickle, difficult to get along with, and rebellious. This portrayal is more of a reflection of the ambivalence and intimidation adults feel about youth than a reality. If we stop to think about it (or just pay attention to the news), adults frequently do the very same things they complain about in regard to adolescents (e.g., risk taking, substance use, moodiness). It is probably more accurate to conceptualize adolescence as an artifact of social engineering (i.e., the enactment of child labor laws, the development of the juvenile justice system, and the advent of compulsory education), rather than a universally experienced psychological stage. Moreover, most adolescents do not experience tumultuous psychological upheaval, identity crisis, or alienation from their parents and family (see Chapters 5 and 10). In fact, most adolescents find considerable identity and security through their involvements with their families. It does appear that adolescents spend less time engaged in daily family routines, but not because they are repelled by processes internal to the family or adolescent, but because of pulls or incentives from the external social environment (e.g., sports, jobs). As a rule of thumb, conflict with parents reaches its height in early adolescence and typically involves struggles around minor autonomy issues and not about core substantive values. Most older adolescents and young adults report feeling warmth and mutual respect for their parents and recognize they bear some responsibility for family interactions.

Still, it is obvious that adolescents go through fairly major developmental transitions, including physiological, neurological, cognitive, and social changes. These changes, along with less than optimal social environmental conditions, create risks for adolescent mental health problems. For example, early sexual maturation for girls is sometimes linked with poorer body image, dieting, ridicule from less mature peers, and associating with older adolescents and age-inappropriate activities that they are not mentally or emotionally mature enough to handle, such as experimenting with drugs or sexual encounters (see also Chapter 2). Adolescents may suffer from the psychological problems already discussed in this chapter or they may qualify for any number of other psychological diagnoses that are used in identifying adult psychopathology. It is beyond the scope of this chapter to describe all the possible psychological maladies that can befall adolescents; instead, the focus here will be on two common and critical concerns: adolescent substance abuse and depression. See the Considering Interesting Questions special feature (Box 12.2) for a discussion of the prevalence of eating disorders in adolescents.

Adolescent Substance Misuse

Adolescents with substance misuse problems are diagnosed using the same criteria that are used for adults. The more serious type of substance use disorder is *substance dependence*, which is characterized by maladaptive substance use despite experiencing physiological symptoms (e.g., tolerance for the drug and taking larger amounts for a longer time, withdrawal symptoms when the drug is not being used) and psychological problems (e.g., repeated unsuccessful attempts to diminish the drug use, inordinate time spent on substance use or recovery, drug use interfering with obligations at home, work, or school; using the substance when it is known to be physically hazardous or dangerous) during the previous year (American Psychiatric Association, 1994). In some literature this is called *chemical dependency*, or *addiction*. Substance abuse is diagnosed when an individual's drug use causes him or her to suffer social and psychological consequences during the previous year, like failing to meet work, school, or family obligations, using drugs when it is physically hazardous to do so, encountering legal problems related to substance use, and continuing to use the substance despite its deleterious impact on interpersonal relationships (American Psychiatric Association, 1994). Because of the adult standards implicit in these criteria, and despite the prolific use of drugs by adolescents, only about 2–4% of adolescents qualify for a substance use diagnosis.

However, the statistics regarding adolescent substance misuse are (or at least should be) incredibly alarming, even though there have been modest decreases in adolescent substance use in the past few years (Johnston, O'Malley, Bachman, & Schulenberg, 2004). Consider first the use of licit substances: alcohol and nicotine, the so-called gateway drugs. Estimates from the Monitoring the Future Survey (MTF; Johnston et al., 2004), a sample of 48,500 eighth-, 10th-, and 12th-grade volunteers in

Considering Interesting Questions

BOX 12.2. How Prevalent are Eating Disorders in Teenage Girls?

Every few years, public awareness of the problem of eating disorders increases, usually because a high-profile celebrity admits to a problem with an eating disorder and seeks treatment. How much should teachers be concerned about eating disorders in their middle-school and high-school students?

There are different kinds of eating disorders and they are most commonly found in females, with only 5–10% of all cases of eating disorders found in males (Committee on Adolescence, 2003). One type, **anorexia nervosa,** is manifested when people stop eating and frequently exercise to excess. Other symptoms of anorexia include loss of dramatic amounts of weight (15% below ideal weight), a refusal to maintain normal weight, a fear of gaining weight, a distorted body image, and lack of menstrual cycles. This disorder actually occurs in less that one-half of 1% of the population, primarily among girls, though some incidence is found in boys who participate in sports with weight restrictions such as wrestling and rock climbing. While anorexia is a serious disorder that is difficult to treat and often requires hospitalization, it is not particularly common.

Somewhat more common is an eating disorder called **bulimia,** sometimes referred to by its most salient characteristics as "binge-and-purge" syndrome. Symptoms of bulimia include binge eating, purging (more than twice a week), and body image problems. Bulimia can create substantial medical complications as a side effect of the frequent regurgitation. Like anorexia, bulimia occurs much more frequently in girls. Sometimes substantially higher rates of bulimia are found in populations of college-age girls living in close proximity such as in dormitories or sororities. It is also not uncommon for some girls to occasionally engage in the binge-and-purge symptoms of bulimia but full-fledged bulimia is estimated to occur in only 1–5% of the population (Committee on Adolescence, 2003).

Although these two eating disorders are relatively uncommon, concerns about weight and body image are very common among teenage girls. Some estimates are that more than two-thirds of high-school girls diet regularly, suggesting elevated concern about weight and appearance (Calderon, Yu, & Jambazian, 2004; Gordon, 2000; Story, Neumark-Sztainer, Sherwood, Stang, & Murray, 1998). A variety of theories have been proposed about why eating disorders occur. One predominant theory is the focus of U.S. culture, as exemplified in media, on unrealistic standards of thinness.

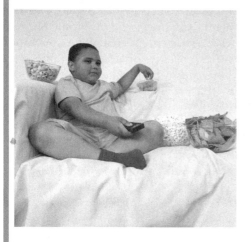

Perhaps the most common weight problem in U.S. children, however, is obesity. Children in the United States eat many more calories than they expend. The ready availability of high-caloric food, bombardment of enticing food images in the media, and generally sedentary lifestyles have resulted in a populace that is overweight. The problem of obesity has major social and physical implications for children and is two to three times more common across all race and ethnic groups than in the 1970s (Koplan, Liverman, & Kraak, 2005). *Obesity* is defined as an excessively high amount of body fat in relation to lean body mass (Stunkard & Wadden, 1993). Although methods for determining obesity in children and adolescents vary, the best estimate is that about 17% of these age groups are obese (Centers for Disease Control and Prevention, 2006).

Obesity is perhaps the most prevalent health problem found in school-age children.

(continued)

> In closing, in the realm of eating disorders, teachers of middle-school and high-school students will most commonly encounter students who are overweight, sedentary, and unhealthy. Many of these students will be experiencing the beginnings of serious health problems related to their obesity such as Type 2 diabetes. In addition, teachers will also encounter teenage girls who find their bodies unacceptable and are making poor nutritional choices as they engage in one fad diet plan after another.

392 schools throughout the United States in 2003, indicate that 77% of high school seniors admit to some use of alcohol during their lifetime, 70% in the year prior to being asked, and almost 43% in the 30 days prior to being asked. Fifty-eight percent of seniors indicate they have been drunk at least once in their lifetime; 31% admit to being drunk some time in the 30 days prior to being asked. Younger adolescents are also in the act; 46% of eighth graders in 2003 indicated they had used alcohol in their lifetime, and 20% admitted to being drunk. Ten percent of eighth graders and 24% of 12th graders disclose they are current cigarette smokers.

The statistics from the MTF study regarding illicit drug use (i.e., marijuana, amphetamines and methamphetamines, tranquilizers, hallucinogens, narcotics, cocaine and crack, and club drugs like Rohypnol, GHB, and ketamine) are similarly grim. Fifty-one percent of 12th graders in 2003 divulged they have used some illicit drug during their lifetime, 39% in the year prior to being asked, and 24% in the 30 days prior to being asked. Since 80–90% of high school seniors reported that marijuana is easy to procure and because it is the most commonly abused illicit drug, the MTF study asked high-school students about their illicit drug use other than marijuana to get an estimate of "harder drug" use. Twenty-eight percent of 12th graders indicated using an illicit drug other than marijuana, nearly 20% in the year prior to being surveyed, and 10% in the 30 days prior to being surveyed. The use of illicit drugs by youth in the United States in the past 30–40 years has been exceptionally high compared to other times in history and compared to other nations (Johnston et al., 2004). If only a fraction of adolescents and young adults continue their substance use and abuse into adulthood, our society could be facing a serious public health problem. In the 1990s, the expense of underage drinking alone exceeded $52 billion, including substance abuse treatment, prevention, other health-care costs, and the costs of crime (Levy, Miller, & Cox, 1999).

What leads to adolescents engaging in substance misuse? There are no simple answers to this question. There are undoubtedly many different paths that result in adolescent substance abuse, depending on an individual's age at onset, gender, family environment, and cultural and socioeconomic background (Chasin, Ritter, Trim, & King, 2003). Family factors seem to play a large role, both through genetic inheritance and socialization. Prenatal and childhood exposure to drugs, particularly alcohol and nicotine, may predispose an individual toward their use. Children with difficult temperaments, who are inclined toward behavioral undercontrol, especially when coupled with inadequate parenting, are at greater risk for developing substance use disorders. Poor academic achievement and estrangement from the positive socializing influences of school can exacerbate an inclination toward substance misuse. Regardless of the cause, the effects of adolescent substance abuse are potentially profound. Adolescent substance abusers generally achieve less academically and vocationally. They tend to be more alienated from family and prosocial peers, which leads to greater family conflict, having more associations with deviant peers, and a tendency to engage in delinquency. Lastly, and perhaps obviously, adolescents who engage in substance misuse are at greater risk for developing substance addictions.

Mood Disorders

Adolescent Depression

There are different types of mood disorders. Some mood disorders have very serious and unpleasant symptoms that come on quickly, others have less serious symptoms that develop gradually but endure for a long time. Some types of mood disorders are "bipolar," which means that the depressed person has had some variation in their mood; sometimes they feel depressed, and at least once, and maybe repeatedly, they experienced an episode of mania in which they became uncontrollably excited. In recent years there has been a flurry of interest in bipolar disorders and controversy regarding the extent to which children and adolescents suffer from them. Bipolar disorders probably begin during childhood and adolescence, but it can be very difficult to confirm the diagnosis and distinguish it from other more common juvenile disorders, and it is probably relatively uncommon (perhaps a 1% prevalence rate) (Hammen & Rudolph, 2003). Consequently, this discussion focuses on the more common "unipolar" depressions, of which there are two types: the more severe major depressive disorder (MDD) and the more chronic dysthmic disorder (DD).

Some of the symptoms of MDD and DD are emotional, some are behavioral/physiological, and some are cognitive. Feeling sad or dysphoric, anhedonia (the loss of interest or pleasure in usual activities), apathy, a sense of hopelessness, and feelings of worthlessness comprise the emotional symptoms of depression. Behavioral/physiological symptoms include sleep disturbance (i.e., insomnia or sleeping too much), feeling anxious and agitated or alternatively feeling lethargic and fatigued, appetite changes that result in rapid weight gain or weight loss, and neglecting hygiene and appearance. In addition, depression also affects peoples' cognitive abilities. People with depression may experience a diminished ability to think or concentrate; they may be overly pessimistic, excessively guilty, and self-denigrating; ruminate over negative events and consider suicide or actually attempt suicide; and when depression is exceedingly severe, they may experience delusions and hallucinations. A diagnosis of MDD is considered when a person feels deep and constant dysphoria in addition to experiencing intense distress from several of the more serious symptoms (especially the behavioral/physiological) for more than 2 weeks. Dysthmic disorder is the more appropriate diagnosis when a child or adolescent experiences only one or two of these symptoms and they don't cause quite as much distress, although they are chronic and never diminish much over the course of 1 year. The kinds of symptoms of depression that children and adolescents have tend to be different, or are at least expressed differently, than the symptoms adults complain about (Fonagy et al., 2002; Hammen & Rudolph, 2003). Children tend to experience fewer behavioral/physiological symptoms of depression; they are unlikely to say they feel hopeless or melancholy and they're more inclined to be irritable and to express somatic complaints (e.g., stomachache, headache). Adolescents, particularly older adolescents, are likely to have symptoms that are more like adults (Fonagy et al., 2002), although they too are more likely to be irritable, to be aggressive, and to complain about boredom.

Full-blown diagnosable depression is relatively infrequent in children—perhaps less than a 3% prevalence rate (Fonagy et al., 2002; Hammen & Rudolph, 2003). However, the prevalence of depression in adolescents is similar to what is found in adults; about 14% of adolescents have had MDD and 11% of adolescents have had DD, and these rates seem to be increasing (Hammen & Rudolph, 2003). Moreover, large proportions of adolescents (more than 20%, maybe as many as 35–40%) have experienced a troublesome depressed mood that is "subclinical," or in other words, doesn't last long enough or that's not quite serious enough to be formally diagnosable as depression (Compas, Ey, & Grant, 1993; Hammen & Rudolph, 2003). More than two times as many girls as boys are diagnosed with depression (Fonagy et al., 2002; Hammen & Rudolph, 2003). Depression in children and adolescents is an internalizing disorder; the symptoms are somewhat self-contained, particularly compared to the disruptive behavior disorders. As a result, child and adolescent depression is not always recognized and treated. To complicate matters even more, between 40 and 70% of children and adolescents with depression also have some other diagnosable psychological problem, especially anxiety, and lots of times ADHD, substance use disorders, or eating disorders (Fonagy et al., 2002; Hammen & Rudolph, 2003). Sometimes these other disorders get attention, but the underlying depression is missed.

Depression can have very negative consequences for child and adolescent development (Fonagy et al., 2002; Hammen & Rudolph, 2003). DD can last 2, 3, 4, or more years, and even though it's the milder form of depression, its chronic nature can result in considerable deterioration in adolescent psychological growth and adjustment. Moreover, if it goes untreated, it can flare up into MDD. MDD can last for 6 months to a year, longer if untreated, and has symptoms that are devastating to adolescents' academic achievement, social development, and psychological adjustment. For example, about 60% of depressed children and adolescents contemplate suicide (Hammen & Rudolph, 2003). Children and adolescents who develop depression are much more likely to experience mood disorders in adulthood and as many as 7% of adolescents who develop major depression commit suicide in adulthood. Children and adolescents who receive proper treatment often recover from depression, but unfortunately many relapse and have repeated bouts of depression.

Many things can cause depression in children and adolescents. Evidence exists that a predisposition for mood disorders can be genetically inherited, particularly the bipolar disorders. Moreover, exposure to unremitting anxiety and/or chronic subclinical depression can ultimately lead to physiological and neurological changes that result in mood disorders. Many, perhaps most, adolescents acquire depression through exposure to social and psychological stressors like traumatic events; poor family relationships (e.g., parental unavailability, disturbed parent–child interactions, family and marital violence); poor, sometimes abusive, peer relationships; and self- or other-imposed pressures to achieve in academics, athletics, or some other activity.

Adolescent Suicide

Suicide is rather rare among children under age 12 (Fonagy et al., 2002), but it is the third leading cause of death among adolescents and young adults. Estimates suggest that between eight and 12 of every 100,000 adolescents (depending on the age range used) commits suicide (American Association of Suicidology, 2006; National Institute of Mental Health, 2003). This is probably an underestimate; perhaps three times as many adolescent deaths are a consequence of self-destructive behavior (Fonagy et al., 2002). Suicide is more common in adolescent boys than girls and more prevalent, or increasing in prevalence, among some populations, particularly gay, lesbian, and bisexual youth, black males, and some American Indian tribes. For every adolescent who commits suicide, as many as 40 to 100 times more attempt it, often repeatedly (Fonagy et al., 2002). In 1999, 20% of adolescent admitted they had contemplated suicide in the previous year (American Association of Suicidology, 2006), and other research has found more than 50% of adolescents claiming to have thought about suicide at one time (Fonagy et al., 2002).

What Can Teachers Do to Support and Assist Troubled Adolescents?

The important message for educators who work with adolescents is that a sizeable proportion of the students they interact with have serious psychological problems. As many as 20–30% are using drugs and/or alcohol on a fairly regular basis. For many of these students, their substance use is not just "normative" drug exploration; it is debilitating abuse that is hindering their development and their capacity to learn and be fully engaged in the academic process. As many as 20% of middle- and high-school students are clinically depressed, and many middle- and high-school students are contemplating suicide.

Treatment for these conditions is quite complicated and beyond the scope of this chapter. Many of these adolescents need medical attention (e.g., detox, medication) and therapy delivered by skilled specialists in adolescent psychology, family dynamics, and substance abuse. Still, it is a giant mistake for teachers to assume there is nothing they can do to address the mental health concerns of adolescents. The worst thing teachers (and other adults for that matter) can do is try to ignore these problems.

To begin with, teachers need to be caring observers of adolescents and know the warning signs of substance abuse, mood disorder, and possible suicidal risk. See the Applying Developmental Theory to Educational Contexts special feature (Box 12.3).

Second, teachers should take action when they observe these warning signs. Many adolescents are quite naïve about mental health issues and may not recognize their troubles as mental health concerns. Moreover, adolescents often associate a great stigma with talking to a counselor; it suggests they might be crazy or weak. So troubled adolescents frequently don't initiate help-seeking behavior. On the other hand, if a teacher or counselor approaches them privately, they are more apt to talk about their problems and concerns. If you don't feel comfortable or qualified to talk with a troubled student, alert another teacher, counselor, or school administrator about the problem.

Last, be bold and be active in the lives of adolescents. Encourage adolescents to develop strong bonds to their school, to be polite and caring to one another, and to develop prosocial and wholesome friendships. Talk with them about drug abuse and encourage abstinence from alcohol and other substance use. Teach them how to be assertive in declining drug use should their peers offer it. Help adolescents develop healthy habits, like regular exercise, good nutrition, and getting sufficient sleep.

Teachers play an important role in the lives of the children and adolescents they educate. Teachers' access to children and adolescents and their knowledge about

---

Applying Developmental Theory to Educational Contexts

BOX 12.3. Warning Signs of Substance Abuse, Mood Disorder, and Suicide Risk

Teachers are in a unique position to observe adolescents in everyday activities. Thus they may have the best opportunity to observe the warning signs of substance abuse, mood disorder, and suicide risk. The indications of substance misuse vary, depending on what drug is being ingested. The following are some major warning signs of substance abuse for teachers (and parents) to note:

- Loss of interest in school
- Irritability, nervousness, tremors
- Drug paraphernalia
- Careless hygiene
- Always tired, drowsiness
- Frequently needing money
- Loss or change of friends
- Impaired mental functioning, confusion, and memory loss
- Specific physical signs
  Bloodshot eyes (cocaine/marijuana)
  Runny nose (cocaine)
  Sleeplessness (meth/cocaine)
  Sensitivity to noise (meth)
  Nervousness (meth/cocaine)
  Slowed respiration (opiates)
  Constricted pupils (opiates)

Warning signs of a mood disorder and possible suicidal risk include:

- Appearing sad, anxious, and/or irritable
- Talking about being worthless and/or hopeless
- Changes in behavior such as social withdrawal
- Declining school performance
- Uncharacteristic acting-out behavior or aggression
- Changes in appearance such as poor hygiene or sudden weight gain or loss
- Constant fatigue, sleep disturbance

---

human development put them in an excellent position to detect children and adolescents who are troubled and to refer them to the mental health services they need. The more teachers know, the more they can get involved; so study children and the troubles they can encounter, stay alert, and get involved. Sure you may make mistakes, but you might also make a significant difference in the life of a student.

■ ■ ■ CHAPTER SUMMARY AND EVALUATION

When trying to assess student behavior, teachers and educators need to keep in mind both the quantity and the quality of the behavior as well as the context in which the behavior occurs. Nonetheless, it is very likely that educators will have contact with students suffering from a variety of mental health problems. Some of these problems, such as pervasive autism and Asperger's syndrome are typically first detected in early childhood. Children with autism exhibit severe deficits in social interaction, greatly impaired communication, and generally poor intellectual functioning. Similar to children with autism, children with Asperger's syndrome display social deficits but do not exhibit the same level of impairment in language and intellectual functioning.

Other mental health issues often do not emerge until the elementary-school years. Some children experience great difficulties with anxiety disorders such as separation anxiety disorder, social phobia, and generalized anxiety disorder. Children with attention-deficit/hyperactivity disorder exhibit difficulty paying attention as well as hyperactivity and impulsivity. Children with conduct disorders repeatedly engage in unacceptable social behavior.

Still other mental health problems, such as substance abuse, depression, and suicide, are more typically encountered in adolescents than in younger children. These problems are by no means rare, with substantial percentages of high-school students reporting substance abuse, more than 20% reporting depression, and about 60% of these depressed students reporting having considered suicide.

Developmental Debates

The mental health topics discussed in this chapter can be considered in terms of the debates first introduced in Chapter 1.

Nature versus Nurture

Some of the developmental disorders described in this chapter are almost certainly biologically determined. For example, there is every indication that autism, Asperger's syndrome, or nonverbal learning disorders have some biological underpinnings, most likely due to differences in brain development. It is also likely that some mood disorders, particularly bipolar disorder, are genetically determined. Moreover, children with robust temperaments, which is also most likely biologically determined, are less vulnerable to developing some of the mental health problems described in this chapter.

Trait-Like Consistency versus Situational Variability

It is important to remember that many situations are more unsettling for children and adolescents than adults because they lack the social and emotional maturity of adults. In addition, many behaviors of children and adolescents are situation-specific and do not occur in all situations. In fact, one theme of this chapter is for educators to always consider the context in which the problem behavior occurs. Moreover, factors beyond the control of children and adolescents can place situational stress on children and adolescents which, in turn, profoundly impacts their mental health. These include family disruption and divorce, child abuse, and alcoholism or mental health problems within the family.

■■■ REVIEW OF KEY TERMS

anorexia nervosa An eating disorder characterized by dramatic loss of weight, refusal to maintain normal weight, and distorted body image.

Asperger's syndrome Children with Asperger's syndrome, who are often average or above average in intellectual abilities, exhibit a variety of symptoms, including awkwardness in social interactions and complex and serious difficulties in learning.

attention-deficit/hyperactivity disorder (ADHD) Students with ADHD exhibit a variety of symptoms including inattentiveness, distractibility, hyperactivity, and impulsivity.

autistic disorder A mental disorder characterized by a variety of symptoms including deficits in social interaction, impairments in communications, and a limited repertoire of activity and interests.

bulimia An eating disorder characterized by binge eating, purging, and body image problems.

conduct disorder (CD) A persistent pattern of unacceptable behavior that violates basic social norms.

generalized anxiety disorder (GAD) Children with GAD express a global and indiscriminant type of anxiety.

oppositional defiant disorder (ODD) Children with ODD are argumentative, disrespectful, and express generally negative moods, including tantrums. These patterns of behavior, although less extreme than those exhibited by children with conduct disorder, persist for more than 6 months.

separation anxiety disorder (SAD) Children with SAD express extreme anxiety and agitation when separated or anticipating separation from attachment figures.

CHAPTER 13

Integrative Review
of Major Concepts

Anyone who writes a textbook on human development faces a dilemma from the outset. Development can be written about from either a chronological or a topical perspective. In a chronological approach, each chapter would focus on a specific period of development (e.g., infancy, early childhood, middle childhood, and adolescence). This text used a more topical approach in that each chapter focused on some important aspect of development, such as biological development, cognitive development, language development, motivation, development, and so on. Because of the sheer amount of information and the complexity of the ideas represented, we believed it was best to take the topical approach to address each important aspect of development in turn. A chronological overview, however, does have merits. So, in this review chapter, we put some of the big ideas together in a brief chronological overview of development. After this chronological review of many of the concepts covered in this book, we review the mechanisms of development, especially as they determine individual differences within developmental levels. If you do not understand any of the points made in this review chapter, you may find it helpful to reread relevant portions of the earlier chapters.

■ ■ ■ THE MAJOR PERIODS OF DEVELOPMENT

Because this text focused on these developmental ideas that would be most important to future educators, developmental concepts particularly significant in childhood and adolescence were emphasized in comparison to those key to infancy and adulthood. As we summarize the major points of the text in the chronological review, we cannot resist presenting some new information in special boxed features to bolster the case that intimate ties exist between education and development.

Prenatal Development

When an egg and sperm unite, a unique combination of DNA is created, with half of the DNA coming from the egg and half from the sperm. In a very real sense, this combination of DNA goes far in determining development. Most critically, it specifies that the organism that is beginning with this single cell is decidedly human. The billions and billions of developments that occur for all humans are specified by this DNA. Typically, however, educators are not interested in DNA's contribution to the *common* developments that define humans as much as they are interested in the role of DNA in determining *differences* between humans. Many differences between humans are determined in large part by genetics. Whether any such differences are determined entirely by genetics, however, is typically difficult and often impossible to determine. The dimension of difference that has received the most attention is intelligence as defined by psychometric intelligence, with some behavior geneticists contending that intelligence is determined by genetics more than anything else. Others believe that environment plays a larger role. We return to the subject of the potential role of genes in determining individual differences later in this chapter.

The single cell that is the merger of egg and sperm quickly divides and becomes multiple cells, with the cellular origins of all major organ systems occurring in the first 3 months of the prenatal period. Because so many systems begin during this first trimester, this is a period of time that is especially susceptible to the potential negative effects of teratogens. That is, various environmental agents (e.g., chemicals, radiation) and disease can affect development at the cellular level at this stage in ways that may have profound negative effects.

The cellular beginnings of organ systems are followed by rapid development of the organs themselves through cell division and then organ growth. Normal growth during the prenatal period is affected by factors such as the nutrition and health of the mother. Normal growth and development is a fragile commodity. It is for this reason that there is so much emphasis on prenatal care and on the education of adolescent girls about responsible lifestyles during pregnancy. For example, as harmful as drug intake, smoking, or alcohol abuse is to any female teenager, such abuses have much greater potential for negative impact on her developing fetus.

Much has been learned about prenatal development, and especially about brain development, in recent decades. Since we suspect that educators will eventually make stronger connections to this expanding literature on prenatal development than they do currently, textbooks on development specialized for educators will eventually include even more information about development before birth.

Infancy

The physical development of the brain continues following birth, although no new brain cells are formed after birth. Indeed, much of brain growth is accomplished by brain cell loss, that is, by elimination of excess capacity.

The concept of "critical period" has become better understood in recent decades. It is now clear that there are experience-expectant brain cells that require stimulation of a particular type at a particular point in development if they are to function normally for the rest of life. Perceptual development, in particular, has been shown to depend very much on appropriate sensory stimulation during infancy. If the needed stimulation does not occur, the capacity is lost forever.

Major areas of the brain become functional as the brain increases in weight and size, with discernible changes in behavior as a function of such brain maturation. For example, the frontal lobe develops a great deal in the first year of life, which is associated with increases in self-regulation skills as well as the development of understandings such as object permanency.

During infancy, and throughout life, brain growth tends to occur in spurts, which translates into discontinuous growth of thinking abilities and emotions. Brain growth is especially rapid during infancy, although the brain will continue to increase in size and weight into adolescence. The efficiency of the central nervous system increases because of development of myelin sheathing, the fatty tissue that insulates nerve cells, and thereby allows faster and more certain transmission of nerve impulses.

Piaget felt that thinking as an internal activity hardly existed during early infancy. That is, he described infants' reactions to their environment as much more *reflexive* than *reflective*. The beginnings of cognition, however, develop during the first 2 years of life, during what Piaget termed the "sensorimotor stage." Infants gradually develop the understanding that objects continue to exist even when they are out of sight (i.e., object permanence). Moreover, symbolic functioning emerges (i.e., the beginnings of language) by the end of the sensorimotor period.

Nonetheless, babies communicate long before they have language. From their earliest days, babies cry differently depending on their need. For example, sudden fright elicits a different cry than slight physical discomfort. Babies also smile differentially, often smiling in reaction to the presence of another human. Babies are biased to attend to social stimuli—for example, to look at perceptual displays that resemble faces and to listen to high-pitched voices, such as mother's voice.

Cognitive scientists have focused on several specific communicative developments that underpin language development. Thus, it is now known that during the first year of life infants come to discriminate speech sounds in the surrounding sound environment from other sounds. In particular, they learn to discriminate the phonemes in their family's and community's language from other sounds. Infants also learn to discriminate the rhythm of language from other rhythms. As speech perception increases, the production of sounds consistent with the surrounding language also increases. Thus babbling during the first year is increasingly filled with sounds that are characteristic of the language the child hears daily. During the second year of life, most children will have entered the single-word stage, with their single-word utterances serving a variety of functions. For example, the utterance "Mommy" can mean "Mommy come here," "Don't do that Mommy," or "I prefer Mommy." The exact meaning sometimes must be inferred from context clues and voice intonation.

That infant utterances can express complex meanings is consistent with the conclusion that by the end of infancy thought is complex. One of the most important discoveries in the past decade or so is that infant thinking is schematic. Thus the 2-year-old has substantial understanding about the events and settings she or he has experienced frequently, with these schematic representations providing a basis for expectations about the present. For example, many U.S. 2-year-olds know exactly what to expect from a visit to McDonald's. That children's schematic knowledge is so much more complex than their language is consistent with one of Vygotsky's key points: thought and language emerge separately. While in adulthood thought very much depends on language, thought and language are not so intimately connected during infancy.

Schematic knowledge develops largely because of social interactions, and, as it does, it affects future social interactions. Thus a mother who is consistently responsive to her child affects the child's representation of the mother–infant relationship and the infant's expectations about how his or her mother will react in the future. An infant who has experienced a responsive mother feels secure in her presence, with this security permitting the child to explore the world beyond mom, so long as mother is there as a secure base to which the child can look for assistance if needed. Such secure relations with a parent (i.e., a secure attachment) permit the child to explore comfortably, promoting the development of a healthy self-concept. The development of a secure attachment during the first year of life fosters feelings in the child that she or he is valuable and self-reliant. In contrast, the lack of a secure relationship with an adult can translate into an emerging self-concept that is negative, one filled with perceptions of being unworthy and incompetent.

The first attachment relationship emerges in the first year and continues to develop during the second year, with parents making increasing self-control demands on children. In the early 20th century, Freud characterized the conflicts surrounding initial attachments and the development of self-control as the oral and anal conflict stages. At midcentury, Erikson reconceived these developments, respectively, as conflicts between trust versus mistrust and autonomy versus shame and doubt. At the end of the 20th century, researchers are digging deeper, attempting to establish the neural and cognitive underpinnings of social relationships between parents and children, as well as between children and children. Although attention to parent–child interactions traditionally have dominated work on the development of social competence, increasing attention is being paid to infant relationships with other children, since responsiveness to other infants increases substantially during the first 2 years of life.

In summary, by the end of infancy, if all has gone well, the child has a larger and more capable brain than she or he possessed at birth. Perceptual, linguistic, conceptual, and social skills have developed substantially. These various systems do not develop in isolation, but rather in relation to one another. For example, the development of some types of perceptual skills (e.g., phoneme perception) affects language development, and the development of particular conceptual understandings (e.g., object permanence) affects social relations (e.g., attachment). Moreover, although biological development is certainly salient during this period of life, biological development very much depends on appropriate environmental stimulation during the first 2 years of life. Thus a very important topic of research has been the exploration of effective ways to intervene during the first 2 years of life to assure optimal development, as taken up in Box 13.1.

Early Childhood

Brain growth continues during the preschool years. Myelination of the nervous system also increases, accounting in part for the increases in speed of information processing between 2 and 5 years of age. It is not easy to separate out the contributions of neural development versus experience in cognitive development, however. For example, traditionally, the increases in short-term memory that occur during early

BOX 13.1. Early Intervention

The breadth of research on early interventions is stunning, with most work on early intervention occurring since 1970. A handbook (Guralnick, 1997a) that summarized comprehensively the research that has been carried out on early intervention included chapters about interventions for all of the following:

- Preterm infants in the newborn intensive care unit
- Low-birthweight infants
- Children at risk for neuromotor problems
- Children prenatally exposed to alcohol and other drugs
- Children of maltreating parents
- Children of parents with mental retardation
- Children with HIV infection
- Children with Down syndrome
- Children with autism
- Children with cerebral palsy and related motor disorders
- Children with communication disorders
- Families of preschoolers with conduct problems
- Deaf children and children with hearing loss
- Children with visual impairments

Some general conclusions emerge from this work. One certainty is that early intervention must focus on the needs of families and effective interventions tend to be based in local communities. Effective interventions tend to be informed by basic research, often including work from several different disciplines. Typically, support from several different agencies is coordinated as part of delivering an intervention.

Is early intervention effective? When all of the data across the many experimental evaluations of early interventions are considered, a great deal of evidence indicates that early intervention produces at least some advantage for the children receiving it (Casto & Mastropieri, 1986; Guralnick, 1997b; Shonkoff & Hauser-Cram, 1987). Even so, critics point to methodological flaws in individual studies that call their results into question. Clearly, it is very hard to conduct excellent experimental research with children who are handicapped or at risk for becoming handicapped.

Thus, as far as the future of research on early intervention is concerned, more experimental tests are needed. Beyond that, however, we need to understand much better than we do the features of intervention programs that are associated with successful implementation and positive effects on development. Much more work is also needed to determine who most benefits from early interventions. Because early intervention is very expensive, it makes sense to determine if there are thresholds of severity beyond which it is unlikely that an intervention can be effective. In addition, much more needs to be known about the comprehensive effects of interventions. For example, in the past, cognitive and language improvement have been measured much more extensively in studies of early intervention than effects on social competence (Guralnick, 1997b). Given what is now known about how social interactions are key in cognitive development (e.g., from a Vygotskian perspective), it is clear that those who want to stimulate the development of cognition and language must also stimulate the development of social competence.

childhood and continue until adolescence have been conceived as reflecting neurological development. We have come to realize, however, that there are alternative explanations of such developments. For example, the child's developing knowledge base permits the young thinker to create bigger and bigger chunks of information, so that both 3-year-olds and 15-year-olds might have 5 ± 2 short-term memory slots, but each slot holds more in the case of the older compared to the younger child. Thus, for the first author of this book, it is trivially easy to remember the number sequence 2305673548162987652154637851 because the sequence can be coded as a familiar identification number (230567354), a relative's phone number (8162987652), and a university account number (15463785). Those of you who do not have these chunks in long-term memory might have more trouble with the sequence since it should involve many more than the 5 ± 2 chunks of information that you can hold in short-term memory. The point to emphasize is that even though it is known that the central nervous system continues to develop during the preschool years, researchers are continuing their efforts to sort out acquisitions that reflect neurological development versus other developments.

The thinking of preschoolers has received a great deal of attention from child development researchers, largely because of the strong claims made by Jean Piaget that early childhood is a different stage of development than middle childhood as defined by differences in the quality of thought possible. Although researchers have confirmed that, consistent with Piaget's concept of the preoperational stage, preschoolers perform less well than older children on conservation and classification tasks, they have also discovered that preschoolers sometimes do conserve and classify. Evidence that preschoolers can learn to conserve and classify went far in discrediting Piaget's characterization of the preschool years as a period of time when thinking is completely different from thinking later in childhood.

Piaget's characterization of preschooler thought as egocentric (i.e., intuitive, strongly influenced by perception) also has given way to more complex conceptions of children's thinking. For example, preschoolers can exhibit considerable understanding of other people—their perceptions, desires, beliefs, and emotions. During the 1960s, when Piagetian theory about children's thinking prevailed in North America, a conception of preschoolers as nonstrategic relative to older children was given as one more example of preschoolers' cognitive inadequacies. In contrast, it is now understood that preschoolers can be strategic, especially when they are in familiar situations doing familiar tasks. Thus developmental shifts in thinking can be understood better as *expansion of abilities* rather than as *qualitatively different abilities* at different times in life. Preschoolers' thinking involves strategies, declarative knowledge, metacognition, and motivational beliefs just as the thinking of elementary-grades children is an articulation of strategies, knowledge, metacognition, and motivations. For example, gender schemas (i.e., knowledge of the complex strategies, knowledge, and motivations that define femaleness and maleness) have their origins in the preschool years. These schemas play a powerful role in organizing and motivating gender-consistent behaviors during middle childhood and adolescence.

Language competencies grow greatly during early childhood, although language development is critically dependent on immersion in language. Syntactic development during the preschool years has commanded a great deal of attention, with documentation of substantial regularity in the acquisition of the various morphemes. The two-word stage is the beginning of syntactical development, with much longer and complex utterances possible by the end of the preschool period. As language production skills improve, so do metalinguistic competencies such as recognition of syntactical versus nonsyntactical constructions.

Expanding language skills as well as increased understanding of the perspectives of others leads to substantial increases in communication skills during early childhood. Social-communication skills and cognition are intertwined as indicated by the ability to predict cognitive competence in early childhood from attachment status during infancy. What mediates this continuity are more productive parent–child interactions both in infancy and early childhood when parents are responsive to their children. Parental responsivity results in secure attachment during infancy and better parent–child problem solving and intellectual interaction during early childhood. Thus, when parents and children are securely attached, they have more productive emergent literacy experiences (e.g., interactions during storybook readings), which help prepare children for more formal literacy instruction in kindergarten and first grade.

Although educational television programming, such as *Sesame Street*, can do much to convey knowledge of some fundamental literacy concepts, such as letters and numbers, much that is important to know about reading is better acquired in interaction with responsive adults. According to Vygotsky, as language develops, it can play a greater role in thought, but for that to happen children must learn how to use language to direct thought. They learn this as they interact with adults who use language to direct the children's thinking and attention as they interact with them. With many such experiences, children internalize the directive role of adults, using self-speech to direct their own thinking and attention. Whereas Piaget viewed children's talk to themselves as a symptom of egocentricity, Vygotsky saw it as an intellectual advance, an early step in the development of directive speech-for-self which is a prominent part of mature thinking.

Early conceptions of development during the early childhood years focused more exclusively on the parent–child relationship than do more recent conceptions. Thus, in describing the phallic stage, Freud placed relationships with parents at the center of moral development. In contrast, Kohlberg borrowed from Piaget's theory to explain development of moral judgment in terms of cognitive development, but also acknowledged the large role that peers play in stimulating thinking about morality. With increasing peer relationships during the preschool years and increasing complexity of children's play, there are increasing opportunities for the types of cognitive conflicts that Kohlberg believed stimulate increases in moral understanding.

In summary, by the end of the preschool years, thinking, language, and social skills have many of the characteristics of adult thinking, language, and social interactions. Throughout the preschool years, thinking, language, and social interactions are increasingly linked. A great deal of development during the preschool years depends greatly on experiences with supportive adults. Thus it is very important to provide the types of educational experiences most likely to foster development during early childhood.

Middle Childhood

Neurological growth and development continues throughout middle childhood; so does myelination. Potential indicators of increases in brain functioning, such as speed of processing and capacity of short-term memory, continue to improve.

For Piaget, the hallmark of middle childhood was the ability to conserve, presumably indicative of the development of concrete operational thinking. Conservation, however, proved not to be an all-or-nothing acquisition, as suggested by Piaget's theory. Instead, some conservations were acquired before others during middle childhood, and some were not acquired until well into adolescence.

Although Piaget's theory was important in stimulating research on cognitive development in the 1960s and 1970s, information-processing perspectives have predominated in discussions of cognitive development in the more recent past. For example, considerable research has documented that strategy use expands during the middle-childhood years (e.g., rehearsal of word lists that are to be remembered). Information-processing theorists studying middle childhood have also demonstrated developmental improvements in inhibition of irrelevant thought, increases in resistance to interference, increased cognitive monitoring and self-regulation, and expanding metacognitive understandings. There are concomitant increases in children's sociocognitive understandings, that is, their views of how other people's minds work, what others are thinking and feeling.

Increasingly, information-processing researchers have been interested in demonstrating the positive effects of strategies instruction on academic competence, with a large body of evidence now pointing to substantial improvements in academic performance, such as in reading comprehension and composition of texts. When students are first taught strategies, their performance of them is anything but automatic. Often strategies use is accompanied by overt verbalization at first, with verbalization increasingly covert as skill in strategies use increases. That is, consistent with Vygotskian theory, during middle childhood, children are capable of self-directive inner speech, and thus thought and language are increasingly intertwined.

Indeed, in general, language development continues to be salient during the middle childhood years. Syntactic skills, vocabulary, and metalinguistic awareness all increase. One form of metalinguistic awareness, phonemic awareness, has proven to be particularly important in early reading. Phonemic awareness is the understanding that words are composed of sounds blended together, sounds that "map to" the constituent letters in words. Phonemic awareness must develop no later than kindergarten or early first grade, if learning to read is to proceed well during the early elementary years. Phonemic awareness can be stimulated by language experiences emphasizing the component sounds of words. This experience can be provided, for example, in games requiring children to say what words would sound like with a different initial, middle, or final letter, such as asking "What would *bam* sound like if it started with *s*?"

Much of reading instruction during the primary years focuses on teaching children how to read words—although the making of meaning is prominent in contemporary reading instruction from the beginning of literacy instruction. Researchers interested in basic reading have documented that learning to read words is most likely if students are explicitly taught decoding skills and given practice using those skills during actual reading and writing. When children are taught to read in school, they are provided a powerful means for increasing their intelligence: Much can be learned by reading. Moreover, good readers often elect not only to read but to reduce other behaviors that are not consistent with maximizing cognitive development (e.g., excessive television viewing).

Provision of strategies instruction and teaching children to read are only two of the ways that schooling can affect the cognitive development of students positively.

In general, intelligent performance is affected positively by schooling. That is, at least in Western cultures, middle childhood marks the beginning of an important factor in cognitive development: formal schooling. Interestingly, even psychoanalytic theorists recognized that middle childhood is largely a period devoted to the development of the competencies valued in the child's culture. For Freud, middle childhood corresponded to latency, which he characterized as a period of relative calm with respect to psychosocial development, a calm that permits attention to other matters, such as the intellectual development that occurs in school. According to Erikson, this is a period in which the child develops a sense of industry (i.e., if he or she is successful in accomplishing the demands of the period, such as the development of elementary literacy and numeracy skills) or inferiority (i.e., if he or she is unsuccessful in meeting demands such as learning to read, write, and solve elementary mathematical problems).

A number of other middle childhood developments might be affected in part by the onset of schooling or the concomitants of schooling, such as increased interactions with other children. Thus Kohlberg noted increases in the conventionality of children's moral judgments during the elementary-school years. Understanding of appropriate and inappropriate social behaviors (i.e., how, when, and where to behave in particular ways) also increases. Play increases in diversity and complexity.

More negatively, the academic self-concept does not fare so well with the onset of schooling. The typical kindergarten or first-grade child believes that he or she can do anything, that learning to read, write, and do math will go well. With every passing year, such perceptions decline, as do the motivations to do things academic. How much decline occurs, however, depends on a child's academic successes and failures and is domain-specific. Thus, by the late elementary-school years, children know whether they are good at math, reading, or writing, with these self-efficacy perceptions affecting their subsequent motivations to read, write, and take mathematics. The declining motivation during middle childhood reflects the operation of several factors: (1) With increasing age, children believe less in personal effort as the determinant of academic performance and believe more in the role of natural ability, which is not under their own control. (2) With increasing grade level during the elementary-school years, school becomes increasingly competitive, with far fewer academic winners than losers.

In summary, during middle childhood, thinking, language, and social skills continue to develop. A significant difference between this period of development and earlier periods is that schooling plays an important role in the cognitive life of the child, mostly for better, but also for worse (e.g., negatively affecting academic motivation). What has been learned about development during middle childhood has permitted many innovations in education. Box 13.2 tells the story of one elementary school that has been at the forefront in developing and implementing innovations based on educational research.

Adolescence

Neurological maturity is achieved by midadolescence (i.e., 16 years of age). For example, the brain reaches its adult weight and size. Even so, many cognitive functions continue to expand throughout adolescence. For example, the diversity of memory strategies increases as the teen years proceed. Inhibition of irrelevant cognitions also continues to increase, as does resistance to cognitive interference and monitoring of

---

BOX 13.2. Benchmark School

Benchmark School, outside of Philadelphia, educates children who experience great difficulties in school. The typical entry-level student has done poorly in 2 years of regular schooling (i.e., typically grades 1 and 2, or 2 years of grade 1), with the most common problem being failure to learn to read. Formal assessments have determined that the child is at least average, and more typically above average in intelligence. The Benchmark student is a smart kid who cannot read.

During the first year or two at Benchmark (see Gaskins & Elliot, 1991, for a book-length description of the school, its programs, and students), students are taught to decode, using an approach to decoding developed at the school. Lessons on decoding continue throughout the elementary years. Right from the start, however, Benchmark students learn that reading is not just about sounding out words but about meaning getting. As decoding skills develop, students read increasingly challenging literature; they are taught to tackle such challenging reading by using the comprehension strategies that work for all elementary children, including prediction, rereading when text does not make sense, constructing mental images, self-questioning, and summarizing. In addition, there is daily instruction in writing, again involving instruction of higher order strategies, such as the planning–translating–revising strategies described in earlier chapters. Content-area instruction is not neglected but rather the strategies that the students learn to read, write, and problem solve are applied to social studies and science texts (Pressley, Gaskins, Wile, Cunicelli, & Sheridan, 1991).

The Benchmark model of instruction is consistent with a model of instruction that has been validated by research (Pressley, Gaskins, Cunicelli, et al., 1991): long-term instruction of strategies well matched to important academic tasks; development of metacognition about strategies through direct explanation, modeling, and scaffolded practice; reinforcement for improvement rather than for outperforming other students in a class, with every effort made to encourage healthy motivational beliefs (e.g., "I can do well if I apply the right strategies, the ones I am learning in school"); and expansion of content knowledge.

Does it work? An 8-year-old who cannot read, which is the status of most entry-level Benchmark students, is at great risk for long-term academic failure. In contrast, most Benchmark students leave the school in an average of 4 years (some stay as long as 7 years) to return to normal schooling. When they do so, typically they are at least average students or better. Virtually all Benchmark alumni graduate from high school; many go on to college. Although no true experiment of Benchmark has ever been conducted (or ever could be), the case is nonetheless strong that Benchmark makes a difference for its students.

---

cognitive functions. Thought of in another way, both fluid and crystallized intelligence increase as adolescence continues.

Piaget, in particular, portrayed adolescence as the time when cognitive development culminates. With the acquisition of formal operations, more elaborate and flexible thinking is possible. More hypothetical thinking also becomes possible, so that adolescents are able to think about things that have never occurred and to think about abstract concepts. Other theorists, inspired by Piaget, also proposed that formal operations would permit functioning not possible during early and middle childhood. For example, Kohlberg proposed that postconventional moral judgment became a possibility during adolescence, in part because of the onset of formal operations during that period.

By the end of his life, Piaget came to realize that formal operations was anything but a universal attainment, with many adolescents not becoming formal operational. In addition, Piaget eventually concluded that formal operational competence was most likely in domains that are very familiar to the thinker. For example, teenage computer "wonks" are much more likely to be flexible and hypothetical in their own thinking about computer programming than in their thinking about other matters. Similarly, Kohlberg eventually came to realize that postconventional moral judgment often did not develop during adolescence. Postconventional thinking is much more likely to develop during early adulthood, that is, after people had opportunities to experience some complex moral interactions requiring serious reflection.

Just as the nervous system becomes fully mature during adolescence, so do the sexual organs and functioning. Psychoanalytically oriented theorists (e.g., Freud, Erikson) and others (e.g., G. Stanley Hall) believed that both sexual and intellectual maturity contributed to the conflicts of adolescence. Freud characterized adolescence as the genital stage, a period characterized by great volatility, due, in part, to the surge in sexual energy experienced with hormonal maturity. Such volatility was termed "storm and stress" by G. Stanley Hall. Erikson was one theorist who elaborated on this idea of conflict during adolescence, making the case that adolescence is a period of identity crisis, with conflicts about potential career directions and personal philosophies.

How does maturing thinking play a role in development according to psychoanalytically oriented theorists? With adolescence, the full range of defense mechanisms become possible. More positively, with the ability to think about unexperienced possibilities, it is possible to imagine oneself in a variety of occupations, to envision alternative sexual identities, and to contemplate alternative life philosophies. Adolescent thinking differs from childhood thinking in many ways.

One of the most striking differences between life in childhood and life in adolescence is that by the end of adolescence peer interactions become very important. These peer relations are critical to development, including intellectual development. For example, Kohlberg emphasized how peer relations permit cognitive conflicts that promote increases in the development of moral thinking. Lawrence Steinberg and his associates documented how peer relations go far in affecting academic achievement in high school in that successful students naturally tend to associate with other successful students.

In summary, during adolescence, biological maturation occurs. Thinking and social relations expand, with cognitive skills and social interactions reciprocally affecting one another. That is, increasing cognitive abilities permits more sophisticated social functioning, with social functioning positively affecting thinking skills. Typically, adolescents in North America attend high school. School reformers are concerned about schooling in America and have considered how schooling during adolescence might occur differently. An alternative conception of high school is discussed in Box 13.3.

Summary and Concluding Comment

Whenever you look at a 19-year-old, it is a marvel to realize that that person began as a single cell almost two decades ago. Almost as marvelous is that it is possible now to articulate in some detail the many different ways the individual has grown and changed. The portrait of development summarized in Figure 13.1 represents the cumulative efforts of thousands of scientists, with almost all of the conclusions offered here the product of research during the second half of the 20th century.

BOX 13.3. Coalition of Essential Schools

Theodore R. Sizer came to school reform well prepared, having served as the headmaster at two distinguished private high schools and then as dean of the Graduate School of Education at Harvard University. He also headed the Coalition of Essential Schools, which has developed a set of principles about how to make high schools more effective. The Coalition has captured the attention of many school reformers in the United States. Ted Sizer recognized that the large, impersonal, comprehensive high schools that characterize U.S. secondary education are not working well for many students or for many teachers. He proposed some revisions (Sizer, 1996, pp. 154–155):

- Rather than worrying about being comprehensive—meaning offering every type of course that students might want—focus on teaching students to use their minds well.
- Students should master essential skills and areas of knowledge. This is a "less is more" approach, with mastery of important content and skills taking precedence over covering of content comprehensively.
- While the goal of essential learning applies to all students, the means for meeting the goal may vary depending on the students.
- Personal attention is important, with teachers having contact with no more than 80 students.
- The school should be a place where the emphasis is on the student as a worker rather than on the teacher as the deliverer of instruction. Coaching (i.e., scaffolding) will be a prominent form of teaching.
- Students should enter high school when they have the prerequisite language and mathematical competencies; they should exit when they have mastered the curriculum. When the students demonstrate they have mastered the curriculum, they graduate regardless of age.
- Teachers should expect much of students but not threaten them. Trust and decency should prevail in the school. Staff members will perform many roles (e.g., teacher, counselor, and manager) as part of committed membership in the school.
- The staff must have sufficient planning time, within the constraint that the essential school not cost much more per pupil than a traditional school. This can be accomplished by eliminating some services that are provided to students in comprehensive secondary schools.
- What results when these principles are put into practice is usually a more communal school, one that is smaller than the typical comprehensive high school, one in which a few teachers work intensely with their students. Sometimes such small schools are created as schools within schools. Does such restructuring positively affect student learning and achievement? The available evidence suggests that restructured schools consistent with the Essential Schools model promote student achievement (MacMullen, 1996). What we like about Sizer's message is that it points out high schools can make a difference in the lives of students.

Beyond mere description of how development occurs, understanding is growing as to how biological development relates to psychological development, and, within psychological development, how shifts in thinking skills affect social behaviors and personality. Great progress has been made in understanding the complexities of development.

What are the processes that account for developmental change? These are taken up in the next section, where we argue that the same mechanisms that account for developmental shifts also account for individual differences at any given developmental level.

Prenatal Period

Conception
Cell differentiation, cell proliferation, and eventual development of organ systems
Intrauterine growth and development until birth

Infancy (0–2 years of age)

Rapid growth of brain and nervous system
- Increasing size and weight of brain, with some growth spurts
- A number of areas of the brain (e.g., frontal lobes) become functional
- Programmed brain cell loss
- Experience-expectant synaptic connections made if appropriate experience occurs during critical period

Myelination of nervous system with increased efficiency of neural transmission
Reflexive reactions gradually give way to reflective reactions
Object permanence develops
Attachment develops during the first year and continues to develop in the second year
- Freud's oral and anal conflicts
- Erikson's crises of trust versus mistrust, autonomy versus shame and doubt

Emergence of symbolic functioning and language
- Increased speech perception during the first year
- Babbling becomes more consistent with sounds in the surrounding language
- One-word stage by the end of the second year, with single words associated with complex meanings

Early Childhood (2–6 years of age)

Brain growth and myelination continues, with speed of information processing and functional short-term memory increasing
Piagetian preoperational period, with thought intuitive and influenced by perception
Use of elementary strategies in familiar situations
Schematic knowledge continues to grow, including gender schematic knowledge
Great growth in language skills
- Syntax
- Vocabulary
- Metalinguistic linguistic understanding
- Increasing articulation of language and thought as proposed by Vygotsky
- Emergent literacy experiences and productive parent–child language interactions

Increasing peer relationships, with cognitive conflicts that stimulate cognitive growth
Development of moral thinking and conscience
- Freudian phallic stage, the beginning of internalization of conscience
- Preconventional moral reasoning as defined by Kohlberg

Middle Childhood (6–11 or 12 years of age)

Brain growth and myelination continues
Piagetian concrete operational period

(continued)

FIGURE 13.1. A chronological summary of human development.

Improvements in information processing
- Speed of information processing and growth of functional short-term memory capacity increase
- Strategy use expands, with children responsive to strategy instruction
- Improved inhibition of irrelevant thinking
- Increased resistance to cognitive interference
- Increased cognitive monitoring and self-regulation
- Expanding metacognitive understandings
- Increased sociocognitive understandings

Language development continues
- Syntax
- Vocabulary
- Metalinguistic awareness (e.g., phonemic awareness, which can be stimulated with language manipulation games if it does not develop on its own)

Academic learning is preeminent (e.g., reading)
- Freud's latency period
- Erikson's crisis of competence versus incompetence
- Academic self-concept becomes more differentiated and generally declines with increasing age
- Academic motivation generally declines with increasing age

Social relationships become more complex
- Play increases in diversity
- Increasing understanding of appropriateness in social behaviors
- Increases in sociocognitive competence allow more productive cognitive conflicts, which, in turn, positively affect cognitive development

Preconventional moral judgments as defined by Kohlberg

Adolescence (11 or 12 years of age to the late teen years)

Biological maturity achieved by midadolescence
- Brain attains adult size and weight
- Sexual maturity

Piagetian formal operational stage, with formal operations most evident when operating in familiar domains
- Increased abstract and hypothetical reasoning
- Increased cognitive flexibility permits more complex thinking—for example, many ego defense mechanisms as defined by Freudians

Improvements in information processing
- Speed of information processing increases
- Functional short-term memory capacity increases
- Strategy diversity expands
- Cognitive inhibition increases
- Resistance to interference increases
- Cognitive monitoring increases

Potential storm and stress
- Freud's genital stage
- Erikson's identity crisis conflict

Peer interactions now are more prominent

FIGURE 13.1. *(continued)*

■ ■ ■ MECHANISMS OF DEVELOPMENT AND THE DETERMINANTS OF INDIVIDUAL DIFFERENCES

The mechanisms of growth and development and the determinants of individual differences can be classified in a number of different ways. One way that has endured, and one that has been used throughout this textbook, is to frame the mechanisms/ determinants as principally part of "nature" or "nurture." As we have learned, however, a clean separation of nature and nurture is impossible, for there are always interactions between biological and environmental factors.

The Nature of Nature

Much of development is determined at the moment of conception. At a minimum, the genes all humans inherit do much to ensure that the biological development of any child will be much like the biological development of other humans. Barring some environmental disruption, such as malnutrition or physical injury, the central nervous system develops in orderly and predictable ways following birth. Developments that are universal include the following:

- Critical and sensitive periods for the development of some perceptual and language skills occur at about the same time for most humans. Indeed, biology biases humans to orient to and process particular types of sensory and linguistic information. These biases go far in assuring that the developing human will experience needed sensation at critical points in his or her development.
- Biology also biases humans to construct meaning and understanding from sensory and linguistic input. Thus, when perceptual arrays are incomplete (e.g., there is a faint image of a ball that is visible) or when linguistic input is sparse (e.g., a person picks up only part of a sentence, "The ball is ____ing on the f____"), humans often fill in the missing pieces based on their prior knowledge in order to see a ball or to know that the speaker must have said, "The ball is rolling on the floor."
- Because the central nervous system develops as it does, most humans will have the conscious capacity to actively manipulate symbols. That is, they will have short-term memory. They will also have the capacity to form enduring memories.
- In general, humans have evolved to be sensitive to information in the environment. That is, the environment makes a difference because of human biology. All humans attend to and learn from social models, can understand explanations, and respond to reinforcements and feedback because their biology equips them—and indeed *biases* them—to do so.

Because of the prominence of behavior genetics research, however, biological determination is typically thought about in terms of the role genes play in determining individual differences in people. Genes specify *reaction ranges* with respect to a number of human characteristics. For example, a person's genes specify neurological development that will permit the individual to be above average, average, or below average in intelligence. In the case of a person whose genes permit above-average intellectual functioning, exactly how much above average will depend on the environment, however. That is, the reaction range for someone who has inherited above-average intelligence might be 115–130, with exact placement in the range depending on the quantity and quality of intellectual stimulation experienced. Similarly, there are genetically specified reaction ranges for more specific intellectual acquisitions (e.g., the ability to read), as well as for personality characteristics and, of course, physical characteristics.

One salient biologically determined characteristic is gender. Biological gender can affect some mental functions (e.g., competence to perform tasks with a spatial component) as well as social interaction patterns. Even so, gender is always one variable among many, in part because how a girl or a boy develops depends largely on environmental variables, with much greater variability *among* girls and *among* boys than *between* girls and boys on average.

Nature matters, with human biology going far in explaining aspects of development that are universal as well as how and why developments occur differently when they do. Human biology, however, always unfolds in an environment, so nothing in human development reflects purely genetic or purely biological mechanisms. Like the fish in the sea that fails to understand it is swimming in water, humans sometimes fail to appreciate that physical attributes, intelligence, personality, and gender-related behaviors are often affected dramatically by a number of environmental factors. One of the great contributions of psychology as a science has been its role in heightening awareness of the many ways that nurture can affect development and behavior.

The Nature of Nurture

There are many ways of conceptualizing how experience matters. One traditional approach is to think about mechanisms of development or change, with each of these mechanisms summarizing how environmental input translates into shifts in behavior and knowledge.

Mechanisms of Change

Psychologists who are interesting in learning, in particular, have been active in characterizing development in terms of the mechanisms that cause change. The typical means of learning are as follows:

OBSERVATIONAL LEARNING

Humans have evolved to learn a great deal from what they observe. They are attuned to the behaviors they see modeled by other people. Sometimes, for example, teachers model strategic behaviors, urging their students to attend to these behaviors and intentionally learn them. More often, however, people do not intend to learn from others, but they nonetheless incidentally learn the individual's behaviors. For example, when the first author's son attended his first University of Wisconsin hockey game, he probably had no intention of learning to scream "Sieve" at the opposing goalie, but after a short period of time he not only learned to scream the word, but did so with the exact rhythm and cadence of the surrounding fans.

With the cognitive revolution in psychology in the 1960s and 1970s, conceptions of modeling broadened. For example, part of modeling can be verbal explanations, which also have a powerful effect on children's learning. Indeed, the scaffolding of instruction, as conceived by Vygotskian-oriented educators, begins with extensive modeling and explaining, followed by additional modeling and explaining as needed. In addition, cognitive psychologists presented evidence that observational learning very much depends on the learner attending to the model. Social learning researchers, in particular, have devoted a great deal of effort to determine what factors account for learner attention. People attend to others who are well respected, but they also attend to people like themselves who are confronting tasks that they themselves must confront soon.

REINFORCEMENT

Any event that follows another event and increases the probability of the first event reoccurring in the future is a reinforcement. Although technically reinforcements are not rewards, many people find it helpful to think of reinforcements as rewards that increase the likelihood of the behavior that occurred just before the reward. Again, with the cognitive revolution, reinforcements came to be thought of in different ways, in particular, with greater emphasis on their informational value. Reinforcements often signal that the individual performed appropriately at a particular time, providing information about where and when to do something. Such feedback can have an effect on the metacognition of learners, increasing what they know about the occasions when particular tactics make sense.

With the cognitive revolution, understanding has also increased about when reinforcement does not work as it is intended and why. In particular, reinforcements can be construed as controlling, so that a reinforced student begins to think "I am doing this activity to get the reward." Once the reward stops, so does the behavior, even if it is a behavior that the child used to perform for no reward at all.

PUNISHMENT

Punishments have the opposite effects of reinforcements. Any event that follows another event and decreases the probability of the first event in the future is a punishment. Punishment as discussed by psychologists corresponds to the concept as used by the layperson.

Cognitive psychologists have also thought about punishment and made the case that punishment is more effective if the child understands the reason for the punishment. The cognitivists have gone even farther, however, arguing that punishment is most effective if punished children are made to understand how their misdeed negatively affected others. These explanations, referred to as "inductions," go far toward decreasing the punished behaviors in the future.

CLASSICAL CONDITIONING

Humans are born with a variety of reflexes and emotions, which can be elicited by particular forms of stimulation. For example, in school settings, failure often elicits anxiety and even fear. Because the failure and accompanying emotion occurs in the context of school, school itself can come to be anxiety arousing. Avoiding school then reduces anxiety.

COGNITIVE CONFLICT

Although it is possible to account for much of development through analyses of the learning mechanisms of observation, reinforcement, punishment, and conditioning, some researchers have favored explaining developmental change with respect to the child's level of development. A key mechanism in promoting developmental change is *cognitive conflict*. Specifically, if a situation is a little bit different than the learner expects based on her or his knowledge and understanding of the world, the learner is motivated to try to understand what is going on. A classic example of this occurs when a nonconserving child is presented with a conservation task such as determining how pouring water from a short, fat beaker into a tall, thin beaker affects the amount of liquid. The nonconserver believes that there is a different amount of liquid when the water is in one of the beakers than when it is in the other. There comes a time, however, when it is very puzzling that water originally in beaker A looks different in beaker B, but when poured back into A once again appears to be the same as before the pouring from A to B. This confusion motivates reflection on the situation and the eventual construction of the understanding that pouring liquid from one beaker to another has no effect on the amount of liquid. Amount of liquid can only be affected by adding or subtracting liquid from the total.

A general principle of instruction that emerges is that cognitive conflict is most likely to stimulate reflection and learning when the task is just a little bit beyond the child's current understanding. This general principle was summarized by Vygotsky as "teaching within the *zone of proximal development*." According to this approach, find out what the child knows already and what she or he can do, then present tasks to him or her that are just a bit beyond the child's current level of functioning. Many motivational frameworks also include the idea that motivation is maximized by presenting students with tasks that are a little bit challenging for them: not so easy that they can be done immediately, nor so difficult that the tasks become frustrating. Piagetian educators, such as those who were inspired by Lawrence Kohlberg's theory of moral judgment and its development, often refer to this as the "plus-one approach." Being exposed to thinking that is a stage beyond the child's current level of functioning has a fascination for the child that increases attention and his or her attempts to understand the thinking.

Some have labeled teaching and learning within the zone of proximal development as "constructivist," rather than involving cultural transmission of information. The constructivist label emphasizes the theme that the child is active in coming to understand the situation. Educators identifying with constructivism as an approach to teaching and learning often believe that modeling and explaining to-be-learned principles for students does not cause the same type of reflection that plus-one approaches stimulate. In this view, modeling, explaining, and reinforcing use of principles that have been explicitly taught does not result in as complete understanding as when learning involves cognitive conflict. The problem is that there is not much evidence for this position that learning via cognitive conflict is better than learning from observation or explanations. Modeling often is the beginning of a constructivist process for the learner. The learner does not fully understand a process simply from watching another person carry out the process, but probably does understand it well enough to try the process. Trying a process results in mistakes, which prompt reflection and gradual construction of understanding.

When students are working in the zone of proximal development, often they are not going to "get it" immediately. They may need support in the form of hints, prompts, and reminders. Such support is at the heart of scaffolding, with the excellent scaffolder providing enough support for the student to make progress but not more than the student actually needs. Discovery in the absence of such support often is uncertain or even unlikely. Constructivist discovery always involves active student thinking, although sometimes the learner requires some prompting in order to begin thinking about a problem in a way that will lead to a solution.

How can individual differences in learners be explained in terms of the learning mechanisms and cognitive conflict? Students are likely to be better informed and more skillful to the extent that they have experienced appropriate models and explanations of information that is important to know. It helps if their efforts to respond to models are reinforced and that appropriate help is provided when it is needed (i.e., when learning is scaffolded). Families differ with respect to the provision of such input, as do schooling environments. Some children experience worlds filled with appropriate modeling and explaining, reinforcing, and scaffolding. Other things being equal, those living in such worlds are far ahead of children coming from less stimulating and responsive environments. Thus the context in which development occurs is key.

Contexts of Development

In the first chapter of this book, we introduced Urie Bronfenbrenner's (1979, 1989) *ecological systems theory*. Bronfenbrenner divided the environment into a microsystem (i.e., contexts making immediate contact with the developing child, such as home or daycare center), a mesosystem (i.e., the context in which microsystem elements are embedded, such as community, school, and church), an exosystem (i.e., elements affecting the child removed from direct experience, such as media and the extended family), and a macrosystem (i.e., the larger culture). In fact, over the course of this textbook, evidence has been reviewed supporting the impact of all levels of the ecological system as Bronfenbrenner described it.

At the microsystem level, a great deal of evidence was summarized about how family and friends affect development. For example, family size can make a difference in the child's development. The microsystem shifts somewhat with development, being defined mostly by the family early in life and increasingly by peers as development proceeds. That said, the elements of the microsystem somewhat codetermine each other. Thus when parent–child interactions during infancy result in a secure attachment, healthy peer relations during the preschool years are more likely. Parents also affect their children's peers by their choice of neighborhood and educational options. In turn, peers can affect a teen's interactions with parents, although more often than not the perspectives and values held by a teen's family are consistent with the perspectives and values held by a teen's peers. The family and friendship relationships that define a child's microsystem of development are strongly interrelated.

Of course, it is not simply the child's family that determines peer relationships. The microsystem is also determined by biology to some extent. For example, males and females interact differently with their families. Moreover, there are different friendship patterns for boys and girls. Gender goes far in determining a child's microcontext. So do other biologically defined variables, such as intelligence. For example, at the extremes, children with mental retardation experience very different family and peer interactions than do children of normal and superior intelligence. Of course, the microsystem in turn does much more to stimulate mental growth in normal and superior children than in retarded children.

With respect to individual differences in children, the microsystem can go far in affecting such differences. How parents react to their children affects them in many ways. Thus securely attached children develop differently than insecurely attached children, enjoying better social relationships that impact favorably on their intellectual development due to their better academic interactions with adults during the preschool years. Authoritative parents provide a healthier context for development than do permissive or authoritarian parents. Peers can support an academic outlook or an anti-intellectual perspective. How family and peers act toward a child and what families and peers believe go a long way in determining how a child develops.

The mesosystem element that has received the greatest consideration in this textbook is school. Schools can be places where instruction is well informed by contemporary research or bastions of tradition, with such curricular decisions having an important impact on what the child learns. Although schools can be organized on cooperative principles and emphasize improvement, more often than not they are based on competition and rewards for doing better than others. Competitive schooling certainly undermines the motivation of many students.

Schooling can be more or less constructivist. That is, the teacher simply can present information and expect students to learn it or the teacher can make presentations that are the start of a constructivist process, during which students work with the ideas and attempt to apply them to meaningful tasks with the aid of teacher scaffolding. In some schools that are decidedly constructivist in their orientation, students are apprentice readers, writers, and problem solvers, taking on meaningful academic tasks (e.g., writing a letter to the author of a book just read by the class) in a cooperative, supportive community. In contrast, in the bastions of tradition, they are merely the doers of tasks that do not make much sense to them, tasks that are defined by drills and workbook pages that the teacher specifies as the assignments for the day.

The mesosystem variable of schooling can go far in determining individual differences between children. Whether a child is a motivated learner or lacks academic motivation often depends on school. Whether a child knows how to comprehend and interpret texts or only knows how to answer literal questions about a text will vary with the type of schooling the child experiences. Whether a child understands what it means to live in a just community and the role of individuals in constructing just communities can vary depending on the social organization of the school.

One exosystem variable that was encountered at different points in this text was television. Heavy doses of entertainment television are associated with academic difficulties. Heavy doses of televised aggression are associated with inappropriate aggressive behavior in children. More positively, educational programming that is well informed by research on learning and development can be effective in stimulating academic development. In short, television viewing affects development and individual differences in cognitive outcomes.

The study of macrosystem effects (i.e., culture) on development has been extensive in the past half century in particular. Often comparisons have been made between different cultures (e.g., Asian vs. American) or within cultures that vary in the degree to which they conform to Western traditions (e.g., cultures in which some children are Western-schooled and other children are not). Even within the United States, academic development has been analyzed as a function of subcultural membership (e.g., black, urban, poor youth vs. white, suburban, middle-class youth). Time and again, culture has proved to be telling in defining psychologically important differences. For example, Asians are more likely to explain their accomplishments as reflecting ability than are Western students. Africans experiencing Western-style schooling think differently than Africans not so educated. In the United States, urban, poor, black youth devalue schooling relative to suburban, white, middle-class students.

Culture is determined not only by place and group membership, but also by when development occurs. The culture that today's grandparents experienced during childhood is dramatically different from the culture in which today's children are raised. Such cohort differences in experience translate into a variety of differences in development, including in fundamental knowledge and capacities tapped by intelligence tests.

In summary, Bronfenbrenner's model was well supported by the evidence presented in this textbook. Context consistently makes a difference in development and goes far in explaining individual differences in development. A variety of differences in this textbook have been explained as a function of family and peer relationships, schooling variables, media exposure, and culture. Something else that became apparent, however, was that with increasing age, students became creators and determiners of their own contexts of development. They decide on how much they will interact with family and friends, whether they will be committed to school, which media will engage them, and the subculture they choose to inhabit. For example, what difference will it make to a middle-school girl if she makes choices designed to make her more popular and attractive to boys instead of choosing a more academic orientation? With a little thought, it will be clear that the environment such a girl elects to be in will dramatically affect her development. Thus we take up next how children are determiners of their own contexts and development—that is, how self-regulation determines environment and development.

The Self-Regulating Child as a Determiner of Development

Self-regulation increases with development. For example, Vygotsky highlighted how internalized speech comes to self-regulate behavior and thought. With advancing age, at least in Western societies, comes increased strategy use and increased self-monitoring of behavior. With advancing age, children inhibit irrelevant and potentially interfering cognitions. Children also acquire a variety of values and beliefs that affect their self-determination. If they come to believe that their accomplishments are due to their personal efforts, this can motivate great effort. If they come to believe that ability mediates academic success, ability they believe they lack, motivation can very much be undermined. Students can either come to value school or believe it is not valuable in their lives, with these beliefs affecting their willingness to engage in academic tasks.

As children mature, they choose their friends and develop their interests. What friends do largely determines what an individual child does. Interests go far in explaining where a child will direct her or his energies, with interests directly affecting the developing knowledge base of the child. As children mature, their knowledge deepens as a function of experience. A child's state of knowledge becomes an important contextual variable, a context that is developed largely through the child's own choices. Thus the child who has been interested in computers since the preschool years and has done things with computers through the elementary- and middle-school years enters high school with a much more elaborated knowledge base about computers than his or her classmates. Such a child is in a better position than his or her peers to understand new information about computers and technology. The prior knowledge provides a basis for expectations that the child may have with respect to a new possibility (e.g., taking the introductory computer course that so many of his classmates take during freshman year of high school), expectations that affect behaviors and decisions (e.g., deciding not to take the class). The knowledge base also provides the basis for interpretations of the world that are not possible for those not having the knowledge base (e.g., the course will have to be low level since it is taught in a computer lab with machines that cannot run state-of-the-technology programs).

This developing knowledge base in no way guarantees clarity of understanding. Indeed, to the extent that the child has acquired prior knowledge that is inconsistent with new knowledge, there is reason to expect misinterpretations and interference in learning the new content.

As this knowledge base is expanding, however, so are communication skills and the ability to understand the perspectives of others, with these also part of the context that is the child's own mind. Expanding interpersonal competencies permit the opportunities to cooperate with others in academic endeavors, and to work on problems together. It has been known for some time that peers and peer interactions can affect cognitive development. We now are coming to understand how thinking can be distributed between minds and how interacting with others can lead to understandings that would not have been reached by any of the thinkers confronting a situation alone—that is, how the context of people thinking together can affect the development of the individual thinkers.

In short, the state of a child's own mind is an important contextual variable helping to determine the experiences the child will have and what the child will gain from those experiences. To the extent that the child has acquired academic interests, attitudes, and beliefs that support trying hard, and prior knowledge that permits understanding of new content, the child is more likely to profit from educational opportunities. Thus an important source of individual differences between children tomorrow is individual differences in their minds today, with the intellectually rich in a better position to become richer, increasing the distance between the academically well endowed and the not so well endowed as development proceeds. Another way to say it is that a child's own mind is an important contextual variable, with some minds better able to profit from experience than others.

Disruptions in Development That Determine Contexts of Development

Most of this book has been about normal development. Development does not always go normally, however. There are very real dangers in the world, with children more susceptible than adults to many of them. Thus environmental toxins and disease can affect the developing fetus as teratogens, altering physical development permanently. Children who are born into poverty are especially susceptible to the potential developmental disruptions associated with malnutrition, parental and child substance abuse, disease, and injury.

Understanding of developmental biology has provided many insights about why, when, and how various factors impact negatively on development. Research that illuminates developmental disruptions also provides some understanding about the challenges that must be overcome if the effects of negative factors are to be minimized. Consider, for example, what is known about childhood cancer now compared to several decades ago.

The most common childhood cancer is leukemia (see Bartel & Thurman, 1992, for this point and what follows). Because of great advances in treatment, most childhood leukemia victims will survive, a reality that motivated developmental psychologists to study childhood leukemia patients and their functioning after treatment for the disease. Brain tumors are the next most common form of childhood cancer and, although the survival probabilities are not as great as for leukemia, the chances of survival are increasing steadily with new understandings about effective treatments. Again, with increased survival, there is increased reason to study such children's development.

An initial problem is that childhood cancer victims fall behind in school because the illness and treatment dramatically disrupt normal life and school attendance. Often treatments produce side effects that preclude normal academic engagement, such as fatigue. The treatments also can affect long-term cognitive development negatively, with radiation because of a brain tumor especially likely to impair cognitive functioning in the long term (Brown & Madan-Swain, 1993). Through study of development, we have learned that how much impairment occurs depends on a number of factors, including the age of the child when the cancer occurs, whether there is postsurgical infection of the nervous system, and how much radiation therapy is administered.

For example, brain tumors during the preschool years, when the brain is developing rapidly, seem to produce more impairment than brain tumors later in childhood. Even in the more favorable situation afforded by leukemia, many more postleukemia students require special educational interventions to keep them at grade level than do children who are free of disease. More positively, with a reduction in recent years in the use of radiation therapy to the head to treat leukemia, there seems to be less impairment, an understanding that motivates research to find ways to treat leukemia and other children's diseases without the use of radiation to the brain. In short, factors that cause harm to children and children's own health are important in that the changes they produce affect the contexts the child will experience. Of course, the inseparability of nature and nurture is transparent when the effects of injury and disease are considered. Humans have evolved so that they are susceptible to particular types of injuries and diseases. This biologically determined susceptibility goes far in determining the contexts that some children experience, with their worlds limited and affected in ways that other children's worlds are not limited or affected. Injury and disease define characteristics of children today that go far in determining psychological and physical growth tomorrow. Just as the state of a child's mind is an important contextual variable affecting development, so is the state of the child's health.

Summary and Concluding Comment

Nature and nurture continuously interact to determine development. The child's biology as determined in part by genes goes far in explaining some aspects of development. More can be understood, however, by thinking about the experiential mechanisms that promote change, including observational learning, reinforcement, punishment, conditioning, and cognitive conflict. Such mechanisms always operate in contexts, however, with the contexts coming to have causal properties, or at least becoming part of a causal chain. Hence, experiencing a responsive mother during infancy is part of the cause of secure attachment. Attendance at a school that strokes students for improvement is part of the cause of high motivation in the school. Watching *Sesame Street* can cause children to learn basic literacy and numeracy facts. Experiencing Western culture and schooling can cause children to develop Western-style thinking.

Children are not passive in all of this, however. As children mature, they increasingly self-regulate, including making choices to embed themselves in particular situations versus others. Thus the child who decides to read a great deal becomes a causal force in her or his own literacy development. More negatively, characteristics over which children have little control also affect development, including health status. The child's characteristics are important contextual variables affecting the child's subsequent development. We focused on children's health as a characteristic defining the context of their development, because a great deal of attention has been paid to that dimension in recent years. We should add, however, that many other child characteristics can affect the contexts that a child experiences as part of development. Thus the gorgeous child will have different opportunities than the homely child. The easygoing child will have different experiences than the impulsive-aggressive child. The athletic child will be admitted to different contexts that affect development than will the clumsy youngster. The many different determinants of individual differences in development are summarized in Figure 13.2.

Do we understand nature and nurture completely? Hardly. Rather, this book has been written after a period of explosive growth in knowledge about development and how development relates to education. The findings summarized here, however, are only the stones in a gateway to additional research on development and education. Every one of the topics covered in this volume will be studied additionally in the near future. Educators who wish to know child development must work hard to stay current, for this is a field in which change is a constant. We plan to keep busy doing research on education and development and keeping abreast of the research of others, for it has proven to be an exciting and stimulating life adventure for us. We hope that at least a few of the readers of this textbook will choose to do research and that many more will make a point of becoming consumers and users of research pertaining to development and education. Do not be surprised if sometime in the new century you encounter a revised version of this text that is very different from the book you have just read. Although we have no doubt that much of what is studied as development in the middle of the 21st century will be classifiable as work on nature, nurture, or nature–nurture interactions, there is no crystal ball that can tell for certain how development and education will be construed in the future.

Genes

Differential learning opportunities
- Exposure to various models of behaviors
- Quality of teaching experiences (i.e., the reinforcements and punishments that occur, explanations and scaffolding provided)—for example, whether learning opportunities are consistently in the zone of proximal development

Differences in social ecology
- Microsystem differences (e.g., quality of home experiences, such as those leading to secure vs. insecure attachments; schooling characteristics, such as whether the school is more cooperative or competitive, more constructivist in orientation or more driven by mastery of low-level skills)
- Mesosystem differences (e.g., peer culture of the community in which the child develops; the church culture and traditions in which the child's development occurs)
- Exosystem differences (e.g., media, extended family)
- Macrosystem differences (e.g., larger culture; the historical period in which a child develops)

Social reactions to biologically determined characteristics of the child such as gender, intelligence, physical attractiveness, temperament, and athletic abilities

Experience of particular contexts of development determined by biologically determined characteristics of the child

Child as determiner of own development
- What strategies does the child use?
- To what degree does the child inhibit irrelevant behaviors and resist interference?
- How often and how well does the child monitor his or her behavior and what is going on around him or her?
- What attributions does the child make about successes and difficulties (e.g., outcomes are due to effort or ability)?
- What are the child's self-efficacy beliefs that determine his or her behavior?
- What are the child's attitudes and values that affect his or her behavior?
- Who does the child select for friends?
- What are the child's interests?
- What prior knowledge does the child have and how pertinent is it to the tasks and settings the child is expected to negotiate (e.g., school)?
- How good are the child's communication skills?

FIGURE 13.2. Determinants of individual differences in development.

References

Abel, E. L. (1998). *Fetal alcohol abuse syndrome*. New York: Plenum Press.

Abi-Nader, J. (1990). "A house for my mother": Motivating Hispanic high school students. *Anthropology and Education Quarterly, 21*, 41–58.

Achenbach, T., & Zigler, E. (1968). Cue-learning and problem-learning strategies in normal and retarded children. *Child Development, 3*, 827–848.

Adamczyk-Robinette, S. L., Fletcher, A. C., & Wright, K. (2002). Understanding the authoritative parenting–early adolescent tobacco use link: The mediating role of peer tobacco use. *Journal of Youth and Adolescence, 31*, 311–318.

Adams, M. J. (1990). *Beginning to read*. Cambridge, MA: Harvard University Press.

Adeyemo, S. A. (2002). A review of the role of the hippocampus in memory. *Psychology and Education: An Interdisciplinary Journal, 39*, 46–63.

Agmon, S., & Schneider, S. (1998). The first stages in the development of the small group: A psychoanalytic understanding. *Group Analysis, 31*, 131–156.

Ainley, M., Hidi, S., & Berndorff, D. (2002). Interest, learning, and the psychological processes that mediate their relationship. *Journal of Educational Psychology, 94*, 545–561.

Ainsworth, M. D. S. (1967). *Infancy in Uganda: Infant care and the growth of love*. Baltimore: Johns Hopkins University Press.

Ainsworth, M. D. S. (1979). Attachment as related to mother–infant interaction. In J. G. Rosenblatt, R. A. Hinde, C. Beer, & M. Busnel (Eds.), *Advances in the study of behavior* (Vol. 9, pp. 1–51). Orlando, FL: Academic Press.

Ainsworth, M. D. S., Blehar, M. C., Waters, E., & Wall, S. (1978). *Patterns of attachment: A psychological study of the Strange Situation*. Hillsdale, NJ: Erlbaum.

Ainsworth, M. S., & Bowlby, J. (1991). An ethological approach to personality development. *American Psychologist, 46*(4), 333–341.

Akhtar, N., Dunham, F., & Dunham, P. J. (1991). Directive interactions and early vocabulary development: The role of joint attentional focus. *Journal of Child Language, 18*, 41–50.

Alan Guttmacher Institute. (1994). *Sex and America's teenagers*. New York: Author.

Alan Guttmacher Institute. (2001). *Teenagers' sexual and reproductive health*. New York: Author.

Albano, A. M., Chorpita, B. F., & Barlow, D. H. (2003). Childhood anxiety disorders. In E. J. Mash & R. A. Barkley (Eds.), *Child psychopathology* (2nd ed., pp. 279–329). New York: Guilford Press.

Albertini, J. A., & Schley, S. (2003). Writing: Characteristics, instruction, and assessment. In M. Marschark & P. E. Spencer (Eds.), *Oxford handbook of deaf studies, language, and education* (pp. 123–135). New York: Oxford University Press.

Alexander, D. (1998). Prevention of mental retardation: Four decades of research. *Mental Retardation and Developmental Disabilities, 4*, 50–58.

Alexander, D. H. T., Walker, H. T., & Money, J. (1964). Studies in the directional sense. *Archives of General Psychiatry, 10*, 337–339.

Alexander, R., Boehme, R., & Cupps, B. (1993). *Normal development of functional motor skills: The first year of life*. San Antonio, TX: Psychological Corporation.

Allen, J. P., & Land, D. (1999). Attachment in adolescence. In J. Cassidy & P. R. Shaver (Eds.), *Handbook of attachment: Theory, research, and clinical applications* (pp. 319–335). New York: Guilford Press.

Allen, J. P., McElhaney, K. B., Land, D. J., Kuperminc, G. P., Moore, C. W., O'Beirne-Kelly, H., et al. (2003). A secure base in adolescence: Markers of attachment security in the mother–adolescent relationship. *Child Development, 74*, 292–307.

Allen, L. S., & Gorski, R. A. (1992). Sexual orientation and the size of the anterior commissure in the human brain. *Proceedings of the National Academy of Sciences USA, 89*, 7199–7202.

Allen, V. L. (Ed.). (1976). *Children as teachers: Theory and research on tutoring*. New York: Academic Press.

Alley, T. R. (1981). Head shape and the perception of cuteness. *Developmental Psychology, 17*, 650–654.

Allington, R. L. (1991a). Effective literacy instruction for at-risk children. In M. S. Knapp & P. M. Shields (Eds.), *Better schooling for the children of poverty: Alternatives to conventional wisdom* (pp. 9–30). Berkeley, CA: McCutchan.

Allington, R. L. (1991b). The legacy of "slow it down and make it more concrete." In J. Zutell & S. McCormick (Eds.), *Learner factors/teacher factors: Issues in literacy research and instruction: Fortieth yearbook of the National Reading Conference* (pp. 19–29). Chicago: National Reading Conference.

Allington, R. L., & McGill-Franzen, A. (1989). School response to reading failure: Chapter 1 and special education students in grades 2, 4, and 8. *Elementary School Journal, 89*, 529–542.

Allison, P. D., & Furstenberg, F. F. (1989). How marital dissolution affects children: Variations by age and sex. *Developmental Psychology, 25*, 540–549.

Allport, G. W., & Odbert, H. S. (1936). Trait names: A psycho-lexical study. *Psychological Monographs, 47*(1, Whole No. 211).

Alonso, E. (1999). A meta-analysis of the metacognition of gifted children. *Dissertation Abstracts International, Section B: The Sciences and Engineering, 60*(4–B), 1877.

Alsaker, F. D. (1992). Being overweight and psychological adjustment. *Journal of Early Adolescence, 12*, 396–419.

Altermatt, E. R., Pomerantz, E. M., Ruble, D. N., & Greulich, F. K. (2002). Predicting changes in children's self-perceptions of academic competence: A naturalistic examination of evaluative discourse among classmates. *Developmental Psychology, 38*, 903–917.

Alvarado, M. C., & Bachevalier, J. (2000). Revisiting the maturation of medial temporal lobe memory functions in primates. *Learning and Memory, 7*(5), 244–256.

American Association of Suicidology. (2006). *Youth suicide fact sheet*. Retrieved from www.suicidology.org/associations/1045/files/Youth2003.pdf.

American Association of University Women (1992). *How schools shortchange girls*. Washington, DC: AAIW Educational Foundation.

American Association of University Women. (1995). *How schools shortchange girls*. New York: Marlowe.

American Association of University Women Educational Foundation. (1998). *Gender gaps: Where schools still fail on children*. Washington, DC: Author.

American Association of University Women Educational Foundation. (2000). *A license for bias: Sex discrimination, schools, and Title IX*. Washington, DC: Author.

American Association of University Women Educational Foundation (2001). *Hostile hallways: Bullying, teasing, and sexual harrassment in schools*. Washington, DC: Author.

American Psychiatric Association. (1994). *Diagnostic and statistical manual of mental disorders* (4th ed.). Washington, DC: Author.

American Psychological Association. (1985). *Standards for educational and psychological testing*. Washington, DC: Author.

Ames, C. (1984). Competitive, cooperative, and individualistic goal structures: A motivational analysis. In R. Ames & C. Ames (Eds.), *Research on motivation in education* (Vol. 1, pp. 117–207). New York: Academic Press.

Ames, C. (1992). Classrooms: Goals, structures, and student motivation. *Journal of Educational Psychology, 84*, 261–271.

Ames, C., & Archer, J. (1988). Achievement goals in the classroom: Students' learning strategies and motivation processes. *Journal of Educational Psychology, 80*, 260–270.

Anastasi, A., & Irbina, S. (1997). *Psychological testing* (7th ed.). Saddle River, NJ: Prentice-Hall.

Anastasiow, N. J. (1990). Implications of the neurobiological model for early intervention. In S. J. Meisels & J. P. Shonkoff (Eds.), *Handbook of early childhood interventions* (pp. 196–216). Cambridge, UK: Cambridge University Press.

Anderman, E. M., Austin, C. C., & Johnson, D. M. (2002). The development of goal orientation. In A. Wigfield & J. S. Eccles (Eds.), *Development of achievement motivation* (pp. 197–220). San Diego, CA: Academic Press.

Anderman, E. M., Eccles, J. S., Yoon, K. S., Roeser, R., Wigfield, A., & Blumenfeld, P. (2001). Learning to value mathematics and reading: Relations to mastery and performance-oriented instructional practices. *Contemporary Educational Psychology, 26*, 76–95.

Anderman, E. M., & Maehr, M. L. (1994). Motivation and schooling in the middle grades. *Review of Educational Research, 64*, 287–309.

Anderman, E. M., Maehr, M. L., & Midgley, C. (1999). Declining motivation after the transition to middle school: Schools can make a difference. *Journal of Research and Development in Education, 32*, 131–147.

Anderman, E. M., & Midgley, C. (1997). Changes in achievement goal orientations, perceived academic competence, and grades across the transition to middle-level schools. *Contemporary Educational Psychology, 22*, 269–298.

Anderson, B., Mead, N., & Sullivan, S. (1986). *Television: What do national assessment results tell us!* Princeton, NJ: Educational Testing Service.

Anderson, D. R., Huston, A. C., Schmitt, K. L., Linebarger, D. L., & Wright, J. C. (2001). Early childhood television viewing and adolescent behavior. *Monographs of the Society for Research in Child Development, 66*(Serial No. 264).

Anderson, J. R. (1984). Spreading activation. In J. R. Anderson & S. M. Kosslyn (Eds.), *Tutorials in learning and memory: Essays in honor of Gordon Bower* (pp. 61–90). San Francisco: Freeman.

Anderson, P., Doyle, L. W., Callanan, C., Carse, E., Casalaz, D., Charlton, M., et al. (2003). Neurobehavioral outcomes of school-age children born extremely low birth weight or very preterm in the 1990s. *Journal of the American Medical Association, 289*, 3264–3272.

Anderson, R. C., Mason, J. M., & Shirey, L. (1984). The reading group: An experimental investigation of a labyrinth. *Reading Research Quarterly, 20*, 6–38.

Anderson, R. C., & Nagy, W. E. (1991). Word meanings. In R. Barr, M. L. Kamil, P. Mosenthal, & P. D. Pearson (Eds.), *Handbook of reading research* (Vol. II, pp. 690–724). New York: Longman.

Anderson, R. C., & Pearson, P. D. (1984). A schema-theoretic view of basic processes in reading. In P. D. Pearson (Ed.), *Handbook of reading research* (pp. 255–292). New York: Longman.

Anderson, R. C., Shirey, L. L., Wilson, P. T., & Fielding, L. G. (1987). Interestingness of children's reading material. In R. E. Snow & M. J. Farr (Eds.), *Aptitude, learning, and instruction: Vol. 3. Conative and affective process analyses* (pp. 287–299). Hillsdale, NJ: Erlbaum.

Anderson, V. (1992). A teacher development project in transactional strategy instruction for teachers of severely reading-disabled adolescents. *Teaching and Teacher Education, 8*, 391–403.

Andre, T., Whigham, M., Hendrickson, A., & Chambers, S. (1999). Competence beliefs, positive affect, and gender stereotypes of elementary students and their parents about science and other school subjects. *Journal of Research in Science Teaching, 36*, 719–747.

Anglin, J. M. (1977). *Word, object, and concept development.* New York: Norton.

Anglin, J. M. (1993). Vocabulary development: A morphological analysis. *Monographs of the Society for Research in Child Development, 58*(Serial No. 238).

Annett, J. (1989). Training skilled performance. In A. M. Colley & J. R. Beech (Eds.), *Acquisition and performance of cognitive skills* (pp. 61–84). Chichester, UK: Wiley.

Antia, S. D., & Kriemeyer, K. H. (2003). Peer interactions of deaf and hard-of-hearing children. In M. Marschark & P. E. Spencer (Eds.), *Oxford handbook of deaf studies, language, and education* (pp. 164–176). New York: Oxford University Press.

Apple, M. W. (1979). *Ideology and curriculum.* London: Routledge & Kegan Paul.

Applebee, A. N., & Langer, J. A. (1983). Instructional scaffolding: Reading and writing as natural language activities. *Language Arts, 60*, 168–175.

Applebee, A. N., Langer, J. A., Nystrand, M., & Gamoran, A. (2003). Discussion-based approaches to developing understanding: Instruction and achievement in middle and high school English. *American Educational Research Journal, 40*, 685–730.

Aram, D., & Nation, J. (1980). Preschool language disorders and subsequent language and academic difficulties. *Journal of Communication Disorders, 13*, 159–198.

Armbruster, B. B. (1984). The problem of "inconsiderate text." In G. G. Duffy, L. R. Roehler, & J. Mason (Eds.), *Comprehension instruction* (pp. 202–217). New York: Longman.

Arnold, D. H., Lonigan, C. J., Whitrhurst, G. J., & Epstein, J. N. (1994). Accelerating language development through picture book reading: Replication and extension to a videotape training format. *Journal of Educational Psychology, 86*, 235–243.

Arnold, D. H., McWilliams, L., & Arnold, E. H. (1998). Teacher discipline and child misbehavior in day care: Untangling causality with correlational data. *Developmental Psychology, 34*, 276–287.

Artzt, A. F., & Armour-Thomas, E. (1992). Development of a cognitive-metacognitive framework for protocol analysis of mathematical problem solving in small groups. *Cognition and Instruction, 9*, 137–175.

Asher, J., & Garcia, G. (1969). The optimal age to learn a foreign language. *Modern Language Journal, 38*, 334–341.

Asher, S. R., & Dodge, K. A. (1986). The identification of socially rejected children. *Developmental Psychology, 22*, 444–449.

Ashton, E. (1983). Measures of play behavior: The influence of sex role stereotyped books. *Sex Roles, 9*, 43–47.

Aslin, R. N. (1981). Experimental influence and sensitive period in perceptual development: A unified model. In R. N. Aslin & F. Peterson (Eds.), *The development of perception* (Vol. 2, pp. 45–93). Orlando, FL: Academic Press.

Aslin, R. N. (1987). Visual and auditory development in infancy. In J. Osofsky (Ed.), *Handbook of infant development* (pp. 5–97). New York: Wiley.

Aslin, R. N., Jurczyk, P. W., & Pisoni, D. B. (1998). Speech and auditory processing during infancy: Constraints on and precursors to language. In W. Damon (Gen. Ed.), D. Kuhn & R. S. Siegler (Vol. Eds.), *Handbook of child psychology* (5th ed., Vol. 2. Cognition, perception, and language (pp. 147–198). New York: Wiley.

Astington, J. W., & Olsen, D. R. (1990). Metacognitive and metalinguistic language: Learning to talk about thought. *Applied Psychology: An International Review, 39*, 77–87.

Atkinson, R. C., & Shiffrin, R. M. (1968). Human memory: A proposed system and its control processes. In K. W. Spence & J. T. Spence (Eds.), *The psychology of*

learning and motivation (Vol. 2, pp. 90–197). New York: Academic Press.

Au, K., & Mason, J. M. (1981). Social organizational factors in learning to read: The balance of rights hypothesis. *Reading Research Quarterly, 27*, 115–152.

August, D., Calderon, M., & Carlo, M. (2000). *Transfer of skills from Spanish to English: A study of young learners* (ED-98-CO-0071). Washington, DC: Center for Applied Linguistics.

Aukett, A., & Wharton, B. (1995). Suboptimal nutrition. In B. Lindström & N. Spencer (Eds.), *Social pediatrics* (pp. 270–296). Oxford, UK: Oxford University Press.

Avenvoli, S., Sessa, F. M., & Steinberg, L. (1999). Family structure, parenting practices, and adolescent adjustment: An ecological examination. In E. M. Hetherington (Ed.), *Coping with divorce, single parenting, and remarriage: A risk and resiliency perspective* (pp. 65–90). Mahwah, NJ: Erlbaum.

Azmitia, M., & Montgomery, R. (1993). Friendship, transactive dialogues, and the development of scientific reasoning. *Social Development, 2*, 202–221.

Bachman, J. G., & Schulenberg, J. (1993). How part-time work intensity relates to drug use: Problem behavior, time use, and satisfaction among high school seniors: Are these consequences or merely correlates? *Developmental Psychology, 29*, 220–235.

Bacon, C. S. (1993). Student responsibility for learning. *Adolescence, 28*, 199–212.

Baddeley, A. (1981). The concept of working memory: A view of its current state and probable future development. *Cognition, 10*, 17–23.

Baddeley, A. (1986). *Working memory.* New York: Oxford University Press.

Baek, H. (2002). A comparative study of moral development of Korean and British children. *Journal of Moral Education, 31*(4), 373–391.

Bagwell, C. L., Newcomb, A. F., & Bukowski, W. M. (1998). Pre-adolescent friendship and peer rejection as predictors of adult adjustment. *Child Development, 69*, 140–153.

Bailey, H. N., Waters, C. A., Pederson, D. R., & Moran, G. (1999). Ainsworth revisited: An empirical analysis of interactive behavior in the home. *Attachment and Human Development, 1*, 191–216.

Bailey, J. M., Bobrow, D., Wolfe, M., & Mikach, S. (1995). Sexual orientation of adult sons of gay fathers. *Developmental Psychology, 31*, 124–129.

Bakan, P. (1969). Hypnotizability, laterality of eye movement, and functional brain asymmetry. *Perceptual and Motor Skills, 28*, 927–932.

Bakeman, R., & Adamson, L. B. (1984). Coordinating attention to people and objects in mother–infant and peer–infant interaction. *Child Development, 55*, 1278–1289.

Baker-Ward, L., Ornstein, P. A., & Holden, D. J. (1984). The expression of memorization in early childhood. *Journal of Experimental Child Psychology, 37*, 555–575.

Bakwin, H. (1973). Reading disability in twins. *Developmental Medicine and Child Neurology, 15*, 184–187.

Ball, S., & Bogatz, G. A. (1970). *The first year of "Sesame Street": An evaluation.* Princeton, NJ: Educational Testing Service.

Baltes, P. B. (1968). Longitudinal and cross-sectional sequences in the study of age and generation effects. *Human Development, 11*, 145–171.

Baltes, P. B., Lindenberger, U., & Staudinger, U. M. (1998). Life-span theory in developmental psychology. In W. Damon (Gen. Ed.) & R. M. Lerner (Vol. Ed.), *Handbook of child psychology: Vol. 1. Theoretical models of human development* (5th ed., pp. 1029–1144). New York: Wiley.

Baltes, P. B., Reese, H. W., & Nesselroade, J. R. (1988). *Life-span developmental psychology: Introduction to research methods.* Monterey, CA: Brooks/Cole.

Bandura, A. (1965). Vicarious processes: A case of no-trial learning. In L. Berkowitz (Ed.), *Advances in experimental social psychology* (Vol. 2, pp. 1–55). New York: Academic Press.

Bandura, A. (1969). *Principles of behavior modification.* New York: Holt.

Bandura, A. (1977). *Social learning theory.* Englewood Cliffs, NJ: Prentice-Hall.

Bandura, A. (1986). *Social foundations of thought and action: A social cognitive theory.* Englewood Cliffs, NJ: Prentice-Hall.

Bandura, A. (1993). Perceived self-efficacy in cognitive development and functioning. *Educational Psychologist, 28*, 117–148.

Bandura, A. (1997). *Self-efficacy: The exercise of control.* New York: Freeman.

Bandura, A. (2002a). Social cognitive theory in cultural context. *Applied Psychology: An International Review, 51*, 269–290.

Bandura, A. (2002b). Social cognitive theory of mass communication. In J. Bryant & D. Zillmann (Eds.), *Media effects: Advances in theory and research* (2nd ed., pp. 121–153). Mahwah, NJ: Erlbaum.

Bandura, A. (2003). On the psychosocial impact and mechanisms of spiritual modeling: Comment. *International Journal for the Psychology of Religion, 13*, 167–173.

Bandura, A., Barbaranelli, C., Caprara, G. V., & Pastorelli, C. (1996). Multifaceted impact of self-efficacy beliefs on academic functioning. *Child Development, 67*, 1206–1222.

Bandura, A., Barbaranelli, C., Vittorio-Caprara, G. V., & Pastorelli, C. (2001). Self-efficacy beliefs as shapers of children's aspirations and career trajectories. *Child Development, 72*, 187–206.

Bandura, A., Grusec, J. E., & Menlove, F. L. (1966). Observational learning as a function of symbolization and incentive set. *Child Development, 37*, 499–506.

Bandura, A., & Jeffrey, R. W. (1973). Role of symbolic coding and rehearsal processes in observational learning. *Journal of Personality and Social Psychology, 26*, 122–130.

Bandura, A., Jeffrey, R. W., & Bachicha, D. L. (1974). Analysis of memory codes and cumulative rehearsal in observational learning. *Journal of Research in Personality, 7*, 295–305.

Bandura, A., & Schunk, D. H. (1981). Cultivating competence, self-efficacy, and intrinsic interest through proximal self-instruction. *Journal of Personality and Social Psychology, 41*, 586–598.

Bandura, A., & Walters, R. H. (1963). *Social learning and personality development.* New York: Holt, Rinehart & Winston.

Banks, J. A., & Banks, C. A. M. (Eds.). (1995). *Handbook of multicultural education.* New York: Macmillan.

Banks, M. S., & Salapatek, P. (1983). Infant visual perception. In M. M. Haith & J. J. Campos (Vols. Eds.) & P. H. Mussen (Gen. Ed.), *Handbook of child psychology: Vol. II. Infancy and developmental psychobiology* (pp. 435–571). New York: Wiley.

Barclay, C. R. (1979). The executive control of mnemonic activity. *Journal of Experimental Child Psychology, 27*, 262–276.

Barden, R. C., Zelko, F., Duncan, S. W., & Masters, J. C. (1980). Children's consensual knowledge about the experiential components of emotion. *Journal of Personality and Social Psychology, 39*, 968–976.

Barkley, R. A. (1997). *Defiant children: A clinician's manual for assessment and parent training* (2nd ed.). New York: Guilford Press.

Barkley, R. A. (2000). *Taking charge of ADHD: The complete, authoritative guide for parents* (rev. ed.). New York: Guilford Press.

Barkley, R. A. (2003). Attention-deficit/hyperactivity disorder. In E. J. Mash & R. A. Barkley (Eds.), *Child psychopathology* (2nd ed., pp. 75–143). New York: Guilford Press.

Barkley, R. A., & Benton, C. M. (1998). *Your defiant child: Eight steps to better behavior.* New York: Guilford Press.

Barkley, R. A., Edwards, G. H., & Robin, A. L. (1999). *Defiant teens: A clinician's manual for assessment and family intervention.* New York: Guilford Press.

Barnett, D., Kidwell, S. L., & Leung, K. H. (1998). Parenting and preschooler attachment among low-income urban African American families. *Child Development, 69*, 1657–1671.

Barnett, W. S. (2002). Early childhood education. In A. Molnar (Ed.), *School reform proposals: The research evidence* (pp. 1–26). Greenwich, CT: Information Age.

Baron-Cohen, S. (2001). Theory of mind and autism: A review. In L. M. Glidden (Ed.), *International review of research in mental retardation: Autism* (Vol. 23, pp. 169–184). San Diego, CA: Academic Press.

Baron-Cohen, S., Wheelwright, S., Lawson, J., Griffin, R., & Hill, J. (2002). The exact mind: Empathizing and systematizing in autism spectrum conditions. In U. Goswami (Ed.), *Blackwell handbook of childhood cognitive development* (pp. 491–508). Oxford, UK: Blackwell.

Barrett, M. D. (1989). Early language development. In A. Slater & C. Bremner (Eds.), *Infant development* (pp. 211–241). London, UK: Erlbaum.

Bartel, N. R., & Thurman, S. K. (1992). Medical treatment and educational problems in children. *Phi Delta Kappan, 74*, 57–61.

Bartsch, K., & Wellman, H. (1989). Young children's attribution of action to beliefs and desires. *Child Development, 60*, 946–964.

Bates, E. (1976). *Language and context.* New York: Academic Press.

Bates, E., Bretherton, L., & Snyder, L. (Eds.). (1988). *From first words to grammar: Individual differences and dissociable mechanisms.* Cambridge, UK: Cambridge University Press.

Bates, E., Dale, P. S., & Thal, D. (1995). Individual differences and their implications for language development. In P. Fletcher & B. MacWhinney (Eds.), *The handbook of child psychology* (pp. 96–151). Oxford, UK: Blackwell.

Bates, E., & Roe, K. (2001). Language development in children with unilateral brain injury. In C. A. Nelson & M. Luciana (Eds.), *Handbook of developmental cognitive neuroscience* (pp. 281–307). Cambridge, MA: MIT Press.

Bates, J. E., Marvinney, D., Kelly, T., Dodge, K. A., Bennett, D. S., & Pettit, G. S. (1994). Child-care history and kindergarten adjustment. *Developmental Psychology, 30,* 690–700.

Bateson, P., & Hinde, R. A. (1987). Developmental changes in sensitivity to experience. In M. H. Bornstein (Ed.), *Sensitive periods in development: Interdisciplinary perspectives* (pp. 19–34). Hillsdale, NJ: Erlbaum.

Batshaw, M. L., & Shapiro, B. (2002). Mental retardation. In M. L. Batshaw (Ed.), *Children with disabilities* (5th ed., pp. 287–305). Baltimore: Brookes.

Batshaw, M. L., & Tuchman, M. (2002). PKU and other inborn errors of metabolism. In M. L. Batshaw (Ed.), *Children with disabilities* (5th ed., pp. 333–346). Baltimore: Brookes.

Bauer, P. J. (1993). Memory for gender-consistent and gender-inconsistent event sequences by twenty-five-month-old children. *Child Development, 64,* 285–297.

Bauer, P. J., Wiebe, S. A., Carver, L. J., Waters, J. M., & Nelson, C. A. (2003). Developments in long-term explicit memory late in the first year of life: Behavioral and electrophysiological indices. *Psychological Science, 14,* 629–635.

Bauer, R. H. (1977a). Memory processes in children with learning disabilities. *Journal of Experimental Child Psychology, 24,* 415–430.

Bauer, R. H. (1977b). Short-term memory in learning disabled and nondisabled children. *Bulletin of the Psychonomic Society, 10,* 128–130.

Baumrind, D. (1972). From each according to her ability. *School Review, 80,* 161–197.

Baumrind, D. (1989). Rearing competent children. In W. Damon (Ed.), *Child development today and tomor-*

row (pp. 349–378). San Francisco: Jossey-Bass.

Baumrind, D. (1991). The influence of parenting style on adolescent competence and substance abuse. *Journal of Early Adolescence, 11,* 56–95.

Baydar, N., & Brooks-Gunn, J. (1991). Effects of maternal employment and child-care arrangements on preschoolers' cognitive and behavioral outcomes: Evidence from the children of the National Longitudinal Survey of Youth. *Developmental Psychology, 27,* 932–945.

Bayley, N. (1969). *Manual for the Bayley Scales of Infant Development.* New York: Psychological Corporation.

Bearer, C. F. (1995). Environmental health hazards: How children are different from adults. *The Future of Children, 5*(1), 11–26.

Bebeau, M. J., & Brabeck, M. M. (1987). Integrating care and justice issues in professional moral education: A gender perspective. *Journal of Moral Education, 16,* 189–203.

Bebko, J. M., & Luhaorg, H. (1998). The development of strategy use and metacognitive processing in mental retardation: Some sources of difficulty. In J. A. Burack, R. M. Hodapp, & E. Zigler (Eds.), *Handbook of mental retardation and development* (pp. 382–407). Cambridge, UK: Cambridge University Press.

Bechtel, W., & Abrahamsen, A. (1991). *Connectionism and the mind.* Cambridge, MA: Basil Blackwell.

Beck, I. L., & McKeown, M. (1991). Conditions of vocabulary acquisition. In R. Barr, M. L. Kamil, P. Mosenthal, & P. D. Pearson (Eds.), *Handbook of reading research* (Vol. II, pp. 789–814). New York: Longman.

Beck, R. W., & Beck, S. H. (1989). The incidence of extended households among middle-aged black and white women. *Journal of Family Issues, 10,* 147–168.

Becker, J. R. (1982). Differential treatment of females and males in mathematics classes. *Journal for Research in Mathematics Education, 12,* 40–53.

Beckwith, L., & Parmelee, A. H. Jr. (1986). EEG patterns of preterm infants: Home environments and later IQ. *Child Development, 57,* 777–789.

Behrend, D. A., Scofield, J., & Kleinknecht, E. E. (2001). Beyond fast mapping: Young children's extensions of novel words and novel facts. *Developmental Psychology, 37*(5), 698–705.

Beker L. T., Farber, A. F., & Comonitski Yanni, C. (2002). Nutri-

tion and children with disabilities. In M. L. Batshaw (Ed.), *Children with disabilities* (5th ed., pp. 141–164). Baltimore: Brookes.

Bell, M. A., & Fox, N. A. (1992). The relations between frontal brain electrical activity and cognitive development during infancy. *Child Development, 63,* 1142–1163.

Bell, M. A., & Fox, N. A. (1994). Brain development over the first year of life: Relations between electroencephalographic frequency and coherence and cognitive and affective behaviors. In G. Dawson & K. W. Fischer (Eds.), *Human behavior and the developing brain* (pp. 314–345). New York: Guilford Press.

Bell, M. A., & Fox, N. A. (1997). Individual differences in object permanence performance at 8 months: Locomotor experience and brain electrical activity. *Developmental Psychobiology, 31,* 287–297.

Bell, R. Q. (1968). A reinterpretation of the direction of effects in studies of socialization. *Psychological Review, 75,* 81–95.

Bell, R. Q., & Harper, L. V. (1977). *Child effects on adults.* Hillsdale, NJ: Erlbaum.

Belmont, J. M., Butterfield, E. C., & Ferretti, R. P. (1982). To secure transfer of training: Instruct self-management skills. In D. K. Detterman & R. J. Sternberg (Eds.), *How and how much can intelligence be increased* (pp. 147–154). Norwood, NJ: Ablex.

Belsky, J., Gilstrap, B., & Rovine, M. (1984). The Pennsylvania Infant and Family Development Project I: Stability and change in mother–infant and father–infant interaction in a family setting. *Child Development, 59,* 692–705.

Belsky, J., Rosenberger, K., & Crnic, K. (1995). The origins of attachment security: "Classical" and contextual determinants. In S. Goldberg, R. Muir, & J. Kerr (Eds.), *Attachment theory: Social, developmental, and clinical perspectives* (pp. 153–183). Hillsdale, NJ: Analytic Press.

Belsky, J., Rovine, M., & Taylor, D. G. (1984). The Pennsylvania Infant and Family Development Project III: The origins of individual differences in infant–mother attachment—Maternal and infant contributions. *Child Development, 55,* 718–728.

Belsky, J., Steinberg, L., & Draper, P. (1991). Childhood experience, interpersonal development, and reproductive strategy: An evolutionary theory of socialization. *Child Development, 62,* 647–670.

Belsky, J., Woodworth, S., & Crnic, K. (1996). Trouble in the second year: Three questions about family interaction. *Child Development, 67,* 556–578.

Bem, S. L. (1974). The measurement of psychological androgyny. *Journal of Consulting and Clinical Psychology, 42,* 155–162.

Bem, S. L. (1977). On the utility of alternative procedures for assessing psychological androgyny. *Journal of Consulting Clinical Psychology, 45*(2), 196–205.

Bem, S. L. (1975). Sex-role adaptability: One consequence of psychological androgyny. *Journal of Personality and Social Psychology, 31,* 634–643.

Bem, S. L. (1989). Genital knowledge and gender constancy in preschool children. *Child Development, 60,* 649–662.

Bem, S. L. (1993). *The lenses of gender: Transforming the debate on sexual inequality.* New Haven, CT: Yale University Press.

Bem, S. L. (1998). *An unconventional family.* New Haven, CT: Yale University Press.

Ben-Chaim, D., Lappan, G., & Houang, R. T. (1988). The effect of instruction on spatial visualization skills of middle school boys and girls. *American Educational Research Journal, 25,* 51–71.

Benenson, J. F., Apostoleris, N. H., & Parnass, J. (1997). Age and sex differences in dyadic and group interaction. *Developmental Psychology, 33,* 538–543.

Bennett, F. C. (1987). The effectiveness of early intervention for infants at increased biologic risk. In M. J. Guralnick & F. C. Bennett (Eds.), *The effectiveness of early intervention for at-risk and handicapped children* (pp. 79–112). Orlando, FL: Academic Press.

Bereiter, C. (1990). Aspects of an educational learning theory. *Review of Educational Research, 60,* 603–624.

Bereiter, C., & Scardamalia, M. (1982). From conversation to composition" The role of instruction in a developmental process. In R. Glaser (Ed.), *Advances in instructional psychology* (Vol. 2, pp. 1–64). Hillsdale, NJ: Erlbaum.

Berg, J. M. (1985). Physical determinants of environmental origin. In A. M. Clarke, A. D. B. Clarke, & J. M. Berg (Eds.), *Mental deficiency: The changing outlook* (4th ed., pp. 99–134). New York: Free Press.

Bergem, T. (1990). The teacher as moral agent. *Journal of Moral Education, 19,* 88–100.

Berk, L. E. (1986). Relationship of elementary school children's private speech to behavioral accompaniment to task, attention, and task performance. *Developmental Psychology, 22*(5), 671–680.

Berk, L. E., & Winsler, A. (1999). *Scaffolding children's learning: Vygotsky and early childhood education.* Washington, DC: National Association for the Education of Young Children.

Berndt, T. J. (1979). Developmental changes in conformity to peers and parents. *Developmental Psychology, 15,* 608–616.

Berndt, T. J. (1982). The features and effects of friendship in early adolescence. *Child Development, 53,* 1447–1460.

Berndt, T. J., & Miller, K. E. (1990). Expectancies, values, and achievement in junior high school. *Journal of Educational Psychology, 82,* 319–326.

Bernthal, J., & Bankson, N. (1993). *Articulation disorders.* Englewood Cliffs, NJ: Prentice-Hall.

Berry, G. (2000). Multicultural media portrayals and the changing demographic landscape: The psychological impact of television representations on the adolescent of color. *Journal of Adolescent Health, 275,* 57–60.

Berthoud-Papandropoulou, I. (1978). An experimental study of children's ideas about language. In A. Sinclair, R. J. Jarvella, & W. J. M. Levelt (Eds.), *The child's conception of language* (pp. 55–64). Berlin: Springer-Verlag.

Berthoud-Papandropoulou, I. (1980). *La réflexion métalinguistique chez l'enfant.* Geneva: Imprimerie Nationale.

Bialystock, E. (1987). Words as things: Development of word concept by bilingual children. *Studies in Second Language Acquisition, 9,* 133–140.

Bialystok, E. (1997). Effects of bilingualism and biliteracy on children's emerging concepts of print. *Developmental Psychology, 33,* 429–440.

Bialystok, E., Shenfield, T., & Codd, J. (2000). Languages, scripts, and the environment: Factors in developing concepts of print. *Developmental Psychology, 36,* 66–76.

Bickham, D. S., Wright, J. C., & Huston, A. C. (2001). Attention, comprehension, and the educa-

tional influences of television. In D. G. Singer & J. L. Singer (Eds.), *Handbook of children and the media* (pp. 101–119). Thousand Oaks, CA: Sage.

Bidell, T. R., & Fischer, K. W. (1992). Cognitive development in educational contexts: Implications for skill theory. In A. Demetriou, M. Shayner, & A. Efklides (Eds.), *Neo-Piagetian theories of cognitive development* (pp. 11–30). New York: Routledge.

Bidell, T. R., & Fischer, K. W. (2000). The role of cognitive structure in the development of behavioral control: A dynamic skills approach. In W. J. Perrig & A. Grob (Eds.), *Control of human behavior, mental processes, and consciousness: Essays in honor of the 60th birthday of August Flammer* (pp. 183–201). Mahwah, NJ: Erlbaum.

Bielinski, J., & Davison, M. L. (1998). Gender differences by item difficulty interactions in multiple-choice mathematics items. *American Educational Research Journal, 35,* 455–476.

Biemiller, A. (2003). Vocabulary: Needed if more children are to read well. *Reading Psychology, 24,* 323–335.

Biemiller, A., & Slonim, N. (2001). Estimating root word vocabulary growth in normative and advantaged populations: Evidence for a common sequence of vocabulary acquisition. *Journal of Educational Psychology, 93,* 498–520.

Bierman, K. L., Smoot, D. L., & Aumiller, K. (1993). Characteristics of aggressive-rejected, aggressive (non-rejected), and rejected (nonaggressive) boys. *Child Development, 64,* 139–151.

Bigler, R. S. (1995). The role of classification skill in moderating environmental influences on children's gender stereotyping: A study of the functional use of gender in the classroom. *Child Development, 66,* 1072–1087.

Bigler, R. S., & Liben, L. S. (1990). The role of attitudes and interventions in gender schematic processing. *Child Development, 61,* 1440–1452.

Bigler, R. S., & Liben, L. S. (1992). Cognitive mechanisms in children's gender stereotyping: Theoretical and educational implications of a cognitively-based intervention. *Child Development, 63,* 1351–1363.

Biller, H. B. (1970). Father absence

and the personality development of the male child. *Developmental Psychology, 2,* 181–201.

Biller, H. B., & Bahm, R. M. (1971). Father absence, perceived maternal behavior, and masculinity of self-concept among junior high boys. *Developmental Psychology, 4,* 178–181.

Billy, J. O. G., & Idry, J. R. (1987). The influence of male and female best friends on adolescent sexual behavior. *Adolescence, 20,* 21–31.

Binet, A., & Simon, T. (1905a). Application des methodes nouvelles au diagnostic du niveau intellectuel chez des enfants normaux et anormaux d'hospice et d'ecole primaire. *L'Annee Psychologique, 11,* 245–336.

Binet, A., & Simon, T. (1905b). Methodes nouvelles pour le disagnostic du niveau intellectuel des anormaux. *L'Annee Psychologique, 11,* 191–244.

Binet, A., & Simon, T. (1905c). Sur la necessite d'établit un diagnostic scientifique des etats inferieurs de l'intelligence. *L'Annee Psychologique, 11,* 163–190.

Birdsong, D. (1999). *Second language acquisition and the critical period hypothesis.* Mahwah, NJ: Erlbaum.

Birdsong, D. (2005). Interpreting age effects in second language acquisition. In J. F. Kroll & A. M. B. de Groot (Eds.), *Handbook of bilingualism: Psycholinguistic approaches* (pp. 109–127). New York: Oxford University Press.

Birenbaum, A. (2002). Poverty, welfare reform, and disproportionate rates of disability among children. *Mental Retardation, 40,* 212–218.

Bishop, E. G., Stacey, S., Corley, R., Plomin, R., DeFries, J. C., & Hewitt, J. K. (2003). Development genetic analysis of general cognitive ability from 1 to 12 years in a sample of adoptees, biological siblings, and twins. *Intelligence, 31,* 31–49.

Bjorklund, D. F. (1989). *Cognitive development.* Monterey CA: Brooks/Cole.

Bjorklund, D. F. (2000). *Children's thinking: Developmental function and individual differences* (3rd ed.). Belmont, CA: Wadsworth Thomson Learning.

Bjorklund, D. F., & Harnishfeger, K. K. (1990). The resources construct in cognitive development: Diverse resources of evidence and a theory of inefficient inhibition. *Developmental Review, 10,* 48–71.

Black, B., & Hazen, N. L. (1990). Social status and patterns of communication in acquainted and unacquainted preschool children. *Developmental Psychology, 13,* 175–183.

Black, J. E., & Greenough, W. T. (1991). Developmental approaches to the memory process. In J. L. Martinez Jr. & R. P. Kesner (Eds.), *Learning and memory: A biological view* (2nd ed., pp. 61–91). San Diego, CA: Academic Press.

Black, K. A. (2000). Gender differences in adolescents' behavior during conflict resolution tasks with best friends. *Adolescence, 35,* 499–512.

Blackman, L. S., & Lin, A. (1984). Generalization training in the educable mentally retarded: Intelligence and its educability revisited. In P. H. Brooks, R. Sperber, & C. McCauley (Eds.), *Learning and cognition in the mentally retarded* (pp. 237–263). Hillsdale, NJ: Erlbaum.

Blackwood, R. (1970). The operant conditioning of verbally mediated self-control in the classroom. *Journal of School Psychology, 8,* 251–258.

Blair, S. L., Blair, M. C. L., & Madamba, A. B. (1999). Racial/ethnic differences in high school students' academic performance: Understanding the interweave of social class and ethnicity in the family context. *Journal of Comparative Family Studies, 30,* 539–555.

Blakenay, R., & Blakenay, C. (1990). Reforming moral misbehaviour. *Journal of Moral Education, 19,* 101–113.

Blarney, P. J. (2003). Development of spoken language by deaf children. In M. Marschark & P. E. Spencer (Eds.), *Oxford handbook of deaf studies, language, and education* (pp. 232–246). New York: Oxford University Press.

Block, J. H. (1977). Another look at sex differentiation in the socialization behaviors of mothers and fathers. In J. Sherman & F. Denmark (Eds.), *Psychology of women: Future directions of research* (pp. 29–87). New York: Psychological Dimensions.

Block, J. H., Block, J., & Gjerde, P. F. (1986). The personality of children prior to divorce: A prospective study. *Child Development, 57,* 827–840.

Bloom, B. S. (1985). *Developing talent in young people.* New York: Ballantine Books.

Bloom, L. (1973). *One word at a time.* The Hague, The Netherlands: Mouton.

Bloom, L. (1998). Language acquisition in its developmental context. In W. Damon (Gen. Ed.), D. Kuhn & R. S. Siegler (Vol. Eds.), *Handbook of child psychology: Vol. 2. Cognition, perception, and language,* pp. 309–370). New York: Wiley.

Bloom, L. (2000). The intentionality model of word learning: How to learn a word, any word. In R. M. Golinkoff, K. Hirsh-Pasek, L. Bloom, L. B. Smith, A. L. Woodward, N. Akhtar, et al. (Eds.), *Becoming a word learner: A debate on lexical acquisition* (pp. 19–50). New York: Oxford University Press.

Bloom, L., Margulis, C., Tinker, E., & Fujita, N. (1996). Early conversations and word learning: Contributions from child and adult. *Child Development, 67,* 3154–3175.

Bloom, L., Rocissano, L., & Hood, L. (1976). Adult–child discourse: Developmental interaction between linguistic processing and linguistic knowledge. *Cognitive Psychology, 8,* 521–552.

Bloom, L., & Tinker, E. (2001). The intentionality model and language acquisition. *Monographs of the Society for Research in Child Development, 66*(Serial No. 267), i–viii, 1–91.

Blumenfeld, P. C. (1992). Classroom learning and motivation: Clarifying and expanding goal theory. *Journal of Educational Psychology, 84,* 272–281.

Bodrova, E., & Leong, D. J. (2003). Learning and development of preschool children from the Vygotskian perspective. In A. Kozulin, B. Gindia, V. S. Ageyev, & S. M. Miller (Eds.), *Vygotsky's educational theory in cultural context* (pp. 156–176). Cambridge, UK: Cambridge University Press.

Bogner, K., Raphael, L. M., & Pressley, M. (2002). How grade-1 teachers motivate literate activity by their students. *Scientific Studies of Reading, 6,* 135–165.

Bohn, C. M., Roehrig, A. D., & Pressley, M. (2004). The first days of school in effective and less effective primary-grades classrooms. *Elementary School Journal, 104,* 269–278.

Boldizar, J. P. (1991). Assessing sex typing and androgyny in children. *Developmental Psychology, 27,* 505–515.

Bomba, P. C., & Siqueland, E. R. (1983). The nature and structure of infant form categories. *Journal of Experimental Child Psychology, 35,* 294–328.

Bond, G. L., & Dykstra, R. (1967). The cooperative research program in first-grade reading instruction. *Reading Research Quarterly, 2,* 5–142.

Booth, A., Brinkerhoff, D., & White, C. (1984). The impact of parental divorce on courtship. *Journal of Marriage and the Family, 46,* 85–94.

Booth, J. R., & Hall, W. S. (1994). Role of the cognitive internal state lexicon in reading comprehension. *Journal of Educational Psychology, 86,* 413–422.

Borja-Alvarez, T., Zarbatany, L., & Pepper, S. (1991). Contributions of male and female guests and hosts to peer group entry. *Child Development, 62,* 1079–1090.

Borkowski, J. G., Carr, M., Rellinger, E. A., & Pressley, M. (1990). Self-regulated strategy use: Interdependence of metacognition, attributions, and self-esteem. In B. F. Jones (Ed.), *Dimensions of thinking: Review of research* (pp. 53–92). Hillsdale, NJ: Erlbaum.

Borkowski, J. G., & Dukewich, T. L. (1996). Environmental covariations and intelligence: How attachment influences self-regulation. In D. K. Detterman (Ed.), *Current topics in human intelligence: Vol. 5. The environment* (pp. 3–15). Norwood, NJ: Ablex.

Borkowski, J. G., & Kurtz, B. E. (1987). Metacognition and executive control. In J. G. Borkowski & J. D. Day (Eds.), *Cognition in special children: Comparative approaches to retardation, learning disabilities, and giftedness* (pp. 123–152). Norwood, NJ: Ablex.

Borkowski, J. G., & Peck, V. A. (1986). Causes and consequences of metamemory in gifted children. In R. J. Sternberg & J. E. Davidson (Eds.), *Conceptions of giftedness* (pp. 182–200). Cambridge, UK: Cambridge University Press.

Borkowski, J. G., Ramey, S. L., & Bristol-Power, M. (2002). *Parenting and the child's world: Influences on academic, intellectual, and social-emotional development.* Mahwah, NJ: Erlbaum.

Borkowski, J. G., Weyhing, R. S., & Carr, M. (1988). Effects of attributional retraining on strategy-based reading comprehension in learning-disabled students. *Journal of Educational Psychology, 80,* 46–53.

Bortfield, H., & Whitehurst, G. J. (2001). Sensitive periods in first language acquisition. In D. B. Bailey Jr., J. T. Bruer, F. J. Symons,

& J. W. Lichtman (Eds.), *Critical thinking about critical periods* (pp. 173–192). Baltimore: Brookes.

Bos, C. S., & Vaughn, S. (1991). *Strategies for teaching students with learning and behavior problems.* Boston: Allyn & Bacon.

Boston, M. B., & Levy, G. D. (1991). Changes and differences in preschoolers' understanding of gender scripts. *Cognitive Development, 6,* 417–432.

Botwinick, J. (1977). Intellectual abilities. In J. E. Birren & K. W. Schaie (Eds.), *The handbook of the psychology of aging* (pp. 580–605). New York: Van Nostrand Reinhold.

Bouchard, T. J. Jr., & Loehlin, J. C. (2001). Genes, evolution, and personality. *Behavior Genetics, 31,* 243–273.

Bouchard, T. J. Jr., & McGue, M. (1981). Familial studies of intelligence: A review. *Science, 212,* 1055–1059.

Bourgeois, J. P. (2001). Synaptogenesis in the neocortex of the newborn: The ultimate frontier for individuation. In C. A. Nelson & M. Luciana (Eds.), *Handbook of developmental cognitive neuroscience* (pp. 23–34). Cambridge, MA: MIT Press.

Bower, G. H. (1972). Mental imagery and associative learning. In L. Gregg (Ed.), *Cognition in learning and memory* (pp. 51–87). New York: Wiley.

Bower, G. H., & Clapper, J. P. (1989). Experimental methods in cognitive science. In M. L. Posner (Ed.), *Foundations of cognitive science.* Cambridge, MA: MIT Press.

Bowers, C. A., & Flinders, D. J. (1990). *Responsive teaching: An ecological approach to classroom patterns of language, culture, and thought.* New York: Teachers College Press.

Bower, G. H., & Hilgard, E. R. (1981). *Theories of learning* (5th ed.). Englewood Cliffs, NJ: Prentice-Hall.

Bowey, J. A., & Tunmer, W. E. (1984). Word awareness in children. In W. E. Tunmer, C. Pratt, & M. L. Herriman (Eds.), *Metalinguistic awareness in children* (pp. 73–91). Berlin: Springer-Verlag.

Bowlby, J. (1969). *Attachment and loss, Volume 1. Attachment.* New York: Basic Books.

Bowlby, J. (1973). *Attachment and loss, Volume 2. Separation.* New York: Basic Books.

Bowlby, J. (1980). *Attachment and loss, Volume 3. Loss.* New York: Basic Books.

Bowles, S., & Gintis, H. (1976). *Schooling in capitalist America: Educational reform and the contradictions of economic life.* New York: Basic Books.

Boyes, M. C., & Chandler, M. (1992). Cognitive development, epistemic doubt, and identity formation in adolescence. *Journal of Youth and Adolescence, 21,* 277–304.

Boysson-Bardies, B. de, Halle, P., Sagart, L., & Durand, C. (1989). A cross-linguistic investigation of vowel formants in babbling. *Journal of Child Language, 16,* 1–17.

Boysson-Bardies, B. de, Vihman, M. M., Roug-Hellichius, L., Durand, C., Landberg, I., & Arao, F. (1992). Material evidence of infant selection from target language: A cross-linguistic study. In C. A. Ferguson, L. Menn, & C. Stoel-Gammon (Eds.), *Phonological development: Models, research, and implications* (pp. 369–91). Timonium, MD: York Press.

Brabeck, M. M. (Ed.) (1989). *Who cares?: Theory, research, and educational implications of the ethic of care.* New York: Praeger.

Bracht, G. H., & Glass, G. V. (1968). The external validity of experiments. *American Educational Research Journal, 5,* 437–474.

Braden, J.P. (2003). Psychological assessment in school settings. In J. R. Graham, J. A. Naglieri (Vol. Eds.) & I. B. Weiner (Ed.-in-Chief), *Handbook of psychology: Vol. 10. Assessment psychology* (pp. 261–290). New York: Wiley.

Bradford, M. R., & Ensley, R. C. (1983). The effects of sex-typed labeling on preschool children's information-seeking and retention. *Sex Roles, 9,* 247–260.

Bradley, L. (1988). Making connections in learning to read and to spell. *Applied Cognitive Psychology, 2,* 3–18.

Bradley, L. (1989). Predicting learning disabilities. In J. Dumont & H. Nakken (Eds.), *Learning disabilities: Vol. 2. Cognitive, social, and remedial aspects* (pp. 1–18). Amsterdam, The Netherlands: Swets.

Bradley, L., & Bryant, P. E. (1983). Categorizing sounds and learning to read—a causal connection. *Nature, 301,* 419–421.

Bradley, L., & Bryant, P. (1991). Phonological skills before and after learning to read. In S. A. Brady & D. P. Shankweiler (Eds.), *Phonological processes in literacy: A tribute to Isabelle Y. Liberman* (pp. 37–45). Hillsdale, NJ: Erlbaum.

Braine, M. D. (1963). The ontogeny of

English phrase structure: The first phase. *Language, 39*, 3–13.

Braine, M. D. (1976). Children's first-word combinations. *Monographs of the Society for Research in Child Development, 41*(No. 164).

Brainerd, C. J. (1978a). Learning research and Piagetian theory. In L. S. Siegel & C. J. Brainerd (Eds.), *Alternatives to Piaget: Critical essays on the theory* (pp. 69–109). New York: Academic Press.

Brainerd, C. J. (1978b). *Piaget's theory of intelligence.* Englewood Cliffs, NJ: Prentice-Hall.

Brainerd, C. J. (1978c). The stage question in cognitive developmental theory. *Behavioral and Brain Sciences, 1*, 173–213.

Brainerd, C. J., & Reyna, V. F. (1993). "Memory independence and memory interference in cognitive development": Correction. *Psychological Review, 100*(2), 319.

Brainerd, C. J., & Reyna, V. F. (1989). Output-interference theory of dual-task deficits in memory development. *Journal of Experimental Child Psychology, 47*, 1–18.

Brainerd, C. J., & Reyna, V. F. (1990a). Can age × learnability interactions explain the development of forgetting? *Developmental Psychology, 26*, 194–204.

Brainerd, C. J., & Reyna, V. F. (1990b). Gist in the grist: Fuzzy-trace theory and the new intuitionism. *Developmental Review, 10*, 3–47.

Brainerd, C. J., & Reyna, V. F. (1992). The memory independence effect: What do the data show? What do the theories claim? *Developmental Review, 12*, 164–186.

Brainerd, C. J., & Reyna, V. F. (1993). "Memory independence and memory interference in cognitive development": Correction. *Psychological Review, 100*(2), 319.

Brainerd, C. J., & Reyna, V. F. (1995). Autosuggestibility and memory development. *Cognitive Psychology, 28*, 65–101.

Braungart-Rieker, J. M., Garwood, M. M., Powers, B. P., & Wang, X. (2001). Parental sensitivity, infant affect, and affect regulation: Predictors of later attachment. *Child Development, 72*, 252–270.

Bray, N. W., Fletcher, K. L., & Turner, L. A. (1997). Cognitive competencies and strategy use in individuals with mental retardation. In W. E. MacLean Jr. (Ed.), *Ellis' handbook of mental deficiency, psychological theory and research* (pp. 197–217). Mahwah, NJ: Erlbaum.

Breggin, P. R. (2001). *Talking back to Ritalin: What doctors aren't telling you about stimulants and ADHD.* New York: Perseus.

Brenneis, C. B. (2000). Evaluating the evidence: Can we find authenticated recovered memory? *Psychoanalytic Psychology, 17*, 61–77.

Bretherton, I. (1995). A communication perspective on attachment relationships and internal working models. In E. Waters, B. E. Vaughn, G. Posada, & K. Kondo-Ikemura (Eds.), *Caregiving, cultural, and cognitive perspectives on secure-base behavior and working-models. Monographs of the Society for Research in Child Development, 60*(Nos. 2–3, Serial No. 244), 310–329.

Bretl, D. J., & Cantor, J. (1988). The portrayal of men and women in U.S. television commercials: A recent content analysis and trends over 15 years. *Sex Roles, 18*(9–10), 595–609.

Brewer, N. (1987). Processing speed, efficiency, and intelligence. In J. G. Borkowski & J. D. Day (Eds.), *Cognition in special children: Comparative approaches to retardation, learning disabilities, and giftedness* (pp. 15–48). Norwood, NJ: Ablex.

Bridgeman, B., & Wendler, C. (1991). Gender differences in predictors of college mathematics performance and in college mathematics course grades. *Journal of Educational Psychology, 83*, 275–284.

Brigham, C. C. (1923). *A study of American intelligence.* Princeton, NJ: Princeton University Press.

Brinton, B., & Fujiki, M. (1982). A comparison of the request–response sequences in the discourse of normal and language-disordered children. *Journal of Hearing and Speech Disorders, 47*, 57–62.

Brinton, B., & Fujiki, M. (1995). Conversational intervention with children with specific language impairment. In M. E. Fey, J. Windsor, & S. F. Warren (Eds.), *Language intervention: Preschool through the elementary years* (pp. 183–212). Baltimore: Brookes.

Broberg, A. G., Wessels, H., Lamb, M. E., & Hwang, C. P. (1997). Effects of day care on the development of cognitive abilities in 8-year-olds: A longitudinal study. *Developmental Psychology, 33*, 62–69.

Brody, E. B., & Brody, N. (1978). *Intelligence: Nature, determinants, and consequences.* New York: Academic Press.

Brody, G. H., Ge, X., Conger, R., Gibbons, F. X., McBride-Murry, V., Gerrard, M., et al. (2001). The influence of neighborhood disadvantage, collective socialization, and parenting on African American children's affiliation with deviant peers. *Child Development, 72*, 1231–1246.

Brody, G. H., Stoneman, Z., & McCoy, J. K. (1992). Associations of maternal and paternal direct and differential behavior with sibling relationships: Contemporaneous and longitudinal analyses. *Child Development, 63*, 391–400.

Brody, L. (1999). *Gender, emotion, and the family.* Cambridge, MA: Harvard University Press.

Brody, N. (1992). *Intelligence.* San Diego, CA: Academic Press.

Bronfenbrenner, U. (1979). *The ecology of human development.* Cambridge, MA: Harvard University Press.

Bronfenbrenner, U. (1989). Ecological systems theory. In R. Vasta (Ed.), *Annals of child development* (Vol. 6, pp. 187–251). Greenwich, CT: JAI Press.

Bronfenbrenner, U. (1992). Ecological systems theory. In R. Vasta (Ed.), *Six theories of child development: Revised formulations and current issues* (pp. 187–249). London: Kingsley.

Bronson, W. (1981). Toddlers' behavior with age-mates: Issues of interaction, cognition, and affect. *Monographs in Infancy, 1*, 127.

Brooks-Gunn, J., & Chase-Lansdale, P. L. (1995). Adolescent parenthood. In M. H. Bornstein (Ed.), *Handbook of parenting: Vol. 3. Status and social conditions of parenting* (pp. 113–149). Hillsdale, NJ: Erlbaum.

Brooks-Gunn, J., & Mathews, W. S. (1979). *He and she: How children develop their sex role identity.* Englewood Cliffs, NJ: Prentice-Hall.

Brophy, J. (1981). Teacher praise: A functional analysis. *Review of Educational Research, 51*, 5–32.

Brophy, J. (1986, October). *On motivating students* (Occasional Paper No. 101). East Lansing: Michigan State University, Institute for Research on Teaching.

Brophy, J. (1987). Socializing students' motivation to learning. In M. L. Maehr & D. A. Kleiber (Eds.), *Advances in motivation and achievement: Enhancing motivation* (Vol. 5, pp. 181–210). Greenwich, CT: JAI Press.

Brophy, J. E. (1998). *Motivating students to learn.* Boston: McGraw-Hill.

Brophy, J. E., & Evertson, C. M. (1976). *Learning from teaching: A developmental perspective.* Boston: Allyn & Bacon.

Brophy, J., & Good, T. (1974). *Teacher–student relationships: Causes and consequences.* New York: Holt, Rinehart & Winston.

Brown, A. L. (1974). The role of strategic behavior in retardate memory. In N. R. Ellis (Ed.), *International review of research in mental retardation* (Vol. 7, pp. 55–111). New York: Academic Press.

Brown, A. L. (1978). Knowing when, where, and how to remember: A problem of metacognition. In R. Glaser (Ed.), *Advances in instructional psychology* (Vol. 1, pp. 77–165). Hillsdale, NJ: Erlbaum.

Brown, A. L., & Campione, J. C. (1978). Permissible inferences from cognitive training studies in developmental research. In W. S. Hall & M. Cole (Eds.), *Quarterly Newsletter of the Institute for Comparative Human Behavior, 2*(3), 46–53.

Brown, A. L., & DeLoache, J. S. (1978). Skills, plans, and self-regulation. In R. S. Siegler (Ed.), *Children's thinking: What develops?* (pp. 3–36). Hillsdale, NJ: Erlbaum.

Brown, A. L., & French, L. (1979). The zone of proximal development: Implications for intelligence testing in the year 2000. *Intelligence, 3,* 253–271.

Brown, A. L., & Palincsar, A. S. (1989). Guided, cooperative learning and individual knowledge acquisition. In L. B. Resnick (Ed.), *Knowing, learning, and instruction: Essays in honor of Robert Glaser* (pp. 393–451). Hillsdale, NJ: Erlbaum.

Brown, B. B. (1989). The role of peer groups in adolescents' adjustment to secondary school. In T. J. Berndt & G. W. Ladd (Eds.), *Peer relationships in child development* (pp. 188–215). New York: Wiley.

Brown, B. B. (1990). Peer groups and peer cultures. In S. S. Feldman & G. R. Elliott (Eds.), *At the threshold: The developing adolescent* (pp. 171–196). Cambridge, MA: Harvard University Press.

Brown, B. B., & Klute, C. (2003). Friendships, cliques, and crowds. In G. R. Adams & M. D. Berzonsky (Eds.), *Blackwell handbook of adolescence* (pp. 330–348). Malden, MA: Blackwell.

Brown, B. B., Lohr, M. J., & McClenahan, E. L. (1986). Early adolescents' perceptions of peer pressure. *Journal of Early Adolescence, 6,* 139–154.

Brown, B. B., Mounts, N., Lamborn, S. D., & Steinberg, L. (1993). Parenting practices and peer group affiliation in adolescence. *Child Development, 64,* 467–482.

Brown, I. (1976). Role of referent concreteness in the acquisition of passive sentence comprehension through abstract modeling. *Journal of Experimental Child Psychology, 22,* 185–189.

Brown, I. (1979). Language acquisition: Linguistic structure and rule-governed behavior. In G. J. Whitehurst & B. J. Zimmerman (Eds.), *The functions of language and cognition* (pp. 141–173). New York: Academic Press.

Brown, J. S., Collins, A., & Duguid, P. (1989). Situated cognition and the culture of learning. *Educational Researcher, 18*(1), 32–42.

Brown, Ra., Pressley, M., & Van Meter, P. (1996). A quasi-experimental validation of transactional strategies instruction with low-achieving grade-2 readers. *Journal of Educational Psychology, 88,* 18–37.

Brown, Ro. (1965). *Social psychology.* New York: Free Press.

Brown, Ro. (1973). *A first language: The early stages.* Cambridge, MA: Harvard University Press.

Brown, Ro., & Bellugi, U. (1964). Three processes in the child's acquisition of syntax. *Harvard Educational Review, 34,* 133–151.

Brown, R. T., & Madan-Swain, A. (1993). Cognitive, neuropsychological, and academic sequelae in children with leukemia. *Journal of Learning Disabilities, 26,* 74–91.

Brown, T. N., Schulenberg, J., Bachman, J. G., O'Malley, P. M., & Johnston, L. D. (2001). Are risk and protective factors for substance use consistent across historical time?: National data from the high school classes of 1976 through 1997. *Prevention Science, 2,* 29–43.

Brownell, C. A., & Brown, E. (1992). Peers and play in infants and toddlers. In V. B. V. Hasselt & M. Hersen (Eds.), *Handbook of social development: A lifespan perspective* (pp. 183–200). New York: Plenum Press.

Brownell, C. A., & Carriger, M. S. (1990). Changes in cooperation and self–other differentiation during the second year. *Child Development, 61,* 1164–1174.

Bruck, M. (1990). Word-recognition skills of adults with childhood diagnoses of dyslexia. *Developmental Psychology, 26,* 439–454.

Bruck, M. (1992). Persistence of dyslexics' phonological awareness deficits. *Developmental Psychology, 28,* 874–886.

Bruer, J. T. (1999). *The myth of the first three years: A new understanding of early brain development and lifelong learning.* New York: Free Press.

Bruer, J. T. (2001). A critical and sensitive period primer. In D. B. Bailey Jr., J. T. Bruer, F. J. Symons, & J. W. Lichtman (Eds.), *Critical thinking about critical periods* (pp. 3–26). Baltimore: Brookes.

Bruner, J. S., Olver, R. R., & Greenfield, P. M. (1966). *Studies in cognitive growth.* New York: Wiley.

Bry, B. H. (1982). Reducing the incidence of adolescent problems through preventive intervention: One- and five-year follow-up. *American Journal of Community Psychology, 10,* 265–276.

Bryant, A. L., Schulenberg, J. E., O'Malley, P. M., Bachman, J. G., & Johnston, L. D. (2003). How academic achievement, attitudes, and behaviors relate to the course of substance abuse during adolescence. *Journal of Research on Adolescence, 13,* 361–397.

Bryk, A. S., & Schneider, B. (2002). *Trust in schools: A core resource for improvement.* New York: Russell Sage.

Buchanen, C. M., Maccoby, E. E., & Dornbusch, S. M. (1991). Caught between parents: Adolescent experience in divorced homes. *Child Development, 62,* 1008–1029.

Budoff, M. (1987). Measures for assessing learning potential. In C. S. Lidz (Ed.), *Dynamic assessment: An interactional approach to evaluating learning potential* (173–195). New York: Guilford Press.

Buhrmester, D. (1992). The developmental courses of sibling and peer relationships. In F. Boer & J. Dunn (Eds.), *Children's sibling relationships: Developmental and clinical issues* (pp. 19–40). Hillsdale, NJ: Erlbaum.

Buhrmester, D. (1996). Need fulfilment, interpersonal competence, and the developmental contexts of early adolescent friendship. In W. M. Bukowski, A. F. Newcomb, & W. W. Hartup (Eds.), *The company they keep: Friendship in childhood and adolescence* (pp. 158–185). Cambridge, UK: Cambridge University Press.

Buhrmester, D., & Furman, W. (1986). The changing functions of children's friendships: A neo-Sullivanian perspective. In V. Derlega & B. Winstead (Eds.), *Friendships and social interactions* (pp. 141–162). New York: Springer-Verlag.

Bukowski, W. M., Gauze, C., Hoza, B., & Newcomb, A. E. (1993). Difference and consistency between same-sex and other-sex peer relationships during early adolescence. *Developmental Psychology, 29,* 255–263.

Bukstein, O. G. (1995). *Adolescent substance abuse: Assessment, prevention, and treatment.* New York: Wiley.

Burack, J. A. (1990). Differentiating mental retardation: The two-group approach and beyond. In R. M. Hodapp, J. A. Burdack, & E. Zigler (Eds.), *Issues in the developmental approach to mental retardation* (pp. 27–48). Cambridge, UK: Cambridge University Press.

Burbules, N. C., & Linn, M. C. (1988). Response to contradiction: Scientific reasoning during adolescence. *Journal of Educational Psychology, 80,* 67–75.

Burgess, D. M., & Streissguth, A. P. (1992). Fetal alcohol syndrome and fetal alcohol effects: Principles for educators. *Phi Delta Kappan, 74,* 24–30.

Burgess, K. B., Marshall, P.J., Rubin, K. H., & Fox, N. A. (2003). Infant attachment and temperament as predictors of subsequent externalizing problems and cardiac physiology. *Journal of Child Psychology and Psychiatry and Allied Disciplines, 44,* 819–831.

Burns, C. W. (2003). Assessing the psychological and educational needs of children with moderate and severe mental retardation. In C. R. Reynolds & R. W. Kamphaus (Eds.), *Handbook of psychological and educational assessment of children: Intelligence, aptitude, and achievement* (2nd ed., pp. 671–684). New York: Guilford Press.

Bus, A. G. (2001). Joint caregiver–child storybook reading: A route to literacy development. In S. B. Neuman & D. K. Dickinson (Eds.), *Handbook of early literacy research* (pp. 179–191). New York: Guilford Press.

Bus, A. G., & van IJzendoorn, M. H. (1988). Mother–child interactions, attachment, and emergent literacy: A cross-sectional study. *Child Development, 59,* 1262–1272.

Bus, A. G., van IJzendoorn, M. H., & Pellegrini, A. D. (1995). Joint book reading makes for success in learning to read: A meta-analysis on intergenerational transmission of literacy. *Review of Educational Research, 65,* 1–21.

Buss, A. H., & Plomin, R. (1984). *Temperament: Early developing personality traits.* Hillsdale, NJ: Erlbaum.

Bussey, K., & Bandura, A. (1984). Influence of gender constancy and social power on sex-linked modeling. *Journal of Personality and Social Psychology, 47,* 1292–1302.

Bussey, K., & Bandura, A. (1992). Self-regulatory mechanisms governing gender development. *Child Development, 63,* 1236–1250.

Bussey, K., & Perry, D. G. (1982). Same-sex imitation. *Sex Roles, 8,* 773–784.

Butkowski, I. S., & Willows, D. M. (1980). Cognitive-motivational characteristics of children varying in reading ability: Evidence for learned helplessness in poor readers. *Journal of Educational Psychology, 72,* 408–422.

Butler, R. W., & Copeland, D. R. (2002). Attentional processes and their remediation in children treated for cancer: A literature review and the development of a therapeutic approach. *Journal of the International Neuropsychological Society, 8,* 115–124.

Butterfield, E. C., & Belmont, J. M. (1977). Assessing and improving the executive cognitive functions of mentally retarded people. In I. Bialar & M. Sternlicht (Eds.), *Psychological issues in mental retardation* (pp. 277–318). New York: Psychological Dimensions.

Caine, D., & Watson J. D. G. (2000). Neuropsychological and neuropathological sequelae of cerebral anoxia: A critical review. *Journal of the International Neuropsychological Society, 6,* 86–99.

Calderon, L. L., Yu, C. K., & Jambazian, P. (2004). Dieting practices in high school students. *Journal of the American Dietetic Association, 104*(9), 1369–1374.

Calhoon, M. B., & Fuchs, L. S. (2003). The effects of peer-assisted learning strategies and curriculum-based measurement on the mathematics performance of secondary students with disabilities. *Remedial and Special Education, 24,* 235–245.

California Assessment Program. (1988). *Annual report: 1985–86.* Sacramento: California State Department of Education.

Calvert, S. L., & Huston, A. C. (1987). Television and children's gender schemata. In L. S. Liben & M. L. Signorella (Eds.), *Children's gender schemata: New directions for child development* (No. 38, pp. 75–88). San Francisco: Jossey-Bass.

Calvin, A. (2000). Use of standardized tests in admissions in post-secondary institutions of higher education. *Psychology, Public Policy, and the Law, 6,* 20–32.

Camara, K. A., & Resnick, G. (1988). Interparental conflict and cooperation: Factors moderating children's post-divorce adjustment. In E. M. Hetherington & J. Arasteh (Eds.), *Impact of divorce, single-parenting, and stepparenting on children* (pp. 169–195). Hillsdale, NJ: Erlbaum.

Camarata, S. (1995). A rationale for naturalistic speech intelligibility intervention. In M. E. Fey, J. Windsor, & S. F. Warren (Eds.), *Language intervention: Preschool through the elementary years* (pp. 63–84). Baltimore: Brookes.

Camp, B. W., & Bash, M. A. S. (1985). *Think aloud: Increasing social and cognitive skills–A problem-solving program for children.* Champaign, IL: Research Press.

Campbell, D. T., & Fiske, D. W. (1959). Convergent and discriminant validation by the multitrait–multimethod matrix. *Psychological Bulletin, 56,* 81–105.

Campbell, D. T., & Stanley, J. C. (1966). *Experimental and quasi-experimental designs for research.* Chicago: Rand-McNally.

Campbell, F. A., & Ramey, C. T. (1995). Cognitive and school outcomes for high-risk African American students in middle adolescence: Positive effects of early intervention. *American Educational Research Journal, 32,* 743–772.

Campbell, J. R., Hombo, C. M., & Mazzeo, J. (2000). *NAEP 1999: Trends in academic progress.* Washington, DC: U.S. Department of Educaton.

Campbell, P. B. (1995). Redefining the "girl problem in mathematics." In W. G. Secada, E. Fennema, & L. B. Adajian (Eds.), *New directions for equity in mathematics education* (pp. 225–241). Cambridge, UK: Cambridge University Press.

Campbell, S. B. (2002). *Behavior problems in preschool children: Clinical and developmental issues* (2nd ed.). New York: Guilford Press.

Canfield, R. L., Kreher, D. A., Cornwell, C., & Henderson, C. R. Jr. (2003). Low-level lead exposure, executive functioning, and learning in early childhood. *Child Neuropsychology, 9,* 35–53.

Cantor, N., Markus, H., Niedenthal, P., & Nurius, P. (1986). On motivation and self-concept. In R. M. Sorrentino & E. T. Higgins (Eds.),

Handbook of motivation and cognition: Vol. 1. Foundations of social behavior (pp. 99–127). New York: Guilford Press.

Caplan, D. (1992). *Language: Structure, processing, and disorders.* Cambridge, MA: MIT Press.

Cardon, L. R., DiLalla, L. F., Plomin, R., DeFries, J. C., & Fulker, D. W. (1990). Genetic correlations between reading performance and IQ in the Colorado Adoption Project. *Intelligence, 14,* 245–257.

Carew, J. (1980). Experience and the development of intelligence in young children at home and in day care. *Monographs of the Society for Research in Child Development, 45*(6–7, Serial No. 187).

Carey, S. (1978). The child as word learner. In M. Halle, J. Bresnan, & G. A. Miller (Eds.), *Linguistic theory and psychological reality* (pp. 264–273). Cambridge, MA: MIT Press.

Carey, S. (1985). *Conceptual change in childhood.* Cambridge, MA: MIT Press.

Carey, S., & Markman, E. M. (1999). Cognitive development. In B. M. Bly, M. Benjamin, & D. E. Rumelhart (Eds.), *Cognitive science: Handbook of perception and cognition* (2nd ed., pp. 201–254). San Diego, CA: Academic Press.

Carlisle, J. F. (2004). Morphological processes that influence learning to read. In C. A. Stone, E. R. Silliman, B. J. Ehren., & K. Apel (Eds.), *Handbook of language and literacy* (pp. 318–339). New York: Guilford Press.

Carlisle, J. F., & Beeman, M. M. (2000). The effects of language of instruction on the reading and writing achievement of first-grade Hispanic children. *Scientific Studies of Reading, 4,* 331–353.

Carlo, M. S., August, D., McLaughlin, B., Snow, C. E., Dressler, C., Lippman, D., et al. (2004). Closing the gap: Addressing the vocabulary needs of English language learners in bilingual and mainstream classrooms. *Reading Research Quarterly, 39,* 188–215.

Carlsen, W. S. (1991). Questioning in classrooms: A sociolinguistic perspective. *Review of Educational Research, 61*(2), 157–178.

Carlson, V., Cicchetti, D., Barnett, D., & Braunwald, K. (1989). Disorganized/disoriented attachment relationships in maltreated infants. *Developmental Psychology, 25,* 525–531.

Carpenter, M., Nagell, K., & Tomasello, M. (1998). Social cognition, joint attention, and communicative competence from 9 to 15 months of age. *Monographs of the Society for Research in Child Development, 63*(4, Serial No. 255).

Carpenter, P. A., & Just, M. A. (1989). The role of working memory in language comprehension. In D. Klahr & K. Kotovsky (Eds.), *Complex information processing: The impact of Herbert A. Simon* (pp. 31–68). Hillsdale, NJ: Erlbaum.

Carpenter, T. P., Fennema, E., Peterson, P. L., & Carey, D. A. (1988). Teachers' pedagogical content knowledge of students' problem solving in elementary arithmetic. *Journal for Research in Mathematics Education, 19,* 385–401.

Carr, M., & Borkowski, J. G. (1989). Attributional training and the generalization of reading strategies with underachieving children. *Learning and Individual Differences, 1,* 327–341.

Carr, M., Borkowski, J. G., & Maxwell, S. E. (1991). Motivational components of underachievement. *Developmental Psychology, 27,* 108–118.

Carr, M., Kurtz, B. E., Schneider, W., Turner, L. A., & Borkowski, J. G. (1989). Strategy acquisition and transfer: Environmental influences on metacognitive development. *Developmental Psychology, 25,* 765–771.

Carringer, D. C. (1974). Creative thinking abilities of Mexican youth: The relationship of bilingualism. *Journal of Cross-Cultural Psychology, 5,* 492–504.

Carroll, D. W. (1994). *Psychology of language* (2nd ed.). Pacific Grove, CA: Brooks-Cole.

Carroll, M., Byrne, B., & Kirsner, K. (1985). Autobiographical memory and perceptual learning: A developmental study using picture recognition, naming latency, and perceptual identification. *Memory and Cognition, 13,* 273–279.

Carskadon, M. A. (Ed.). (2002). *Adolescent sleep patterns: Biological, social and psychological influences.* New York: Cambridge University Press.

Carver, L. J., & Bauer, P. J. (2001). The dawning of a past: The emergence of long-term explicit memory in infancy. *Journal of Experimental Child Psychology, 130,* 726–745.

Case, R. (1978). Intellectual development from birth to adulthood: A neo-Piagetian investigation. *Journal of Experimental Child Psychology, 18,* 382–397.

Case, R. (1985). *Intellectual development: Birth to adulthood.* Orlando, FL: Academic Press.

Case, R. (1991). A developmental approach to the design of remedial instruction. In A. McKeough & J. L. Lupart (Eds.), *Toward the practice of theory-based instruction* (pp. 117–147). Hillsdale, NJ: Erlbaum.

Case, R. (1992). Neo-Piagetian theories of child development. In R. J. Sternberg & C. A. Berg (Eds.), *Intellectual development* (pp. 161–196). New York: Cambridge University Press.

Case, R. (1995). Capacity-based explanations of working memory growth: A brief history and reevaluation. In F. E. Weinert & W. Schneider (Eds.), *Memory performance and competencies: Issues in growth and development* (pp. 23–44). Hillsdale, NJ: Erlbaum.

Case, R. (1999). Neo-Piagetian theories of intellectual development. In H. Beilin & P. B. Pufall (Eds.), *Piaget's theory: Prospects and possibilities* (pp. 61–104). Hillsdale, NJ: Erlbaum.

Case, R., & Kurland, D. M. (1980). A new measure for determining children's subjective organization of speech. *Journal of Experimental Child Psychology, 30,* 206–222.

Case, R., Kurland, D. M., & Goldberg, J. (1982). Operational efficiency and the growth of short-term memory span. *Journal of Experimental Child Psychology, 33,* 386–404.

Casey, B. J., Thomas, K. M., & McCandliss, B. (2001). Applications of magnetic resonance to the study of development. In C. A. Nelson & M. Luciana (Eds.), *Handbook of developmental cognitive neuroscience* (pp. 137–147). Cambridge, MA: MIT Press.

Caspi, A., Elder, G. H. Jr., & Bem, D. J. (1987). Moving against the world: Life-course patterns of explosive children. *Developmental Psychology, 23,* 308–313.

Casserly, P. (1980). An assessment of factors affecting female participation in advanced placement programs in mathematics, chemistry, and physics. In L. H. Fox, L. Brody, & D. Tobin (Eds.), *Women and the mathematical mystique* (pp. 138–163). Baltimore: Johns Hopkins University Press.

Cassidy, J., & Asher, S. R. (1992). Loneliness and peer relations in young children. *Child Development, 63,* 350–365.

Cassidy, J., & Shaver, P. R. (Eds.) (1999). *Handbook of attachment: Theory, research, and clinical applications.* New York: Guilford Press.

Castellino, D. R., Lerner, J. V., Lerner, R. M., & von Eye, A. (1998). Maternal employment and education: Predictors of young adolescent career trajectories. *Applied Developmental Science, 2*, 114–126.

Casto, G., & Mastropieri, M. A. (1986). The efficacy of early intervention programs: A meta-analysis. *Exceptional Children, 52*, 417–424.

Cattell, R. B. (1987). *Intelligence: Its structure, growth, and action.* Amsterdam, The Netherlands: North-Holland.

Cattell, R. B., & Horn, J. L. (1978). A check on the theory of fluid and crystallized intelligence with description of new subtest designs. *Journal of Educational Measurement, 15*, 139–164.

Catts, H. (1989). Defining dyslexia as a developmental language disorder. *Annals of Dyslexia, 39*, 50–64.

Caughy, M. O., DiPietro, J. A., & Strobino, D. M. (1994). Day-care participation as a protective factor in the cognitive development of low-income children. *Child Development, 65*, 457–471.

Cazden, C. B. (1988). *Classroom discourse: The language of teaching and learning.* Portsmouth, NH: Heinemann.

Ceci, S. J. (1991). How much does schooling influence general intelligence and its cognitive components?: A reassessment of the evidence. *Developmental Psychology, 27*, 703–722.

Centers for Disease Control and Prevention. (2000). Blood lead levels in young children: United States and selected states, 1996–1999. *Morbidity and Mortality Weekly Report, 49*, 1133–1137.

Centers for Disease Control and Prevention. (2004). *Defining overweight and obesity.* Available online at www.cdc.gov/nbccdphp/dnpa/obesity.

Centers for Disease Control and Prevention. (2006). *Defining overweight and obesity.* Retrieved at www.cdc.gov/nccdphp/dnpa/obesity.

Chaiklin, S. (2003). The zone of proximal development in Vygotsky's analysis of learning and instruction. In A. Kozulin, B. Gindia, V. S. Ageyev, & S. M. Miller (Eds.), *Vygotsky's educational theory in cultural context* (pp. 39–64). Cambridge, UK: Cambridge University Press.

Chan, C. K. K., Burtis, P. J., Scardamalia, M., & Bereiter, C. (1992). Constructive activity in learning from text. *American Educational Research Journal, 29*, 97–118.

Chan, L. K. S. (1996). Motivational orientations and metacognitive abilities of intellectually gifted students. *Gifted Child Quarterly, 40*, 184–193.

Chao, R. K. (2001). Extending research on the consequences of parenting style for Chinese Americans and European Americans. *Child Development, 72*, 1832–1843.

Chamberlain, P., & Moore, K. J. (2002). Chaos and trauma in the lives of adolescent females with antisocial behavior and delinquency. In R. Greenwald (Ed.), *Trauma and juvenile delinquency: Theory, research, and interventions* (pp. 79–108). Binghamton, NY: Haworth.

Chang, V. (1999). Lead abatement and prevention of developmental disabilities. *Journal of Intellectual and Developmental Disability, 24*, 161–168.

Chapman, M., & Lindenberger, U. (1989). Concrete operations and attentional capacity. *Journal of Experimental Child Psychology, 47*, 236–258.

Chapman, M., Skinner, E. A., & Baltes, P. B. (1990). Interpreting correlations between children's perceived control and cognitive performance: Control, agency, or means–ends beliefs? *Developmental Psychology, 26*, 246–253.

Chase, H. (1973). The effects of intrauterine and postnatal undernutrition on normal brain development. *Annals of the New York Academy of Sciences, 205*, 231–244.

Chassin, L., Ritter, J., Trim, R. S., & King, K. M. (2003). Adolescent substance use disorders. In E. J. Mash & R. A. Barkley (Eds.), *Child psychopathology* (2nd ed., pp. 199–230). New York: Guilford Press.

Chen, C., & Stevenson, H. W. (1988). Cross-linguistic differences in digit span of preschool children. *Journal of Experimental Child Psychology, 46*, 150–158.

Chen, C., & Stevenson, H. W. (1989). Homework: A cross-cultural examination. *Child Development, 60*(3), 551–561.

Chen, P. P. (2002). Exploring the accuracy and predictability of the self-efficacy beliefs of seventh-grade mathematics students. *Learning and Individual Differences, 14*, 77–90.

Cherney, I. D., & Ryalls, B.O. (1999). Gender-linked differences in the incidental memory of children and adults. *Journal of Experimental Child Psychology, 72*, 305–328.

Chess, S., & Thomas, A. (1987). *Origins and evolution of behavior disorders: From infancy to early adult life.* Cambridge, MA: Harvard University Press.

Cheyne, J. A., & Walters, R. H. (1969). Intensity of punishment, timing of punishment, and cognitive structure as determinants of response inhibition. *Journal for Experimental Child Psychology, 7*, 231–244.

Chi, M. T. H. (1977). Age differences in memory span. *Journal of Experimental Child Psychology, 23*, 266–281.

Chi, M. T. H. (1978). Knowledge structure and memory development. In R. S. Siegler (Ed.), *Children's thinking: What develops?* (pp. 73–96). Hillsdale, NJ: Erlbaum.

Child Trends DataBank. (2004). *Children in poverty.* Available online at www.childtrendsdatabank. org/indicators/4Poverty.cfm. Also available at U.S. Census Bureau, Current Population Reports, Series P60–222, Detailed Poverty Tables, Table 3, online at ferret.bls.census.gov/macro/032004/pov/toc.htm.

Childs, C. P., & Greenfield, P. M. (1980). Informal modes of learning and teaching: the case of Zinecanteco weaving. In N. Warren (Ed.), *Studies in cross-cultural psychology* (Vol. 2, pp. 269–316). London: Academic Press.

Chipeur, H. M., Rovine, M. J., & Plomin, R. (1990). LISREL modeling: Genetic and environmental influences on IQ revisited. *Intelligence, 14*, 11–29.

Cho, S., & Ahn, D. (2003). Strategy acquisition and maintenance of gifted and nongifted young children. *Exceptional Children, 69*, 497–505.

Chodorow, N. J. (1978). *The reproduction of mothering: Psychoanalysis and the sociology of gender.* Berkeley and Los Angeles: University of California Press.

Chodorow, N. J. (1989). *Feminism and psychoanalytic theory.* New Haven, CT: Yale University Press.

Chomitz, V. R., Cheung, L. W. Y., & Lieberman, E. (1995). The role of lifestyle in preventing low birth weight. *The Future of Children, 5*(1), 121–138.

Chomsky, N. (1957). *Syntactic structures.* The Hague, The Netherlands: Mouton.

Chomsky, N. (1959). Review of B. F.

Skinner's *Verbal behavior. Language, 35,* 16–58.

Chomsky, N. (1965). *Aspects of the theory of syntax.* Cambridge, MA: MIT Press.

Chomsky, N. (1980a). Initial states and steady states. In M. Paittelli-Palmarini (Ed.), *Language and learning: The debate between Jean Piaget and Noam Chomsky* (pp. 97–130). Cambridge, MA: Harvard University Press.

Chomsky, N. (1980b). Rules and representations. *Behavioral and Brain Sciences, 3,* 1–61.

Chong, S. C. F., Werker, J. F., Russell, J. A., & Carroll, J. M. (2003). Three facial expressions mothers direct to their infants. *Infant and Child Development, 12,* 211–232.

Christophersen, E. R. (1989). Injury control. *American Psychologist, 44,* 237–241.

Christophersen, E. R., & Mortweet, S. L. (2001). *Treatments that work with children: Empirically supported strategies for managing childhood problems.* Washington, DC: American Psychological Association.

Cicchetti, D., Cummings, E. M., Greenberg, M. T., & Marvin, R. S. (1990). An organizational perspective on attachment beyond infancy: Implications for theory, measurement, and research. In M. T. Greenberg, D. Cicchetti, & E. M. Cummings (Eds.), *Attachment in the preschool years: Theory, research, and intervention* (pp. 3–49). Chicago: University of Chicago Press.

Cillessen, A. H. N., & Bukowski, W. M. (2000). *Recent advances in the measurement of acceptance and rejection in the peer system.* San Francisco: Jossey-Bass.

Clark, E. V. (1973). What's in a word?: On the child's acquisition of semantics in his first language. In T. E. Moore (Ed.), *Cognitive development and the acquisition of language* (pp. 65–110). New York: Academic Press.

Clark, J. M., & Paivio, A. (1991). Dual coding theory and education. *Educational Psychology Review, 3,* 149–210.

Clark, R. M. (1983). *Family life and school achievement: Why poor black children succeed or fail.* Chicago: University of Chicago Press.

Clarke-Stewart, K. A., Lowe-Vandell, D., Burchinal, M., O'Brien, M., & McCartney, K. (2002). Do regulable features of child-care homes affect children's development? *Early Childhood Research Quarterly, 17,* 52–86.

Clay, M. M., & Cazden, C. B. (1990). A Vygotskian interpretation of Reading Recovery. In L. C. Moll (Ed.), *Vygotsky and education: Instructional implications and applications of sociohistorical psychology* (pp. 206–222). Cambridge, UK: Cambridge University Press.

Cleary, T. J., & Zimmerman, B. J. (2001). Self-regulation differences during athletic practice by experts, non-experts, and novices. *Journal of Applied Sport Psychology, 13,* 186–206.

Clement, J., Brown, D. E., & Zeitsman, A. (1989). Not all preconceptions are misconceptions: Finding "anchoring conceptions" for grounding instruction on students' intuition. *International Journal of Science Education, 11,* 554–565.

Cobb, P., Wood, T., Yackel, E., Nicholls, J., Wheatley, G., Trigatti, B., et al. (1991). Assessment of a problem centered second-grade mathematics project. *Journal for Research in Mathematics Education, 22,* 3–29.

Cochran-Smith, M. (1984). *The making of a reader.* Norwood, NJ: Ablex.

Cohen, A. D. (1974). The Culver City Spanish immersion program: The first two years. *Modern Language Journal, 58,* 95–105.

Cohen, A. D. (1975). *Progress report on the Culver City Spanish immersion program: The third and fourth year* (Workpapers in Teaching English as a Second Language, 9). University of California, Los Angeles, 47–65, Educational Resources Information Center, 121 093.

Cohen, A. D., & Horowitz, R. (2002). What should teachers know about bilingual learners and the reading process? In J. A. H. Sullivan (Ed.), *Literacy and the second language learner* (pp. 29–53). Greenwich, CT: Information Age.

Cohen, J. (1988). *Statistical power analysis for the behavioral sciences* (rev. ed.). Hillsdale, NJ: Erlbaum.

Cohler, B. J. (1994). Memory recovery and the use of the past: A commentary on Lindsay and Read from psychoanalytic perspectives. *Applied Cognitive Psychology, 8*(4), 365–378.

Cohn, D. A. (1990). Child–mother attachment of 6-year-olds and social competence at school. *Child Development, 61,* 152–162.

Coie, J. D., & Dodge, K. A. (1998). Aggression and antisocial behavior. In N. Eisenberg (Ed.), *Handbook of child psychology: Vol. 3. Social, emotional, and personality development*

(5th ed., pp. 779–862). New York: Wiley.

Coie, J. D., Dodge, K. A., & Coppotelli, H. (1982). Dimensions and types of social status: A cross-age perspective. *Developmental Psychology, 18,* 557–70.

Coie, J. D., Dodge, K. A., & Kupersmidt, J. B. (1990). Peer group behavior and social status. In S. R. Asher & J. D. Coie (Eds.), *Peer rejection in childhood* (pp. 17–59). New York: Cambridge University Press.

Colapinto, J. (2001). *As nature made him: The boy who was raised as a girl.* New York: Perennial.

Cole, C., & Rodman, H. (1987). When school-age children care for themselves: Issues for family-life educators and parents. *Family Relations, 26,* 92–96.

Cole, M. (1998). Cognitive development and formal schooling: The evidence from cross-cultural research. In D. Faulkner, K. Littleton, & M. Woodhead (Eds.), *Learning relationships in the classroom* (pp. 31–53). London: Routledge.

Cole, M., Gay, J., Glick, J., & Sharp, D. (1971). *The cultural context of learning and thinking.* New York: Basic Books.

Cole, M., & Scribner, S. (1977). Cross-cultural studies of memory and cognition. In R. V. Kail & J. W. Hagen (Eds.), *Perspectives on the development of memory and cognition* (pp. 239–271). Hillsdale, NJ: Erlbaum.

Coles, R. (1970). *Erik H. Erikson: The growth of his work.* Boston: Little, Brown.

Collaer, M. L., & Hines, M. (1995). Human behavioral sex differences: A role for gonadal hormones during early development? *Psychological Bulletin, 118,* 55–107.

Collier, V. P. (1992). A synthesis of studies examining long-term language minority student data on academic achievement. *Bilingual Research Journal, 16,* 187–212.

Collier, V. P. (1995). Acquiring a second language for school. *Directions in Language and Education, 1,* 3–14. (ERIC ED 394 301)

Collins, A., Brown, J. S., & Newman, S. E. (1989). Cognitive apprenticeship: Teaching the crafts of reading, writing, and mathematics. In L. B. Resnick (Ed.), *Knowing, learning, and instruction: Essays in honor of Robert Glaser* (pp. 453–494). Hillsdale, NJ: Erlbaum.

Collins, A. M., & Loftus, E. F. (1975).

A spreading-activation theory of semantic processing. *Psychological Review, 82,* 407–428.

Collins, A. M., & Quillian, M. R. (1969). Retrieval time from semantic memory. *Journal of Verbal Learning and Verbal Behavior, 8,* 240–247.

Collins, C. (1991). Reading instruction that increases thinking abilities. *Journal of Reading, 34*(7), 510–516.

Collins, W. A., Harris, M. L., & Susman, A. (1995). Parenting during middle childhood. In M. H. Bornstein (Ed.), *Handbook of parenting: Vol. 1. Children and parenting* (pp. 65–89). Hillsdale, NJ: Erlbaum.

Collins, W. A., Maccoby, E. E., Steinberg, L., Hetherington, E. M., & Bornstein, M. H. (2000). Contemporary research on parenting: The case for nature and nurture. *American Psychologist, 55,* 218–232.

Collins, W. A., Wellman, H., Keniston, A. H., & Westby, S. D. (1978). Age-related aspects of comprehension and inference from a televised dramatic narrative. *Child Development, 49,* 389–399.

Coltrane, S. (1998). *Gender and families.* Thousand Oaks, CA: Pine Forge Press.

Columbo, J., & Bundy, R. S. (1981). A method for the measurement of infant auditory selectivity. *Infant Behavior and Development, 4,* 229–231.

Comber, L. C., & Keeves, J. P. (1973). *Science education in nineteen countries.* Stockholm: Almqvist & Wiksell.

Committee on Adolescence. (2003). Identifying and treating eating disorders. *Pediatrics, 111*(1), 204–211.

Compas, B. E., Ey, S., & Grant, K. E. (1993). Taxonomy, assessment, and diagnosis of depression during adolescence. *Psychological Bulletin, 114,* 323–344.

Compas, B. E., Hinden, B. R., & Gerhardt, C. A. (1995). Adolescent development: Pathways and processes of risk and resilience. *Annual Review of Psychology, 46,* 265–293.

Comstock, G. (1989). *The evaluation of American television.* Newbury Park, CA: Sage.

Comstock, G. (1991). *Television and the American child.* Orlando, FL: Academic Press.

Comstock, G., & Paik, H. (1991). *Television and the American child.* San Diego, CA: Academic Press.

Comunian, A. L., & Gielen, U. P. (Eds.). (2000). *International perspectives on human development.* Lengerich, Germany: Pabst Science.

Conger, R. D., Conger, K. J., Elder, G. H. Jr., Lorenz, F. O., Simons, R. L., & Whitbeck, L. B. (1992). A family process model of economic hardship and adjustment of early adolescent boys. *Child Development, 63,* 526–541.

Conger, R. D., Conger, K. J., Elder, G. H. Jr., Lorenz, F. O., Simons, R. L., & Whitbeck, L. B. (1993). Family economic stress and adjustment of early adolescent girls. *Developmental Psychology, 29,* 206–219.

Connell, J., & Wellborn, J. (1991). Competence, autonomy, and relatedness: A motivational analysis of self-system processes. In M. R. Gunner & L. A. Sroufe (Eds.), *Self processes and development* (pp. 43–77). Mahwah, NJ: Erlbaum.

Conrad, R. (1979). *The deaf school child.* London: Harper & Row.

Constantino, G. (1992). Overcoming bias in the educational assessment of Hispanic students. In K. F. Geisinger (Ed.), *Psychological testing of Hispanics* (pp. 89–98). Washington, DC: American Psychological Association.

Conti-Ramsden, G., & Friel-Patti, S. (1983). Mothers' discourse adjustments to language-impaired and non-language-impaired children. *Journal of Speech and Hearing Disorders, 48,* 360–367.

Cook, T. D. (2002). Randomized experiments in educational policy research: A critical examination of the reasons the educational evaluation community has offered for not doing them. *Educational Evaluation and Policy Analysis, 24*(3), 175–199.

Cook, V. (1997). The consequences of bilingualism for cognitive processing. In A. M. B. de Groot & J. F. Kroll (Eds.), *Tutorials in bilingualism* (pp. 279–300). Mahwah, NJ: Erlbaum.

Copeland-Mitchell, J., Denham, S. A., & DeMulder, E. K. (1997). Q-sort assessment of child–teacher attachment relationships and social competence in the preschool. *Early Education and Development, 8,* 27–39.

Cordeiro, P. (1988). Children's punctuation: An analysis of errors in period placement. *Research in the Teaching of English, 22,* 62–75.

Cornelius, G., & Hornett, D. (1990). The play behavior of hearing-impaired kindergarten children. *American Annals of the Deaf, 135,* 316–321.

Coscia, J. M., Ris, M. D., Succop, P. A., & Dietrich, K. N. (2003). Cognitive development of lead exposed children from ages 6 to 15 years: An application of growth curve analysis. *Child Neuropsychology, 9,* 10–21.

Costello, E. J., Compton, S. N., Keeler, G., & Angold, A. (2003). Relationships between poverty and psychopathology: A natural experiment. *Journal of the American Medical Association, 290,* 2023–2029.

Coté, J. E. (1994). *Adolescent storm and stress: An evaluation of the Mead–Freeman controversy.* Hillsdale, NJ: Erlbaum.

Covington, M. V. (1987). Achievement motivation, self-attributions, and the exceptional learner. In J. D. Day & J. G. Borkowski (Eds.), *Intelligence and exceptionality* (pp. 355–389). Norwood, NJ: Ablex.

Covington, M. V. (1992). *Making the grade: A self-worth perspective on motivation and school reform.* New York: Cambridge University Press.

Covington, M. V. (1998) *The will to learn: A guide for motivating young people.* New York: Cambridge University Press.

Covington, M. V. (2000). Goal theory, motivation, and school achievement: An integrative review. *Annual Review of Psychology, 51,* 171–200.

Covington, M. V. (2004). Self-worth theory: Goes to college or do our motivation theories motivate? In D. M. McInerney & S. Van Etten (Eds.), *Big theories revisited* (pp. 91–114). Greenwich, CT: Information Age.

Covington, M. V., & Omelich, C. L. (1979a). Effort: The double-edged sword in school achievement. *Journal of Educational Psychology, 71,* 169–182.

Covington, M. V., & Omelich, C. L. (1979b). It's best to be able and virtuous too: Student and teacher evaluative responses to successful effort. *Journal of Educational Psychology, 71,* 688–700.

Covington, M. V., & Omelich, C. L. (1981). As failures mount: Affective and cognitive consequences of ability demotion in the classroom. *Journal of Educational Psychology, 73,* 796–808.

Covington, M. V., & Omelich, C. L. (1984). Task-oriented versus competitive learning structures: Motivational and performance consequences. *Journal of Educational Psychology, 6,* 1038–1050.

Covington, M. V., & Roberts, B. (1994). Self-worth and college achievement: Motivational and personality correlates. In P. R. Pintrich, D. R. Brown, & C. E. Weinstein (Eds.), *Student motivation, cognition, and learning: Essays in honor of Wilbert J. McKeatchie* (pp. 157–187). Hillsdale, NJ: Erlbaum.

Cowan, N. (2002). Childhood development of working memory: An examination of two basic parameters. In P. Graf & N. Ohta (Eds.), *Lifespan development of human memory* (pp. 39–57). Cambridge, MA: MIT Press.

Cowan, N., Saults, J. S., & Elliot, E. M. (2002). The search for what is fundamental in the development of working memory. In R. V. Kail & H. W. Reese (Eds.), *Advances in child development and behavior* (Vol. 29, pp. 1–49). San Diego, CA: Academic Press.

Cowan, N., Saults, J. S., Elliott, E. M., & Moreno, M. V. (2002). Deconfounding serial recall. *Journal of Memory and Language, 46*(1), 153–177.

Cox, E. (1988). Explicit and implicit moral education. *Journal of Moral Education, 17,* 92–97.

Coyle, T. R., Read, L. E., Gaultney, J. F., & Bjorklund, D. F. (1998). Giftedness and variability in strategic processing on a multitrial memory task: Evidence for stability in gifted cognition. *Learning and Individual Differences, 10,* 273–290.

Craig, H. K., & Evans, J. (1989). Turn exchange characteristics of SLI children's simultaneous and nonsimultaneous speech. *Journal of Speech and Hearing Disorders, 54,* 334–347.

Crain-Thoreson, C., & Dale, P. S. (1992). Do early talkers become early readers?: Linguistic precocity, preschool language, and emergent literacy. *Developmental Psychology, 28,* 421–429.

Cramer, K. A., Post, T. R., & delMas, R. C. (2002). Initial fraction learning by fourth- and fifth-grade students: A comparison of the effects of using commercial curricula with the effects of using the Rational Number Project Curriculum. *Journal for Research in Mathematics Education, 33*(2), 111–144.

Crandall, V. C. (1969). Sex differences in expectancy of intellectual and academic reinforcement. In C. P. Smith (Ed.), *Achievement-related behaviors in children* (pp. 11–45). New York: Russell Sage Foundation.

Cratty, B. J. (1986). *Perceptual and motor development in infants and children* (3rd ed). Englewood Cliffs, NJ: Prentice-Hall.

Crawford, K. (1998). Learning and teaching mathematics in the information era. In D. Faulkner, K. Littleton, & M. Woodhead (Eds.), *Learning relationships in the classroom* (pp. 293–309). London: Routledge.

Crick, N. R., & Werner, N. E. (1998). Response decision processes in relational and overt aggression. *Child Development, 69,* 1630–1639.

Crockenberg, S. B. (1981). Infant irritability, mother responsiveness, and social support influences on the security of infant–mother attachment. *Child Development, 52,* 857–865.

Crockenberg, S. B., & Litman, C. (1990). Autonomy as competence in 2-year-olds: Maternal correlates of child defiance, compliance, and self-assertion. *Developmental Psychology, 26,* 961–971.

Cronbach, L. J. (1951). Coefficient alpha and the internal structure of tests. *Psychometrica, 16,* 297–334.

Cronbach, L. J. (1990). *Essentials of psychological testing* (5th ed.). New York: Harper & Row.

Crone, D. A., & Whitehurst, G. J. (1999). Age and schooling effects on emergent literacy and early reading skills. *Journal of Educational Psychology, 91,* 604–614.

Crouter, A. C., MacDermid, S. M., McHale, S. M., & Perry-Jenkins, M. (1990). Parental monitoring and perceptions of children's school performance and conduct in dual- and single-earner families. *Developmental Psychology, 26,* 649–657.

Crowell, J. A., Fraley, R. C., & Shaver, P. R. (1999). Measurement of individual differences in adolescent and adult attachment. In J. Cassidy & P. R. Shaver (Eds.), *Handbook of attachment: Theory, research, and clinical applications* (pp. 434–465). New York: Guilford Press.

Crutcher, K. A. (1991). Anatomical correlates of neuronal plasticity. In J. L. Martinez Jr. & R. P. Kesner (Eds.), *Learning and memory: A biological view* (2nd ed., pp. 93–146). San Diego, CA: Academic Press.

Crystal, D. (1987). *The Cambridge encyclopedia of language*. Cambridge, UK: Cambridge University Press.

Crystal, D. (1995). *The Cambridge encyclopedia of the English language*. Cambridge, UK: Cambridge University Press.

Crystal, D. S., & Stevenson, H. W.

(1991). Mothers' perceptions of children's problems with mathematics: A cross-national comparison. *Journal of Educational Psychology, 83*(3), 372–376.

Csikszentmihalyi, M., & Larson, R. (1984). *Being adolescent: Conflict and growth in the teenage years*. New York: Basic Books.

Cummings, E. M., & Davies, P. T. (1994). Maternal depression and child development. *Journal of Child Psychology and Psychiatry, 35,* 73–112.

Curtiss, S., Katz, W., & Tallal, P. (1992). Delay versus deviance in the language acquisition of language-impaired children. *Journal of Speech and Hearing Research, 35,* 373–383.

Cutting, L. E., & Denckla, M. B. (2003). Attention: Relationships between attention-deficit hyperactivity disorder and learning disabilities. In H. L. Swanson, K. R. Harris, & S. Graham (Eds.), *Handbook of learning disabilities* (pp. 125–139). New York: Guilford Press.

Dabbs, J. (1980). Left–right differences in cerebral blood flow and cognition. *Psychophysiology, 17,* 548–551.

Dai, D. Y. (2002). Are gifted girls motivationally disadvantaged?: Review, reflection, and redirection. *Journal for the Education of the Gifted, 25,* 315–358.

Dale, P. S., Dionne, G., Eley, T. C., & Plomin, R. (2000). Lexical and grammatical development: A behavioral genetic perspective. *Journal of Child Language, 27,* 619–642.

Dalgarno, B. (2001). Interpretations of constructivism and consequences for computer assisted learning. *British Journal of Educational Technology, 32*(2), 183–194.

Dalgarno, B. (2002). The potential of 3D virtual learning environments: A constructivist analysis. *Electronic Journal of Science and Technology, 5*(2).

d'Anna, C. A., Zechmeister, E. B., & Hall, J. W. (1991). Toward a meaningful definition of vocabulary size. *Journal of Reading Behavior, 23,* 109–122.

Darling, N., & Steinberg, L. (1993). Parenting style as context: An integrative model. *Psychological Bulletin, 113,* 487–496.

Dasen, P. R. (1984). The cross-cultural study of intelligence: Piaget and the Baoule. *International Journal of Psychology, 19,* 407–434.

Davidson, E. S., Yasuna, A., & Tower,

A. (1979). The effects of television cartoons on sex-role stereotyping in young girls. *Child Development, 50,* 597–600.

Davis, A., Gardner, B., Gardner, M., & Warner, W. (1941). *Deep south.* Chicago: University of Chicago Press.

Dawson, T. L. (2002). A comparison of three developmental stage scoring systems. *Journal of Applied Measurement, 3*(2), 146–189.

Day, J. D. (1983). The zone of proximal development. In M. Pressley & J. R. Levin (Eds.), *Cognitive strategy research: From basic research to educational applications* (pp. 83–103). New York: Springer-Verlag.

Day, J. D., Borkowski, J. G., Dietmeyer, D. L., Howsepian, B. A., & Saenz, D. S. (1994). Possible selves and academic achievement. In L. Winegar & J. Valsiner (Eds.), *Children's development within social contexts* (pp. 181–201). Hillsdale, NJ: Erlbaum.

Day, J. D., Cordon, L. B., & Kerwin, M. L. (1989). Informal instruction and development of cognitive skills: A review and critique of research. In C. B. McCormick, G. Miller, & M. Pressley (Eds.), *Cognitive strategy research: From basic research to educational applications* (pp. 83–103). New York: Springer-Verlag.

de Fiorini, L. G. (1998). The feminine in psychoanalysis: A complete construction. *Journal of Clinical Psychoanalysis, 7,* 421–439.

de Houwer, A. (1987). Gender marking in a young Dutch–English bilingual child. In *Proceedings of the 1987 Child Language Seminar* (pp. 53–65). York, UK: University of York.

de Houwer, A. (1990). *Acquisition of two languages from birth: A case study.* New York: Cambridge University Press.

de Houwer, A. (1995). Bilingual language acquisition. In P. Fletcher & B. MacWhinney (Eds.), *The handbook of child language* (pp. 219–250). Oxford, UK: Blackwell.

De Wolff, M., & van IJzendoorn, M.H. (1997). Sensitivity and attachment: A meta-analysis on parental antecedents of infant attachment. *Child Development, 68,* 571–591.

DeBaryshe, B. D., Patterson, G. R., & Capaldi, D. M. (1993). A performance model for academic achievement in early adolescent boys. *Developmental Psychology, 29,* 795–804.

Debowski, S., Wood, R. E., & Bandura, A. (2001). Impact of guided exploration and enactive exploration on self-regulatory mechanisms and information acquisition through electronic search. *Journal of Applied Psychology, 86,* 1129–1141.

Decasper, A., & Fifer, W. P. (1980). On human bonding: Newborns prefer their mother's voices. *Science, 208*(1), 174–176.

Deci, E. L., & Ryan, R. M. (1985). *Intrinsic motivation and self-determination in human behavior.* New York: Plenum Press.

deCharms, R. (1968). *Personal causation.* New York: Academic Press.

deCharms, R. (1992). Personal causation and the origin concept. In C. P. Smith, J. W. Atkinson, D.C. McClelland, & J. Veroff (Eds.), *Motivation and personality: Handbook of thematic content analysis* (pp. 325–333). New York: Cambridge University Press.

Decker, S. N., & Vandenberg, S. G. (1985). Colorado twin study of reading disability. In D. B. Gray & J. Kavanaugh (Eds.), *Biobehavioral measures of dyslexia* (pp. 123–135). Baltimore: York.

DeFries, J. C., Fulker, D. W., & LaBuda, M. C. (1987). Evidence for a genetic aetiology in reading disability of twins. *Nature, 329,* 537–539.

DeFries, J. C., Olson, R. K., Pennington, B. F., & Smith, S. D. (1991). Colorado Reading Project: An update. In D. Duane & D. Gray (Eds.), *The reading brain: The biological basis of dyslexia* (pp. 53–87). Parkton, MD: York Press.

Dehaene, S., Tzourio, N., Frak, V., Raynaud, L., Cohen, L., Mehler, J., et al. (2000). Cerebral activations during number multiplication and comparison: A PET study. *Neuropsychologia, 34,* 1097–1106.

de Jong, T., & van Joolingen, W. R. (1998). Scientific discovery learning with computer simulations of conceptual domains. *Review of Educational Research, 68*(2), 179–201.

Delaney-Black, V., Covington, C., Templin, T., Kershaw, T., Nordstrom-Klee, B., Ager, J., et al. (2000). Expressive language development of children exposed to cocaine prenatally: Literature review and report of a prospective cohort study. *Journal of Communication Disorders, 33,* 463–481.

Delgado-Gaitan, C. (1990). *Literacy for empowerment: The role of parents in children's education.* New York: Falmer Press.

Delgado-Gaitan, C. (1992). School matters in the Mexican-American home: Socializing children to education. *American Educational Research Journal, 29,* 495–513.

De Lisi, R., & Golbeck, S. L. (1999). Implications of Piagetian theory for peer learning. In A. M. O'Donnell & A. King (Eds.), *Cognitive perspectives on peer learning* (pp. 3–37). Mahwah, NJ: Erlbaum.

DeLoache, J. S., Cassidy, D. J., & Brown, A. L. (1985). Precursors of mnemonic strategies in very young children's memory. *Child Development, 56,* 125–137.

Delpit, L., & Dowdy, J. K. (Eds.). (2002). *The skin that we speak: Thoughts on language and culture in the classroom.* New York: New Press.

DeMeis, D. K., Hock, E., & McBride, S. L. (1986). The balance of employment and motherhood: Longitudinal study of mothers' feelings about separation from their first-born infants. *Developmental Psychology, 22,* 627–632.

Dempster, F. N. (1981). Memory span: Sources of individual and developmental differences. *Psychological Bulletin, 89,* 63–100.

Dempster, F. N. (1985). Short-term memory development in childhood and adolescence. In C. J. Brainerd & M. Pressley (Eds.), *Basic processes in memory development: Progress in cognitive development research* (pp. 209–248). New York: Springer-Verlag.

Dempster, F. N. (1993). Resistance to interference: Developmental changes in a basic processing mechanism. In M. L. Howe & R. Pasnak (Eds.), *Emerging themes in cognitive development: Vol. 1. Foundations* (pp. 3–27). New York: Springer-Verlag.

DeMulder, E. K., Denham, S., Schmidt, M., & Mitchell, J. (2000). Q-sort assessment of attachment security during the preschool years: Links from home to school. *Developmental Psychology, 36,* 274–282.

Denckla, M. B., & Rudel, R. G. (1976). Rapid "automatized" naming (R.A.N.): Dyslexia differentiated from other learning disabilities. *Neuropsychologica, 14,* 471–479.

Denzin, N. K., & Lincoln, Y. S. (Eds.). (2000). *Handbook of qualitative research* (2nd ed.). Thousand Oaks, CA: Sage.

Department of Health and Human Services, Administration for Children and Families (2002). *Child Maltreatment 2002.* Available online at acf.hhs.gov/programs/cb/publications/cmreports.htm.

DeRosier, M. E., & Kupersmidt, J. B.

(1991). Costa Rican children's perceptions of their social networks. *Developmental Psychology, 27,* 656–662.

DeRosier, M. E., & Thomas, J. M. (2003). Strengthening sociometric prediction: Scientific advances in the assessment of children's peer relations. *Child Development, 74,* 1379–1392.

Derry, S. J., DuRussel, L. A., & O'Donnell, A. M. (1998). Individual and distributed cognitions in interdisciplinary teamwork: A developing case study and emerging theory. *Educational Psychology Review, 10*(1), 25–56.

Deshler, D. D., & Schumaker, J. B. (1988). An instructional model for teaching students how to learn. In J. L. Graden, J. E. Zins, & M. J. Curtis (Eds.), *Alternative educational delivery systems: Enhancing instructional options for all students* (pp. 391–411). Washington, DC: National Association of School Psychologists.

Detterman, D. K. (1979). Memory in the mentally retarded. In N. R. Ellis (Ed.), *Handbook of mental deficiency: Psychological theory and research* (pp. 727–760). Hillsdale, NJ: Erlbaum.

Dev, P. C. (1998). Intrinsic motivation and the student with learning difficulties. *Journal of Research and Development in Education, 31,* 98–108.

deVillers, P. A., & deVilliers, J. G. (1992). Language development. In M. H. Bornstein & M. E. Lamb (Eds.), *Developmental psychology: An advanced textbook* (pp. 337–418). Hillsdale, NJ: Erlbaum.

Dewey, J. (1913). *Interest and effort in education.* Boston: Riverside Press.

Dewey, J. (1933). *How we think: A restatement of the relation of reflective thinking to the education process.* Boston: Heath.

Diamond, A. (1990a). Developmental time course in human infants and infant monkeys, and the neural bases of inhibitory control in reaching. In A. Diamond (Ed.), *The development and neural bases of higher cognitive functions* (pp. 637–676). New York: New York Academy of Science.

Diamond, A. (1990b). Rate of maturation of the hippocampus and the developmental progression of children's performance on the delayed non-matching to sample and visual paired comparison tasks. In A. Diamond (Ed.), *The development and neural bases of higher cognitive functions* (pp. 394–433). New York: New York Academy of Science.

Diamond, A. (1991). Frontal lobe involvement in cognitive changes during the first year of life. In K. R. Gibson & A. C. Petersen (Eds.), *Brain maturation and cognitive development: Comparative and cross-cultural perspectives* (pp. 127–180). New York: Aldine de Gruyter.

Diamond, A. (2001). A model for studying the role of dopamine in the prefrontal cortex during early development in humans: Early and continuously treated phenylketonuria. In C. A. Nelson & M. Luciana (Eds.), *Handbook of developmental cognitive neuroscience* (pp. 433–472). Cambridge, MA: MIT Press.

Diamond, A., Werker, J. F., & Lalonde, C. (1994). Toward understanding commonalities in the development of object search: Detour navigation, categorization, and speech perception. In G. Dawson & K. W. Fischer (1994), *Human behavior and the developing brain* (pp. 380–426). New York: Guilford Press.

Diamond, M. (1982). Sexual identity: Monozygotic twins reared in discordant sex roles and a BBC followup. *Archives of Sexual Behavior, 11,* 181–185.

Diamond, M., & Sigmundson, H. K. (1999). Sex reassignment at birth. In S. J. Ceci & W. M. Williams (Eds.), *The nature–nurture debate* (pp. 55–75). Malden, MA: Blackwell.

Diamond, M. C. (1988). *Enriching heredity: The impact of the environment on the anatomy of the brain.* New York: Free Press.

Diamond, M. C. (1991). Environmental influences on the young brain. In K. R. Gibson & A. C. Petersen (Eds.), *Brain maturation and cognitive and cross-cultural perspectives* (pp. 107–124). New York: Aldine de Gruyter.

Diamond, M. C. (1992, October). Plasticity of the brain: Enrichment versus impoverishment. In C. Clark & K. King (Eds.), *Television and the preparation of the mind for learning.* Washington, DC: U.S. Department of Health and Human Services.

Diana v. State Board of Education. C-70–37 RFP (N. D. Cal. June 18, 1973). (stipulated settlement.)

Diaz, R. M. (1983). Thought and two languages: The impact of bilingualism on cognitive development. In E. Norbeck, D. Price-Williams, & W. McCord (Eds.), *Review of research in education* (Vol. 10, pp. 23–54). Washington, DC: American Educational Research Association.

Diaz, R. M., Padilla, K. A., &

Weathersby, E. K. (1991). The effects of bilingualism on preschoolers' private speech. *Early Childhood Research Quarterly, 6,* 377–393.

Dishion, T. J. (1990). The family ecology of boys' peer relations in middle childhood. *Child Development, 61,* 874–892.

Dittman, R. W., Kappes, M. E., & Kappes, M. H. (1992). Sexual behavior in adolescent and adults females with congenital adrenal hyperplasia. *Psychoneuroendocrinology, 17,* 1–18.

Divine-Hawkins, P. (1981). *Family day care in the United States: National Day Care Home Study final report, executive summary.* Washington, DC: U.S. Government Printing Office.

Dobbing. J. (1974). The later growth of the brain and its vulnerability. *Pediatrics, 53,* 2–6.

Dodge, K. A., Coie, J. D., Pettit, G. S., & Price, J. M. (1990). Peer status and aggression in boys' groups: Developmental and contextual analyses. *Child Development, 61,* 1289–1309.

Dodge, K. A., & Crick, N. R. (1990). Social information-processing bases of aggressive behavior in children. *Personality and Social Psychology Bulletin, 16*(1), 8–22.

Dodge, K. A., Schlundt, D. C., Schocken, L., & Delugach, J. D. (1983). Social competence and children's sociometric status: The role of peer group entry strategies. *Merrill–Palmer Quarterly, 29,* 309–336.

Doherty, W. J., & Needle, R. H. (1991). Psychological adjustment and substance use among adolescents before and after parental divorce. *Child Development, 62,* 328–337.

Dolezal, S. E., Welsh, L. M., Pressley, M., & Vincent, M. (2003). How do grade-3 teachers motivate their students? *Elementary School Journal, 103,* 239–267.

Dollard, J. (1949). *Caste and caste in a small southern town* (3rd ed.). New York: Anchor Books.

Donlon, T. F. (1992). Legal issues in the educational testing of Hispanics. In K. F. Geisinger (Ed.), *Psychological testing of Hispanics* (pp. 55–78). Washington, DC: American Psychological Association.

Dornbusch, S. M., Ritter, P. L., Leiderman, P. H., Roberts, D. F., & Fraleigh, M. J. (1987). The relation of parenting style to adolescent school performance. *Child Development, 58,* 1244–1257.

Douvan, E., & Adelson, J. (1966). *The adolescent experience.* New York: Wiley.

Doyle, K. W., Wolchik, S. A., Dawson-McClure, S. R., & Sandler, I. N. (2003). Positive events as a stress buffer for children and adolescents in families in transition. *Journal of Clinical Child and Adolescent Psychology, 32,* 536–545.

Doyle, W. (1986). Classroom organization and management. In M. C. Wittrock (Ed.), *Handbook of research on teaching* (3rd ed., pp. 392–431). New York: Macmillan.

Dreyfus, A., Jungwirth, E., & Eliovitch, R. (1990). Applying the "cognitive conflict" strategy for conceptual change: Some implications, difficulties, and problems. *Science Education, 74,* 555–569.

Driver, R., Asoko, H., Leach, J., Mortimer, E., & Scott, P. (1998). Constructing scientific knowledge in the classroom. In D. Faulkner, K. Littleton, & M. Woodhead (Eds.), *Learning relationships in the classroom* (pp. 258–275). London: Routledge.

Duckworth, E. (Ed.). (2001). *Tell me more: Listening to learners explain.* New York: Teachers College Press.

Duda, J. L., & Nicholls, J. G. (1992). Dimensions of achievement motivation in schoolwork and sport. *Journal of Educational Psychology, 84,* 290–299.

Dudycha, G. J., & Dudycha, M. M. (1941). Childhood memories: A review of the literature. *Psychological Bulletin, 38,* 668–682.

Duit, R. (1991). Students' conceptual frameworks: Consequences for learning science. In S. M. Glynn, R. H. Yeany, & B. K. Britton (Eds.), *The psychology of learning science* (pp. 65–85). Hillsdale, NJ: Erlbaum.

Dunlap, L. K., & Dunlap, G. (1989). A self-monitoring package for teaching subtraction with regrouping to students with learning disabilities. *Journal of Applied Behavior Analysis, 22,* 309–314.

Dunn, J. (1992). Siblings and development. *Current Directions in Psychological Science, 1,* 6–9.

Dunn, J. (1993). *Young children's close relationships.* Newbury Park, CA: Sage.

Dunn, J. (2002). Sibling relationships. In P. K. Smith & C. H. Hart (Eds.), *Blackwell handbook of childhood social development* (pp. 223–237). Oxford, UK: Blackwell.

Dunn, J., & Kendrick, C. (1982). Siblings and their mothers: Developing relationships within the family. In M. C. Lamb & B. Sutton-Smith (Eds.), *Sibling relationships* (pp. 39–60). Hillsdale, NJ: Erlbaum.

Dunn, J., Kendrick, C., & MacNamee, R. (1981). The reaction of first-born children to the birth of a sibling: Mother's reports. *Journal of Child Psychology and Psychiatry, 22,* 1–18.

Dunn, J., & McGuire, S. (1994). Young children's nonshared experiences: A summary of studies in Cambridge and Colorado. In E. M. Hetherington, D. Reiss, & R. Plomin (Eds.), *Separate social worlds of siblings: The impact of nonshared environment on development* (pp. 111–128). Hillsdale, NJ: Erlbaum.

DuPaul, G. J., & Stoner, G. (1999a). *Assessing ADHD in the schools* [Videotape]. New York: Guilford Press.

DuPaul, G. J., & Stoner, G. (1999b). *Classroom interventions for ADHD* [Videotape]. New York: Guilford Press.

DuPaul, G. J., & Stoner, G. (2003). *ADHD in the schools: Assessment and intervention strategies* (2nd ed.). New York: Guilford Press.

Duran, B. J., & Weffer, R. E. (1992). Immigrants' aspirations, high school process, and academic outcomes. *American Educational Research Journal, 29,* 163–181.

Durgunoglu, A., Nagy, W. E., & Hancin-Bhatt, B. J. (1993). Cross-language transfer of phonological awareness. *Journal of Educational Psychology, 85,* 453–465.

Durkin, D. (1966). The achievement of pre-school readers: Two longitudinal studies. *Reading Research Quarterly, 1,* 5–36.

Durso, F. T., & Coggins, K. A. (1991). Organized instruction for the improvement of word knowledge skills. *Journal of Educational Psychology, 83,* 109–112.

Dweck, C. S. (1978). Achievement. In M. E. Lamb (Ed.), *Social and personality development* (pp. 268–276). New York: Holt, Rinehart & Winston.

Dweck, C. S. (1986). Motivational processes affecting learning. *American Psychologist, 41,* 1040–1048.

Dweck, C. (1987, April). *Children's theories of intelligence: Implications for motivation and learning.* Paper presented at the annual meeting of the American Educational Research Association, Washington, DC.

Dweck, C. S. (2002a). Beliefs that make smart people dumb. In R. Sternberg (Ed.), *Why smart people can be so stupid* (pp. 24–41). New Haven, CT: Yale University Press.

Dweck, C. S. (2002b). Messages that motivate: How praise molds students' beliefs, motivation, and performance (in surprising ways). In J. Aronson (Ed.), *Improving academic achievement: Impact of psychological factors on education* (pp. 37–60). San Diego, CA: Academic Press.

Dweck, C. S., Davidson, W., Nelson, S., & Enna, B. (1978). Sex differences in learned helplessness: II. The contingencies of evaluative feedback in the classroom. III. An experimental analysis. *Developmental Psychology, 14,* 268–276.

Dweck, C. S., & Leggett, E. L. (1988). A social-cognitive approach to motivation and personality. *Psychological Review, 95,* 256–273.

Eaton, W. O., & Enns, L. R. (1986). Sex differences in human motor activity level. *Psychological Bulletin, 100,* 19–28.

Eccles, J. (1983). Expectancies, values, and academic behaviors. In J. T. Spence (Ed.), *Achievement and achievement motives* (pp. 75–146). San Francisco: Freeman.

Eccles, J. S. (1984). Sex differences in achievement patterns. In T. Sonderegger (Ed.), *Nebraska Symposium on Motivation* (Vol. 32, pp. 97–132). Lincoln: University of Nebraska Press.

Eccles, J. S. (1989). Bringing young women to math and science. In M. Crawford & M. Gentry (Eds.), *Gender and thought: Psychological perspectives* (pp. 36–58). New York: Springer-Verlag.

Eccles, J. S. (1993). School and family effects on the ontogeny of children's interests, self-perceptions, and activity choices. In J. E. Jacobs (Ed.), *Nebraska symposium on motivation: Developmental perspectives on motivation* (Vol. 40, pp. 145–208). Lincoln: University of Nebraska Press.

Eccles, J. S. (1999). The development of children ages 6 to 14. *The Future of Children, 9*(2), 30–44.

Eccles, J. S., & Blumenfeld, P. (1985). Classroom experience and student gender: Are there differences and do they matter? In L. C. Wilkinson & C. B. Marrett (Eds.), *Gender influences in classroom interaction* (pp. 79–114). New York: Academic Press.

Eccles, J. S., Freedman-Doan, C., Frome, P., Jacobs, J., & Yoon, K. S. (2000). Gender-role socialization in the family: A longitudinal approach. In T. Eckes & H. M. Trautner (Eds.), *The developmental social psychology of gender* (pp. 333–360). Mahwah, NJ: Erlbaum.

Eccles, J. S., & Jacobs, J. (1986). Social forces shape math participation. *Signs, 11,* 367–380.

Eccles, J., MacIver, D., & Lange, L. (1986, April). *Classroom practice and motivation to study math.* Paper presented at the annual meeting of the American Educational Research Association, San Francisco.

Eccles, J. S., & Midgley, C. (1989). Stage/environment fit: Developmentally appropriate classrooms for early adolescents. In R. E. Ames & C. Ames (Eds.), *Research on motivation in education* (Vol. 3, pp. 139–186). New York: Academic Press.

Eccles, J. S., Midgley, C., & Wigfield, A. (1993). Development during adolescence: The impact of stage-environment fit on young adolescents' experiences in schools and in families. *American Psychologist, 48,* 90–101.

Eccles, J. S., & Wigfield, A. (2002). Motivational beliefs, values, and goals. *Annual Review of Psychology, 53,* 109–132.

Eccles, J. S., Wigfield, A., Midgley, C., Reuman, D., Mac Iver, D., & Feldlaufer, H. (1993). Negative effects of traditional middle schools on students' motivation. *Elementary School Journal, 93,* 553–574.

Eccles, J., Wigfield, A., Flanagan, C., Miller, C., Reuman, D., & Yee, D. (1989). Self-concepts, domain values, and self-esteem: Relationships and changes in early adolescence. *Journal of Personality, 57,* 283–310.

Eccles, J. S., Wigfield, A., & Schiefele, U. (1998). Motivation to succeed. In N. Eisenberg (Vol. Ed.) & W. Damon (Ed.-in-Chief), *Handbook of child psychology: Vol. 3. Social, emotional, and personality development* (pp. 1017–1095). New York: Wiley.

Eccles-Parson, J., Adler, T. F., & Kaczala, C. M. (1982). Socialization of achievement attitudes and beliefs: Parental influences. *Child Development, 53,* 310–321.

Eckenrode, J., Laird, M., & John, D. (1993). School performance and disciplinary problems among abused and neglected children. *Developmental Psychology, 29,* 53–62.

Eckerman, C. O., & Stein, M. R. (1982). The toddler's emerging skills. In K. H. Rubin & H. S. Ross (Eds.), *Peer relationships and social skills in childhood* (pp. 41–71). New York: Springer-Verlag.

Eden, G. F., & Zeffiiro, T. A. (1998). Neural systems affected in developmental dyslexia revealed by functional neuroimaging. *Neuron, 21,* 279–282.

Eder, D., with Evans, C. C., & Parker, S. (1995). *School talk: Gender and adolescent culture.* New Brunswick, NJ: Rutgers University Press.

Edmonds, R. R. (1979). Effective schools for the urban poor. *Educational Leadership, 37*(1), 15–24.

Edwards, R., & Edwards, J. (1987). Corporal punishment. In A. Thomas & J. Grimes (Eds.), *Children's needs: Psychological perspectives* (pp. 127–131). Washington, DC: National Association of School Psychologists.

Egeland, B., & Hiester, M. (1995). The long-term consequences of infant day-care and mother–infant attachment. *Child Development, 66,* 474–485.

Eghbalieh, B., Crinella, F. M., Hunt, L. E., & Swanson, J. M. (2000). Prenatal stimulant exposure affects alerting and executive control in six- and seven-year-olds. *Journal of Attention Disorders, 4,* 5–13.

Ehri, L. C. (2004). Teaching phonemic awareness and phonics: An explanation of the National Reading Panel meta-analyses. In P. McCardle & V. Chhabra (Eds.), *The voice of evidence in reading research* (pp. 153–186). Baltimore: Brookes.

Ehri, L. C., Nunes, S., Willows, D., Schuster, B., Yaghoub-Zadeh, Z., & Shanahan, T. (2001). Phonemic awareness instruction helps children learn to read: Evidence from the National Reading Panel's meta-analysis. *Review of Educational Research, 71,* 393–447.

Eimas, P. D., Siqueland, E. R., Jusczyk, P., & Vigorito, J. (1971). Speech perception in infants. *Science, 171,* 303–306.

Eisenberg, N., & Fabes, R. A. (1994). Mothers' reactions to children's negative emotions: Relations to children's temperament and anger behavior. *Merrill–Palmer Quarterly, 40,* 138–156.

Eisenberg, N., Wolchik, S. A., Hernandez, R., & Pasternack, J. F. (1985). Parental socialization of young children's play: A short-term longitudinal study. *Child Development, 56,* 1506–1513.

Eitzen, D. S. (1992). Problem students: The sociocultural roots. *Phi Delta Kappan, 73,* 584–590.

Eley, T. C., Bishop, D. V. M., Dale, P. S., Oliver, B., Petrill, S. A., Price, T. S., et al. (1999). Genetic and environmental origins of verbal and performance components of cognitive delay in 2-year-olds. *Developmental Psychology, 35,* 1122–1131.

El-Dinary, P. B., Pressley, M., &

Schuder, T. (1992). Teachers learning transactional strategies instruction. In C. K. Kinzer & D. J. Leu (Eds.), *Literacy research, theory, and practice: Views from many perspectives: 41st yearbook of the National Reading Conference* (pp. 453–462). Chicago: National Reading Conference.

Elicker, J., Englund, M., & Sroufe, L. A. (1992). Predicting peer competence and peer relationships in childhood from early parent–child relationships. In R. Parke & G. Ladd (Eds.), *Family-peer relationships: Modes of linkage* (pp. 77–106). Hillsdale, NJ: Erlbaum.

Elliott, E. S., & Dweck, C. S. (1988). Goals: An approach to motivation and achievement. *Journal of Personality and Social Psychology, 54,* 5–12.

Ellis, N. R. (Ed.). (1979). *Handbook of mental deficiency: Psychological theory and research.* Hillsdale, NJ: Erlbaum.

Emde, R. N. (1992). Individual meaning and increasing complexity: Contributions of Sigmund Freud and Rene Spitz to developmental psychology. *Developmental Psychology, 28,* 347–359.

Emde, R. N. (1998). Individual meaning and increasing complexity: Contributions of Sigmund Freud and Rene Spitz to developmental psychology. *Psychotherapie Psychosomatik Medizinische Psychologie, 53,* 79–82.

Emde, R. N., & Hewitt, J. K. (Eds.). (2001). *Infancy to early childhood: Genetic and environmental influences on developmental change.* New York: Oxford University Press.

Emler, N., & Dickinson, J. (1993). The child as sociologist: The development of implicit theories of role categories and social organization. In M. Bennett (Ed.), *The child as psychologist: An introduction to the development of social cognition* (pp. 168–190). New York: Harvester Wheatsheaf.

Emmer, E. T., Evertson, C. M., & Worsham, M. E. (2001). *Classroom management for secondary teachers* (6th ed.). Boston: Pearson/Allyn & Bacon.

Emmerich, W., Goldman, K., Kirsh, B., & Sharabany, R. (1977). Evidence for a transitional phase in the development of gender constancy. *Child Development, 48,* 930–936.

Engel, S. (1986). *Learning to reminisce: A developmental study of how young children talk about the past.* Unpublished PhD dissertation, City University of New York, Graduate Center.

Enright, R. D. (1994) The moral development of forgiveness. In B. Puka (Ed.), *Reaching out: Caring, altruism, and prosocial behavior* (pp. 219–248). New York: Garland.

Enright, R. D. (2001). *Forgiveness is a choice: A step-by-step process for resolving anger and restoring hope.* Washington, DC: American Psychological Association.

Enright, R. D., & Fitzgibbons, R. P. (2000). *Helping clients forgive: An empirical guide for resolving anger and restoring hope.* Washington, DC: American Psychological Association.

Enright, R. D., Lapsley, D. K., & Levy, V. M. (1983). Moral education strategies. In M. Pressley & J. R. Levin (Eds.), *Cognitive strategy research: Educational applications* (pp. 43–83). New York: Springer-Verlag.

Enright, R. D., & The Human Development Study Group. (1994). Piaget on the moral development of forgiveness: Identity or reciprocity? *Human Development, 37,* 63–80.

Entwisle, D., & Hayduk, L. (1978). *Too great expectations: The academic outlook of young children.* Baltimore: Johns Hopkins University Press.

Epstein, S. (1994). Integration of the cognitive and the psychodynamic unconscious. *American Psychologist, 49,* 709–724.

Erickson, F. (1987). Transformation and school success: The politics and culture of educational achievement. *Anthropology and Education Quarterly, 18,* 335–356.

Erickson, G. L., & Erickson, L. J. (1984). Females and science achievement: Evidence, explanation, and implications. *Science Education, 68,* 63–89.

Erickson, F., & Mohatt, G. (1982). Cultural organization of participation structures in two classrooms of Indian students. In G. Spindler (Ed.), *Doing the ethnography of schooling* (pp. 133–174). New York: Holt, Rinehart & Winston.

Erickson, M. F., Sroufe, L. A., & Egeland, B. (1985). The relationship between quality of attachment and behavior problems in preschool in a high-risk sample. In I. Bretherton & E. Waters (Eds.), Growing points of attachment theory and research (pp. 147–166). *Monographs of the Society for Research in Child Development, 50*(1–2, Serial No. 209).

Erikson, E. (1943). Observations on the Yurok: Childhood and world image. *American Archaeology and Ethnology, 35,* 257–302.

Erikson, E. (1945). Childhood and tradition in two American Indian tribes. *In psychoanalytic study of the child* (Vol. 1, pp. 319–350). New York: International Universities Press.

Erikson, E. (1963). *Childhood and society.* New York: Norton.

Erikson, E. (1968). *Identity: Youth and crisis.* New York: Norton.

Erikson, E., & Coles, R. (Eds.). (2000). *The Erik Erikson reader.* New York: Norton.

Eron, L. D. (1987). The development of aggression from the perspective of a developing behaviorism. *American Psychologist, 42,* 435–442.

Erting, C. J., Prezioso, C., & O'Grady Hynes, M. (1990). The interactional context of deaf mother–infant communication. In V. Volterra & C. J. Erting (Eds.), *From gesture to language in hearing and deaf children* (pp. 97–106). Berlin: Springer-Verlag.

Espy, K. A., Moore, I. M., Kaufmann, P. M., Kramer, J. H., Mattha, K., & Hutter, J. J. (2001). Chemotherapeutic CNS prophylaxis and neuropsychologic change in children with acute lymphoblastic leukemia: A prospective study. *Journal of Pediatric Psychology, 26,* 1–9.

Estes, D., Wellman, H. M., & Woolley, J. D. (1989). Children's understanding of mental phenomenon. In H. W. Reese (Ed.), *Advances in child development and behavior* (Vol. 22, pp. 41–87). San Diego, CA: Academic Press.

Estrada, M. T. (1990). *Improving academic performance through enhancing possible selves.* Unpublished master's thesis, University of Notre Dame, Notre Dame, IN.

Ethington, C. A. (1992). Gender differences in a psychological model of mathematics achievement. *Journal for Research in Mathematics Education, 23,* 166–181.

Evans, G. W. (2004). The environment of childhood poverty. *American Psychologist, 59,* 77–92.

Evans, J. A., & Hamerton, J. L. (1985). Chromosomal anomalies. In A. M. Clarke, A. D. B. Clarke, & J. M. Berg (Eds.), *Mental deficiency: The changing outlook* (pp. 135–213). New York: Free Press.

Evans, M. A. (2001). Shyness in the classroom and home. In R. W. Crozier & L. E. Alden (Eds.), *International handbook of social anxiety: Concepts, research and interventions relating to the self and shyness* (pp. 159–183). New York: Wiley.

Evans, M. A., Fitzsimmons, M., &

McDermid, B. (1995, April). *A longitudinal study of reticence: Kindergarten through grade three.* Paper presented at the biennial meeting of the Society for Research in Child Development, Indianapolis.

Evertson, C. M. (1989). Classroom organization and management. In M. C. Reynolds (Ed.), *Knowledge base for the beginning teacher* (pp. 59–70). New York: Pergamon Press.

Evertson, C. M., Emmer, E. T., & Worsham, M. E. (2002). *Classroom management for elementary teachers* (6th ed.). Boston: Pearson/Allyn & Bacon.

Fabiani, M., & Wee, E. (2001). Age-related changes in working memory function: A review. In C. Nelson & M. Luciana (Eds.), *Handbook of developmental cognitive neuroscience* (pp. 473–488). Cambridge, MA: MIT Press.

Fagot, B. I. (1974). Sex differences in toddlers' behavior and parental reaction. *Developmental Psychology, 10,* 554–558.

Fagot, B. I. (1978). The influence of sex of child on parental reactions to toddler children. *Child Development, 49,* 459–465.

Fagot, B. I. (1981). Male and female teachers: Do they treat boys and girls differently? *Sex Roles, 7,* 263–271.

Fagot, B.I. (1985). Changes in thinking about early sex role development. *Developmental Review, 5,* 83–98.

Fagot, B. I., & Hagan, R. (1991). Observation of parent reactions to sex-stereotyped behaviors: Age and sex effects. *Child Development, 62,* 617–628.

Fagot, B. I., & Kavanagh, K. (1993). Parenting during the second year: Effects of children's age, sex, and attachment classification. *Child Development, 64,* 258–271.

Fagot, B. I., & Leinbach, M. D. (1989). The young child's gender schema: Environmental input, internal organization. *Child Development, 60,* 663–672.

Fagot, B. I., & Leinbach, M. D. (1993). Gender role development in young children: From discrimination to labeling. *Developmental Review, 13,* 86–106.

Falbo, T., & Polit, D. F. (1986). Quantitative review of the only child literature: Research evidence and theory development. *Psychological Bulletin, 100,* 176–189.

Fan, X., & Chen, M. (2001). Parental involvement and students' academic achievement: A meta-analysis. *Educational Psychology Review, 13*(1), 1–22.

Fantuzzo, J., Boruch, R., Beriama, A., Atkins, M., & Marcus, S. (1997). Domestic violence and children: Prevalence and risk in five major U.S. cities. *Journal of the American Academy of Child and Adolescent Psychiatry, 36*(1), 116–122.

Fantz, R. L., & Nevis, S. (1967). Pattern preferences and perceptual-cognitive development in early infancy. *Merrill–Palmer Quarterly, 13*, 77–108.

Farkas, G., Sheehan, D., & Grobe, R. P. (1990). Coursework mastery and school success: Gender, ethnicity, and poverty groups within an urban school district. *American Educational Research Journal, 27*, 807–827.

Farnham-Diggory, S. (1992). *The learning-disabled child.* Cambridge, MA: Harvard University Press.

Farran, D. C. (2001). Critical periods and early interventions. In D. B. Bailey Jr., J. T. Bruer, F. J. Symons, & J. W. Lichtman (Eds.), *Critical thinking about critical periods* (pp. 233–266). Baltimore: Brookes.

Farrell, E., Peguero, G., Lindsey, R., & White, R. (1988). Giving voice to high school students: Pressure and boredom, ya know what I'm sayin'? *American Educational Research Association, 25*, 489–502.

Fauber, R., Forehand, R., Thomas, A. M., & Wierson, M. (1990). A mediational model of the impact of marital conflict on adolescent adjustment in intact and divorced families: The role of disrupted parenting. *Child Development, 61*, 1112–1123.

Feagans, L. V., Kipp, E., & Blood, I. (1994). The effects of otitis media on the attention skills of day-care-attending toddlers. *Developmental Psychology, 30*, 701–708.

Feeney, J. A., & Noller, P. (1990). Attachment style as a predictor of romantic relationships. *Journal of Personality and Social Psychology, 58*, 281–291.

Feinfield, K. A., Lee, P. P., Flavell, E. R., Green, F. L., & Flavell, J. H. (1999). Young children's understanding of intention. *Cognitive Development, 14*, 463–486.

Feldhusen, J. F. (1986). A conception of giftedness. In R. J. Sternberg & J. E. Davidson (Eds.), *Conceptions of giftedness* (pp. 112–127). Cambridge, UK: Cambridge University Press.

Feldhusen, J. F., & Kolloff, M. B. (1981). Me: A self-concept scale for

gifted students. *Perceptual and Motor Skills, 53*, 319–323.

Feldman, D. H. (1979). The mysterious case of extreme giftedness. In A. H. Passow (Ed.), *The gifted and the talented: Their education and development* (pp. 335–351). Chicago: University of Chicago Press.

Feldman, D. H. (1982). *Developmental approaches to giftedness and creativity.* San Francisco: Jossey-Bass.

Feldman, D. H. (1988). *Nature's gambit: Child prodigies and the development of human potential.* New York: Basic Books.

Feldman, D. H. (2003). Cognitive development in childhood. In I. B. Weiner (Series Ed.), R. M. Lerner, M. A. Easterbrooks, & J. Mistry (Vol. Eds.), *Handbook of psychology: Vol. 6. Developmental psychology* (pp. 195–210). New York: Wiley.

Feldman, D. H., with A. C. Benjamin. (1986). Giftedness as a developmentalist sees it. In R. J. Sternberg & J. E. Davidson (Eds.), *Conceptions of giftedness* (pp. 285–305). Cambridge, UK: Cambridge University Press.

Feltz, D. L., Landers, D. M., & Becker, B. J. (1988). A revised meta-analysis of the mental practice literature on motor skill performance. In D. Druckman & J. A. Swets (Eds.), *Enhancing human performance: Issues, theories and techniques: Background papers* (pp. 1–65). Washington, DC: National Research Council.

Fennema, E. (1974). Sex differences in mathematics learning: Why??? *Elementary School Journal, 75*, 183–190.

Fennema, E., & Franke, M. L. (1992). Teachers' knowledge and its impact. In D. A. Grouws (Ed.), *Handbook of research on mathematics teaching and learning* (pp. 147–164). New York: Macmillan.

Fernald, A. (1991). Prosody in speech to children: Prelinguistic and linguistic features. In R. Vasta (Ed.), *Annals of child development* (Vol. 8, pp. 43–80). Greenwich, CT: JAI Press.

Fernald, A., & Kuhl, P. (1987). Acoustic determinants of infant preference for motherese speech. *Infant Behavior and Development, 10*, 279–293.

Fernandez, R. J., & Samuels, M. A. (1986). Intellectual dysfunction: Mental retardation and dementia. In M. A. Samuels (Ed.), *Manual of neurologic therapeutics* (pp. 30–50). Boston: Little, Brown.

Feurstein, R. (1980). *Instrumental en-*

richment: An intervention program for cognitive modifiability. Baltimore: University Park Press.

Fey, M. E. (1986). *Language intervention with young children.* Newton, MA: Allyn & Bacon.

Fey, M. E., Windsor, J., & Warren, S. F. (1995). *Language intervention: Preschool through the elementary years.* Baltimore: Brookes.

Field, T. (1979). Differential cardiac responses of 3-month-old infants to mirror and peer. *Infant Behavior and Development, 2*, 179–184.

Fillmore, L. W. (1991). When learning a second language means losing the first. *Early Childhood Research Quarterly, 6*, 323–346.

Fincham, F. D., Hokoda, A., & Sanders, R., Jr. (1989). Learned helplessness, text anxiety, and academic achievement: A longitudinal analysis. *Child Development, 60*, 138–145.

Finkelhor, D. (1991). *National Youth Victimization Prevention Survey.* Los Altos, CA: Sociometrics Corp.

Finkelhor, D., Ormrod, R., Turner, H., & Hamby, S. L. (2005). The victimization of children and youth: A comprehensive, national survey. *Child Maltreatment: Journal of the American Professional Society on the Abuse of Children, 10*(1), 5–25.

Flavell, J. H. (1985). *Cognitive development.* Englewood Cliffs, NJ: Prentice-Hall.

Finn, J. D., & Cox, D. (1992). Participation and withdrawal among fourth-grade pupils. *American Educational Research Journal, 29*, 141–162.

Firestone, W. A. (1991). Educators, researchers, and the effective schools movement. In J. R. Bliss, W. A. Firestone, & C. E. Richards (Eds.), *Rethinking effective schools research and practice* (pp. 12–27). Englewood Cliffs, NJ: Prentice-Hall.

Fischer, K. W. (1980). A theory of cognitive development: The control and construction of hierarchies of skills. *Psychological Review, 87*, 477–531.

Fischer, K. W., & Rose, S. P. (1994). Dynamic development of coordination of components in brain and behavior: A framework for theory and research. In G. Dawson & K. W. Fischer (1994), *Human behavior and the developing brain* (pp. 3–66). New York: Guilford Press.

Fischer, K. W., & Rose, S. P. (1996). Dynamic growth cycles of brain and cognitive development. In R. W. Thatcher, G. R. Lyon, J. Rumsey,

& N. Krasnegor (Eds.), *Developmental neuroimaging: Mapping the development of brain and behavior* (pp. 263–279). San Diego, CA: Academic Press

Fischer, K. W., Shaver, P. R., & Carnochan, P. (1989). A skill approach to emotional development: From basic- to subordinate-category emotions. In W. Damon (Ed.), *Child development today and tomorrow* (pp. 107–136). San Francisco: Jossey-Bass/Pfeiffer

Fischer, K. W., Shaver, P. R., & Carnochan, P. (1990). How emotions develop and how they organise development. *Cognition and Emotion, 4,* 81–127.

Fitzgerald, J. (1995a). English-as-a-second-language learners' cognitive reading processes: A review of the research in the United States. *Review of Educational Research, 65,* 145–190.

Fitzgerald, J. (1995b). English-as-a-second-language reading instruction in the United States: A research review. *Journal of Reading Behavior, 27,* 115–152.

Fitzgerald, J., & Markham, L. (1987). Teaching children about revision in writing. *Cognition and Instruction, 4,* 3–24.

Fivush, R. (1994). Constructing narrative, emotion, and self in parent–child conversations about the past. In U. Neisser & R. Fivush (Eds.), *The remembering self: Construction and accuracy in the self-narrative* (pp. 136–157). Cambridge, UK: Cambridge University Press.

Flanagan, C. A., & Eccles, J. S. (1993). Changes in parents' work status and adolescents' adjustment at school. *Child Development, 64,* 246–257.

Flannery, D. J., Rowe, D. C., & Gulley, B. L. (1993). Impact of pubertal status, timing, and age on adolescent sexual experience and delinquency. *Journal of Adolescent Research, 8,* 21–40.

Flavell, J. H. (1971). Stage-related properties of cognitive development. *Cognitive Psychology, 2,* 421–453.

Flavell, J. H. (1972). An analysis of cognitive-developmental sequences. *Genetic Psychology Monographs, 86,* 279–350.

Flavell, J. H., Beach, D. H., & Chinsky, J. M. (1966). Spontaneous verbal rehearsal in a memory task as a function of age. *Child Development, 37,* 283–299.

Flavell, J. H., Everett, B. A., Croft, K., & Flavell, E. R. (1981). Young children's knowledge about visual perception: Further evidence for the Level 1–Level 2 distinction. *Developmental Psychology, 17,* 99–103.

Flavell, J. H., Green, F. L., Herrera, C., & Flavell, E. R. (1991). Young children's knowledge about visual perception: Lines of sight must be straight. *British Journal of Developmental Psychology, 9,* 73–87.

Flavell, J. H., & Miller, P. H. (1998). Social cognition. In D. Kuhn & R. S. Siegler (Vol. Eds.) & W. Damon (Ed.-in-Chief), *Handbook of child psychology: Vol. 2. Cognition, perception, and language* (pp. 851–898). New York: Wiley.

Flavell, J. H., Miller, P. H., & Miller, S. M. (1993). *Cognitive development* (3rd ed.). Englewood Cliffs, NJ: Prentice-Hall.

Flerx, V. C., Fidler, D. S., & Rodgers, R. W. (1976). Sex role stereotypes: Developmental aspects and early intervention. *Child Development, 47,* 998–1007.

Fletcher, A. C., Darling, N. E., Steinberg, L., & Dornbusch, S. M. (1995). The company they keep: Relation of adolescents' adjustment and behavior to their friends' perceptions of authoritative parenting in the social network. *Developmental Psychology, 31,* 300–310.

Fletcher, P., & Ingham, R. (1995). Grammatical impairment. In P. Fletcher & B. MacWhinney (Eds.), *The handbook of child language* (pp. 603–622). Oxford, UK: Blackwell.

Flood, J. (1977). Parental styles in reading episodes with young children. *Reading Teacher, 30,* 864–867.

Florsheim, P. (Ed.). (2003). *Adolescent romantic relations and sexual behavior: Theory, research, and practical implications.* Mahwah, NJ: Erlbaum.

Flower, L., & Hayes, J. (1980). The dynamics of composing: Making plans and juggling constraints. In L. Gregg & E. Steinberg (Eds.), *Cognitive processes in writing* (pp. 31–50). Hillsdale, NJ: Erlbaum.

Flowers, D. L., Wood, F. B., & Naylor, C. E. (1991). Regional cerebral bloodflow correlates of language processes in reading disability. *Archives of Neurology, 48,* 637–643.

Fodor, J. A. (1983). *The modularity of mind.* Cambridge, MA: MIT Press.

Foersterling, F. (1985). Attribution retraining: A review. *Psychological Bulletin, 98,* 495–512.

Fogel, A. (1979). Peer- vs. mother-directed behavior in 1- to 3-month-old infants. *Infant Behavior and Development, 2,* 215–226.

Foley, D. E. (1991). Reconsidering anthropological explanations of ethnic school failure. *Anthropology and Education Quarterly, 22,* 60–86.

Foley, J., & Thompson, L. (2003). *Language learning: A lifelong process.* New York: Oxford University Press.

Fonagy, P., Steele, H., & Steele, M. (1991). Maternal representations of attachment during pregnancy predict the organization of infant-mother attachment at one year of age. *Child Development, 62,* 891–905.

Fonagy, P., & Kurtz, A. (2002), Disturbance of conduct. In P. Fonagy, M. Target, D. Cottrell, J. Phillips, & Z. Kurtz, *What works for whom?: A critical review of treatments for children and adolescents* (pp. 106–193). New York: Guilford Press.

Fonagy, P., Target, M., Cottrell, D., Phillips, J., & Kurtz, Z. (2002). *What works for whom?: A critical review of treatments for children and adolescents.* New York: Guilford Press.

Ford, D. H. (1987). *Humans as self-constructing living systems: A developmental perspective on behavior and personality.* Hillsdale, NJ: Erlbaum.

Fordham, S. (1988). Racelessness as a factor in black students' school success: Pragmatic strategy or pyrrhic victory? *Harvard Educational Review, 58,* 54–84.

Fordham, S., & Ogbu, J. U. (1986). Black students' school success: Coping with the burden of "acting white." *Urban Review, 18,* 176–206.

Fottland, H. (2000). Childhood cancer and the interplay between illness, self-evaluation and academic experiences. *Scandinavian Journal of Educational Research, 44,* 253–273.

Foundas, A. L. (2001). The anatomical basis of language. *Topics in Language Disorders, 21,* 1–19

Fox, B. A. (1993). *The human tutorial dialogue project.* Hillsdale NJ: Erlbaum.

Fox, N. A., & Bell, M. A. (1990). Electrophysiological indices of frontal lobe development: Relations to cognitive and affective behavior in human infants over the first year of life. In A. Diamond (Ed.), *The development and neural bases of higher cognitive functions* (pp. 677–704). New York: New York Academy of Sciences.

Fox, R. (1991). Developing awareness of mind reflected in children's narrative writing. *British Journal of Developmental Psychology, 9,* 281–298.

Francis, P. L., Self, P. A., & Horowitz,

F. D. (1987). The behavioral assessment of the neonate: An overview. In J. D. Osofsky (Ed.), *Handbook of infant development* (pp. 723–779). New York: Wiley.

Frankel, K. A., & Bates, J. E. (1990). Mother–toddler problem-solving: Antecedents in attachment, home behavior, and temperament. *Child Development, 61,* 810–819.

Fredricks, J. A., Blumenfeld, P. C., & Paris, A. H. (2004). School engagement: Potential of the concept, state of the evidence. *Review of Educational Research, 74,* 59–109.

Freedman-Doan, C., Wigfield, A., Eccles, J., Blumenfeld, P., Arbreton, A., & Harold, R. D. (2000). What am I best at?: Grade and gender differences in children's beliefs about ability improvement. *Journal of Applied Developmental Psychology, 21,* 379–402.

Freeman, D. (1983). *Margaret Mead and Samoa: The making and unmaking of an anthropological myth.* Cambridge, MA: Harvard University Press.

French, D. C., Jansen, E. A., & Pidada, S. (2002). United States and Indonesian children's and adolescents' reports of relational aggression by disliked peers. *Child Development, 73,* 1143–1150.

Freud, A. (1936). *The ego and the mechanisms of defense.* New York: International Universities Press.

Freud, S. (1938). *An outline of psychoanalysis.* London: Hogarth Press.

Frey, K. S., & Ruble, D. N. (1987). What children say about classroom performance: Sex and grade differences in perceived competence. *Child Development, 58,* 1066–1078.

Fried, P. A. (2002). Conceptual issues in behavioral teratology and their application in determining long-term sequelae of prenatal marihuana exposure. *Journal of Child Psychology and Psychiatry and Allied Disciplines, 43,* 81–102.

Fried, P. A., & Watkinson, B. (1990). 36- and 48-month-neurobehavioral follow-up of children prenatally exposed to marijuana, cigarettes, and alcohol. *Journal of Developmental and Behavioral Pediatrics, 11,* 49–58.

Friedman, L. (1989). Mathematics and the gender gap: A meta-analysis of recent studies on sex differences in mathematical tasks. *Review of Educational Research, 59,* 185–213.

Frisancho, A. R. (1995). *Human adaptation and accommodation.* Ann Arbor: University of Michigan Press.

Frisch, H. L. (1977). Sex stereotypes in adult–infant play. *Child Development, 48,* 1671–1675.

Fuchs, D., & Fuchs, L. S. (1986). Test procedure bias: A meta-analysis of examiner familiarity effects. *Review of Educational Research, 56,* 243–262.

Fuchs, L. S., & Fuchs, D. (2003). Enhancing the mathematical problem solving of students with mathematics disabilities. In H. L. Swanson, K. R. Harris, & S. Graham (Eds.), *Handbook of learning disabilities* (pp. 306–322). New York: Guilford Press.

Fuchs, L. S., Fuchs, D., Yazdian, L., & Powell, S. R. (2002). Enhancing first-grade children's mathematical development with peer-assisted learning strategies. *School Psychology Review, 31,* 569–583.

Fuhrer, U., & Josephs, I. E. (1998). The cultivated mind: From mental mediation to cultivation. *Developmental Review, 18*(3), 279–312.

Fuligni, A. L., & Eccles, J. S. (1993). Perceived parent–child relationships and early adolescents' orientation toward peers. *Developmental Psychology, 29,* 622–632.

Fulk, B. M. (1996a). The effects of combined strategy and attribution training on LD adolescents' spelling performance. *Exceptionality, 6,* 13–27.

Fulk, B. M. (1996b). Reflections on "The effects of combined strategy and attribution training on LD adolescents' spelling performance." *Exceptionality, 6,* 59–63.

Furman, W. (1995). Parenting siblings. In M. H. Bornstein (Ed.), *Handbook of parenting: Vol. 1. Children and parenting* (pp. 143–162). Hillsdale, NJ: Erlbaum.

Furman, W., & Bierman, K. I. (1984). Children's conceptions of friendship: A multimethod study of developmental changes. *Developmental Psychology, 20,* 925–931.

Furrer, C., & Skinner, E. (2003). Sense of relatedness as a factor in children's academic engagement and performance. *Journal of Educational Psychology, 95,* 148–162.

Furth, H. G. (1964). Research with the deaf: Implications for language and cognition. *Psychological Bulletin, 62,* 145–164.

Furth, H. G. (1966). *Thinking without language.* New York: Free Press.

Furuno, S., O'Reilly, K., Inatsuka, T., Hosaka, C., Allman, T., & Zeisloft-Falbey, B. (1987). *Hawaii early learning profile.* Palo Alto, CA: VORT Corporation.

Fuson, K. C., Carroll, W. M., & Drueck, J. V. (2000). Achievement results for second and third graders using the standards-based curriculum everyday mathematics. *Journal for Research in Mathematics Education, 31*(3), 277–295.

Fuster, J. M. (1989). *The prefrontal cortex: Anatomy, physiology, and neuropsychology of the frontal lobe.* New York: Raven Press.

Gagné, R. M., & Dick, W. (1983). Instructional psychology. *Annual Review of Psychology, 34,* 261–295.

Galaburda, A. M. (1983). Developmental dyslexia: Current anatomical research. *Annals of Dyslexia, 33,* 41–53.

Galaburda, A. M., Sherman, G. F., Rosen, G. D., Aboitz, F., & Geschwind, N. (1985). Developmental dyslexia: Four consecutive patients with cortical anomalies. *Archives of Neurology, 35,* 812–817.

Gallagher, T. M. (1981). Contingent query sequences within adult–child discourse. *Journal of Child Language, 8*(1), 51–62.

Gallagher, T. M., & Darnton, B. (1978). Conversational aspects of the speech of language-disordered children: Revision behaviors. *Journal of Speech and Hearing Research, 21,* 118–135.

Gallaway, C., & Woll, B. (1994). Interaction and childhood deafness. In C. Galloway & B. Richards (Eds.), *Input and interaction in language acquisition* (pp. 197–218). Cambridge, UK: Cambridge University Press.

Galotti, K. M. (1989). Gender differences in self-reported moral reasoning: A review and new evidence. *Journal of Youth and Adolescence, 18,* 475–488.

Galotti, K. M., Kozberg, S. F., & Farmer, M. C. (1991). Gender and developmental differences in adolescents' conceptions of moral reasoning. *Journal of Youth and Adolescence, 20,* 13–30.

Galton, F. (1869). *Hereditary genius: An inquiry into its laws and consequences.* London: Macmillan.

Garcia, E. E. (1991). *The education of linguistically and culturally diverse students: Effective instructional practices.* Santa Cruz, CA: National Center for Research on Cultural Diversity and Second Language Learning.

Garcia, E. E. (1993). Curriculum and instruction: Revision for constant relevancy. *Education and Urban Society, 25,* 270–284.

Gardner, E. (1975). *Fundamentals of neurology* (6th ed.). Philadelphia: Saunders.

Gardner, H. (1983). *Frame of mind: The theory of multiple intelligences.* New York: Basic Books.

Gardner, H. (1993). *Multiple intelligences: The theory in practice*. New York: Basic Books.

Gardner, H. (1999). *Intelligence reframed: Multiple intelligences for the 21st century*. New York: Basic Books.

Gardner, W., & Rogoff, B. (1982). The role of instruction in memory development: Some methodological choices. *Quarterly Newsletter of the Laboratory of Comparative Human Cognition, 4*, 6–12.

Garlick, D. (2002). Understanding the nature of the general factor of intelligence: The role of individual differences in neural plasticity as an explanatory mechanism. *Psychological Review, 109*, 116–136.

Garner, R. (1992). Learning from school texts. *Educational Psychologist, 27*, 53–63.

Garner, R., Alexander, P. A., Gillingham, M. G., Kulikowich, J. M., & Brown, R. (1991). Interest and learning from text. *American Educational Research Journal, 28*, 643–660.

Garner, R., Gillingham, M. G., & White, C. S. (1989). Effects of "seductive details" on macroprocessing and microprocessing in adult and children. *Cognition and Instruction, 6*, 41–57.

Garvey, C. (1974). Requests and responses in children's speech. *Journal of Child Language, 2*, 41–60.

Gaskins, I. W., & Elliot, T. T. (1991). *Implementing cognitive strategy instruction across the school: The benchmark manual for teachers*. Cambridge, MA: Brookline Books.

Gates, B. (Guest Ed.). (1990). Special Issue: Perspectives on morality and moral education east and west. *Journal of Moral Education, 19*(3).

Gaulin, S. J. C. (1995). Does evolutionary theory predict sex differences in the brain? In M. S. Gazzaniga (Ed.), *The cognitive neurosciences* (pp. 1211–1225). Cambridge, MA: MIT Press.

Gayan, J., & Olson, R. K. (2003). Genetic and environmental influences on individual differences in printed word recognition. *Journal of Experimental Child Psychology, 84*, 97–123.

Ge, X., Conger, R. D., & Elder, G. H. Jr. (1996). Coming of age too early: Pubertal influences on girls' vulnerability to psychological distress. *Child Development, 67*, 3386–3400.

Geary, D. C. (1998). *Male, female: The evolution of human sex differences*. Washington, DC: American Psychological Association.

Geary, D. C., & Brown, S. C. (1991).

Cognitive addition: Strategy choice and speed-of-processing differences in gifted, normal, and mathematically disabled children. *Developmental Psychology, 27*, 398–406.

Geisenger, K. F. (1992). Fairness and selected psychometric issues in the psychological testing of Hispanics. In K. F. Geisinger (Ed.), *Psychological testing of Hispanics* (pp. 17–42). Washington, DC: American Psychological Association.

Geisinger, K. F. (2003). Testing and assessment in cross-cultural psychology. In J. R. Graham & J. A. Naglieri (Vol. Eds.), I. B. Weiner (Ed.-in-Chief), *Handbook of psychology: Vol. 10. Assessment psychology* (pp. 95–117). New York: Wiley.

Gelman, R. (1972). Logical capacity of very young children: Number invariance rules. *Child Development, 43*(1), 75–90.

Gelman, R., & Baillargeon, R. (1983). A review of some Piagetian concepts. In J. H. Flavell & E. M. Markman (Eds.), *Handbook of child psychology: Vol. 3. Cognitive development* (pp. 167–230). New York: Wiley.

Gelman, R., Massey, C. M., & McManus, M. (1991). Characterizing supporting environments for cognitive development: Lessons from children in a museum. In L. Resnick, J. M. Levine, & S. D. Teasley (Eds.), *Perspectives on socially shared cognition* (pp. 226–256). Washington, DC: American Psychological Association.

Gelman, S. A., & Koenig, M. A. (2003). Theory-based categorization in early childhood. In D. H. Rakison & L. M. Oakes (Eds.), *Early category and concept development: Making sense of the blooming, buzzing confusion* (pp. 330–359). New York: Oxford University Press.

Genesee, F. (1981). Cognitive and social consequences of bilingualism. In R. G. Gardner & R. Kalin (Eds.), *A Canadian social psychology of ethnic relations*. London: Methuen.

Genesee, F. (1985). Second language learning through immersion: A review of U.S. programs. *Review of Educational Research, 55*, 541–562.

Genesee, F. (1987). *Learning through two languages: Studies of immersion and bilingual education*. Cambridge, MA: Newbury House.

Genesee, F., Lindholm-Leary, K., Saunders, W. M., & Christian, D. (Eds.). (2006). *Educating English language learners: A synthesis of research evidence*. New York: Cambridge University Press.

Gentry, M., Gable, R. K., & Rizza, M. (2002). Students' perceptions of classroom activities: Are there grade-level and gender differences? *Journal of Educational Psychology, 94*, 539–544.

George, C., & Main, M. (1979). Social interactions of young abused children: Approach, avoidance, and aggression. *Child Development, 50*, 306–318.

Georgieff, M. K., & Rao, R. (2001). The role of nutrition in cognitive development. In C. A. Nelson & M. Luciana (Eds.), *Handbook of developmental cognitive neuroscience* (pp. 491–504). Cambridge, MA: MIT Press.

Gershoff, E. T. (2002). Parental corporal punishment and associated child behaviors and experiences: A meta-analytic and theoretical review. *Psychological Bulletin, 128*, 539–579.

Gersten, R., & Baker, S. (2001). Teaching expressive writing to students with learning disabilities: A meta-analysis. *Elementary School Journal, 101*, 251–272.

Gersten, R., Fuchs, L. S., Williams, J. P., & Baker, S. (2001). Teaching reading comprehension strategies to students with learning disabilities: A review of research. *Review of Educational Research, 71*, 279–320.

Geva, E., & Siegel, L. S. (1998). Orthographic and cognitive factors in the concurrent development of basic reading skills in two languages. *Reading and Writing: An Interdisciplinary Journal, 12*, 1–31.

Geva, E., Wade-Wooley, L., & Shany, M. (1993). The concurrent development of spelling and decoding in two different orthographies. *Journal of Reading Behavior, 25*, 383–406.

Ghatala, E. S. (1986). Strategy-monitoring training enables young learners to select effective strategies. *Educational Psychologist, 21*, 43–54.

Ghatala, E. S., Levin, J. R., Pressley, M., & Goodwin, D. (1986). A componential analysis of the effects of derived and supplied strategy-utility information on children's strategy selections. *Journal of Experimental Child Psychology, 41*, 76–92.

Gibbs, J. C., Arnold, K. D., & Burkart, J. E. (1984). Sex differences in the expression of moral judgment. *Child Development, 55*, 1040–43.

Gibbs, J. C., Basinger, K. S., & Fuller, D. (1992). *Moral maturity: Measuring the development of sociomoral reflection*. Hillsdale, NJ: Erlbaum.

Gibbs, J. C., Basinger, K. S., & Grime, R. L. (2003). Moral judgment maturity: From clinical to standard measures. In S. J. Lopez & C. R. Snyder (Eds.), *Positive psychological assessment: A handbook of models and measures* (pp. 361–373). Washington, DC: American Psychological Association.

Gibbs, J. C., Widaman, K. F., & Colby, A. (1982). Construction and validation of a simplified, group-administrable equivalent to the Moral Judgment Interview. *Child Development, 53*, 895–910.

Gibson, E. J. (1969). *Principles of perceptual learning and development.* New York: Appleton–Century–Crofts.

Gibson, E. J. (1991). *The odyssey in learning and perception.* Cambridge, MA: MIT Press.

Gibson, E. J., & Spelke, E. S. (1983). The development of perception. In J. H. Flavell & E. M. Markman (Eds.), *Handbook of child psychology: Vol. 3. Cognitive development* (4th ed., pp. 1–76). New York: Wiley.

Gibson, K. R. (1991a). Basic neuroanatomy for the nonspecialist. In K. R. Gibson & A. C. Petersen (Eds.), *Brain maturation and cognitive development: Comparative and cross-cultural perspectives* (pp. 13–25). New York: Aldine de Gruyter.

Gibson, K. R. (1991b). Myelination and behavioral development: A comparative perspective on questions of neoteny, altriciality and intelligence. In K. R. Gibson & A. C. Petersen (Eds.), *Brain maturation and cognitive development: Comparative and cross-cultural perspectives* (pp. 29–63). New York: Aldine de Gruyter.

Gibson, K. R., & Petersen, A. C. (1991). Introduction. In K. R. Gibson & A. C. Petersen (Eds.), *Brain maturation and cognitive development: Comparative and cross-cultural perspectives* (pp. 3–12). New York: Aldine de Gruyter.

Gibson, M. A. (1988). *Accomodation without assimilation: Sikh immigrants in an American high school.* Ithaca, NY: Cornell University Press.

Gibson, M. A., & Ogbu, J. U. (Eds.). (1991a). *Minority status and schooling: A comparative study of immigrant and involuntary minorities.* New York: Garland Press.

Gibson, M. A., & Ogbu, J. U. (1991b). The dynamics of educational decision making: A comparative study of Sikhs in Britain and the United States. In M. A. Gibson & J. U. Ogbu (Eds.), *Minority status and schooling: A comparative study of immigrant and involuntary minorities* (pp. 63–95). New York: Garland Press.

Gick, M. L., & Holyoak, K. J. (1980). Analogical problem solving. *Cognitive Psychology, 12*, 306–355.

Gick, M. L., & Holyoak, K. J. (1983). Schema induction and analogical transfer. *Cognitive Psychology, 15*, 1–38.

Giest, H., & Lompscher, J. (2003). Formation of learning activity and theoretical thinking in science teaching. In A. Kozulin, B. Gindia, V. S. Ageyev, & S. M. Miller (Eds.), *Vygotsky's educational theory in cultural context* (pp. 267–288). Cambridge, UK: Cambridge University Press.

Gilger, J. W., & Wise, S. E. (2004). Genetic correlates of language and literacy impairments. In C. A. Stone, E. R. Silliman, B. J. Ehren, & K. Apel (Eds.), *Handbook of language and literacy* (pp. 25–48). New York: Guilford Press.

Gillam, R., & Johnston, J. (1992). Spoken and written language relationships in language/learning impaired and normally achieving school-age children. *Journal of Speech and Hearing Research, 35*, 1303–1315.

Gillam, R., McFadden, T. U., & van Kleeck, A. (1995). Improving narrative abilities: Whole language and language skills approaches. In M. E. Fey, J. Windsor, & S. F. Warren (Eds.), *Language intervention: Preschool through the elementary years* (pp. 145–182). Baltimore: Brookes.

Gilliam, W. S., & Zigler, E. F. (2000). A critical meta-analysis of evaluations of state-funded preschool from 1997 to 1998: Implications for policy, service delivery and program evaluation. *Early Childhood Research Quarterly, 15*, 441–473.

Gilligan, C. (1982). *In a different voice: Psychological theory and women's development.* Cambridge, MA: Harvard University Press.

Gilligan, C., & Attanucci, J. (1988). Two moral orientations. In C. Gilligan, J. V. Ward, & J. M. Taylor with B. Bardige (Eds.), *Mapping the moral domain: A contribution of women's thinking to psychological theory and education* (pp. 73–86). Cambridge, MA: Harvard University Press.

Gindis, B. (2003). Remediation through education: Sociocultural theory and children with special needs. In A. Kozulin, B. Gindia, V. S. Ageyev, & S. M. Miller (Eds.), *Vygotsky's educational theory in cultural context* (pp. 200–221). Cambridge, UK: Cambridge University Press.

Ginsburg, G. S., & Bronstein, P. (1993). Family factors related to children's intrinsic/extrinsic motivational orientation and academic performance. *Child Development, 64*, 1461–1474.

Ginsburg, H. J., & Miller, S. M. (1982). Sex differences in children's risk-taking behavior. *Child Development, 53*, 426–428.

Glaser, B., & Strauss, A. (1967). *The discovery of grounded theory.* Chicago: Aldine.

Glasgow, K. L., Dornbusch, S. M., Troyer, L., Steinberg, L., & Ritter, P. I. (1997). Parenting styles, adolescents' attributions, and educational outcomes in nine heterogenous high schools. *Child Development, 68*, 507–523.

Glass, D. C., Neulinger, J., & Brim, O. G. (1974). Birth order, verbal intelligence, and educational aspiration. *Child Development, 45*, 807–811.

Gleason, J. B. (1973). Code switching in children's language. In T. E. Moore (Ed.), *Cognitive development and the acquisition of language.* Oxford, UK: Academic Press.

Glover, J. A. (1989). The "testing" phenomenon: Not gone but nearly forgotten. *Journal of Educational Psychology, 81*, 392–399.

Gnepp, J. (1989). Children's use of personal information to understand other people's feelings. In C. Saarni & P. L. Harris (Eds.), *Children's understanding of emotion* (pp. 151–177). Cambridge, UK: Cambridge University Press.

Goelman, H. (1986). The language environments of family day care. In S. Kilmer (Ed.), *Advances in early education and day care* (Vol. 4, pp. 153–179). Greenwich, CT: JAI Press.

Gold, D., & Andres, D. (1978). Developmental comparisons between ten-year-old children with employed and unemployed mothers. *Child Development, 49*, 75–84.

Goldberg, S. (1983). Parent–infant bonding: Another look. *Child Development, 54*, 1355–1382.

Goldberg, S. (1995). Introduction. In S. Goldberg, R. Muir, & J. Kerr (Eds.), *Attachment theory: Social, developmental, and clinical perspectives* (pp. 1–11). Hillsdale, NJ: Analytic Press.

Goldberg, S., Blumberg, S. L., & Kriger, A. (1982). Menarche and interest in infants: Biological and social influences. *Child Development, 53*, 1544–1550.

Goldberg, S., & DeVitto, B. A. (1983). *Born too soon: Preterm birth and early development.* San Francisco: Freeman.

Goldberger, A. S. (1977). On Thomas's model for kinship correlations. *Psychological Bulletin, 84*(6), 1239–1244.

Goldfield, B. A., & Reznick, J. S. (1990). Early lexical acquisition: Rate, content, and the vocabulary spurt. *Journal of Child Language, 17,* 171–183.

Goldin-Meadow, S. (1985). Language development under atypical learning conditions. In K. E. Nelson (Ed.), *Children's language* (Vol. 5, pp. 197–245). Hillsdale, NJ: Erlbaum.

Goldin-Meadow, S., & Mylander, C. (1984). Gestural communication in deaf children: The effects and noneffects of parental input on early language development. *Society for Research in Child Development Monographs, 49*(No. 207).

Goldman-Rakic, P. S., Isseroff, A., Schwartz, M. L., & Bugbee, N. M. (1983). The neurobiology of cognitive development. In M. M. Haith & J. J. Campos (Vol. Eds.) & P. H. Mussen (Gen. Ed.), *Handbook of child psychology: Vol. 2. Infancy and developmental psychobiology* (pp. 281–344). New York: Wiley.

Goldsmith, H. H., & Alansky, J. A. (1987). Maternal and infant temperamental predictors of attachment: A meta-analytic review. *Journal of Consulting and Clinical Psychology, 55*, 805–816.

Goleman, D. (1990, March 6). As a therapist, Freud fell short. *New York Times*, pp. C1, C12.

Golombok, S., & Hines, M. (2002). Sex differences in social behavior. In P. K. Smith & C. H. Hart (Eds.), *Blackwell handbook of childhood social development* (pp. 117–136). Oxford, UK: Blackwell.

Golombok, S., & Tasker, F. (1996). Do parents influence the sexual orientation of their children?: Findings from a longitudinal study of lesbian families. *Developmental Psychology, 32*, 3–11.

Gombert, E. (1991). *Metalinguistic development.* Chicago: University of Chicago Press.

Gooden, W. E. (1989). Development of black men in early adulthood. In R. L. Jones (Ed.), *Black adult development and aging* (pp. 63–89). Berkeley, CA: Cobb & Henry.

Goodman, J. F. (1990). Infant intelligence: Do we, can we, should we assess it? In C. R. Reynolds & R. W. Kamphaus (Eds.), *Handbook of psychological and educational assessment of children: Intelligence and achievement* (pp. 183–208). New York: Guilford Press.

Goodman, R. A. (1983). *Mead's "Coming of Age in Samoa": A dissenting view.* Oakland, CA: Pipperline Press.

Goodwyn, S. W., & Acredolo, L. P. (1993). Symbolic gesture versus word: Is there a modality advantage for onset of symbol use? *Child Development, 64*(3), 688–701.

Gopnik, A., Meltzoff, A., & Kuhl P. (1999). *The scientist in the crib: Minds, brains, and how children learn.* New York: Morrow.

Gordon, R. A. (2000). *Eating disorders: Anatomy of a social epidemic.* Malden, MA: Blackwell.

Gorsuch, R. L. (1983). *Factor analysis* (2nd ed.). Mahwah, NJ: Erlbaum.

Goswami, U. (2004). Neuroscience and education. *British Journal of Educational Psychology, 74*, 1–14.

Goswami, U., & Bryant, P. (1992). Rhyme, analogy, and children's reading. In P. B. Gough, L. C. Ehri, & R. Treiman (Eds.), *Reading acquisition* (pp. 49–63). Hillsdale, NJ: Erlbaum.

Gottesman, I. I. (1963). Genetic aspects of intelligent behavior. In N. Ellis (Ed.), *Handbook of mental deficiency* (pp. 253–296). New York: McGraw-Hill.

Gottesman, I. I., & Hanson, D. R. (2005). Human development: Biological and genetic processes. *Annual Review of Psychology, 56*, 263–286.

Gottfredson, D. C., Gottfredson, G. D., & Hybl, L. G. (1993). Managing adolescent behavior: A multiyear, multischool study. *American Educational Research Journal, 30*, 179–215.

Gottfried, A. E., Gottfried, A. W., & Bathurst, K. (1988). Maternal employment, family environment, and children's development: Infancy through the school years. In A. E. Gottfried & A. W. Gottfried (Eds.), *Maternal employment, family environment, and children's development: Infancy through the school years* (pp. 11–58). New York: Plenum Press.

Gottlieb, G. (1974). *Aspects of neurogenesis.* New York: Academic Press.

Gottlieb, G. (1995). Some conceptual deficiencies in "developmental" behavior genetics. *Human Development, 38*, 131–141.

Gottman, J. M. (1977). Toward a definition of social isolation in children. *Child Development, 48*, 513–517.

Gottman, J. M. (1986). The world of coordinated play: Same- and cross-sex friendship in young children. In J. M. Gottman & J. G. Parker (Eds.), *Conversations of friends: Speculations on affective development* (pp. 139–191). Cambridge, UK: Cambridge University Press.

Gould, S. J. (1981). *The mismeasure of man.* New York: Norton.

Graber, J. A., Peterson, A. C., & Brooks-Gunn, J. (1996). Pubertal processes: Methods, measures, and models. In J. A. Graber, J. Brooks-Gunn, & A. C. Petersen (Eds.), *Transitions through adolescence* (pp. 23–53). Mahwah, NJ: Erlbaum.

Graf, P., & Schacter, D. L. (1985). Implicit and explicit memory for new associations in normal and amnesic subjects. *Journal of Experimental Psychology: Learning, Memory, and Cognition, 11*, 501–518.

Graham, S. (1990). The role of production factors in learning disabled students' compositions. *Journal of Educational Psychology, 82*, 781–791.

Graham, S., & Harris, K. R. (1987). Improving composition skills of inefficient learners with self-instructional strategy training. *Topics in Language Disorders, 7*, 66–77.

Graham, S., & Harris, K. R. (1988). Instructional recommendations for teaching writing to exceptional children. *Exceptional Children, 54*, 506–512.

Graham, S., & Harris, K. R. (2003). Students with learning disabilities and the process of writing: A meta-analysis of SRSD studies. In H. L. Swanson, K. R. Harris, & S. Graham (Eds.), *Handbook of learning disabilities* (pp. 323–344). New York: Guilford Press.

Graham, S., Hudley, C., & Williams, E. (1992). Attributional and emotional determinants of aggression among African-American and Latino young adolescents. *Developmental Psychology, 28*, 731–740.

Graham, S., & MacArthur, C. (1988). Improving learning disabled students' skill at revising essays produced on a word processor: Self-instructional strategy training. *Journal of Special Education, 22*, 133–152.

Graham, S., & Taylor, A. Z. (2002). Ethnicity, gender, and the development of achievement values. In A. Wigfield & J. S. Eccles (Eds.), *Development of achievement motivation* (pp. 121–146). San Diego, CA: Academic Press.

Graham, S., & Weiner, B. (1996). Theories and principles of motivation. In D. C. Berliner & R. C. Calfee (Eds.), *Handbook of educational psychology* (pp. 63–84). New York: Macmillan.

Grant, J. P. (1989). *The state of the world's children*. New York: Oxford University Press.

Grayson, D. A. (1989). Twins reared together: Minimizing shared environmental effects. *Behavior Genetics, 19*, 593–603.

Graziano, W. G., Varca, P. E., & Levy, J. C. (1982). Race of examiner effects and the validity of intelligence tests. *Review of Educational Research, 52*, 469–498.

Green, S. K. (2002). Using an expectancy–value approach to examine teachers' motivational strategies. *Teaching and Teacher Education, 18*, 989–1005.

Green, S. K., & Gredler, M. E. (2002). A review and analysis of constructivism for school-based practice. *School Psychology Review, 31*(1), 53–70.

Greenbaum, J., & Graf, P. (1989). Preschool period development of implicit and explicit remembering. *Bulletin of the Psychonomic Society, 27*(5), 417–420.

Greenburg, M. T. (1999). Attachment and psychopathology in childhood. In J. Cassidy & P. R. Shaver (Eds.), *Handbook of attachment: Theory, research, and clinical applications* (pp. 469–496). New York: Guilford Press.

Greenberger, E., & Goldberg, W. A. (1989). Work, parenting, and the socialization of children. *Developmental Psychology, 25*, 22–35.

Greenberger, E., O'Neil, R., & Nagel, S. (1994). Linking workplace and homeplace: Relations among the nature of adults' work and their parenting behaviors. *Developmental Psychology, 30*, 990–1002.

Greenfield, P. M. (1984). A theory of the teacher in the learning activities of everyday life. In B. Rogoff & J. Lave (Eds.), *Everyday cognition: Its development in social context* (pp. 117–138). Cambridge, MA: Harvard University Press.

Greenfield, P. M., Keller, H., Filigni, A., & Maynard, A. (2003). Cultural pathways through universal development. *Annual Review of Psychology, 54*, 461–490.

Greenfield, P. M., & Savage-Rumbaugh, E. S. (1990). Grammatical combination in *Pan paniscus*: Processes of learning and invention in the evolution and development of language. In S. T. Parker & K. R. Gibson (Eds.), *"Language" and intelligence in monkeys and apes* (pp. 540–578). Cambridge, UK: Cambridge University Press.

Greenough, W. T. (1993). Experience and brain development. *Child Development, 58*, 539–559.

Greenough, W. T., Black, J. E., & Wallace, C. S. (1987). Experience and brain development. *Child Development, 58*, 539–559.

Greenough, W. T., & Juraska, J. M. (1986). *Developmental neuropsychobiology*. Orlando, FL: Academic Press.

Greenwood, C. R., Delquadri, J. C., & Hall, R. V. (1989). Longitudinal effects of classwide peer tutoring. *Journal of Educational Psychology, 81*, 371–383.

Griffith, D. R. (1992). Prenatal exposure to cocaine and other drugs: Developmental and educational prognoses. *Phi Delta Kappan, 74*, 30–34.

Griffith, P. L. (1991). Phonemic awareness helps first graders invent spellings and third graders remember correct spellings. *Journal of Reading Behavior, 23*, 215–233.

Grinder, R. E. (1985). The gifted in our midst: By their divine deeds, neuroses, and mental test scores we have known them. In F. D. Horowitz & M. O'Brien (Eds.), *The gifted and talented: Developmental perspectives* (pp. 5–35). Washington, DC: American Psychological Association.

Grosjean, F. (1982). *Life with two languages: An introduction to bilingualism*. Cambridge, MA: Harvard University Press.

Gross-Glenn, K., Duara, R., Yoshii, F., Barker, W. W., Chen, J. Y., Apicella, A., et al. (1988). PET-scan reading studies of familial dyslexics [Abstract]. *Journal of Clinical and Experimental Neuropsychology, 10*, 34–35.

Grossman, H., & Grossman, S. H. (1994). *Gender issues in education*. Needham Heights, MA: Allyn & Bacon.

Guay, F., Marsh, H. W., & Boiven, M. (2003). Academic self-concept and academic achievement: Developmental perspectives on their causal ordering. *Journal of Educational Psychology, 95*, 124–136.

Guba, E. G. (Ed.). (1990). *Paradigm dialog*. Newbury CA: Sage.

Guzzetti, B. J., Snyder, T. E., Glass, G. V., & Gamas, W. S. (1993). Promoting conceptual change in science: A comparative meta-analysis of instructional interventions from reading education and science education. *Reading Research Quarterly, 28*, 117–159.

Grusec, J. E., & Goodnow, J. J. (1994). Impact of parental discipline methods on the child's internalization of values: A reconceptualization of current points of view. *Developmental Psychology, 30*, 4–19.

Guba, E. G., & Lincoln, Y. S. (1982). Epistemological and methodological bases of naturalistic inquiry. *Educational Communication and Technology Journal, 30*, 233–252.

Guralnick, M. J. (1997a). *The effectiveness of early intervention*. Baltimore: Brookes.

Guralnick, M. J. (1997b). Second-generation research in the field of early intervention. In M. J. Guralnick (Ed.), *The effectiveness of early intervention* (pp. 3–20). Baltimore: Brookes.

Guttentag, R. E. (1989). Age differences in dual-task performance: Procedures, assumptions, and results. *Developmental Review, 9*, 146–170.

Haberlandt, K. (1980). Story grammar and reading time of story constituents. *Poetics, 9*, 99–116.

Hack, M., Klein, N. K., & Taylor, H. G. (1995). Long-term developmental outcomes of low birth weight infants. *The Future of Children, 5*(1), 176–196.

Hacker, D. J., & Tenent, A. (2002). Implementing reciprocal teaching in the classroom: Overcoming obstacles and making modifications. *Journal of Educational Psychology, 94*, 699–718.

Hadwin, J., & Perner, J. (1991). Pleased and surprised: Children's cognitive theory of emotion. *British Journal of Developmental Psychology, 9*, 215–234.

Haenen, J., Schrijnemakers, H., & Stufkens, J. (2003). Sociocultural theory and the practice of teaching historical concepts. In A. Kozulin, B. Gindia, V. S. Ageyev, & S. M. Miller (Eds.), *Vygotsky's educational theory in cultural context* (pp. 246–266). Cambridge, UK: Cambridge University Press.

Hakuta, K. (1986). *Mirror of language: The debate on bilingualism*. New York: Basic Books.

Hakuta, K. (1999). The debate on bilingual education. *Journal of Developmental and Behavioral Pediatrics, 20*(1), 36–37.

Hakuta, K. (2001). A critical period for second language acquisition. In

D. B. Bailey Jr., J. T. Bruer, F. J. Symons, & J. W. Lichtman (Eds.), *Critical thinking about critical periods* (pp. 193–205). Baltimore: Brookes.

Hakuta, K., & D'Andrea, D. (1992). Some properties of bilingual maintenance and loss in Mexican background high-school students. *Applied Linguistics, 13,* 72–99.

Hale, G. A., & Lewis, M. (1979). *Attention and cognitive development.* New York: Plenum Press.

Hale, N. G. Jr. (1995). *The rise and crisis of psychoanalysis in the United States: Freud and the Americans, 1917–1985.* New York: Oxford University Press.

Hall, C. R., Rodgers, W. M., & Barr, K. A. (1990). The use of imagery by athletes in selected sports. *Sport Psychologist, 4,* 1–10.

Hall, G. S. (1904). *Adolescence: Vol. 1.* New York: Appleton.

Hall, G. S. (1905). *Adolescence: Vol. 2.* New York: Appleton.

Halpern, D. F. (1992). *Sex differences in cognitive abilities* (2nd ed.). Hillsdale, NJ: Erlbaum.

Halpern, D. F. (2000). *Sex differences in cognitive abilities* (3rd ed.). Mahwah, NJ: Erlbaum.

Hamers, J. F., & Blanc, M. H. A. (1989). *Bilinguality and bilingualism.* Cambridge, UK: Cambridge University Press.

Hamilton, C. E. (2000). Continuity and discontinuity of attachment from infancy through adolescence. *Child Development, 71,* 690–694.

Hammen, C., & Rudolph, K. D. (2003). Childhood mood disorders. In E. J. Mash & R. A. Barkley (Eds.), *Child psychopathology* (2nd ed., pp. 233–278). New York: Guilford Press.

Hanna, E., & Meltzoff, A. N. (1993). Peer imitation by toddlers in laboratory, home, and day-care contexts: Implications for social learning and memory. *Developmental Psychology, 29,* 701–710.

Hannah, C. L., & Shore, B. M. (1995). Metacognition and intellectual ability: Insights from the study of learning disabled gifted students. *Gifted Child Quarterly, 39,* 95–109.

Hanson, S. L., & Ginsburg, A. L. (1988). Gaining control: Values and high school success. *American Educational Research Journal, 25,* 334–365.

Harkins, J. E., & Bakke, M. (2003). Technologies for communication: Status and trends. In M. Marschark & P. E. Spencer (Eds.), *Oxford handbook of deaf studies, language, and ed-*

ucation (pp. 406–419). New York: Oxford University Press.

Harkness, S., & Super, C. M. (1985). Child–environment interaction in the socialization of affect. In M. Lewis & C. Saarni (Eds.), *The socialization of emotions* (pp. 21–36). New York: Plenum Press.

Harms, T., Cryer, D., & Clifford, R. M. (1990). *Infant/toddler environment rating scale.* New York: Teachers College Press.

Harnishfeger, K. K., & Bjorklund, D. F. (1993). The ontogeny of inhibition mechanisms: A renewed approach to cognitive development. In M. L. Howe & R. Pasnak (Eds.), *Emerging themes in cognitive development, Volume 1. Foundations* (pp. 28–49). New York: Springer-Verlag.

Haroutunian-Gordon, S. (1991). *Turning the soul: Teaching through conversation in the high school.* Chicago: University of Chicago Press.

Harper, L. V., & Huie, K. S. (1985). The effects of prior group experience, age, and familiarity on the quality and organization of preschoolers' social relationships. *Child Development, 56,* 704–717.

Harrell, R., Capp, R., Davis, D., Peerless, J., & Ravitz, L. (1981). Can nutritional supplements help mentally retarded children? *Proceedings of the National Academy of Science, 78,* 574–578.

Harris, K. R. (1988, April). *What's wrong with strategy intervention research?: Intervention integrity.* Paper presented at the annual meeting of the American Educational Research Association, New Orleans.

Harris, K. R., & Graham, S. (1992). Self-regulated strategy development: A part of the writing process. In M. Pressley, K. R. Harris, & J. T. Guthrie (Eds.), *Promoting academic competence and literacy in school* (pp. 277–309). San Diego, CA: Academic Press.

Harris, M., Jones, D., Brookes, S., & Grant, J. (1986). Relations between the non-verbal context of maternal speech and rate of language development. *British Journal of Developmental Psychology, 4,* 261–268.

Harris, P. L., Brown, E., Marriott, C., Whittall, S., & Harmer, S. (1991). Monsters, ghosts, and witches: Testing the limits of the fantasy–reality distinction. *British Journal of Developmental Psychology, 9,* 105–123.

Harris, P. L., & Gross, D. (1988). Children's understanding of real and apparent emotion. In J. W.

Astington, P. L. Harris, & D. R. Olsen (Eds.), *Developing theories of mind* (pp. 295–314). Cambridge, UK: Cambridge University Press.

Harris, P. L., Olthof, T., & Terwogt, M. M. (1981). Children's knowledge of emotion. *Journal of Child Psychology and Psychiatry, 22,* 247–261.

Harris, P. L., Olthof, T., Terwogt, M. M., & Hardman, C. E. (1987). Children's knowledge of situations that provoke emotion. *International Journal of Behavioral Development, 10,* 319–343.

Harrison, G. A., Tanner, J. M., Pilbeam, D. R., & Baker, P. T. (1988). *Human biology: An introduction to human evolution, variation, growth, and adaptability.* Oxford, UK: Oxford University Press.

Harry, B. (1992). An ethnographic study of cross-cultural communication with Puerto Rican-American families in the special education system. *American Educational Research Journal, 29,* 471–494.

Hart, B. (1991). Input frequency and children's first words. *First Language, 11,* 289–300.

Hart, B., & Risley, T. R. (1995). *Meaningful differences in the everyday experience of young American children.* Baltimore: Brookes.

Hart, B., & Risley, T. R. (1999). *The social world of children: Learning to talk.* Baltimore: Brookes.

Hart, H. H. (Ed.). (1970). *SummerHill: For and against.* New York: Hart.

Harter, M. R. (1991). Event-related potential indices: Learning disabilities and visual processing. In J. E. Obrzut & G. W. Hynd (Eds.), *Neuropsychological foundations of learning disabilities: A handbook of issues, methods, and practice* (pp. 437–473). San Diego, CA: Academic Press.

Harter, S. (1990). Cause, correlates, and the functional role of self-worth: A life-span perspective. In R. J. Sternberg & J. Kolligian (Eds.), *Competence considered* (pp. 67–97). New Haven, CT: Yale University Press.

Harter, S. (1992). The relationship between perceived competence, affect, and motivational orientation within the classroom: Processes and patterns of change. In A. K. Boggiano & T. S. Pittman (Eds.), *Achievement and motivation: A social-developmental perspective* (pp. 77–114). New York: Cambridge University Press.

Harter, S., Marold, D. B., & Whitesell, N. R. (1992). A model of psychosocial risk factors leading to suicidal ideation in young adolescents. *Development and Psychopathology, 4,* 167–188.

Harter, S., Whitesell, N. R., & Kowalski, P. (1992). Individual differences in the effects of educational transitions on young adolescent's perceptions of competence and motivational orientation. *American Educational Research Journal, 29,* 777–807.

Hartup, W. W. (1983). Peer relations. In P. H. Mussen (Ed.), *Handbook of child psychology* (4th ed., Vol. 4, pp. 103–196). New York: Wiley.

Hartup, W. W. (1989). Social relations and their developmental significance. *American Psychologist, 44,* 120–126.

Hartup, W. W. (1996a). The company they keep: Friendships and their developmental significance. *Child Development, 67,* 1–13.

Hartup, W. W. (1996b). Cooperation, close relationships, and cognitive development. In W. M. Bukowski, A. F. Newcomb, & W. W. Hartup (Eds.), *The company they keep: Friendship in childhood and adolescence* (pp. 213–237). Cambridge, UK: Cambridge University Press.

Hartup, W. W. (2005). Peer interaction: What causes what? *Journal of Abnormal Child Psychology, 33*(3), 387–394.

Hartup, W. W., Daiute, C., Zajac, R., & Sholl, W. (1995). *Collaboration in creative writing by friends and nonfriends.* Unpublished manuscript, University of Minnesota. (Cited in Hartup, 1996b)

Harvey, E. (1999). Short-term and long-term effects of early parental employment on children of the National Longitudinal Survey of Youth. *Developmental Psychology, 35,* 445–459.

Hasselhorn, M. (1986). *Differentielle Bedingunsanalyse verbaler Gedächtnisleitungen bei Schulkindern.* Frankfurt: Lang.

Haubenstricker, J., & Seefeldt, V. (1986). Acquisition of motor skills during childhood. In V. Seefeldt (Ed.), *Physical activity and well-being* (pp. 41–102). Reston, VA: American Alliance for Health, Physical Education, Reaction and Dance.

Hay, D. F. (1984). Social conflict in early childhood. In G. Whitehurst (Ed.), *Annals of child development* (Vol. 1, pp. 1–44). Greenwich, CT: JAI Press.

Hay, D. F., Nash, A., & Pedersen, J. (1983). Interaction between six-month-old peers. *Child Development, 54,* 557–562.

Hayes, J. R., Waterman, D. A., & Robinson, C. S. (1977). Identifying relevant aspects of a problem text. *Cognitive Science, 1,* 297–313.

Hayward, C., Killen, J. D., Wilson, D. M., & Hammer, L. D. (1997). Psychiatric risk associated with early puberty in adolescent girls. *Journal of the American Academy of Child and Adolescent Psychiatry, 36,* 255–262.

Hazan, C., & Shaver, P. (1987). Romantic love conceptualized as an attachment process. *Journal of Personality and Social Psychology, 52,* 511–524.

Heath, S. B. (1989). Oral and literate traditions among black Americans living in poverty. *American Psychologist, 44,* 367–373.

Hebb, D. O. (1949). *The organization of behavior.* New York: Wiley.

Heine, S. J., Kitzyama, S., Lehman, D. R., Takata, T., Ide, E., Leung, C., & et al. (2001). Divergent consequences of success and failure in Japan and North America: An investigation of self-improving motivations and malleable selves. *Journal of Personality and Social Psychology, 81,* 599–615.

Hemmings, R. (1973). *Children's freedom: A. S. Neill and the evolution of the Summerhill idea.* New York: Schocken Books.

Henderlong, J., & Lepper, M. R. (2002). The effects of praise on children's intrinsic motivation: A review and synthesis. *Psychological Bulletin, 128*(5), 774–795.

Henderson, V. L., & Dweck, C. S. (1990). Motivation and achievement. In S. S. Feldman & G. R. Elliott (Eds.), *At the threshold: The developing adolescent* (pp. 308–329). Cambridge, MA: Harvard University Press.

Henry, L. A., & MacLean, M. (2002). Working memory performance in children with and without intellectual disabilities. *American Journal on Mental Retardation, 107*(6), 421–432.

Henry, L. A., & Millar, S. (1991). Memory span increases with age: A test of two hypotheses. *Journal of Experimental Child Psychology, 51,* 459–484.

Henry, M., & Renaud, H. (1972). Examined and unexamined lives. *Research Reporter, 7,* 5–8.

Herdt, G. H., & Davidson, J. (1988). The Sambia "Turnim-Man": Sociocultural and clinical aspects of gender formation in male pseudohermaphrodites with 5 alpha-reductase deficiency in Papua New Guinea. *Archives of Sexual Behavior, 17,* 33–56.

Herman, L. M. (2002). Exploring the cognitive world of the bottlenosed dolphin. In C. Allen & M. Bekoff (Eds.), *The cognitive animal: Empirical and theoretical perspectives on animal cognition* (pp. 275–283). Cambridge, MA: MIT Press.

Herman, L. M., & Uyeyama, R. R. (1999). The dolphin's grammatical competency: Comments on Kako. *Animal Learning and Behavior, 27,* 18–23.

Herman, P. A., Anderson, R. C., Pearson, P. D., & Nagy, W. E. (1987). Incidental acquisition of word meaning from expositions with varied text features. *Reading Research Quarterly, 22,* 263–284.

Herrnstein, R. J., & Murray, C. (1994). *The bell curve: Intelligence and class structure in American life.* New York: Free Press.

Hershenson, M., Munsinger, H., & Kessen, W. (1965). Preferences for shapes of intermediate variability in the newborn human. *Science, 147,* 630–631.

Hertzog, C. (1989). Influences of cognitive slowing on age differences in intelligence. *Developmental Psychology, 25,* 636–651.

Hess, R. D., Chih-Mei, C., & McDevitt, T. M. (1987). Cultural variations in family beliefs about children's performance in mathematics: Comparisons among People's Republic of China, Chinese-American, and Caucasian-American families. *Journal of Educational Psychology, 79,* 179–188.

Hesse, E. (1999). The Adult Attachment Interview: Historical and current perspectives. In J. Cassidy & P. R. Shaver (Eds.), *Handbook of attachment: Theory, research, and clinical applications* (pp. 395–433). New York: Guilford Press.

Hesse, E., & van IJzendoorn, M. H. (1999). Propensities towards absorption are related to lapses in the monitoring of reasoning or discourse during the Adult Attachment Interview: A preliminary investigation. *Attachment and Human Development, 1,* 67–91.

Hetherington, E. M. (1972). Effects of father absence on personality development in adolescent daughters. *Developmental Psychology, 7,* 313–326.

Hetherington, E. M. (1989). Coping with family transitions: Winners, losers, and survivors. *Child Development, 60,* 1–14.

Hetherington, E. M., Bridges, M., & Insabella, G. M. (1998). What matters?, What does not?: Five perspectives on the association between marital transitions and children's adjustment. *American Psychologist, 53,* 167–184.

Hetherington, E. M., Clingempeel, W. G., & Associates (1992). Coping with marital transitions: A family systems perspective. *Monographs of the Society for Research in Child Development*(2–3, Serial No. 227).

Hetherington, E. M., & Frankie, G. (1967). Effect of parental dominance, warmth, and conflict on imitation in children. *Journal of Personality and Social Psychology, 6,* 119–125.

Hewitt, J., & Scardamalia, M. (1998). Design principles for distributed knowledge building processes. *Educational Psychology Review, 10*(1), 75–96.

Hewson, P. W., & Thorley, R. (1989). The conditions of conceptual change in the classroom. *International Journal of Science Education, 11,* 541–553.

Hidi, S. (1990). Interest and its contribution as a mental resource for learning. *Review of Educational Research, 60,* 549–571.

Hidi, S. (2001). Interest, reading, and learning: Theoretical and practical considerations. *Educational Psychology Review, 13*(3), 191–209.

Hidi, S., & Baird, W. (1988). Strategies for increasing text-based interest and students' recall of expository text. *Reading Research Quarterly, 23,* 465–483.

Hier, D. B., & Crowley, W. F. (1982). Spatial ability in androgen-deficient men. *New England Journal of Medicine, 306,* 1202–1205.

Hier, D. B., LeMay, M., Rosenberger, P. B., & Perlo, V. P. (1978). Developmental dyslexia: Evidence for a subgroup with a reversal of cerebral asymmetry. *Archives of Neurology, 35,* 90–92.

Higgins, A. (1987). A feminist perspective on moral education. *Journal of Moral Education, 16,* 240–247.

Hilliard, A. G. III, & Amankwatia, N. B. II (2003). No mystery: Closing the achievement gap between Africans and excellence. In T. Perry, C. Steele, & A. Hilliard III (Eds.), *Young, gifted, and black: Promoting high achievement among African-American students* (pp. 131–165). Boston: Beacon Press.

Hines, M., Golombok, S., Rust, J., Johnston, K. J., Golding, J., & Avon Longitudinal Study of Parents and Children Study Team. (2002). Testosterone during pregnancy and gender role behavior of preschool children: A longitudinal, population study. *Child Development, 73,* 1678–1687.

Hines, M., & Kaufman, F. R. (1994). Androgen and the development of human sex-typical behavior: Rough-and-tumble play and sex of preferred playmates in children with congenital adrenal hyperplasia (CAH). *Child Development, 65,* 1042–1053.

Hinshaw, S. P., & Lee, S. S. (2003) Conduct and oppositional defiant disorders. In E. J. Mash & R. A. Barkley (Eds.), *Child psychopathology* (2nd ed., pp. 144–198). New York: Guilford Press.

Hinsley, D., Hayes, J. R., & Simon, H. A. (1977). From words to equations. In P. Carpenter & M. Just (Eds.), *Cognitive processes in comprehension* (pp. 84–106). Hillsdale, NJ: Erlbaum.

Hirsh-Pasek, K., & Golinkoff, R. M. (1991). Language comprehension: A new look at some old themes. In N. Krasnegor, D. Rumbaugh, M. Studdert-Kennedy, & R. Schiefelbusch (Eds.), *Biological and behavioral aspects of language acquisition* (pp. 301–320). Hillsdale, NJ: Erlbaum.

Hitch, G. J., Halliday, M. S., Schaafstal, A. M., & Heffernan, T. M. (1991). Speech, "inner speech," and the development of short-term memory: Effects of picture-labeling on recall. *Journal of Experimental Child Psychology, 51,* 220–234.

Hitchcock, G., & Hughes, D. (1989). *Research and the teacher: A qualitative introduction to school-based research.* New York: Routledge.

Hock, E., & DeMeis, D. K. (1990). Depression in mothers of infants: The role of maternal employment. *Developmental Psychology, 26,* 285–291.

Hock, M., Schumaker, J., & Deshler, D. (2003). *Possible selves: Nurturing student motivation,* Lawrence, KS: Edge Enterprises.

Hoff, E. (2001). *Language development.* Monterrey, CA: Wadsworth Thompson Learning.

Hoff, E. (2003). Language development in childhood. In I. B. Weiner (Gen. Ed.), R. M. Lerner, M. A. Easterbrooks, & J. Mistry (Vol. Eds.), *Handbook of psychology, Volume 6, Developmental psychology* (pp. 171–193). New York: Wiley.

Hoff, E., & Naigles, L. (2002). How children use input to acquire a lexicon. *Child Development, 73,* 418–433.

Hoffman, H. S. (1969). Stimulus factors in conditioned suppression. In B. A. Campbell & R. M. Church (Eds.), *Punishment and aversive behavior* (pp. 185–234). New York: Appleton–Century–Crofts.

Hoffman, L. W. (1977). Changes in family roles, socialization, and sex differences. *American Psychologist, 32,* 644–658.

Hoffman, L. W. (1979). Maternal employment: 1979. *American Psychologist, 34,* 859–865.

Hoffman, L. W. (1989). Effects of maternal employment in the two-parent family. *American Psychologist, 44,* 283–292.

Hoffman, L. W. (2000). Maternal employment: Effects of social context. In R. D. Taylor & M. C. Wang (Eds.), *Resilience across contexts: Family, work, culture, and community* (pp. 147–176). Mahwah, NJ: Erlbaum.

Hoffman, M. L. (1970). Moral development. In P. H. Mussen (Ed.), *Carmichael's manual of child psychology* (3rd ed., Vol. 2, pp. 261–360). New York: Wiley.

Hoffman, M. L. (2001). Toward a comprehensive empathy-based theory of prosocial moral development. In A. C. Bohart & D. Stipek (Eds.), *Constructive and destructive behavior: Implications for family, school, and society* (pp. 61–86). Washington, DC: American Psychological Association.

Hoffmann, C. (1991). *An introduction to bilingualism.* London: Longman

Hogan, K., Nastasi, B. K., & Pressley, M. (2000). Discourse patterns and collaborative scientific reasoning in peer- and teacher-guided discussions. *Cognition and Instruction, 17,* 379–432.

Hogan, K., & Pressley, M. (1997a). Scaffolding scientific competencies within classroom communities of inquiry. In K. Hogan & M. Pressley (Eds.), *Scaffolding student instruction* (pp. 74–107). Cambridge, MA: Brookline Books.

Hogan, K., & Pressley, M. (Eds.). (1997b). *Scaffolding student instruction.* Cambridge, MA: Brookline Books.

Holloway, S. D. (1988). Concepts of ability and effort in Japan and the United States. *Review of Educational Research, 58,* 327–345.

Honig, A. S. (1995). Choosing child care for young children. In M. H. Bornstein (Ed.), *Handbook of parenting: Vol. 4. Applied and practical parenting* (pp. 411–435). Mahwah, NJ: Erlbaum.

Hops, H., & Finch, M. (1985). Social competence and skill: A reassessment. In B. H. Schneider, K. H. Rubin, & J. E. Ledingham (Eds.), *Children's peer relations: Issues in assessment and intervention* (pp. 23–40). New York: Springer-Verlag.

Horn, J. L. (1985). Remodeling old models of intelligence. In B. Wolman (Ed.), *Handbook of intelligence* (pp. 267–300). New York: Wiley.

Horn, J. L., & Cattell, R. B. (1967). Age differences in fluid and crystallized intelligence. *Acta Psychologica, 26*, 107–129.

Horn, J. L., & Hofer, S. M. (1992). Major abilities and development in the adult period. In R. J. Sternberg & C. A. Berg (Eds.), *Intellectual development* (pp. 44–99). Cambridge, UK: Cambridge University Press.

Horn, J. L., & Stankov, L. (1982). Auditory and visual factors of intelligence. *Intelligence, 6*, 165–185.

Horney, K. (1967). *Feminine psychology.* New York: Norton.

Hort, B. E., Leinbach, M. D., & Fagot, B. I. (1991). Is there coherence among the cognitive components of gender acquisition? *Sex Roles, 24*, 195–207.

Horton, J. C. (2001). Critical periods in the development of the visual system. In J. B. Bailey Jr., J. T. Bruer, F. J. Symons, & J. W. Lichtman (Eds), *Critical thinking about critical periods* (pp. 45–65). Baltimore: Brookes.

Horton, M. S. (1982). *Category familiarity and taxonomic organization in young children.* Unpublished doctoral dissertation, Stanford University, Stanford, CA.

Howe, K. R. (1988). Against the quantitative–qualitative incompatibility thesis. *Educational Researcher, 17*(8), 10–16.

Howe, M. L., & Courage, M. L. (1993). On resolving the enigma of infantile amnesia. *Psychological Bulletin, 113*, 305–326.

Howes, C. (1987a). Peer interaction of young children. *Monographs of the Society for Research in Child Development, 53*(1, Serial No. 217).

Howes, C. (1987b). Social competence with peers in young children: Developmental sequences. *Developmental Review, 7*, 252–272.

Howes, C. (1988). Relations between early child care and schooling. *Developmental Psychology, 24*, 53–57.

Howes, C. (1990). Can the age of entry into child care and the quality of child care predict adjustment in kindergarten? *Developmental Psychology, 26*, 292–303.

Howes, C. (1996). The earliest friendships. In W. M. Bukowski, A. F. Newcomb, & W. W. Hartup (Eds.), *The company they keep: Friendship in childhood and adolescence* (pp. 66–86). Cambridge, UK: Cambridge University Press.

Howes, C., & Matheson, C. C. (1992). Sequences in the development of competent play with peers: Social and pretend play. *Developmental Psychology, 28*, 961–974.

Howes, C., Inger, O., & Matheson, C. C. (1992). *The collaborative construction of pretend: Social pretend play functions.* Albany: State University of New York Press.

Howlin, P., & Rutter, M. (1987). The consequences of language delay for other aspects of development. In W. Yule & M. Rutter (Eds.), *Language development and disorders* (pp. 271–294). Oxford, UK: Mac Keith Press.

Hoysniemi, J., Harmalainen, P., & Turkki, L. (2003). Using peer tutoring in evaluating the usability of a physically interactive computer game with children. *Interacting with Computers, 15*, 203–225.

Hoyt, S., & Scherer, D. G. (1998). Female juvenile delinquency: Misunderstood by the juvenile justice system, neglected by social science. *Law and Human Behavior, 22*, 81–107.

Hrabowski, F. A. III, Maton, K. I., Greene, M. L., & Greif, G. L. (2002). *Beating the odds: Raising academically successful African American young women.* New York: Oxford University Press.

Hrabowski, F. A., III, Maton, K. I., & Greif, G. L. (1998). *Beating the odds: Raising academically successful African American males.* New York: Oxford University Press.

Hudley, C., & Graham, S. (1993). An attributional intervention to reduce peer-directed aggression among African-American boys. *Child Development, 64*, 124–138.

Hudson, J., & Nelson, K. (1983). Effects of script structure on children's story recall. *Developmental Psychology, 19*, 625–635.

Hudson, J. A. (1990). Constructive processing in children's event memory. *Developmental Psychology, 26*, 180–187.

Hudson, J. A., & Shapiro, L. R. (1991). From knowing to telling: The development of children's scripts, stories, and personal narratives. In A. McCabe & C. Peterson (Eds.), *Developing narrative structure* (pp. 89–136). Hillsdale, NJ: Erlbaum.

Hudson, J. A., & Slackman, E. A. (1990). Children's use of scripts in inferential text processing. *Discourse Processes, 13*, 375–385.

Hudson, L. M., Forman, E. R., & Briuon-Meisels, S. (1982). Role-taking as a predictor of prosocial behavior in cross-age tutors. *Child Development, 53*, 1320–1329.

Huebner, A. J., & Mancini, J. A. (2003). Shaping structured out-of-school time use among youth: The effects of self, family, and friend systems. *Journal of Youth and Adolescence, 32*, 453–463.

Hulme, C., & MacKenzie, S. (1992). *Working memory and severe learning difficulties.* Hillsdale, NJ: Erlbaum.

Humes, A. (1983). Putting writing research into practice. *Elementary School Journal, 81*, 3–17.

Hunt, E., Lunneborg, C., & Lewis, J. (1975). What does it mean to be high verbal? *Cognitive Psychology, 7*, 194–227.

Hunter-Blanks, P., Ghatala, E. S., Pressley, M., & Levin, J. R. (1988). Comparison of monitoring during study and during testing on a sentence-learning task. *Journal of Educational Psychology, 80*, 279–283.

Huntley, M. A., Rasmussen, C. L., Villarubi, R. S., Sangtong, J., & Fey, J.T. (2000). Effects of standards-based mathematics education: A study of the core-plus mathematics project algebra and functions strand. *Journal for Research in Mathematics Education, 31*(3), 328–361.

Huston, A. C. (1983). Sex typing. In E. M. Hetherington (Vol. Ed.) & P. H. Mussen (Gen. Ed.), *Handbook of child psychology: Vol. 4. Socialization, personality, and social development* (pp. 387–467). New York: Wiley.

Huston, A. C., & Wright, J. C. (1998). Mass media and children's development. In I. E. Sigel & K. A. Renninger (Vol. Eds.) & W. Damon (Ed.-in-Chief), *Handbook of child psychology: Vol. 4. Child psychology in practice* (pp. 999–1058). New York: Wiley.

Hutchins, E. (1991). The social organization of distributed cognition. In L. Resnick, J. M. Levine, & S. D. Teasley (Eds.), *Perspectives on socially shared cognition* (pp. 283–307). Washington, DC: American Psychological Association.

Huttenlocher, J., Haight, W., Bryk, A., Seltzer, M., & Lyons, T. (1991). Early vocabulary growth: Relation to language input and gender. *Developmental Psychology, 27,* 236–248.

Huttenlocher, J., Vasilyeva, M., Cymerman, E., & Levine, S. (2001). Language input and child syntax. *Cognitive Psychology, 45,* 337–374.

Huttenlocher, P. R. (1979). Synaptic density in human frontal cortex-developmental changes and effects of aging. *Brain Research, 163,* 195–205.

Huttenlocher, P. R. (2002). *Neural plasticity: The effects of environment on the development of cerebral cortex.* Cambridge, MA: MIT Press.

Hyde, J. S., Fennema, E., & Lamon, S. J. (1990). Gender differences in mathematics performance: A meta-analysis. *Psychological Bulletin, 107,* 139–155.

Hyde, J. S., & Linn, M. C. (1988). Gender differences in verbal ability: A meta-analysis. *Psychological Bulletin, 104,* 53–69.

Hyde, J. S., & Plant, E. A. (1995). Magnitude of psychological gender differences: Another side to the story. *American Psychologist, 50,* 159–161.

Hyman, I. A. (1990). *Reading, writing, and the hickory stick: The appalling story of physical and psychological abuse in American schools.* San Diego, CA: Lexington Books.

Hyman, I. A., & Wise, J. H. (Eds.). (1977). *Corporal punishment in American education.* Philadelphia: Temple University Press.

Hymel, S., Rubin, K. H., Rowden, L., & LeMare, L. (1990). Children's peer relationships: Longitudinal prediction of internalizing and externalizing problems from middle to late childhood. *Child Development, 61,* 2004–2021.

Hymel, S., Vaillancourt, T., McDougall, P., & Renshaw, P. D. (2002). Peer acceptance and rejection in childhood. In P. K. Smith & C. H. Hart (Eds.), *Blackwell handbook of childhood social development* (pp. 265–284). Oxford, UK: Blackwell.

Hymes, D. (1974). *Foundations in sociolinguistics.* Philadelphia: University of Pennsylvania Press.

Hynd, G. W., & Semrud-Clikeman, M. (1989). Dyslexia and brain morphology. *Psychological Bulletin, 106,* 447–482.

Iarocci, G., & Burack, J. A. (1998). Understanding the development of attention in persons with mental retardation: Challenging the myths. In J. A. Burack, R. M. Hodapp, & E. Zigler (Eds.), *Handbook of mental retardation and development* (pp. 349–

381). Cambridge, UK: Cambridge University Press.

Imperato-McGinley, J., Peterson, R. E., Gautier, T., & Sturla, E. (1979). Androgens and the evolution of male-gender identity among male pseudohermaphridites with 5a-reductase deificiency. *New England Journal of Medicine, 300,* 1233–1237.

Inciardi, J. A., Surratt, H. L., & Saum, C. A. (1997). *Cocaine-exposed infants: Social, legal, and public health issues.* Thousand Oaks, CA: Sage.

Infant Health and Development Program. (1990). Enhancing the outcomes of low-birth-weight premature infants. *Journal of the American Medical Association, 263,* 3035–3042.

Ingram, D. (1976). *Phonological disability in children.* London: Arnold.

Ingram, T. (1963). Delayed development of speech with special references to dyslexia: The association of speech retardation and educational difficulties. *Proceedings of the Royal Society of Medicine, 56,* 199–203.

Inhelder, B., Sinclair, H., & Bovet, M. (1974). *Learning and the development of cognition.* Cambridge, MA: Harvard University Press.

Isabella, R. A., & Belsky, J. (1991). Interactional synchrony and the origins of infant–mother attachment: A replication study. *Child Development, 62,* 373–384.

Iwasa, N. (1992). Postconventional reasoning and moral education in Japan. *Journal of Moral Education, 21,* 3–16.

Jackson, N. E., & Butterfield, E. C. (1986). A conception of giftedness designed to promote research. In R. J. Sternberg & J. E. Davidson (Eds.), *Conceptions of giftedness* (pp. 151–181). Cambridge, UK: Cambridge University Press.

Jackson, N. E., & Myers, M. G. (1982). Letter naming time, digit span, and precocious reading achievement. *Intelligence, 6,* 311–329.

Jacobs, J. E. (1991). Influence of gender stereotypes on parent and child mathematics attitudes. *Journal of Educational Psychology, 83,* 518–527.

Jacobs, J. E., Lanza, S., Osgood, W., Eccles, J. S., & Wigfield, A. (2002). Changes in children's self-competence and values: Gender and domain differences across grades one through twelve. *Child Development, 73,* 509–527.

Jacobs, J. E., & Wigfield, A. (1989). Sex equity in mathematics and science education: Research–policy links. *Educational Psychology Review, 1,* 39–56.

Jacobsen, B., Lowery, B., & DuCette, J. (1986). Attributions of learning disabled children. *Journal of Educational Psychology, 78,* 59–64.

Jacobson, J. L., & Frye, K. F. (1991). Effect of maternal support on attachment: Experimental evidence. *Child Development, 62,* 572–582.

Jacobson, J. L., & Wille, D. E. (1986). The influence of attachment pattern on developmental changes in peer interaction from the toddler to the preschool period. *Child Development, 57,* 338–347.

Jacobson, K. C., & Crockett, L. J. (2000). Parental monitoring and adolescent adjustment: An ecological perspective. *Journal of Research on Adolescence, 10,* 65–97.

Jacoby, R., & Glauberman, N. (1995). *The bell curve debate: History, documents, and opinion.* New York: Times Books.

Jaffee, S., & Hyde, J. S. (2000). Gender differences in moral orientation: A meta-analysis. *Psychological Bulletin, 126*(5), 703–726.

Jausovec, N. (1994). Can giftedness be taught? *Roeper Review, 16,* 210–214.

Jausovec, N. (1998). Are gifted individuals less chaotic thinkers? *Personality and Individual Differences, 25,* 253–267.

Jensen, A. R. (1969). How much can we boost IQ and scholastic achievement? *Harvard Educational Review, 39,* 1–123.

Jensen, A. R. (1972). *Genetics and education.* New York: Harper & Row.

Jensen, A. R. (1973). *Educability and group differences.* New York: Harper & Row.

Jensen, A. R. (1976, December). Test bias and construct validity. *Phi Delta Kappan,* pp. 340–346.

Jensen, A. R. (1980). *Bias in mental testing.* New York: Free Press.

Jensen, A. R. (1992). Understanding *g* in terms of information processing. *Educational Psychology Review, 4,* 271–308.

Jernigan, T. L., Hesselink, J. R., Sowell, E., & Tallal, P. A. (1991). Cerebral structure on magnetic resonance imaging in language- and learning-impaired children. *Archives of Neurology, 48,* 539–545.

Jiménez, R. T. (1997). The strategic reading abilities and potential of five low-literacy Latina/o readers in the middle school. *Reading Research Quarterly, 32,* 224–243.

Jiménez, R. T., Garcia, G. E., & Pearson, P. D. (1995). Three children, two languages, and strategic reading: Case studies in bilingual/monolingual reading. *American Ed-*

ucational *Research Journal, 32,* 31–61.

Jiménez, R. T., Garcia, G. E., & Pearson, P. D. (1996). The reading strategies of bilingual Latino/a students who are successful English readers: Opportunities and obstacles. *Reading Research Journal, 27,* 427–471.

Johnson, B., & Moore, H. A. (1968). Injured children and their parents. *Children, 15,* 147–152.

Johnson, D., Maruyama, G., Johnson, R., Nelson, D., & Skon, L. (1981). Effects of cooperative, competitive, and individualistic goal structures on achievement: A meta-analysis. *Psychological Bulletin, 89,* 47–62.

Johnson, D., & Myklebust, H. R. (1967). *Learning disabilities: Educational principles and practice.* New York: Grune & Stratton.

Johnson, D. K. (1988). Adolescents' solutions to dilemmas in fables: Two moral orientations—Two problem-solving strategies. In C. Gilligan, J. V. Ward, & J. M. Taylor, with B. Bardige (Eds.), *Mapping the moral domain: A contribution of women's thinking to psychological theory and education* (pp. 49–72). Cambridge, MA: Harvard University Press.

Johnson, D. W., & Johnson, R. (1985a). Classroom conflict: Controversy over debate in learning groups. *American Educational Research Journal, 22,* 237–256.

Johnson, D. W., & Johnson, R. (1985b). Motivational processes in cooperative, competitive, and individualistic learning situations. In C. Ames & R. Ames (Eds.), *Research on motivation in education* (Vol. 2, pp. 249–286). New York: Academic Press.

Johnson, J. L., & Leff, M. (1999). Children of substance abusers: An overview of research findings. *Pediatrics, 103,* 1089–1099.

Johnson, J. S., & Newport, E. L. (1989). Critical period effects in second language learning: The influence of maturational state on the acquisition of English as a second language. *Cognitive Psychology, 21,* 60–99.

Johnson, M. H., Dziurawiec, S., Ellis, H., & Morton, J. (1991). Newborns' preferential tracking of face-like stimuli and its subsequent decline. *Cognition, 40,* 1–19.

Johnson, R. E. (2003). Aging and the remembering of text. *Developmental Review, 23*(3), 261–346.

John-Steiner, V., & Mahn, H. (2003).

Sociocultural contexts for teaching and learning. In I. B. Weiner (Ed.-in-Chief), W. M. Reynolds & G. E. Miller (Vol. Eds.), *Handbook of psychology: Vol. 7. Educational psychology* (pp. 125–175). New York: Wiley.

Johnston, L. D., O'Malley, P. M., Bachman, J. G., & Schulenberg, J. E. (2004). *Monitoring the Future national results on adolescent drug use: Overview of key findings, 2003* (NIH Publication No. 04-5506). Bethesda, MD: National Institute on Drug Abuse.

Jones, C. H., Slate, J. R., Blake, P. C., & Sloas, S. (1995). Relationship of study skills, conceptions of intelligence, and grade level in secondary school students. *High School Journal, 79,* 25–32.

Jones, M. G., & Gerig, T. M. (1994). Silent sixth-grade students: Characteristics, achievement, and teacher expectations. *Elementary School Journal, 95,* 169–182.

Jones, M. G., & Wheatley, J. (1988). Factors influencing the entry of women into science and related fields. *Science Education, 72,* 127–142.

Jones, M. G., & Wheatley, J. (1990). Gender differences in teacher–student interactions in science classrooms. *Journal of Research in Science Teaching, 27,* 861–874.

Jones, R. (2004). Listen and learn. *Nature Reviews Neuroscience, 4,* 699.

Joseph, J., Noble, K., & Eden, G. (2001). The neurobiological basis of reading. *Journal of Learning Disabilities, 34,* 566–579.

Juel, C. (1988). Learning to read and write: A longitudinal study of 54 children from first through fourth grades. *Journal of Educational Psychology, 80,* 417–447.

Juel, C., Griffith, P. L., & Gough, P. B. (1986). Acquisition of literacy: A longitudinal study of children in first and second grade. *Journal of Educational Psychology, 78,* 243–255.

Jusczyk, P. W., Pisoni, D. B., & Mullenix, J. (1992). Some consequences of talker variability on speech processing by 2-month-old infants. *Cognition, 43*(2), 253–291..

Just, M. A., & Carpenter, P. A. (1992). A capacity theory of comprehension: Individual differences in working memory. *Psychological Review, 99,* 122–149.

Juvonen, J. (1988). Outcome and attributional disagreements between students and their teachers. *Journal of Educational Psychology, 80,* 330–336.

Kagan, J. (1982). *Psychological research on the human infant: An evaluative summary.* New York: W. T. Grant Foundation.

Kagan, J., Moss, H., & Sigel, I. (1963). Psychological significance of types of conceptualization. *Monographs of the Society for Research in Child Development, 28*(2, Serial No. 86).

Kahle, J. (1984). *Girl-friendly science.* Paper presented at the annual meeting of the American Association for the Advancement of Science, New York. (Cited in Eccles, 1989.)

Kail, R. V. (1992). Processing speed, speech rate, and memory. *Developmental Psychology, 28,* 899–904.

Kail, R. V. (2000). Speed of information processing: Developmental changes and links to intelligence. *Journal of School Psychology, 38,* 51–61.

Kail, R. V., & Leonard, L. B. (1986). Word-finding abilities in language-impaired children. *ASHA Monographs, 25.* Rockville, MD: American Speech, Hearing, and Language Association.

Kail, R. V., & Park, Y.-S. (1994). Processing time, articulation time, and memory span. *Journal of Experimental Child Psychology, 57,* 281–291.

Kako, E. E. (1999). Elements of syntax in the systems of three language-trained animals. *Animal Learning and Behavior, 27,* 1–14.

Kamii, C. K. (1985). *Young children reinvent arithmetic.* New York: Teachers College Press.

Kamil, M. L. (2004). Vocabulary and comprehension instruction: Summary and implications of the National Reading Panel report. In P. McCardle & V. Chhabra (Eds.), *The voice of evidence in reading research* (pp. 213–234). Baltimore: Brookes.

Kamphaus, R. W. (1993). *Clinical assessment of children's intelligence.* Boston: Allyn & Bacon.

Kamphaus, R. W. (2003). Clinical assessment practice with the Kaufman Assessment Battery for Children (K-ABC). In C. R. Reynolds & R. W. Kamphaus (Eds.), *Handbook of psychological and educational assessment of children* (pp. 204–216). New York: Guilford Press.

Kamphaus, R. W., Kaufman, A. S., & Harrison, P. L. (1990). Clinical assessment practice with the Kaufman Assessment Battery for Children (K-ABC). In C. R. Reynolds & R. W. Kamphaus (Eds.), *Handbook of psychological and educa-*

tional assessment of children: Intelligence and achievement (pp. 259–276). New York: Guilford Press.

Kandel, E. R., Schwartz, J. H., & Jessell, T. M. (1995). Essentials of neural science and behavior. Norwalk, CT: Appleton & Lange.

Kandel, E. R., Schwartz, J. H., & Jessell, T. M. (2000). Principles of neural science (4th ed.). New York: McGraw-Hill/Appleton Lange.

Kanevsky, L. (1995). Learning potentials of gifted students. Roeper Review, 17, 157–163.

Kanfer, F., & Zich, J. (1974). Self-control training: The effect of external control on children's resistance to temptation. Developmental Psychology, 10, 108–115.

Karabenick, S. A., & Newman, R. S. (Eds.). (2006). Help seeking in academic setting: Goals, groups, and contexts. Mahwah, NJ: Erlbaum.

Karchmer, M. A., & Mitchell, R. E. (2003). Demographic and achievement characteristics of deaf and hard-of-hearing students. In M. Marschark & P. E. Spencer (Eds.), Oxford handbook of deaf studies, language, and education (pp. 21–37). New York: Oxford University Press.

Katcher, A. (1955). The discrimination of sex differences by young children. Journal of Genetic Psychology, 87, 131–143.

Katz, L. F., & Gottman, J. M. (1991). Marital discord and child outcomes: A social psychophysiological approach. In J. Gerber & K. A. Dodge (Eds.), The development of emotion regulation and dysregulation (pp. 129–155). Cambridge, UK: Cambridge University Press.

Katz, R. B., Shankweiler, D., & Liberman, I. Y. (1981). Memory for item order and phonetic recoding in the beginning reader. Journal of Experimental Child Psychology, 32, 474–484.

Katzir, T., & Pare-Blagoev, J. (2006). Applying cognitive neuroscience research to education: The case of literacy. Educational Psychologist, 41(1), 53–74.

Kaufman, A. S. (1990). Assessing adolescent and adult intelligence. Boston: Allyn & Bacon.

Kaufman, A. S., & Kaufman, N. L. (1983). The Kaufmann Assessment Battery for Children (K-ABC). Circle Pines, MN: American Guidance Services.

Kaufman, A. S., Reynolds, C. R., & McLean, J. E. (1989). Age and WAIS-R intelligence in a national sample of adults in the 20- to 74-year-old age range: A cross-sectional analysis with education level controlled. Intelligence, 13, 235–253.

Kavale, K. A., & Forness, S. R. (1992). History, definition, and diagnosis. In N. N. Singh & I. L. Beale (Eds.), Learning disabilities: Nature, theory, and treatment (pp. 3–43). New York: Springer-Verlag.

Kavale, K. A., & Forness, S. R. (1995). The nature of learning disabilities: Critical elements of diagnosis and classification. Mahwah, NJ: Erlbaum.

Kavale, K. A., & Forness, S. R. (1996). Social skills deficits and learning disabilities: A meta-analysis. Journal of Learning Disabilities, 29, 226–237.

Kazdin, A. E. (1994). Interventions for aggressive and antisocial children. In L. D. Eron, J. H. Gentry, & P. Schlegel (Eds.), Reason for hope: A psychological perspective on violence and youth (pp. 341–382). Washington, DC: American Psychological Association.

Keating, D. P. (1990). Adolescent thinking. In S. S. Feldman & G. R. Elliott (Eds.), At the threshold: The developing adolescent (54–89). Cambridge, MA: Harvard University Press.

Keating, D. P., & Bobbitt, B. (1978). Individual and developmental differences in cognitive processing components of mental ability. Child Development, 49, 155–169.

Keene, E., & Zimmerman, S. (1997). Mosaic of thought: Teaching comprehension in a reader's workshop. Portsmouth, NH: Heinemann.

Keeney, F. J., Cannizzo, S. R., & Flavell, J. H. (1967). Spontaneous and induced verbal rehearsal in a recall task. Child Development, 38, 953–966.

Keller, C. E., & Sutton, J. P. (1991). Specific mathematics disorders. In J. E. Obrzut & G. W. Hynd (Eds.), Neuropsychological foundations of learning disabilities (pp. 549–571). San Diego, CA: Academic Press.

Keller, H., & Scholmerich, A. (1987). Infant vocalizations and parental reactions during the first four months of life. Developmental Psychology, 23, 62–67.

Kendall, P. C. (Ed.). (1991). Child and adolescent therapy: Cognitive-behavioral procedures. New York: Guilford Press.

Kent, R. D., & Miolo, G. (1995). Phonetic abilities in the first year of life. In P. Fletcher & B. MacWhinney (Eds.), The handbook of child psychology (pp. 303–334). Oxford, UK: Blackwell.

Kerestes, M., & Youniss, J. E. (2003). Rediscovering the importance of religion in adolescent development. In R. M. Lerner, F. Jacobs, & D. Weretlieb (Eds.), Handbook of applied developmental science: Promoting positive child, adolescent, and family development through research, policies, and programs: Vol. 1. Applying (pp. 165–184). Thousand Oaks, CA: Sage.

Kerwin, M. L. E., & Day, J. D. (1985). Peer influences on cognitive development. In J. B. Pryor & J. D. Day (Eds.), The development of social cognition (pp. 211–228). New York: Springer-Verlag.

Kerr, M., Stattin, H., Biesecker, G., & Ferrer-Wreder, L. (2003). Relationships with parents and peers in adolescence. In R. M. Lerner, M. A. Easterbrooks, J. Mistry (Vol. Eds.) & I. B. Weiner (Ed.-in-Chief), Handbook of psychology: Vol. 6. Developmental psychology (pp. 395–419). New York: Wiley.

Kessen, W. (1975). Childhood in China. New Haven, CT: Yale University Press.

Ketcham, R., & Snyder, R. T. (1977). Self-attitudes of the intellectually and socially advantaged student: Normative study of the Piers–Harris Children's Self-Concept Scale. Psychological Reports, 40, 111–116.

Khalfa, J. (1994). What is intelligence? Cambridge, UK: Cambridge University Press.

Kieffer-Renaux, V., Bulteau, C., Grill, J., Kalifa, C., Viguier, D., & Jambaque, I. (2000). Patterns of neuropsychological deficits in children with medulloblastoma according to craniospatial irradiation doses. Developmental Medicine and Child Neurology, 42, 741–745.

Kiernan, C. (1985). Behaviour modification. In A. M. Clarke, A. D. B. Clarke, & J. M. Berg (Eds.), Mental deficiency: The changing outlook (pp. 465–511). New York: Free Press.

Kilpatrick, J., Martin, W. G., & Schifter, D. (2003). A research companion to principles and standards for school mathematics. Reston, VA: National Council of Teachers of Mathematics.

Kimball, M. M. (1989). A new perspective on women's math achievement. Psychological Bulletin, 105, 198–214.

Kintsch, W. (1982). Text representations. In W. Otto & S. White (Eds.), Reading expository material (pp. 87–102). New York: Academic Press.

Kintsch, W., & Greene, E. (1978). The role of culture-specific schemata in the comprehension and recall of stories. *Discourse Processes, 1*, 1–13.

Kintsch, W., Mandel, T. S., & Kozminsky, E. (1977). Summarizing scrambled stories. *Memory and Cognition, 5*, 547–552.

Kintsch, W., & Yarbrough, C. J. (1982). Role of rhetorical structure in text comprehension. *Journal of Educational Psychology, 74*, 828–834.

Kistner, J. A., Osborne, M., & LeVerrier, L. (1988). Causal attributions of learning-disabled children: Developmental patterns and relation to academic progress. *Journal of Educational Psychology, 80*, 82–89.

Kitsantas, A., & Zimmerman, B. J. (1998). Self-regulation of motoric learning: A strategic cycle view. *Journal of Applied Sport Psychology, 10*, 220–239.

Kitsantas, A., & Zimmerman, B. J. (2002). Comparing self-regulatory processes among novice, non-expert, and expert volleyball players: A microanalytic study. *Journal of Applied Sport Psychology, 14*, 91–105.

Klainen, S., & Fensham, P. J. (1987). Learning achievement in upper secondary school chemistry in Thailand: Some remarkable sex reversals. *International Journal of Science Education, 9*, 217–227.

Klainen, S., Fensham, P. J., & West, L. H. T. (1989). Successful achievements by girls in physics learning. *International Journal of Science Education, 11*, 101–112.

Klausmeier, H. J. (1990). Conceptualizing. In B. F. Jones & L. Idol (Eds.), *Dimensions of thinking and cognitive instruction* (pp. 93–138). Hillsdale, NJ: Erlbaum.

Kliegl, R., Smith, J., & Baltes, P. B. (1990). On the locus and process of magnification of age differences during mnemonic training. *Developmental Psychology, 26*, 894–904.

Kline, M., Tschann, J. M., Johnson, J. R., & Wallerstein, J. S. (1989). Children's adjustment in joint and sole physical custody families. *Developmental Psychology, 25*, 430–438.

Klinger, L. G., Dawson, G., & Renner, P. (2003). Autistic disorder. In E. J. Mash & R. A. Barkley (Eds.), *Child psychopathology* (2nd ed., pp. 409–454). New York: Guilford Press.

Klingner, J. K., Vaughn, S., & Schumm, J. S. (1998). Collaborative strategic reading during social studies in heterogeneous fourth-grade classrooms. *Elementary School Journal, 99*, 3–22.

Kloosterman, P. (1988). Self-confidence and motivation in mathematics. *Journal of Educational Psychology, 80*, 345–351.

Knapp, M. S., & Associates. (1995). *Teaching for meaning in high poverty schools.* New York: Teachers College Press.

Knoors, H., & Vervloed, M. P. J. (2003). Educational programming for deaf children with multiple disabilities: Accommodating special needs. In M. Marschark & P. E. Spencer (Eds.), *Oxford handbook of deaf studies, language, and education* (pp. 82–94). New York: Oxford University Press.

Kobak, R. R., & Sceery, A. (1988). Attachment in late adolescence: Working models, affect regulation, and representations of self and others. *Child Development, 59*, 135–146.

Koballa, T. R. (1988). Persuading girls to take elective physical science courses in high school: Who are the credible communicators? *Journal of Research in Science Teaching, 25*, 465–478.

Koch, J. (2003). Gender issues in the classroom. In W. M. Reynolds (Vol. Ed.) & I. B. Weiner (Ed.-in-Chief), *Handbook of psychology: Vol. 7. Educational psychology* (pp. 259–281). New York: Wiley.

Kochanska, G. (2001). Emotional development in children with different attachment histories: The first three years. *Child Development, 72*, 474–490.

Kohlberg, L. (1966). A cognitive-developmental analysis of children's sex-role concepts and attitudes. In E. E. Maccoby (Ed.), *The development of sex differences* (pp. 82–173). Stanford, CA: Stanford University Press.

Kohlberg, L. (1969). Stage and sequence: The cognitive-developmental approach to socialization. In D. Goslin (Ed.), *Handbook of socialization theory and research* (pp. 347–480). New York: Rand-McNally.

Kohlberg, L. (1981). *The philosophy of moral development: Moral stages and the idea of justice: Essays on moral development, Vol. 1.* San Francisco: Harper & Row.

Kohlberg, L. (1984). *The psychology of moral development: Essays on moral development, Vol. 2.* San Francisco: Harper & Row.

Kohlberg, L., Levine, C., & Hewer, A. (1983). Moral stages: A current formulation and a response to critics. *Contributions to Human Development, 10.* Basal, Switzerland: Karger.

Kohlberg, L., & Mayer, R. (1972). Development as the aim of education: The Dewey view. *Harvard Educational Review, 42*, 449–496.

Kohlberg, L., Yaeger, J., & Hjertholm, E. (1968). Private speech: Four studies and a review of theories. *Child Development, 39*, 691–736.

Kolb, B., & Gibb, R. (2001). Early brain injury, plasticity, and behavior. In C. A. Nelson & M. Luciana (Eds.), *Handbook of developmental cognitive neuroscience* (pp. 175–190). Cambridge, MA: MIT Press.

Komarovsky, M. (1985). *Women in college: Shaping new feminine identities.* New York: Basic Books.

Konner, M. (1991). Universals of behavioral development in relation to brain myelination. In K. R. Gibson & A. C. Petersen (Eds.), *Brain maturation and cognitive development: Comparative and cross-cultural perspectives* (pp. 181–223). New York: Aldine de Gruyter.

Koocher, G. P., & Keith-Spiegel, P. C. (1990). *Children, ethics, and the law.* Lincoln: University of Nebraska Press.

Koolstra, C. M., van der Voort, T. H. A., & van der Kamp, L. J. T. (1997). Television's impact on children's reading comprehension and decoding skills: A 3-year panel study. *Reading Research Quarterly, 32*, 128–152.

Koplan, J. P., Liverman, C. T., & Kraak, V. A. (Eds.). (2005). *Committee on Prevention of Obesity in Children and Youth.* Washington, DC: Institute of Medicine.

Kosslyn, S. M., Margolis, J. A., Barrett, A. M., Goldknopf, E. J., & Daly, P. F. (1990). Age differences in imagery abilities. *Child Development, 61*, 995–1010.

Krauss, R. H., & Glucksberg, S. (1969). The development of communication. *Child Development, 40*, 255–266.

Kress, G. (1982). *Learning to write.* London: Routledge & Kegan Paul.

Kuczaj, S. A. (1977). The acquisition of regular and irregular past tense forms. *Journal of Verbal Learning and Verbal Behavior, 16*, 589–600.

Kuhn, D., Amsel, E., & O'Loughlin, M. (1988). *The development of scientific thinking skills.* San Diego, CA: Academic Press.

Kumar, D., & Sherwood, R. (1997). Hypermedia in science and mathematics: Applications in teacher education, problem solving and student testing. *Journal of Educational Computing Research, 17*(3), 249–262.

Kumar, R., O'Malley, P. M., Johnston,

L. D., Schulenberg, J. E., & Bachman, J. G. (2002). Effects of school-level norms on student substance use. *Prevention Science, 3,* 105–124.

Kupersmidt, J. B., & Coie, J. D. (1990). Preadolescent peer status, aggression, and school adjustment as predictors of externalizing problems in adolescence. *Child Development, 61,* 1350–1362.

Kurdek, L. A., & Fine, M. A. (1994). Family acceptance and family control as predictors of adjustment in young adolescents: Linear, curvilinear, or interactive effects. *Child Development, 65,* 1137–1146.

Kurdek, L. A., & Krile, D. (1982). A developmental analysis of the relation between peer acceptance and both interpersonal understanding and perceived social self-competence. *Child Development, 53,* 1485–1491.

Kurdek, L. A., & Siesky, A. E. (1980). Sex role self concepts of single divorced parents and their children. *Journal of Divorce, 3,* 249–261.

Kurtines, W., & Grief, E. B. (1974). The development of moral thought: Review and evaluation of Kohlberg's approach. *Psychological Bulletin, 81,* 453–470.

Kurtz, B. E. (1990). Cultural influences on children's cognitive and metacognitive development. In W. Schneider & F. E. Weinert (Eds.), *Interactions among aptitudes, strategies, and knowledge in cognitive performance* (pp. 177–199). New York: Springer-Verlag.

Kurtz, B. E., Schneider, W., Carr, M., Borkowski, J. G., & Rellinger, E. (1990). Strategy instruction and attributional beliefs in West Germany and the United States: Do teachers foster metacognitive development? *Contemporary Educational Psychology, 15,* 268–283.

Kutnick, P. (1988). "I'll teach you!": Primary school teachers' attitudes to and use of moral education in the curriculum. *Journal of Moral Education, 17,* 40–51.

Kutnick, P. (1990). A survey of primary school teachers' understanding and implementation of moral education in Trinidad and Tobago. *Journal of Moral Education, 19,* 48–57.

Labouvie-Vief, G. (1989). Modes of knowledge and the organization of development. In M. L. Commons, J. D. Sinnott, F. A. Richards, & C. Armon (Eds.), *Adult development* (Vol. 2, pp. 43–62). New York: Praeger.

Labouvie-Vief, G. (1990). Wisdom as integrated thought: Historical and developmental perspectives. In R. J. Sternberg (Ed.), *Wisdom: Its nature, origins, and development* (pp. 52–83). New York: Cambridge University Press.

Labouvie-Vief, G. (2003). Without gender, without self. In U. M. Staudinger & U. Lindenberger (Eds.), *Understanding human development: Dialogues with lifespan psychology* (pp. 401–412). Dordrecht, The Netherlands: Kluwer Academic.

Labov, W. (2003). When ordinary children fail to read. *Reading Research Quarterly, 38,* 128–131.

Ladd, G. W. (1990). Having friends, keeping friends, making friends, and being liked by peers in the classroom: Predictors of children's early school adjustment? *Child Development, 61,* 1081–1100.

Ladd, G. W., & Burgess, K. B. (1999). Charting the relationship trajectories of aggressive, withdrawn, and aggressive/withdrawn children during early grade school. *Child Development, 70,* 910–929.

Ladd, G. W., Price, J. M., & Hart, C. H. (1988). Predicting preschoolers' peer status from their playground behaviors. *Child Development, 59,* 986–992.

Laible, D. J., & Thompson, R. A. (2000). Mother–child discourse, attachment security, shared positive affect, and early conscience development. *Child Development, 71,* 1424–1440.

Lally, R., Mangione, P. L., & Honig, A. S. (1988). The Syracuse University Family Development Research Program: Long-range impact of an early intervention with low-income children and their families. In D. Powell (Ed.), *Parent education as early childhood intervention: Emerging directions in theory, research, and practice* (pp. 79–104). Norwood, NJ: Ablex.

Lambert, W. E. (1974). Culture and language as factors in learning and education. In F. Aboud & R. D. Mead (Eds.), *Cultural factors in learning* (pp. 91–122). Bellingham: Washington State College.

Lambert, W. E. (1977). The effects of bilingualism on the individual: Cognitive and socio-cultural consequences. In P. Hornby (Ed.), *Bilingualism: Psychological, social, and educational implications* (pp. 15–28). New York: Academic Press.

Lamborn, S. D., Mounts, N. S., Steinberg, L., & Dornbusch, S. M. (1991). Patterns of competence and adjustment among adolescents from authoritative, authoritarian, indulgent, and neglectful families. *Child Development, 62,* 1049–1065.

Lampert, M. (2001). *Teaching problems and the problems of teaching.* New Haven, CT: Yale University Press.

Lange, G., MacKinnon, C. E., & Nida, R. E. (1989). Knowledge, strategy, and motivational contributions to preschool children's object recall. *Developmental Psychology, 25,* 772–779.

Langeveld, N. E., Ibbink, M. C., Last, B. F., Grootenhuis, M. A., Voute, P. A., & De Haan, R. J. (2003). Educational achievement, employment and living situation in long-term young adult survivors of childhood cancer in the Netherlands. *Psycho-Oncology, 12,* 213–225.

Langlois, J. H., & Downs, C. (1980). Mothers, fathers, and peers as socialization agents of sex-typed play behavior in young children. *Child Development, 51,* 1217–1247.

Lantolf, J. P. (2003). Intrapersonal communication and internalization in the second language classroom. In A. Kozulin, B. Gindia, V. S. Ageyev, & S. M. Miller (Eds.), *Vygotsky's educational theory in cultural context* (pp. 349–370). Cambridge, UK: Cambridge University Press.

Larry P. v. Riles, 343 F. Supp. 1306 (N. D. Cal. 1979), aff'd 502 F. 2d (9th Cir. 1974); 495 F. Supp. 926 (N. D. Cal. 1979), aff'd. in part and rev'd in part, 793 F. 2d 969 (9th Cir. 1984)

Larsen, J. P., Hoien, T., Lundberg, I., & Ødegaard, S. (1990). MRI evaluation of the size and symmetry of the planum temporale in adolescents with developmental dyslexia. *Brain and Language, 39,* 289–301.

Larson, K. A., & Gerber, M. M. (1992). Metacognition. In N. N. Singh & I. L. Beale (Eds.), *Learning disabilities: Nature, theory, and treatment* (pp. 126–169). New York: Springer-Verlag.

Lasky, R. E. (1974). The ability of six-year-olds, eight-year-olds, and adults to abstract visual patterns. *Child Development, 45,* 626–632.

Last, C. G. (1989). Anxiety disorders. In T. H. Ollendick & M. Hersen (Eds.), *Handbook of child psychopathology* (pp. 219–227). New York: Plenum Press.

Lauren, L., & Allen, L. (1999). Factors that predict success in an early literacy intervention project. *Reading Research Quarterly, 34*(4), 404–424.

LaVoie, J. C. (1973). Punishment and

adolescent self-control. *Developmental Psychology, 8,* 16–24.

LaVoie, J. C. (1974). Cognitive determinants of resistance to deviation in seven-, nine-, and eleven-year-old children of low and high maturity of moral judgment. *Developmental Psychology, 10,* 393–403.

Lawlor, S., Richman, S., & Richman, C. L. (1997). The validity of using the SAT as a criterion for black and white students' admission to college. *College Student Journal, 31,* 507–515.

Laybaert, J., & Alegria, J. (2003). The role of cued speech in language development of deaf children. In M. Marschark & P. E. Spencer (Eds.), *Oxford handbook of deaf studies, language, and education* (pp. 261–274). New York: Oxford University Press.

Lazar, I., Darlington, R., Murray, H., Royce, J., & Sipper, A. (1982). Lasting effects of early childhood education: A report from the consortium for longitudinal studies. *Monographs of the Society for Research in Child Development, 47* (2–3, Whole No. 195).

Leaper, C. (1991). Influence and involvement in childhood discourse: Age, gender, and partner effects. *Child Development, 62,* 797–811.

Leaper, C. (1994). Exploring the correlates and consequences of gender segregation: Social relationships in childhood, adolescence, and adulthood. In C. Leaper (Ed.), *New directions for child development* (No. 65, pp. 67–86). San Francisco: Jossey-Bass.

Leaper, C. (2000). Gender, affiliation, assertion, and the interactive context of parent–child play. *Developmental Psychology, 36,* 381–393.

Leaper, C., Anderson, K. J., & Sanders, P. (1998). Moderators of gender effects on parents' talk to their children: A meta-analysis. *Developmental Psychology, 3*(4), 3–27.

Leaper, C., Tenenbaum, H. R., & Shaffer, T. G. (1999). Communication patterns of African-American girls and boys from low income urban backgrounds. *Child Development, 70,* 1489–1503.

Lederberg, A. R. (2003). Expressing meaning: From communicative intent to building a lexicon. In M. Marschark & P. E. Spencer (Eds.), *Oxford handbook of deaf studies, language, and education* (pp. 247–260). New York: Oxford University Press.

Lederberg, A. R., & Mobley, C. E. (1990). The effect of hearing impairment on the quality of attachment and mother–infant interaction. *Child Development, 61,* 1596–1604.

Lee, C. D. (2003). Cultural modeling: CHAT as a lens for understanding instructional discourse based on African American English discourse patterns. In A. Kozulin, B. Gindia, V. S. Ageyev, & S. M. Miller (Eds.), *Vygotsky's educational theory in cultural context* (pp. 393–410). Cambridge, UK: Cambridge University Press.

Lee, O., & Brophy, J. (1996). Motivational patterns observed in sixth-grade science classrooms. *Journal of Research in Science Teaching, 33,* 303–318.

Lee, S. J. (1994). Behind the model-minority stereotype: Voices of high- and low-achieving Asian American students. *Anthropology and Education Quarterly, 25,* 413–429.

Leekam, S. (1993). Children's understanding of mind. In M. Bennett (Ed.), *The development of social cognition: The child as psychologist* (pp. 26–61). New York: Guilford Press.

LeMare, L. J., & Rubin, K. H. (1987). Perspective taking and peer interaction: Structural and developmental analyses. *Child Development, 58,* 306–315.

Lenneberg, E. (1967). *Biological foundations of language.* New York: Wiley.

Leonard, L. B. (1995). Phonological impairment. In P. Fletcher & B. MacWhinney (Eds.), *The handbook of child language* (pp. 573–602). Oxford, UK: Blackwell.

Leonard, L., Bortolini, U., Caselli, M. C., McGregor, K., & Sabbadini, L. (1992). Morphological deficits in children with specific language impairments: The status of features in the underlying grammar. *Language Acquisition, 2,* 151–179.

Leopold, W. (1939). *Speech development of a bilingual child: A linguist's record. Vol. 1. Vocabulary growth in the first two years.* Evanston, IL: Northwestern University Press.

Leopold, W. (1947). *Speech development of a bilingual child: A linguist's record: Vol. 2. Sound learning in the first two years.* Evanston, IL: Northwestern University Press.

Leopold, W. (1949a). *Speech development of a bilingual child: A linguist's record: Vol. 3. Grammar and general problems.* Evanston, IL: Northwestern University Press.

Leopold, W. (1949b). *Speech development of a bilingual child: A linguist's record: Vol. 4. Diary from age 2.* Evanston, IL: Northwestern University Press.

Lepper, M. R. (1983). Extrinsic reward and intrinsic motivation: Implications for the classroom. In J. M. Levine & M. C. Wang (Eds.), *Teacher and student perceptions: Implications for learning.* Hillsdale, NJ: Erlbaum.

Lepper, M. R. (1995). Theory by the numbers?: Some concerns about meta-analysis as a theoretical tool. *Applied Cognitive Psychology, 9,* 411–422.

Lepper, M. R., Aspinwall, L. G., Mumme, D. L., & Chabey, R. W. (1990). Self-perception and social-perception processes in tutoring: Subtle social control strategies of expert tutors. In J. M. Olson & M. P. Zanna (Eds.), *Self-inference processes: The Ontario Symposium* (pp. 217–237). Hillsdale, NJ: Erlbaum.

Lepper, M. R., Corpus, J. H., & Iyengar, S. S. (2005). Intrinsic and extrinsic motivational orientations in the classroom: Age differences and academic correlates. *Journal of Educational Psychology, 97*(2), 184–196.

Lepper, M. R., Greene, D., & Nisbett, R. E. (1973). Undermining children's intrinsic interest with extrinsic rewards: A test of the "over-justification" hypothesis. *Journal of Personality and Social Psychology, 28,* 129–137.

Lepper, M. R., & Hodell, M. (1989). Intrinsic motivation in the classroom. In C. Ames & R. Ames (Eds.), *Research on motivation in education: Vol. 3. Goals and cognitions* (pp. 73–105). San Diego, CA: Academic Press.

Lepper, M. R., Keavney, M., & Drake, M. (1996). Intrinsic motivation and extrinsic rewards: A commentary on Cameron and Pierce's meta-analysis. *Review of Educational Research, 66,* 5–32.

Lepper, M. R., & Malone, T. W. (1987). Intrinsic motivation and instructional effectiveness in computer-based education. In R. E. Snow & M. J. Farr (Eds.), *Aptitude, learning, and instruction: Vol. 3. Conative and affective process analyses* (pp. 255–286). Hillsdale, NJ: Erlbaum.

Lerner, J. W., Lowenthal, B., & Lerner, S. W. (1995). *Attentional deficit disorder: Assessment and teaching.* Pacific Grove, CA: Brooks/Cole.

Lerner, R. M. (2002). *Concepts and theories of human development* (3rd ed.). Mahwah, NJ: Erlbaum.

Lerner, R. M., & Busch-Rossnagel, N. (Eds.). (1981). *Individuals as producers of their own development: A lifespan perspective*. New York: Academic Press.

Lerner, R. M., Easterbrooks, M. A., & Mistry, J. (Eds.). (2003). *Handbook of psychology: Vol. 6. Developmental psychology*. New York: Wiley.

Lerner, R. M., & Galambos, N. L. (1985). Maternal role satisfaction, mother–child interaction, and child temperament: A process model. *Developmental Psychology, 21,* 1157–1164.

Lerner, R. M., & Galambos, N. L. (1986). Child development and family change: The influence of maternal employment in infants and toddlers. In L. P. Lipsett & C. Rovee-Collier (Eds.), *Advances in infancy research* (Vol. 4, pp. 40–86). Norwood, NJ: Ablex.

Lerner, R. M., & Galambos, N. L. (1988). The influence of maternal employment across life: The New York Longitudinal Study. In A. E. Gottfried & A. W. Gottfried (Eds.), *Maternal employment and children's development: Longitudinal research* (pp. 59–83). New York: Plenum Press.

Lerner, R. M., Hertzog, C., Hooker, K. A., Hassibi, M., & Thomas, A. (1988). A longitudinal study of negative emotional states and adjustment from early childhood through adolescence. *Child Development, 58,* 356–368.

Lerner, R. M., & Lerner, J. (1977). Effects of age, sex, and physical attractiveness on child–peer relations, academic performance, and elementary school adjustment. *Developmental Psychology, 13,* 585–590.

Lester, B. M., Kotelchuck, M., Spelke, E., Sellers, M. J., & Klein, R. E. (1974). Separation protest in Guatemalan infants: Cross-cultural and cognitive findings. *Developmental Psychology, 10,* 79–85.

Letendre, G. K. (2000). *Learning to be adolescent: Growing up in U.S. and Japanese middle schools*. New Haven, CT: Yale University Press.

Leung, K., Lau, S., & Lam, W. L. (1998). Parenting styles and academic achievement: A cross-cultural study. *Merrill–Palmer Quarterly, 44,* 157–172.

LeVay, S. (1991). A difference in hypothalamic structure between heterosexual and homosexual men. *Science, 253,* 1034–1037.

Levin, T., Sabar, N., & Libman, Z. (1991). Achievements and attitudinal patterns of boys and girls in science. *Journal of Research in Science Teaching, 28,* 315–328.

Levine, H. G. (1993). Context and scaffolding in developmental studies of mother–child problem-solving dyads. In S. Chaiklin & J. Lave (Eds.), *Understanding practice: Perspectives on activity and context* (pp. 306–326). New York: Cambridge University Press.

Levine, S. C., Huttenlocher, L., Taylor, A., & Langrock, A. (1999). Early sex differences in spatial skill. *Developmental Psychology, 35,* 940–949.

Levitt, M. J., Guacci-Franco, N., & Levitt, J. L. (1993). Convoys of social support in childhood and early adolescence: Structure and function. *Developmental Psychology, 29,* 811–818.

Levitt, M. J., Guacci-Franco, N., & Levitt, J. L. (1994). Social support and achievement in childhood and early adolescence: A multicultural study. *Journal of Applied Developmental Psychology, 15,* 207–222.

Levy, D. T., Miller, T. R., & Cox K. C. (1999). *Costs of underage drinking*. Available online at www.udetc.org/documents/costunderagedrinking.pdf. Calverton, MD: Pacific Institute for Research and Evaluation.

Levy, G., & Fivush, R. (1993). Scripts and gender: A new approach for examining gender role development. *Developmental Review, 13,* 126–146.

Levy, G. D. (1999). Gender-typed and non-gender-typed category awareness in toddlers. *Sex Roles, 41,* 851–873.

Levy, Y. (1985). Theoretical gains from the study of bilingualism: A case report. *Language Learning, 35,* 541–554.

Lewis, B. A., & Freebairn, L. (1992). Residual effects of preschool phonology disorders in grade school, adolescence and adulthood. *Journal of Speech and Hearing Research, 35*(4), 819–831.

Lewis, B. A., Freebairn, L. A., & Taylor, H. G. (2000). Follow-up of children with early expressive phonology disorders. *Journal of Learning Disabilities, 33*(5), 433–444.

Lewis, C., & Carpendale, J. (2002). Social cognition. In P. K. Smith & C. H. Hart (Eds.), *Blackwell handbook of childhood social development* (pp. 375–393). Oxford, UK: Blackwell.

Lewis, M., Feiring, C., & Rosenthal, S. (2000). Attachment over time. *Child Development, 71,* 707–720.

Lewis, M. D. (1993). Emotion–cognition interactions in early infant development. *Cognition and Emotion, 1,* 145–170.

Lewontin, R. C. (1974). *The genetic basis of evolutionary change*. New York: Columbia University Press.

Lewontin, R. C., Rose, S., & Kamin, L. J. (1984). *Not in our genes: Biology, ideology, and human nature*. New York: Pantheon Books.

Liben, L. S., & Signorella, M. L. (1993). Gender-schematic processing in children: The role of initial interpretations of stimuli. *Developmental Psychology, 29,* 141–149.

Liberman, I. Y., Mann, V. A., Shankweiler, D., & Werfelman, M. (1982). Children's memory for recurring linguistic and nonlinguistic material in relation to reading ability. *Cortex, 18,* 367–375.

Licht, B. (1983). Cognitive–motivational factors that contribute to the achievement of learning-disabled children. *Journal of Learning Disabilities, 16,* 483–490.

Licht, B. (1992). Achievement-related beliefs in children with learning disabilities. In L. J. Meltzer (Ed.), *Strategy assessment and instruction for students with learning disabilities: From theory to practice* (pp. 195–220). Austin, TX: PRO-ED.

Licht, B. G., & Dweck, C. S. (1984). Determinants of academic achievement: The interaction of children's achievement orientation with skill area. *Developmental Psychology, 20,* 628–636.

Lichtman, J. W. (2001). Developmental neurobiology overview. In J. B. Bailey Jr., J. T. Bruer, F. J. Symons, & J. W. Lichtman (Eds.), *Critical thinking about critical periods* (pp. 27–43). Baltimore: Brookes.

Lickona, T. (1991). *Educating for character: How our schools can teach respect and responsibility*. New York: Bantam Books.

Lieberman, A., Weston, D., & Pawl, J. (1991). Preventive intervention and outcome with anxiously attached dyads. *Child Development, 62,* 199–209.

Lieberman, M., Doyle, A. B., & Markiewicz, D. (1999). Developmental patterns in security of attachment to mother and father in late childhood and early adolescence: Associations with peer relations. *Child Development, 70,* 202–213.

Lieberman, P. (1984). *The biology and evolution of language*. Cambridge, MA: Harvard University Press.

Lieberman, P. (1989). Some biological constraints on universal grammar and learnability. In M. L. Rice & R. L. Schiefelbusch (Eds.), *The teachability of language* (pp. 199–225). Baltimore: Brookes.

Lincoln, Y. S., & Guba, E. G. (1985). *Naturalistic inquiry*. Newbury Park, CA: Sage.

Lindauer, P., & Petrie, G. (1997). A review of cooperative learning: An alternative to everyday instructional strategies. *Journal of Instructional Psychology, 24*, 183–187.

Lindholm, K. J., & Padilla, A. M. (1978). Child bilingualism: Report on language mixing, switching and translations. *Linguistics, 16*, 23–44.

Lindsay, D. S., & Read, J. D. (2006). Adults' memories of long-past events. In L. G. Nilsson & N. Ohta (Eds.), *Memory and society: Psychological perspectives* (pp. 51–72). New York: Psychology Press.

Linebarger, D. L. (2001). Learning to read from television: The effects of using captions and narration. *Journal of Educational Psychology, 93*, 288–298.

Linebarger, D. L., Kosanic, A., Greenwood, C. R., & Doku, N. S. (2004). Effects of viewing the television program *Between the Lions* on the emergent literacy skills of young children. *Journal of Educational Psychology, 96*(2), 297–308.

Lipka, J., & McCarty, T. L. (1994). Changing the culture of schooling: Navajo and Yup'ik cases. *Anthropology and Education Quarterly, 25*, 266–284.

Lipson, M. Y. (1983). The influence of religious affiliation on children's memory for text information. *Reading Research Quarterly, 18*, 448–457.

Livesley, W. J., & Bromley, D. B. (1973). *Person perception in childhood and adolescence*. London: Wiley.

Livingston, M. S., Rosen, G. D., Drislane, F. W., & Galaburda, A. M. (1991). Physiological and anatomical evidence for a magnocellular deficit in developmental dyslexia. *Proceedings of the National Academy of Sciences of the U.S.A., 88*, 7943–7947.

Lobel, T. E., Bempechat, J., Gewirtz, J. C., Shoken-Topaz, T., & Bashe, E. (1993). The role of gender-related information and self-endorsement of traits in preadolescents' inferences and judgments. *Child Development, 64*, 1285–1294.

Locke, J. L. (2002). Vocal development in the human infant: Functions and phonetics. In M. L. Kelly & F. Windsor (Eds.), *Investigations in clinical phonetics and linguistics* (pp. 243–256). Mahwah, NJ: Erlbaum.

Locke, J. L., & Mather, P. L. (1989). Genetic factors in the ontogeny of spoken language: Evidence from monozygotic and dizygotic twins. *Journal of Child Language, 16*, 553–559.

Lockhart, P. J. (2001). Fetal alcohol spectrum disorders for mental health professionals—A brief review. *Current Opinion in Psychiatry, 14*, 463–469.

Lockheed, M. E. (1985). Some determinants and consequences of sex segregation in the classroom. In L. C. Wilkinson, & C. B. Marrett (Eds.), *Gender influences on classroom interaction* (pp. 167–184). Orlando, FL: Academic Press.

Locurto, C. (1988). On the malleability of IQ. *The Psychologist, 11*, 431–435.

Locurto, C. (1990). The malleability of IQ as judged from adoption studies. *Intelligence, 14*, 275–292.

Locurto, C. (1991a). Beyond IQ in preschool programs? *Intelligence, 15*, 295–312.

Locurto, C. (1991b). Hands on the elephant: IQ, preschool programs, and the rhetoric of innoculation—A reply to commentaries. *Intelligence, 15*, 335–349.

Locurto, C. (1991c). *Sense and nonsense about IQ: The case for uniqueness*. New York: Praeger.

Loeber, R., & Dishion, T. J. (1984). Boys who fight at home and school: Family conditions influencing cross-setting consistency. *Journal of Consulting and Clinical Psychology, 52*, 759–778.

Loehlin, J. C., & Nichols, R. C. (1976). *Heredity, environment, and personality*. Austin: University of Texas Press.

Logie, R. H. (1995). *Visuo-spatial working memory*. Hillsdale, NJ: Erlbaum.

Lomawaima, K. T. (1995). Educating native Americans. In J. A. Banks & C. A. M. Banks (Eds.), *Handbook of research on multicultural education* (pp. 331–347). New York: Macmillan.

Lonigan, C. J., & Whitehurst, G. J. (1998). Relative efficacy of parent and teacher involvement in a shared-reading intervention for preschool children from low-income backgrounds. *Early Childhood Research Quarterly, 13*, 263–290.

Lopez, R. (1997). The practical impact of current research and issues in intelligence test interpretation and use for multicultural populations. *School Psychology Review, 26*, 249–254.

Lorsbach, T. C., & Morris, A. K. (1991). Direct and indirect testing of picture memory in second and sixth grade children. *Contemporary Educational Psychology, 16*, 18–27.

Lorsbach, T. C., & Worman, L. J. (1989). The development of explicit and implicit forms of memory in learning disabled children. *Contemporary Educational Psychology, 14*, 67–76.

Lorsbach, T. C., & Worman, L. J. (1990). Episodic priming in children with learning disabilities. *Contemporary Educational Psychology, 15*, 93–102.

Lou, H. C., Henriksen, L., & Bruhn, P. (1984). Focal cerebral hypoperfusion in children with dysphasia and/or attention deficit disorder. *Archives of Neurology, 41*, 825–829.

Loveland, K. K., & Olley, J. G. (1979). The effect of external reward on interest and quality of task performance in children of high and low intrinsic motivation. *Child Development, 50*, 1207–1210.

Lubinski, D., & Benbow, C. P. (1994). The study of mathematically precocious youth: The first three decades of a planned 50–year study of intellectual talent. In R. F. Subotnik & K. D. Arnold (Eds.), *Beyond Terman: Contemporary longitudinal studies of giftedness and talent* (pp. 255–281). Norwood, NJ: Ablex.

Lucas, T., & Katz, A. (1994). Reframing the debate: The roles of native languages in English-only programs for language minority students. *TESOL Quarterly, 28*(3), 537–561.

Ludeke, R. J., & Hartup, W. W. (1983). Teaching behaviors of 9- and 11-year-old girls in mixed-age and same-age dyads. *Journal of Educational Psychology, 75*, 909–914.

Luecke-Aleksa, D., Anderson, D. R., Collins, P. A., & Schmitt, K. L. (1995). Gender constancy and television viewing. *Developmental Psychology, 31*, 773–780.

Lueptow, L. B., Garovich, L., & Lueptow, M. B. (2001). Social change and the persistence of sex typing, 1974–1997. *Social Forces, 80*, 1–36.

Luhmer, K. (1990). Moral education in Japan. *Journal of Moral Education, 19*, 172–181.

Lundberg, I. (1991). Phonemic awareness can be developed without reading instruction. In S. A. Brady

& D. P. Shankweiler (Eds.), *Phonological processes in literacy: A tribute to Isabelle Y. Liberman* (pp. 47–53). Hillsdale, NJ: Erlbaum.

Luria, A. R. (1961). *The role of speech in the regulation of normal and abnormal behavior.* New York: Pergamon Press.

Luria, A. R. (1973). *The working brain: An introduction of neuropsychology.* New York: Pergamon Press.

Luria, A. R. (1982). *Language and cognition.* New York: Wiley.

Lyons, N. P. (1988). Two perspectives: On self, relationships, and morality. In C. Gilligan, J. V. Ward, & J. M. Taylor, with B. Bardige (Eds.), *Mapping the moral domain: A contribution of women's thinking to psychological theory and education* (pp. 21–48). Cambridge, MA: Harvard University Press.

Lyons-Ruth, K., Alpern, L., & Repacholi, B. (1993). Disorganized infant attachment classification and maternal psychosocial problems as predictors of hostile-aggressive behavior in the preschool classroom. *Child Development, 64,* 572–585.

Lyons-Ruth, K., Connell, D. B., Grunebaum, H. U., & Botein, S. (1990). Infants at social risk: Maternal depression and family support services as mediators of infant development and security of attachment. *Child Development, 61,* 85–98.

Lytton, H., & Romney, D. M. (1991). Parents' differential socialization of boys and girls: A meta-analysis. *Psychological Bulletin, 109,* 267–296.

MacArthur, C., Schwartz, S., & Graham, S. (1991). Effects of a reciprocal peer revision strategy in special education classrooms. *Learning Disabilities Research and Practice, 6*(4), 201–210.

Maccoby, E. E. (1988). Gender as a social category. *Developmental Psychology, 24,* 755–765.

Maccoby, E. E. (1990). Gender and relationships: A developmental account. *American Psychologist, 45,* 513–520.

Maccoby, E. E. (1998). *The two sexes: Growing up apart, coming together.* Cambridge, MA: Belknap Press of Harvard University Press.

Maccoby, E. E. (2002). Perspectives on gender development. In W. W. Hartup & R. K. Silbereisen (Eds.), *Growing points in developmental science: An introduction* (pp. 202–222). Philadelphia: Psychology Press.

Maccoby, E. E., & Jacklin, C. N. (1974). *The psychology of sex differences.* Stanford, CA: Stanford University Press.

Maccoby, E. E., & Jacklin, C. N. (1987). Gender segregation in childhood. In H. W. Reese (Ed.), *Advances in child development and behavior* (Vol. 20, pp. 239–287). New York: Academic Press.

Maccoby, E. E., & Martin, J. A. (1983). Socialization in the context of the family: Parent–child interaction. In P. H. Mussen (Gen. Ed.) & E. M. Hetherington (Vol. Ed.), *Handbook of child psychology: Vol. 4. Socialization, personality, and social behavior* (4th ed., pp. 1–102). New York: Wiley.

Mackey, W. F., & Beebe, V. N. (1977). *Bilingual schools for a bicultural community: Miami's adaptation to the Cuban refugees.* Rowley, MA: Newbury House.

MacKinnon, D. W. (1978). *In search of human effectiveness.* Buffalo, NY: Creative Education Foundation.

MacKinnon-Lewis, C., Volling, B. L., Lamb, M. E., Dechman, K., Rabiner, D., & Curtner, M. E. (1994). A cross-contextual analysis of boys' social competence: From family to school. *Developmental Psychology, 30,* 325–333.

MacMillan, D. L., & Knopf, E. D. (1971). Effects of instructional set on perceptions of event outcomes by EMR and nonretarded children. *American Journal of Mental Deficiency, 76,* 185–189.

MacMillan, D. L., & Reschly, D. J. (1997). Issues of definition and classification. In W. E. MacLean Jr. (Ed.), *Ellis' handbook of mental deficiency, psychological theory and research* (pp. 47–74). Mahwah, NJ: Erlbaum.

MacMullen, M. M. (1996). The coalition of essential schools: A national research context. In T. R. Sizer (Ed.), *Horace's hope: What works for the American high school* (pp. 160–176). Boston: Houghton-Mifflin.

MacPherson, E. M., Candee, B. L., & Hohman, R. J. (1974). A comparison of three methods for eliminating disruptive classroom behavior. *Journal of Applied Behavior Analysis, 7,* 287–297.

Madison, P. (1969). *Personality development in college.* Reading, MA: Addison-Wesley.

Maehr, M. L., & Anderman, E. M. (1993). Reinventing schools for early adolescents: Emphasizing task goals. *Elementary School Journal, 93,* 593–610.

Mahoney, M. J. (1991). *Human change processes: The scientific foundation of psychotherapy.* New York: Basic Books.

Main, M., & Cassidy, J. (1988). Categories of response to reunion with the parent at age six: Predictable from infant attachment classifications and stable over a 1-month period. *Developmental Psychology, 24,* 415–426.

Main, M., & Hesse, E. (1990). Parents' unresolved traumatic experiences are related to infant disorganized attachment status: Is frightened and/or frightening parental behavior the linking mechanism? In M. T. Greenberg, D. Cicchetti, & E. M. Cummings (Eds.), *Attachment in the preschool years* (pp. 161–182). Chicago: University of Chicago Press.

Main, M., Kaplan, N., & Cassidy, J. (1985). Security in infancy, childhood, and adulthood: A move to the level of representation. In I. Bretherton & E. Waters (Eds.), Growing points of attachment theory and research. *Monographs of the Society for Research in Child Development, 50*(1–2, Serial No. 209), 66–104.

Maisto, S. A., Carey, K. B., & Bradizza, C. M. (1999). Social learning theory. In K. E. Leonard & H. T. Blane (Eds.), *Psychological theories of drinking and alcoholism* (2nd ed., pp. 106–163). New York: Guilford Press.

Malinowski, B. (1927). *Sex and repression in savage society.* New York: Humanities Press.

Malakoff, M., & Hakuta, K. (1991). Translation skill and metalinguistic awareness in bilinguals. In E. Bialystok (Ed.), *Language processing in bilingual children* (pp. 141–166). Cambridge, UK: Cambridge University Press.

Malcolm, S. (1984). *Equity and excellence: Compatible goals.* Washington, DC: American Association for the Advancement of Science.

Mallory, M. E. (1989). Q-sort definition of ego identity status. *Journal of Youth and Adolescence, 18,* 399–412.

Mandler, J. M. (1978). A code in the node: The use of a story schema in retrieval. *Discourse Processes, 1,* 14–35.

Mandler, J. M. (1984). *Stories, scripts, and scenes: Aspects of schema theory.* Hillsdale, NJ: Erlbaum.

Mandler, J. M. (1987). On the psychological reality of story structure. *Discourse Processes, 10,* 1–29.

Mandler, J. M., & DeForest, M. (1979). Is there more than one way to recall a story? *Child Development, 50,* 886–889.

Mandler, J. M., & Goodman, M. S.

(1982). On the psychological validity of story structure. *Journal of Verbal Learning and Verbal Behavior, 21*, 507–523.

Mandler, J. M., & Johnson, N. S. (1977). Remembrance of things parsed: Story structure and recall. *Cognitive Psychology, 9*, 111–151.

Mandler, J. M., Scribner, S., Cole, M., & DeForest, M. (1980). Cross-cultural invariance in story recall. *Child Development, 51*, 19–26.

Mangelsdorf, S. C., & Frosch, C. A. (2000). Temperament and attachment: One construct or two? In H. W. Reese (Ed.), *Advances in child development and behavior* (Vol. 27, pp. 181–220). San Diego, CA: Academic Press.

Mangelsdorf, S., Gunnar, M., Kestenbaum, R., Lang, S., & Andreas, D. (1990). Infant proneness-to-distress temperament, maternal personality, and mother–infant attachment: Associations and goodness of fit. *Child Development, 61*, 820–831.

Mann, V. A. (1984). Review: Reading skill and language skill. *Developmental Review, 4*(1), 1–15.

Manning, B. H. (1988). Application of cognitive behavior modification: First and third graders' self-management of classroom behaviors. *American Educational Research Journal, 25*, 193–212.

Manning, B. H. (1990). Cognitive self-instruction for an off-task fourth grader during independent academic tasks: A case study. *Contemporary Educational Psychology, 15*, 36–46.

Manning, B. H. (1991). *Cognitive self-instruction for classroom processes.* Albany: State University of New York Press.

Manning, B. H., Glasner, S. E., & Smith, E. R. (1996). The self-regulated learning aspect of metacognition: A component of gifted education. *Roeper Review, 18*, 217–223.

Maosen, L. (1990). Moral education in the People's Republic of China. *Journal of Moral Education, 19*, 159–171.

Maple, S. A., & Stage, F. K. (1991). Influence on the choice of math/science major by gender and ethnicity. *American Educational Research Journal, 28*, 37–60.

Marantz, S. A., & Mansfield, A. F. (1977). Maternal employment and the development of sex role stereotyping in five- to eleven-year-old girls. *Child Development, 48*, 668–673.

Maratsos, M. (1989). Innateness and plasticity in language acquisition. In M. Rice & R. L. Shiefelbusch (Eds.), *The teachability of language* (pp. 105–125). Baltimore: Brookes.

Marcia, J. E. (2002). Identity and psychosocial development in adulthood. *Identity, 2*, 7–28.

Marcia, J. E. (1966). Development and validation of ego-identity status. *Journal of Personality and Social Psychology, 3*, 551–558.

Marcia, J. E. (1994). The empirical study of ego identity. In H. A. Bosma, T. L. G. Graafsma, H. D. Grotevant, & D. J. De Levita (Eds.), *Identity and development: An interdisciplinary approach* (pp. 67–80). Thousand Oaks, CA: Sage.

Marcus, D. E., & Overton, W. F. (1978). The development of cognitive gender constancy and sex-role preferences. *Child Development, 49*, 434–444.

Marcus, G. F., Pinker, S., Ullman, M., Hollander, M., Rosen, T. J., & Xu, F. (1992). Overregulation in language acquisition. *Monographs of the Society for Research in Child Development, 57*(4), 1–182.

Marks, M., Pressley, M., Coley, J. D., Craig, S., Gardner, R., DePinto, W., et al. (1993). Three teachers' adaptations of reciprocal teaching in comparison to traditional reciprocal teaching. *Elementary School Journal, 94*, 267–283.

Markman, E. M., & Callanan, M. A. (1983). An analysis of hierarchical classification. In R. Sternberg (Ed.), *Advances in the psychology of human intelligence* (Vol. 2, pp. 325–365). Hillsdale, NJ: Erlbaum.

Markon, K. E., Krueger, R. F., Bouchard, T. J. Jr., & Gottesmann, I. I. (2002). Normal and abnormal personality traits: Evidence for genetic and environmental relationships in the Minnesota Study of Twins Reared Apart. *Journal of Personality, 70*, 661–693.

Markovits, H., Benenson, J., & Dolenszky, E. (2001). Evidence that children and adolescents have internal models of peer interactions that are gender differentiated. *Child Development, 72*, 879–886.

Markus, H., & Nurius, P. (1986). Possible selves. *American Psychologist, 41*, 954–969.

Marr, M. B. (1997). Cooperative learning: A brief review. *Reading and Writing Quarterly, 13*, 7–20.

Marschark, M. (1993). *Psychological development of deaf children.* New York: Oxford University Press.

Marsh, H. W. (1989). Effects of attending single-sex and coeducational high schools on achievement, attitudes, behaviors, and sex differences. *Journal of Educational Psychology, 81*, 70–85.

Marsh, H. W. (1990a). Causal ordering of academic self-concept and academic achievement: A multiwave, longitudinal panel analysis. *Journal of Educational Psychology, 82*, 646–656.

Marsh, H. W. (1990b). The structure of academic self-concept: The Marsh/Shavelson model. *Journal of Educational Psychology, 82*, 623–636.

Marsh, H. W. (1992). Content specificity of relations between academic achievement and academic self-concept. *Journal of Educational Psychology, 84*, 35–42.

Marsh, H. W., & Ayotte, V. (2003). Do multiple dimensions of self-concept become more differentiated with age?: The differential distinctiveness hypothesis. *Journal of Educational Psychology, 95*(4), 687–706.

Marsh, H. W., Chessor, D., Craven, R., & Roche, L. (1995). The effects of gifted and talented programs on academic self-concept: The big fish strikes again. *American Educational Research Journal, 32*, 285–319.

Marsh, H. W., & Craven, R. G. (1991). Self–other agreement on multiple dimensions of preadolescent self-concept: Inferences by teachers, mothers, and fathers. *Journal of Educational Psychology, 83*, 393–404.

Marsh, H. W., Craven, R. G., & Debus, R. (1991). Self-concepts of young children 5 to 8 years of age: Measurement and multidimensional structure. *Journal of Educational Psychology, 83*, 377–392.

Marsh, H. W., Craven, R. G., & Debus, R. (1999). Separation of competency and affect components of multiple dimensions of academic self-concept: A developmental perspective. *Merrill–Palmer Quarterly, 45*, 567–601.

Marsh, H. W., & Hau, K. T. (2003). Big-fish–little-pond effect on academic self-concept: A cross-cultural (26-country) test of the negative effects of academically selective schools. *American Psychologist, 58*, 364–376.

Marsh, H. W., & Yeung, A. S. (1997a). Causal effects of academic self-concept on academic achievement: Structural equation models of longitudinal data. *Journal of Educational Psychology, 89*, 41–54.

Marsh, H. W., & Yeung, A. S. (1997b). Coursework selection: Relations to academic self-concept and achievement. *American Educational Research Journal, 34,* 691–720.

Martin, B. (1975). Parent–child relations. In F. D. Horowitz, E. M. Hetherington, S. Scarr-Salapatek, & G. M. Siegel (Eds.), *Review of child development research* (Vol. 4, pp. 463–540). Chicago: University of Chicago Press.

Martin, C. L. (1989). Children's use of gender-related information in making social judgments. *Developmental Psychology, 25,* 80–88.

Martin, C. L. (1993). New directions for investigating children's gender knowledge. *Developmental Reiew, 13,* 184–204.

Martin, C. L. (2000). Cognitive theories of gender development. In E. Eckes & H. M. Trautner (Eds.), *The developmental social psychology of gender* (pp. 19–121). Mahwah, NJ: Erlbaum.

Martin, C. L., Eisenbud, L., & Rose, H. (1995). Children's gender-based reasoning about toys. *Child Development, 66,* 1453–1471.

Martin, C. L., & Halverson, C. F. (1981). A schematic processing model of sex typing and stereotyping in children. *Child Development, 52,* 1119–1134.

Martin, C. L., & Halverson, C. F. (1983). The effect of sex-typing schemas on young children's memory. *Child Development, 54,* 563–574.

Martin, C. L., & Halverson, C. F. (1987). The roles of cognition in sex-roles and sex-typing. In D. B. Carter (Ed.), *Current conceptions of sex roles and sex-typing: Theory and research* (pp. 123–137). New York: Praeger.

Martin, C. L., Ruble, D. N., & Szjrybalo, J. (2002). Cognitive theories of early gender development. *Psychological Bulletin, 128,* 903–933.

Martin, C. L., Wood, C. H., & Little, J. K. (1990). The development of gender stereotype components. *Child Development, 61,* 1861–1904.

Martin, J., & Martin, W. (1983). *Personal development: Self-instruction for personal agency.* Calgary, Alberta, Canada: Detselig Enterprises.

Martin, J. H., Brust, J. C. M., & Hilal, S. (1991). Imaging the living brain. In E. R. Kandel, J. H. Schwartz, & T. M. Jessel (Eds.), *Principles of neural science* (pp. 309–324). New York: Elsevier.

Martindale, C. (1991). *Cognitive psychology: A neural-network approach.* Pacific Grove, CA: Brooks/Cole.

Martinez, M. E. (1992). Interest enhancements to science experiments: Interactions with student gender. *Journal of Research in Science Teaching, 29,* 167–177.

Martinez, M. E. (2000). *Education as the cultivation of intelligence.* Mahwah, NJ: Erlbaum.

Marvin, R. S., & Britner, P. A. (1999). Normative development: The ontogeny of attachment. In J. Cassidy & P. R. Shaver (Eds.), *Handbook of attachment: Theory, research, and clinical applications* (pp. 44–67). New York: Guilford Press.

Mascolo, M. F., Li, J., Fink, R., & Fischer, K. (2002). Pathways to excellence: Value presuppositions and the development of academic and affective skills in educational contexts. In M. Ferrari (Ed.), *The pursuit of excellence through education* (pp. 113–146). Mahwah, NJ: Erlbaum.

Mash, E. J., & Dozois, D. J. A. (2003). Child psychopathology: A developmental-systems perspective. In E. J. Mash & R. A. Barkley (Eds.), *Child psychopathology* (2nd ed., pp. 3–72). New York: Guilford Press.

Mason, C. A., Cauce, A. M., Gonzales, N., & Hiraga, Y. (1996). Neither too sweet nor too sour: Problem peers, maternal control, and problem behavior in African American adolescents. *Child Development, 67,* 2115–2130.

Mason, C. L., & Kahle, J. B. (1988). Student attitudes toward science and science-related careers: A program designed to promote a stimulating gender-free learning environment. *Journal of Research in Science Teaching, 26,* 25–39.

Masson, J. M. (1984). *The assault on truth: Freud's suppression of the seduction theory.* New York: Farrar, Straus, & Giroux.

Mastropieri, M. A., Scruggs, T. E., & Graetz, J. E. (2003). Reading comprehension instruction for secondary students: Challenges for struggling students and teachers. *Learning Disability Quarterly, 26,* 103–116.

Mastropieri, M. A., Scruggs, T. E., Spencer, V., & Fontana, J. (2003). Promoting success in high school world history: Peer tutoring versus guided notes. *Learning Disabilities Research and Practice, 18,* 52–65.

Mastropieri, M. A., Sweda, J., & Scruggs, T. E. (2000). Putting mnemonic strategies to work in an inclusive classroom. *Learning Disabilities Research and Practice, 15,* 69–74.

Matas, L., Arend, R. A., & Sroufe, L. A. (1978). Continuity of adaptation in the second year: The relationship between quality of attachment and later competence. *Child Development, 49,* 547–556.

Mather, N., & Goldstein, S. (2002). Learning disabilities and challenging behaviors: A guide to intervention and classroom management. *Education and Treatment of Children, 25*(3), 366–370.

Mathison, S. (1988). Why triangulate? *Educational Researcher, 17*(2), 13–17.

Matsuzawa, T. (1990). Spontaneous sorting in human and chimpanzee. In S. T. Parker & K. R. Gibson (Eds.), *"Language" and intelligence in monkeys and apes* (pp. 451–468). Cambridge, UK: Cambridge University Press.

Mayer, R. (2003). Memory and information processes. In I. B. Weiner (Series Ed.), W. M. Reynolds & G. E. Miller (Vol. Eds.), *Handbook of psychology: Vol. 7. Educational psychology* (pp. 47–58). New York: Wiley.

Mayer, R. E. (1981). Frequency norms and structural analysis of algebra story problems into families, categories, and templates. *Instructional Science, 10,* 135–175.

Mayer, R. E. (1982). Memory for algebra story problems. *Journal of Educational Psychology, 74,* 199–216.

McAnarney, E. R., & Schreider, C. (1984). *Identifying social and psychological antecedents of adolescent pregnancy.* New York: Grant Foundation.

McCall, R., Beach, S. R., & Lan, S. (2000). The nature and correlates of underachievement among elementary school children in Hong Kong. *Child Development, 71,* 785–801.

McCall, R. B., Evahn, C., & Kratzer, L. (1992). *High school underachievers: What do they achieve as adults?* Newbury Park, CA: Sage.

McCarthy, K. A., & Nelson, K. (1981). Children's use of scripts in story recall. *Discourse Processes, 4,* 59–70.

McCarthy, K. F., & Valdez, R. B. (1986). *Current and future effects of Mexican immigration in California: Executive summary* (Rand Corporation Series, R-3365/1-CR). Santa Monica, CA: Rand Corporation.

McCarthy, R. A., & Warrington, E. K. (1990). *Cognitive neuropsychology: A clinical introduction.* San Diego, CA: Academic Press.

McCarty, T. L., Lynch, R. H., Wallace,

S., & Benally, A. (1991). Classroom inquiry and Navajo learning styles: A call for reassessment. *Anthropology and Education Quarterly, 22,* 42–59.

McCauley, C., Kellas, G., Dugas, J., & DeVillis, R. F. (1976). Effects of serial rehearsal training of memory search. *Journal of Educational Psychology, 68,* 474–481.

McClelland, J. L., & Rumelhart, D. E. (1981). An interactive activation model of context effects in letter perception: Part 1. An account of basic findings. *Psychological Review, 88,* 375–407.

McClelland, J. L., & Rumelhart, D. E. (1988). *Explorations in parallel distributed processing: A handbook of models, programs, and exercises.* Cambridge, MA: MIT Press.

McConaghey, M. J. (1979). Gender permanence and the genital basis of gender: Stages in the development of constancy of gender identity. *Child Development, 50,* 1223–1226.

McConnell, K., Ryser, G., & Higgins, J. (2000). *Practical ideas that really work for students with ADHD.* Austin, TX: PRO-ED.

McCormick, C. B. (2003). Metacognition and learning. In I. B. Weiner (Ed.-in-Chief), W. M. Reynolds & G. E. Miller (Vol. Eds.), *Handbook of psychology: Vol. 7. Educational psychology* (pp. 79–102). New York: Wiley.

McCormick, C. B., & Pressley, M. (1997). *Educational psychology: Learning, instruction, and assessment.* New York: Longman.

McCrae, R. R., & Allik, J. (Eds.). (2002). *The five-factor model across cultures.* New York: Kluwer Academic/Plenum Press.

McDonald, S. M. (1989). Sex bias in the representation of male and female characteristics in children's picture books. *Journal of Genetic Psychology, 150,* 389–401.

McDonnell, J., & Ferguson, B. (1989). A comparison of time delay and decreasing prompt hierarchy strategies in teaching banking skills to students with moderate handicaps. *Journal of Applied Behavior Analysis, 22,* 85–91.

McElwain, N. L., Cox, M. J., Burchinal, M. R., & Macfie, J. (2003). Differentiating among insecure mother–infant attachment classifications: A focus on child–friend interaction and exploration during solitary play at 36 months. *Attachment and Human Development, 5,* 136–164.

McGregor, K. K. (2004). Developmental dependencies between lexical semantics and reading. In C. A. Stone, E. R. Silliman, B. J. Ehren., & K. Apel (Eds.), *Handbook of language and literacy* (pp. 302–317). New York: Guilford Press.

McGregor, K. K., & Leonard, L. B. (1995). Intervention for word-finding deficits in children. In M. E. Fey, J. Windsor, & S. F. Warren (Eds.), *Language intervention: Preschool through the elementary years* (pp. 85–106). Baltimore: Brookes.

McGuire, K. D., & Weisz, J. R. (1982). Social cognition and behavior correlates of preadolescent chumship. *Child Development, 53,* 1478–1484.

McHale, S. M., Dariotis, K. K., & Kauh, T. J. (2003). Social development and social relationship in middle childhood. In I. B. Weiner (Ed.-in Chief) & R. M. Lerner, M. A. Easterbrooks, & J. Mistry (Vol. Eds.), *Handbook of psychology: Vol. 6, Developmental psychology* (pp. 241–265). New York: Wiley.

McHale, S. M., & Pawletko, T. M. (1992). Differential treatment of siblings in two family contexts. *Child Development, 63,* 68–81.

McIntire, M. (1974). *A modified model for the description of language acquisition in a deaf child.* Unpublished master's thesis, California State University, Northridge.

McKeown, M. G. (1985). The acquisition of word meaning from context by children of high and low ability. *Reading Research Quarterly, 20,* 482–496.

McKoon, G., & Ratcliff, R. (1979). Priming in episodic and semantic memory. *Journal of Verbal Learning and Verbal Behavior, 18,* 463–480.

McLanahan, S., & Teitler, J. (1999). *The consequences of father absence: Parenting and child development in "nontraditional" families.* Mahwah, NJ: Erlbaum.

McLaughlin, B. (1977). Second-language learning in children. *Psychological Bulletin, 84,* 438–459.

McLaughlin, B. (1978). *Second-language acquisition in childhood.* Hillsdale, NJ: Erlbaum.

McLaughlin, B. (1984). *Second-language acquisition in childhood: Vol. 1. Preschool children* (2nd ed.). Hillsdale, NJ: Erlbaum.

McLoyd, V. C. (1979). The effects of extrinsic rewards of differential value on high and low intrinsic interest. *Child Development, 50,* 1010–1019.

McLoyd, V. C. (1998). Socioeconomic disadvantage and child development. *American Psychologist, 53*(2), 185–204.

McLoyd, V. C., & Wilson, L. (1990). Maternal behavior, social support, and economic conditions as predictors of psychological distress in children. *New Directions for Child Development, 46,* 49–69.

McMaster, K. L., Fuchs, D., & Fuchs, L. S. (2002). Using peer tutoring to prevent early reading failure. In J. S. Thousand, R. A. Villa, & A. I. Nevin (Eds.), *Creativity and collaborative learning: The practical guide to empowering students, teachers, and families* (2nd ed., pp. 235–246). Baltimore: Brookes.

McNamee, G. D. (1979). The social interaction origins of narrative skills. *Quarterly Newsletter of the Laboratory of Comparative Human Cognition, 1,* 63–68.

McTear, M. F. (1985). Pragmatic disorders: A case study of conversational disability. *British Journal of Disorders of Communication, 20,* 129–142.

Mead, M. (1961). *Coming of age in Samoa.* New York: Morrow Quill.

Mead, M. (1963). *Sex and temperament in three primitive societies.* New York: Morrow Quill.

Meadow-Orlans, K. P. (1987). An analysis of the effectiveness of early intervention programs for hearing-impaired children. In M. J. Guralnick & F. C. Bennett (Eds.), *The effectiveness of early intervention for at-risk and handicapped children* (pp. 325–362). New York: Academic Press.

Meadows, A. (Ed.). (1991). *Caring for America's children.* Washington, DC: National Research Council.

Meece, J. L. (1987). The influence of school experiences on the development of gender schemata. *New Directions for Child Development, 38,* 57–73.

Meece, J. L., Blumenfeld, P. C., & Hoyle, R. H. (1988). Students' goal orientations and cognitive engagement in classroom activities. *Journal of Educational Psychology, 80,* 514–523.

Meeus, W., Iedema, J., Helsen, M., & Vollebergh, W. (1999). Patterns of adolescent identity development: Review of literature and longitudinal analysis. *Developmental Review, 19,* 419–461.

Mehan, H. (1979). *Social organization in the classroom.* Cambridge, MA: Harvard University Press.

Mehan, H., Hubbard, L., & Villanueva, I. (1994). Forming academic identities: Accommodation without assimilation among involuntary minorities. *Anthropology and Education Quarterly, 25,* 91–117.

Mehler, J., & Christophe, A. (1995). Maturation and learning of language in the first year of life. In M. S. Gazzaniga (Ed.), *The cognitive neurosciences* (pp. 943–954). Cambridge, MA: MIT Press.

Mehler, J., Jusczyk, P., Lambertz, G., Halsted, N., Bartonici, J., & Amiel-Tison, C. (1988). A precursor of language acquisition in young infants. *Cognition, 29,* 143–178.

Meichenbaum, D. (1977) *Cognitive behavior modification.* New York: Plenum Press.

Meichenbaum, D., & Biemiller, A. (1998). *Nurturing independent learners: Helping students take charge of their learning.* Cambridge, MA: Brookline Books.

Meichenbaum, D., & Goodman, J. (1971). Training impulsive children to talk to themselves: A means of developing self-control. *Journal of Abnormal Child Psychology, 77,* 115–126.

Meier, R. P., & Newport, E. L. (1990). Out of the hands of babes: On a possible sign advantage in language acquisition. *Language, 66,* 1–23.

Meisel, J. (1984). *Zum Erwerb von Worstellungsregularitäten und Kasusmarkierungen.* Hamburg, Germany: Universität Hamburg Romanisches Seminar.

Meisel, J. M. (1995). Parameters in acquisition. In P. Fletcher & B. MacWhinney (Eds.), *The handbook of child language* (pp. 10–35). Oxford, UK: Blackwell.

Meisels, S. J., & Plunkett, J. W. (1988). Developmental consequences of preterm birth: Are there long-term effects? In P. B. Baltes, D. L. Featherman, & R. M. Lerner (Eds.), *Life-span development and behavior* (Vol. 9, pp. 87–128). Hillsdale, NJ: Erlbaum.

Melson, G. F., Ladd, G. W., & Hsu, H. (1993). Maternal support networks, maternal cognitions, and young children's social and cognitive development. *Child Development, 64,* 1401–1417.

Meltzoff, A. N. (1985). Immediate and deferred imitation in fourteen- and twenty-four-month-old infants. *Child Development, 56,* 62–72.

Meltzoff, A. N. (2002). Imitation as a mechanism of social cognition: Origins of empathy, theory of mind, and the representation of action. In U. Goswami (Ed.), *Blackwell handbook of childhood cognitive development* (pp. 6–25). Malden, MA: Blackwell.

Meltzoff, A. N., & Gopnik, A. (1989). On linking nonverbal imitation, representation, and language learning in the first two years of life. In G. E. Speidel & K. E. Nelson (Eds.), *The many faces of imitation in language learning* (pp. 23–51). New York: Springer-Verlag.

Meltzoff, A. N., & Moore, M. K. (1977). Imitation of facial and manual gestures by human neonates. *Science, 198,* 75–78.

Meltzoff, A. N., & Moore, M. K. (1983). Newborn infants imitate adult facial gestures. *Child Development, 54,* 702–709.

Meltzoff, A. N., & Prinz, W. (Eds.). (2002). *The imitative mind: Development, evolution, and brain bases.* New York: Cambridge University Press.

Mensh, E., & Mensh, H. (1991). *The IQ mythology.* Carbondale: Southern Illinois University Press.

Mercer, J. R. (1979). *System of multicultural pluralistic assessment (SOMPA): Technical manual.* San Antonio, TX: Psychological Corporation.

Merighi, J., Edison, M., & Zigler, E. (1990). The role of motivational factors in the functioning of mentally retarded individuals. In R. M. Hodapp, J. A. Burack, & E. Zigler (Eds.), *Issues in the developmental approach to retardation* (pp. 114–134). New York: Cambridge University Press.

Metz, S. S., & Campbell, P. B. (1987). What does it take to increase the number of women majoring in engineering? In *ASEE Council Annual Conference Proceedings* (pp. 882–887). Washington, DC: American Society for Engineering Education.

Meyer, D., Schvaneveldt, R. W., & Ruddy, M. G. (1975). Loci of contextual effects on word recognition. In P. M. A. Rabbitt & S. Dornic (Eds.), *Attention and performance* (Vol. 5, pp. 98–118). London: Academic Press.

Meyer, D. K., Turner, J. C., & Spencer, C. A. (1997). Challenge in a mathematics classroom: Students' motivation and strategies in project-based learning. *Elementary School Journal, 97,* 501–521.

Meyer, M., & Fienberg, S. (1992). *Assessing evaluation studies: The case of bilingual education strategies.* Washington, DC: National Academy Press.

Meyer-Bahlburg, H. F. L., Ehrhardt, A. A., Rosen, L. R., Gruen, R. S., Veridiano, N. P., Vann, F. H., et al. (1995). Prenatal estrogens and the development of homosexual orientation. *Developmental Psychology, 31,* 12–21.

Midgley, C. (1993). Motivation and middle level schools. In P. Pintrich & M. Maehr (Eds.), *Advances in motivation and achievement* (Vol. 8, 217–274). Greenwich, CT: JAI Press.

Midgley, C., Anderman, E., & Hicks, L. (1995). Differences between elementary and middle school teachers and students: A goal theory approach. *Journal of Early Adolescence, 15,* 90–113.

Miles, H. L. W. (1990). The cognitive foundations for reference in a signing orangutan. In S. T. Parker & K. R. Gibson (Eds.), *"Language" and intelligence in monkeys and apes* (pp. 511–539). Cambridge, UK: Cambridge University Press.

Miller, B. C., & Moore, K. (1990). Adolescent sexual behavior, pregnancy, and parenting: Research through the 1980s. *Journal of Marriage and the Family, 52,* 1025–1044.

Miller, G. A. (1956). The magical number seven, plus or minus two: Some limits on our capacity to process information. *Psychological Review, 63,* 81–97.

Miller, G. A. (1977). *Spontaneous apprentices: Children and language.* New York: Seabury Press.

Miller, P. H., Woody-Ramsey, J., & Aloise, P. A. (1991). The role of strategy effortfulness in strategy effectiveness. *Developmental Psychology, 27,* 738–745.

Miller, P. J. (1994). Narrative practices: Their role in socialization and self-construction. In U. Neisser & R. Fivush (Eds.), *The remembering self: Construction and accuracy in the self-narrative* (pp. 158–179). Cambridge, UK: Cambridge University Press.

Miller, S. A. (1987). *Developmental research methods.* Englewood Cliffs, NJ: Prentice-Hall.

Miller, S. M. (2003). How literature discussion shapes thinking: ZPDs for teaching/learning habits of the heart and mind. In A. Kozulin, B. Gindia, V. S. Ageyev, & S. M. Miller (Eds.), *Vygotsky's educational theory in cultural context* (pp. 289–316). Cambridge, UK: Cambridge University Press.

Miller, S. M., Boyer, B. A., & Rodoletz, M. (1990). Anxiety in children: Nature and development. In M. Lewis & S. M. Miller (Eds.), *Handbook of developmental psychopathology* (pp. 191–207). New York: Plenum Press.

Minuchin, P. P., & Shapiro, E. K. (1983). The school as a context for social development. In P. H. Mussen (Gen. Ed.) & E. M. Hetherington (Vol. Ed.), *Handbook of child psychology: Vol. 4. Socialization, personality, and social development* (4th ed., pp. 197–274). New York: Wiley.

Mischel, W. (1968). *Personality and assessment.* New York: Wiley.

Mistry, J., & Saraswathi, T. S. (2003). The cultural context of child development. In R. M. Lerner, M. Ann, & J. Mistry (Eds.), *Handbook of psychology: Vol. 6. Developmental psychology* (pp. 269–291). Hoboken, NJ: Wiley.

Mody, M. (2004). Neurobiological correlates of language and reading impairments. In C. A. Stone, E. R. Silliman, B. J. Ehren, & K. Apel (Eds.), *Handbook of language and literacy* (pp. 49–72). New York: Guilford Press.

Moely, B. E., Olson, F. A., Halwes, T. G., & Flavell, J. H. (1969). Production deficiency in young children's clustered recall. *Developmental Psychology, 1,* 26–34.

Mohr, D. M. (1978). Development of attributes of personal identity. *Developmental Psychology, 14,* 427–428.

Money, J. (1987). Sin, sickness, or status?: Homosexual gender identity and psychoneuroendocrinology. *American Psychologist, 42,* 384–399.

Money, J. (1988). *Gay, straight, and in-between: The sexology of erotic orientation.* New York: Oxford University Press.

Money, J., & Ehrhardt, A. (1972). *Man and woman, boy and girl.* Baltimore: Johns Hopkins University Press.

Money, J., Schwartz, M., & Lewis, V. G. (1984). Adult erotosexual status and fetal hormonal masculization and demasculization: 46 XX congenital virilizing adrenal hyperplasia and 46 XY androgen-insensitivity syndrome compared. *Psychoneuroendocrinology, 9,* 405–414.

Money, J., & Tucker, P. (1975). *Sexual signatures: On being a man or a woman.* Boston: Little, Brown.

Moon, C. R., Panneton-Cooper, T., & Fifer, W. P. (1993). Two-day-olds prefer their native language. *Infant Behavior and Development, 16,* 495–500.

Moore, J. L., & Rocklin, T. R. (1998). The distribution of distributed cognition: Multiple interpretations and uses. *Educational Psychology Review, 10*(1), 97–113.

Moran, C. E., & Hakuta, K. (1995). Bilingual education: Broadening research perspectives. In J. A. Banks & C. A. M. Banks (Eds.), *Handbook of research on multicultural education* (pp. 445–462). New York: Macmillan.

Moran, G., Pederson, D. R., Pettit, P., & Krupka, A. (1992). Maternal sensitivity and infant–mother attachment in a developmentally delayed sample. *Infant Behavior and Development, 15,* 427–442.

Morehead, D. M., & Ingram, I. (1973). The development of base syntax in normal and linguistically deviant children. *Journal of Speech and Hearing Research, 16,* 330–352.

Morgan, B., & Gibson, K. R. (1991). Nutritional and environmental interactions in brain development. In K. R. Gibson & A. C. Petersen (Eds.), *Brain maturation and cognitive development: Comparative and cross-cultural perspectives* (pp. 91–106). New York: Aldine de Gruyter.

Morgan, M. (1987). Television, sex-role attitudes, and sex-role behavior. *Journal of Early Adolescence, 7,* 269–282.

Morizot, J., & LeBlanc, M. (2000). Le role des pairs dans l'emergence et le developement de la conduite delinquante: Ine recension critique des ecrits. *Revue Canadienne de Psycho-Education, 29,* 87–117.

Morrison, F. J., Griffith, E. M., & Alberts, D. M. (1997). Nature–nurture in the classroom: Entrance age, school readiness, and learning in children. *Developmental Psychology, 33,* 254–262.

Morrison, F. J., Smith, L., & Dow-Ehrensberger, M. (1995). Education and cognitive development: A natural experiment. *Developmental Psychology, 31,* 789–799.

Morrow, L. M. (1989). *Literacy development in the early years: Helping children read and write.* Boston: Allyn & Bacon.

Morrow, L. M., Pressley, M., Smith, J. K., & Smith, M. (1997). The effect of a literature-based program integrated into literacy and science instruction with children from diverse backgrounds. *Reading Research Quarterly, 32*(1), 54–76.

Morse, L. W., & Handley, H. M. (1985). Listening to adolescents: Gender differences in science classroom interactions. In L. C. Wilkinson & C. B. Marrett (Eds.), *Gender influences on classroom interaction* (pp. 37–56). Orlando, FL: Academic Press.

Moshman, D. (1982). Exogenous, endogenous, and dialectical constructivism. *Developmental Review, 2,* 371–384.

Moss, E. (1992). The socioaffective context of joint cognitive activity. In L. T. Winegar & J. Valsiner (Eds.), *Children's development within social context: Vol. 2. Research and methodology* (pp. 117–154). Hillsdale, NJ: Erlbaum.

Moss, E., & St. Laurent, D. (2001). Attachment at school age and academic performance. *Developmental Psychology, 37,* 863–874.

Mosteller, F., & Boruch, R. (2002). *Evidence matters: Randomized trials in education research.* Washington, DC: Brookings Institute.

Mowrer, D. E. (1980). Phonological development during the first year of life. In N. J. Lass (Ed.), *Speech and language advances in basic research and practice* (Vol. 4, pp. 99–137). New York: Academic Press.

Muir-Broaddus, J. E. (1995). Gifted underachievers: Insights from the characteristics of strategic functioning associated with giftedness and achievement. *Learning and Individual Differences, 7,* 189–206.

Muniz-Swicegood, M. (1994). The effects of metacognitive reading strategy training on the reading performance and fluent reading analysis strategies of third grade bilingual students. *Bilingual Research Journal, 18,* 83–97.

Munsinger, H., & Weir, M. W. (1967). Infants' and young children's preference for complexity. *Journal of Experimental Child Psychology, 5,* 69–73.

Murphy, G. L. (2002). *The big book of concepts.* Cambridge, MA: MIT Press.

Murphy, K., McKone, E., & Slee, J. (2003). Dissociations between implicit and explicit memory in children: The role of strategic processing and the knowledge base. *Journal of Experimental Child Psychology, 84,* 124–165.

Murphy, L. L., Plake, B. S., Impara, J. C., & Spies, R. A. (Eds.). (2002). *Tests in print VI.* Lincoln, NE: Buros.

Myers, D., & Dynarski, D. (2003). *Random assignment in program evaluation and intervention research: Questions and answers.* Washington, DC: U.S. Department of Education.

Nagy, W., & Anderson, R. (1984). How many words are there in printed school English? *Reading Research Quarterly, 19,* 304–330.

Nagy, W., Anderson, R., & Herman, P. (1987). Learning word meanings from context during normal reading. *American Educational Research Journal, 24,* 237–270.

Nagy, W., Herman, P., & Anderson, R. (1985). Learning words from context. *Reading Research Quarterly, 20,* 233–253.

Naigles, L., & Hoff-Ginsberg, E. (1995). Input to verb learning: Evidence for the plausibility of syntactic bootstrapping. *Developmental Psychology, 5,* 827–837.

Nairne, J. S. (2003). Sensory and working memory. In I. B. Weiner (Ed.-in-Chief), A. F. Healy & R. W. Proctor (Vol. Eds.), *Handbook of psychology: Vol. 4. Experimental psychology* (pp. 423–444). New York: Wiley.

Naito, M. (1990). Repetition priming in children and adults: Age-related dissociation between implicit and explicit memory. *Journal of Experimental Child Psychology, 50,* 462–484.

Nanez, J. E., Padilla, R. V., & Maez, B. L. (1992). Bilinguality, intelligence, and cognitive information processing. In R. V. Padilla & A. H. Benavides (Eds.), *Critical perspectives on bilingual education research* (pp. 42–69). Tempe, AZ: Bilingual Press.

National Center for Education Statistics. (2003). *Trends in international mathematics and science study.* Washington, DC: U.S. Department of Education.

National Commission on Children. (1991). *Beyond rhetoric: A new American agenda for children and families.* Washington, DC: U.S. Government Printing Office.

National Institute of Mental Health. (2003). *In harm's way: Suicide in America.* Washington, DC: Author.

National Reading Panel. (2000). *Report of the National Reading Panel: Teaching children to read: An evidence-based assessment of the scientific research literature on reading and its implications for reading instruction: Reports of the subgroups.* Washington, DC: National Institutes of Health, National Institute of Child Health and Human Development.

Needleman, H. L. (1992). Childhood exposure to lead: A common cause of school failure. *Phi Delta Kappan, 74,* 35–37.

Needleman, H. L., & Bellinger, D. (1991). The health effects of low level exposure to lead. *Annual Review of Public Health, 12,* 111–140.

Neely, J. H. (1976). Semantic priming and retrieval from lexical memory: Evidence for facilitatory and inhibitory processes. *Memory and Cognition, 4,* 648–654.

Neely, J. H. (1977). Semantic priming and retrieval from lexical memory: Roles of inhibitionless spreading

activation and limited capacity attention. *Journal of Experimental Psychology, 106,* 226–254.

Neill, A. S. (1960). *Summerhill: A radical approach to child rearing.* New York: Hart.

Neisser, U. (1967). *Cognitive psychology.* New York: Appleton–Century–Crofts.

Nelson, C. A. (1995). The ontogeny of human memory: A cognitive neuroscience perspective. *Development Psychology, 31*(5), 723–738.

Nelson, C. A., & Bosquet, M. (2000). Neurobiology of fetal and infant development: Implications for infant mental health. In C. H. Zeanah Jr. (Ed.), *Handbook of infant mental health* (pp. 37–59). New York: Guilford Press.

Nelson, K. (1973). Structure and strategy in learning to talk. *Monographs of the Society for Research in Child Development, 38*(Serial No. 149).

Nelson, K. (1978). How children represent their world in and out of language. In R. S. Siegler (Ed.), *Children's thinking: What develops?* (pp. 255–273). Hillsdale, NJ: Erlbaum.

Nelson, K. (1993a). Events, narratives, and memory: What develops? In C. A. Nelson (Ed.), *Memory and affect in development: Minnesota Symposium on Child Psychology* (Vol. 26, pp. 1–24). Hillsdale, NJ: Erlbaum.

Nelson, K. (1993b). Explaining the emergence of autobiographical memory in early childhood. In A. F. Collins, S. E. Gathercole, M. A. Conway, & P. E. Morris (Eds.), *Theories of memory* (pp. 355–385). Hillsdale, NJ: Erlbaum.

Nelson, K., & Gruendel, J. (1981). Generalized event representations: Basic building blocks of cognitive development. In A. Brown & M. Lamb (Eds.), *Advances in developmental psychology* (Vol. 1, pp. 231–247). Hillsdale, NJ: Erlbaum.

Nettelbeck, T., & Wilson, C. (1997). Speed of information processing and cognition. In W. E. MacLean Jr. (Ed.), *Ellis' handbook of mental deficiency, psychological theory and research* (pp. 245–274). Mahwah, NJ: Erlbaum.

Neves, D. M., & Anderson, J. R. (1981). Knowledge compilation: Mechanisms for the automatization of cognitive skills. In J. R. Anderson (Ed.), *Cognitive skills and their acquisition* (pp. 251–272). Hillsdale, NJ: Erlbaum.

Neville, H. J., & Bruer, J. T. (2001). Language processing: How experi-

ence affects brain organization. In D. B. Bailey Jr., J. T. Bruer, F. J. Symons, & J. W. Lichtman (Eds.), *Critical thinking about critical periods* (pp. 151–172). Baltimore: Brookes.

Newborg, J., Stock, J. R., & Wnek, L. (1984). *Battelle Developmental Inventory.* Allen, TX: LINC Associates.

Newcomb, A. F., & Bagwell, C. L. (1995). Children's friendship relations: A meta-analytic review. *Psychological Bulletin, 117,* 306–347.

Newcomb, A. F., & Brady, J. E. (1982). Mutuality in boys' friendship relations. *Child Development, 53,* 392–395.

Newcomb, A. F., Bukowski, W., & Pattee, L. (1993). Children's peer relations: A meta-analytic review of popular, rejected, neglected, controversial, and average sociometric status. *Psychological Bulletin, 113,* 99–128.

Newcomer, P., & Barenbaum, E. (1991). The written composing ability of children with learning disabilities: A review of the literature from 1980 to 1990. *Journal of Learning Disabilities, 24,* 578–593.

Newman, L. S. (1990). Intentional and unintentional memory in young children: Remembering versus playing. *Journal of Experimental Child Psychology, 50,* 243–258.

Newman, P., & Newman, B. (1978). Identity formation and the college experience. *Adolescence, 13,* 311–326.

Newman, R. S., & Goldin, L. (1990). Children's reluctance to seek help with schoolwork. *Journal of Educational Psychology, 82,* 92–100.

Newman, R. S., & Schwager, M. T. (1992). Student perceptions and academic help seeking. In D. H. Schunk & J. L. Meece (Eds.), *Student perceptions in the classroom* (pp. 209–228). Hillsdale NJ: Erlbaum.

Newmann, F. M. (1991). Promoting higher order thinking in social studies: Overview of a study of 16 high school departments. *Theory and Research in Social Education, 19,* 324–340.

Newport, E. L. (1990). Maturational constraints on language learning. *Cognitive Science, 14,* 11–28.

Newson, J., & Newson, E. (1986). Family and sex roles in middle childhood. In D. J. Hargreaves & S. M. Colley (Eds.), *The psychology of sex roles* (pp. 142–158). London: Harper & Row.

NICHD Early Child Care Research Network. (1997). The effects of infant child care on infant–mother attachment security: Results of the NICHD study of early child care. *Child Development, 68,* 860–879.

NICHD Early Child Care Research Network. (2001). Child care and family predictors of preschool attachment and stability from infancy. *Developmental Psychology, 37,* 847–862.

Nicholls, A., & Kirkland, J. (1996). Maternal sensitivity: A review of attachment literature definitions. *Early Childhood Development and Care, 120,* 55–65.

Nicholls, J. G. (1978). The development of the concepts of effort and ability, perception of academic attainment, and the understanding that difficult tasks require more than ability. *Child Development, 49,* 800–814.

Nicholls, J. G. (1984). Achievement motivation: Conceptions of ability, subjective experience, task choice, and performance. *Psychological Review, 91*(3), 328–346.

Nicholls, J. G. (1989). *The competitive ethos and democratic education.* Cambridge, MA: Harvard University Press.

Nicholls, J. G. (1990). What is ability and why are we mindful of it?: A developmental perspective. In R. Sternberg & J. Kolligian (Eds.), *Competence considered* (pp. 11–40). New Haven, CT: Yale University Press.

Nicholls, J. G., & Miller, A. (1983). The differentiation of the concepts of difficulty and ability. *Child Development, 54,* 951–959.

Nicholls, J. G., & Miller, A. (1985). Differentiation of the concepts of luck and skill. *Developmental Psychology, 21,* 76–82.

Nicholls, J. G., & Nelson, J. R. (1992). Students' conceptions of controversial knowledge. *Journal of Educational Psychology, 84,* 224–230.

Nicholls, J. G., & Thorkildsen, T. A. (1987, October). *Achievement goals and beliefs: Individual and classroom differences.* Paper presented at the annual meeting of the Society for Experimental Social Psychology, Charlottesville, NC.

Ninio, A. (1980). Picture-book reading in mother–infant dyads belonging to two subgroups in Israel. *Child Development, 51,* 587–590.

Niparko, J. K., & Blankenhorn, R. (2003). Cochlear implants in young children. *Mental Retardation and Developmental Disabilities Research Reviews, 9,* 267–275.

Noddings, N. (1984). *Caring: A femi-*nine approach to ethics and moral education.* Berkeley and Los Angeles: University of California Press.

Noddings, N. (1996). Learning to care and to be cared for. In A. M. Hoffman (Ed.), *Schools, violence, and society* (pp. 185–198). Westport, CT: Praeger/Greenwood Press.

Nolen, S. B. (1988). Reasons for studying: Motivational orientations and study strategies. *Cognition and Instruction, 5,* 269–287.

Nolen-Hoeksema, S., Wolfson, A., Mumme, D., & Guskin, K. (1995). Helplessness in children of depressed and nondepressed mothers. *Developmental Psychology, 31,* 377–387.

Nolte, R. Y., & Singer, H. (1985). Active comprehension: Teaching a process of reading comprehension and its effects on reading achievement. *Reading Teacher, 39,* 24–31.

Norwood, G. R. (1985). A society that promotes drug abuse: The effects on pre-adolescence. *Childhood Education, 61,* 267–271.

Nucci, L. P. (2003a). The development of moral reasoning. In U. Goswami (Ed.), *Blackwell handbook of childhood cognitive development* (pp. 303–325). Malden, MA: Blackwell.

Nucci, L. P. (2003b). Morality, religion and public education in pluralist democracies: A reply to Kunzman. *Journal of Moral Education, 32*(3), 263–270.

Numminen, H., Service, E., & Ruoppila, I. (2002). Working memory, intelligence and knowledge base in adult persons with intellectual disability. *Research in Developmental Disabilities, 23,* 105–118.

Nussbaum, J., & Novick, S. (1982). Alternative frameworks, conceptual conflict and accommodation: Toward a principled teaching strategy. *Instructional Science, 11,* 183–200.

Oakes, J. (1985). *Keeping track: How schools structure inequality.* New Haven, CT: Yale University Press.

Oakland, T., & Parmelee, R. (1985). Mental measurement of minority-group children. In B. B. Wolman (Ed.), *Handbook of intelligence: Theories, measurements, and applications* (pp. 699–736). New York: Wiley.

Ochoa, S. H. (2003). Assessment of culturally and linguistically diverse children. In C. R. Reynolds & R. W. Kamphaus (Eds.), *Handbook of psychological and educational assessment of children* (pp. 563–583). New York: Guilford Press.

Ochs, E., & Schieffelin, B. (1995). The impact of language socialization on grammatical development. In P.

Fletcher & B. MacWhinney (Eds.), *The handbook of child psychology* (pp. 73–94). Oxford, UK: Blackwell.

Oczkus, L. D. (2003). *Reciprocal teaching at work: Strategies for improving reading comprehension.* Newark, DE: International Reading Association.

Oden, G. C. (1987). Concept, knowledge, and thought. *Annual Review of Psychology, 38,* 203–227.

O'Donnell, A. M., & King, A. (1999). *Cognitive perspectives on peer learning.* Mahwah, NJ: Erlbaum.

O'Donnell, C. R., Lydgate, T., & Fo, W. S. O. (1979). The buddy system: Review and follow-up. *Child Behavior Therapy, 1,* 161–169.

Ogbu, J. U. (1974). *The next generation: An ethnography of education in an urban neighborhood.* New York: Academic Press.

Ogbu, J. U. (1978). *Minority education and caste: The American system in cross-cultural perspective.* New York: Academic Press.

Ogbu, J. U. (1981). Origins of human competence: A cultural–ecological perspective. *Child Development, 52,* 413–429.

Ogbu, J. U. (1987). Variability in minority school performance: A problem in search of an explanation. *Anthropology and Education Quarterly, 18,* 312–334.

Ogbu, J. U. (1991). Immigrant and involuntary minorities in comparative perspective. In M. A. Gibson & J. U. Ogbu (Eds.), *Minority status and schooling: A comparative study of immigrant and involuntary minorities* (pp. 3–33). New York: Garland Press.

Ogbu, J. U. (1997). Understanding the school performance of urban blacks: Some essential background knowledge. In H. J. Walberg & O. Reyes (Eds.), *Children and youth: Interdisciplinary perspectives: Issues in children's and families' lives* (Vol. 7, pp. 190–222). Thousand Oaks, CA: Sage.

Ogbu, J. U., with Davis, A. (2003). *Black American students in an affluent suburb: A study of academic disengagement.* Mahwah, NJ: Erlbaum.

Ogbu, J. U., & Stern, P. (2001). Caste status and intellectual development. In R. J. Sternberg & E. L. Grigorenko (Eds.), *Environmental effects on cognitive abilities* (pp. 3–37). Mahwah, NJ: Erlbaum.

O'Heron, C. A., & Orlofsky, J. L. (1990). Stereotypic and nonstereotypic sex role trait and behavior orientations, gender identity, and psychological adjustment. *Jour-*

nal of Personality and Social Psychology, 58(1), 134–143.

Okonkwo, R. (1997). Moral development and culture in Kohlberg's theory: A Nigerian (Igbo) evidence. *IFE Psychologia: An International Journal, 5*(2), 117–128.

Oksaar, E. (1977). On becoming trilingual. In C. Molony (Ed.), *Deutsch in Kontaki mit anderen Sprachen* (pp. 296–306). Kronberg, Germany: Scriptor Verlag.

Oller, D. K., & Eilers, R. E. (1988). The role of audition in babbling. *Child Development, 59*, 441–449.

Olson, G. M., & Olson, J. S. (2003). Human-computer interaction: Psychological aspects of the human use of computing. *Annual Review of Psychology, 54*, 491–516.

Olson, R. K., Kliegl, R., Davidson, B. J., & Foltz, G. (1985). Individual and developmental differences in reading disability. In G. E. MacKinnon & T. G. Waller (Eds.), *Reading research: Advances in theory and practice* (Vol. 4, pp. 1–64). Orlando, FL: Academic Press.

Olweus, D. (1980). Familial and temperamental determinants of aggressive behavior in adolescent boys: A causal analysis. *Developmental Psychology, 16*, 644–660.

Olweus, D. (1993). *Bullying at school: What we know and what we can do.* Oxford, UK: Blackwell.

Olweus, D. (2003). Social problems in school. In A. Slater & G. Bremner (Eds.), *An introduction to developmental psychology* (pp. 434–454). Malden, MA: Blackwell.

107th Congress. (2002). *The No Child Left Behind act of 2001.* Washington, DC: U.S. Congress.

Orlofsky, J. L., & O'Heron, C. A. (1987). Stereotypic and nonstereotypic sex role trait and behavior orientations: Implications for personal adjustment. *Journal of Personality and Social Psychology, 52*(5), 1034–1042.

Ornstein, P. A., Naus, M. J., & Liberty, C. (1975). Rehearsal and organizational processes in children's memory. *Child Development, 46*, 818–830.

Ornstein, R. (1977). *The psychology of consciousness.* New York: Harcourt, Brace, Jovanovich.

Ornstein, R. (1978). The split and whole brain. *Human Nature, 1* 76–83.

Osborne, R., & Freyberg, P. (1985). *Learning in science: The implications of children's science.* London: Heinemann.

O'Sullivan, J. T., & Pressley, M. (1984). Completeness of instruction and strategy transfer. *Journal of Experimental Child Psychology, 38*, 275–288.

Osterman, K. (2000). Students' need for belonging in the school community. *Review of Educational Research, 70*, 323–367.

Oyama, S. (1976). Sensitive period for the acquisition of a nonnative phonological system. *Journal of Psycholinguistic Research, 5*, 261–283.

Padron, Y. (1992). The effect of strategy instruction on bilingual students' cognitive strategy use in reading. *Bilingual Research Journal, 16*, 35–52.

Pagliaro, A. M., & Pagliaro, L. A. (1996). *Substance abuse among children and adolescents.* New York: Wiley.

Paivio, A. (1971). *Imagery and verbal processes.* New York: Holt, Rinehart & Winston.

Paivio, A. (1986). *Mental representations: A dual-coding approach.* New York: Oxford University Press.

Palincsar, A. S. (1998). Social constructivist perspectives on teaching and learning. *Annual Review of Psychology, 49*, 345–375.

Palincsar, A. S. (2003). Ann L. Brown: Advancing a theoretical model of learning and instruction. In B. J. Zimmerman & D. H. Schunk (Eds.), *Educational psychology: A century of contributions* (pp. 459–475). Mahwah, NJ: Erlbaum.

Palincsar, A. S., & Brown, A. L. (1984). Reciprocal teaching of comprehension-fostering and monitoring activities. *Cognition and Instruction, 1*, 117–175.

Palincsar, A. S., & Herrenkohl, L. R. (1999). Designing collaborative contexts: Lessons from three research programs. In A. M. O'Donnell & A. King (Eds.), *Cognitive perspectives on peer learning: The Rutgers Invitational Symposium on Education Series* (pp. 151–177). Mahwah, NJ: Erlbaum.

Palladino, P., Poli, P., Masi, G., & Marcheschi, M. (2000). The relation between metacognition and depressive symptoms in preadolescents with learning disabilities: Data in support of Borkowski's model. *Learning Disabilities Research and Practice, 15*, 142–148.

Palmer, S. L., Gajjar, A., Reddick, W. E., Glass, J. O., Kun, L. E., Wu, S., et al. (2003). Predicting intellectual outcome among children treated with 35–40 Gy craniospinal irradiation for medulloblastoma. *Neuropsychology, 17*, 548–555.

Palmonari, A., Pombeni, M. L., & Kirchler, E. (1989). Peer groups and evolution of the self-system in adolescence. *European Journal of Psychology of Education, 4*, 3–15.

Panksepp, J. (1986). The neurochemistry of behavior. *Annual Review of Psychology, 7*, 77–108.

Papanicolaou, A. C., Pugh, K. R., Simos, P. G., & Mencl, W. E. (2004). Functional brain imaging: An introduction to concepts and applications. In P. McCardle & V. Chhabra (Eds.), *The voice of evidence in reading research* (pp. 383–416). Baltimore: Brookes.

Parents in Action on Special Education v. Hannon et al. (1980, July). No. 74 C 3586, United States District of Illinois, Eastern Division, slip opinion.

Paris, S. G., Lipson, M. Y., & Wixson, K. K. (1983). Becoming a strategic reader. *Contemporary Educational Psychology, 8*, 293–316.

Park, H.-S., & Gaylord-Ross, R. (1989). A problem-solving approach to social skills training in employment settings with mentally retarded youth. *Journal of Applied Behavior Analysis, 22*, 373–380.

Park, K. A., & Waters, E. (1989). Security of attachment and preschool friendships. *Child Development, 60*, 1076–1081.

Park, K. J. (2001). Attachment security of 12 month old Korean infants: Relations with maternal sensitivity and infants' temperament. *Early Child Development and Care, 167*, 27–38.

Parke, R. D. (1969). Effectiveness of punishment as an interaction of intensity, timing, agent nurturance and cognitive structuring. *Child Development, 40*, 213–236.

Parke, R. D. (1974). Rules, roles, and resistance to deviation in children: Explorations in punishment, discipline and self-control. In A. D. Pick (Ed.), *Minnesota Symposium on Child Psychology* (Vol. 8, pp. 111–144). Minneapolis: University of Minnesota Press.

Parke, R. D. (2002). Fathers and families. In M. H. Bornstein (Ed.), *Handbook of parenting: Vol. 3. Being and becoming a parent* (2nd ed., pp. 27–73). Mahwah, NJ: Erlbaum.

Parke, R. D., & Buriel, R. (1998). Socialization in the family: Ethnic and ecological perspectives. In N. Eisenberg (Ed.), *Handbook of child psychology: Vol. 3. Social, emotional, and personality development* (5th ed., pp. 463–552). New York: Wiley.

Parke, R. D., & Collmer, C. W. (1975). Child abuse: An interdisciplinary analysis. In E. M. Hetherington, J. W. Hagen, R. Kron, & A. H. Stein (Eds.), *Review of child development research* (Vol. 5, pp. 509–590). Chicago: University of Chicago Press.

Parke, R. D., & Slaby, R. G. (1983). The development of aggression. In M. Hetherington (Vol. Ed.) & P. H. Mussen (Gen. Ed.), *Handbook of child psychology: Vol. 4. Socialization, personality, and social development* (4th ed., pp. 547–642). New York: Wiley.

Parke, R. D., & Suomi, S. J. (1980). Adult male–infant relationships: Human and nonprimate evidence. In K. Immelmann, G. Barlow, M. Main, & L. Petrinovich (Eds.), *Behavioral development: The Bielefeld Interdisciplinary Project* (pp. 700–725). New York: Cambridge University Press.

Parke, R. D., & Walters, R. H. (1967). Some factors influencing the efficacy of punishment training for inducing response inhibition. *Monographs of the Society for Research in Child Development, 32*(1, Serial No. 109).

Parker, L. E., & Lepper, M. R. (1992). Effects of fantasy contexts on children's learning and motivation: Making learning more fun. *Journal of Personality and Social Psychology, 62*, 625–633.

Parker, S. T., & Gibson, K. R. (Eds.) (1990). *"Language" and intelligence in monkeys and apes.* Cambridge, UK: Cambridge University Press.

Parkin, A. J., & Streete, S. (1988). Implicit and explicit memory in young children and adults. *British Journal of Psychology, 79*, 361–369.

Parten, M. (1932). Social participation among preschool children. *Journal of Abnormal and Social Psychology, 27*, 243–269.

Parsons, J., & Ruble, D. N. (1977). The development of achievement-related expectancies. *Child Development, 48*, 1075–1079.

Pascarella, E. T., & Terenzini, P. T. (1991). *How college affects students.* San Francisco: Jossey-Bass.

Pascual-Leone, J. (1970). A mathematical model for the transition rule in Piaget's developmental stages. *Acta Psychologica, 32*, 301–345.

Pastor, D. L. (1981). The quality of mother–infant attachment and its relationship to toddler's initial so-

ciability with peers. *Developmental Psychology, 17*, 326–335.

Patrick, B. C., Skinner, E. A., & Connell, J. A. (1993). What motivates children's behavior and emotion?: Joint effects of perceived control and autonomy in the academic domain. *Journal of Personality and Social Psychology, 65*, 781–791.

Patterson, C. J. (1992). Children of lesbian and gay parents. *Child Development, 63*, 1025–1042.

Patterson, C. J. (2002). Lesbian and gay parenthood. In M. H. Bornstein (Ed.), *Handbook of parenting: Vol. 3. Being and becoming a parent* (2nd ed., pp. 317–338). Mahwah, NJ: Erlbaum.

Patterson, C. J. (2003). Children of gay and lesbian parents. In L. D. Garnets & D. C. Kimmel (Eds.), *Psychological perspectives on lesbian, gay, and bisexual experiences* (2nd ed., pp. 497–548). New York: Columbia University Press.

Patterson, C. J., & Mischel, W. (1976). Effects of temptation-inhibiting and task-facilitating plans on self-control. *Journal of Personality and Social Psychology, 33*, 209–217.

Patterson, G. R. (1976). The aggressive child: Victim and architect of a coercive system. In L. A. Hamerlynck, L. C. Handy, & E. J. Mash (Eds.), *Behavior modification and families: Vol. 1. Theory and research* (pp. 267–316). New York: Brunner/Mazel.

Patterson, G. R. (1986). Performance models for antisocial boys. *American Psychologist, 41*, 432–444.

Patterson, G. R. (1996). Some characteristics of a developmental theory for early-onset delinquency. In M. F. Lenzenweger & J. J. Haugard (Eds.), *Frontiers of developmental psychopathology* (pp. 81–124). New York: Oxford University Press.

Patterson, G. R., DeBaryshe, B. D., & Ramsey, E. (1989). A developmental perspective on antisocial behavior. *American Psychologist, 44*, 329–335.

Patterson, G. R., & Fleischman, M. J. (1979). Maintenance of treatment effects: Some considerations concerning family systems and follow-up data. *Behavior Therapy, 10*, 168–185.

Paul, P. V. (2003). Processes and components of reading. In M. Marschark & P. E. Spencer (Eds.), *Oxford handbook of deaf studies, language, and education* (pp. 97–109). New York: Oxford University Press.

Payne, A. C., Whitehurst, G. J., &

Angell, A. L. (1994). The role of home literacy environment in the development of language ability in preschool children from low-income families. *Early Childhood Research Quarterly, 9*, 427–440.

Peal, E., & Lambert, W. E. (1962). The relation of bilingualism to intelligence. *Psychological Monographs, 546*, 1–23.

Pearson, B. Z. (1993). Predictive validity of the Scholastic Aptitude Test (SAT) for Hispanic bilingual students. *Hispanic Journal of the Behavioral Sciences, 15*, 342–356.

Pearson, B. Z., Fernandez, S. C., Lewedeg, V., & Oller, D. K. (1997). The relation of input factors to lexical learning by bilingual infants. *Applied Psycholinguistics, 18*, 41–58.

Pearson, D. A., & Lane, D. M. (1991). Auditory attention switching: A developmental study. *Journal of Experimental Child Psychology, 51*, 320–334.

Pederson, D. A., & Moran, G. (1995). Maternal behavior Q-set. In E. Waters, B. E. Vaughn, G. Posada, & K. Kondo-Ikemura (Eds.), Caregiving, cultural, and cognitive perspectives on secure-base behavior and working-models. *Monographs of the Society for Research in Child Development, 60*(Nos. 2–3, Serial No. 244), 247–254.

Pederson, D. R., Gleason, K. E., Moran, G., & Bento, S. (1998). Maternal attachment representations, maternal sensitivity, and the infant–mother attachment relationship. *Developmental Psychology, 34*, 925–933.

Pederson, D. R., Moran, G., Sitko, C., Campbell, K., Ghesquire, K., & Acton, H. (1990). Maternal sensitivity and security of infant–mother attachment: A Q-sort study. *Child Development, 61*, 1974–1983.

Pellegrini, A. D., Perlmutter, J. C., Galda, L., & Brody, G. H. (1990). Joint reading between black Head Start children and their mothers. *Child Development, 61*, 443–453.

Pennington, B. F. (1989). Using genetics to understand dyslexia. *Annals of Dyslexia, 39*, 81–93.

Pennington, B. F., Groisser, D., & Welsh, M. C. (1993). Contrasting cognitive deficits in attention deficit hyperactivity disorder versus reading disability. *Developmental Psychology, 29*, 511–523.

Pennington, B. F., Van Orden, G. C., Smith, S. D., Green, P. A., & Haith, M. M. (1990). Phonological processing skills and deficits in adult dyslexics. *Child Development, 61,* 1753–1778.

Pennock-Román, M. (1992). Interpreting test performance in selective admissions for Hispanic students. In K. F. Geisinger (Ed.), *Psychological testing of Hispanics* (pp. 99–136). Washington, DC: American Psychological Association.

Pepler, D. J., & Rubin, K. H. (Eds.). (1991). *The development and treatment of childhood aggression.* Hillsdale, NJ: Erlbaum.

Perez, B. (2004). *Becoming biliterate: A study of two-way bilingual immersion education.* Mahwah, NJ: Erlbaum.

Perfetti, C. A. (1992). The representation problem in reading acquisition. In P. B. Gough, L. C. Ehri, & R. Treiman (Eds.), *Reading acquisition* (pp. 145–174). Hillsdale, NJ: Erlbaum.

Perfetti, C. A., Beck, I., Bell, L., & Hughes, C. (1987). Phonemic knowledge and learning to read are reciprocal: A longitudinal study of first grade children. *Merrill–Palmer Quarterly, 33,* 283–319.

Perlman, S. M. (1973). Cognitive abilities of children with hormone abnormalities: Screening by psychoeducational tests. *Journal of Learning Disabilities, 6,* 21–29.

Perner, J. (1991). *Understanding the representational mind.* Cambridge, MA: MIT Press.

Perry, D. G., & Bussey, K. (1979). The social learning theory of sex differences: Imitation is alive and well. *Journal of Personality and Social Psychology, 37,* 1699–1712.

Perry, M., VanderStoep, S. W., & Yu, S. L. (1993). Asking questions in first-grade mathematics classes: Potential influences on mathematical thought. *Journal of Educational Psychology, 85*(1), 31–40.

Pesenti, M., Thioux, M., Seron, X., & DeVolder, A. (2000). Neuroanatomical substrates of Arabic number processing, numerical comparison, and simple addition: A PET study. *Journal of Cognitive Neuroscience, 12,* 461–479.

Peterson, D. (1988). The epidemiology of sudden infant death syndrome. In J. Culbertson, H. Krous, & R. D. Bendell (Eds.), *Sudden infant death syndrome: Medical aspects and psychological management* (pp. 3–17). Baltimore: Johns Hopkins University Press.

Petitto, L. A., Holowka, S., Sergio, L. E., Levy, B., & Ostry, D. J. (2004). Baby hands that move to the rhythm of language: Hearing babies acquiring sign languages babble silently on the hands. *Cognition, 93,* 43–73.

Petitto, L. A., Holowka, S., Sergio, L. E., & Ostry, D. J. (2001). Language rhythms in baby hand movements. *Nature, 413,* 35–36.

Petitto, L. A., & Marantette, P. F. (1991). Babbling in the manual mode: Evidence for the ontogeny of language. *Science, 251,* 299–322.

Pfundt, H., & Duit, R. (1991). *Bibliography: Students' alternative frameworks and science education* (3rd ed.). Kiel, Germany: IPN.

Phelps, L. (1999). Low-level lead exposure: Implications for research and practice. *School Psychology Review, 28,* 477–492.

Phelps, M. E., Mazziotta, J. C., & Huang, S.-C. (1982). Study of cerebral function with positron computed tomography. *Journal of Cerebral Blood Flow Metabolism, 2,* 113–162.

Philips, S. U. (1983). *The invisible culture: Communication in classroom and community on the Warm Springs Indian reservation.* New York: Longman.

Phinney, J. S. (1989). Stages of ethnic identity development in minority group adolescents. *Journal of Early Adolescence, 9,* 34–49.

Piaget, J. (1926). *The language and thought of the child.* London: Routledge & Kegan Paul.

Piaget, J. (1929). *The child's conception of the world.* London: Routledge & Kegan Paul.

Piaget, J. (1962). *Play, dreams, and imitation in childhood.* New York: Norton.

Piaget, J. (1965). *The moral judgment of the child.* New York: Free Press. (Original work published in French in 1932)

Piaget, J. (1967). *Biologie et connaissance.* Paris: Gallimard.

Piaget, J. (1970). Piaget's theory. In P. H. Mussen (Ed.), *Carmichael's Manual of child psychology* (3rd ed., Vol. 1, pp. 703–732). New York: Wiley.

Piaget, J. (1972). Intellectual evolution from adolescence to adulthood. *Human Development, 15,* 1–12.

Piaget, J. (1983). Piaget's theory. In W. Kesson (Vol. Ed.) & P. H. Mussen (Gen. Ed.), *History, theory, and methods: Vol. 1. Handbook of child psychology* (pp. 103–128). New York: Wiley.

Piaget, J. (1995). *Sociological studies.* New York: Routledge.

Piaget, J., & Inhelder, B. (1973). *Memory and intelligence.* New York: Basic Books.

Pillemer, D. B., & White, S. H. (1989). Childhood events recalled by children and adults. In H. W. Reese (Ed.), *Advances in child development and behavior* (Vol. 21, pp. 297–340). San Diego, CA: Academic Press.

Pinker, S. (1994). *The language instinct: How the mind creates language.* New York: Morrow.

Pintrich, P. R., & De Groot, E. V. (1990). Motivational and self-regulated learning components of classroom academic performance. *Journal of Educational Psychology, 82,* 33–40.

Plake, B. S., Impara, J. C., & Spies, R. A. (Eds.). (2003). *The fifteenth mental measurements yearbook.* Lincoln, NE: Buros.

Pleiss, M. K. & Feldhusen, J. F. (1995). Mentors, role models, and heroes in the lives of gifted children. *Educational Psychologist, 30*(3), 159–169.

Plomin, R., DeFries, J. C., & Fulker, D. W. (1988). *Nature and nurture during infancy and early childhood.* New York: Cambridge University Press.

Plomin, R., DeFries, J. C., & McClearn, G. E. (1990). *Behavioral genetics: A primer* (2nd ed.). New York: Freeman.

Plomin, R., Defries, J. C., McClearn, G. E., & McGuffin, P. (Eds.). (2000). *Behavioral genetics.* San Francisco: Freeman.

Plomin, R., & McClearn, G. E. (Eds.). (1993). *Nature, nature, and psychology.* Washington, DC: American Psychological Association.

Plomin, R., & Walker, S. O. (2003). Genetics and educational psychology. *British Journal of Educational Psychology, 73,* 3–14.

Plutchik, R. (1995). A theory of ego defenses. In H. R. Conte & R. Plutchik (Eds.), *Ego defenses: Theory and measurement* (pp. 13–37). New York: Wiley.

Poissonet, C., LaValle, M., & Burdi, A. (1988). Growth and development of adipose tissue. *Journal of Pediatrics, 113,* 1–9.

Polit, D. F., & Falbo, T. (1987). Only children and personality development: A quantitative review. *Journal of Marriage and the Family, 49,* 309–325.

Pollitt, E. (1990). *Malnutrition and infection in the classroom.* Paris: UNESCO.

Polya, G. (1954a). *Mathematics and plausible reasoning: Induction and analogy in mathematics.* Princeton, NJ: Princeton University Press.

Polya, G. (1954b). *Mathematics and plausible reasoning: Induction and* analogy in mathematics: Patterns of plausible inference. Princeton, NJ: Princeton University Press.

Pomerantz, E. M., & Ruble, D. N. (1998). The role of maternal control in the development of sex differences in child self-evaluative factions. Child Development, 69, 458–478.

Popenoe, J. (1970). Inside Summerhill. New York: Hart.

Porter, A. C. (1991). Good teaching of worthwhile mathematics to disadvantaged students. In M. S. Knapp & P. M. Shields (Eds.), Better schooling for the children of poverty: Alternatives to conventional wisdom (pp. 125–148). Berkeley, CA: McCutchan.

Posada, G., Gao, Y., Wu, F., Posada, R., Tascon, M., Schöelmerich, A., et al. (1995). The secure-base phenomenon across cultures: Children's behavior, mothers' preferences, and experts' concepts. In E. Waters, B. E. Vaughn, G. Posada, & K. Kondo-Ikemura (Eds.), Caregiving, cultural, and cognitive perspectives on secure-base behavior and working-models. Monographs of the Society for Research in Child Development, 60(Nos. 2–3, Serial No. 244), 27–48.

Posner, G. J., Strike, K. A., Hewson, P. W., & Gertzog, W. A. (1982). Accommodation of a scientific conception: Toward a theory of conceptual change. Science Education, 66, 211–227.

Posner, M. I., & Keele, S. W. (1968). On the genesis of abstract ideas. Journal of Experimental Psychology, 77, 353–363.

Posner, M. I., & Keele, S. W. (1970). Retention of abstract ideas. Journal of Experimental Psychology, 83, 304–308.

Posner, M. I., & Rothbart, M. K. (2005). Influencing brain networks: Implications for education. Trends in Cognitive Sciences, 9(3), 99–103.

Powell, R. E., Locke, D. C., & Spinthall, N. A. (1991). Female offenders and their guards: A programme to promote moral and ego development of both groups. Journal of Moral Education, 20, 191–203.

Power, D., & Leigh, G. R. (2003). Curriculum: Cultural and communicative contexts. In M. Marschark & P. E. Spencer (Eds.), Oxford handbook of deaf studies, language, and education (pp. 38–51). New York: Oxford University Press.

Power, F. C., & Power, M. R. (1992). A raft of hope: Democratic education and the challenge of pluralism. Journal of Moral Education, 21, 193–205.

Powlishta, K. K., Sen, M. G., Serbin, L. A., Poulin-Dubois, D., & Eichstedt, J. A. (2001). From infancy through middle childhood: The role of cognitive and social factors in becoming gendered. In R. K. Inger (Ed.), Handbook of psychology of women and gender (pp. 116–132). New York: Wiley.

Pratt, A. C., & Brady, S. (1988). Relation of phonological awareness to reading disability in children and adults. Journal of Educational Psychology, 80, 319–323.

Prechtl, H. F. R. (1986). New perspectives in early human development. European Journal of Obstetrics, Gynecology, and Reproductive Biology, 21, 347–354.

Pressley, G. M. (1976). Mental imagery helps eight-year-olds remember what they read. Journal of Educational Psychology, 68, 355–359.

Pressley, M. (1977). Imagery and children's learning: Putting the picture in developmental perspective. Review of Educational Research, 47, 586–622.

Pressley, M. (1979). Increasing children's self-control through cognitive interventions. Review of Educational Research, 49, 319–370.

Pressley, M. (Ed.). (2002). Teaching service and alternative teacher education: Notre Dame's Alliance for Catholic Education. South Bend, IN: University of Notre Dame Press.

Pressley, M., & Afflerbach, P. (1995). Verbal protocols of reading: The nature of constructively responsive reading. Hillsdale, NJ: Erlbaum.

Pressley, M., Allington, R. L., Wharton-McDonald, R., Block, C. C., & Morrow, L. M. (2001). Learning to read: Lessons from exemplary first-grade classrooms. New York: Guilford Press.

Pressley, M., Borkowski, J. G., & O'Sullivan, J. T. (1984). Memory strategy instruction is made of this: Metamemory and durable strategy use. Educational Psychologist, 19, 94–107.

Pressley, M., Borkowski, J. G., & O'Sullivan, J. T. (1985). Children's metamemory and the teaching of strategies. In D. L. Forrest-Pressley, G. E. MacKinnon, & T. G. Waller (Eds.), Metacognition, cognition, and human performance (pp. 111–153). Orlando, FL: Academic Press.

Pressley, M., Dolezal, S. E., Raphael, L. M., Mohan, L., Roehrig, A. D., & Bogner, K. (2003). Motivating primary-grade students. New York: Guilford Press.

Pressley, M., Dolezal, S., Raphael, L. M., Mohan, L., Roehrig, A., & Bogner, K. (2003). Increasing academic motivation in primary-grades classrooms. Catholic Education: A Journal of Inquiry and Practice, 6.

Pressley, M., & El-Dinary, P. B. (1997). What we know about translating comprehension-strategies instruction research into practice. Journal of Learning Disabilities, 30(5), 486–488, 512.

Pressley, M., El-Dinary, P. B., Gaskins, I., Schuder, T., Bergman, J. L., Almasi, J., et al. (1992). Beyond direct explanation: Transactional instruction of reading comprehension strategies. Elementary School Journal, 92, 513–556.

Pressley, M., Forrest-Pressley, D., Elliott-Faust, D. L., & Miller, G. E. (1985). Children's use of cognitive strategies, how to teach strategies, and what to do if they can't be taught. In M. Pressley & C. J. Brainerd (Eds.), Cognitive learning and memory in children: Progress in cognitive development research (pp. 1–47). New York: Springer-Verlag.

Pressley, M., Gaskins, I. W., Cunicelli, E. A., Bardick, N. J., Schaub-Matt, M., Lee, D. S., et al. (1991). Strategy instruction at Benchmark School: A faculty interview study. Learning Disability Quarterly, 14, 19–48.

Pressley, M., Gaskins, I. W., Wile, D., Cunicelli, E. A., & Sheridan, J. (1991). Teaching literacy strategies across the curriculum: A case study at Benchmark School. In S. McCormick & J. Zutell (Eds.), 40th yearbook of the National Reading Conference (pp. 219–228). Chicago: National Reading Conference.

Pressley, M., & Ghatala, E. S. (1989). Metacognitive benefits of taking a test for children and young adolescents. Journal of Experimental Child Psychology, 47, 430–450.

Pressley, M., & Ghatala, E. S. (1990). Self-regulated learning: Monitoring learning from text. Educational Psychologist, 25, 19–34.

Pressley, M., & Grossman, L. R. (Eds.). (1994). Recovery of memories of childhood sexual abuse [Special issue]. Applied Cognitive Psychology, 8(4).

Pressley, M., Heisel, B. E., McCormick, C. G., & Nakamura, G.

V. (1982). Memory strategy instruction with children. In C. J. Brainerd & M. Pressley (Eds.), *Progress in cognitive development research: Vol. 2. Verbal processes in children* (pp. 125–159). New York: Springer-Verlag.

Pressley, M., & Levin, J. R. (1977a). Developmental differences in subjects' associative learning strategies and performance: Assessing a hypothesis. *Journal of Experimental Child Psychology, 24*, 431–439.

Pressley, M., & Levin, J. R. (1977b). Task parameters affecting the efficacy of a visual imagery learning strategy in younger and older children. *Journal of Experimental Child Psychology, 24* 53–59.

Pressley, M., Levin, J. R., & Ghatala, E. S. (1984). Memory strategy monitoring in adults and children. *Journal of Verbal Learning and Verbal Behavior, 23*, 270–288.

Pressley, M., Levin, J. R., Ghatala, E. S., & Ahmad, M. (1987). Test monitoring in young grade-school children. *Journal of Experimental Child Psychology, 43*, 96–111.

Pressley, M., & MacFadyen, J. (1983). The development of mnemonic mediator usage at testing. *Child Development, 54*, 474–479.

Pressley, M., with McCormick, C. B. (1995). *Advanced educational psychology for educators, researchers, and policymakers.* New York: HarperCollins.

Pressley, M., Raphael, L., Gallagher, J. D., & DiBella, J. (2004). Providence–St. Mel School: How a school that works for African-American students works. *Journal of Educational Psychology, 96*, 216–235.

Pressley, M., Ross, K. A., Levin, J. R., & Ghatala, E. S. (1984). The role of strategy utility knowledge in children's strategy decision making. *Journal of Experimental Child Psychology, 38*, 491–504.

Prince, G. (1978). Putting the other half of the brain to work. *Training: The Magazine of Human Resources Development, 15*, 57–61.

Pulkkinen, L. (1982). Self-control and continuity in childhood and delayed adolescence. In P. Baltes & O. Brin (Eds.), *Life span development and behavior* (Vol. 4, pp. 64–107). New York: Academic Press.

Purcell, P., & Stewart, L. (1990). Dick and Jane in 1989. *Sex Roles, 22*, 177–185.

Purcell-Gates, V. (1995). *Other people's worlds: The cycle of low literacy.* Cambridge, MA: Harvard University Press.

Putallaz, M. (1987). Maternal behavior and children's sociometric status. *Child Development, 58*, 324–340.

Putnam, R., Lampert, M., & Peterson, P. L. (1990). Alternative perspectives on knowing mathematics in elementary schools. In C. B. Cazden (Ed.), *Review of research in education* (Vol. 16, pp. 57–150). Washington, DC: American Educational Research Association.

Qin, Z., Johnson, D. W., & Johnson, R. T. (1995). Cooperative versus competitive efforts and problem solving. *Review of Educational Research, 65*, 129–143.

Quay, S. (1993). *Bilingual evidence against the principle of contrast.* Paper presented at the 67th annual meeting of the Linguistic Society of America, Los Angeles.

Quiggle, N. L., Garber, J., Panak, W. F., & Dodge, K. A. (1992). Social information processing in aggressive and depressed children. *Child Development, 63*, 1305–1320.

Quigley, S. P., & Paul, P. V. (1984). *Language and deafness.* San Diego, CA: College Hill Press.

Rabinowitz, M., Freeman, K., & Cohen, S. (1992). Use and maintenance of strategies: The influence of accessibility to knowledge. *Journal of Educational Psychology, 84*, 211–218.

Rabinowitz, M., & Glaser, R. (1985). Cognitive structure and process in high competent performance. In F. D. Horowitz & M. O'Brien (Eds.), *The gifted and talented: Developmental perspectives* (pp. 75–98). Washington, DC: American Psychological Association.

Rack, J. P., Snowling, M. J., & Olson, R. K. (1992). The nonword reading deficit in developmental dyslexia: A review. *Reading Research Quarterly, 27*, 28–53.

Radford, J. (1990). *Child prodigies and exceptional early achievers.* New York: Free Press.

Radke-Yarrow, M., Zahn-Waxler, C., & Chapman, M. (1983). Children's prosocial dispositions and behavior. In E. M. Hetherington (Vol. Ed.) & P. H. Mussen (Gen. Ed.), *Handbook of child psychology: Vol. 4. Socialization, personality, and social development* (pp. 469–545). New York: Wiley.

Rais-Bahrami, K., Short, B. L., & Batshaw, M. L. (2002). Premature and small-for-dates infants. In M. L. Batshaw (Ed.), *Children with disabilities* (5th ed., pp. 85–106). Baltimore: Brookes.

Rallison, M. L. (1986). *Growth disorders in infants, children, and adolescents.* New York: Wiley.

Ramey, C. T. (1992). High-risk children and IQ: Altering intergenerational patterns. *Intelligence, 16*, 239–256.

Ramey, C. T., & Campbell, F. A. (1987). The Carolina Abecedarian Project: An educational experiment concerning human malleability. In J. J. Gallagher & C. T. Ramey (Eds.), *The malleability of children.* Baltimore: Brookes.

Ramey, C. T., Campbell, F. A., & Ramey, S. L. (1999). Early intervention: Successful pathways to improving intellectual development. *Developmental Neuropsychology, 16*, 385–392.

Ramey, C. T., Ramey, S. L., & Lanzi, R. G. (2001). Intelligence and experience. In R. J. Sternberg & E. L. Grigorenko (Eds.), *Environmental effects on cognitive abilities* (pp. 83–115). Mahwah, NJ: Erlbaum.

Randhawa, B. S., Beamer, J. E., & Lundberg, I. (1993). Role of mathematics self-efficacy in the structural model of mathematics achievement. *Journal of Educational Psychology, 85*, 41–48.

Rathunde, K., & Csikszentmihalyi, M. (1991). Adolescent happiness and family interaction. In K. Pillemer & K. McCartney (Eds.), *Parent–child relations throughout life* (pp. 143–162). Hillsdale, NJ: Erlbaum.

Ratner, H. H. (1980). The role of social context in memory development. In M. Perlmutter (Ed.), *Children's memory: New directions for child development* (Vol. 10, pp. 49–67). San Francisco: Jossey-Bass.

Ratner, H. H. (1984). Memory demands and the development of young children's memory. *Child Development, 55*, 2173–2191.

Rawls, J. (1971). *A theory of justice.* Cambridge, MA: Harvard University Press.

Rayner, K., & Pollatsek, A. (1989). *The psychology of reading.* Englewood Cliffs, NJ: Prentice-Hall.

Raz, S., Lauterbach, M. D., Hopkins, T. L., Glogowski, B. K., Porter, C. L., Riggs, W. W., et al. (1995). A female advantage in cognitive recovery from early cerebral insult. *Developmental Psychology, 31*, 958–966.

Redd, W. H., Morris, E. K., & Martin, J. A. (1975). Effects of positive and negative adult–child interaction on children's social preferences. *Journal of Experimental Child Psychology, 19*, 153–164.

Redlinger, W., & Park, T. Z. (1980). Language mixing in young bilinguals. *Journal of Child Language, 3,* 449–455.

Reed, S. K. (1972). Pattern recognition and categorization. *Cognitive Psychology, 3,* 382–407.

Reese, E., Haden, C., & Fivush, R. (1993). Mother–child conversations about the past: Relations of style and memory over time. *Cognitive Development, 8,* 141–148.

Reid, M. K., & Borkowski, J. G. (1987). Causal attributions of hyperactive children: Implications for teaching strategies and self-control. *Journal of Educational Psychology, 79,* 296–307.

Reis, S. M., & Renzulli, J. S. (2004). Current research on the social and emotional development of gifted and talented students: Good news and future possibilities. *Psychology in the Schools, 41,* 119–130.

Renick, M. J., & Harter, S. (1989). Impact of social comparisons on the developing self-perceptions of learning disabled students. *Journal of Educational Psychology, 81,* 631–638.

Renninger, K. A. (1990). Children's play interests, representation, and activity. In R. Fivush & J. Hudson (Eds.), *Knowing and remembering in young children* (pp. 127–165). Cambridge, MA: Cambridge University Press.

Renninger, K. A., & Wozniak, R. H. (1985). Effect of interest on attentional shift, recognition, and recall in young children. *Developmental Psychology, 21,* 624–632.

Renzulli, J. S. (1986). The three-ring conception of giftedness: A developmental model for creative productivity. In R. J. Sternberg & J. E. Davidson (Eds.), *Conceptions of giftedness* (pp. 53–92). Cambridge, UK: Cambridge University Press.

Research Advisory Committee. (1989). The mathematics education of underserved and underrepresented groups: A continuing challenge. *Journal for Research in Mathematics Education, 20,* 371–375.

Resnick, L. B., Levine, J. M., & Teasley, S. D. (Eds.). (1991). *Perspectives on socially shared cognition.* Washington, DC: American Psychological Association.

Resnick, S. M., Berenbaum, S. A., Gottesman, I. I., & Bouchard, T. J. (1986). Early hormonal influences on cognitive functioning in congenital adrenal hyperplasia. *Developmental Psychology, 22,* 191–198.

Rest, J. (1968). *Developmental hierarchy in preference and comprehension of moral judgment.* Unpublished doctoral dissertation, University of Chicago.

Rest, J. (1979). *Development in judging moral issues.* Minneapolis: University of Minnesota Press.

Rest, J., Thoma, S., & Edwards, L. (1997). Designing and validating a measure of moral judgment: Stage preference and stage consistency approaches. *Journal of Educational Psychology, 89*(1), 5–28.

Rest, J. R., Barnett, R., Bebeau, M., Deemer, D., Getz, I., Moon, Y., et al. (1986). *Moral development: Advances in research and theory.* New York: Praeger.

Reyna, V. F. (1995). Interference effects in memory and reasoning: A fuzzy-trace theory analysis. In F. N. Dempster & C. J. Brainerd (Eds.), *Interference and inhibition in cognition* (pp. 29–59). San Diego, CA: Academic Press.

Reyna, V. F., & Brainerd, C. J. (1995). Fuzzy-trace theory: An interim synthesis. *Learning and Individual Differences, 7,* 1–75.

Reynolds, A. J. (2000). *Success in early intervention: The Chicago Child–Parent Centers.* Lincoln: University of Nebraska Press.

Reynolds, C. R., & Kaiser, S. M. (1990a). Bias in assessment of aptitude. In C. R. Reynolds & R. W. Kamphaus (Eds.), *Handbook of psychological and educational assessment of children: Intelligence and achievement* (pp. 611–653). New York: Guilford Press.

Reynolds, C. R., & Kaiser, S. M. (1990b). Test bias in psychological assessment. In T. B. Gutkin & C. R. Reynolds (Eds.), *The handbook of school psychology* (pp. 487–525). New York: Wiley.

Reynolds, C. R., & Kaiser, S. M. (2003). Bias in assessment of aptitude. In C. R. Reynolds & R. W. Kamphaus (Eds.), *Handbook of psychological and educational assessment of children: Intelligence, aptitude, and achievement* (2nd ed., pp. 519–562). New York: Guilford Press.

Reynolds, C. R., & Kamphaus, R. W. (Eds.). (2003). *Handbook of psychological and educational assessment of children: Intelligence, aptitude, and achievement.* New York: Guilford Press.

Reynolds, C. R., & Ramsay, M. C. (2003). Bias in psychological assessment: An empirical review and recommendations. In J. R. Graham, J. A. Naglieri (Vol. Eds.) & I. B.

Weiner (Ed.-in-Chief), *Handbook of psychology: Vol. 10. Assessment psychology* (pp. 67–94). New York: Wiley.

Rice, M. L., Huston, A. C., Truglio, R., & Wright, L. C. (1990). Words from *Sesame Street*: Learning vocabulary while viewing. *Developmental Psychology, 26,* 421–428.

Richardson, S. A., & Koller, H. (1985). Epidemiology. In A. M. Clarke, A. D. B. Clarke, & J. M. Berg (Eds.), *Mental deficiency: The changing outlook* (4th ed., pp. 356–400). New York: Free Press.

Richert, E. S. (1991). Rampant problems and promising practices in identification. In N. Colangelo & G. A. Davis (Eds.), *Handbook of gifted education* (pp. 81–96). Boston: Allyn & Bacon.

Rief, S. F. (2003). *The ADHD book of lists: A practical guide for helping children and teens with attention deficit disorders.* San Francisco: Jossey-Bass.

Rigby, K. (2002). Bullying in childhood. In P. K. Smith & C. H. Hart (Eds.), *Blackwell handbook of childhood social development* (pp. 549–568). Oxford, UK: Blackwell.

Ring, M. M., & Reetz, L. (2000). Modification effects on attributions of middle school students with learning disabilities. *Learning Disabilities Research and Practice, 15,* 34–42.

Ringness, T. A. (1961). Self concept of children of low, average, and high intelligence. *American Journal of Mental Deficiency, 65,* 453–461.

Riordan, J. E., & Noyce, P. E. (2001). The impact of two standards-based mathematics curricula on student achievement in Massachusetts. *Journal for Research in Mathematics Education, 32*(4), 368–398.

Ripple, C. H., & Zigler, E. (2003). Research, policy, and the federal role in prevention initiatives for children. *American Psychologist, 58,* 482–490.

Rips, L. J., Shoben, E. J., & Smith, E. E. (1973). Semantic distance and the verification of semantic relations. *Journal of Verbal Learning and Verbal Behavior, 12,* 1–20.

Risberg, J. (1986). Regional cerebral blood flow in neuropsychology. *Neuropsychologia, 24,* 135–140.

Rist, R. C. (1970). Student social class and teacher expectations: The self-fulfilling prophecy in ghetto education. *Harvard Educational Review, 40,* 411–451.

Ritter, K. (1978). The development of knowledge of an external retrieval cue strategy. *Child Development, 49,* 1227–1230.

Rivera v. City of Wichita Falls, 665 F. 2d 531 (1982).

Roberton, M. A. (1984). Changing motor patterns during childhood. In J. R. Thomas (Ed.), *Motor development during childhood and adolescence* (pp. 48–90). Minneapolis: Burgess.

Roberts, T. A., & Kraft, R. H. (1989). Developmental differences in the relationship between reading comprehension and hemispheric alpha patterns: An EEG study. *Journal of Educational Psychology, 81*, 322–328.

Robinson, C. S., & Hayes, J. R. (1978). Making inferences about relevance in understanding problems. In R. Revlin & R. E. Mayer (Eds.), *Human reasoning* (pp. 195–206). Washington, DC: Winston.

Robinson, J. A., & Kingsley, M. E. (1977). Memory and intelligence: Age and ability differences in strategies and organization of recall. *Intelligence, 1*, 318–330.

Robinson, T. R., Smith, S. W., Miller, M. D., & Brownell, M. T. (1999). Cognitive behavior modification of hyperactivity–impulsivity and aggression: A meta-analysis of school-based studies. *Journal of Educational Psychology, 91*, 195–203.

Robison, D., & Gonzalez, L. S. (1999). Children born premature: A review of linguistic and behavioral outcomes. *Infant Toddler Intervention, 9*, 373–390.

Rodriguez, O. (1992). Introduction to technical and societal issues in the psychological testing of Hispanics. In K. F. Geisinger (Ed.), *Psychological testing of Hispanics* (pp. 11–16). Washington, DC: American Psychological Association.

Roediger, H. L. III (1990). Implicit memory: Retention without remembering. *American Psychologist, 45*, 1043–1056.

Roediger, H. L., Guynn, M. J., & Jones, T. C. (1994). Implicit memory: A tutorial review. In G. d'Ydewalle & P. Eelen (Eds.), *International perspectives on psychological science: Vol. 2. The state of the art* (pp. 67–94). Hillsdale, NJ: Erlbaum Associates.

Roeser, R. W., Eccles, J. S., & Sameroff, A. J. (2000). School as a context of early adolescents' academic and social–emotional development. *Elementary School Journal, 100*, 443–479.

Rogers, H., & Saklofske, D. H. (1985). Self-concept, locus of control and performance expectations of learning disabled children. *Journal of Learning Disabilities, 18*, 273–278.

Rogoff, B. (1990). *Apprenticeship in thinking: Cognitive development in social context.* New York: Oxford University Press.

Rogoff, B. (1998). Cognition as a collaborative process. In W. Damon (Ed.-in-Chief), D. Kuhn & R. S. Siegler (Vol. Eds.), *Handbook of child psychology* (pp. 679–744). New York: Wiley.

Rogoff, B., Turkanis, C. G., & Bartlett, L. (2001). *Learning together: Children and adults in a school community.* Oxford, UK: Oxford University Press.

Rogoff, B., & Waddell, K. J. (1982). Memory for information organized in a scene by children from two cultures. *Child Development, 53*(5), 1224–1228.

Rohner, R. P., Kean, K. J., & Cournoyer, D. E. (1991). Effects of corporal punishment, perceived caretaker warmth, and cultural beliefs on the psychological adjustment of children in St. Kitts, West Indies. *Journal of Marriage and the Family, 53*, 681–693.

Rohwer, W. D. Jr. (1980). An elaborative conception of learner differences. In R. E. Snow, P. A. Federico, & W. E. Montague (Eds.), *Aptitude, learning, and instruction: Vol. 2. Cognitive process analysis of learning and problem solving* (pp. 23–46). Hillsdale, NJ: Erlbaum.

Rohwer, W. D. Jr., Ammon, P. R., & Cramer, P. (1974). *Understanding intellectual development.* Hinsdale, IL: Dryden Press.

Rohwer, W. D. Jr., & Litrownik, J. (1983). Age and individual differences in the learning of a memorization procedure. *Journal of Educational Psychology, 75*, 799–810.

Roizen, N. J. (2002). Down syndrome. In M. L. Batshaw (Ed.), *Children with disabilities* (5th ed., pp. 307–320). Baltimore: Brookes.

Rollins, B. C., & Thomas, D. L. (1979). Parental support, power, and control techniques in the socialization of children. In W. R. Burr, R. Hill, F. I. Nye, & I. L. Reiss (Eds.), *Contemporary theories about the family: Research-based theories* (Vol. 1, pp. 317–364). New York: Free Press.

Romaine, S. (1995). *Bilingualism* (2nd ed.). Oxford, UK: Blackwell.

Romo, H. D., & Falbo, T. (1996). *Latino high school graduation: Defying the odds.* Austin: University of Texas Press.

Roodenrys, S., Hulme, C., & Brown, G. (1993). The development of short-term memory span: Separable effects of speech rate and long-term memory. *Journal of Experimental Child Psychology, 56*, 431–442.

Rosch, E. (1973). On the internal structure of perceptual and semantic categories. In T. Moore (Ed.), *Cognitive development and the acquisition of language* (pp. 111–144). New York: Academic Press.

Rosch, E. (1975). Cognitive representations of semantic categories. *Journal of Experimental Psychology: General, 104*, 192–233.

Rosch, E. (1978). Principles of categorization. In E. Rosch & B. Lloyd (Eds.), *Cognition and categorization* (pp. 9–31). Hillsdale, NJ: Erlbaum.

Rosch, E., & Mervis, C. (1975). Family resemblance studies in the internal structure of categories. *Cognitive Psychology, 7*, 575–605.

Rosen, G. D. (2006). *The dyslexic brain: New pathways in neuroscience discovery.* Mahwah, NJ: Erlbaum.

Rosen, M. G. (1985). Factors during labor and delivery that influence brain disorders. In J. Freeman (Ed.), *Prenatal and perinatal factors associated with brain disorders* (NIH Publication No. 85-1149, pp. 237–262). Washington, DC: U.S. Department of Health and Human Services.

Rosenblatt, L. M. (1978). *The reader, the text, the poem: The transactional theory of the literary work.* Carbondale: Southern Illinois University Press.

Rosengren, K. E., & Windahl, S. (1989). *Media matter: TV use in childhood and adolescence.* Norwood, NJ: Ablex.

Rosenquist, C., Conners, F. A., & Roskos-Ewoldsen, B. (2003). Phonological and visuo-spatial working memory in individuals with intellectual disability. *American Journal of Mental Retardation, 108*, 403–413.

Rosenshine, B. V. (1979). Content, time, and direct instruction. In P. L. Peterson & H. J. Walberg (Eds.), *Research on teaching: Concepts, findings, and implications* (pp. 28–56). Berkeley, CA: McCutchan.

Rosenshine, B., & Meister, C. (1994). Reciprocal teaching: A review of nineteen experimental studies. *Review of Educational Research, 64*(4), 479–530.

Rosenthal, R., & Jacobson, L. (1968). *Pygmalion in the classroom: Teacher expectation and pupils' intellectual development.* New York: Holt, Rinehart & Winston.

Rosenthal, T. L., & Zimmerman, B. J. (1978). *Social learning and cognition.* New York: Academic Press.

Roser, N., & Martinez, M. (1985).

Roles adults play in preschool responses to literature. *Language Arts, 62,* 485–490.

Rosinski-McClendon, M. K., & Newhoff, M. (1987). Conversational responsiveness and assertiveness in language-impaired children. *Language, Speech, and Hearing Services in Schools, 18,* 53–62.

Ross, A. O. (1981). *Child behavior therapy.* New York: Wiley.

Ross, B. H. (1984). Remindings and their effects in learning a cognitive skill. *Cognitive Psychology, 16,* 371–416.

Ross, B. M., & Millson, C. (1970). Repeated memory of oral prose in Ghana and New York. *International Journal of Psychology, 5,* 173–181.

Ross, H. S., & Lollis, S. P. (1987). Communication within infant social games. *Developmental Psychology, 23,* 241–248.

Ross, L. E., & Ross, S. M. (1984). Oculomotor functioning and the learning and cognitive processes of the intellectually handicapped. In P. H. Brooks, R. Sperber, & C. McCauley (Eds.), *Learning and cognition in the mentally retarded* (pp. 217–235). Hillsdale, NJ: Erlbaum.

Roth, M. A., & Parker, J. G. (2001). Affective and behavioral responses to friends who neglect their friends for dating partners: Influences of gender, jealousy and perspective. *Journal of Adolescence, 24,* 281–296.

Rothbart, M. K., & Rothbart, M. (1976). Birth order, sex of child, and maternal help-giving. *Sex Roles, 2,* 39–46.

Rothganger, H. (2003). Analysis of the sounds of the child in the first year of age and a comparison to the language. *Early Human Development, 75,* 55–69.

Rotter, J. B. (1954). *Social learning and clinical psychology.* Englewood Cliffs, NJ: Prentice-Hall.

Rourke, B. P. (1995). *Syndrome of nonverbal learning disabilities: Neurodevelopmental manifestations.* New York: Guilford Press.

Rourke, B. P., Ahmad, S. A., & Collins, D. W. (2002). Child clinical/pediatric neuropsychology: Some recent advances. *Annual Review of Psychology, 53,* 309–339.

Rovet, J., & Netley, C. (1982). Processing deficits in Turner's syndrome. *Developmental Psychology, 18,* 77–94.

Rubin, K. H., Bukowski, W., & Parker, J. G. (1998). Peer interactions, relationships, and groups. In N. Eisenberg (Vol. Ed.) & W. Damon (Gen. Ed.), *Handbook of child psychology: Vol. 3. Social, emotional, and personality development* (5th ed., pp. 619–700). New York: Wiley.

Rubin, K. H., & Coplan, R. J. (1992). Peer relationships in childhood. In M. H. Bornstein & M. E. Lamb (Eds.), *Developmental psychology: An advanced textbook* (3rd ed., pp. 519–578). Hillsdale, NJ: Erlbaum.

Rubin, K. H., LeMare, L. J., & Lollis, S. (1990). Social withdrawal in childhood: Developmental pathways to peer rejection. In S. R. Asher & J. D. Coie (Eds.), *Peer rejection in childhood* (pp. 77–249). New York: Cambridge University Press.

Rubin, K. H., Maioni, T. L., & Hornung, M. (1976). Free play behaviors in middle- and lower-class preschoolers: Parten and Piaget revisited. *Child Development, 47,* 414–419.

Rubin, K. H., Stewart, S. L., & Chen, X. (1995). Parents of aggressive and withdrawn children. In M. H. Bornstein (Ed.), *Handbook of parenting: Vol. 1. Children and parenting* (pp. 255–284). Hillsdale, NJ: Erlbaum.

Ruble, D. N. (1983). The development of social-comparison processes and their role in achievement-related self-socialization. In E. T. Higgins, D. N. Ruble, & W. Hartup (Eds.), *Social cognition and social development* (pp. 134–157). New York: Cambridge University Press.

Ruble, D. N., Boggiano, A. K., Feldman, N. S., & Loebl, J. H. (1980). Developmental analysis of the role of social comparison in self-evaluation. *Developmental Psychology, 16,* 105–115.

Ruble, D. N., & Brooks-Gunn, J. (1982). The experience of menarche. *Child Development, 53,* 1557–1566.

Ruble, D. N., & Martin, C. L. (1998). Gender development. In N. Eisenberg (Vol. Ed.) & W. Damon (Ed.-in-Chief), *Handbook of child psychology: Vol. 3. Social, emotional, and personality development* (5th ed., pp. 933–1016). New York: Wiley.

Rulon, D. (1992). The just community: A method for staff development. *Journal of Moral Education, 21,* 217–224.

Rutter, D. R., & Durkin, K. (1987). Turn-taking in mother–infant interaction: An examination of vocalizations and gaze. *Developmental Psychology, 23,* 54–61.

Rutter, M. (2002a). The interplay of nature, nurture, and developmental influences. *Archives of General Psychiatry, 59,* 996–1000.

Rutter, M. (2002b). Nature, nurture, and development: From evangelism through science toward policy and practice. *Child Development, 73,* 1–21.

Ryan, J. J., & Smith, J. W. (2003). Assessing the intelligence of adolescents with the Wechsler Adult Intelligence Scale–Third edition (WAIS-III). In C. R. Reynolds & R. W. Kamphaus (Eds.), *Handbook of psychological and educational assessment of children: Intelligence, aptitude, and achievement* (2nd ed., pp. 147–173). New York: Guilford Press.

Saab, N., van Joolingen, W., & van Hout-Wolters, B. (2005). Communications in collaborative discovery learning. *British Journal of Educational Psychology, 75*(4), 603–621.

Sabar, N., & Levin, T. (1989). Still waters run deep. *Journal of Research in Science Teaching, 26,* 727–735.

Saccuzzo, D. P., Johnson, N. E., & Guertin, T. L. (1994). Information processing in gifted versus nongifted African Americans, Latino, Filipino, and white children: Speeded versus nonspeeded paradigms. *Intelligence, 19,* 219–243.

Sadeh, A., Gruber, R., & Raviv, A. (2002). Sleep, neurobehavioral functioning, and behavior problems in school-age children. *Child Development, 73,* 405–417.

Sadker, M., & Sadker, D. (1994). *Failing at fairness: How America's schools cheat girls.* New York: Scribners.

Sadoski, M. (1983). An exploratory study of the relationship between reported imagery and the comprehension and recall of a story. *Reading Research Quarterly, 19,* 110–123.

Sadoski, M. (1985). The natural use of imagery in story comprehension and recall: Replication and extension. *Reading Research Quarterly, 20,* 658–667.

Sadoski, M., & Paivio, A. (2001). *Imagery and text: A dual coding theory of reading and writing.* Mahwah, NJ: Erlbaum.

Sadoski, M., Paivio, A., & Goetz, E. T. (1991). A critique of schema theory in reading and a dual coding alternative. *Reading Research Quarterly, 26*(4), 463–484.

Safyer, A. W., & Hauser, S. T. (1995). A developmental view of defenses: Empirical approaches. In H. R. Conte & R. Plutchik (Eds.), *Ego defenses: Theory and measurement* (pp. 120–138). Oxford, UK: Wiley.

Salili, F., Chiu, C.-Y., & Lai, S. (2001).

The influence of culture and context on students' motivational orientation and performance. In F. Salili & C.-Y. Chiu (Eds.), *Student motivation: The culture and context of learning* (pp. 221–247). Dordrecht, The Netherlands: Kluwer.

Saltaris, C. (2002). Psychopathy in juvenile offenders: Can temperament and attachment be considered as robust developmental precursors? *Clinical Psychology Review, 22,* 729–752.

Salthouse, T. A. (1982). *Adult cognition: An experimental psychology of human aging.* New York: Springer-Verlag.

Salthouse, T. A. (1985). Speed of behavior and its implications for cognition. In J. E. Birren & K. W. Schaie (Eds.), *Handbook of the psychology of aging* (2nd ed., pp. 400–426). New York: Van Nostrand Reinhold.

Salthouse, T. A. (1988). The role of processing resources in cognitive aging. In M. I. Howe & C. J. Brainerd (Eds.), *Cognitive development in adulthood* (pp. 185–239). New York: Springer-Verlag.

Salthouse, T. A. (1992). The information-processing perspective on cognitive aging. In R. J. Sternberg & C. A. Berg (Eds.), *Intellectual development* (pp. 261–277). Cambridge, UK: Cambridge University Press.

Sameroff, A. J. (1975). Early influences on development: Fact or fancy? *Merrill–Palmer Quarterly, 21,* 267–294.

Sameroff, A. J., & Fiese, B. H. (1990). Transactional regulation and early intervention. In S. J. Meisels & J. P. Shonkodf (Eds.), *Handbook of early childhood intervention* (pp. 119–149). Cambridge, UK: Cambridge University Press.

Sampaio, R. C., & Truwit, C. L. (2001). Myelination in the developing human brain. In C. A. Nelson & M. Luciana (Eds.), *Handbook of developmental cognitive neuroscience* (pp. 35–58). Cambridge, MA: MIT Press.

Samuels, H. R. (1980). The effect of older siblings on infant locomotor exploration of a new environment. *Child Development, 51,* 607–609.

Sandoval, J. H., & Mille, M. P. W. (1980). Accuracy judgments of WISC-R items' difficulty for minority groups. *Journal of Consulting and Clinical Psychology, 48,* 249–253.

Sandnabba, N. K., & Ahlberg, C. (1999). Parents' attitudes and expectations about children's cross-gender behavior. *Sex Roles, 40,* 249–262.

Santrock, J. W., & Warshak, R. A. (1979). Father custody and social development in boys and girls. *Journal of Social Issues, 35,* 112–135.

Santrock, J. W., Warshak, R., Lindbergh, C., & Meadows, L. (1982). Children's and parents' observed social behaviors in stepfather families. *Child Development, 53,* 472–480.

Sattler, J. M. (1992). *Assessment of children* (rev. 3rd ed.). San Diego, CA: Author.

Sattler, J. M. (2002). *Assessment of children.* La Mesa CA: Author.

Sawyer, D. J., & Butler, K. (1991). Early language intervention: A deterrent to reading disability. *Annals of Dyslexia, 41,* 55–79.

Saye, K. B. (2003). Preschool intellectual assessment. In C. R. Reynolds & R. W. Kamphaus (Eds.), *Handbook of psychological and educational assessment of children: Intelligence, aptitude, and achievement* (2nd ed., pp. 187–203). New York: Guilford Press.

Sayfer, A. W., & Hauser, S. T. (1995). A developmental view of defenses: Empirical approaches. In H. R. Conte & R. Plutchik (Eds.), *Ego defenses: Theory and measurement* (pp. 120–138). New York: Wiley.

Scarborough, H. S. (1989). Prediction of reading disability from familial and individual differences. *Journal of Educational Psychology, 81,* 101–108.

Scarborough, H. S. (1990). Very early language deficits in dyslexic children. *Child Development, 61,* 1728–1743.

Scarborough, H. S. (2001). Connecting early language and literacy to later reading (dis)abilities: Evidence, theory, and practice. In S. B. Neuman & D. K. Dickinson (Eds.), *Handbook of early literacy research* (pp. 97–110). New York: Guilford Press.

Scarborough, H. S., & Dobrich, W. (1990). Development of children with early language delay. *Journal of Speech and Hearing Research, 33,* 70–83.

Scardamalia, M., & Bereiter, C. (1986). Research on written composition. In M. C. Wittrock (Ed.), *Handbook of research on teaching* (3rd ed., pp. 778–803). New York: Macmillan.

Scarr, S. (1992). Developmental theories for the 1990s: Development and individual differences. *Child Development, 63,* 1–19.

Scarr, S., Eisenberg, M., & Dieter-Deckard, R. (1994). Measurement of quality in child care centers. *Early Childhood Research Quarterly, 9,* 131–151.

Scarr, S., & Kidd, K. K. (1983). Developmental behavior genetics. In M. M. Haith & J. J. Campos (Eds.) & P. H. Mussen (Gen. Ed.), *Handbook of child psychology: Vol. 2. Infancy and developmental psychobiology* (pp. 345–433). New York: Wiley.

Scarr, S., & McCartney, K. (1983). How people make their own environments: A theory of genotype-environment effects. *Child Development, 54,* 424–435.

Scarr, S., & Weinberg, R. A. (1976). IQ test performance of black children adopted by white families. *American Psychologist, 31,* 726–739.

Scarr, S., & Weinberg, R. A. (1983). The Minnesota Adoption Studies: Genetic differences and malleability. *Child Development, 54,* 260–268.

Schacter, D. L. (1987). Implicit memory: History and current status. *Journal of Experimental Psychology: Learning, Memory, and Cognition, 13,* 501–518.

Schacter, D. L. (1992). Understanding implicit memory: A cognitive neuroscience perspective. *American Psychologist, 47,* 559–569.

Schacter, D. L., Chiu, C. Y. P., & Ochsner, K. N. (1993). Implicit memory: A selective review. *Annual Review of Neuroscience, 16,* 159–182.

Schade, J. P., & van Groeningen, W. B. (1961). Structural organization of the human cerebral cortex: I. Maturation of the middle frontal gyrus. *Acta Anatomica, 47,* 74–85.

Schaffer, H. R. (1971). *The growth of sociability.* Baltimore: Penguin Books.

Schaffer, H. R., & Emerson, P. E. (1964). Patterns of response to physical contact in early human behavior. *Journal of Child Psychology and Psychiatry, 5,* 1–13.

Schaie, K. W. (1959). Cross-sectional methods in the study of psychological aspects of aging. *Journal of Gerontology, 14,* 208–215.

Schaie, K. W. (1980). Age changes in intelligence. In R. L. Sprott (Ed.), *Age, learning ability, and intelligence* (pp. 41–77). New York: Van Nostrand.

Schaie, K. W. (1990). Intellectual development in adulthood. In J. E. Birren & K. W. Schaie (Eds.), *Handbook of the psychology of aging* (3rd ed., pp. 291–309). San Diego, CA: Academic Press.

Schaie, K. W. (2002). The impact of

longitudinal studies on understanding development from young adulthood to old age. In H. W. Hartup & R. K. Silbereisen (Eds.), *Growing points in developmental science: An introduction* (pp. 307–328). Philadelphia: Psychology Press.

Schaie, K. W., & Labouvie-Vief, G. (1974). Generational versus ontogenetic components of change in adult cognitive behavior: A fourteen year cross sequential study. *Developmental Psychology, 10,* 305–320.

Schaie, K. W., & Parham, I. A. (1977). Cohort-sequential analyses of adult intellectual development. *Developmental Psychology, 13,* 649–653.

Schatz, E. K., & Baldwin, R. S. (1986). Context clues are unreliable predictors of word meanings. *Reading Research Quarterly, 21,* 439–453.

Schau, C. G., Kahn, L., Diepold, J. H., & Cherry, F. (1980). The relationship of parental expectations and preschool children's verbal sex-typing to their sex-typed toy play behavior. *Child Development, 51,* 607–609.

Schick, B. (2003). The development of American sign language and manually coded English system. In M. Marschark & P. E. Spencer (Eds.), *Oxford handbook of deaf studies, language, and education* (pp. 219–231). New York: Oxford University Press.

Schiefelbusch, R. L., & Bricker, D. D. (1979). *Early language: Acquisition and intervention.* Baltimore: University Park Press.

Schiefele, U. (1992). Topic interest and levels of text comprehension. In K. A. Renninger, S. Hidi, & A. Krapp (Eds.), *The role of interest in learning and development* (pp. 151–182). Hillsdale, NJ: Erlbaum.

Schirmer, B. R., & Williams, C. (2003). Approaches to teaching reading. In M. Marschark & P. E. Spencer (Eds.), *Oxford handbook of deaf studies, language, and education* (pp. 110–122). New York: Oxford University Press.

Schlyter, S. (1990). The acquisition of tense and aspect. In J. Meisel (Ed.), *Two first languages: Early grammatical development in bilingual children* (pp. 87–122). Dordrecht, The Netherlands: Foris.

Schmeiser, C. B. (1992). Reactions to technical and societal issues in testing Hispanics. In K. F. Geisinger (Ed.), *Psychological testing of Hispanics* (pp. 79–88). Washington, DC: American Psychological Association.

Schmidt, C. R., Ollendick, T. H., & Stanowicz, L. B. (1988). Developmental changes in the influence of assigned goals on cooperative and competition. *Developmental Psychology, 24,* 574–579.

Schmidt-Hellerau, C. (1997). Libido and lethe: Fundamentals of a formalized conception of metapsychology. *International Journal of Psycho-Analysis, 78,* 683–697.

Schmittau, J. (2003). Cultural-historical theory and mathematics education. In A. Kozulin, B. Gindia, V. S. Ageyev, & S. M. Miller (Eds.), *Vygotsky's educational theory in cultural context* (pp. 225–245). Cambridge, UK: Cambridge University Press.

Schneider, B., & Stevenson, D. (1999). *The ambitious generation: America's teenagers: Motivated but directionless.* New Haven, CT: Yale University Press.

Schneider, B. H., Atkinson, L., & Tardif, C. (2001). Child–parent attachment and children's peer relations: A quantitative review. *Developmental Psychology, 37,* 86–100.

Schneider, W., & Pressley, M. (1997). *Memory development between two and twenty* (2nd ed.). Mahwah, NJ: Erlbaum.

Schneirla, T. C. (1957). The concept of development in developmental psychology. In D. B. Harris (Ed.), *The concept of development: An issue in the study of human behavior* (pp. 78–108). Minneapolis: University of Minnesota Press.

Schon, D. A. (1983). *The reflective practitioner: How professionals think in action.* London: Temple Smith.

Schon, D. A. (1987). *Educating the reflective practitioner.* San Francisco: Jossey-Bass.

Schonert-Reichl, K. A. (1999). Relations of peer acceptance, friendship adjustment, and social behavior to moral reasoning during early adolescence. *Journal of Early Adolescence, 19*(2), 249–279.

Schraw, G., Flowerday, T., & Lehman, S. (2001). Increasing situational interest in the classroom. *Educational Psychology Review, 13*(3), 211–224.

Schraw, G., & Lehman, S. (2001). Situational interest: A review of the literature and directions for future research. *Educational Psychology Review, 13*(1), 23–52.

Schunk, D. H. (1989). Social cognitive theory and self-regulated learning. In B. J. Zimmerman & D. H. Schunk (Eds.), *Self-regulated learning and academic achievement* (pp. 83–110). New York: Springer-Verlag.

Schunk, D. H. (1990). Goal setting and self-efficacy during self-regulated learning. *Educational Psychologist, 25,* 71–86.

Schunk, D. H. (1991). Self-efficacy and academic motivation. *Educational Psychologist, 26,* 207–232.

Schunk, D. H., Hanson, A. R., & Cox, P. D. (1987). Peer-model attributes and children's achievement behaviors. *Journal of Educational Psychology, 79,* 54–61.

Schunk, D. H. & Pajares, F. (2004). Self-efficacy in education revisted: Empirical and applied evidence. In D. M. McInerney & S. Van Etten (Eds.), *Big theories revisited* (pp. 115–138). Greenwich, CT: Information Age.

Schwartz, D., Dodge, K. A., & Coie, J. D. (1993). The emergence of chronic peer victimization in boys' play groups. *Child Development, 64,* 1755–1772.

Schwartz, S. J. (2001). The evolution of Eriksonian and neo-Eriksonian identity theory and research: A review and integration. *Identity, 1,* 7–58.

Scollon, R., & Scollon, S. (1981). *Narrative literacy and face in inter-ethnic communication.* Norwood, NJ: Ablex.

Scott, C. M. (1995). Syntax for school-age children: A discourse perspective. In M. E. Fey, J. Windsor, & S. F. Warren (Eds.), *Language intervention: Preschool through the elementary years* (pp. 107–144). Baltimore: Brookes.

Scott, C. M. (2004). Syntactic contributions to literacy learning. In C. A. Stone, E. R. Silliman, B. J. Ehren, & K. Apel (Eds.), *Handbook of language and literacy* (pp. 340–362). New York: Guilford Press.

Scott, D. T. (1987). Premature infants in later childhood: Some recent followup results. *Seminary Perinatology, 11,* 191–199.

Scribner, S., & Cole, M. (1981). *The psychology of literacy.* Cambridge, MA: Harvard University Press.

Scrimsher, S., & Tudge, J. (2003). The teaching/learning relationship in the first years of school: Some revolutionary implications of Vygotsky's theory. *Early Education and Development, 14,* 293–312.

Searls, D. T., Mead, N. A., & Ward, B. (1985). The relationship of students' reading skills to TV watching, leisure time reading, and homework. *Journal of Reading, 29,* 158–162.

Sebald, H., & White, B. (1980). Teenagers' divided reference groups: Uneven alignment with parents and peers. *Adolescence, 15,* 579–584.

Secada, W. G. (1991). Selected conceptual and methodological issues for studying the mathematics education of the disadvantaged. In M. S. Knapp & P. M. Shields (Eds.), *Better schooling for the children of poverty: Alternatives to conventional wisdom* (pp. 149–168). Berkeley CA: McCutchan.

Seidel, J. F. (1992). Children with HIV-related developmental difficulties. *Phi Delta Kappan, 74,* 38–40, 56.

Seidman, E., Allen, L., Aber, J. L., Mitchell, C., & Feinman, J. (1994). The impact of school transitions in early adolescence on the self-system and perceived social context of poor urban youth. *Child Development, 65,* 507–522.

Seifer, R., Schiller, M., Sameroff, A. J., Resnick, S., & Riordan, K. (1996). Attachment, maternal sensitivity, and infant temperament during the first year of life. *Developmental Psychology, 32,* 12–25.

Seitz, V., Rosenbaum, L. K., & Apfel, N. H. (1985). Effects of family support intervention: A ten-year followup. *Child Development, 56,* 376–391.

Selfridge, O. G. (1959). Pandemonium: A paradigm for learning. In D. V. Blake & A. M. Uttley (Eds.), *Proceeding of the symposium on the mechanization of thought processes.* London: H. M. Stationery Office.

Selman, R. L. (1976). Social-cognitive understanding: A guide to educational and clinical practice. In T. Lickona (Ed.), *Moral development and behavior: Theory, research, and social issues* (pp. 299–316). New York: Holt.

Selman, R. L. (1980). *The growth of interpersonal understanding.* New York: Academic Press.

Selman, R. L. (1981). The child as a friendship philosopher. In S. R. Asher & J. M. Gottman (Eds.), *The development of children's friendships* (pp. 242–272). New York: Cambridge University Press.

Selman, R. L., Schorin, M. Z., Stone, C., & Phelps, E. (1983). A naturalistic study of children's understanding. *Developmental Psychology, 19,* 82–102.

Semb, G. B., Ellis, J. A., & Araujo, J. (1993). Long-term memory for knowledge learned in school. *Journal of Educational Psychology, 85,* 305–316.

Serbin, L. A., & O'Leary, K. D. (1975, December). How nursery schools teach girls to shut up. *Psychology Today, 9,* 56–58, 102–103.

Serbin, L. A., & Sprafkin, C. (1986). The salience of gender and the process of sex-typing in three to seven year olds. *Child Development, 57,* 1188–1199.

Sedlak, A. (1988). *National incidence and prevalence of child abuse and neglect: 1988, Revised report.* Rockville, MD: Westat.

Segel, E. (1986). "As the twig is bent . . .": Gender and childhood reading. In E. A. Flynn & P. P. Schweickart (Eds.), *Gender and reading: Essays on readers, texts, and contexts* (pp. 165–186). Baltimore: Johns Hopkins University Press.

Service, V., Lock, A., & Chandler, P. (1989). Individual differences in early communicative development: A social constructivist perspective. In S. von Tetzchner, L. S. Siegel, & L. Smith (Eds.), *The social and cognitive aspects of normal and atypical language development* (pp. 23–49). New York: Springer-Verlag.

Shakin, M., Shakin, D., & Sternglanz, S. H. (1985). Infant clothing: Sex labeling for strangers. *Sex Roles, 12,* 955–963.

Shantz, C. U., & Hartup, W. W. (Eds.). (1992). *Conflict in child and adolescent development.* New York: Cambridge University Press.

Sharabany, R., Gershoni, R., & Hofman, J. E. (1981). Girlfriend: Boyfriend: Age and sex differences in intimate friendship. *Developmental Psychology, 17,* 691–703.

Sharp, A. M. (1987). What is a "community of inquiry"? *Journal of Moral Education, 16,* 37–45.

Sharp, D., Cole, M., & Lave, C. (1979). Education and cognitive development: The evidence from experimental research. *Monographs of the Society for Research in Child Development, 44*(Serial No. 178).

Shatz, M. (1983). Communication. In J. H. Flavell & E. M. Markman (Eds.), *Handbook of child psychology: Vol. 3. Cognitive development* (4th ed., pp. 841–889). New York: Wiley.

Shatz, M., & Gelman, R. (1973). The development of communication skills: Modification in the speech of young children as a function of listener. *Monographs of the Society for Research in Child Development, 38*(5, Serial No. 152).

Shavelson, R. J., & Towne, L. (Eds.). (2002). *Scientific research in education.* Washington, DC: National Academy Press.

Shaywitz, B. A., Shaywitz, S. E., Pugh, K. R., Mencl, W. E., Fulbright, R. K., Skudlarski, P., et al. (2002). Disruption of posterior brain systems for reading in children with developmental dyslexia. *Biological Psychiatry, 52,* 101–110.

Shaywitz, S. E. (2003). *Overcoming dyslexia: A new and complete science-based program for overcoming reading problems at any level.* New York: Knopf.

Shaywitz, S. E., & Shaywitz, B. A. (1992). Learning disabilities and attention deficits in the school setting. In L. J. Meltzer (Ed.), *Strategy assessment and instruction for students with learning disabilities: From theory to practice* (pp. 221–241). Austin, TX: PRO-ED.

Shaywitz, S. E., & Shaywitz, B. A. (2004). Neurobiologic basis for reading and reading disability. In P. McCardle & V. Chhabra (Eds.), *The voice of evidence in reading research* (pp. 417–442). Baltimore: Brookes.

Shaywitz, S. E., & Shaywitz, B. A. (2005). Dyslexia (specific reading disability). *Biological Psychiatry, 57,* 1301–1309.

Shaywitz, S. E., Shaywitz, B. A., Fletcher, J. M., & Escobar, M. D. (1990). Prevalence of reading disability in boys and girls: Results of the Connecticut Longitudinal Study. *Journal of the American Medical Association, 264,* 998–1002.

Shaywitz, S. E., Shaywitz, B. A., Fulbright, R. K., Skudlarski, P., Mencl, W. E., Constable, R. T., et al. (2003). Neural systems for compensation and persistence: Young adult outcome of childhood reading disability. *Biological Psychiatry, 54,* 25–33.

Shea, D. L., Lubinski, D., & Benbow, C. P. (2001). Importance of assessing spatial ability in intellectually talented young adolescents: A 20-year longitudinal study. *Journal of Educational Psychology, 93,* 604–614.

Shea, J. D. C. (1981). Changes in interpersonal distances and categories of play behavior in the early weeks of preschool. *Developmental Psychology, 17,* 417–425.

Sheehy, A., Gasser, T., Molinari, L., & Largo, R. H. (1999). An analysis of variance of the pubertal and midgrowth spurts for length and width. *Annals of Human Biology, 26,* 309–331.

Shell, D. F., Murphy, C. C., & Bruning, R. H. (1989). Self-efficacy and outcome expectancy mechanisms in reading and writing achievement. *Journal of Educational Psychology, 81,* 91–100.

Shepard, R. N., & Metzler, J. (1971). Mental rotation of three-dimensional objects. *Science, 171,* 701–703.

Shepard, T. H. (1998). *Catalog of teratogenic agents* (9th ed.). Baltimore: Johns Hopkins University Press.

Shirey, L. L., & Reynolds, R. E. (1988). Effect of interest on attention and learning. *Journal of Educational Psychology, 80,* 159–166.

Shonkoff, J. P., & Hauser-Cram, P. (1987). Early intervention for learning disabled infants and their families: A quantitative analysis. *Pediatrics, 80,* 650–658.

Shonkoff, J. P., & Marshall, P. C. (1990). Biological bases of developmental dysfunction. In S. J. Meisels & J. P. Shonkoff (Eds.), *Handbook of early childhood intervention* (pp. 35–52). Cambridge, UK: Cambridge University Press.

Shonkoff, J. P., & Phillips, D. A. (2000). *From neurons to neighborhoods: The science of early childhood development.* Washington, DC: National Academy Press.

Short, E. J., & Ryan, E. B. (1984). Metacognitive differences between skilled and less skilled readers: Remediating deficits through story grammar and attribution training. *Journal of Educational Psychology, 76,* 225–235.

Shriberg, L., Kwiatkowski, J., Best, S., Hengst, J., & Tereselic-Weber, B. (1986). Characteristics of children with phonologic disorders of unknown origin. *Journal of Speech and Hearing Disorders, 51,* 140–161.

Shulman, S., Bar-Ilan, U., & Ramat-Gen, I. (2003). Conflict and negotiation in adolescent romantic relationships. In P. Florsheim (Ed.), *Adolescent romantic relations and sexual behavior: Theory, research, and practical implications* (pp. 109–135). Mahwah, NJ: Erlbaum.

Shurkin, J. N. (1992). *Terman's kids: The groundbreaking study of how the gifted grow up.* Boston: Little, Brown.

Sidorowicz, L. S., & Lunney, G. S. (1980). Baby X revisited. *Sex Roles, 6,* 67–73.

Sigman, M., Neumann, C., Jansen, A. A. J., & Bwibo, N. (1989). Cognitive abilities of Kenyan children in relation to nutrition, family characteristics, and education. *Child Development, 60,* 1463–1474.

Signorella, M. L., Bigler, R. S., & Liben, L. (1993). Developmental differences in children's gender schemata about others: A meta-analytic review. *Developmental Review, 13,* 106–126.

Signorella, M. L., & Liben, L. S.

(1984). Recall and reconstruction of gender-related pictures: Effects of attitude, task difficulty, and age. *Child Development, 55,* 393–405.

Signorielli, N., & Lears, M. (1992). Children, television, and conceptions about chores: Attitudes and behavior. *Sex Roles, 27,* 157–170.

Silver, E. A. (1987). Foundations of cognitive theory and research for mathematics problem solving instruction. In A. Schoenfeld (Ed.), *Cognitive science and mathematics education* (pp. 33–60). Hillsdale, NJ: Erlbaum.

Silver, E. J., Bauman, L. J., Coupey, S. M., Doctors, S. R., & Boeck, M. A. (1990). Ego development and chronic illness in adolescents. *Developmental Psychology, 59,* 305–310.

Silverstein, B., & Krate, R. (1975). *Children of the dark ghetto: A developmental psychology.* Oxford, UK: Praeger.

Sim, T. N., & Koh, S. F. (2003). Domain conceptualization of adolescent susceptibility to peer pressure. *Journal of Research on Adolescence, 13,* 58–80.

Simmons, R. G., Blyth, D. A., & McKinney, K. L. (1983). The social and psychological effects of puberty on white females. In J. Brooks-Gunn & A. C. Pertersen (Eds.), *Girls at puberty: Biological and psychosocial aspects* (pp. 229–272). New York: Plenum Press.

Simmons, R. G., Burgeson, R., & Reef, M. J. (1988). Cumulative change at entry to adolescence. In M. R. Gunnar & W. A. Collins (Eds.), *Development during the transition to adolescence: Minnesota Symposium on Child Psychology* (Vol. 21, pp. 123–150). Hillsdale, NJ: Erlbaum.

Simon, H. A. (1974). How big is a chunk? *Science, 183,* 482–488.

Simons, R. L., Lorenz, F. O., Wu, C., & Conger, R. D. (1993). Social network and marital support as mediators and moderators of the impact of stress and depression on maternal behavior. *Developmental Psychology, 29,* 368–391.

Singer, D., & Singer, J. (2001). *Handbook of children and the media.* Thousand Oaks, CA: Sage.

Sizer, T. R. (1996). *Horace's hope: What works for the American high school.* New York: Houghton-Mifflin.

Skaalvik, E. M. (1990). Gender differences in general academic self-esteem and in success expectations on defined academic problems. *Journal of Educational Psychology, 82,* 593–598.

Skinner, B. F. (1953). *Science and human behavior.* New York: Free Press.

Skinner, B. F. (1977). Corporal punishment. In I. A. Hyman & J. H. Wise (Eds.), *Corporal punishment in American education* (pp. 335–336). Philadelphia: Temple University Press.

Skinner, E. A. (1991). Development and perceived control: A dynamic model of action in context. In M. R. Gunnar & L. A. Sroufe (Eds.), *Self processes in development: Minnesota Symposium in Child Psychology* (Vol. 23, pp. 167–216). Chicago: University of Chicago Press.

Skinner, E. A., & Belmont, M. J. (1993). Motivation in the classroom: Reciprocal effects of teacher behavior and student engagement across the school year. *Journal of Educational Psychology, 85,* 571–581.

Skinner, E. A., Wellborn, J. G., & Connell, J. P. (1990). What it takes to do well in school and whether I've got it: A process model of perceived control and children's engagement and achievement in school. *Journal of Educational Psychology, 82,* 22–32.

Skinner, E. A., Zimmer-Gembeck, M. J., & Connell, J. P. (1998). Individual differences and the development of perceived control. *Monographs of the Society for Research in Child Development, 63*(2–3, Serial No. 220).

Skuse, D. H. (1984). Extreme deprivation in early childhood: II. Theoretical issues and a comparative review. *Journal of Child Psychology and Psychiatry, 25,* 543–572.

Slaby, R. G., & Crowley, C. G. (1977). Modification of cooperation and aggression through teacher attention to children's speech. *Journal of Experimental Child Psychology, 23,* 442–458.

Slaby, R. G., & Frey, K. S. (1975). Development of gender constancy and selective attention to same sex models.l *Child Development, 46,* 849–856.

Slavin, R. (1985a). An introduction to cooperative learning research. In R. Slavin, S. Sharan, S. Kagan, R. H. Lazarowitz, C. Webb, & R. Schmuck (Eds.), *Learning to cooperate, cooperating to learn* (pp. 5–15). New York: Plenum Press.

Slavin, R. (1985b). Team-assisted individualization: Combining cooperative learning and individualized instruction in mathematics. In R. Slavin, S. Sharan, S. Kagan, R. H. Lazarowitz, C. Webb, & R. Schmuck (Eds.), *Learning to cooperate, cooper-*

ating to learn (pp. 177–209). New York: Plenum Press.

Slavin, R. (1995). *Cooperative learning*. Boston: Allyn & Bacon.

Slavin, R. E. (1991). Synthesis of research on cooperative learning. *Educational Leadership*, 71–77.

Slavin, R. E., Hurley, E. A., & Chamberlain, A. (2003). Cooperative learning and achievement: Theory and research. In I. B. Weiner (Ed.-in-Chief), W. M. Reynolds & G. E. Miller (Vol. Eds.), *Handbook of psychology: Vol. 7. Educational psychology* (pp. 177–198). Hoboken, NJ: Wiley.

Slavin, R. E., Karweit, N. L., & Wasik, B. A. (1994). *Preventing early school failure: Research, policy, and practice*. Boston: Allyn & Bacon.

Smetana, J. G. (1993). Understanding of social rules. In M. Bennett (Ed.), *The child as psychologist: An introduction to the development of social cognition* (pp. 111–141). New York: Harvester Wheatsheaf.

Smith, C., & Lloyd, B. (1978). Maternal behavior and perceived sex of infant: Revisited. *Child Development, 49*, 1263–1265.

Smith, C. L., & Tager-Flusberg, H. (1982). Metalinguistic awareness and language development. *Journal of Experimental Child Psychology, 34*, 449–468.

Smith, E. E., & Medin, D. L. (1981). *Categories and concepts*. Cambridge, MA: Harvard University Press.

Smith, G., Spiker, D., Peterson, C., Cicchetti, D., & Justice, P. (1984). Use of megadoses of vitamins with minerals in Down syndrome. *Journal of Pediatrics, 105*, 228–234.

Smith, M. L., & Glass, G. V. (1987). *Research and evaluation in education and the social sciences*. Englewood Cliffs, NJ: Prentice-Hall.

Smith-Hefner, N. J. (1993). Education, gender, and generational conflict among Khmer refugees. *Anthropology and Education Quarterly, 24*, 135–158.

Snarey, J. R. (1985). Cross-cultural universality of social-moral development: A critical review of Kohlbergian research. *Psychological Bulletin, 97*, 202–232.

Snitzer, H. (1964). *Living at Summerhill*. New York: Macmillan.

Snow, C. E. (1987). Relevance of the notion of a critical period to language acquisition. In M. H. Bornstein (Ed.), *Sensitive periods in development: Interdisciplinary perspectives* (pp. 183–209). Hillsdale, NJ: Erlbaum.

Snow, C. E. (2002). Second language

learners and understanding the brain. In S. M. Kosslyn & A. M. Galaburda (Eds.), *The languages of the brain* (pp. 151–165). Cambridge, MA: Harvard University Press.

Snow, C. E., Barnes, W. S., Chandler, J., Goodman, I. F., & Hemphill, L. (1991). *Unfulfilled expectations: Home and school influences on literacy*. Cambridge, MA: Harvard University Press.

Snow, C. E., Burns, S. M., & Griffin, P. (Eds.). (1998). *Preventing reading difficulties in young children*. Washington, DC: National Research Council, National Academy Press.

Snow, C. E., & Hoefnagel-Hohle, M. (1978). The critical period for language acquisition: Evidence from second language learning. *Child Development, 49*, 1114–1128.

Snow, M. A., Galvan, J. L., & Campbell, R. N. (1983). The pilot class of the Culver City Spanish immersion program: A followup report, or whatever happened to the class of '78? In K. M. Bailey, M. H. Long, & S. Peck (Eds.), *Second language acquisition studies* (pp. 115–125). Rowley, MA: Newbury House.

Snow, M. E., Jacklin, C. N., & Maccoby, E. E. (1983). Sex-of-child differences in father–child interaction at one year of age. *Child Development, 54*, 227–232.

Snowling, M. (2000). *Dyslexia: A cognitive developmental perspective*. London: Blackwell.

Sodian, B., & Schneider, W. (1990). Children's understanding of cognitive cuing: How to manipulate cues to fool a competitor. *Child Development, 61*, 697–704.

Solomon, J., & George, C. (1999). The measurement of attachment security in infancy and childhood. In J. Cassidy & P. R. Shaver (Eds.), *Handbook of attachment: Theory, research, and clinical applications* (pp. 287–316). New York: Guilford Press.

Sommerfeld, M. (1992). "Micro-society" schools tackle real-world woes. *Education Week, 12*, 1, 14.

Sommers, R. K., Logsdon, B., & Wright, J. (1992). A review and critical analysis of treatment research related to articulation and phonological disorders. *Journal of ommunication Disorders, 25*, 3–22.

Sowell, E. J. (1989). Effects of manipulative materials in mathematics instruction. *Journal for Research in Mathematics Education, 20*, 498–505.

Spearman, C. (1904). "General intelligence" objectively determined and measured. *American Journal of Psychology, 15*, 201–293.

Spence, J. T., Helmreich, R., & Stapp, J. (1975). Ratings of self and peers on sex role attributes and their relation to self-esteem and conceptions of masculinity and femininity. *Journal of Personality and Social Psychology, 32*(1), 29–39.

Spencer, P. E., & Marschark, M. (2003). Cochlear impants: Issues and implications. In M. Marschark & P. E. Spencer (Eds.), *Oxford handbook of deaf studies, language, and education* (pp. 434–448). New York: Oxford University Press.

Spiegel, H. M. L., & Bonwit, A. M. (2002). HIV infection in children. In M. L. Batshaw (Ed.), *Children with disabilities* (5th ed., pp. 123–139). Baltimore: Brookes.

Spitz, H. H. (1986a). Preventing and curing mental retardation by behavioral intervention: An evaluation of some claims. *Intelligence, 10*, 197–207.

Spitz, H. H. (1986b). *The raising of intelligence: A selected history of attempts to raise retarded intelligence*. Hillsdale, NJ: Erlbaum.

Spitz, H. H. (1991a). Commentary on Locurto's "Beyond IQ in preschool programs?" *Intelligence, 15*, 327–334.

Spitz, H. H. (1991b). Review of *The Milwaukee Project: Preventing mental retardation in children at risk*. *American Journal on Mental Retardation, 95*, 482–490.

Spitz, H. H. (1992). Does the Carolina Abecedarian Early Intervention Project prevent sociocultural mental retardation? *Intelligence, 16*, 225–237.

Spitz, R. A., & Wolf, K. M. (1946). The smiling response: A contribution to the ontogenesis of social relations. *Genetic Psychology Monographs, 34*, 57–125.

Spivack, G., & Shure, M. B. (1982). The cognition of social adjustment: Interpersonal cognitive problem solving thinking. In B. B. Lahey & A. E. Kazdin (Eds.), *Advances in clinical child psychology* (Vol. 5, pp. 323–372). New York: Plenum Press.

Spreen, O., Risser, A. T., & Edgell, D. (1995). *Developmental neuropsychology*. New York: Oxford University Press.

Springer, S. P., & Deutsch, G. (1989). *Left brain, right brain* (3rd ed.). New York: Freeman.

Squire, L. R. (1992). Memory and hippocampus: A synthesis from findings with rats, monkeys and humans. *Psychological Review, 99*(2), 195–231.

Squire, L. R. (2004). Memory systems

of the brain: A brief history and current perspective. *Neurobiology of Learning and Memory, 82*(3), 171–177.

Sroufe, L. A. (1996). *Emotional development: The organization of emotional life in the early years.* Cambridge, UK: Cambridge University Press.

Sroufe, L. A., Carlson, E., & Schulman, S. (1993). Individuals in relationships: Development from infancy through adolescence. In D. C. Funder, R. D. Parke, C. Tomlinson-Keasey, & K. Widaman (Eds.), *Studying lives through time: Personality and development* (pp. 315–342). Washington, DC: American Psychological Association.

Sroufe, L. A., Egeland, B., & Kreutzer, T. (1990). The fate of early experience following developmental change: Longitudinal approaches to individual adaptation in childhood. *Child Development, 61,* 1363–1373.

Sroufe, L. A., Fox, N. E., & Pancake, V. R. (1983). Attachment and dependency in developmental perspective. *Child Development, 54,* 1335–1354.

Stahl, S. A., & Miller, P. D. (1989). Whole language and language experience approaches for beginning reading: A quantitative research synthesis. *Review of Educational Research, 59,* 87–116.

Stams, G. J., Juffer, F., & van IJzendoorn, M. H. (2002). Maternal sensitivity, infant attachment, and temperament in early childhood predict adjustment in middle childhood: The case of adopted children and their biologically unrelated parents. *Developmental Psychology, 38,* 806–821.

Stanley, J. C., & Benbow, C. P. (1986). Youth who reason exceptionally well mathematically. In R. J. Sternberg & J. E. Davidson (Eds.), *Conceptions of giftedness* (pp. 361–387). Cambridge, UK: Cambridge University Press.

Stanovich, K. E. (1986). Matthew effects in reading: Some consequences of individual differences in the acquisition of literacy. *Reading Research Quarterly, 21,* 360–407.

Stanovich, K. E. (1988). Explaining the differences between the dyslexic and the garden-variety poor reader: The phonological–core variable-difference model. *Journal of Learning Disabilities, 21,* 590–604.

Stanovich, K. E., & Cunningham, A. E. (1993). Where does knowledge come from: Specific associations between print exposure and infor-

mation acquisition. *Journal of Educational Psychology, 85,* 211–229.

Steele, C. M. (1992, April). Race and the schooling of black Americans. *Atlantic Monthly,* pp. 68–78.

Steele, C. M. (2004). Through the back door to theory. *Psychological Inquiry, 14,* 314–317.

Steele, C. M., & Aronson, J. (1995). Stereotype threat and the intellectual test performance of African Americans. *Journal of Personality and Social Psychology, 69,* 797–811.

Steele, C. M., & Aronson, J. (2004). Stereotype threat does not live by Steele and Aronson (1995) alone. *American Psychologist, 59,* 47–48.

Steele, H., Steele, M., & Fonagy, P. (1996). Associations among attachment classifications of mothers, fathers, and their infants. *Child Development, 67,* 541–555.

Stein, J., Schettler, T., Wallinga, D., & Valenti, M. (2002). In harm's way: Toxic threats to child development. *Journal of Developmental and Behavioral Pediatrics, 23,* 13–22.

Stein, M. A., Efron, L. A., Schiff, W. B., & Glanzman, M. (2002). Attention deficits and hyperactivity. In M. L. Batshaw (Ed.), *Children with disabilities* (5th ed., pp. 389–416). Baltimore: Brookes.

Stein, N. L., & Glenn, C. G. (1979). An analysis of story comprehension in elementary school children. In R. O. Freedle (Eds.), *New directions in discourse processing* (Vol. 2, pp. 53–120). Norwood, NJ: Ablex.

Stein, N. L., & Nezworski, G. (1978). The effects of organization and instructional set on story memory. *Discourse Processes, 1,* 177–193.

Steinberg, L. (1997). *You and your adolescent, Revised edition: A parent's guide for ages 10–20.* New York: HarperResource.

Steinberg, L. (2001). We know some things: Parent–adolescent relationships in retrospect and prospect. *Journal of Research on Adolescence, 11,* 1–19.

Steinberg, L., Brown, B., & Dornbusch, S. M. (1996). *Beyond the classroom: Why school reform has failed and what parents need to do.* New York: Simon & Schuster.

Steinberg, L., & Cauffman, E. (1995). The impact of employment on adolescent development. In R. Vasta (Ed.), *Annals of child development: A research annual* (Vol. 11, pp. 131–166). London: Kingsley.

Steinberg, L., & Dornbusch, S. M. (1991). Negative correlates of part-time employment during adolescence: Replication and elaboration.

Developmental Psychology, 27, 304–313.

Steinberg, L., Dornbush, S. M., & Brown, B. B. (1992). Ethnic differences in adolescent achievement: An ecological perspective. *American Psychologist, 47*(6), 723–729.

Steinberg, L., Elmen, J. D., & Mounts, N. S. (1989). Authoritative parenting, psychosocial maturity, and academic success among adolescents. *Child Development, 60,* 1424–1436.

Steinberg, L., Fegley, S., & Dornbusch, S. M. (1993). Negative impact of part-time work on adolescent adjustment: Evidence from a longitudinal study. *Developmental Psychology, 29,* 171–180.

Steinberg, L., Lamborn, S. D., Darling, N., Mounts, N. S., & Dornbusch, S. M. (1994). Over-time changes in adjustment and competence among adolescents from authoritative, indulgent, and neglectful families. *Child Development, 65,* 754–770.

Steinberg, L., Lamborn, S. D., Dornbusch, S. M., & Darling, N. (1992). Impact of parenting practices on adolescent achievement: Authoritative parenting, school involvement, and encouragement to succeed. *Child Development, 63,* 1266–1281.

Steinberg, L., & Silverberg, S. B. (1986). The vicissitudes of autonomy in early adolescence. *Child Development, 57,* 841–851.

Steiner, H. H., & Carr, M. (2003). Cognitive development in gifted children: Toward a more precise understanding of emerging differences in intelligence. *Educational Psychology Review, 15,* 215–246.

Stern, J. (1985). Biochemical aspects. In A. M. Clarke, A. D. B. Clarke, & J. M. Berg (Eds.), *Mental deficiency: The changing outlook* (pp. 135–212). New York: Free Press.

Stern, M., & Karraker, K. H. (1989). Sex stereotyping of infants: A review of gender labeling studies. *Sex Roles, 20,* 501–522.

Sternberg, R. J. (1981). A componential theory of intellectual giftedness. *Gifted Child Quarterly, 25,* 86–93.

Sternberg, R. J. (1987). Most vocabulary is learned from context. In M. G. McKeown & M. E. Curtis (Eds.), *The nature of vocabulary acquisition* (pp. 89–105). Hillsdale, NJ: Erlbaum.

Sternberg, R. J. (1994). *Encyclopedia of human intelligence.* New York: Macmillan.

Sternberg, R. J. (1985). *Beyond IQ: A*

triarchic theory of human intelligence. Cambridge, UK: Cambridge University Press.

Sternberg, R. J. (2003). Contemporary theories of intelligence. In I. B. Weiner (Ed.-in-Chief), W. M. Reynolds & G. E. Miller (Vol. Eds.), *Handbook of psychology: Vol. 7. Educational psychology* (pp. 23–46). New York: Wiley.

Sternberg, R. J., & Davidson, J. E. (1983). Insight in the gifted. *Educational Psychologist, 18,* 51–57.

Sternberg, R. J., & Detterman, D. K. (Eds.). (1986). *What is intelligence?: Contemporary viewpoints on its nature and definition.* Norwood, NJ: Ablex.

Sternberg, R. J., & Powell, J. S. (1983). Comprehending verbal comprehension. *American Psychologist, 38,* 878–893.

Stetsenko, A., Little, T. D., Oettingen, G., & Baltes, P. B. (1995). Agency, control, and means–ends beliefs about school performance in Moscow children: How similar are they to beliefs in Western children? *Developmental Psychology, 31,* 285–299.

Stevens, L. J., & Price, M. (1992). Meeting the challenges of educating children at risk. *Phi Delta Kappan, 74,* 18–23.

Stevens, R. J., & Slavin, R. E. (1995a). The cooperative elementary school: Effects on students' achievement, attitudes, and social relations. *American Educational Research Journal, 32,* 321–351.

Stevens, R. J., & Slavin, R. E. (1995b). Effects of a cooperative learning approach in reading and writing on academically handicapped and nonhandicapped students. *Elementary School Journal, 95,* 241–262.

Stevenson, H. W. (1992). Learning from Asian schools. *Scientific American, 267,* 70–75.

Stevenson, H. W. (1990). The Asian advantage: The case of mathematics. In J. J. Shields (Ed.), *Japanese schooling: Patterns of socialization, equality, and political control* (pp. 85–95). University Park: Pennyslvania State University Press.

Stevenson, H. W., Lee, S., & Mu, X. (2000). Successful achievement in mathematics: China and the United States. In C. F. M. van Lieshout & P. G. Heymans (Eds.), *Developing talent across the lifespan* (pp. 167–183). New York: Psychology Press.

Stevenson, M. R., & Black, K. N. (1988). Parental absence and sex role development: A meta-analysis. *Child Development, 59,* 793–814.

Stevenson-Hinde, J., & Shouldice, A.

(1995). Maternal interactions and self-reports related to attachment classifications at 4.5 years. *Child Development, 66,* 583–596.

Stevenson-Hinde, J., & Verschueren, K. (2002). Attachment in childhood. In P. K. Smith & C. H. Hart (Eds.), *Blackwell handbook of childhood social development* (pp. 182–204). Oxford, UK: Blackwell

Stewart, K. (2002). *Helping a child with nonverbal learning disorder or Asperger's syndrome: A parent's guide.* Oakland, CA: New Harbinger.

Stewart, R. B., & Marvin, R. S. (1984). Sibling relations: The role of conceptual perspective taking in the ontogeny of sibling caregiving. *Child Development, 55,* 1322–1332.

Stifter, C. A., Coulehan, C. M., & Fish, M. (1993). Linking employment to attachment: The mediating effects of maternal separation anxiety and interactive behavior. *Child Development, 64,* 1451–60.

Stillings, N. A., Feinstein, M. H., Garfield, J. L., Rissland, E. L., Rosenbaum, D. A., Weisler, S. E., et al. (1987). *Cognitive science: An introduction.* Cambridge, MA: MIT Press.

Stipek, D., & Kowalski, P. (1989). Learned helplessness in task-orienting versus performance-orienting test conditions. *Journal of Educational Psychology, 81,* 384–391.

Stipek, D., & Mac Iver, D. (1989). Developmental change in children's assessment of intellectual competence. *Child Development, 60,* 521–538.

Stipek, D. J. (1996). Motivation and instruction. In D. C. Berliner & R. C. Calfee (Eds.), *Handbook of educational psychology* (pp. 85–113). New York: Macmillan.

Stipek, D. J., & Daniels, D. H. (1988). Declining perceptions of competence: A consequence of changes in the child or in the educational environment? *Journal of Educational Psychology, 80,* 352–356.

Stipek, D. J., & Gralinski, J. H. (1991). Gender differences in children's achievement-related beliefs and emotional responses to success and failure in mathematics. *Journal of Educational Psychology, 83,* 361–371.

Stipek, D. J., & Hoffman, J. M. (1980). Children's achievement-related expectancies as a function of academic performance histories and sex. *Journal of Educational Psychology, 72,* 861–865.

Stocker, C., Dunn, J., & Plomin, R. (1989). Sibling relationships: Links with child temperament, maternal

behavior, and family structure. *Child Development, 60,* 715–727.

Stolberg, A. L., & Anker, J. M. (1984). Cognitive and behavioral changes in children resulting from parental divorce and consequent environmental changes. *Journal of Divorce, 8,* 184–197.

Stone, C. A. (1993). What is missing in the metaphor of scaffolding? In E. A. Forman, N. Minnick, & C. A. Stone (Eds.), *Contexts for learning: Sociocultural dynamics in children's development* (pp. 169–183). New York: Oxford University Press.

Stone, C. A. (1998). What is missing in the metaphor of scaffolding? In D. Faulkner, K. Littleton, & M. Woodhead (Eds.), *Learning relationships in the classroom* (pp. 156–167). London: Routledge.

Storch, S. A., & Whitehurst, G. J. (2001). The role of family and home in the literacy development of children from low-income backgrounds. In P. R. Britto & J. Brooks-Gunn (Eds.), *The role of family literacy environments in promoting young children's emerging literacy skills. New directions for child and adolescent development.* (pp. 53–71). San Francisco: Jossey-Bass/Pfeiffer.

Storfer, M. D. (1990). *Intelligence and giftedness: The contributions of heredity and early environment.* San Francisco: Jossey-Bass.

Story, M., Neumark-Sztainer, D., Sherwood, N., Stang, J., & Murray, D. (1998). Dieting status and its relationship to eating and physical activity behaviors in a representative sample of U.S. adolescents. *Journal of the American Dietetic Association, 98,* 1127–1132.

Strage, A. (1997). Agency, communion, and achievement motivation. *Adolescence, 32,* 299–312.

Strange, W., & Jenkins, J. (1978). Role of linguistic experience in the perception of speech. In R. D. Walk & H. L. Pick (Eds.), *Perception and experience.* New York: Plenum Press.

Strauss, A. L., & Corbin, J. (1998). *Basics of qualitative research: Techniques and procedures for developing grounded theories* (2nd ed.). Thousand Oaks, CA: Sage.

Strauss, M. S. (1979). Abstraction of prototypical information by adults and 10-month-olds. *Journal of Experimental Psychology: Human Learning and Memory, 5,* 618–632.

Streissguth, A. P., & Connor, P. D. (2001). Fetal alcohol syndrome and other effects of prenatal alcohol: Developmental cognitive neuroscience implications. In C. A. Nelson

& M. Luciana (Eds.), *Handbook of developmental cognitive neuroscience* (pp. 505–518). Cambridge, MA: MIT Press.

Stromswold, K. (1995). The cognitive and neural bases of language acquisition. In M. S. Gazzaniga (Ed.), *The cognitive neurosciences* (pp. 855–870). Cambridge, MA: MIT Press.

Stromswold, K. (1998). The genetics of spoken language disorders. *Human Biology, 70*, 297–324.

Stromswold, K. (2001). The heritability of language: A review and metaanalysis of twin, adoption, and linkage studies. *Language, 77*(4), 647–723.

Stuart, M., & Masterson, J. (1992). Patterns of reading and spelling in 10-year old children related to prereading phonological abilities. *Journal of Experimental Child Psychology, 54*, 168–187.

Stunkard, A. J., & Wadden, T. A. (Eds.). (1993). *Obesity: Theory and therapy* (2nd ed.). New York: Raven Press.

Subrahmanyam, K., Greenfield, P., Kraut, R., & Gross, E. (2001). The impact of computer use on children's and adolescents' development. *Journal of Applied Developmental Psychology, 22*, 7–30.

Sugarman, S. (1983). *Children's early thought: Developments in classification*. Cambridge, MA: Cambridge University Press.

Sulloway, F. J. (1992). *Freud: Biologist of the mind*. Cambridge, MA: Harvard University Press.

Sulzby, E., & Teale, W. (1991). Emergent literacy. In R. Barr, M. L. Kamil, P. B. Mosenthal, & P. D. Pearson (Eds.), *Handbook of reading research* (Vol. 2, pp. 727–758). New York: Longman.

Sutton-Smith, B., & Rosenberg, B. G. (1970). *The sibling*. New York: Holt, Rinehart & Winston.

Swaab, D. F., Gooren, L. J. G., & Hofman, M. A. (1992). The human hypothalamus in relation to gender and sexual orientation. *Progress to Brain Research, 93*, 205–219.

Swadi, H. (1992). Drug abuse in children and adolescents: An update. *Archives of Disease in Childhood, 67*, 1245–1246.

Swain, M., & Lapkin, S. (1982). *Evaluating bilingual education: A Canadian case study*. Clevedon, UK: Multilingual Matters.

Swain, M., & Wesche, M. (1973). Linguistic interaction: Case study of a bilingual child. *Working Papers on Bilingualism, 1*, 10–34.

Swanson, H. L. (1999). What develops in working memory?: A life span perspective. *Developmental Psychology, 35*(4), 986–1000.

Swanson, H. L. (2003). Age-related differences in learning disabled and skilled readers' working memory. *Journal of Experimental Child Psychology, 85*, 1–31.

Swanson, H. L., & Cooney, J. B. (1991). Learning disabilities and memory. In B. Y. L. Wong (Ed.), *Learning about learning disabilities* (pp. 104–127). San Diego, CA: Academic Press.

Swanson, H. L., & Sáez, L. (2003). Memory difficulties in children and adults with learning disabilities. In H. L. Swanson, K. R. Harris, & S. Graham (Eds.), *Handbook of learning disabilities* (pp. 182–198). New York: Guilford Press.

Symons, D., Clark, S., Isaksen, G., & Marshall, J. (1998). Stability of Q-sort attachment security from age two to five. *Infant Behavior and Development, 21*, 785–791.

Taber, K. S. (1992). Girls' interactions with teachers in mixed physics classes: Results of classroom observation. *International Journal of Science Education, 14*, 163–180.

Taitz, L. A. (1983). *The obese child*. Boston: Blackwell.

Takahashi, T., Nowakowski, R. S., & Caviness, V. S. Jr. (2001). Neocortical neurogenesis regulation, control points, and a strategy for structural variation. In C. A. Nelson & M. Luciana (Eds.), *Handbook of developmental cognitive neuroscience* (pp. 3–22). Cambridge, MA: MIT Press.

Tamis-LeMonda, C. S., Bornstein, M. H., Kahana-Kalman, R., Baumwell, L., & Cyphers, L. (1998). Predicting variation in the timing of linguistic milestones in the second year: An event-history approach. *Journal of Child Language, 28*, 127–152.

Tannen, D. (1990). *You just don't understand: Women and men in conversation*. New York: Macmillan.

Tannenbaum, A. J. (1983). *Gifted children: Psychological and educational perspectives*. New York: Macmillan.

Tannenbaum, A. J. (1986). Giftedness: A psychosocial approach. In R. J. Sternberg & J. E. Davidson (Eds.), *Conceptions of giftedness* (pp. 21–52). Cambridge, UK: Cambridge University Press.

Tanner, J. M. (1962). *Growth of adolescence* (2nd ed.). Oxford, UK: Blackwell Scientific Publications.

Tanner, J. M. (1970). Physical growth. In P. H. Mussen (Ed.), *Carmichael's manual of child psychology* (3rd ed., Vol. 1, pp. 77–155). New York: Wiley.

Tappan, M. B. (1998). Sociocultural psychology and caring pedagogy: Exploring Vygotsky's "hidden curriculum." *Educational Psychologist, 33*, 23–33.

Tarver, S. G., Hallahan, D. P., Kauffman, J. M., & Ball, D. W. (1976). Verbal rehearsal and selective attention in children with learning disabilities: A developmental lag. *Journal of Experimental Child Psychology, 22*, 375–385.

Tasbihsazan, R., Nettelbeck, T., & Kirby, N. (2003). Predictive validity of the Fagan Test of Infant Intelligence. *British Journal of Developmental Psychology, 21*, 585–597.

Tashakkori, A., & Teddlie, C. (Eds.). (2003). *Handbook of mixed methods in social and behavioral sciences*. Thousand Oaks, CA: Sage.

Tavris, C., & Wade, C. (1984). *The longest war: Sex differences in perspective* (2nd ed.). San Diego, CA: Harcourt, Brace, Jovanovich.

Taylor, D., & Strickland, D. (1986). *Family storybook reading*. Exeter, NH: Heinemann Educational Books.

Taylor, E. (1995). Unexpected death in infancy. In B. Linström & N. Spencer (Eds.), *Social pediatrics* (pp. 297–309). Oxford, UK: Oxford University Press.

Taylor, G. H., Klein, N., & Hack, M. (2000). School-age consequences of birth weight less than 750 g: A review and update. *Developmental Neuropsychology, 17*, 289–321.

Taylor, M. (1996). A theory of mind perspective on social cognitive development. In R. Gelman & T. Kit-Fong (Eds.), *Perceptual and cognitive development: Handbook of perception and cognition* (2nd ed., pp. 283–329). San Diego, CA: Academic Press.

Taylor, M. C., & Hall, J. A. (1982). Psychological androgyny: A review and reformulation of theories, methods, and conclusions. *Psychological Bulletin, 92*, 347–366.

Taylor, R. D., Casten, R., & Flickinger, S. M. (1993). Influence of kinship social support on the parenting experiences and psychosocial adjustment of African-American adolescents. *Developmental Psychology, 29*, 382–388.

Teale, W. H. (1978). Positive environments for learning to read: What studies of early readers tell us. *Language Arts, 55*, 922–932.

Tepper, C. A., & Cassidy, K. W. (1999). Gender differences in emotional language in children's picture books. *Sex Roles, 40*, 265–280.

Terman, L. M. (1925). *Genetic studies of genius: Mental and physical traits of a thousand gifted children.* Stanford, CA: Stanford University Press.

Teman, L. M., & Childs, H. G. (1912). A tentative revision and extension of the Binet–Simon Measuring Scale of Intelligence. *Journal of Educational Psychology, 3*, 61–74, 133–143, 198–208, 277–289.

Terman, L. M., & Oden, M. H. (1947). *The gifted child grows up: Twenty-five years' followup of a superior group.* Stanford, CA: Stanford University Press.

Terman, L. M., & Oden, M. H. (1959). *The gifted group in midlife: Thirty years followup of the superior child.* Stanford, CA: Stanford University Press.

Terwogt, M. M., & Harris, P. L. (1993). Understanding of emotion. In M. Bennett (Ed.), *The development of social cognition: The child as psychologist* (pp. 62–86). New York: Guilford Press.

Tessler, M. (1986). *Mother–child talk in a museum: The socialization of a memory.* New York: City University of New York, Graduate Center.

Teti, D. (2001). Retrospect and prospect in the psychological study of sibling relationships. In J. McHale & W. Grolnick (Eds.), *Retrospect and prospect in the psychological study of families* (pp. 193–224). Mahwah, NJ: Erlbaum.

Teti, D. M., Nakagawa, M., Das, R., & Wirth, O. (1991). Security of attachment between preschoolers and their mothers: Relations among social interaction, parenting stress, and mothers' sorts of the attachment Q-set. *Developmental Psychology, 27*, 440–447.

Tharp, R. G. (1982). The effective instruction of comprehension: Results and description of the Kamehameha Early Education Program. *Reading Research Quarterly, 27*, 503–527.

Tharp, R. G., & Gallimore, R. (1988). *Rousing minds to life: Teaching, learning, and schooling in social context.* New York: Cambridge University Press.

Thibaut, J. P. (1997). Similarité et catégorisation. *Année Psychologique, 97*, 701–736.

Thomas, A., & Chess, S. (1977). *Temperament and development.* New York: Brunner/Mazel.

Thomas, A., & Chess, S. (1986). The New York Longitudinal Study: From infancy to early adult life. In R. Plomin & J. Dunn (Eds.), *The study of temperament: Changes, continuities, and challenges* (pp. 39–52). Hillsdale, NJ: Erlbaum.

Thomas, E. (1990). Filial piety, social change and Singapore youth. *Journal of Moral Education, 19*, 192–206.

Thomas, J. R. (1984). Children's motor skill development. In J. R. Thomas (Ed.), *Motor development during childhood and adolescence* (pp. 91–104). Minneapolis, MN: Burges.

Thomas, J. R., & French, K. E. (1985). Gender differences across age in motor performance: A meta-analysis. *Psychological Bulletin, 98*, 260–282.

Thomas, J. R., Nelson, J. K., & Church, G. (1991). A developmental analysis of gender differences in health related physical fitness. *Pediatric Exercise Science, 3*, 28–42.

Thomas, W. P., & Collier, V. (1997). *School effectiveness for language minority students* (NCBE Resource Collection Series No. 9). Washington, DC: George Washington University, National Clearinghouse for Bilingual Education.

Thompson, D. R., & Senk, S. L. (2001). The effects of curriculum on achievement in second-year algebra: The example of the University of Chicago school mathematics project. *Journal for Research in Mathematics Education, 32*(1), 58–84.

Thompson, M. S., Entwisle, D. R., Alexander, K. L., & Sundius, M. J. (1992). The influence of family composition on children's conformity to the student role. *American Educational Research Journal, 29*, 405–424.

Thompson, R. A. (1999). Early attachment and later development. In J. Cassidy & P. R. Shaver (Eds.), *Handbook of attachment: Theory, research, and clinical applications* (pp. 265–286). New York: Guilford Press.

Thompson, R. A., Easterbrooks, M. A., & Walker, P. (2003). Social and emotional development in infancy. In R. M. Lerner, M. A. Easterbrooks, J. Mistry (Vol. Eds.) & I. B. Weiner (Ed.-in-Chief), *Handbook of psychology: Vol. 6. Developmental psychology* (pp. 91–112). New York: Wiley.

Thompson, S. K., & Bentler, P. M. (1971). The priority of cues in sex discrimination by children and adults. *Developmental Psychology, 5*, 181–185.

Thompson, V. D. (1974). Family size: Implicit policies and assumed psychological outcomes. *Journal of Social Issues, 30*, 93–124.

Thomson, J. B., & Raskind, W. H. (2003). Genetic influences on reading and writing disabilities. In H. L. Swanson, K. R. Harris, & S. Graham (Eds.), *Handbook of learning disabilities* (pp. 256–279). New York: Guilford Press.

Thorkildsen, T. A. (1989). Justice in the classroom: The student's view. *Child Development, 60*, 323–334.

Thorkildsen, T. A. (1993). Those who can, tutor: High-ability students' conceptions of fair ways to organize learning. *Journal of Educational Psychology, 85*, 182–190.

Thorkildsen, T. A., Nolen, S. B., & Fournier, J. (1994). What is fair?: Children's critiques of practices that influence motivation. *Journal of Educational Psychology, 86*(4), 475–486.

Thorkildsen, T. A., Sadonis, A., & White-McNulty, L. (2004). Epistemology and adolescents' conceptions of procedural justice in school. *Journal of Educational Psychology, 96*(2), 347–359.

Thorndike, R. L., Hagen, E. P., & Sattler, J. M. (1986). *Stanford–Binet intelligence scale: Technical manual* (4th ed.). Chicago: Riverside Press.

Thyer, B. A., & Myers, L. L. (1998). Social learning theory: An empirically-based approach to understanding human behavior in the social environment. *Journal of Human Behavior in the Social Environment, 1*, 33–52.

Tipper, S. P., Bourque, T. A., Anderson, S. H., & Brehaut, J. C. (1989). Mechanisms of attention: A developmental study. *Journal of Experimental Child Psychology, 48*, 353–378.

Todorov, T. (1984). *Mikhail Bakhtin: The dialogical principle.* Minneapolis: University of Minnesota Press.

Tomasello, M. (1994). Can an ape understand a sentence?: A review of *Language comprehension in ape and child*, by E. S. Savage-Rumbaugh et al. *Language and Communication, 14*, 377–390.

Tomasello, M. (2000). Do young children have adult syntactic competence? *Cognition, 74*, 209–253.

Tomasello, M. (2003). *Constructing a language: A usage-based theory of language acquisition.* Cambridge, MA: Harvard University Press.

Tomasello, M., & Farrar, M. J. (1986). Joint attention and early language. *Child Development, 57*, 1454–1463.

Tomasello, M., & Mannle, S. (1985). Pragmatics of sibling speech to one-year-olds. *Child Development, 56,* 911–917.

Tomasello, M., & Todd, J. (1983). Joint attention and lexical acquisition style. *First Language, 4,* 197–212.

Tomporowski, P. D., & Tinsley, V. (1997). Attention in mentally retarded persons. In W. E. MacLean Jr. (Ed.), *Ellis' handbook of mental deficiency, psychological theory and research* (pp. 219–244). Mahwah, NJ: Erlbaum.

Toppino, T. C., Kasserman, J. E., & Mracek, W. A. (1991). The effect of spacing repetitions on the recognition memory of young children and adults. *Journal of Experimental Child Psychology, 51,* 123–138.

Torgesen, J. K. (1975). Problems and prospects in the study of learning disabilities. In M. Hetherington & J. Hagen (Eds.), *Review of research in child development* (Vol. 5, pp. 385–440). Chicago: University of Chicago Press.

Torgesen, J. K. (1977). Memorization processes in reading-disabled children. *Journal of Educational Psychology, 69,* 571–578.

Torgesen, J. K. (1991). Learning disabilities: Historical and conceptual issues. In B. Y. L. Wong (Ed.), *Learning about learning disabilities* (pp. 3–37). San Diego, CA: Academic Press.

Torgesen, J. K., & Goldman, T. (1977). Verbal rehearsal and short-term memory in reading disabled children. *Child Development, 48,* 56–60.

Trautwein, U., & Koeller, O. (2003). The relationship between homework and achievement: Still much of a mystery. *Educational Psychology Review, 15,* 115–145.

Traynor, P. (2003). Effects of computer-assisted-instruction on different learners. *Journal of Instructional Psychology, 30*(2), 137–143.

Troia, G. A. (2004). Phonological processing and its influence on literacy learning. In C. A. Stone, E. R. Silliman, B. J. Ehren, & K. Apel (Eds.), *Handbook of language and literacy* (pp. 271–301). New York: Guilford Press.

Trueba, H. T. (1988). Culturally based explanations of minority students' academic achievement. *Anthropology and Education Quarterly, 19,* 270–287.

Tsao, F. M., Liu, H. M., & Kuhl, P. K. (2004). Speech perception in infancy predicts language development in the second year of life: A longitudinal study. *Child Development, 75,* 1067–1084.

Tudge, J., & Scrimsher, S. (2003). Lev

S. Vygotsky on education: A cultural-historical, interpersonal, and individual approach to development. In B. J. Zimmerman & D. H. Schunk (Eds.), *Educational psychology: A century of contributions* (pp. 207–228). Mahwah, NJ: Erlbaum.

Tulving, E. (1983). *Elements of episodic memory.* Oxford, UK: Oxford University Press.

Turkeltaub, P. E., Eden, G., Jones, K., & Zeffiro, T. (2002). Meta-analysis of the functional neuroanatomy of single-word reading: Method and validation. *NeuroImage, 16,* 765–780.

Turkeltaub, P. E., Gareau, L., Flowers, D. L., Zeffiro, T. A., & Eden, G. F. (2003). Development of neural mechanisms for reading. *Nature Neuroscience, 10,* 1038–1065.

Turner, J. C., Midgley, C., Meyer, D. K., Gheen, M., Anderman, E. M., Kang, Y., et al. (2002). The classroom environment and students' reports of avoidance strategies in mathematics: A multimethod study. *Journal of Educational Psychology, 94,* 88–106.

Turner, P. J., & Gervai, J. (1995). A multidimensional study of gender typing in preschool children and their parents: Personality, attitudes, preferences, behavior, and cultural differences. *Developmental Psychology, 31,* 759–772.

Turner-Bowker, D. M. (1996). Gender stereotyped descriptions in children's picture books: Does "Curious Jane" exist in literature? *Sex Roles, 35,* 461–488.

Tuss, P., Zimmer, J., & Ho, H. Z. (1995). Causal attributions of underachieving fourth grade students in China, Japan, and the United States. *Journal of Cross-Cultural Psychology, 26,* 408–425.

Twenge, J. M. (2000). The age of anxiety?: Birth cohort change in anxiety and neuroticism, 1952–1993. *Journal of Personality and Social Psychology, 79,* 1007–1021.

Tychsen, L. (2001). Critical periods for development of visual acuity, depth perception, and eye tracking. In J. B. Bailey Jr., J. T. Bruer, F. J. Symons, & J. W. Lichtman (Eds.), *Critical thinking about critical periods* (pp. 67–80). Baltimore: Brookes.

Tyson, P., & Tyson, R. L. (1990). *Psychoanalytic theories of development.* New Haven, CT: Yale University Press.

Tzuriel, D. (1992). The development of ego identity at adolescence among Israeli Jews and Arabs. *Journal of Youth and Adolescence, 21,* 551–571.

Udry, J. R., & Campbell, B. C. (1994). Getting started on sexual behavior. In A. S. Rossi (Ed.), *Sexuality across the life course* (pp. 187–207). Chicago: University of Chicago Press.

Underwood, M. K. (2002). Sticks and stones and social exclusion: Aggression among girls and boys. In P. K. Smith & C. H. Hart (Eds.), *Blackwell handbook of childhood social development* (pp. 533–548). Oxford, UK: Blackwell.

Underwood, M. K., Schockner, A. E., & Hurley, J. C. (2001). Children's responses to same- and other-gender peers: An experimental investigation with 8-, 10-, and 12-year-olds. *Developmental Psychology, 37,* 262–272.

Unger, R., & Crawford, M. (1992). *Women and gender: A feminist psychology.* New York: McGraw-Hill.

United States of America v. State of South Carolina, 434 U.S. 1026 (1978).

U.S. Bureau of the Census. (1997). *Statistical abstract of the United States* (117th ed.). Washington, DC: U.S. Government Printing Office.

Urberg, K. A. (1982). The development of the concepts of masculinity and femininity in young children. *Sex Roles, 8,* 659–668.

Urberg, K. A., Luo, Q., Pilgrim, C., & Degirmencioglu, S. M. (2003). A two-stage model of peer influence in adolescent substance use: Individual and relationship-specific differences in susceptibility to influence. *Addictive Behaviors, 28,* 1243–1256.

Urdan, T., & Midgley, C. (2001). Academic self-handicapping: What we know, what more there is to learn. *Educational Psychology Review, 13*(2), 115–138.

Urdan, T., & Midgley, C. (2003). Changes in the perceived classroom goal structure and pattern of adaptive learning during early adolescence. *Contemporary Educational Psychology, 28*(4), 524–551.

Vaillant, G. E. (1971). Theoretical hierarchy of adaptive ego mechanisms. *Archives of General Psychiatry, 24,* 107–118.

Vaillant, G. E. (1975). Natural history of male psychological health: III. Empirical dimensions of mental health. *Archives of General Psychiatry, 32*(4), 420–426.

Vaillant, G. E. (1976). Natural history of male psychological health: V. The relation of choice of ego mechanism of defense to adult adjustment. *Archives of General Psychiatry, 33*(5), 535–545.

Valdez-Menchaca, M. C., & Whitehurst, G. J. (1992). Accelerating language development through picture book reading: A systematic extension to Mexican day care. *Developmental Psychology, 28,* 1106–1114.

Valencia, R. R., & Suzuki, L. A. (2001). *Intelligence testing and minority students: Foundation, performance factors, and assessment issues.* Thousand Oaks, CA: Sage.

Valenzuela, A. (1999). *Subtractive schooling: U.S. Mexican youth and the politics of caring.* Albany: State University of New York Press.

van Daalen-Kapteijns, M. M., & Elshout-Mohr, M. (1981). The acquisition of word meanings as a cognitive learning process. *Journal of Verbal Learning and Verbal Behavior, 20,* 386–389.

van den Boom, D. C. (1994). The influence of temperament and mothering on attachment and exploration: An experimental manipulation of sensitive responsiveness among lower-class mothers and irritable infants. *Child Development, 65,* 1457–1477.

van den Boom, D. C. (1995). Do first-year intervention effects endure?: Follow-up during toddlerhood of a sample of Dutch irritable infants. *Child Development, 66,* 1798–1816.

Van Houten, R., & Rolider, A. (1989). An analysis of several variables influencing the efficacy of flash card instruction. *Journal of Applied Behavior Analysis, 22,* 111–118.

van IJzendoorn, M. H. (1995). Adult attachment representations, parental responsiveness, and infant attachment: A meta-analysis on the predictive validity of the adult attachment interview. *Psychological Bulletin, 117,* 397–403.

van IJzendoorn, M. H., Juffer, F., & Duyvesteyn, M. G. C. (1995). Breaking the intergenerational cycle of insecure attachment: A review of the effects of attachment-based interventions on maternal sensitivity and infant security. *Journal of Child Psychology and Psychiatry, 36,* 225–248.

Van Laar, C. (2000). The paradox of low achievement but high self-esteem in African-American students: An attributional account. *Educational Psychology Review, 12,* 33–61.

Van Ness, H. (1981). Social control and social organization in an Alaskan Athabaskan classroom: A microethngraphy of "getting ready" for reading. In H. Trueba, G. Guthrie, & K. Au (Eds.), *Culture and*

the *bilingual classroom* (pp. 120–138). Rowley, MA: Newbury House.

Vance, Y. H., & Eiser, C. (2002). The school experience of the child with cancer. *Child Care, Health and Development, 28,* 5–19.

Vandell, D. L., Henderson, V. K., & Wilson, K. S. (1988). A longitudinal study of children with daycare experiences of varying quality. *Child Development, 59,* 1286–92.

Vandell, D. L., Minnett, A. M., & Santrock, J. W. (1987). Age differences in sibling relationships during middle childhood. *Journal of Applied Developmental Psychology, 8,* 247–257.

Vandell, D. L., & Mueller, E. C. (1980). Peer play and friendships during the first two years. In H. C. Foot, A. J. Chapman, & J. R. Smith (Eds.), *Friendships and social relations in children* (pp. 181–208). Chichester, UK: Wiley.

Vandell, D. L., & Ramanan, J. (1992). Effects of early and recent maternal employment on children from low-income families. *Child Development, 63,* 938–949.

Vandell, D. L., Wilson, K. S., & Buchanen, N. R. (1980). Peer interaction in the first year of life: An examination of its structure, content, and sensitivity to toys. *Child Development, 51,* 481–488.

vanLehn, K. (1990). *Mind bugs: The origins of procedural misconceptions.* Cambridge MA: MIT Press.

Vaughn, V. C., & Litt, I. F. (1990). *Child and adolescent development: Clinical implications.* Philadelphia: Saunders.

Vellutino, F. R. (1979). *Dyslexia: Theory and research.* Cambridge, MA: MIT Press.

Vellutino, F. R., & Fletcher, J. M. (2005). Developmental dyslexia. In M. J. Snowling & C. Hulme (Eds.), *The science of reading: A handbook* (pp. 362–378). Malden, MA: Blackwell.

Vernon, P. A. (1991). Studying intelligence the hard way. *Intelligence, 15,* 389–395.

Viadero, D. (1994, March 16). Jittery students are put to test with new S.A.T. *Education Week,* pp. 1, 12.

Vihman, M. M. (1992). Early syllables and the construction of phonology. In C. A. Ferguson, L. Menn, & C. Stoel-Gammon (Eds.), *Phonological development: Models, research, and implications* (pp. 393–422). Timonium, MD: York Press.

Volterra, V., & Taeschner, T. (1978). The acquisition and development of language by bilingual children. *Journal of Child Language, 5,* 311–326.

von Glaserfeld, E. (1995). *Radical constructivism: A way of knowing and learning.* Bristol, PA: Falmer Press.

Vorhees, C. V. (1986). Principles of behavioral teratology. In E. P. Riley & C. V. Vorhees (Eds.), *Handbook of behavioral teratology* (pp. 23–48). New York: Plenum Press.

Vouloumanos, A., & Werker, J. F. (2004). Tuned to the signal: The privileged status of speech for young infants. *Developmental Science, 7,* 270–276.

Vurpillot, E. (1968). The development of scanning strategies and their relation to visual differentiation. *Journal of Experimental Child Psychology, 6,* 632–650.

Vygotsky, L. S. (1962). *Thought and language.* Cambridge, MA: MIT Press.

Vygotsky, L. S. (1978). *Mind in society: The development of higher psychological processes.* Cambridge, MA: Harvard University Press.

Vygotsky, L. S. (1987). *Thinking and speech* (Ed. & Trans. by N. Minick). New York: Plenum Press.

Waddington, C. H. (1961). Genetic assimilation. *Advances in Genetics, 10,* 257–293.

Wade, S. E., & Adams, R. B. (1990). Effects of importance and interest on recall of biographic text. *Journal of Reading Behavior, 22,* 331–353.

Waggoner, D. (1991). *Undereducation in America.* New York: Auburn House.

Wagner, D. A. (1974). The development of short-term and incidental memory: A cross-cultural study. *Child Development, 45,* 389–396.

Wagner, D. A. (1978). Memories of Morocco: The influence of age, schooling, and environment on memory. *Cognitive Psychology, 10,* 1–28.

Wagner, D. A., & Spratt, J. E. (1987). Cognitive consequences of contrasting pedagogies: The effects of Quranic preschooling in Morocco. *Child Development, 58,* 1207–1219.

Wahler, R. G., & Dumas, J. E. (1989). Attentional problems in dysfunctional mother–child interactions: An interbehavioral model. *Psychological Bulletin, 105,* 116–130.

Walberg, H. J., Harnisch, D., & Tsai, S. L. (1986). Elementary school mathematics productivity in twelve countries. *British Educational Research Journal, 12,* 237–248.

Waldrop, M. F., & Halverson, C. F. (1975). Intensive and extensive peer behavior: Longitudinal and cross-sectional analyses. *Child Development, 46,* 19–26.

Walford, G. (1983). Science education

and sexism in the Soviet Union. *School Science Review, 65*, 213–224.

Walker, L. J. (1984). Sex differences in the development of moral reasoning: A critical review. *Child Development, 55*, 677–691.

Walker, L. J. (1989). A longitudinal study of moral reasoning. *Child Development, 60*, 157–166.

Walker, L. J., & Moran, T. J. (1991). Moral reasoning in a communist Chinese society. *Journal of Moral Education, 20*, 139–155.

Wallerstein, J. S., & Corbin, S. B. (1989). Daughters of divorce: Report from a ten-year followup. *American Journal of Orthopsychiatry, 59*, 593–604.

Wallerstein, J. S., Corbin, S. B., & Lewis, J. M. (1988). Children of divorce: A ten-year study. In E. M. Hetherington & J. Arasteh (Eds.), *Impact of divorce, single-parenting, and stepparenting on children* (pp. 197–214). Hillsdale, NJ: Erlbaum.

Wallerstein, J. S., & Kelly, J. B. (1980). *Surviving the breakup: How children and parents cope with divorce.* New York: Basic Books.

Wallerstein, J. S., & Lewis, J. M. (2004). The unexpected legacy of divorce: Report of a 25-year study. *Psychoanalytic Psychology, 21*(3), 353–370.

Walters, G. C., & Grusec, J. E. (1977). *Punishment.* San Francisco: Freeman.

Wang, Q. (2003). Infantile amnesia reconsidered: A cross-cultural analysis. *Memory, 11*, 65–80.

Ward, L. P., & McCune, S. K. (2002). The first weeks of life. In M. L. Batshaw (Ed.), *Children with disabilities* (5th ed., pp. 69–84). Baltimore: Brookes.

Ward, M. J., & Carlson, E. A. (1995). Associations among adult attachment representations, maternal sensitivity, and infant–mother attachment in a sample of adolescent mothers. *Child Development, 66*, 69–79.

Wark, G. R., & Krebs, D. L. (1996). Gender and dilemma differences in real-life moral judgment. *Developmental Psychology, 32*(2), 220–230.

Washington v. Davis, 426 U.S. 229 (1976).

Wasserman, G. A., Factor-Litvak, P., Liu, X., Todd, A. C., Kline, J. K., Slavkovich, V., et al. (2003). The relationship between blood lead, bone lead and child intelligence. *Child Neuropsychology, 9*, 22–34.

Wasserman, J. D. (2003). Assessment of intellectual functioning. In J. R. Graham, J. A. Naglieri (Vol. Eds.) &

I. B. Weiner (Ed.-in-Chief), *Handbook of psychology: Vol. 10. Assessment psychology* (pp. 417–442). New York: Wiley.

Wasik, B. A., & Slavin, R. E. (1993). Preventing early reading failure with one-to-one tutoring: A review of five programs. *Reading Research Quarterly, 28*, 178–200.

Waterman, A., & Goldman, J. (1976). A longitudinal study of ego identity development in a liberal arts college. *Journal of Youth and Adolescence, 5*, 361–369.

Waters, E. (1995). The attachment Q-set. In E. Waters, B. E. Vaughn, G. Posada, & K. Kondo-Ikemura (Eds.), Caregiving, cultural, and cognitive perspectives on secure-base behavior and working-models. *Monographs of the Society for Research in Child Development, 60*(Nos. 2–3, Serial No. 244), 234–246.

Waters, E., & Deane, K. E. (1985). Defining and assessing individual differences in attachment relationships: Q-methodology and the organization of behavior in infancy and early childhood. In I. Bretherton & E. Waters (Eds.), Growing points of attachment theory and research (pp. 41–65). *Monographs of the Society for Research in Child Development, 50*(1–2, Serial No. 209), 41–65.

Waters, E., Merrick, S., Treboux, D., Crowell, J., & Albersheim, L. (2000). Attachment security in infancy and early adulthood: A twenty-year longitudinal study. *Child Development, 71*, 684–689.

Waters, E., Vaughn, B. E., Posada, G., & Kondo-Ikemura, K. (Eds.). (1995). Caregiving, cultural, and cognitive perspectives on secure-base behavior and working models: New growing points of attachment theory and research. *Monographs of the Society for Research in Child Development, 60*(Serial No. 244).

Waters, E., Weinfield, N. S., & Hamilton, C. E. (2000). The stability of attachment security from infancy to adolescence and early adulthood: General discussion. *Child Development, 71*, 703–706.

Waters, E., Wippman, J., & Sroufe, L. A. (1979). Attachment, positive affect, and competence in the peer group: Two studies in construct validation. *Child Development, 50*, 821–829.

Watson, D. J. (1989). Defining and describing whole language. *Elementary School Journal, 90*, 129–141.

Watson, J. B. (1927, March). What to do when your child is afraid [Inter-

view with Beatrice Black]. *Children,* pp. 25–27.

Watson, J. B., & Rayner, R. (1920). Conditioned emotional reactions. *Journal of Experimental Psychology, 3*, 1–14.

Watts, W. J. (1979). The influence of language on the development of quantitative, spatial, and social thinking in deaf children. *American Annals of the Deaf, 12*, 45–56.

Waxman, S. R., & Booth, A. E. (2000). Principles that are invoked in the acquisition of words, but not facts. *Cognition, 77*(2), B33–B43.

Webb, N. L. (1992). Assessment of students' knowledge of mathematics: Steps toward a theory. In D. A. Grouws (Ed.), *Handbook of research on mathematics teaching and learning* (pp. 661–683). New York: Macmillan.

Webb, N. M. (1984). Sex differences in interaction and achievement in cooperative small groups. *Journal of Educational Psychology, 76*, 33–34.

Webb, N. M. (1989). Peer interaction and learning in small groups. *International Journal of Educational Research, 13*, 21–39.

Webb, N. M., & Kenderski, C. M. (1985). Gender differences in small-group interaction and achievement in high- and low-achieving classes. In L. C. Wilkinson & C. B. Marrett (Eds.), *Gender influences on classroom interaction* (pp. 209–236). Orlando, FL: Academic Press.

Weed, K., Ryan, E. B., & Day, J. (1990). Metamemory and attributions as mediators of strategy use and recall. *Journal of Educational Psychology, 82*, 849–855.

Weeks, T. E. (1971). Speech registers in young children. *Child Development, 42*, 1119–1131.

Weikart, D. (1989). *Quality preschool programs: A long-term social investment* (Occasional Paper, Project on Social Welfare and the American Future, No. 5). New York: Ford Foundation.

Weikart, D. P., & Schweinhart, L. J. (1992). High/Scope Preschool Program outcomes. In J. McCord & R. E. Tremblay (Eds.), *Preventing antisocial behavior* (pp. 67–86). New York: Guilford Press.

Weinberg, R. A., Scarr, S., & Waldman, I. D. (1992). The Minnesota Transracial Adoption Study: A followup of IQ test performance at adolescence. *Intelligence, 16*, 117–135.

Weiner, B. (1979). A theory of motivation for some classroom experiences. *Journal of Educational Psychology, 71*, 3–25.

Weiner, B. (1991). Metaphors in motivation and attribution. *American Psychologist, 46*(9), 921–930.

Weiner, B. (2001). Intrapersonal and interpersonal theories of motivation from an attribution perspective. In F. Salili & C.-Y. Chiu (Eds.), *Student motivation: The culture and context of learning* (pp. 17–30). Dordrecht, The Netherlands: Kluwer.

Weiner, B. (2003). The classroom as courtroom. *Social Psychology of Education, 6*, 3–15.

Weinert, F. E. (1979). Entwicklungspsychologische Lern- under Gedächynisforschung. Entwicklungsabhängigkeit des Lernens und des Gedächnisforschung. In L. Montada (Ed.), *Brennpunkte der Entwicklungspsychologie* (pp. 61–76). Stuttgart, Germany: Kohlhammer.

Weinfield, N. S., Sroufe, L. A., Egeland, B., & Carlson, E. A. (1999). The nature of individual differences in infant–caregiver attachment. In J. Cassidy & P. R. Shaver (Eds.), *Handbook of attachment: Theory, research, and clinical applications* (pp. 68–88). New York: Guilford Press.

Weinfield, N. S., Sroufe, L. A., & Egeland, B. (2000). Attachment from infancy to early adulthood in a high-risk sample: Continuity, discontinuity, and their correlates. *Child Development, 71*, 695–702.

Weinraub, M., Jaeger, E., & Hoffman, L. W. (1988). Predicting infant outcomes in families of employed and non-employed mothers. *Early Childhood Research Quarterly, 3*, 361–378.

Weinstein, R. S. (2002). *Reaching higher: The power of expectations in schooling.* Cambridge, MA: Harvard University Press.

Weisner, T. S., & Garnier, H. (1992). Nonconventional family life-styles and school achievement: A 12-year longitudinal study. *American Educational Research Journal, 29*, 605–632.

Weiss, B., Dodge, K. A., Bates, J. E., & Pettit, G. S. (1992). Some consequences of early harsh discipline: Child aggression and a maladaptive social information processing style. *Child Development, 63*, 1321–1335.

Weiss, L. G., Saklofske, D. H., & Prifitera, A. (2003). Clinical interpretation of the Wechsler Intelligence Scale for Children–Third edition (WISC-III) index scores. In C. R. Reynolds & R. W. Kamphaus (Eds.), *Handbook of psychological and educational assessment of children: Intelligence, aptitude, and achievement* (2nd ed., pp. 115–146). New York: Guilford Press.

Weiss, L. H., & Schwarz, J. C. (1996). The relationship between parenting types and older adolescents' personality, academic achievement, adjustment, and substance use. *Child Development, 67*, 2101–2114.

Weitzman, N., Birns, B., & Friend, R. (1985). Traditional and nontraditional mothers' communication with their daughters and sons. *Child Development, 56*, 894–898.

Wellman, H. M. (1990). *The child's theory of mind.* Cambridge, MA: MIT Press.

Wellman, H. M. (2002). Understanding the psychological world: Developing a theory of mind. In U. Goswami (Ed.), *Blackwell handbook of childhood cognitive development* (pp. 167–187). Oxford, UK: Blackwell.

Wellman, H. M., & Estes, D. (1986). Early understanding of mental entities: A reexamination of childhood realism. *Child Development, 57*, 910–923.

Wells, A. S., & Crain, R. L. (1997). *Stepping over the color line: African-American students in white suburban schools.* New Haven, CT: Yale University Press.

Wentzel, K. R. (1991a). Relations between social competence and academic achievement in early adolescence. *Child Development, 62*, 1066–1078.

Wentzel, K. R. (1991b). Social competence at school: Relation between social responsibility and academic achievement. *Review of Educational Research, 61*, 1–24.

Wentzel, K. R. (1998). Social relationships and motivation in middle school: The role of parents, teachers, and peers. *Journal of Educational Psychology, 90*, 202–209.

Wentzel, K. R. (2003). Sociometric status and adjustment in middle school: A longitudinal study. *Journal of Early Adolescence, 23*, 5–28.

Wentzel, K. R., & Asher, S. R. (1995). The academic lives of neglected, rejected, popular, and controversial children. *Child Development, 66*, 754–763.

Werker, J. F. (1995). Exploring developmental changes in cross-language speech perception. In L. R. Gleitman & M. Liberman (Eds.), *Language: An invitation to cognitive science* (pp. 87–106). Cambridge, MA: MIT Press.

Werker, J. F., & Pegg, J. E. (1992). Infant speech perception and phonological acquisition. In C. A. Fergu-son, L. Menn, & C. Stoel-Gammon (Eds.), *Phonological development: Models, research, and implications* (pp. 285–311). Timonium, MD: York Press.

Werner, E. E. (1990). Protective factors and individual resilience. In S. J. Meisels & J. P. Shonkoff (Eds.), *Handbook of early childhood interventions* (pp. 97–116). Cambridge, UK: Cambridge University Press.

Werner, E. E., & Smith, R. S. (1982). *Vulnerable but invincible: A longitudinal study of resilient children and youth.* New York: McGraw-Hill.

Werner, H., & Kaplan, E. (1952). The acquisition of word meanings: A developmental study. *Monographs of the Society for Research in Child Development, 15*(1, Serial No. 51).

Wertsch, J. V. (1979). From social interaction to higher psychological processes: A clarification and application of Vygotsky's theory. *Human Development, 22*, 1–22.

Wertsch, J. V. (1985). *Vygotsky and the social formation of mind.* Cambridge, MA: Harvard University Press.

Wertsch, J. V. (1991). *Voices of the mind: A sociocultural approach to mediated action.* Cambridge, MA: Harvard University Press.

Westermeyer, J. (1992). Substance use disorders: Predictions for the 1990s. *American Journal on Drug and Alcohol Abuse, 18*, 1–11.

Wetzler, S. E., & Sweeney, J. A. (1986). Childhood amnesia: An empirical demonstration. In D. C. Rubin (Ed.), *Autobiographical memory* (pp. 191–201). Cambridge, UK: Cambridge University Press.

White, R. W. (1959). Motivation reconsidered: The concept of competence. *Psychological Review, 66*, 297–333.

Whitehurst, G. J., Arnold, D. S., Epstein, J. N., Angel, A. L., Smith, M., & Fischel, J. E. (1994). A picture book reading intervention in day care and home for children from low-income families. *Developmental Psychology, 30*, 679–689.

Whitehurst, G. J., Epstein, J. N., Angel, A. L., Payne, A. C., Crone, D. A., & Fischel, J. E. (1994). Outcomes of an emergent literacy intervention in Head Start. *Journal of Educational Psychology, 86*, 542–555.

Whitehurst, G. J., Falco, F. L., Lonigan, C. J., Fischel, J. E., DeBaryshe, B. D., Valdez-Menchaca, M. C., et al. (1988). Accelerating language development through picturebook reading. *Developmental Psychology, 24*, 552–559.

Whitehurst, G. J., & Valdez-Menchaca,

M. C. (1988). What is the role of reinforcement in early language acquisition? *Child Development, 59,* 430–440.

Whitehurst, G. J., Zevenbergen, A. A., Crone, D. A., Schultz, M. D., Velting, O. N., & Fischel, J. E. (1999). Outcomes of an emergent literacy intervention from Head Start through second grade. *Journal of Educational Psychology, 91,* 261–272.

Whitley, B. E. Jr. (1983). Sex-role orientation and self-esteem: A critical meta-analytic review. *Journal of Personality and Social Psychology, 44,* 765–778.

Whitley, B. E. Jr., McHugh, M. C., & Frieze, I. H. (1986). Assessing the theoretical models for sex differences in causal attributions of success and failure. In J. S. Hyde & M. C. Linn (Eds.), *The psychology of gender: Advances through meta-analysis* (pp. 67–101). Baltimore: Johns Hopkins University Press.

Whitman, T. L. (1990). Self-regulation and mental retardation. *American Journal on Mental Retardation, 94,* 347–362.

Wigfield, A. (1994). Expectancy-value theory of achievement motivation: A developmental perspective. *Educational Psychology Review, 6,* 49–78.

Wigfield, A., & Eccles, J. (1992). The development of achievement task values: A theoretical analysis. *Developmental Review, 12,* 265–310.

Wigfield, A., & Eccles, J. S. (2000). Expectancy-value theory of achievement motivation. *Contemporary Educational Psychology, 25,* 68–81.

Wigfield, A., Eccles, J. S., Mac Iver, D., Reuman, D. A., & Midgley, C. (1991). Transitions during early adolescence: Changes in children's domain-specific self-perceptions and general self-esteem across the transition to junior high school. *Developmental Psychology, 27,* 552–565.

Wiig, E. H. (1992). Linguistic transitions in children and adolescents with language learning disabilities: Characteristics and training. In S. A. Vogel (Ed.), *Educational alternatives for students with learning disabilities* (pp. 43–63). New York: Springer-Verlag.

Wilkinson, L. C., & Marrett, C. B. (Eds.). (1985). *Gender influences on classroom interaction.* Orlando, FL: Academic Press.

Wilks, J. (1986). The relative importance of parents and friends in adolescent decision making. *Journal of Youth and Adolescence, 15,* 323–334.

Williams, R. L. (1972, September). *The BITCH-100: A culture-specific test.* Paper presented at the annual meeting of the American Psychological Association, Honolulu, HI.

Willig, A. (1985). A meta-analysis of selected studies on the effectiveness of bilingual education. *Review of Educational Research, 55,* 269–317.

Wilson, P. (1991). Trauma of Sioux Indian high school students. *Anthropology and Education Quarterly, 22,* 367–383.

Wilson, S. (1982). Heritability. *Journal of Applied Problems, 19,* 71–85.

Wimmer, H., Landerl, K., Linortner, R., & Hummer, P. (1991). The relationship of phonemic awareness to reading acquisition: More consequence than precondition but still important. *Cognition, 40,* 219–249.

Winne, P. H., Woodlands, M. H., & Wong, B. Y. L. (1982). Comparability of self-concept among learning disabled, normal, and gifted students. *Journal of Learning Disabilities, 15,* 470–475.

Winsler, A., Diaz, R. M., & Montero, I. (1997). The role of private speech in the transition from collaborative to independent task performance in young children. *Early Childhood Research Quarterly, 12,* 59–79.

Witlein, H., Moore, C., Goodenough, D., & Cox, P. (1977). Field-dependence and field-independence: Cognitive styles and their educational implications. *Reviews of Educational Research, 47,* 1–64.

Wohlwill, J. F. (1973). *The study of behavioral development in children.* New York: Academic Press.

Wolf, M. (1986). Rapid alternating stimulus naming in developmental dyslexias. *Brain and Language, 27,* 360–379.

Wolf, M. (1991). The word-retrieval deficit hypothesis and developmental dyslexia. *Learning and Individual Differences, 3,* 205–223.

Wolf, M. (Ed.). (2001). *Dyslexia, fluency, and the brain.* Timonium, MD: York Press.

Wolf, M., & Bowers, P. G. (1999). The double-deficit hypothesis for the developmental dyslexias. *Journal of Educational Psychology, 91,* 415–438.

Wolf, M., & Obregon, M. (1992). Early naming deficits, developmental dyslexia, and a specific deficit hypothesis. *Brain and Language, 42,* 219–247.

Wolff, P. H. (1969). The natural history of crying and other vocalizations in early infancy. In B. M. Foss

(Ed.), *Determinants of infant behavior* (Vol. 4, pp. 81–109). London: Menthuen.

Woll, B., & Ladd, P. (2003). Deaf communities. In M. Marschark & P. E. Spencer (Eds.), *Oxford handbook of deaf studies, language, and education* (pp. 151–163). New York: Oxford University Press.

Wollheim, R. (1989). *Sigmund Freud.* Cambridge, UK: Cambridge University Press.

Woloshyn, V. E., Paivio, A., & Pressley, M. (1994). Using elaborative interrogation to help students acquire information consistent with prior knowledge and information inconsistent with prior knowledge. *Journal of Educational Psychology, 86,* 79–89.

Wong, B. Y. L., Harris, K. R., Graham, S., & Butler, D. L. (2003). Cognitive strategies instruction research in learning disabilities. In H. L. Swanson, K. R. Harris, & S. Graham (Eds.), *Handbook of learning disabilities* (pp. 1383–1402). New York: Guilford Press.

Wood, R., & Bandura, A. (1989). Impact of conceptions of ability on self-regulatory mechanisms and complex decision-making. *Journal of Personality and Social Psychology, 56,* 407–415.

Wood, S. S., Bruner, J. S., & Ross, G. (1976). The role of tutoring in problem solving. *Journal of Child Psychology and Psychiatry, 17,* 89–100.

Wozniak, R. (1972). Verbal regulation of motor behavior: Soviet research and non-Soviet replications. *Human Development, 15,* 13–57.

Wright, J. C., Huston, A. C., Murphy, K. C., St. Peters, M., Pinon, M., Scantlin, R., et al. (2001). The relations of early television viewing to school readiness and vocabulary of children from low income families: The Early Window Project. *Child Development, 72*(5), 1347–1366.

Wunsch, M. J., Conlon, C. J., & Scheidt, P. C. (2002). Substance abuse: A preventable threat to development. In M. L. Batshaw (Ed.), *Children with disabilities* (5th ed., pp. 107–122). Baltimore: Brookes.

Yakolev, P. L., & Lecours, A.-R. (1967). The myelogenetic cycles of regional maturation of the brain. In A. Minkowski (Ed.), *Regional development of the brain in early life* (pp. 3–70). Oxford, UK: Blackwell.

Yoakum, C. S., & Yerkes, R. M. (1920). *Army mental tests.* New York: Holt.

Yoshida, M., Fernandez, C., & Stigler,

J. W. (1993). Japanese and American students' differential recognition memory for teachers' statements during a mathematics lesson. *Journal of Educational Psychology, 85,* 610–617.

Young, W. C., Goy, R. W., & Phoenix, C. H. (1964). Hormones and sexual behavior. *Science, 143,* 212–218.

Younger, A. J., & Daniels, T. M. (1992). Children's reasons for nominating their peers as withdrawn: Passive withdrawal versus active isolation. *Developmental Psychology, 28,* 955–960.

Youngstrom, E. A., Glutting, J. J., & Watkins, M. W. (2003). Stanford-Binet Intelligence Scale: Fourth edition (SB4): Evaluating the empirical bases for interpretation. In C. R. Reynolds & R. W. Kamphaus (Eds.), *Handbook of psychological and educational assessment of children: Intelligence, aptitude, and achievement* (2nd ed., pp. 217–242). New York: Guilford Press.

Youniss, J., & Smollar, J. (1985). *Adolescent relations with mothers, fathers, and friends.* Chicago: University of Chicago Press.

Yuill, N. (1993). Understanding of personality and dispositions. In M. Bennett (Ed.), *The development of social cognition: The child as psychologist* (pp. 87–110). New York: Guilford Press.

Zabalia, M. (2002). Action et imagerie mentale chez l'enfant [Action and mental imagery in children]. *L'année Psychologique, 102*(3), 409–422.

Zachau-Christiansen, B., & Ross, E. M. (1975). *Babies: Human development during the first year.* London: Wiley.

Zajonc, R. B., Markus, H., & Markus, G. B. (1979). The birth order puzzle. *Journal of Personality and Social Psychology, 37,* 1325–1341.

Zald, D. H., & Iacono, W. G. (1998). The development of spatial working memory abilities. *Developmental Neuropsychology, 14*(4), 563–578.

Zarbatany, L., Hartmann, D. P., & Rankin, D. B. (1990). The psychological functions of preadolescent peer activities. *Child Development, 61,* 1067–1080.

Zeamon, D., & House, B. J. (1979). A review of attention theory. In N. R. Ellis (Ed.), *Handbook of mental deficiency: Psychological theory and research* (pp. 63–120). Hillsdale, NJ: Erlbaum.

Zebrack, B. J., & Chesler, M. A. (2002). Quality of life in childhood cancer survivors. *Psycho-Oncology, 11,* 132–141.

Zecker, L. B. (2004). Learning to read and write in two languages: The development of early biliteracy abilities. In C. A. Stone, E. R. Silliman, B. J. Ehren, & K. Apel (Eds.), *Handbook of language and literacy* (pp. 248–265). New York: Guilford Press.

Zeffiro, T., & Eden, G. (2000). The neural basis of developmental dyslexia. *Annals of Dyslexia, 50,* 3–30.

Zeffiro, T., & Eden, G. (2001). The cerebellum and dyslexia: Perpetrator or innocent bystander? *Trends in Neuroscience, 24,* 512–513.

Zetlin, A., & Murtaugh, M. (1990). Whatever happened to those with borderline IQs? *American Journal of Mental Deficiency, 94,* 463–469.

Zevenbergen, A. A., Whitehurst, G. J., & Zevenbergen, J. A. (2003). Effects of a shared-reading intervention on the inclusion of evaluative devices in narratives of children from low-income families. *Journal of Applied Developmental Psychology, 24,* 1–15.

Zigler, E. F., & Balla, D. (Eds.). (1982). *Mental retardation: The developmental-difference controversy.* Hillsdale, NJ: Erlbaum.

Zigler, E. F., Finn-Stevenson, M., & Hall, N. W. (2002). *The first three years and beyond.* New Haven, CT: Yale University Press.

Zigler, E. F., & Hodapp, R. M. (1986). *Understanding mental retardation.* Cambridge, UK: Cambridge University Press.

Zigler, E. F., & Styfco, S. J. (1993). *Head start and beyond.* New Haven, CT: Yale University Press.

Zigler, E. F., & Styfco, S. J. (1994). Head Start: Criticisms in a constructive context. *American Psychologist, 49*(2), 127–132.

Zigler, E. F., & Styfco, S. J. (2003). The federal commitment to preschool education: Lessons from and for Head Start. In A. J. Reynolds, M. C. Wang, H. J. Walberg (Eds.), *Early childhood programs for a new century* (pp. 3–33). Washington, DC: Child Welfare League of America.

Zimiles, H. & Lee, V. E. (1991). Adolescent family structure and educational progress. *Developmental Psychology, 27,* 314–320.

Zimmerman, B. J. (1989a). Models of self-regulated learning and academic achievement. In B. J. Zimmerman & D. H. Schunk (Eds.), *Self-regulated learning and academic achievement* (pp. 1–25). New York: Springer-Verlag.

Zimmerman, B. J. (1989b). A social cognitive view of self-regulated academic learning. *Journal of Educational Psychology, 81,* 329–339.

Zimmerman, B. J. (1990a). Self-regulated learning and academic achievement: An overview. *Educational Psychologist, 25,* 3–18.

Zimmerman, B. J. (1990b). Self-regulating academic learning and achievement: The emergence of a social-cognitive perspective. *Educational Psychology Review, 2,* 173–201.

Zimmerman, B. J. (2002). Achieving academic excellence: A self-regulatory perspective. In M. Ferrari (Ed.), *The pursuit of excellence through education* (pp. 85–110). Mahwah, NJ: Erlbaum.

Zimmerman, B. J., & Bandura, A. (1994). Impact of self-regulatory influences on writing course attainment. *American Educational Research Journal, 31,* 845–862.

Zimmerman, B. J., Bandura, A., & Martinez-Pons, M. (1992). Self-motivation for academic attainment: The role of self-efficacy beliefs and personal goal setting. *American Educational Research Journal, 29,* 663–676.

Zimmerman, B. J., & Schunk, D. H. (2003). Albert Bandura: The scholar and his contributions to educational psychology. In B. J. Zimmerman & D. H. Schunk (Eds.), *Educational psychology: A century of contributions* (pp. 431–457). Mahwah, NJ: Erlbaum.

Zucker, K. J. (2001). Biological influences on psychosexual differentiation. In R. K. Unger (Ed.), *Handbook of psychology of women and gender* (pp. 101–115). New York: Wiley.

Zucker, K. J., Bradley, S. J., & Lowry-Sullivan, C. B. (1996). Traits of separation anxiety in boys with gender identity disorder. *Journal of the American Academy of Child and Adolescent Psychiatry, 35,* 791–798.

Zuckerman, G. (2003). The learning activity in the first years of schooling: The developmental path toward reflection. In A. Kozulin, B. Gindia, V. S. Ageyev, & S. M. Miller (Eds.), *Vygotsky's educational theory in cultural context* (pp. 177–199). Cambridge, UK: Cambridge University Press.

Zuckerman, M. (1991). *Psychobiology of personality.* Cambridge, UK: Cambridge University Press.

Index

Page numbers followed by *f* indicate figure.